DR   Fischer, Mary
267.5   Ellen.
.C4
F567   Nicolae Ceausescu
1989

$42.50

DATE		

NICOLAE
CEAUŞESCU

NICOLAE CEAUŞESCU

A Study in Political Leadership

Mary Ellen Fischer

Lynne Rienner Publishers • Boulder & London

Published in the United States of America in 1989 by
Lynne Rienner Publishers, Inc.
1800 30th St., Boulder, Colorado 80301

and in the United Kingdom by
Lynne Rienner Publishers, Inc.
3 Henrietta Street, Covent Garden, London WC2E 8LU

Library of Congress Cataloging-in-Publication Data
Fischer, Mary Ellen
  Nicolae Ceauşescu : a study in political leadership.
  Bibliography: p.
  Includes index.
  1. Ceauşescu, Nicolae. 2. Romania—Politics and
government—1944– . 3. Romania—Presidents—
Biography. I. Title.
DR267.5.C4F567 1989   949.8'03'0924 [B]   89-36391
ISBN 0-931477-83-2 (alk. paper)

British Cataloguing in Publication Data
A Cataloguing in Publication record for this book
is available from the British Library.

Printed and bound in the United States of America

The paper used in this publication meets the requirements of
the American National Standard for Permanence of Paper for
Printed Library Materials Z39.48–1984.

*To my mother
and the memory of my father*

Contents

Preface

Since the completion of this manuscript a number of developments have occurred in Romania, most notably the open letter criticizing Ceauşescu's policies, signed by Gheorghe Apostol, Alexandru Bîrlădeanu, Constantin Pârvulescu, Silviu Brucan (former ambassador to the United States), Corneliu Mănescu (former ambassador to the United Nations and president of its General Assembly), and Grigore Răceanu (a pre-war member of the Romanian Communist Party). The letter is a devastating indictment of Ceauşescu for human rights violations and economic mismanagement, especially his "systematization" campaign of rural resettlement, his disregard for the constitution, and his food exports, which threaten the "biological existence" of the nation. His policies, they lament, discredit socialism.

Ceauşescu's initial reaction was to have the police harass and isolate the signers and charge Răceanu's son, a diplomat who had served in Washington, with espionage. This typical reaction may indeed forestall further protests, but the unprecedented open criticism of Ceauşescu by former colleagues within the RCP leadership may also open a new stage in Romanian politics. At a time when Soviet and Romanian diplomats seem to have reversed roles in Washington—when it is the Soviet embassy that is wooing its emigrés and seeking trade and cultural relations as the Romanians did in the 1960s and 1970s—it seems that no changes should be dismissed as impossible. This latest protest could signal significant opposition within the RCP and augur the end of Ceauşescu's rule, but it is difficult to be optimistic after so many years of watching the success of his Machiavellian strategies to preserve his own power. At present, I can only hope that this book provides the reader with some understanding of Romania over the past few decades and help in analyzing future developments.

The faults of this study are, of course, my own. For its merits, however, there are many organizations and individuals to thank. The Romanian Ministry of Education, at the suggestion of the Romanian embassy in Washington, supported my initial attempts to learn Romanian at Sinaia in 1973. The International Research and Exchanges Board (IREX) in 1974–1975 and the Council for International Exchange of Scholars in 1978 enabled me to live and conduct research in Romania. Funds to support travel to and in Romania have also been provided by the Joint Committee on Eastern Europe of the ACLS and SSRC, by the Romanian Academy, and by the Skidmore College Faculty Research Fund; the last has also given extensive support in the acquisition of research materials, and I should like to thank especially the dean of the faculty at Skidmore, Eric J. Weller.

The National Council for Soviet and East European Research provided me with time for research and writing at an earlier stage of this project, and the Romanian research staff at Radio Free Europe in Munich has offered me hospitality and access to archives and library materials at various times since 1973. Much of the research and writing took place in or near the Russian Research Center at Harvard University, and I am particularly grateful to its director, Adam B. Ulam, and associate director, Marshall I. Goldman, for their support and encouragement over the years. The Society for Romanian Studies has helped to create a bond among scholars in this country who are interested in Romania, and I should like to thank my colleagues in that organization for their enlightening papers and comments as well as their friendship.

Inside Romania, the National Council for Science and Technology, the Academy of Social and Political Sciences, and the Ştefan Gheorghiu Academy provided support and research facilities, and a number of individuals within those organizations were exceedingly helpful and kind to me. Many other Romanian citizens have talked with me and confided in me over the years, sometimes at considerable risk to themselves. I dare not mention their names, but they know they have my deep gratitude.

The following individuals also deserve my thanks for a variety of reasons best known to themselves: Walter M. Bacon, Jr., Steve Barr, MaryBelle Fisher, Anneli Ute Gabanyi, Nicki Nichols Gamble, the late Vlad Georgescu, Barbara Jelavich, Tad Kuroda, Patricia Ann Lee, David Marcell, Paul Michelson, the late Joseph C. Palamountain, Jr., Lynne Rienner, Michael Shafir, Claire Walker, and Joanna Zangrando. Finally, I should like to thank my husband, Erwin L. Levine, who has contributed far more than he realizes to the completion of this book.

Mary Ellen Fischer

Introduction

When Gheorghe Gheorghiu-Dej died in March 1965 after a short illness, he was succeeded as leader of the Romanian Workers' Party (RWP)[1] by Nicolae Ceauşescu, a relatively unknown figure inside and outside Romania. Ceauşescu's youth, small stature, and gawky appearance made him conspicuous among his colleagues in photographs taken at the funeral. He was the youngest Party leader in Eastern Europe, and he looked even younger than his forty-seven years.

Within a decade, however, this unprepossessing individual had established himself as the omniscient and omnipotent ruler of Romania, the object of a leadership cult similar in many ways to the cults of Stalin and Mao Zedong. He had also become an international statesman, well known and widely admired for his maverick and activist foreign policy, which if not totally independent of the USSR, was at least exceptional among members of the Soviet bloc. Under his leadership, Romania often failed to follow Moscow's guidelines in Comecon and the Warsaw Pact, at the United Nations, and in inter-bloc negotiations in Helsinki and Geneva. Indeed, in 1968 Ceauşescu made himself a national hero by denouncing the Warsaw Pact intervention in Czechoslovakia as "a great mistake" and "a shameful moment" in the history of the communist movement and by creating detachments of armed "patriotic guards" to resist foreign (presumably Soviet) occupation.[2] Such overt anti-Soviet actions were simply unheard of in Eastern Europe—or were followed by swift retaliation as in Hungary in 1956. Yet the USSR took no steps to punish Romania or its leader.

A number of Ceauşescu's other statements were also welcomed by the Romanian population during the early years of his rule. For example, he constantly stressed the need for legality, constitutionality, and democratic participation in the political process. On economic issues, he promised not only rapid growth but also greater equality, higher living standards, and an end to corruption. In April 1968 he denounced the Stalinist excesses of Gheorghiu-Dej and promised Romanians a new era free from abuses of police power. Many Romanians began to regard this new leader, if not with actual

1

optimism, then at least with the hope that their future would prove better than the past.

Meanwhile Ceauşescu was using his political skills to remove his major rivals in the Romanian Communist Party (RCP) leadership, and after 1969 he was largely unchallenged by those colleagues who remained in office. During the early 1970s his leadership cult gradually intensified until, in 1974, the office of President of the Republic was created especially for him, and he was sworn into office in a nationally televised ceremony more like a royal coronation than a presidential inauguration. By this time Ceauşescu was perhaps the best-known leader in Eastern Europe, an independent Soviet ally, who was on good terms not only with his own population, but also with Washington and Beijing, with Israel and the Arab states, and with most of the Third World.

Until the late 1970s Ceauşescu presided over a country experiencing rapid economic growth, some improvement in living standards, and extraordinary successes in foreign policy, and thus his prestige was not entirely undeserved. But by the mid-1980s the economic and foreign policy successes that had characterized the first years of his rule had evaporated. After 1979 Romanian living standards were drastically reduced by Ceauşescu's decision to pay off, not merely to service, the country's foreign debt. To do so, he increased Romanian exports at the expense of internal consumption and reduced imports even of goods necessary for domestic industries. Food became scarce, and severe cutbacks in energy allocations for the population made homes and public buildings dark and cold due to restrictions on electricity and heat. Petroleum rationing meant that private automobiles, which had proliferated during the 1970s as symbols of the rising living standards, now sat idle—constant reminders of the newly imposed hardships. Romanians compared the food and energy shortages of the 1980s with those they had suffered during World War II, and in private many blamed Ceauşescu for the difficulties.

Meanwhile, Romanian foreign relations deteriorated into a series of quarrels with states inside and outside the Soviet bloc. The post-Brezhnev leaders in Moscow were embarrassed by Ceauşescu's leadership cult and annoyed by his resistance to *perestroika* (restructuring) and *glasnost* (openness). Friction between Ceauşescu and Mikhail Gorbachev was evident when the Soviet leader came to Bucharest in mid-1987 for a visit that had been long postponed, in part as a sign of Soviet displeasure. By then Budapest had begun to protest the treatment of Hungarians in Romania, and a rift had developed between the two small Soviet allies. In addition, Romanian pollution threatened the previously friendly relationships with other neighbors, such as Bulgaria and Yugoslavia. Outside the bloc, Romanian relations with the West had deteriorated after 1979 over economic and human rights issues; for example, U.S. criticism of human rights violations in Romania throughout the 1980s finally led Ceauşescu himself to end

Romania's most-favored-nation (MFN) trade status in the spring of 1988. Ceauşescu, who had been President Richard Nixon's special friend in the Soviet bloc during the era of détente, was now regarded in Washington as an oppressive dictator.

What happened to produce the drastic contrast between the successes and optimism of the 1960s and 1970s and the failures of the 1980s? And why has the public adulation of Ceauşescu inside Romania continued and intensified despite the growing disillusionment and eventual despair of the population in the face of his policy choices? For the leadership cult has continued. Ceauşescu remains publicly infallible: successes are his alone, and failures the fault of those who do not carry out his instructions correctly. In addition, his personalized power has come to include many members of his family, including his wife, Elena—nepotism, as well as leader worship, is characteristic of Ceauşescu's rule.

The focus of this study is Ceauşescu himself, his background, his personality and character, the political environment in which he operates, his own political views and techniques, and his methods of leadership and control as he has revealed them publicly in his actions and in the Romanian press. It is my contention that a combination of Romanian political culture and tradition, the Marxist-Leninist ideology and Party organization, and Ceauşescu himself were all crucial elements in the evolution of Romanian politics and society after 1965. However, Ceauşescu's own strengths and weaknesses were largely responsible for the successes and promises of the early years, the leadership cult, and then the failures of the 1980s. Obviously factors external to Romania were also relevant, among them the international economic environment—rising interest rates, for example, or changes in the balance of trade in petroleum and petroleum products—and political developments such as the end of détente and the death of Brezhnev. Other individuals and groups inside Romania contributed to the cult and the disastrous economic decisions. But Ceauşescu exercised an inordinate amount of power and proved incapable of adjusting his strategies in the face of new developments. As a result, he must shoulder much of the blame for the general deterioration.

These points will form the center of my argument: Ceauşescu's very skill at political control produced a situation in which there was no effective opposition to his will. His policy preference for rapid industrialization at the expense of living standards precluded widespread popular support except on foreign policy. His refusal to tolerate opposition or listen to advice that questioned his own priorities led him to abandon his brief experiments with broader participation and leadership based on support rather than coercion. His lack of genuine charisma brought the fake charisma of the cult. Finally, his inability to understand the complexities of economic development issues, his rejection of advice from experts, and his reliance on coercion rather than positive economic incentives produced the economic disasters.

Now in his seventies, Ceauşescu continues to make choices that are leading Romania further down the path to disintegration. For example, the RCP under Ceauşescu is destroying the social and cultural fabric of the country by razing and rebuilding Romanian towns and villages to fit the president's image of what the country should become. Although dozens of new town centers had risen throughout the country as symbols of modernity in the 1970s, at that time buildings of historical interest were usually carefully preserved and incorporated into the new areas, and these new centers increased the goods and services available to the population. In the 1980s, in contrast, when the old center of Bucharest was razed to provide space for a gigantic project of public buildings in honor of Ceauşescu, many churches and other historical monuments were deliberately destroyed.

Not only Bucharest is threatened: Literally thousands of villages throughout the country are to be destroyed in a "systematization" campaign to consolidate the population into larger and more efficient communities with multistory apartment buildings rather than private homes. This would destroy the traditional culture and values of many Romanian peasants, and it would be even more devastating for the minority nationalities, such as the Hungarians, whose group identity would be threatened by the destruction of their churches and other symbols of ethnic unity and their relocation into new Romanian towns. Ceauşescu began his rule in the mid-1960s with overtures to the ethnic minorities and promises to preserve their culture and give them full equality as citizens of socialist Romania; twenty years later he seemed determined to end their existence as distinct groups in Romanian society. He had also promised the ethnic Romanians that he would preserve their national independence and raise their level of economic development to that of advanced socialism. Instead, he began to threaten their national heritage and to move the economy backward toward primitive communism.

In order to understand this seemingly irrational and destructive behavior, and to grasp the broader issues of the evolution of Romania under Ceauşescu and Ceauşescu as leader of Romania, we must start by examining the factors that produced Ceauşescu's personality, political perceptions, and choices. Thus, Chapter 1 surveys this background—the Romanian political environment, the communist movement in Romania, and Ceauşescu's own childhood and personal experiences before and during World War II. These experiences formed the basis of his political beliefs and policy choices, and we cannot understand Ceauşescu without looking at this period. Unfortunately, much of the information we have on those years has been affected by the propaganda of the leadership cult, and myths have been created around his person and his activities. Even so, the myths in themselves are worth examining because they tell us what Ceauşescu wishes to portray of his early life and the lessons he would like us to draw from his example. This in turn tells us about his later beliefs and priorities.

Chapter 2 then provides the background to one of the most fascinating aspects of Ceauşescu's political career: how he rose to the top position in the Romanian Communist Party. To outside observers Ceauşescu was not an obvious choice in 1965 to head the RCP. Despite his status as a first-generation revolutionary and his years in prison with Gheorghiu-Dej for communist activity, he had formidable rivals for the top position. A number of individuals in the Romanian Political Bureau (Chivu Stoica, Ion Gheorghe Maurer, and Gheorghe Apostol, for example) had more seniority in the Party and had been personally closer to Gheorghiu-Dej than had Ceauşescu. Even in his own age group Ceauşescu was rivaled by Alexandru Drăghici, for many years minister of the interior and thus in control of the secret police (*Securitate*). Why was this awkward young man the choice, apparently of Gheorghiu-Dej, and certainly of the 1965 Political Bureau? What aspects of his background and personality led the Party elite to accept him as first secretary? Chapter 2 concentrates on the years from 1944 to 1965 to analyze the background to Ceauşescu's bid for power and the lessons of Gheorghiu-Dej's leadership for his apprentice and protégé. Ceauşescu's major policy choices—autonomy in foreign policy and rapid industrialization of the domestic economy—merely continued and intensified lines of development established under Gheorghiu-Dej. The influence of his mentor was therefore crucial in the formation of Ceauşescu's political priorities.

Once the new first secretary was elected, the next issue becomes his consolidation of power, the focus of Chapters 3 through 6. How was Ceauşescu able to establish his domination over the Party, eliminate his rivals, and become the unchallenged ruler of Romania? These years of leadership transition from 1965 to 1969 are among the most important of his rule. It was then that he laid the foundations for his total dominance of the political process. He began to demonstrate his skill at personnel manipulation with methods that would change over time but that would be extremely effective in achieving and maintaining control over the RCP and the entire political system. During this period many of his other political techniques emerged, particularly his nationalist and populist appeals for the participation of all citizens in achieving the goals of socialist Romania. In addition, these first years of Ceauşescu's rule contain lessons for anyone involved in a struggle for power in a Leninist party, and Ceauşescu's undoubted success in consolidating power makes his combination of strategies a model that other new leaders might wish to consider. These were the years of optimism, looked back on later by many Romanians as a golden age when Ceauşescu was promising everything to everyone, and many believed him. We cannot understand Romania in the 1970s and 1980s unless we remember the 1960s.

Indeed, many of the policy themes expressed by Gorbachev in the Soviet Union as part of his policy of *glasnost* were frequently emphasized by Ceauşescu during his first years as Party leader. *Glasnost* implies open and frank discussion, and Ceauşescu often called for "broad exchanges of opinions" (*schimburi largi de opinii*) and "open confrontation of viewpoints" (*confruntarea deschisă a punctelor de vedere*).[3] The similarities between the two men in the first years of leading their parties are striking—for example, their initial assumption of the policy center, allowing both conservatives and reformers to find cause to hope in the new leader; their appeals to legality and efficiency; and their criticism and rehabilitation of carefully selected past leaders. However, neither leader would like to admit any similarities. Gorbachev moved very quickly to dissociate himself from the immediate past and to stake out a claim as a reformer. Ceauşescu has been adamantly opposed to Gorbachev's *perestroika* (restructuring); he has his own word, *perfecţionarea* (perfecting) and explicitly rejects the applicability of *perestroika* in Romania. *Glasnost* he prefers simply to ignore. Of course, the two men are very different in their backgrounds, education, and personalities, and there is no reason to assume that Gorbachev's eventual policy choices will resemble those of Ceauşescu. But some of the political strategies that served Ceauşescu so well are already being utilized, consciously or unconsciously, by Gorbachev as he consolidates his power.

By 1969 Ceauşescu had clearly come to dominate the Romanian Communist Party, and thereafter the most obvious feature of his rule inside Romania was the extreme adulation accorded him by his colleagues and the mass media. This adulation gradually came to include many of the characteristics of a religious cult, with an iconography (portraits of Ceauşescu), a Bible (his collected speeches), an infallible leader, and rituals of mass worship. By the mid-1970s no Romanian official could deliver a report or write an article without referring to President Ceauşescu's political insight and leadership as the major source of inspiration and guidance. Chapter 7 examines the Ceauşescu cult in some detail, first placing it into the broader context of leadership cults in Leninist parties to seek its causes and effects, and then examining the cult inside Romania by studying the major features of its image, its appeal to various groups in the Romanian population, its development in the first half of the 1970s, and, as a case study in Ceauşescu's methods of manipulation, his control over the propagators of the cult, the journalists of the mass media.

Although the leadership cult has been the most prominent public feature of Ceauşescu's rule, the crucial technique that has contributed to his control over the Romanian political system has been his manipulation of Party personnel. This is the focus of Chapter 8, which examines the entire Party, its Central Committee, the county first secretaries, and the top leadership over more than two decades of Ceauşescu's rule to evaluate his strategies toward those groups in the 1960s, the 1970s, and after 1980. Ceauşescu treated each of these groups differently, and his strategies changed over time according to his personal needs and policy priorities.

Chapter 9 evaluates a number of major policies from the second decade of Ceauşescu's rule, focusing first on those that related to his early promises of legality, equality, and participatory democracy. As it turned out, Ceauşescu's view of popular participation did not mean popular influence over policy choices, and after 1975 his promises of legality and participatory democracy became bitter jokes in Romania. A number of protests took place in the late 1970s, but they were quickly isolated and rendered ineffective by a variety of responses such as imprisonment, exile, or concessions followed by reprisals. The feelings of grievance were particularly strong among the ethnic Hungarians, and the nationality policies of the RCP, analyzed in the second section of this chapter, became a matter of international controversy. The chapter concludes with a discussion of the economic deterioration and political stalemate of the 1980s.

Finally, Chapter 10 offers an overview of the Ceauşescu era and suggests the potential effects of his leadership on the future of Romania. Any analysis of a leader who is still in power must necessarily be both premature and tentative—most of the material on which biographies are usually based is simply not available—and Ceauşescu is a particularly difficult case. He has been the subject of approved biographies so laudatory as to be unreliable[4] and the object of vitriolic attacks by political enemies or defectors.[5] When he became Party leader in Romania in 1965 he was relatively unknown; he then became part of a traditionally private collective leadership in a communist state; and later he became the object of a leadership cult that created a history and image of him shaped to fulfill regime needs rather than to reveal an accurate picture of his life. Unlike some Soviet leaders, his personality is not outgoing and he is not given to jokes or spontaneous remarks that could fill in some minor details about his character. And, of course, there is no inquisitive press in Romania to seek out and publish details of his political or personal life that are not part of the approved image.

This study of Ceauşescu is not, therefore, a biography in the ordinary sense. It is not a chronological study of his life or his political career. Nor is it a history of the Romanian Socialist Republic during the Ceauşescu period, since a number of excellent studies of Romanian politics[6] and foreign policy[7] have already been written. Instead, I focus on Ceauşescu's successes and ultimate failures, his strategies of leadership and political control inside Romania, and his role as a political leader and public figure, evaluating his actions and seeking their origins in his background and in his own writings. Most of the sources I have used are public, and the most important single source has been the published record of Ceauşescu's rule contained in the RCP daily newspaper, *Scînteia*, through which Ceauşescu communicates directly to the Party instructions about priorities, comments on performance, and reports on personnel changes, recent events, and the changing Party line. The basic guide to Ceauşescu's personal goals and political priorities is the multi-volume collection of his speeches, in which he has expressed his views to a variety of Romanian audiences over more than two decades.[8] I have supplemented these Romanian sources with the work of Western scholars and journalists, as well as visits to Romania and conversations with Romanian officials and scholars.

This book began in the early 1970s, when many individuals, including myself, were somewhat optimistic about Romania's future under Ceauşescu's rule. He had criticized his Stalinist predecessor and promised to develop the economy and raise living standards through institutionalized, democratic political processes—under Party guidance, of course, but improvement seemed possible. Instead, as we shall see, Ceauşescu dashed these hopes and, while maintaining himself and his Party in power, failed to implement the broader goals for Romanian society that are still promised frequently in RCP documents and by Ceauşescu himself. As a result, this work now documents the disastrous results of Ceauşescu's personal power in Romania and reflects the widespread disappointment inside and outside Romania with Ceauşescu and his methods of rule.

1

The Background:
Youth and Revolution

Nicolae Ceaușescu's fundamental political beliefs, values, and expectations—
and therefore his political behavior—were shaped in part by the political
culture of Romania.[1] The ideology of Marx as interpreted and revised by
Lenin, Stalin, Mao Zedong, and Gheorghiu-Dej also helped to mold
Ceaușescu's view of the world and his strategies for political action. Finally,
Ceaușescu's personal background and political experience were crucial in the
formation of his leadership techniques. This chapter presents a brief survey of
the major features of the Romanian environment and the Romanian Marxist
movement[2] and then turns to Ceaușescu's personal life and examines his
childhood and revolutionary activity as well as the myths about this period
that have sprung up as a result of the leadership cult.

The Romanian Environment

Nicolae Ceaușescu lived his entire life in Romania and inevitably looked to
his surroundings for lessons about the nature of society and politics.
Romania's late entrance into World War I on the side against Germany was a
major gamble that led to devastating losses in 1916 but brought windfall
profits after 1918. Greater Romania (*România Mare*) was created at the end of
the war by negotiations among the victorious powers, and the small prewar
Kingdom of Romania—consisting of the principalities of Wallachia and
Moldavia (not united until 1859 and fully independent only since the war
against Turkey in 1877–1878 when Russia and Romania had fought as
allies)—more than doubled in size and population with the addition of the
following territories: Transylvania, the Banat, and Bucovina from the former
Austro-Hungarian Empire; Bessarabia, from the former Russian Empire; and
Northern Dobrogea from Bulgaria. Along with these new territories,
Romania acquired substantial numbers of national minorities—the 1930
census showed that almost 30 percent of the population of Greater Romania
was not ethnically Romanian—and many of these other ethnic groups were

by no means reconciled to Romanian rule. The political unity and internal stability of the new state were therefore quite fragile.

The country's geographical position in Eastern Europe on the periphery of major European empires had taught Romanian leaders to pay tribute (tangible or intangible) to whichever empire held temporary hegemony over the area. With the almost simultaneous collapse of the Ottoman, Austro-Hungarian, and Russian empires as a result of World War I came the creation of a number of small states in Eastern Europe, including Greater Romania, and the hegemony of a relatively distant capital—Istanbul, Vienna, or St. Petersburg—was replaced by the hostility of smaller but closer neighbors. Because each neighbor had a significant minority population inside Romania, there was considerable enmity toward the new state, and it is not surprising that Romanian nationalism in defense of Greater Romania played an important role in the country's domestic and foreign policies between the world wars when both Gheorghiu-Dej and Ceauşescu first became politically active. In fact, many observers of Romanian affairs have concluded that the "overriding motive force" in Romanian history has been nationalism.[3] The emphasis on national unity and independence by the two leaders since 1960 merely reflects the prevailing political tradition.

Another recurring goal of the Romanian elite has been industrialization. Indeed, disputes among Romanian academics and politicians throughout the last century have tended to focus on how, not whether, to industrialize. There were bitter quarrels over the issue of protectionism between National Liberals and Conservatives (then the two major parties) before World War I, and among National Liberals, Social-Democrats, and National Peasant leaders in the interwar period, but all these parties assumed the necessity of industrialization. The National Liberal Party, which governed from 1922 to 1928, was an avid protector of Romanian capital and infant industries. Even the National Peasant Party (NPP), which might have been expected to introduce policies to stimulate agricultural investment at the expense of industry, "was not very 'peasantist' either in its composition or in its activities."[4] When it assumed power in 1928, the NPP welcomed investment by foreign capitalists and adopted agrarian legislation that laid the party open to the charge of favoring the richer peasants and village bourgeoisie. Not even the leader of the fascist Iron Guard, Corneliu Zelea Codreanu, was totally hostile to industrialization. On the contrary, this leader of what was essentially an anti-bourgeois protest movement based on national rebirth "not only praised industry but even exhorted his fellow Romanians to compete with Jews in the art of entrepreneurship."[5]

With implicit or explicit agreement, then, that industrialization must come to Romania, the disagreements during the interwar period focused on the methods the state should use to stimulate industrialization, and specifically on whether to protect Romanian industries against foreign capital. The National Liberal Party's policies of economic nationalism and limited foreign investment apparently did succeed in reducing the share of foreign capital in the economy from 52 percent in 1912–1913 to 36 percent in 1929, but these policies were severely criticized for slowing economic growth: During the 1920s Romania's industrial growth rates were notably lower than those of its Balkan neighbors, and by 1929 per capita gross material product had barely reached the levels of 1913.[6] The National Peasant Party removed most restrictions on foreign capital in 1928, but the onset of the Great Depression reduced the availability of foreign investment funds, and Romania over the next decade and a half faced a series of economic and political crises. The country succumbed first to a royal dictatorship under King Carol II, then to the Iron Guard, and finally to a military dictator, Ion Antonescu, who ruled Romania as a German ally during World War II. The lessons of the 1920s were not learned by Gheorghiu-Dej and Ceauşescu, however: John Lampe and Marvin Jackson have characterized Romanian economic strategies since 1960 as a return to the National Liberal policies of "import substitution and a diversification of trade, all to avoid dependence."[7]

The failure of successive governments to achieve industrial growth meant that Romania before World War II was a country predominantly of peasants; as late as 1950, 75 percent of the Romanian population was engaged in agriculture. Ceauşescu's birth and early childhood in a peasant home placed him in the mainstream of Romanian society. As he frequently reminds us, the life of the Romanian peasant before World War II was not easy, and we can see why he left home in the 1930s and why he might reject attempts to preserve village traditions in the 1980s. At the beginning of this century, the disparity in land ownership in Romania between large and small holdings was the greatest in Europe including Russia, and this situation helped to produce a violent peasant revolt in 1907 that was harshly suppressed. In the last year of World War I, however, the most extensive land reform in interwar Europe (excluding the Soviet Union) was begun and carried out over the next decade.[8]

The reform stemmed from a variety of reasons: in part from promises made by the National Liberals before 1914 in order to compete with the old Conservative Party; in part from the need for improved morale in the army after the severe military defeats of 1916 (King Ferdinand himself promised land reform in the spring of 1917 to motivate the peasant army to fight); and in part from growing fear of bolshevism. The reform changed land ownership, but unfortunately did little to increase the size of farming units or to consolidate the holdings. Even worse, the frequent delays in settling ownership rights discouraged investment as well as the purchase and consolidation of the land by more efficient farmers.[9] Many of the resulting landholdings thus remained too small and scattered to be economically viable, and Romanian peasants exacerbated the problem by their tradition of dividing land among male children. The agrarian reform therefore did not produce a productive class of prosperous farmers; instead, it allowed rural overpopulation, underemployment, and low productivity to continue and in some ways actually delayed the painful transformation of poor or landless peasants into industrial workers. Given this background, it is not surprising that Ceauşescu demands large cooperative farms rather than small private plots.

A major purpose of the land reform, however, was not to improve the social and economic situation of the peasants but rather to preserve them from political radicalism. In other words, political stability was more important than economic development. This fear of political instability stemmed in part from the fragility of national unity and independence in the face of hostile minorities and neighbors, but another factor involved the governing elites' relationship with the Romanian masses. What Michael Shafir has termed the most striking feature of Romanian society and politics was the contrast between the *pays légal* and the *pays réel:* Western constitutional forms *(pays légal)* grafted onto a corporate, patriarchal, and status-based society *(pays réel)*. However we characterize the division in Romania—a contrast of form and substance, a "gap between the social elite and the peasantry," an "abyss between urban and rural Romania," or a "moral and psychological chasm between the oligarchic, bureaucratic elite and the lower classes"—the country consisted of two worlds differing in political, economic, social, educational, and cultural experiences and values.[10] The political result of this duality was an electoral system so corrupt as to guarantee the election of the party in power. The political elites did not dare to risk a transfer of real power to the masses, and so the interior minister simply ensured that the proper candidates won. Rather than being held responsible to the voters, the Cabinet in effect dominated them.[11] Both Gheorghiu-Dej and Ceauşescu continued this tradition.

The political system was not only corrupt, it was also personalized. The parties revolved around personalities and clans: The Brătianu family controlled the National Liberals, for example, and the National Peasants were led by individuals such as Iuliu Maniu, Ion Mihalache, Alexandru Vaida-Voevod, and Constantin Stere, each with his own loyalists. As Joseph Rothschild described the situation, "A leader was followed for the sake of the power, influence, and positions he could command and distribute, and so his death would entail a severe crisis for his party, and perhaps even dissolution."[12] This helps to explain the determination of the RCP leadership to remain united in 1965 when Gheorghiu-Dej died and indicates that Ceauşescu's nepotism and personalization of power merely carried to an extreme previous tendencies in Romanian politics. The National Liberal Party, for example, never fully recovered from the deaths in 1927 of Ion Brătianu and King Ferdinand, a strong supporter of the party's nationalist and protectionist policies, and in 1928 the National Peasants under Iuliu Maniu gained power.

Three years earlier, in 1925, King Ferdinand's son and heir to the throne,

Carol, had renounced his rights to succession for personal reasons—his desire to live with Magda Lupescu rather than with his wife, Princess Helen. Carol had gone into exile, and at Ferdinand's death in 1927 Carol's five-year-old son Michael became king. In 1930, however, when Romania was facing the consequences of the international economic crisis, Carol abruptly returned to Romania and took the throne. The prime minister and leader of the National Peasant Party, Iuliu Maniu, agreed provisionally to Carol's return, but when Carol was not reconciled with his wife and brought back Lupescu instead, Maniu resigned. From then until 1940 Romanian politics at the top level was largely dominated by Carol who, although he did lend state support to industrial projects and achieve important growth in some areas, was no more successful in bridging the gap between *pays légal* and *pays réel* or improving the overall economic situation than the party politicians had been. As in the rest of Eastern Europe, the one area in which the Romanian interwar governments were successful was in education, but ironically the spread of mass literacy and the increased opportunities for higher education only contributed to instability. Many of those who graduated failed to find employment that they considered suitable to their new status, and they joined the growing numbers of discontented but politically conscious and articulate.[13]

The deteriorating economic situation throughout Eastern Europe during the 1930s contributed to the growth of radical protest movements, and many of their adherents came from among those discontented students or unemployed graduates. Romania was no exception. Codreanu, the leader of Romanian fascism, saw a vision of the Archangel Michael calling on him to save his nation and named his organization the League of the Archangel Michael. Also known as the Iron Guard, it was a protest movement of the radical right rather than the left, appealing to the nationalism and religious mysticism of Romanian peasants and intellectuals. The Iron Guard's overt anti-Semitism and xenophobia found support in the political environment of interwar Romania and interwar Europe, and its increasing use of violence gave it political influence far beyond its electoral support (16 percent in 1937).[14]

A political stalemate resulted from the 1937 elections, and King Carol took advantage of the situation to establish a royal dictatorship. During 1938 he dissolved the political parties, including the Iron Guard, and even managed to rid himself of Codreanu, who was arrested, tried, imprisoned, and shot in what was reported to be an escape attempt. A year later, in September 1939, the Guard retaliated by assassinating Carol's prime minister, Armand Călinescu, and the king in turn carried out mass reprisals. Carol appeared to be in control of the internal situation, but he could not prevent the Soviet seizure of Bessarabia in June 1940 or Hitler's decision later that summer in the Vienna *Diktat* to give Northern Transylvania back to Hungary. The discontent in Romania over the country's dismemberment was so great that in September Carol was forced to abdicate in favor of his son, Michael. Real power, however, lay with General (later Marshal) Ion Antonescu, who ruled with the support of the Iron Guard and the Germans. Then in January 1941 Antonescu forcibly suppressed the Iron Guardists, and many of them fled to Germany or abroad. Hitler, who wanted an effective military ally with an efficient economy, acquiesced in the destruction of the Guard, and Romania remained a German ally until August 1944.

One party or regime after another—parliamentary, royal, fascist, military—failed to achieve its goals for Romania during the period between the world wars when Ceauşescu was growing up. First, the fragile national unity of Greater Romania was never solidified, and the country was dismembered during and after 1940. Second, like the other small states of Eastern Europe, its independence in international affairs was destroyed by the rise of two new empires; German and then Soviet troops occupied Romania and forced the small state into a close alliance as both Hitler and Stalin sought to control the country's natural resources. Finally, industrial and agricultural growth was stifled for a variety of domestic and international reasons: Small-scale peasant agriculture continued to dominate the Romanian economy until after World War II, and whatever industrialization did occur before the war did not strengthen the country sufficiently to prevent its disintegration in the face of internal and external hostility.

The inability of successive Romanian governments to preserve national unity and independence and to implement a program of industrial development was matched by their failure to regularize constitutional procedures.[15] Romania was not unusual in this respect, as many young parliamentary systems in Europe and elsewhere succumbed to economic difficulties during the 1930s. The deep gulf between the elites and the rest of society induced politicians to fear instability above all else. This fear created alliances among various elite groups and also stimulated electoral corruption to exclude non-elites from attaining power. At the same time, the split strengthened traditional ties of family and friendship on both sides, as a means either of preserving elite status or of mitigating the worst hardships of non-elite status.

The frustrated expectations of the interwar decades intensified the desire of many Romanians for the basic national goals of unity, independence, and industrial growth. Although in some ways Ceauşescu would attempt to escape his past and bring radical change to Romania, he adopted these traditional interwar goals as his priorities. Failure to make significant progress toward these goals before World War II had (1) widened the gap between elites and non-elites, (2) prevented any evolution toward an open and institutionalized political process, and (3) reinforced the importance of personal, informal ties of family and friendship as mechanisms of survival. One irony of the Ceauşescu era has been that his intensified efforts to fulfill these traditional goals have had similar unfortunate results.

The Romanian Communist Party Before 1945[16]

The experience of the Romanian Communist Party in the interwar period was also one of failure and frustrated expectations. Before the Soviet army entered Romania in 1944, the communists were not a significant political force. In fact, the RCP was perhaps the only communist party in Eastern Europe never to play an important role in interwar politics. It was one of the smallest parties in the Comintern, and its political front, the Workers' and Peasants' Bloc, only once gained more than 2 percent of the vote in parliamentary elections—2.5 percent in 1931, and the results were almost immediately invalidated.[17] Ceauşescu was politically active in the RCP by 1933 and experienced for himself the dangers, exhilarations, and hardships of this frustrating revolutionary movement. After he became Party leader, he often acknowledged that his period was a time of RCP weakness, but he always blamed the Party's failures on the interference of the Comintern leaders in Moscow. This criticism created a new Party historiography in Romania that helped Ceauşescu to separate the interests of the RCP from those of the Soviet Union and to begin the process of uniting Romanian communism and Romanian nationalism. This tendency to blame outside interference for internal difficulties would become a basic feature of Ceauşescu's rule and gain him considerable support in Romania in the 1960s and 1970s.

In fact, Comintern interference did have disastrous effects on the RCP during the interwar years. But just as important in the RCP's failure to attract support was the lack of an effective social base for a Marxist party in Romania. As a movement seeking revolutionary change, the communists had to appeal to disaffected groups; as Marxists, they should have found most of their support among the workers. In fact, they targeted three major groups—workers, peasants, and ethnic minorities—but each presented recruitment difficulties.

Romania had a tiny industrial proletariat and a still smaller trade union movement. In 1930, less than 10 percent of the active population was engaged in industry, and most of that group worked in small shops rather than in the large enterprises that were more appropriate for trade union activity and the development of a militant class consciousness open to communist influence.[18] Also, first-generation workers tended to retain close ties to their native villages, which slowed the growth of proletarian consciousness still further. By 1938, total trade union membership in Romania was a mere 80,000.[19] Ceauşescu himself left his village for a shoemaker's shop in Bucharest, and he evidently was first moved to political action by national and economic grievances rather than by trade unionist motives.

Another factor detracting from RCP working-class support was the existence of a serious political rival, the Romanian Socialist Party, a larger and more moderate group from which the RCP split in 1921. Even worse, the communists were hampered in their efforts to organize the proletariat by their own illegality: In 1924 the Party was outlawed and, according to Comintern reports, over "eight hundred members of the Party were arrested and an entirely new party apparatus had to be erected."[20] Thereafter they had to work through a series of front organizations for their activities, such as the Workers' and Peasants' Bloc during elections. Despite these disadvantages, the Romanian working class did provide the RCP with small circles of adherents in industrial centers throughout the country where individuals like Gheorghiu-Dej first began their revolutionary activity.

Because the overwhelming majority of the Romanian population consisted of peasants, the RCP should have had some opportunity to attract support within this group. However, during the 1920s the peasants tended to support the agrarian program of their own National Peasant Party, and the agrarian reform following World War I initially did lessen the appeal of radicalism to the new peasant landowners despite the small size of their holdings. In addition, the RCP was in constant struggle with the Comintern over agrarian policy: The RCP leaders were influenced by the agrarian theories of Constantin Dobrogeanu-Gherea, a prominent Party member who had rejected peasant violence. The Comintern attempted to impose more radical solutions modeled on Soviet practice, but no policy was consistently applied or attracted many Romanian peasants.[21] Peasant radicalism did intensify in Romania during the 1930s for a variety of reasons, including the long-term failure of the agrarian reform to improve the living standards of most peasants and disillusionment with the National Peasant government, which failed to relieve their plight in 1928–1930 as it worsened in the international economic depression. The beneficiaries of this peasant radicalism, however, were not the communists but the fascists, as most Romanian peasants—and here Ceauşescu was an exception—found the religious nationalism of the Iron Guard more attractive than the international atheism of the Romanian Communist Party.

The strongest and most numerous supporters of the RCP were to be found among the third targeted group: the non-Romanian nationalities, especially in the economically advanced areas such as Transylvania and the Banat. In the relatively honest elections of 1928, 66 percent of the communist vote came from these areas, which accounted for only 23 percent of the population of Greater Romania.[22] Although votes for the communists could be attributed in part to the existence of some large-scale industrial and mining enterprises in these former territories of Austria-Hungary, RCP membership was also heavily skewed toward the minorities. The Hungarians, less than 8 percent of the population of Greater Romania, made up over a quarter of the RCP members in the 1930s; the comparable figures for Jews were 4 percent of the population and 18 percent of the Party. Russians, Ukrainians, and Bulgarians had a share in RCP membership over three times greater than their share in the total population. The Romanians were the reverse: They made up 72 percent of the population and only 23 percent of the Party.[23] Clearly the RCP found it easier to attract the ethnic minorities than the Romanian majority.

This brings us to what was probably the most important single reason—aside from the lack of a social base—for the failure of the Romanian Communist Party to attract substantial Romanian support in the interwar years: the national question. The fragile unity of Greater Romania was threatened throughout the period by ethnic minorities unwilling to accept their incorporation into this new state and looking for ways in which to express their discontent. One way to protest was to vote communist, and they did this in numbers disproportionate to their share in the overall population. In addition, Party policies attracted the minorities. For example, the Third Congress of the RCP in September 1924 adopted the "Marxist-Leninist principle of self-determination of nationalities up to [and including] separation from the state."[24] Needless to say, detachment of the newly acquired provinces was not popular with ethnic Romanians, and the RCP's relative success among the national minorities only intensified the Party's difficulties in attracting Romanians, who came to identify the communists with the enemies of Greater Romania. These enemies included the ethnic minorities themselves and, standing behind them and encouraging them, the Soviet Union.

Fear of bolshevism had seized the Romanian elites in the aftermath of the 1917 Russian revolution and had helped to stimulate the agrarian reform in Romania. The threat of revolution and class conflict was then compounded by the demands of the new Soviet state for the return of Bessarabia, annexed by Russia in 1812 and retaken by the Romanians after World War I. Any challenge to existing borders was viewed as a danger to the very survival of Greater Romania, and so what had been a *Bolshevik* threat to the Romanian elites eventually turned into a *Russian* threat against the entire Romanian nation. Most observers agree on the crucial impact of this threat on the development of the RCP after 1918. R.V. Burks, for example, concluded: "It was not the absence of the characteristic social and economic problems which produced communism elsewhere in the Balkans that accounts for the weakness of the Rumanian party. It was rather the fact that it was impossible to identify the national interests of ethnic Rumanians with Soviet communism."[25]

Not only Party membership and policies but also some of the leaders of the RCP rendered it vulnerable to the accusation that it supported the desires of the Soviets and the various minorities for the dismemberment of Greater Romania. In the early days of Romanian Marxism, for example, its main theoretician was Constantin Dobrogeanu-Gherea, a Jew forced to flee his native Russia in 1875 because of revolutionary activity. He came to share the leadership of the Romanian Marxist movement with Christian Rakovsky, a Bulgarian from the Dobrogea and later a leading member of the Soviet Communist Party.[26] The ethnicity and political backgrounds of both Gherea and Rakovsky rendered them suspect in Romania, and the policies they advocated often could be interpreted as inimical not only to the Romanian government but also to Romanian national interests. Both men, for example, opposed Romanian participation in the Second Balkan War in 1913 and the annexation of the southern Dobrogea. They also were lifelong enemies of the Russian Empire, describing it as a predatory neighbor, but in 1916, as in 1913, neither was willing to support the Romanian war effort.[27] During 1917 Rakovsky became a firm supporter of the Bolsheviks and immediate, violent revolution, and after the Bolshevik Revolution he called for the incorporation of Bessarabia into the Soviet state, by force if necessary. In early 1919, as head of the Soviet Ukraine, he planned an invasion of Romania to support Bela Kun's socialist republic in Hungary, and later, in 1921 and 1924, he successfully opposed Soviet *de jure* recognition of Romanian rights to Bessarabia. Rakovsky's actions merely reinforced the growing mistrust in Romania of any individuals or political movements associated with communism.[28]

This mistrust was intensified still further by the factional struggles within the Romanian Marxist movement. Factionalism, not unusual in Marxist revolutionary parties,[29] appeared very early in the Romanian Party. The Social Democratic Party of Romania, founded formally in 1893, had its first factional split in 1899, when a majority of the members decided that Romania was not ripe for socialism and changed the name of the Party from Social Democrat to National Democrat. This would not be the last time that Romanian Marxists would substitute nationalism for the class struggle in recruiting support. The change was not very successful, however, for a year later a number of important members deserted to the Liberal Party. Although individuals such as Gherea remained loyal, Marxism as an organized movement largely disappeared from the Romanian scene until the arrival of Rakovsky in 1905.

Until then the Party had relied largely upon intellectuals for its membership, but Rakovsky saw the need to build a trade union movement and recruit within its ranks. With Gherea he began to publish *România muncitoare*, and in 1910 a new party was established, the Romanian Social-Democratic Party (RSDP).[30] The threat of war soon became the overriding issue on the political scene, and Gherea and Rakovsky were united in their opposition. This alienated them from the West European Social Democrats who supported their respective governments in the war effort. Instead the Romanian leaders drew closer to Lenin and Trotsky, who also denounced the war, and the influence of the Russian Social Democrats began to be felt in Romania. Eventually, once the Bolshevik Revolution took place and the war ended, issues of internal development—most specifically, the nature and timing of the Romanian revolution—began to take priority. It was on these questions that Gherea and Rakovsky could not agree.

The two men actually represented divergent tendencies in twentieth-century Marxism, and the Bolshevik Revolution drove them into different camps. The split resembled the Menshevik-Bolshevik division in Russian Social Democracy, with Gherea taking the Menshevik view that the "bourgeois order" had to be established before the "socialist order" could be attempted. He was quite suspicious of events in Russia from 1917 on, and not long before his death in 1920 he warned that a premature attempt at socialism might bring disaster.[31] His recommendations on agrarian policy were particularly controversial and influential; his most famous work, *Neoiobăgia* [Neo-Serfdom], argued against peasant violence and advocated the development of small-scale capitalism in the countryside. He died too soon for an open break to occur with Rakovsky, but his successors in the Romanian movement, including his son Alexandru Dobrogeanu-Gherea, would spend the two decades between the wars in struggles with the Comintern, and often with Rakovsky.[32] These disagreements formed the background to Ceauşescu's first years in the Party and taught him firsthand about the dangers of factionalism and foreign interference.

As early as July 1917 the rift in Romanian Marxism became public when the RSDP denounced Rakovsky's Committee in Odessa as "not in accord with the past and present policies of the Rumanian social democracy."[33] Nevertheless, Rakovsky continued to recruit Romanians to fight for the Bolsheviks and the rift began to widen. The Party was renamed the Romanian Socialist Party (RSP) in November 1918, and the formation of the Comintern in March 1919 aroused demands among the Romanian maximalists for affiliation and immediate revolution in Romania. The RSP leadership, hoping to avoid either joining or breaking off relations with the Comintern, drafted a moderate, compromise program in May 1919 and sent it to Moscow without requesting affiliation. But the growing hostility of other parties in the Comintern made any attempt at compromise impossible.

When the Romanian army crushed Bela Kun's communist revolution in Hungary during 1919, the Transylvanian Socialists did nothing despite orders from the Comintern to sabotage the Romanian war effort. Had they acted, the Socialists would have been considered traitors to Greater Romania, substantiating the suspicions of many Romanians and rendering themselves and their Party vulnerable to arrest and destruction. Instead, they gave priority to their own interests in Romania, drawing the wrath of some members of the Comintern, especially the Hungarian and Bulgarian parties whose nations had lost territory to Romania in the war. The Romanian elections of May 1919 intensified the hostility, for the Bucovinian and Transylvanian Socialists cooperated with the People's Party of General Alexandru Averescu, who had commanded the Romanian Army during the war.

A delegation of Romanian Socialists finally went to Moscow in November 1920 to negotiate affiliation with the Comintern. Severely criticized by their Comintern colleagues, they defended themselves by stressing the difficulties of working among a non-socialist and Western-oriented people indifferent to communism.[34] Despite the harsh words spoken on both sides, the delegates evidently returned to Romania having promised that their Party would soon affiliate with the Comintern, whose decisions would then be binding upon the Romanian Party. Meanwhile, the radical members of the RSP had continued their maximalist activities, including a general strike in October 1920 and the terrorist bombing of the Senate building in Bucharest in December that killed many people and further polarized the Party.

When the Romanian delegation returned from Moscow in January 1921, its members held a preliminary meeting to try to persuade Party members to accept Comintern affiliation. By this time there were three major groups within the Romanian Marxist movement: the minimalists, who wished to retain the 1919 program advocating legal evolution toward communism; the maximalists, influenced by Rakovsky and supportive of Bolshevik tactics; and the centrists, who favored affiliation with the Comintern "provided this did not overlook the 'specific' (i.e., national) interests of the Romanian movement and did not infringe its independence."[35] It was soon clear that the last was an untenable position. At the January meeting the maximalists won a plurality, and those opposed to Comintern affiliation decided to leave the Party if such affiliation were formally approved. A congress was then called for May, and the major item on the agenda was to be relations with the Comintern.

What is now celebrated as the First Congress of the RCP opened on 8 May 1921. Police raids and arrests ended the meeting early, on 12 May, but the decision had been made the day before to declare affiliation with the Comintern and change the name to Romanian Communist Party.[36] The resulting schism in Romanian Marxism had disastrous effects on Party organization and membership. It was not until the Second Congress in October 1922 that the leading positions of the RCP could all be filled and the various requirements for formal Comintern affiliation completed. Although current Romanian historiography portrays the RCP as the largest group to emerge from the congress, contemporary Comintern sources indicate that the RSP had over 45,000 members before the split, and the RCP had only about 2,000 members by 1922.[37] This time acceptance of Comintern orders had proved devastating to the communist movement in Romania.

Nevertheless, Comintern interference did not cease in 1921. It continued throughout the interwar years as the Moscow organization repeatedly insisted on policies that were in the interest of the Soviet Union but not Romania, thus provoking opposition within the RCP. The most divisive issues included the national question, political alliances with other political groups against the fascists, and Soviet friendship with Germany from 1939 to 1941.

On the national question, for example, the Fifth Congress of the Comintern in June and July 1924 passed a resolution that criticized the Versailles Treaty for creating "a number of small imperialist states . . . by the annexation of large territories with foreign populations." The Comintern then called for "the political separation of oppressed peoples from Poland, Rumania, Czechoslovakia, Yugoslavia, and Greece" and reproved "certain Communist parties" for "deviations" on this issue. Specifically, Bessarabia, Bucovina, and the Western Ukraine were to be united with the Soviet Union, and Transylvania and the Dobrogea taken from Romania and made independent entities.[38] It was in this context that the Third Congress of the RCP in September 1924 accepted the right of the ethnic minorities to secede from Greater Romania,[39] the disastrous nationality policy that made it almost impossible to recruit members among ethnic Romanians.

Later, during the early 1930s, Comintern directives precluded RCP cooperation with other anti-fascist parties and denounced any non-communist groups as fascist. Henry Roberts has summarized the disastrous results as follows:

> In retrospect this ultra-Left tactic of the early 1930s must be regarded as a disaster . . . The veering from Right to Left in the Comintern in the 1920s had brought no results but had merely caused the local parties to be regarded as altogether untrustworthy and treacherous political allies. . . . The Rumanian Communist party . . . by its irresponsible behavior . . . enabled the parties of the Right to use the Communist label as a means of discrediting all working class activity.[40]

The official line on this issue later shifted to allow cooperation with other groups throughout the 1930s, but even so the Party had attracted no significant support by 1940 when the Comintern dealt Romanian communism another blow: criticizing the RCP for anti-German activities and demanding that it retract its slogan "defense of the frontiers" as both anti-German and anti-Soviet.[41] The Romanian communists had opposed Hungary's seizure of Northern Transylvania under Hitler's Vienna *Diktat*, whereas the Comintern was defending the provisions of that *Diktat* (issued by their partner in the Nazi-Soviet Pact), and the Soviet Union's annexation of Bessarabia. Comintern support for Germany ended abruptly when Hitler invaded the USSR the following year, but its 1940 directives and their subsequent reversal were further proof to Romanians that the RCP was merely the agent of an enemy power bent on the dismemberment of Greater Romania. As Michael Shafir has observed: "In their endeavors to project Marxism as an ethnically and socially subversive doctrine, inter-war Romanian politicians found a reliable ally in the Comintern."[42]

Ceauşescu's criticism of the Comintern came early in his tenure. On the forty-fifth anniversary of the Party in 1966, he gave a major speech on Party history in which he blamed the interwar weakness of the RCP on the Comintern. He complained, for example, that Comintern officials often made demands that revealed their ignorance of the situation in Romania and that they appointed "people outside the country" to the RCP leadership, including the post of general secretary. The inclusion of such foreigners, he said, led to "erroneous theses and slogans" and caused serious "harm" to Romania's "revolutionary struggles."[43] Indeed, from 1924 to 1944 the RCP general secretaries were not ethnic Romanians.[44]

Ceauşescu singled out the national question for special criticism, rejecting the Comintern's description of Romania as "a typical multi-national state" and insisting that Marxism-Leninism gave different peoples the right to self-determination—not to encourage "the disintegration of established national states" but, on the contrary, to allow "the liberation of the oppressed peoples and their constitution into sovereign national states."[45] Ceauşescu showed himself a nationalist, determined that the Romanian people would be "liberated" in their own "sovereign national state." At the same time, he pointed out that the RCP eventually corrected its stand on the national question, and in 1938 and 1939 took "a firm stand . . . in defense of national unity . . . independence and sovereignty." Of course, Soviet policy also changed in those years, but Ceauşescu implied that the RCP, left to its own devices, had arrived at the correct decision. The conclusions for 1966 were obvious: Reject outside interference.

Ceauşescu also took the interwar RCP to task for its "sectarian attitude" in refusing to cooperate with other leftists against "the rising fascist organizations." He did not specify when that policy changed, but he placed considerable emphasis on the positive results in the mid-1930s, when the RCP did cooperate with other parties against the fascists and when he himself became politically active. By 1971 Party historians were claiming what Ceauşescu had only hinted at in his 1966 speech: The RCP had actually preceded the Comintern in cooperating with other leftist groups against the fascists.[46] Ceauşescu's final denunciation of the Comintern was as direct as his remarks on the national question: He rejected the Comintern directives of 1940 for creating "profound confusion and disorientation in the Party" with "grave repercussions" on all its activities.[47]

There is no reason to disagree with Ceauşescu's negative assessment of Comintern influence on the RCP in the interwar period. What Ceauşescu ignores are the other factors that kept the RCP weak during the interwar period: the lack of a social base, the internal factionalism (exacerbated no doubt by Comintern interference), and the perception of communism as inimical to Romania's national interests. Of course, Ceauşescu in 1966 was asserting his claim to autonomy by focusing blame on Moscow rather than on circumstances inside Romania. His (and Gheorghiu-Dej's) rejection of Soviet interference in Romanian affairs clearly had roots in the interwar period and was being supported by a new Party historiography of that period.

Despite its weakness, the Romanian Communist Party did manage to organize strikes during those years. The most famous, which acquired legendary status after World War II, was that of the Griviţa railroad workers in 1933 near Bucharest. The Grivița episode was significant not so much for its effect on domestic conditions but because it brought Gheorghe Gheorghiu-Dej, the future general secretary of the RCP and Ceaușescu's political mentor, to national prominence. Gheorghiu-Dej was one of those few Party members who were ethnic Romanians and who came from the tiny industrial proletariat. Born 8 November 1901 in Bîrlad, he was the son of a worker and, according to a 1948 biography,[48] became a shoemaker's apprentice at age eleven. He then worked in a timber mill in Dărmănești, a textile mill in Buhuși, and in coopers' shops in Piatra Neamț and Moinești. In 1920 he took part in a general strike in the Trotuș Valley before moving to Galați; he lost his first job there because he agitated for better working conditions, and he eventually became an electrician in a railroad yard. In short, Gheorghiu-Dej began to acquire his impeccable revolutionary credentials at an early age with his proletarian background, menial jobs, and active role in the class struggle of the Romanian workers.

In 1930 he joined the outlawed Communist Party and a year later left Galați for Dej, still as a railroad worker. As government employees, the railroad workers were not allowed to strike; hence, they were particularly disaffected. In 1932 they held a general meeting in Bucharest; Gheorghiu-Dej attended as representative from Dej and was also elected to the Central Action Committee. It was at this point in his career that he added "Dej" to his name. Arrested along with a number of other prominent labor organizers the night of 14 February 1933 when a government crackdown revoked earlier agreements with the workers, Gheorghiu-Dej was in prison during the most violent of the Grivița demonstrations.[49] Nevertheless, he was brought to trial, gained national publicity as one of the major instigators of the disorders, and received a twelve-year prison sentence.

During his long imprisonment (until summer 1944) Gheorghiu-Dej did not lose touch with the Party; he was elected to its Central Committee in 1935. In addition, he was imprisoned near Cîmpina in Doftana, a prison that, like the Grivița strike, would become famous in the postwar historiography of the RCP. The Romanian authorities in 1936 decided to put all the communists and leftists in Doftana together in order to control them more effectively, but the result was precisely the reverse: Doftana became "a higher Party school of education and toughening for Party cadres," from which the subsequent leaders of the RCP, including both Gheorghiu-Dej and Ceaușescu, graduated "with honor." A police report from September 1936 described the activity: "At Doftana the Communists, although isolated in their cells, carry on political work . . . hold daily conferences and . . . discuss subjects of communist agitation. . . . The prisoners are organized in a collective which includes all communist prisoners. . . . In addition, there is a communist cell . . . which leads the collective."[50]

The Doftana prisoners were allowed visitors and reading matter, and even forbidden material was successfully smuggled in to them. The authorities permitted the prisoners to set up a small handicraft shop to sell wood carvings and toys on the outside. The money, ostensibly used for extra food and other material needs, actually helped support the political activity. Even in Doftana's dreaded "H" section punishment cells, where prisoners were kept in total darkness and solitary confinement, it was possible to communicate from one cell to the next between inspection rounds. Various questions could be discussed or lectured on—Marxism, political economy, the Soviet revolution, a particular work of Lenin—passed from cell to cell, sentence by sentence. So Gheorghiu-Dej's time in prison was not wasted, and he could claim additional credentials as a revolutionary who had suffered imprisonment for his Party.

Nevertheless, prison is an ineffective place from which to lead a revolution, and Gheorghiu-Dej and his colleagues had little influence in Romanian politics during the interwar years. The Romanian Communist Party was a tiny group (the term "organization" is too strong to be appropriate), its activities banned by the government, and many of its leaders in jail. It was weakened by internal factions and struggles with the Comintern, which often forced its Romanian comrades to accept policies inimical to their country's interests. The RCP did not have an effective social base because the proletariat was minute and largely disorganized, the peasants were attracted to other political movements, and the support from the national minorities mitigated against support from ethnic Romanians. In addition, the Party was identified in the eyes of most Romanians with the interests of national enemies, internal and external, particularly the hated Russians who claimed Bessarabia. As a result, in the interwar period the Romanian Communist Party was never able to achieve that synthesis of nationalism and communism that would become characteristic of its policies and its historiography after 1960.

Ceauşescu's Early Life

Nicolae Ceauşescu was among that small group of ethnic Romanians attracted to the RCP before World War II. The essential outline of Ceauşescu's life is quite clear: Born in a peasant home, he went to Bucharest at age 11 to find work, joined the Romanian Communist Party as a teenager in the mid-1930s, spent many years in prison in Romania, and was released in 1944 as the Soviet army entered the country. Thereafter he worked as an organizer for the RCP and rose rapidly in its hierarchy, becoming a Central Committee secretary and candidate member of the Political Bureau in 1954. By 1955 he was a full member of the Political Bureau, and ten years later he succeeded Gheorghiu-Dej as Party leader. Unfortunately, detailed information on Ceauşescu's early years is quite limited. Several biographies have appeared since 1970, but they have been supported or commissioned in some way by the Romanian government and therefore reflect the image of Ceauşescu deliberately created during his rule.[51]

In Romania a mythology has sprung up around Ceauşescu with respect to the major events of his life and his own reactions to them. The content of the Ceauşescu mythology—indeed of any mythology—is not necessarily true of false. Myths may be fact or fiction. What is important about myths is that they are intended to convey certain lessons to those who are taught about them. In other words, they are intended to affect the behavior of believers.

Political myths are usually intended to render acceptable the rule of the individual whose actions are mythologized. Not only individuals but also political movements may have myths. The Griviţa strike and Doftana prison, for example, are part of the mythology of the Romanian Communist Party, justifying the rule of the RCP by the suffering and sacrifice of those who resisted the old regime. Although these particular episodes served to enhance the prestige of Gheorghiu-Dej as a participant in both experiences, it was the events that became myths, not his individual actions. By contrast, the Ceauşescu mythology focuses on him as an individual, and the mythology of great events becomes personalized.

We must be careful to distinguish between myth and memory as we examine Ceauşescu's life, and keep in mind that neither term necessarily denotes what did or did not occur. But the myths about Ceauşescu should be explored for, as Marcus Cunliffe has observed about George Washington: "The real man and his legend have important elements in common."[52] In addition, the myths about Ceauşescu and the image of him they create reveal the lessons that he and his colleagues wish to convey to potential supporters. Different aspects of the myth may appeal to different groups in the population and elicit varying responses. For example, Ceauşescu the revolutionary should appeal to Party members and elicit emulation, or Ceauşescu the royal president may appeal to Romanian peasants to evoke obedience. Indeed, the advantage of an image is its flexibility: its shape can change depending on the facet presented or the angle of view. If the mythmakers are successful, the supporters may include all citizens of Romania, whether members of the Party or not.

Nicolae Ceauşescu was born the third of ten children, on 26 January 1918, in Scorniceşti, a small village set in the low rolling hills of Olt County between the provincial capitals of Piteşti and Slatina. Photographs of his parents, Andruţa and Alexandra Ceauşescu, appeared in *Scînteia* from time to time in the early 1970s; these two elderly people revealed not only the features of the Romanian president—Nicolae was clearly their son—but also the dress, hunched stature, and weatherbeaten faces typical of poor Romanian peasants of their generation. Such distinctive traits could only have been acquired by decades of hard physical labor and economic scarcity. When the father died in 1971, the mother reportedly insisted on a church funeral. The atheist son might have been somewhat embarrassed by this devotion to religion, but the revolutionary son was proud of his peasant origins demonstrated so clearly by the traditional dress and appearance of his parents. Ceauşescu's impoverished and difficult childhood has become part of the Ceauşescu mythology: One lesson intended is that in Romania any individual, through hard work and devotion to the RCP, can rise from poverty and obscurity to become president.[53]

In 1970 a French biographer of Ceauşescu, Michel-Paul Hamelet, was shown the tiny house in which Ceauşescu was raised. He describes a typical peasant house, similar to others in the village and to thousands of homes throughout Romania, even to the enormous brick stove for heating and cooking and the embroidered hangings on the walls.[54] There is no reason to doubt the authenticity of the house or of Hamelet's description. Interviews granted to Hamelet at the time, however, seem less reliable. A number of villagers, including Nicolae's sister Elena, indicated that the Ceauşescu children hired out as agricultural laborers while school was not in session. One employer in particular remembered Nicolae for his "great spirit of organization." Hamelet was told that the young boy often went to school barefooted and never had money to buy books—he borrowed those of this friends and still was first in the class. One of his teachers described him as "an attentive, disciplined pupil, gifted with a very broad memory, brilliant in mathematics and, in addition, a very good comrade." His sister Elena recalled him as the child in the family who "endured the hardships with the best humor" and was "never violent" except in the cause of justice.

Although we must certainly view some of these statements with skepticism, they add another dimension to the Ceauşescu mythology, giving him admirable personal qualities such as intelligence, diligence, patience, endurance, and good humor, to name but a few. His later achievements leave no doubt as to his shrewdness or diligence, but we must look for better evidence of the other positive qualities before accepting these statements as memory rather than myth. In any case, the granting of the interviews and the subsequent publication of these biographical details inside Romania and abroad indicate that these aspects of the mythology are actively promoted by the Romanian Communist Party.

As late as 1975 Scorniceşti was simply a large village with traditional one-story homes strung out for several miles along a paved road. By 1982, however, it had become Ceauşescu's model town for his new Romania, with apartment buildings along the main street, several factories, half a dozen schools, and broad parks. Needless to say, there was also a small museum honoring the town's most famous son. In 1970 his sister Elena's husband, Vasile Barbulescu, was president of the Scorniceşti agricultural cooperative. His status, like that of the village, improved in subsequent years: In 1982 he became first secretary of Olt County, which by 1985 was praised repeatedly as a model of agricultural development for the rest of Romania. The inhabitants of Scornicești had prospered as Ceaușescu's glory spread from himself to his family and eventually to his place of birth.

The entire region of Oltenia was to share in the new mythology. The pre-Ceaușescu image of his native region in the minds of most Romanians was that of an agricultural backwater inhabited by ignorant peasants whose Oltenian accents immediately indicated to listeners that they were stupid, lazy, and illiterate. The open-air village museum in Bucharest reinforces this impression: Among dozens of elaborately decorated houses of wood, brick, and stone moved piece by piece to the site to illustrate the traditional architecture of the various regions of Romania, Oltenia is represented by huts that are simply mounds of earth—like mud caves, very practical to build and keep warm or cool but not very attractive or sophisticated. Because Ceaușescu's own pronunciation still retains traces of his Oltenian origin that bring scornful smiles to the faces of urban Romanian intellectuals, the Ceaușescu mythology is attempting to mold the Oltenian image into one more appropriate for the birthplace of a great leader. The region is now portrayed as the purest source of Romanian ethnicity—not only of Romania's heritage but also of human habitation. In 1976 Romanian scholars claimed to have found in Bugiulești, not far from Scornicești, remnants of "the earliest human presence on the continent of Europe" and, even more amazing, "one of the first decisive examples of anthropogenesis on the path to homo sapiens."[55]

Like his peasant and Oltenian origins, Ceaușescu's revolutionary activities have been mythologized. Undoubtedly an active communist in his teens, he spent long years in prison as a result. But the actual events of those years and his reactions to them are often impossible to distinguish from the myths that have developed. Ceaușescu's formal education stopped with elementary school and, like four of his six brothers, he left Scornicești for a city job.[56] In 1929 the eleven-year-old Nicolae went to Bucharest as a shoemaker's apprentice. The first definite report of his left-wing activities came in June 1933 when he represented the "democratic" youth of Bucharest at an anti-fascist conference and was elected to the national Anti-Fascist Committee, a front organization for the RCP. This was, of course, during that period when the Comintern forbade foreign communist parties to cooperate with other political groups, even against the fascists. At the meeting, Ceaușescu drew attention for his youth and "ardor" and spoke so quickly that his words were later described as a "turbulent, Carpathian torrent." Several future members of the Romanian Academy present remember wondering who the youth was who spoke so well.[57]

Ceaușescu's first political action may have focused on the issue of anti-fascism, but he was soon active in protesting the economic grievances of the workers. He was first arrested on 23 November 1933 for inciting a strike and distributing pamphlets against the order of the State. He was quickly released, but before the end of the year had joined both the Union of Communist

Youth (UCY) and the RCP. In June 1934 he was arrested again for collecting signatures protesting the Craiova trial of the Griviţa railroad workers, among whom, of course, was Gheorghiu-Dej. Whether or not Gheorghiu-Dej heard at the time of young Nicolae Ceauşescu we do not know. It is not likely, although he probably learned about the demonstration. But he surely knew later when and why Ceauşescu had been arrested, and it must have contributed to the eventual rapport between the older revolutionary and his younger protégé.

Ceauşescu was jailed for a third time in August 1934 and again in September when, according to Hamelet and records in the Party Museum in Bucharest, the phrase "dangerous communist agitator" was placed on his police file. Apparently he had been sent home to Scorniceşti several times before, but this time he was exiled from the city of Bucharest and required to live with his parents in the village, signing in each day at the local post office. He soon tired of the confinement, however, returned illegally to Bucharest, and went underground. During 1935 his parents were repeatedly harassed by the police and questioned about their son. He maintained indirect contact through his sister Nicolina and reportedly spent much of his time studying Marxism, history, and politics.[58] By 1936 he was a secretary of the Prahova Regional Committee of the UCY.

The police finally caught up with him early in that year; his arrest report described him as an "active distributor" of communist and anti-fascist propaganda, "long known" to police and judicial authorities. He was brought to trial with a group of "anti-fascists" in May 1936 at Braşov. The defendants evidently decided to turn the trial into a public protest against fascist influence in Romania. One of the accused, V. Tarnovski, became so vehement in his protests that the court excluded him from the trial. The official court record then explains that another of the accused, N. Ceauşescu, declared his support of Tarnovski and "incited the other defendants to follow his example, gesturing and offending the judges by his irreverent . . . attitude."[59] Ceauşescu was immediately given a six-month sentence for his interruption and excluded from the rest of the trial.

The event received wide publicity, and the defense attorney managed to obtain a press interview for Tarnovski and Ceauşescu. The journalist, Eugen Jebeleanu, later a prominent poet whose career under Ceauşescu certainly did not suffer from this early contact, described the two different personalities quite vividly.[60] Tarnovski smiled resignedly and spoke little. Whatever his ethnicity, his Slavic name would have reinforced most Romanian readers in their belief that these leftists were enemies of Greater Romania. Ceauşescu, in contrast, was undoubtedly an ethnic Romanian, and he "spoke clearly, a bit too fast, as if he wanted to get all his words out at once." Jebeleanu described him as small and dark, with sparkling eyes "like two peppercorns," and repeatedly emphasized his youth, his enthusiasm, and his courage. The reporter was quite impressed by Ceauşescu's appearance and personality and expressed hope that this "child" with a "young and generous heart" would receive a light sentence. On 6 June the judgment came: Ceaușescu received two years in prison, plus six months for contempt of court, a fine of 2,000 lei, and a year of forced residence with his parents. He was still only eighteen. The sentence was indeed light, the publicity and experience extremely valuable, and the Jebeleanu interview became part of the Ceaușescu mythology.

But Ceaușescu's revolutionary experience was just beginning. He was sent to Doftana prison, once known as the "Romanian Bastille" for the horrors inflicted on its inmates and later known as the "Marxist University" in the mythology of the Romanian revolution. Ceaușescu appeared there in 1936, just when the authorities placed the communists and other leftists together for more efficient control. Of course, as we have seen,[61] the result was not what the government had hoped: Gheorghiu-Dej, Chivu Stoica, Ceaușescu and others were concentrated in one place where they could communicate and organize much more effectively. Indeed, this group of Doftana "graduates" would form the nucleus of Gheorghiu-Dej's postwar supporters in his successful bid to gain control of the RCP. Ceaușescu's time in prison, therefore, was invaluable: He associated himself with Gheorghiu-Dej and the mythology of the Romanian communist movement.

He was released on 8 December 1938 and soon afterward became a secretary of the Central Committee (CC) of the UCY. His police file from those days bears the label "Person Dangerous to Public Order." In August 1939 the police reported that "the well-known communist, Nicolae Ceaușescu, member of the CC of the youth group," was spreading communist slogans at a meeting organized by the guild of Bucharest leather and footwear workers. Secret police records of the meeting reportedly show that "communist Lenuța Petrescu [the future Elena Ceaușescu], a worker of the 'Jacquard' factory," spoke to the workers demanding "bread" and "justice."[62] Thus his future wife joined the Ceaușescu mythology as a communist militant who shared with him the hardships of illegal political action. Nicolae and Elena did know each other before the war, but the exact nature of their relationship is not certain. It did not have much time to develop, for within a year Ceaușescu was once more in prison, this time until 1944. In September 1939 he was elected general secretary of the UCY and as a result was tried *in absentia* by a Bucharest court and sentenced to three years and 200 days in prison. He continued to work underground until July 1940, when he was finally caught and sent to Jilava, a prison near the capital.[63]

Ceaușescu thus entered Jilava shortly after the Soviet Union seized Bessarabia—not an event to endear members of the Romanian Communist Party to their jailors. However, later in the summer Hitler's Vienna *Diktat* gave Northern Transylvania back to Hungary, and in September King Carol abdicated, leaving Antonescu and the Iron Guard jointly ruling what remained of Greater Romania in the name of the young King Michael. The autumn of 1940 was marked by growing violence carried out by the Iron Guardists against a variety of individuals and groups perceived as enemies. During the night of 26–27 November they broke into Jilava and murdered a number of political prisoners. The communist prisoners should logically have been among the first to be killed and yet they, including Ceauşescu, survived.

The account of this massacre in Ceauşescu's official biographies credits Ceauşescu with saving himself and the other communists. According to this version, the young Nicolae had attempted a new strategy in Jilava from the very beginning of his imprisonment. At Doftana he had not been popular with the guards, who regarded him as "recalcitrant" and accused him of "subversive activity in the prison." In Jilava, however, he spent a great deal of time trying to win over the guards, mostly soldiers, to the communist cause by emphasizing the need for national resistance to the Vienna *Diktat*. Donald Catchlove puts it this way: "Ceauşescu, it might seem, was an incurable pollyanna, unable to resist the challenge of converting the unconvertible." But he apparently did manage to establish some rapport with the soldiers. The Iron Guardists who broke into the prison were able to kill 64 inmates, but when the murderers reached the communists' cells, the soldiers protected the prisoners. It is possible, of course, that the Guardists had exhausted their need for bloodshed and/or the soldiers organized themselves to resist just as the violence neared the communist prisoners. But the Ceauşescu mythology has it otherwise: "That night of blood and terror was . . . a tribute to the persuasion and perseverance of Nicolae Ceauşescu and the other communists in their talks with the military guards."[64] This version portrays Ceauşescu as he evidently likes to see himself: the *enfant terrible*, revolutionary but appealing in his sincerity and enthusiasm, and a skillful propagandist, persuading the soldiers that their true interests lay in supporting the communists rather than the Iron Guard. Indeed, the official story may be true; the Ceauşescu it describes is quite similar to Jebeleanu's impressions at the 1936 trial.

During the war Ceauşescu was interned in various prisons until, in August 1943, he was moved to the concentration camp at Tîrgu Jiu, where he would remain until the Soviet army entered the country. One of the largest in Romania, the camp was built in 1939 for Polish refugees, but in 1941 became an internment center for Romanian political prisoners. Almost six thousand people were kept in a series of long open dormitories, or barracks, each holding 250–300 internees. Only a small proportion of the camp's inmates were communists; most of the major political parties were well represented, and there were also a number of non-political scholars, writers, and artists. Ceauşescu was reportedly able to get into the same building with Gheorghiu-Dej, Chivu Stoica, and Ion Gheorghe Maurer, a lawyer who had defended communists and other leftists and who would become prominent as prime minister under both Gheorghiu-Dej and Ceauşescu. Maurer was released before the others and helped them to maintain contact with the underground movement outside the camp.[65]

At Tîrgu Jiu it was much easier to communicate inside the camp and with the outside world than it had been in the prisons. The guards did not maintain strict discipline—the war began to turn against Romania in early 1943 at the battle of Stalingrad—and the rules were relaxed in order to alleviate the economic hardship and labor shortages that prevailed throughout Romania. For example, work teams of prisoners were sent to do essential construction and repairs in the vicinity, and Ceauşescu reportedly became the leader of one such group specializing in electrical work. (Hamelet was told that there are still homes around Tîrgu Jiu where electricity was installed by Ceauşescu himself.[66]) At the same time that he was wiring homes, he was reportedly serving as a liaison between the RCP members in the camp and those in hiding outside. Thus Ceauşescu, though considerably younger than Gheorghiu-Dej and his other close associates, shared many of their experiences at Doftana and Tîrgu Jiu. He therefore became included in the mythology of their revolution before he began to establish his own myths.

Conclusion

Just twenty-six years old when the Soviet army entered Romania in 1944, Ceauşescu had established impeccable credentials as a communist and revolutionary. His early experience, both personal and political, was a blend of two very different environments: the Romanian political culture, with its frustrated desire for national unity, independence, and industrial development; and the revolutionary tradition of the Romanian Communist Party, with its ideological basis in Marxism-Leninism-Stalinism and its history of weakness, factionalism, and quarrels with the Comintern. Despite the differences between the dominant political culture and Romanian Marxism, these two environments did have several priorities in common, and it is not surprising that these became the fundamental features of Ceauşescu's rule.

One priority on which most interwar Romanian politicians, communist or non-communist, could agree was the need for industrialization, and Ceauşescu both as a Romanian and as a Marxist would come to define the future of his nation in terms of industrial growth. A second vital issue was nationalism; the national question was even more important than economic growth to many Romanians in the interwar years, and Comintern insistence on positions detrimental to Romanian unity was a major cause of RCP weakness. This issue, and other interference by the Comintern, divided the Party and helped to prevent it from playing a significant role in the political process. Ceauşescu learned at first hand the importance of the national question and the dangers of foreign interference, and he would give top priority to unity and independence throughout his rule. A third feature of

Ceaușescu's rule that emerged from both the Romanian and the RCP environments was his eventual failure to accept constitutional processes of discussion and compromise, or indeed any policy influence from the population, as we shall see. Unity—both national and Party—took precedence over democracy, in Ceaușescu's eyes, which had seen the quarrels of Romanian party politics and the weakness and factionalism of the RCP before World War II. Given his experiences, it was only to be expected that he would adopt the Leninist strategy of a highly centralized Party dominating the political system. During the first decade of his rule, Ceaușescu would manage to create a synthesis of Romanian Marxism and Romanian nationalism by giving priority to rapid industrialization and national independence—both to be achieved through his personal leadership of the RCP.

In her biography of East Germany's Walter Ulbricht, Carola Stern ended the chapter on his early life by discussing what Marxism meant to the young Ulbricht. Her conclusions could describe Ceaușescu as well:

> Ulbricht believes in Marxism, the kind of narrow-gauge Marxism he learned . . . while serving his apprenticeship. It is the only kind of Marxism he understands, and it constitutes his one genuine contact with culture . . . For the twenty-year-old Ulbricht, Marxism was the key to the world. It gave meaning to life . . . Ulbricht was an eager young man, but he lacked the basic tools for thinking . . . The uneducated youngster swallowed Marxist ideology whole . . . Here was a seemingly simple, convincing formula that enabled him to categorize and explain everything he learned, heard, and saw. Here was "truth" . . . Come what may, Ulbricht holds fast to his early beliefs: . . . the world still turns according to the same Marxist "laws" he studied fifty years ago. Small wonder that Ulbricht's enemies say he is pig-headed . . . The older he gets, the more obvious it becomes that to him [the goals of the Communist Party] . . . represent the highest ideals to which mankind can aspire. If necessary, he will try to ram them down the throats of dissenters.[67]

The young Ceaușescu was eager, but like Ulbricht he lacked the "basic tools for thinking." He found truth in the Romanian Communist Party fifty years ago and has yet to question his assumptions. Instead, he feels no compunction about imposing his views on others and, like Ulbricht, "ram[s] them down the throats of dissenters." Ceaușescu's writings reveal a narrow view of Marxism that he learned in Marxist revolutionary circles. Not an intellectual, not even educated through primary school, Ceaușescu understands the outlines of Marxism, its materialist laws, its simplification of the complex development of human history, rather than its subtle philosophical ponderings of human capacities and alienation. In his youth, he studied other communists' interpretations of the mature Marx and, most notably, the Stalinist doctrine of rapid and autarkic industrialization as it was being applied in the Soviet Union. This was to dominate Ceauşescu's understanding of post-revolutionary socialism.

Onto this he grafted Romania: building socialism in one nation. Emerging from the Romanian environment, he viewed the national community as primary and saw the flowering of communism in the context of individual nation-states. This has been a fundamental difference between Ceauşescu and the other Party leaders in Eastern Europe. The Romanian leader decided that Marxism had to be altered in the Romanian context, just as Lenin had adapted it to the Russian context, and Ceauşescu eagerly accepted that synthesis of Marxism and Romanian nationalism that separated him and his Party from the USSR in the eyes of most Romanians and created the possibility of popular support for a Marxist regime in his country.

Ceauşescu's early life reveals certain features of his personality that also would affect his later policy choices and political style. Like Lenin, Stalin, and Mao, Ceauşescu is a first-generation revolutionary. Therefore he has always been an activist, impatient with slow processes of development and eager to speed the course of history, by force if necessary, both before and after the revolution. Here again, the Romanian context influenced his choice of methods: disregard for institutionalized political procedures and reliance on personal and family ties in maintaining his power. Yet his speeches and policy choices over the years show that Ceauşescu initially stressed the efficacy of *agitprop* and other populist measures to move the people to implement his goals; like Mao, he emphasized voluntarism harnessed by the Party activist and bolstered by correct education for the masses. The 1970s, however, saw a change in his strategies of rule as power became more personalized and centralized around him.

Ceauşescu is unquestionably a self-made man who displayed tenacity and intelligence in overcoming the poverty of his childhood by hard work and enthusiasm. Yet he expects as much from everyone, demanding full commitment to revolutionary ethics—by which he means economic sacrifice for the common good, personal integrity, and a tightly knit nuclear family. Again, this is reminiscent of Ulbricht and his Ten Commandments of Socialist Morality proclaimed in 1958: For example," . . . Thou shalt strive to increase thine output, be economical, and uphold Socialist work discipline. Thou shalt lead a clean, decent life and respect thy family."[68] Yet even this "socialist morality" has pragmatic goals. Ceauşescu's stress on honesty, the work ethic, and protection of state property is directly connected to increased economic efficiency, and his strict attitude toward family life— condemnation of divorce, abortion, adultery—is part of an attempt to raise the birth rate. As a first-generation revolutionary, Ceauşescu is impatient to achieve rapid industrialization and demands heavy sacrifices from all citizens toward that goal.

Ceauşscu's lack of formal education helps to explain his mistrust of intellectuals and experts, which would become a crucial aspect of his rule. He has no understanding of the thought processes of scientists or artists and no patience with individuals who wish to devote themselves to pure research or personal creativity. As Stern put it in describing Ulbricht, his "terrifyingly simple world has no room for the individualist, the flabby-muscled, the hedonist, the Christian, the doubter, the bourgeois, the dreamer, or the artist."[69] Ceauşescu has repeated again and again that education and research must relate directly to the production process and that artists and writers should devote themselves to educating workers and peasants so that all contribute more effectively to the socialist development of Romania. As a materialist and pragmatist, Ceauşescu expects science and culture to serve the masses and all citizens to be instruments of society in the creation of socialism.

The dominant political culture of Romania has responded positively to some of Ceauşescu's priorities, such as economic growth and national independence. However, the speed with which he has tried to achieve his goals and the economic sacrifices demanded from the population have not been widely supported, and Romanian political culture has been unfriendly to the communist movement on a variety of issues. The interwar weakness of the RCP testifies to the hostility of the environment. The Party lacked a social base and failed to identify itself with the Romanian nation on the major issues mobilizing Romanians to political action between the wars: national unity and sovereignty. It is perhaps not surprising that Ceauşescu and the Romanian communist elite, in trying to bridge the gap between the RCP and the dominant political culture after 1970, turned what under Gheorghiu-Dej had been a series of myths about the Party and its past into a systematic cult of leader worship. The idol created was multifaceted: a peasant hero to appeal to the majority of Romanians who were born peasants; a revolutionary hero to appeal to the communist political elite; and a Romanian national hero to bridge the gap between the rulers and the ruled in contemporary Romania by identifying the RCP at long last with national unity and sovereignty in the person of Ceauşescu.

2

Apprenticeship:
The Gheorghiu-Dej Era, 1944-1965

After his release from the concentration camp at Tîrgu Jiu in August 1944, Ceauşescu began immediately to work for the Party. For the next two decades, his personal story would reflect the evolution of the RCP and the power of his mentor, Gheorghiu-Dej, from whom he would learn a number of important lessons on dealing with rivals both inside and outside the Party leadership. In this period of apprenticeship, Ceauşescu would gain experience in Party activity from bottom to top and learn to emulate the political maneuvering and policy decisions of his predecessor.

The RCP: 1944–1948

During the late 1940s, Ceauşescu and his colleagues were involved in three simultaneous struggles, each with life and death implications for those involved. First, the Romanian Communist Party was fighting to seize control of the country, a goal now made feasible by Soviet military occupation. To do this, the RCP needed to defeat its political rivals, the non-communist parties such as the Liberals and National Peasants, get rid of the king, and establish a monopoly over the political system. Second, there was a struggle within the RCP itself, as a number of individuals and factions including Gheorghiu-Dej and his friends positioned themselves for eventual control of the Party. The communist movement had always been torn by ideological, ethnic, social, and geographical differences, and the divisions were intensified by the war. Third was incipient conflict between Romanian and Soviet communists reminiscent of the Comintern battles of the 1920s and 1930s. Not always were the interests of the RCP identical with Moscow's guidelines, and the Romanian communists had to maintain Stalin's support while adjusting some of his policies to fit their own needs.

These three struggles would continue to characterize Romanian politics in subsequent decades and would always be interrelated because Moscow would try to impose its version of communist rule on Romania and would support certain individuals or groups within the RCP in order to assure Soviet influence. In the first years after the war, both the Romanian Communist Party as a movement and individual communist leaders survived by aligning themselves with Soviet interests. Not until the mid-1950s and later, when the RCP and Gheorghiu-Dej had won their separate battles for control of the country and the Party, were they in any position to challenge Soviet wishes directly. By then survival in Romanian politics had come to mean support for the ruling Romanian leader, not for someone in Moscow, but neither Gheorghiu-Dej nor Ceauşescu would ever forget the insecurity of those early years of RCP factionalism.

The Takeover

The first struggle to be resolved was the RCP's control of the political process. The timing of Romanian developments was similar to the rest of Eastern Europe where the Soviet army provided support for its political allies. The RCP took over somewhat more slowly than its counterparts in Poland and Bulgaria, for example, but slightly faster than in Czechoslovakia.[1] Yet the Romanian communists labored under a number of severe historical disadvantages, previously discussed, in attempting to seize power: little support during the interwar period, lack of a recruiting base, non-Romanian members and leaders, and ideological disagreements exacerbated by Comintern interference. World War II simply compounded these disadvantages.

In 1944 the Romanian communist leaders were separated not only ideologically and ethnically but also geographically. Some were in exile in the Soviet Union, most notably Ana Pauker and Vasile Luca; some, like Gheorghiu-Dej and Ceauşescu, were in prison in Romania; and still others, including Lucreţiu Pătrăşcanu, were in Romania, not in prison but in hiding underground or living in quasi-legality under the Antonescu regime. This geographical separation was characteristic of other East European communist parties during and after the war, but in Romania it was especially divisive, and it exacerbated existing rivalries. As a result, factionalism continued to plague the Party.

Just as debilitating was the perpetual hostility of Romanian nationalism. Unfortunately for the Romanian communists, their country was at war against Stalin, not Hitler. Romania was a German ally, fighting in the Ukraine and the Caucasus for Bessarabia and hoping that Hitler would force Hungary to return Northern Transylvania once Romania proved the more effective military partner. Romanian nationalism therefore tended to support the war effort, though not with any great enthusiasm as losses increased and Soviet troops approached the Romanian border. Minimal enthusiasm for the war, however, did not translate into resistance. In contrast to countries such as Yugoslavia, Czechoslovakia, or France, where the local communist parties added to their membership and prestige by playing a role in the anti-German resistance movements, in Romania those few communist leaders who retained their freedom did not organize extensive sabotage or guerrilla activity against the Germans to which they could point with pride after the war.[2] Consequently, the war and subsequent Soviet military occupation reinforced Romanian hostility toward Russians and communists alike. When the Soviet army entered Romania in the spring of 1944, the RCP had only about a thousand members.[3]

Despite these difficulties, Soviet support and occupation enabled the Romanian communists to gain control of the political system in less than four years.[4] Indeed, the very weakness of the Party compelled the rival leaders to cooperate until the non-communist politicians had been eliminated through arrests, exile, or intimidation. On 23 August 1944, now celebrated as a major national holiday in Romania, Marshal Antonescu was arrested and Romania withdrew from the war against the Soviet Union; two days later the new government declared war on Germany. Although King Michael, with the help of a number of non-communist politicians, actually arrested Antonescu, the RCP later insisted that it played the decisive role and eventually credited Gheorghiu-Dej with planning the action. Although some communists were in contact with the non-communist politicians in planning the arrest,[5] Gheorghiu-Dej was not directly involved, and Ceauşescu was not yet of the stature to play a role—otherwise, he would surely have let us know.

During the next year Soviet and Romanian troops fought together against Nazi Germany, and the Soviet army occupied all of Romania. A coalition government was formed that, through Soviet pressure and intimidation of non-communist politicians, gradually came to include mainly communists and their allies. In the spring of 1946 Antonescu was tried and executed, and that fall elections were organized to produce a victory for the communist front. The Liberal and National Peasant parties were dissolved in the summer of 1947, and in November their leaders were put on trial and given life sentences. In December 1947 King Michael was forced into exile, and the country became the Romanian People's Republic with a constitution modeled on that of the Soviet Union. Two months later a congress was held to unite the RCP with its rival party of the left, the Socialists. The new party was named the Romanian Workers' Party (RWP), and Gheorghiu-Dej was elected general secretary. Countrywide elections were held in March, and in April the newly established Grand National Assembly began to nationalize the economy. By mid-1948 the communists ruled Romania and could begin to implement their policies. Although covert hostility toward the ruling elite would never cease to be a problem in Romania, the struggle of the RCP against overt anti-communist political forces was largely over. In the years following 1948, it would be the conflict within the Party that would assume major importance as Gheorghiu-Dej proceeded to establish his control of the new organization.

The Leadership

That intra-Party struggle for dominance, however, had its roots in this earlier period. In fact, two events in 1944, before the Soviet army arrived in Bucharest, had a major impact on the subsequent evolution of the Party: a meeting in the Tîrgu Jiu prison infirmary in April and the arrest of Antonescu in August. These episodes were so significant that they eventually were used by the Party to demonstrate its right to rule Romania and the right of Gheorghiu-Dej to lead the Party. One of the functions of history in a communist state is to justify the right of the regime or individual leader to rule,[6] and historians are expected to turn important events out of the past into myths with lessons for contemporary behavior. Ceauşescu would learn the value of this technique from Gheorghiu-Dej, and would create his own version of Party historiography after 1965.

The version of the Tîrgu Jiu meeting generally accepted during the Gheorghiu-Dej era[7] asserts that on 4 April 1944 he and a number of colleagues, including Chivu Stoica and Emil Bodnaraş, met in the prison infirmary. Gheorghiu-Dej and his prisoner comrades demanded the removal of RCP General Secretary Ştefan Foriş, whom they considered a police informer. Those at the meeting evidently did dismiss Foriş as a traitor—electing a provisional secretariat of Emil Bodnaraş, Constantin Pârvulescu, and Iosif Rangheţ to replace him—and then they instructed Bodnaraş, Lucreţiu Pătrăşcanu, and Ion Gheorghe Maurer to negotiate with the other political parties, including the Liberals and National Peasants, in an effort to end the war against the USSR and initiate action against Germany.

Both decisions were important. Helping the other political parties to overthrow Antonescu later enhanced the RCP's bid for support inside Romania and, more immediately, forced Stalin to acknowledge the king's new government and the communists who were already in the country. The decision to remove Foriş also helped the local communists because it was made jointly by Party leaders both inside and outside prison and so tended to unify the various groups in Romania. Also, it gave them several months to strengthen their own influence in the Party organizations before the RCP leaders who had spent the war in the USSR could arrive in Romania.[8] Finally, although Gheorghiu-Dej was not elected to the Party leadership in April 1944, he evidently helped to initiate these important decisions, thus reinforcing his own leading role within the RCP.[9]

As years passed, the Romanian media gradually came to portray Gheorghiu-Dej as playing the key role in the Foriş decision. By 1964, the last year of Gheorghiu-Dej's life when Romania consolidated its resistance to economic integration in Comecon, the 1944 change in Party leadership had acquired anti-Soviet implications: Party historiography described Gheorghiu-Dej as a defender of Romanian interests for identifying the clique of traitors headed by Foriş and directing those outside the camp to remove them all from the Party.[10] Four years later, however, the official view changed: In April

1968 Ceauşescu denounced Gheorghiu-Dej for the "assassination" of Foriş, who was now deemed "innocent" of being an enemy agent.[11] In 1968, of course, Ceauşescu was using the criticism of Gheorghiu-Dej to weaken his own rivals such as Chivu Stoica and Bodnaraş, heroes of the Gheorghiu-Dej mythology, but this criticism also allowed Ceauşescu to dissociate himself from his predecessor and to install himself as the RCP's new hero.

Just as important as the Foriş episode in the mythology of Gheorghiu-Dej's revolution was the arrest of Antonescu on 23 August. Shifting interpretations of the event illustrate the changing priorities of RCP historiography over four decades.[12] During the immediate postwar years, 23 August—the date Romania joined the Soviet side—was used to emphasize Romania's new friendship with the Soviet Union. In 1945, for example, Soviet officers played a prominent part in the celebrations, and although *Scînteia* praised the RCP for its crucial role in encouraging and aiding the king to take action, Gheorghiu-Dej was not mentioned at all. In later years King Michael was forgotten, and Gheorghiu-Dej was given the primary credit in order to reinforce his claim to Party leadership against rivals such as Ana Pauker and Vasile Luca, who in August 1944 were still in the Soviet Union. By the 1948 celebrations *Scînteia* was still stressing the RCP-Soviet alliance, but also paying particular attention to Gheorghiu-Dej. During the rest of his rule, his personal role increased and that of the Soviet army faded away. Then, under Ceauşescu, both Gheorghiu-Dej and the Soviet army were ignored, and 23 August became a day of "social and national, anti-fascist and anti-imperialist liberation," in which the RCP led the Romanian nation to freedom.[13]

Gheorghiu-Dej needed to enhance his role in the events of 1944. Although he has been widely credited with being head of the Party after the removal of Foriş, it is only in retrospect that he led the RCP during this early period. Sources such as *Scînteia* indicate that Gheorghiu-Dej was merely one of several important individuals even before the return of Pauker and Luca. For example, although the first issue of *Scînteia* on 21 September 1944 contained photographs of two RCP leaders, Gheorghiu-Dej, and his close friend and supporter, Chivu Stoica, they were not featured; they were pictured on page three with a report of their election as honorary president and president, respectively, of a meeting of railroad workers. The next day, in contrast, Constantin Pârvulescu appeared prominently on the first page of the Party daily and was identified as general secretary of the RCP.[14] For the next few weeks, *Scînteia* gave Pârvulescu titular precedence in formal RCP documents, but two other ethnic Romanians, Gheorghiu-Dej and Lucreţiu Pătrăşcanu, received the most attention in its pages.

Pătrăşcanu, the major rival to Gheorghiu-Dej among those communists who had remained in Romania during the war, had a privileged background quite different from that of either Gheorghiu-Dej or Ceauşescu. Born in 1900 in Bacău, the son of a writer and professor, Pătrăşcanu graduated from the

Law Faculty of the University of Bucharest in 1922 with high honors and then studied political economy and philosophy at the University of Leipzig, where he completed a doctoral thesis on the 1921 agrarian reform in Romania. He went on to study in France, was one of five communists elected to the Romanian parliament in 1931 (the elections were invalidated so he never served), and represented the RCP at the Thirteenth Session of the Comintern Executive Committee in 1933. Pătrăşcanu published several important analyses of the Romanian political economy; during the interwar period he represented communist defendants in court and was arrested a number of times himself.[15]

Along with Maurer and Bodnaraş, he negotiated on behalf of the RCP with the anti-fascist parties from April until August 1944 and was the only communist included in the government immediately following the arrest of Antonescu. He served as minister without portfolio from 23 August to 4 November and then as minister of justice until early 1948. In these early postwar years, Pătrăşcanu was prominent enough to be considered the head of the RCP by such diverse observers as the British attaché in Bucharest and Princess Ileana, sister to Carol II.[16]

The public activities of Pătrăşcanu and Gheorghiu-Dej revealed their respective sources of strength within the communist movement. Pătrăşcanu, the educated intellectual and minister in the king's government, was given front-page publicity in *Scînteia* for his activities in the Council of Ministers, and he signed two rather scholarly articles on the economics of industrialization in Romania. Gheorghiu-Dej, the uneducated Party activist, was the featured speaker at a number of mass demonstrations of workers. Pătrăşcanu usually was pictured in a suit and tie, clean-shaven and rather neat in appearance. Gheorghiu-Dej looked a disreputable contrast: He varied his appearance, sometimes in work clothes, sometimes in a suit, but he managed to appear rumpled and ill at ease no matter how he was dressed. His "five o'clock shadow" often made him look unshaven and sinister in photographs.[17]

Nicolae Ceauşescu also appeared in *Scînteia* frequently during these early weeks. He was back to his prewar activity, writing articles and speaking at meetings of young people, urging them to support the RCP, and heading the newly legalized Union of Communist Youth. His first article appeared on 22 September 1944; titled "The United Front of Youth," it praised the young Romanians fighting beside the "liberating" Soviet army to free Northern Transylvania from the Hitlerites and the Hungarians. The battle, Ceauşescu pointed out, was only begun, for they would have to organize in the factories and educate Romanian young people to the class struggle. Meanwhile, it was urgent to support the alliance between Romania and the Soviet Union: "Only in this way will we earn the full friendship of the Soviet people and youth, a friendship which is so dear to us." These were the themes he repeated again and again during that first year.

Ceauşescu's appeals were always emotional rather than intellectual, unlike the restrained, rational, historical arguments of some of his more highly educated colleagues, such as Miron Constantinescu or even Alexandru Drǎghici.[18] On 14 October 1944, for example, he wrote about his own generation—the persecution and prison terms faced by young people who had fought for progress and social justice. The Iron Guard, he asserted, had tried to turn the Romanian younger generation against their parents, to make them enemies of culture, of science, of civilization. He, in turn, promised them a better life based on new norms of behavior. Education, including vocational schools, would be free and open to all regardless of nationality, sex, or social status; students would be able to take what courses they wished and would have better food and dormitory conditions. In addition, the vote would be extended to everyone at age 18, irrespective of sex or nationality.

Ceauşescu chose his issues and his rhetoric carefully. He created a vision of a better future, emphasizing education as the path to high status for young people and guaranteeing this right to them by access to political power, their vote. It was also during these early months that, according to accounts written after 1970, he was reunited with Elena Petrescu, "the young militant who had waited for him since those days so long ago . . . The prisons had separated them, but not divided them. They were married as soon as Nicolae Ceauşescu was free."[19] The pictures of Ceauşescu that sometimes appeared with his articles or speeches showed an exceedingly skinny and awkward individual; yet his prominence—he was clearly one of the most promising of the next generation of Party leaders—seemed to guarantee room at the top for young Romanians.

Meanwhile the top leadership of the RCP in these first weeks was composed of ethnic Romanians who had spent the war in Romania: Pǎtrǎşcanu, Gheorghiu-Dej, Pârvulescu, Chivu Stoica, and Gheorghe Apostol. The last two were prominent trade unionists who had been close colleagues of Gheorghiu-Dej before and during the years in Romanian prisons. Chivu Stoica, perhaps the closest longtime associate of Gheorghiu-Dej, was born in 1908 in Buzău; like Ceauşescu, he left a peasant home to find work in the city. He found a job in heavy industry (a Ploieşti metallurgical plant from 1926 to 1928) and then with the railroad, becoming involved in the Griviţa strike in 1933 as secretary of the strike committee. Indeed, Chivu Stoica took part in the violence while Gheorghiu-Dej was in jail. He was arrested, tried with Gheorghiu-Dej and the others, sentenced to a long term in Doftana, and so became part of RCP mythology.[20]

Gheorghe Apostol (born 1913) was trained at a trade school for railroad workers and followed his father in that calling. Apostol became involved in the communist movement during the 1930s and spent the years from 1936 to 1944 in prisons and internment camps inside Romania. He was with Gheorghiu-Dej, Chivu Stoica, and Ceauşescu in Tîrgu Jiu. These four men, along with Alexandru Drǎghici, would form the inner core of the

Gheorghiu-Dej group that would dominate the RWP leadership from the early 1950s until the death of Gheorghiu-Dej in 1965.[21]

In September 1944, therefore, Gheorghiu-Dej had a nucleus of supporters in Bucharest consisting of uneducated Romanian workers who had been Party activists before the war and who had spent many years in Romanian jails. His potential rival was Lucreţiu Pătrăşcanu, the intellectual whose revolutionary credentials were as impressive (for different reasons) as those of Gheorghiu-Dej himself.

Then, in early October, Ana Pauker and Vasile Luca returned to Bucharest from exile in the Soviet Union and began to participate in the RCP leadership. On 6 October *Scînteia* listed the Party leaders as Pârvulescu, Luca, Pauker, and Gheorghiu-Dej, in that order, although the arrangement of names varied during subsequent weeks and months. Pătrăşcanu also continued to play an important public role, becoming minister of justice in November when Gheorghiu-Dej joined the government as minister of communications. With a year, however, Pârvulescu and Pătrăşcanu were eclipsed by Pauker, Luca, and Gheorghiu-Dej.

A distinction is often made in analyses of the East European communist leaders between "home" communists (those who spent World War II in their own country) and "Soviet" communists (those who were in exile in the USSR during the war). The groupings can be significant, indicating as they do certain common experiences that may create unity among individuals. Two such groups were distinguishable in the RCP after World War II. But the power alignments within the Party often cut across that division, and personal relations more often cemented Party alliances than did background characteristics such as ethnicity, education, or exile.

Any categorization of the RCP would have to define Gheorghiu-Dej as a "home" communist and Pauker and Luca as "Soviets." Actually, neither Pauker nor Luca was "Soviet" in any sense except their place of residence during World War II. Their credentials as Romanian nationals were, however, almost as weak. Pauker (born 1893) was Jewish, from Iaşi, and Luca (born 1898) was a Hungarian from Transylvania.[22] Both were arrested and imprisoned a number of times in Romania in the 1920s and 1930s before ending up in the USSR, where they formed an "External Bureau" and during the war claimed the right to lead the RCP from exile.

Ana Pauker had special claims to prominence. She was first arrested for revolutionary activity in 1918, and in 1921 was a founding member of the RCP along with her husband, Marcel Pauker. He was executed by Stalin in the late 1930s, but Stalin's displeasure evidently did not extend to the wife who luckily was still in a Romanian jail. She went to the Soviet Union soon afterward in an exchange of prisoners and survived the war to return in triumph with Luca and the Soviet army. In Bucharest she was treated with the greatest of respect, and the worshipful coverage of her activities in *Scînteia* was surpassed in devotion only by the paper's treatment of Stalin himself. By November 1944 the Pauker–Luca–Gheorghiu-Dej triumvirate had emerged at the top of the RCP, but it was Pauker who spoke on the anniversary of the Bolshevik Revolution. She was praised under the headline: "Comrade Ana Pauker Shows Us the Way."[23] Both Ceauşescu and Emil Bodnaraş later declared that Gheorghiu-Dej was Party leader during the 1940s in name only: The real authority, they said, rested with Ana Pauker.[24] This may have been true, but Gheorghiu-Dej certainly appeared at the time to be almost her equal. It was he, for example, who went to Moscow in January 1945, bringing back promises of Soviet economic aid in return for Romanian military support for the "Glorious Red Army."[25]

Early in 1945 Bodnaraş began to play a more powerful role. Long regarded in the West as Stalin's major agent in Romania, Bodnaraş was a rather enigmatic figure who did not fit easily into any category in the Party leadership and whose role was by no means clear or predictable. He remained in the RCP inner circle throughout his life, making the transition with Gheorghiu-Dej to an autonomous foreign policy and continuing as a member of the Ceauşescu group until his death in 1976. Born in 1904 in Suceava, of Ukrainian and German parents, he graduated from a lyceum, took courses in law at the University of Iaşi, and completed Artillery Officers School in Timişoara. According to Romanian sources,[26] Bodnaraş revolted against the "regressive spirit" of the army and was condemned in 1932 to ten years in prison, where he met Gheorghiu-Dej and became a communist. According to most Western sources,[27] he defected to the USSR in 1932 with military documents, returned to Romania in 1933 on a secret mission, was caught and imprisoned, and then escaped to the Soviet Union, where he remained until 1942. It is probable that he did leave Romania for the USSR in 1932; but it is possible that he returned soon thereafter, and he may very well have spent a number of years in Romanian prisons as he claimed.[28] In any case, he certainly had close ties to the Soviets. He took part in the major events of 1944 as a member of the provisional RCP secretariat appointed in the prison infirmary in April, and he organized the paramilitary Guards of Patriotic Defense to support a communist takeover in Bucharest. It was to Bodnaraş and his troops that Antonescu was entrusted as prisoner in August, on the assumption that they would succumb neither to bribes nor to patriotic appeals for his release.[29] In March 1945, ten days after the Soviets had forced the king to accept Petru Groza, their nominee as prime minister, Bodnaraş was installed as general secretary in Groza's office.[30]

While Bodnaraş exercised power behind the scenes and Pătrăşcanu faded into the background, both Pauker and Gheorghiu-Dej actively competed for public prominence. The stalemate between them (with Luca a close third) was not resolved at the Party Conference of October 1945.[31] Although Pârvulescu was promoted to the titular post of president of the Central Control Commission, no new general secretary was publicly named by *Scînteia*. Instead, a Secretariat was established consisting of Gheorghiu-Dej,

Pauker, Teohari Georgescu,[32] and Luca; significantly, Pătrăşcanu was not included. Gheorghiu-Dej presented the Political Report to the Conference, but Pauker gave the report on the Party Statutes; presumably she was in charge of Party organizations and cadres. The new Political Bureau consisted of seven members (the four secretaries, Chivu Stoica, and two others); the Central Committee (CC) had twenty-seven full members (including Ceauşescu and Pătrăşcanu) and eight candidate members.

At this time, Ceauşescu was involved in local Party work in Ilfov County, but he soon went to Constanţa and by November 1946 was a regional secretary in his home area of Oltenia. As he later described his experiences, he was sent to areas devastated by war and famine;[33] and not withstanding his distance from the top-level rivalry in Bucharest, he must have been aware of what was happening to some extent. While he watched Gheorghiu-Dej from afar, Ceauşescu gained experience in political action at the grassroots level.

In these years before 1948, the RCP's focus was on consolidating Party power; the leaders thus maintained their unity, with Gheorghiu-Dej and Ana Pauker continuing to share precedence at the top. The two were usually named before everyone else, but with him first in alphabetical order. In 1945 Gheorghiu-Dej added public works to his ministerial responsibility for communications, and in 1946 he became minister of national economy, renamed industry and commerce the next year. Whatever his exact title, he remained in charge of the economy during this period; in that capacity he oversaw reparations payments to the USSR and visited Moscow several times, evidently availing himself of the opportunity to convince Stalin of his loyalty. Ana Pauker also went to Moscow a number of times, although apparently on Party business. She was reportedly responsible for recruitment of Party members during this period; though she was quite successful in the short run (the Party grew from about 1,000 members in 1944 to 800,000 by February 1948, see Table 2.1), a subsequent purge of "opportunists" provided her colleagues with a basis for complaints against her.[34]

One clear change did occur within the party leadership before 1948: the decline of Pătrăşcanu. Although he remained minister of justice, Pătrăşcanu simply did not receive the coverage or the homage given to the others, and in early 1948 he just disappeared. Later it was revealed that he had been arrested, and he eventually became the only top figure in the RWP to be executed (in 1954) on the orders of his colleagues. Meanwhile, in November 1947 Pauker became minister of foreign affairs and Luca minister of finance, and in December Bodnaraş was named minister of national defense. That same month the king was finally forced by Soviet pressure to leave the country, which cleared the way for a People's Republic. At last the communist leaders could focus on internal rivalries rather than on threats external to the Party, and Pătrăşcanu became the first victim.

In January 1948 preparations were intensified for a congress to unite the

Table 2.1 Romanian Communist Party Membership

Date	Total Membership	Workers (%)	Peasants (%)	Intellectuals (%)
October 1945	256,863	54	32	
November 1946	675,000	46		
1947	714,000			
February 1948	800,000	42		
Post-Feburary 1948	1,060,000	39		
July 1950	720,000	37	(300,000 expelled by now)	
1955	595,393	42	41	12
June 1960	834,600	51	22	11
Late 1961	900,000	52	22	
April 1962	919,873			
December 1964	1,377,847	44	33	9
July 1965	1,450,000	44	34	10
December 1965	1,518,000	40	32	22
May 1967	1,676,000	41	30	
December 1967	1,730,000	42	30	
March 1968	1,761,000	42	28	23
March 1969	1,860,000			
August 1969	1,924,500	43	28	23
March 1970	1,999,720	43	26	
December 1970	2,089,085	44	25	
June 1972	2,230,000	46	24	23
March 1973	2,300,000			
December 1973	2,386,819	40	28[a]	27
November 1974	2,480,000	48	22	21
December 1974	2,500,000	50	20	22
December 1976	2,655,000	83.5[b]		16.5
September 1977	2,700,000	51	19	22
December 1977	2,747,110			
December 1978	2,842,064	53	24	8
November 1979	2,930,000	54	18	29
December 1980	3,044,336	55		
December 1981	3,150,812	55	20	21
December 1982	3,262,125	56	16	21
December 1983	3,370,343	56	16	21
November 1984	3,400,000	56	16	21
December 1984	3,465,069	56	16	21
December 1985	3,557,205	61	15	20
December 1986	3,639,344	55	16	21
December 1987	3,709,735	55	15.5	20.5

Sources: 1945: Museum of the History of the RCP, Bucharest; 1946–1948, 1961, and the expulsions by 1950; Ceaușescu, Scînteia, 13 December 1961; 1950: Fischer-Galați, Romania, p. 76; 1955 and 1960: Gheorghiu-Dej, Articles and Speeches, p. 66; 1962– 1964: Scînteia, 17 April 1965; 1965: Congresul al IX-lea, pp. 71–72, and Scînteia, 14 April 1966; May 1967, and March–December 1970: Rolul conducator al Partidului, p. 338; 1972; Conferința naționalăal PCR, 19–21 iulie 1972, p. 59; November 1974: Congresul al XI-lea, p. 69; November 1979: Congresul al XII-lea, pp. 59–60. Remaining data are from Scînteia of the following dates: 7 December 1967, 25 April 1968, 12 March 1969, 7 August 1969; 3 April 1974, 25 July 1975, 7 April 1977, 24 September 1977, 24 March 1978, 30 March 1979, 28 March 1981, 1–2 April 1982, 31 March 1983, 20 November 1984, 3 April 1985, 8–9 April 1986, 28 March 1987, 1–2 April 1988.
Note: Blanks indicate that data was not available for those years.
[a]Those occupied in agriculture.
[b]Workers and peasants.

RCP and the Social Democrats.[35] The congress was to open on 22 February, and a top-level Romanian delegation led by Groza, Gheorghiu-Dej, and Pauker left for the USSR on the fourth. While in Moscow, they signed a Treaty of Friendship, Collaboration, and Mutual Assistance and attended a dinner given in their honor by Stalin. Then, on 11 February, the front page of *Scînteia* revealed significant differences between the placement of the Romanian leaders in Moscow for the departure photograph and the precedence given them in the photo caption added in Bucharest. The photograph clearly showed four individuals in the front row: from left to right, Groza, Molotov, Gheorghiu-Dej, and Vishinsky. Pauker and Luca were standing in the second row, visible behind and between the others. Because of their positions (Pauker was on the far left) the *Scînteia* caption listed her first, then Groza, Luca, Molotov, Gheorghiu-Dej, and the rest. The Soviets had controlled the physical placement shown in the photograph, and they identified Gheorghiu-Dej as head of the RCP and put him second only to Prime Minister Groza in the Romanian delegation. In contrast, *Scînteia* gave precedence to Pauker and Luca. Stalin seemed to have given his blessing to Gheorghiu-Dej but there was resistance—or at least confusion—in Bucharest.

Gheorghiu-Dej's new stature became clearer at the congress, where he was elected general secretary of the new Romanian Workers' Party[36] and presented the General Political Report.[37] Ana Pauker also was featured—she gave the closing speech—and she and Luca were elected to the Secretariat and Political Bureau. Pătrăşcanu, however, was criticized during the sessions and was not elected to any of the Party bodies. His picture had appeared in *Scînteia* as recently as 12 February, when he greeted the delegates returning from Moscow, and he had been making speeches and writing articles in connection with judicial reforms. Not until June did a Central Committee plenum publicly denounce him for advocating cooperation with the bourgeoisie and the entire peasantry and for underemphasizing the role of the proletariat in Romania;[38] the implication was that he had urged slower methods of collectivizing agriculture and imposing the Soviet model on the economy, a "right-wing" deviation reminiscent of the criticisms then being leveled against Tito by the Soviet Central Committee. All the other top RCP leaders were elected to the Grand National Assembly in the elections that followed the Congress, and they kept the same ministerial positions in the new government.

Ceauşescu was elected a candidate member of the new RWP Central Committee, a demotion from 1945, but then this group had to make room for the Socialists as well. By now he was no longer head of the Union of Communist Youth but a local Party official; as such, he was elected to the Grand National Assembly in March, this time from the number-two seat in Olt County. The former juvenile delinquent and revolutionary had come home in triumph.

By mid-1948 the Romanian communist movement, Gheorghiu-Dej, and

Ceaușescu all had enhanced their positions significantly. The Party had established its control over the political process, and Gheorghiu-Dej had made himself first—though not yet dominant—among his colleagues in the Party leadership and had removed Pătrășcanu. Ceaușescu had become nationally known as a young communist and was learning from Gheorghiu-Dej the elements not only of local Party work but also of intra-Party struggle. In the next decade the younger man would watch his mentor consolidate his control over the Party, eject his remaining rivals, and then create a new leadership group around himself—a group in which Ceaușescu would play a crucial role.

Gheorghiu-Dej Takes Control: 1948–1955

The two years following the First Congress of the Romanian Workers' Party were eventful ones for Romania. In 1948 the economy—including industry, banking, insurance, mining, and transport—was nationalized, the State Planning Commission and the first national plan were instituted, the judiciary and the security forces were reorganized, and Marxism became the accepted philosophy in higher education. In March 1949 the Party Central Committee announced its intent to create a "socialist" agriculture, and by July the first "agricultural production cooperatives" had been set up.[39] These economic changes were accompanied by a political "verification" within the Party to eliminate members who had joined for inappropriate reasons. The Political Bureau announced the measures on 21 November 1948, and by July 1950 about "300,000 foreign elements, careerists, [and] Iron Guardists" had been expelled.[40]

Then, in September 1950, a territorial reorganization of the entire country began. About 40 counties (*judeţe*) were combined to form 28 regions, and a new tier of administrative units—districts (177) or towns (148)—was created at an intermediate level between the regions and the 4,052 localities (*comune*). At the time this seemed evidence of Sovietization: adopting the same three-level system in Romania that existed in the USSR. But the reform also had important implications in the struggle for control of the RWP. Ana Pauker's influence over Party membership and cadre appointments had been weakened by the "verification," and Gheorghiu-Dej now could use the restructuring to place his supporters in positions of authority. Ceaușescu learned this lesson well: The example of 1950, and his experience in 1960 when Gheorghiu-Dej put him in charge of a minor territorial reorganization, provided Ceaușescu with a pattern for his own territorial reform of the entire country.[41] In 1968 he reintroduced the old *judeţ* system, and the resulting turnover in personnel proved crucial to his consolidation of power.

By 1952 Gheorghiu-Dej was strong enough to remove his major rivals, and the methods he used provided Ceauşescu with another example of political skill that the younger man would copy in 1965–1968. A CC plenum held 29 February–1 March 1952 criticized Vasile Luca for mistakes and fraud in applying the recent currency reform, and on 9 March 1952 *Scînteia* announced that Luca was being removed as minister of finance. (He remained a vice-president of the Council of Ministers, however, and kept his posts in the Party Political Bureau and Secretariat.) Other changes followed at the ministerial level and just below. On 28 May *Scînteia* announced that Luca and Teohari Georgescu were no longer vice-presidents of the Council of Ministers and that Alexandru Drăghici had replaced Georgescu as minister of the interior, a position the latter had held since November 1944. The next day a new Party leadership list was published that did not include Pauker, Luca, or Georgescu. Half a dozen other ministerial changes were reported in the next few days, but Pauker remained minister of foreign affairs until early July and vice-president of the Council of Ministers until September. Unlike Luca, who was brought to trial and had his death sentence commuted to life imprisonment, she simply lived in retirement in Bucharest until her death in 1960.[42]

During these maneuvers Ceauşescu appeared from time to time in his role as deputy minister of the armed forces, but he played no public role in the intra-Party struggle. His propaganda work with the UCY and his several years of local Party work must have been effective, because Gheorghiu-Dej had begun to use him in particularly difficult assignments. When the campaign to collectivize agriculture was announced in March 1949, Ceauşescu was sent to the Ministry of Agriculture as a deputy minister. A year later he moved on to the same position in the Ministry of Armed Forces. Bodnaraş, who became minister of national defense in December 1947, had brought in a number of new deputy ministers and begun to reorganize the army according to Soviet patterns. But he made extensive use of career officers in the first two years, and it was not until March 1950 that Party loyalists such as Ceauşescu occupied all the deputy minister posts.[43]

When Gheorghiu-Dej ousted his major rivals in May 1952, he promoted Ceauşescu to full membership in the Central Committee and also to the Party Orgburo. This body (when elected, Ceauşescu was its eleventh member) had been created in 1950 to deal with Party organizations and discipline, but it was abolished in August 1953 after the ouster of the Pauker-Luca group.[44] In the post-1965 succession struggle, Ceauşescu would make repeated use of this Gheorghiu-Dej technique: Both leaders created and abolished top Party organs to strengthen themselves and weaken their rivals.

While with the Ministry of Armed Forces, the young Ceauşescu appeared on a number of occasions in connection with his military duties. Because contacts between the Soviet and Romanian armed forces were extensive, his public appearances often involved Soviet holidays or military delegations from the other socialist states. His speeches emphasized loyalty to Stalin, the Soviet Union, and the Soviet army, as well as the need to defend the independence of Romania against (usually) U.S. imperialism. He also denounced Pauker, Luca, and Georgescu, first as right deviationists, and then as counterrevolutionaries, in accordance with the evolving Party line.[45] In March 1953 Ceauşescu went to Stalin's funeral with Gheorghiu-Dej and half a dozen other RWP leaders; a year later he would become a member of the top Party leadership, an indirect beneficiary of the demands for change emanating from Stalin's successors in Moscow.

As long as Stalin was alive, there was no possibility of conflict between Bucharest and Moscow; survival in Bucharest depended on total loyalty to Stalin and his policies. However, Stalin's death brought collective leadership to the Soviet Union and produced uncertainty throughout the communist world about the future. Gheorghiu-Dej, in control of the Romanian political process and dominant within the Party, now faced a new problem: potential disagreement between himself and the new Soviet leaders over the future of Romania.

Gheorghiu-Dej proved to be more successful than some other East European leaders at minimizing the effects of the Soviet political succession. At first he continued with Stalinist trials of "spies" and "terrorists,"[46] and he allowed no changes in the Romanian party leadership until April 1954. Then, as Soviet pressure to introduce collective leadership in Romania intensified, Gheorghiu-Dej took one final step to ensure his continued personal control of the Party: He had Lucreţiu Pătrăşcanu tried secretly between 6 and 13 April 1954 as a spy and counterrevolutionary. A death sentence, pronounced on 14 April, was implemented on the night of 16–17 April, more than six years after Pătrăşcanu's original arrest.[47] The execution eliminated a potential focal point for opposition to Gheorghiu-Dej, and on 19 April the Romanian leader complied with Soviet demands to separate the top positions in Party and state. Scînteia reported the decision the next day: In order "to strengthen the collective leadership of the Party and state," the Secretariat would henceforth consist of four secretaries (including a first secretary) who would not hold state positions. Gheorghiu-Dej resigned as general secretary, but remained president of the Council of Ministers, and his longtime friend and colleague, Gheorghe Apostol, was elected first secretary of the RWP. The other three secretaries were new—Nicolae Ceauşescu, Mihai Dalea, and János Fazekas— and Ceauşescu and Drăghici were made candidate members of the Political Bureau.[48] Thus Ceauşescu joined the Party leadership after Pătrăşcanu's execution and could later proclaim his innocence in the entire affair.

Other East European countries also separated the top positions in Party and state in compliance with the demands of the post-Stalin Soviet leadership. In Hungary and Poland the division weakened the Stalinist leaders, Mátyás Rákosi and Bolesław Bierut. In Budapest, the Party split between Rákosi and Imre Nagy, resulting in Soviet military intervention in 1956 and the success of another contender for power, János Kádár. In Warsaw, Bierut's death complicated the intra-Party power struggle, which was won eventually by Władysław Gomułka; Khrushchev, presented with a *fait accompli*, was persuaded that Gomułka was acceptable, and Poland managed to avoid a military confrontation. Both Kádár and Gomułka, like Pătrăşcanu, had been arrested and imprisoned during the Stalinist trials of the late 1940s, and Nagy also had been removed in disgrace during that period. In Romania, however, Gheorghiu-Dej was able to prevent any post-Stalin split in the Party by executing Pătrăşcanu: After his death, there were no prominent non-Stalinist alternatives like Nagy, Kádár, or Gomułka. The ousted leaders who remained alive—Pauker, Luca, Georgescu—were perceived to have been as close or closer to Stalin than Gheorghiu-Dej himself.

Except for the separation of the top positions in Party and state, there were few signs of post-Stalinist restructuring in Romania. Gheorghiu-Dej avoided personnel changes by asserting that his Party had already purged itself of its Stalinists when Pauker and Luca were ousted in 1952. The Party did introduce some changes in economic priorities, such as a reduction in the high rate of investment and greater emphasis on agriculture and consumer goods. However, these shifts should probably not be attributed to demands from Moscow but rather to the Romanian regime's insecurity and need to pacify the Romanian population in a time of uncertainty. There were certainly no attempts to decentralize the economy or to enact major reforms.

Nevertheless, in the three years following Stalin's death Gheorghiu-Dej did preside over a series of other developments that would become important in retrospect. For example, the Soviet Union dissolved the Soviet-Romanian joint-stock companies in the summer of 1954 by selling all its shares to the Romanian government. These companies had been set up during the 1940s in such fields as oil production, natural gas, transport, chemicals, coal, construction, insurance, and banking. At the beginning of 1954 the Romanian economy was more closely tied to the USSR than that of any other state in Eastern Europe[49]; after that year, however, only the petroleum and uranium companies remained jointly owned, and even these were sold in 1955 and 1956. In fact, because there was no decentralization in the Romanian economy, no permanent relaxation in cultural affairs, and no significant change in political leadership, Stalin's death seemed to have more influence on Romanian-Soviet relations than on internal Romanian developments.

The Second Congress of the Romanian Workers' Party[50] in December 1955 demonstrated that Gheorghiu-Dej was in firm control of the political system. Just two months earlier he had taken back the post of first secretary and turned the Council of Ministers over to Chivu Stoica; this allowed Gheorghiu-Dej to oversee the congress and to give the major report of the Central Committee. The personnel changes at the congress made it clear that he already had consolidated his control several years earlier. The 1955 Political Bureau, for example, although considerably different from that chosen by the First Congress in 1948, contained the same nine individuals elected in May 1952 when Pauker and Luca were removed: Gheorghe Gheorghiu-Dej, Gheorghe Apostol, Emil Bodnaraş, Petre Borilă, Iosif Chişinevschi, Chivu Stoica, Miron Constantinescu, Alexandru Moghioroş, and Constantin Pârvulescu. Only Nicolae Ceauşescu and Alexandru Drăghici were added, and even they had been candidate members since April 1954. The other top Party body, the CC Secretariat, saw some continuity in 1955 as Ceauşescu and Fazekas remained secretaries, but turnover here was greater. Because Apostol and Mihai Dalea moved to other posts and Gheorghiu-Dej and Chişinevschi returned, no one had served continuously in the Secretariat since 1952. Changes in this body, however, often involved new responsibilities, rather than promotions or demotions, because individuals could simply move back and forth from Party to state. As it turned out, those officials who had reached the top Party leadership during or after May 1952 kept their high status at the Second Congress, though not necessarily the same job. Ceauşescu's personnel strategies would often follow a similar pattern.

The dominance of Gheorghiu-Dej that produced continuity at the top of the RWP in December 1955 simultaneously brought change to the Party as a whole and also to its Central Committee. The entire RWP was much smaller than it had been at the First Congress. The verification process had reduced its size considerably in 1949 and 1950, but the numbers had continued to drop until by the Second Congress membership was only 56 percent of the 1948 figure, and the Party had reached a post-1946 low (see Table 2.1). Consequently, Gheorghiu-Dej could begin to reshape the organization; at the 1955 congress he called for more members, and by 1960 the total size had increased 40 percent (see Table 2.2).

Party growth in Romania has been most rapid during a bid for popular support such as occurred in the mid-1940s when the communists were desperately recruiting anyone who would join, or during the Comecon dispute in 1962–1965 when the RWP was appealing for internal support to establish its autonomy from the USSR in economic policy. In addition, new leaders have encouraged Party membership when they found it useful to add members of their own choosing to strengthen their personal positions. Gheorghiu-Dej did this in 1955–1960 and Ceauşescu in 1965–1969, and these two periods reveal secondary peaks in annual growth (see Table 2.2).

Not only the general (or first) secretary but also some of his colleagues or subordinates have made use of recruitment into the Party for personal strength. Ana Pauker evidently had been in charge of cadre policy during the earliest period of growth, but she was not able to use this to her permanent advantage. Those individuals whom she had accepted or promoted were removed or her influence over them neutralized by the verification campaign. In light of events after 1965, we should not be surprised to discover that the

Table 2.2 Percentage Increases in RCP Membership, 1955–1987

Time Period	Total Increase	Average Annual Increase
December 1955–June 1960	40	8.8
June 1960–April 1962	10	5.0
April 1962–December 1964	50	20.0
December 1964–December 1965	10	10.0
July 1965–August 1969	33	8.2
August 1969–November 1974	29	5.5
November 1974–November 1979	18	3.6
November 1979–November 1984	16	3.2
December 1984–December 1987	7	2.3

Sources: Computed from data in Table 2.1.

growth in Party membership that began in 1955 was overseen by Nicolae Ceauşescu. At the Second Congress, it was he who presented the report on changes in the Party statutes, presumably as the CC secretary for organizations and cadres. He spent much of his speech discussing the need to increase the size of the Party, but insisted that only those who would be politically and morally reliable could be accepted as members.[51] Certainly his control over Party appointments for much of the next decade gave him a powerful base for his claim to the top position after the death of Gheorghiu-Dej.

The pattern of Central Committee growth is somewhat different from that of Party size. At the CC level the needs of the first secretary and his personal bid for power within the Party are primary, not secondary. This becomes clear if we examine Central Committee size and turnover at the Second Congress. CC membership jumped from 56 to 96, an increase of 71 percent (see Table 2.3); presumably Gheorghiu-Dej used the congress to add his supporters. Ceauşescu again learned from his mentor: The only Congress to surpass the Second in the proportional increase in CC membership was Ceauşescu's first congress in 1965, when the new CC was 78 percent larger than its predecessor elected in 1960.

Membership turnover in the Central Committee also reflects the personal priorities of the Party leader. The CC contains the political and economic elite of Romania, and it has tended to be a rather stable body. In view of the many changes between 1948 and 1955, however, it was only to be expected that the Second Congress would re-elect the lowest proportion of CC members (61 percent) of any party congress until Ceauşescu's circulation of elites began to affect that body in 1979. The turnover between 1948 and 1955, combined with the large increase in size, produced a new CC in which 64 percent of the members were not re-elected from 1948. This was by far the highest share of new members of any Central Committee, even including the late Ceauşescu period (see Table 2.4). Examining the retention of full

Table 2.3 Changes in RCP and Central Committee Size at Party Congresses, 1948–1984

| | | Central Committee | | | | | Party | |
	Full Members	Change From Last Congress (%)	Candidate Members	Change From Last Congress (%)	Total	Change From Last Congress (%)	Change From Last Congress Total	(%)
1948	41		15		56		1,060,000	
1955	61	+49	35	+133	96	+71	595,393	−44
1960	79	+30	31	+11	110	+15	834,600	+40
1965	121	+53	75	+142	196	+78	1,450,000	+74
1969	165	+36	120	+60	285	+45	1,924,500	+33
1974	205	+24	156	+30	361	+27	2,500,000	+30
1979	245	+20	163	+4	408	+13	2,920,000	+17
1984	265	+8	181	+11	446	+9	3,400,000	+16

Sources: Scînteia, 24 February 1948, 29 December 1955, 26 June 1960; Congresul al IX-lea, pp. 735–738; Congresul al X-lea, pp. 751–755; Congresul al XI-lea, pp. 834–839; Congresul al XII-lea, pp. 892–898; Scînteia, 23 November 1984.

Table 2.4 Percentage Turnover of the Central Committee at Each Party Congress, Full and Candidate Members

| | Previous Central Committee | | New Central Committee | |
	Re-elected	Not Re-elected	Re-elected From Previous Term	Newly Elected
1955	61	39	36	64
1960	73	25	65	35
1965	84	16	48	52
1969	68	31	48	52
1974	65	30	55	45
1979	52	44	46	54
1984	52	46	47	53

Sources: Same as Table 2.3.

Note: Individuals who lost membership by election to the Central Revisory Commission were not dropped, but were not continuing members; hence they were not counted here, and the percentages for the previous Central Committees do not always total 100.

members separately from that of candidate members clarifies the situation further: While the percentage of full members re-elected was the lowest of the post-1948 era (see Table 2.5), the percentage of candidate members retained or promoted to full membership was higher in 1955 than at any other congress (see Table 2.6). These figures of course reflect the expulsions of the late 1940s and early 1950s and the elimination of Gheorghiu-Dej's opponents. But it seems that Gheorghiu-Dej had had a considerable number of supporters among the candidate members of the CC as early as 1948, and they remained in 1955 to form the core of his new Party.[52]

At the Third Party Congress in 1960, the Central Committee would grow by only 15 percent; almost three quarters of the 1955 members would be re-elected, and only 35 percent of the 1960 CC would be new. The continuity at the level of general secretary thus would carry over to the Central Committee. The stability in 1960 might have been predicted at the end of 1955, when Gheorghiu-Dej's power in Romania seemed unassailable. In February 1956, however, barely two months after the Second Congress, the foundations of Gheorghiu-Dej's control were shaken, once again by a threat emanating from Moscow. The events of 1956 were disquieting enough even in Romania to have a major long-term impact on the Romanian Party leader and his policies.

Interlude: 1956–1958

Khrushchev's denunciation of Stalin at the Soviet Twentieth Party Congress in February 1956 produced instability throughout Eastern Europe, most notably in Poland and Hungary. The speech also created divisions within the RWP, but only in 1957 and again in 1961 and 1968 did the extent of those disagreements become public. The de-Stalinization initiated in Moscow must have reinforced the growing resentment of Gheorghiu-Dej and his close supporters at Soviet interference. Simultaneously, as was later learned, it encouraged those in the RWP who favored change and galvanized them into activity behind the scenes. Nonetheless, Gheorghiu-Dej was able to maintain his personal control of the Romanian political system, despite Khrushchev and the changes within the Soviet leadership. Like the New Course after Stalin's death, Khrushchev's anti-Stalin stance affected Romanian-Soviet relations more than it did internal Romanian developments. Ironically, the main impact inside Romania was to threaten Gheorghiu-Dej and strengthen his determination to prevent the very reforms advocated by the Soviet leader—reforms that might create alternatives to Gheorghiu-Dej within the Romanian Party.[53] Gorbachev would have a similar effect on Ceauşescu.

There was a period in the spring of 1956, however, when signs of change did appear in at least two areas. First, there was a brief cultural thaw;

Table 2.5 Percentage Turnover of the Central Committee at Each Party Congress, Full Members

	Previous Central Committee			New Central Committee	
	Re-elected Full Member	Elected Candidate Member	Not Re-elected	Re-elected From Previous Term[a]	Newly Elected
1955	46	10	44	43	57
1960	75	0	21	77	23
1965	89	0	11	72	28
1969	75	1	22	75	25
1974	72	1	21	81	19
1979	61	2	29	68	32
1984	56	0	41	65	35

Sources: Same as Table 2.3.

Note: Individuals who lost membership by election to the Central Revisory Commission were not dropped, but were not continuing members; hence they were not counted here, and the percentage for the previous Central Committees do not always total 100.

[a]Includes promotions from candidate membership.

Table 2.6. Percentage Turnover of the Central Committee at Each Party Congress, Candidate Members

	Previous Central Committee				New Central Committee	
	Promoted To Full Member	Re-elected Candidate Member	Total Retained	Total Not Retained	Re-elected From Previous Term	Newly Elected
1955	44	31	75	25	26	74
1960	40	29	69	31	32	68
1965	48	23	71	29	11	89
1969	40	16	56	44	12	88
1974	35	20	55	43	22	78
1979	21	19	40	60	18	82
1984	21	24	45	52	22	78

Sources: Same as Table 2.3

Note: Individuals who lost membership by election to the Central Revisory Commission were not dropped, but were not continuing members; hence they were not counted here, and the percentages for the previous Central Committees do not always total 100.

restrictions on Romanian writers and artists and on imports of art and literature were relaxed.[54] Second, reforms in judicial procedures and organization were passed by the Grand National Assembly in late March. The sequence of events surrounding this GNA session was rather unusual. A CC plenum was held in Bucharest 23–25 March at which Gheorghiu-Dej reported on the Twentieth Congress and Khrushchev's revelations. No speeches from that plenum were published, however, and not until 29 March did a shortened version of Gheorghiu-Dej's report appear in *Scînteia*. The published version did criticize Stalin, focusing on the cult of personality, and acknowledged that many of the Soviet leader's earlier achievements were partially negated by the excesses of the cult. In Romania, Gheorghiu-Dej asserted, the Stalinists had been removed in 1952. The secrecy surrounding the plenum and the delay in printing the report conveyed the impression that there were serious disagreements within the RWP, and later Central Committee meetings (June 1957, December 1961, April 1968) confirmed this impression and filled in some of the details.

At the time, the most striking development was a temporary new order of precedence that emerged from the plenum. In an unexplained departure from previous practice, *Scînteia* on 28 March began listing the RWP leadership alphabetically (which put Gheorghiu-Dej halfway down the list despite his position as first secretary). The judicial reforms were passed by the Grand National Assembly on 29 March, and the discussion in the parliament of those reforms connected them explicitly to the need for legality and openness, and so by implication to some of Khrushchev's criticisms of Stalin. During April 1956 it seemed that collective leadership and de-Stalinization—a return to Leninist norms, as Khrushchev had put it—were being introduced in Romania, an impression reinforced in articles celebrating Lenin's birthday that appeared later in the month.[55] Also in April the Political Bureau evidently criticized the Ministry of Internal Affairs for "abuses," for "eluding Party control," and for "deficiencies in cadre policy" and decided to increase Party control and guidance "over the activity of security, militia, prosecuting, and judicial bodies," to rehabilitate "unjustly sentenced persons," and generally to "strengthen legality."[56]

These attempts to impose collective leadership on Gheorghiu-Dej and restrictions on the security forces were ended, like the cultural thaw, by the tumultuous events of autumn 1956: The Hungarian uprising in Budapest produced echoes in Transylvania that put an end to any relaxation of political or cultural control. Not only were nationalist protests heard within the Hungarian minority, but anti-Russian demonstrations surfaced among ethnic Romanians, including student demands for the elimination of required Russian language courses in schools and universities. Although the various demonstrations were quickly suppressed, the Romanian government did show some signs of conciliation: The students were told that "compulsory attendance" in "certain subjects" would be reconsidered. Promises were made to the Hungarian community as well, although its autonomy would actually be reduced in the next decade; not until the early years of Ceauşescu's rule would the ethnic minorities' status improve. Clearly, national sentiment— both Romanian and Hungarian—had not been eliminated in the first decade of communist rule. To alleviate the general discontent, wages were raised slightly and the economic development plan was revised to devote more resources to consumer goods.[57]

The events of 1956 produced few concessions to reformist demands in Romania, but had serious repercussions within the Party leadership. In the spring of 1957, Iosif Chişinevschi and Miron Constantinescu were removed from their posts in the Political Bureau. At the time, they were charged with anti-Party activity going back to the 1930s, but the emphasis was on their support for Ana Pauker and Vasile Luca before 1952 and also their own factional activity in 1956, which, it was later implied, might have split the Party and produced the same disastrous situation in Romania as in Hungary.[58] Little was revealed in 1957, but more details on their mistakes were given at a CC plenum in December 1961 by a number of speakers, including Gheorghiu-Dej, Ceauşescu, Drăghici, and Petre Borilă,[59] all of whom blamed Chişinevschi and Constantinescu for weakening the Party during 1956. Borilă in particular discussed their "anti-Party" activity—they "attacked" Gheorghiu-Dej personally, "slandered" the RWP and its policies, and "tried to orient the discussions of the Twentieth Party Congress" in an "anarchist" and "liberalist" direction that would have released "petty-bourgeois elements" in society. The two men, along with Constantin Pârvulescu,[60] were accused in 1961 of having formed a faction in 1956 by meeting secretly outside of regular Party sessions. Apparently they were trying to implement real collective leadership in Romania by limiting Gheorghiu-Dej's power, and when he blamed the excesses of Stalin and the cult of personality in Romania on Pauker and Luca exclusively, they criticized his report on the Twentieth Party Congress. They were well placed to do so—Chişinevschi and Constantinescu had accompanied Gheorghiu-Dej to the Congress—but the fourth member of that delegation was Borilă, so he was the appropriate member of the Political Bureau to refute their criticisms in 1961.

The combination of Chişinevschi and Constantinescu was a strange one: Both undoubtedly had close ties to Pauker and Luca, both were longtime communists and intellectuals, and both had been CC secretaries and had worked in *agitprop* and cultural affairs.[61] However, there were serious differences between them. Chişinevschi was Jewish, from Bessarabia, evidently had spent the war in the USSR, and had gained a reputation for being extremely conservative in cultural matters. Constantinescu, in contrast, was an ethnic Romanian from Transylvania (Arad) who spent the war in Romanian prisons and by 1956 had developed a reputation as a reformer. Constantinescu, the first editor of *Scînteia*, was reported to be in charge of the CC section for organizations in the mid-1940s under Ana Pauker; as such, he was criticized in 1957 for applying her policies and allowing "opportunists" to join the Party. He was also close to Gheorghiu-Dej, however, serving under him in a variety of economic positions later in the 1940s and then taking over for him as president of the State Planning Commission in 1949. He held that position until 1955 and supervised economic affairs from the CC Secretariat (1952–1954) and the Council of Ministers (1954–1957). When trouble threatened in Transylvania in the fall of 1956, Constantinescu was sent to negotiate with the protesters. On 5 November he talked to a Cluj student meeting and promised to end compulsory Russian courses and improve the students' living conditions; soon after, he was made minister of education.

Constantinescu's opposition in the spring of 1956 and his conciliatory gestures in Transylvania began to pose a threat to Gheorghiu-Dej for at least two reasons. First, Constantinescu's background was remarkably similar to that of Pătrăşcanu—an ethnic Romanian intellectual with long years of service to Romanian communism—giving him a potential power base within the Party. Indeed, he has been described as the "one man after Pătrăşcanu capable of rallying reformist tendencies around himself."[62] Second, and perhaps even more dangerous, Khrushchev could now be expected to support reform within Romania.

The politics of intra-Party struggle in Romania were still closely tied to events in Moscow. Malenkov had originally forced collective leadership on Gheorghiu-Dej in the spring of 1954, but the Romanian leader carefully eliminated Pătrăşcanu and then postponed the Second Party Congress long enough for Malenkov to be defeated by Khrushchev. Two months later came the new threat posed by Khrushchev's sudden criticism of Stalin at the Twentieth Party Congress in Moscow. Indeed, the timing of Constantinescu's removal indicates the plausibility of Khrushchev's support for him as a reformer: The Romanian Central Committee plenum overlapped with the Soviet leadership crisis of June 1957, when Khrushchev was fully occupied removing his own "anti-Party" group of Malenkov, Molotov, and Kaganovich—like the Constantinescu-Chişinevschi pair, an unlikely combination of reformers and conservatives. Khrushchev was therefore confronted with a *fait accompli* in Bucharest, and it was very difficult for him to object because Gheorghiu-Dej was careful to use the same language against his opponents that Khrushchev was using in Moscow.[63]

In 1957, therefore, Gheorghiu-Dej was able to preempt another potential challenge to his leadership and maintain his personal power despite the Soviets. Then in late 1961, when Khrushchev launched another de-Stalinization campaign at the Soviet Twenty-second Congress, Gheorghiu-Dej responded with his own Central Committee plenum attacking Pauker, Luca, Constantinescu, and Chişinevschi as Romanian Stalinists and revealing in more detail his own version of Party history. Again Soviet actions had threatened his control of the RWP, but by 1961 there were no ripples of opposition in Romania. Gheorghiu-Dej had already learned his lesson: After 1957 he tolerated no further interference from Khrushchev. Meanwhile, Ceauşescu was watching closely and absorbing some important lessons for his own future behavior.

The Independent Stalinist: 1958–1965

In 1958 Gheorghiu-Dej appeared to be the ideal Soviet ally. He had established the Romanian Workers' Party firmly in control of Romania and with Stalin's blessing had made himself its undisputed leader. In foreign policy he had always followed Moscow's lead, demonstrating unequivocal loyalty by providing strong political and military support for the suppression of the 1956 Hungarian revolution. In domestic affairs he was reluctant to adopt the reformist policies advocated first by Malenkov and then by Khrushchev, but he had avoided the crises that had occurred elsewhere in Eastern Europe. Partly as a reward for loyalty, partly to indicate confidence in the Romanians as allies, and partly to fulfill promises made in the aftermath of the Hungarian events, Khrushchev removed Soviet troops from Romania in 1958. In the same year the RWP leadership introduced a plan for rapid and broadly based industrialization: A return to the high investment rates and emphasis on heavy industry of the early 1950s. Then in 1959 the campaign to collectivize agriculture, halted in 1951, was resumed and was completed by 1962. All of these developments at the time reinforced an image of Gheorghiu-Dej as a loyal Stalinist, trusted by the leaders in Moscow to remake Romania in the Soviet image. In fact, this series of events produced major shifts in Romanian domestic and foreign policy that would sharply distinguish the last years of his rule from the earlier period and gain him in Moscow the reputation of a disloyal nationalist. The removal of Soviet troops made possible the autonomous foreign policy that the economic development plans required.[64]

At first no serious discrepancy appeared between Soviet goals for Romania and those of Gheorghiu-Dej; the Soviets acquiesced in the new plans, and relations between Khrushchev and Gheorghiu-Dej remained cordial, if not warm. Khrushchev, however, had concluded from the events of 1956 that Stalinist coercion of the USSR's allies should be replaced by the more effective tie of economic integration within Comecon, the economic community of Eastern Europe. He thus began to pursue joint preparation of national plans by these small countries at the formulation stage, with increased specialization by each Comecon member in certain types of production. For Romania this would mean focusing on agriculture and related food industries, as well as petroleum and petrochemical products, rather than continuing the RWP's chosen path of stressing heavy industry. Recognizing that the proposed planning process would threaten their own control and the country's economic sovereignty, the Romanian leaders began to oppose the integration plans within Comecon. The years from 1960, when the conflict between Khrushchev and Gheorghiu-Dej became apparent to both leaders, until 1964, when the latter emerged at least temporarily victorious in his resistance, reveal gradually increasing friction between the two allies and, simultaneously, a growing rapprochement between the Romanian government and its citizens.

A number of factors combined fortuitously to allow Gheorghiu-Dej to resist Soviet demands. First, the Sino-Soviet dispute came into the open; Not only was Khrushchev preoccupied with a neighbor much larger than Romania, but China was available as an alternative ally and model of development. Indeed, Soviet control within the socialist bloc was permanently loosened by the quarrel with China, never again to reach the level of the Stalin years. Second, the Romanians were at the time largely self-sufficient in the production of energy. Unlike the other East European states, they produced their own oil and gas and had potential hydroelectric resources. They did import iron ore and coking coal from the Soviet Union, but the Soviets had less economic leverage over them than over the rest of Eastern Europe. Third, the Romanians could export raw materials (mostly agricultural products) to the West to pay for hard currency imports, and so they were able to reorient a substantial amount of trade away from the Soviet bloc starting in 1958. Finally, the Romanian Party's unity provided strength for resistance; the leadership clearly supported Gheorghiu-Dej and his policies—surprising in view of the diversity in ethnic, social, and educational backgrounds to be found in the early 1960s among the fifteen men in the RWP Political Bureau and Secretariat.[65]

The Party leadership was far from homogeneous, but there were two distinguishable groups: Gheorghiu-Dej, Ceauşescu, Chivu Stoica, Apostol, and Drăghici were all ethnic Romanians, with proletarian or peasant backgrounds, no formal education, and war years spent in Romanian prisons. Bodnaraş, Borilă, Dumitru Coliu, Leonte Răutu, and Leonte Sălăjan, not ethnic Romanians, had some higher education and a number of years spent in the Soviet Union. (The remaining five men did not fit clearly into either group.) The Romanian Political Bureau therefore contained those class, ethnic, and educational groupings often found within the communist parties of Eastern Europe, but it is perhaps surprising that these differences still existed in Romania in 1965, after Gheorghiu-Dej had surrounded himself with loyalists. The RWP leadership was indeed united around Gheorghiu-Dej, but not as the result of ethnic or social homogeneity.

In fact, the Romanian leadership in the early 1960s was homogeneous in only two respects: longevity in office and prewar illegal communist activity. Of the nine full members of the Political Bureau, five had been members before 1952, two joined in that year, and the two newcomers, Ceauşescu and Drăghici, became full members in 1955. Thirteen of the fifteen were Central

Committee members by 1948, and all except Ştefan Voitec and Mihai Dalea had joined the RCP by 1936. Eight of the thirteen prewar communists had suffered long years in prison in Romania, and the remaining five had escaped into exile in the USSR. These two common background characteristics of the Party leadership indicate the bases of group unity and the priorities of Gheorghiu-Dej in selecting his close subordinates: (1) personal loyalty to Gheorghiu-Dej, demonstrated by long years of service with him, and (2) a deep commitment to the socialist development of Romania, proven by imprisonment or exile.

These bonds were strong enough to maintain group solidarity in the face of ethnic diversity and Soviet pressure. The instinctive attitude toward the USSR of all of these men must at one time have been positive—after all, during the illegal days of the RCP the Communist Party of the Soviet Union was the only outside source of support, and it was the Soviet army that established the RCP in power. Yet at the same time these men were probably a bit wary of blindly following Soviet advice. The prewar RCP had not always found the Comintern line to be advantageous within Romania, to say the least, and postwar economic exploitation by the Soviets, who had regarded Romania as an enemy, severely battered an already devastated economy. However, Gheorghiu-Dej himself had administered reparations payments very efficiently as minister of national economy, so at one time even he had placed his international socialist obligations above national interests (although arguably he simply yielded to the inevitable in accepting and implementing Stalin's demands).

As longtime communists, the Party leadership looked at Marxism within the Romanian context and quite naturally adopted the Soviet model of economic development[66]—including the priority development of heavy industry and the policy of industrial protectionism[67]—albeit with resulting hardships on the population. The correctness of this model had been convincingly demonstrated to the Romanians by the Soviet victory over Germany; no wonder Bucharest rejected a Comecon policy that would relegate Romania to production of agricultural products and deny it the heavy industrial base needed for communism. Once the Romanian communists reaffirmed the admired Soviet model in their 1958 industrialization plan, they were forced by subsequent Soviet opposition to become anti-Soviet. In other words, the Soviet leaders themselves ironically opposed Romanian emulation of the Soviet path under Stalin. The Comecon dispute should therefore be viewed not as a nationalist controversy between Soviets and Romanians but as a quarrel among Marxist-Leninists over the correct path of socialist development for Romania and who would define that path.

Within this context, the division of the RWP Political Bureau into "prison" and "exile" groups becomes less important. Gheorghiu-Dej and his "prison" colleagues were surely determined to preserve their control over the Romanian economy, but it would have been those individuals with the closest ties to the USSR—the "exiles"—who were most offended by Khrushchev's refusal to sanction Romanian emulation. With the "exiles" therefore forced to defend Romanian sovereignty and the monopoly of the RWP over economic decisions, the Comecon dispute served to unify rather than split the RWP leadership. From the Romanian viewpoint, both national aspirations and socialist economic development demanded the same line of policy.

The quarrel with the Soviets also brought the RWP increased support from the Romanian population, and here nationalism was crucial. The regime's growing independence of the USSR was accompanied by a reduced emphasis on cultural ties. For example, the Slavic "Romîn" was gradually replaced by "Român." In the 1963–1964 academic year, the Institute for Russian Studies in Bucharest was merged into the new Institute for Foreign Languages, and Russian was no longer compulsory in elementary and secondary schools. The Russian Bookstore was renamed the Universal Bookstore, and many streets, buildings, and institutions were given Romanian instead of Russian names. In 1964 the celebration of the Soviet Revolution was downgraded, and the Soviet-Romanian Friendship Month was reduced to ten "Days of Soviet Culture." A final insult to the Soviets was the publication in December 1964 of Marx's manuscript *Notes About the Romanians*, in which he criticized the Russian government for helping to crush Romanian revolutionary movements in the nineteenth century and for seizing Bessarabia in an agreement with Turkey.[68] All of these measures were essentially symbolic, but they were extremely popular inside Romania.

As a complement to the derussification measures, a new emphasis on Romanian political and cultural traditions appeared. Individuals prominent in prewar Romania—such as Titu Maiorescu, Nicolae Iorga, Nicolae Titulescu, and even Octavian Goga—were rehabilitated; although none was highly praised at this time, their contributions to Romanian culture and independence were once again recognized in their own country. In addition, greater receptivity to cultural contacts with the West accompanied the increased economic relations. During 1963 plays, books, films, exhibitions, lecturers, and tourists from Britain, the United States, France, and Italy were allowed into the country, and in August jamming of the Voice of America, Radio Free Europe, and other Western radio stations ceased. In February 1964 Gheorghiu-Dej spoke out in favor of broader contacts with Western culture, and the next month the Writers' Union accepted all "anti-bourgeois" literature, including Proust, Joyce, and Kafka. The same month *Scînteia* announced that Romania was joining PEN (the International Association of Poets, Essayists, and Novelists), which *Izvestia* had condemned in January as anti-communist.[69] In the fall of 1964 musical repertoires included Schoenberg, Berg, and other representatives of atonalism; jazz became acceptable; and an exhibition of abstract art opened in Bucharest.

Indeed, 1964 was a crucial year for Soviet-Romanian relations. The

Sino-Soviet dispute was intensifying, and during the spring the Romanian leaders made an attempt to mediate between the two giants. The talks broke down, and in April the RWP held a Central Committee plenum that issued what became known as Romania's "Declaration of Independence." The statement called for close unity among bloc members, but pointedly omitted any reference to the vanguard role of the Soviet Party. Instead, the Romanians pointed to the failure of the Comintern in the 1920s and 1930s to show that "solution of problems by an international center is no longer suitable" and "interference in our internal affairs was detrimental . . . to the party's links with the masses." Having thus rejected interference by any supranational organ (specifically the Comintern, but by implication Comecon), they emphatically declared their complete independence within the socialist bloc: "No one can decide what is and is not correct for other countries or parties. It is up to every Marxist-Leninist party, it is a sovereign right of each socialist state, to work out, choose or change the forms and methods of socialist construction."[70]

Although obviously not very happy about the Romanian position, the Soviet government chose to do very little about it. The presence of delegations from *all* communist parties in Bucharest for the twentieth anniversary celebrations in August 1964, and at Gheorghiu-Dej's funeral in March 1965, was visible proof of Romania's success. Two days after Khrushchev's removal from office in October 1964, the new Soviet leaders acquiesced in the Romanian industrialization plans by signing an agreement for extensive technical assistance. By the end of 1964 a truce had been declared, with the Romanians as temporary victors. Gheorghiu-Dej had not only created a socialist state in Romania but, at the time of his death in early 1965, he had also gained at least temporary autonomy for his country. The Romanian Workers' Party was no longer the instrument of Moscow it had been under Stalin.

Given the importance of Gheorghiu-Dej in the evolution of Romania after World War II, it is remarkable that he remains such a shadowy and controversial figure. Ruling communist parties often keep the personal lives of their leaders quite private, even secret, and the RWP under Gheorghiu-Dej was no exception. Unfortunately, this scarcity of information makes it difficult to evaluate the personal role and priorities of this individual who maintained himself and his Party in power through the anti-Titoist purges of the 1940s, the Stalinist trials of the early 1950s, Soviet insistence on de-Stalinization and collective leadership later in the decade, and Khrushchev's attempts at Comecon integration in the 1960s. Clearly Gheorghiu-Dej was a skillful politician, and Ceauşescu learned a great deal from him about controlling and directing the Romanian Workers' Party. But the older man remains an enigmatic figure, who apparently changed from a subservient instrument of Soviet power into a leader determined to minimize Soviet influence in his country.

Although Gheorghiu-Dej was at times both pragmatic and flexible in adapting to current political needs, he was not simply an opportunist. On at least one issue he never wavered: his devotion to the socialist development of Romania as *he* defined it. His commitment to his version of Marxism was demonstrated by the ideological formulations in which he spoke and wrote and also by his long years of service to the communist movement in Romania, including more than a decade in prison. He believed that his revolution in Romania during the 1940s required subservience to Soviet demands because the USSR was then crucial to the RCP's seizure of power. In the 1950s, however, the policies of Malenkov and then Khrushchev threatened the Romanian leader's personal control of the RWP and RWP control of the Romanian political system.

Like many politicians, Gheorghiu-Dej came to identify himself and his personal power as the force most likely to implement his ideological goals in his country. He then built up an apparatus of control—Party, government, secret police, military—and he used these hierarchies in both policy and personnel matters in such a way as to ensure his continued rule. This drive— first to acquire unchallenged power and then to implement his vision for Romania through coercion and terror whenever he deemed them necessary— provided Ceaușescu with an example to follow.

Moscow's threat to Gheorghiu-Dej's power after Stalin's death weakened his loyalty to the Soviet Union and eventually led him to reject Moscow's right to define the path to socialism for other parties. To Gheorghiu-Dej, Marxism meant the Stalinist model: rapid development of heavy industry financed largely through internal resources, most notably the suppression of living standards. In the 1940s he could accomplish this goal only with Soviet support, and so he was a loyal ally. Two decades later he had more confidence in his own decisions than in those made in Moscow, and he decided he could move toward his own goal only if he resisted Soviet pressure. As a result, he rejected Khrushchev's plans for Comecon integration. But it was not Gheorghiu-Dej who changed. It was Soviet plans for Romania.

During his two decades near or at the top of the Romanian communist movement, the accomplishments of Gheorghiu-Dej were considerable. First, he brought about fundamental changes in the politics, economics, and social structure of his country in accordance with his own definitions of Marxist development and with Soviet support. Second, when he disagreed with Soviet interpretations of Romania's needs, he started his Party and his country on the path toward autonomy. Finally, the RWP's new attitude toward the Soviet Union generated a measure of popular support for his regime and created the potential for a new relationship between the Romanian Workers' Party and the Romanian population in which coercion could be replaced at least in part by voluntary acceptance.

Gheorghiu-Dej himself never seriously attempted to alter his methods of rule to take advantage of that potential support. He was an intensely private man who appeared rarely in public and shunned publicity. He also died within a year of the April 1964 declaration of independence, and some changes might have been forthcoming. But there were no indications that he anticipated any style of leadership different from that which he had used for so many years— the Stalinist method of competing hierarchies of coercion in which the Party was first but not omnipotent. His successor, Ceauşescu, would introduce his own style of leadership, and his personal rule would differ in a number of ways from that of Gheorghiu-Dej. But even Ceauşescu would follow the lead of his predecessor in the content of his major policies: the Stalinist economic model achieved through autonomy in foreign policy. Indeed, Ceauşescu's policies, as well as many of his strategies for maintaining his personal control of the political system, can be viewed as extensions of those established by Gheorghiu-Dej. In that sense, the impact of Gheorghiu-Dej on Romania has long outlived his personal power. Ceauşescu's apprenticeship was successful.

3

Succession:
1965 and the Ninth Party Congress

On 20 March 1965 *Scînteia*, the daily newspaper of the Romanian Workers' Party, appeared with a black frame and the announcement that the RWP first secretary and president of the Council of State, Gheorghe Gheorghiu-Dej, had died the preceding day of a "grave illness." The accompanying medical bulletin specified the cause of death as a rapidly developing cancer that had spread to lungs and liver. *Scînteia* reported that Gheorghiu-Dej had first shown signs of lung disease in late January; despite treatment his liver became enlarged during February, and foreign experts were called in to confirm the conclusions of the Romanian doctors; the illness progressed rapidly, and on the afternoon of 19 March the Party leader lapsed into a coma and died. Three days later, on 22 March 1965, the Central Committee elected Nicolae Ceauşescu first secretary and recommended Chivu Stoica as president of the Council of State.

None of Gheorghiu-Dej's colleagues was in a strong position when the unquestioned ruler died. Not even Ceauşescu, who had supervised Party organizations and cadre appointments for a number of years in the CC secretariat, could expect to take his place without difficulty. Those surrounding Gheorghiu-Dej in the Party leadership, including Ceauşescu, had made public statements over the years in connection with their official duties, but they had continued in office by carefully echoing the prevailing Party line on every occasion. Although Ceauşescu's infrequent speeches in 1963 and 1964 were already quite nationalistic in content,[1] they merely reflected the new positions taken by RWP documents. Because differences in personalities and priorities among the various individuals in the Political Bureau were not made public, it was not obvious when Gheorghiu-Dej died that Ceauşescu's election as first secretary would enable him to dominate Romanian politics.

The struggle for political succession has frequently been termed the "Achilles' heel" of communist systems. Leninist parties lack clear lines along which power devolves from one individual to another, and this period of change and uncertainty may weaken the regime, at least temporarily.[2] As a result, the new leadership must attempt to reassure and mollify the population in order to preserve stability. This was true in the Romanian succession of the 1960s, and also during much of the prolonged period of change from Brezhnev to his successors in the USSR during the early 1980s. Ceauşescu's techniques in gaining and consolidating the top position provide a successful model for succession in Leninist parties. Hence it is worth examining these years from 1965 to 1969 in some detail, even though Ceauşescu's personality and priorities often had to be masked and compromised during this period because of personal and Party weakness.

In Romania in 1965 there was not the urgent need for the new leaders to dissociate themselves from their predecessor that had accompanied Khrushchev's forcible removal in late 1964. Instead, Gheorghiu-Dej's natural death allowed the RWP leaders to focus on providing an orderly transition. As a result, they promised caution and compromise in domestic affairs; they stressed continuity in foreign policy, warning that any outside challenge to their authority would be rejected; and they emphasized collective leadership and Party unity, while promising both consumer satisfaction and military strength. In other words, until the succession was decided and the ability of the Party to preserve its rule was assured, the new leaders acted so as to preempt the opposition of groups outside the Party and even sought approval from the citizenry. In consequence, they made overtures to various social and occupational categories inside the country—workers, peasants, intellectuals, economic managers, Party administrators, the national minorities—and used promises instead of threats. They tailored their policies to appeal to those whose neutrality or support they were seeking, and the larger and more diffuse the group, the more public were the attempts to win its approval.

Meanwhile, Ceauşescu and the other top leaders were positioning themselves for dominance within the Party. Maneuvering for individual succession in a Leninist party takes place in private and begins long before the death of the former leader. Outside observers usually see only the waves created by movements behind the scenes. Anyone who hopes to lead a Leninist party must focus on gaining the support of a small number of colleagues in the top decisionmaking body, usually the Political Bureau. That support may be difficult to achieve if there are a number of aspirants to the highest position. Next—or perhaps first, depending upon the individual's institutional power base—the ambitious newcomer must be sure of the support of the Party apparatus, those full-time Party officials who oversee lower-level Party jobs as well as elections to the Party congress and Central Committee. Although the Political Bureau is the crucial forum, both Stalin and Khrushchev, and Ceauşescu as well, used the Party apparatus and Central Committee to oust their rivals and gain control. Recognizing he needed the support of the Party at all levels, Ceauşescu actively sought that support in 1965.[3]

Leaders of communist parties have made use of various power bases to maintain themselves and their movements in control. Three of the most important have been (1) prestige as the leader of the revolution; (2) coercion, or even terror; and (3) foreign support. Revolutionary prestige has been important to a number of rulers following their own revolutions; Lenin, Mao, Tito, and Castro come immediately to mind. Coercion and terror have been just as widespread; the key name here is, of course, Stalin. Finally, foreign support was crucial in Eastern Europe, where in most cases the Soviet army made it possible for the local communist party to seize and retain political control. All three sources of strength were used by Gheorghiu-Dej: Soviet occupation aided Party rule; the secret police employed Stalin's intimidation tactics; and Gheorghiu-Dej drew on his extensive communist activities to create for himself the aura of a revolutionary.

But none of these sources of power was available to Nicolae Ceauşescu when Gheorghiu-Dej died. Despite Ceauşescu's years of Party activity, there were others with greater seniority; he could not claim to be the leader of Romanian communism, responsible for placing Romania on the path of socialist development. His four years as deputy minister in the military hierarchy were outweighed by the control of a major rival, Alexandru Drăghici, over the Ministry of Internal Affairs and hence the security forces. Nor could Ceauşescu use Soviet support to implement his policies; by 1965 Romania's independent course in foreign policy was firmly established, and many of Ceauşescu's international priorities would turn out to be anti-Soviet. Eventually, much of his success would be facilitated by his opposition to the USSR, resulting in increased support for him personally and for his Party. But that would not be clear until after the events in Czechoslovakia in 1968.

Lacking the traditional sources of strength in 1965, Ceauşescu thus was forced to find other strategies not only to preserve the RWP's power but also to, establish himself at the top of the Party. It would take him just over four years to consolidate his control, formalized finally by the Tenth Congress in August 1969. During those years, he would shrewdly combine four methods in order to gain his ends: (1) manipulation of personnel and of organizational responsibilities to enhance his power in the Party and the Party's power in society; (2) policy compromise within the new collective leadership and policy ambiguity toward outside constituencies; (3) promises to institutionalize the political process in both Party and state and to guarantee socialist legality; and (4) political techniques such as participatory reforms and populist appeals to the Romanian masses stressing Romanian traditions and nationalism. Personnel manipulation eventually would allow him to impose his own priorities as regime policies. Meanwhile, he needed to induce compliance, and policy compromise and ambiguity were crucial in this attempt. The third and fourth techniques revealed his desire for cooperation—not just obedience—from the Romanian population. Both techniques were important traits of the 1965–1969 period, but during the 1970s, when Ceauşescu ceased to compromise in his policies and his personal goals became clear (and unacceptable) to most Romanians, he would gradually abandon his promises of legality and institutionalization, while his mass mobilization techniques would intensify almost to a frenzy. Nevertheless, all four strategies were visible in the first few months after the death of Gheorghiu-Dej, a period that set the stage for the next four years.

Death and Transition: March–July 1965

After Gheorghiu-Dej's death, the hierarchy within the leadership went through several stages before settling on a provisional order. The first notice that Gheorghiu-Dej was ill did not appear in *Scînteia* until 18 March; a brief medical bulletin at the bottom of page one indicated he was suffering from a pulmonary affliction with complications. He had not been seen in public since he voted with the other members of the Political Bureau in the national elections of 8 March, but a lull had seemed natural after the round of campaign speeches. Along with the medical bulletin, it was announced that the newly elected Grand National Assembly (GNA) would meet that day. On 19 March *Scînteia* acknowledged Gheorghiu-Dej's worsened condition and reported that the GNA had re-elected him president of the Council of State in his absence, on the nomination of Ceauşescu, and that Chivu Stoica had nominated Ion Gheorghe Maurer for re-election as president of the Council of Ministers, a post he had held since 1960.[4] Gheorghiu-Dej's death at 5:43 p.m. that day was reported over the radio almost within the hour, and a later report that evening listed those present at his death: the fourteen surviving members of the Party leadership, two vice-presidents of the Council of Ministers, and the dead leaders' son-in-law. The leadership was frozen in equality: alphabetical order within rank.[5]

We can only guess at behind-the-scenes activity during the next two days. Ceauşescu must have felt confident of his support at lower levels of the Party, but he needed to convince his colleagues in the Political Bureau that he should be elected first secretary. Of the full members of that group, he, Apostol, and Chivu Stoica were probably the only ones not barred from the top post by ethnicity (as were Bodnaraş, Borilă, Coliu, and Maurer) or background (Drăghici, still minister of internal affairs, must have appeared threatening to everyone). Chivu Stoica evidently did not have the abilities to hold the job, and Apostol may have appeared too strong a personality to his colleagues. The young and diminutive Ceauşescu, on the other hand, could intimidate no one with either his intelligence or his verbal skills. Indeed, given his background—his lack of education and his organizational skills— the Party position in a collective leadership seemed the natural place for him.

In any case, the alphabetical order continued until after the Central Committee met on 22 March 1965 and accepted the Political Bureau's recommendation of Ceauşescu. At the same session, Alexandru Bîrlădeanu was promoted from candidate to full member of the Political Bureau, and three new CC secretaries were chosen: Leonte Răutu, Paul Niculescu-Mizil, and Ilie Verdeţ. In addition, the CC recommended that the Grand National Assembly elect Chivu Stoica to the titular position of president of the Council of State; Ceauşescu and Chivu Stoica would thus split Gheorghiu-Dej's positions between them. Alphabetical order was abandoned the next day, and Ceauşescu and Maurer (already president of the Council of Ministers) were listed first and second, respectively. (Chivu Stoica briefly remained listed in alphabetical order until the GNA met to make him head of state.) The new hierarchy was finally solemnized—fittingly enough, at Gheorghiu-Dej's funeral—after the GNA meeting on 24 March. Nicolae Ceauşescu, Chivu Stoica, and Ion Gheorghe Maurer were listed ahead of the rest in that order, comprising a new triumvirate that would last until December 1967. Collective leadership appeared to be a reality.

At the funeral there were large crowds and much weeping, according to foreign correspondents, who also commented on the presence of Anastas Mikoyan, Zhou Enlai, and Alexander Rankovic, senior representatives of the USSR, China, and Yugoslavia; their presence attested to Romania's neutrality in the quarrels within the communist bloc. Only Albania was absent. There was even a special deputy from France's President Charles de Gaulle.[6] Four members of the Romanian Political Bureau gave brief but revealing eulogies. Chivu Stoica spoke first, rather emotionally, confining himself to glowing praise of Gheorghiu-Dej and revealing some unease by repeatedly stressing the need for close unity around the Party and state leadership. Gheorghe Apostol spoke next, also with emotion and tragic phrases. Not surprisingly, he emphasized the importance of his constituency, the trade unions, in maintaining the unity of the working class under Party leadership.

The third speaker, Maurer, then praised Gheorghiu-Dej for those qualities most closely associated with Maurer himself. For example, the man who had negotiated Roman's re-orientation of foreign trade, and who was known to have a more favorable attitude toward consumer interests than did some of the other leaders, praised Gheorghiu-Dej for achieving a synthesis of national tradition and Marxism-Leninism; he then gave as much weight to the dead leader's contributions to the "people's happiness" as to his "building socialism." He also emphasized Gheorghiu-Dej's care to maintain "ties with the masses" and his "modesty" and respect for "collective work." Maurer's eulogy reinforced his own image as an advocate of moderation and compromise. Differences in nuance were already appearing among the leaders.

The last speaker, Ceauşescu, revealed his major concern: the Party. As CC secretary for cadres and organizations under Gheorghiu-Dej, his influence was strong at lower levels of the Party apparatus; this, and his new position as first secretary, meant that he could expect to influence the selection of Central Committee members at the July 1965 Party congress. Ceauşescu frequently referred to the leading role of the Party and to the Central Committee and the Party organizations. He also emphasized the need for collective work and unity and warned against "foreign concepts and opportunists and splitting elements." Unlike the other speakers, he discussed foreign policy, managing to make his statements extremely ambiguous by praising "proletarian internationalism" (the phrase indicating loyalty to the USSR) while also repeating much of the Romanians' April 1964 declaration of independence.

These funeral eulogies set the stage for the period from March to July when the new leadership was establishing the basic lines of domestic and foreign policy in preparation for the Party congress. Ceauşescu was by far the most visible of the leaders, and he quickly became the official spokesman as he authoritatively addressed various professional groups including scientists, writers and artists, the Ministry of Internal Affairs, Party activists in the armed forces, and Bucharest city and regional Party conferences. Although these speeches, as well as the decisions of the CC plenums held in mid-April and late May, promised a great deal of policy continuity—sometimes ambiguity—the statements also raised hopes that change was coming. Foreign newspapers were particularly dramatic in expressing hope for improvement. A series of dispatches from David Binder to the *New York Times* the first week in April appeared under titles such as "Rumania Easing Art Restrictions," "Theater Thriving in Rumanian Thaw," and "Rumania to Help Farming Families," and the *Washington Post* titled an Anatole Shub article on 23 May "Rumania Destalinizing Without a Lot of Fuss." Romanians or foreigners who wished to believe that the new leaders were promising a cultural thaw or a political de-Stalinization were able to find support for such beliefs in their actions. At the same time, there were many indications of continuity, particularly with respect to the political monopoly of the RWP.

The Party

Emphasis on the leading role of the Romanian Workers' Party, strong during Gheorghiu-Dej's tenure, intensified after his death. Editorials appeared almost daily in *Scînteia* with such titles as "The Party: Burning Heart and Conscience of the People," and a number of specific steps were taken to increase its influence. Because the lower Party organs and the Central Committee were Ceauşescu's major sources of support, we can assume that he initiated proposed revisions in the Party statutes[7] to emphasize the power of the Party over state officials, give the primary party organizations responsibility for culture and ethics in addition to political and economic activity, and place the military political directorate directly under the Central Committee.

The new collective leadership also took steps to increase and broaden

Party membership, but it is not clear that Ceauşescu was behind these measures. The RWP had already grown by almost 50 percent during a recruitment drive initiated in April 1962 (see Table 2.1). Then the CC plenum of 14–15 April 1965 announced success in attracting peasants and intellectuals and emphasized the need to enroll even more intellectuals.[8] The candidate stage in membership was eliminated, and the recommendation process was equalized for all social classes to make it easier for non-workers to join. Former members of the Social Democratic or Socialist parties were now to receive seniority as RCP members from the date of their membership in their original party, an especially important measure in areas where the other parties had been most popular, as in Transylvania.[9] Also, Party members who could show revolutionary credentials but had not joined a party were to be given seniority according to the date they had become active. Finally, those who had been members of foreign communist parties and had later become Romanian citizens would be allowed to join the RWP (with CC approval) with seniority based on their original party membership. Henceforth, it seemed, the RWP would contain a greater preponderance of minority groups as well as intellectuals.

Later, when Ceauşescu controlled recruitment priorities, he would favor workers and ethnic Romanians rather than intellectuals and minorities, so other members of the collective leadership in 1965 must have imposed their priorities. But Ceauşescu at the time had important reasons to acquiesce in reassuring the national minorities about his intentions: He played a major role in implementing the policies of Gheorghiu-Dej, who had demonstrated assimilationist tendencies in the aftermath of the 1965 disturbances by merging the Romanian and Hungarian universities in Cluj in 1959 and diluting the ethnic concentration of Hungarians in the Hungarian Autonomous Region in 1960. The ethnic minorities could have been expected to feel uneasy when Ceauşescu was selected as Party leader. Hence these overtures to the nationalities fit into his general strategy of conciliating as many groups as possible while consolidating his power over the Romanian polity.

Other trends clearly showed Ceauşescu's influence. The correct content of Party education shifted from the classics of Marxism-Leninism to "concrete problems" of socialist construction—from theory to practice—and by mid-April Party documents associated with Gheorghiu-Dej were no longer being mentioned as worthy of study.[10] Changes in internal Party organization included a new Party statute forbidding a member to hold more than one office requiring full-time service; the significance of this change would become apparent at the Party congress when some of Ceauşescu's rivals would be weakened by being forced to choose between two positions. In addition, a new emphasis on "Party democracy" enhanced the influence of the Central Committee as the Political Bureau and CC secretaries were required to report to the CC, and the Party Control Commission was renamed the

Central Collegium and gave up some of its functions (judging those who broke Party rules, for example) to the CC. Because Ceauşescu's major rivals were in the Political Bureau and he presumably had considerable support on the CC, these aspects of Party "democratization" worked to his advantage.

Other Policies

While the new leaders were strengthening the role and political base of the Party, they were also making overtures to specific occupational groups to preempt any opposition during this period of potential weakness. Ceauşescu spoke to the scientific elite in the name of the Party leadership on 7 May and to writers and artists on 19 May.[11] His opening sentence to the scientific establishment was characteristically pragmatic: "We should like to have an exchange of opinions regarding the development of scientific research and the contributions of scientists and teachers to the practical activity of building socialism in our country," and he called for the "open confrontation of views" in order to help production. In terms of scientific investment priorities, he was ambiguous, suggesting disagreement or compromise among the new Party leaders; for example, he advocated both fundamental and applied research. On one issue he was not ambiguous: He praised the progressive traditions of his homeland and the pioneers of Romanian science. The response of the scientists was predictably cautious—neither enthusiastic nor critical.

The meeting with writers and artists was strikingly similar in approach. Ceauşescu explained that the Political Bureau wanted an "exchange of opinions" on cultural activity and expressed as his own the view that both artistic value and social content were necessary in any type of creative work. He recognized the need for "diversity in styles of art and . . . forms of artistic expression" and reiterated his dialectical view of culture: "Art has always developed in the struggle between the new and the old, and especially . . . between realism and . . . opposing trends." Realism, in his view, always won out, but he implied that the struggle was necessary and proper. In retrospect we can see that he prejudged the issue, but at the time his acceptance of conflict was a striking contrast to previous practice.

His ambiguity (which generated a mixture of hope and skepticism) continued: He acknowledged the importance of world culture and discussions with foreign artists and writers, but warned that publications must help to educate the people in artistic taste and must reflect Marxist-Leninist analysis. Later, when he spoke at the Bucharest city Party conference,[12] he would be even more cautious: Contact with universal culture, he warned, "demands a critical attitude of distinguishing what is right and useful" from "what must be rejected." In his remarks to the writers and artists, however, he was somewhat conciliatory, dispensing hope that the new collective leadership would indeed be more lenient in defining permissible forms of expression. He also referred specifically to Romanian, Hungarian, and German artists and writers and their contributions to Romanian culture. This reference contributed to the general impression that an attempt at rapprochement with the national minorities was under way, an attempt viewed with considerable skepticism by those groups.

Ambiguity in cultural policy was accompanied by promises of "socialist legality." A new constitution was proposed that declared Romania to be a Socialist Republic rather than a People's Republic.[13] One provision created a constitutional commission in the Grand National Assembly to check on the constitutionality of new laws; such GNA commissions would proliferate over the next decade as the assembly became a focus for the new emphasis on popular participation in decisionmaking. The new constitution also placed a twenty-four-hour limit on the time that a citizen could be held without being charged; after that, a warrant would be necessary based on evidence of a crime. Not long before the draft constitution was published, however, Ceaușescu met with the workers of the Ministry of Internal Affairs and "assessed highly" the work of "security and militia organs," urging them to "show constant vigilance" and to "set an example of social conduct."[14] He warned against the dangers of imperialism in contemporary society and implied that there would be no reduction in police power. The emphasis on legality, therefore, was also part of the attempt to attract broader support for the collective leadership through policy ambiguity; Ceaușescu and his colleagues raised hopes that important changes were in the offing, but they provided no means by which legality could be ensured and the hope fulfilled—and they praised the very organs that had been responsible for violations of legality in the past.

One clearly articulated aspect of the 1965 constitution was its patriotism. The combination of Romanianization and derussification that had proved so popular in the early 1960s was continued in the new document. In both organization and language, it abandoned Gheorghiu-Dej's 1952 version in several ways and returned to the Romanian constitution of 1938. For example, the grateful references to the Soviet Union and its army were removed, and the role of the RCP in the birth of the Romanian People's Republic was portrayed as decisive. The very change in the name of the state from the Romanian People's Republic (RPR) to the Romanian Socialist Republic (RSR) and of the Party from the Romanian Workers' Party to the Romanian Communist Party elevated both state and Party to a level of ideological equality with their Soviet counterparts.

Despite this constitutional display of patriotism, the new leaders were rather cautious in their foreign policy. Annual trade agreements had been signed with most of the East European countries in January and February, and it is significant that machinery now made up a large share of Romanian exports to these states.[15] This allowed the Romanians to export their agricultural products and raw materials to the West for hard currency, diversifying their trade still further, and implied Moscow's acquiescence in Bucharest's plans for industrial growth. Two agreements signed with the USSR after the death of Gheorghiu-Dej confirmed Soviet acceptance[16]; on their part, the Romanians were careful to fulfill their obligations by attending meetings of the Warsaw Treaty Organization in January and May. Also during May, however, a new cultural accord was signed with China, replacing the agreement of 1951; the post–Gheorghiu-Dej leaders were continuing his policy of neutrality in the Sino-Soviet dispute. Extensive trade contacts with the West during the first half of 1965—especially with France and the United States—indicated that the Romanians were indeed exporting raw materials for hard currency to buy industrial equipment. Thus the foreign policy of the new leaders was clearly an extension of the Gheorghiu-Dej line established by 1964; military alignment with the Soviet bloc, neutrality in the Sino-Soviet quarrel, and diversity in trade relations to facilitate Romania's industrial development.

These major policy trends between March and July 1965 were introduced by a collective leadership characterized by caution, unanimity on most issues, and the public role of Ceauşescu as first among equals. His statements were geared to promote maximum support for the Party and its new leaders, and Party membership policy was designed to increase its size and to appeal to minority groups and intellectuals. The ambiguity of the scientific and cultural pronouncements allowed everyone to hope for the best; the new emphasis on socialist legality, which could be expected to appeal to the population at large, was accompanied by reassurances to the Ministry of Internal Affairs; and the regime's foreign policy was a continuation of Gheorghiu-Dej's popular independent stance.

Although Ceauşescu was the most visible member of the Political Bureau, the others were also quite active, and their public statements reveal no serious disagreements.[17] There were differences; for example, as might have been expected of a close friend, Chivu Stoica frequently referred to Gheorghiu-Dej and his Third RWP Congress of 1960. But the major themes of all the leaders were the same: In economic production, their goals were heavy industry, quality products, realistic planning, and scientific research. In foreign policy, they stressed both the unity of the socialist countries and the April 1964 declaration. In domestic politics, the leading role of the Party, collective work, and Party democracy were the constant themes.

Nicolae Ceauşescu was allowed to play the most prominent role, but he was not praised or even mentioned by the others and was not more than first within a collective leadership. We can look back and see how a number of changes strengthened the Party in society and Ceauşescu's sources of support—the apparatus and the Central Committee—within the Party. We can also infer from what came later that Maurer and Bîrlădeanu were promoting the new emphasis on diversity in science, culture, and education. At the time, however, Ceauşescu was stating these priorities very effectively and appeared to be fully convinced of their necessity. There was reason for all segments of Romanian society in these months before the Party congress to hope that real changes were on the way. The very formality of the group in its protocol following Gheorghiu-Dej's death supports the assumption that decisions were reached by discussion within the Political Bureau and that during this initial transition period collective leadership in Romania was a reality.

The Ninth Party Congress: 19–24 July 1965

By 1980 the Ninth Party Congress of the Romanian Communist Party would be celebrated with great ceremony on its fifteenth anniversary as the beginning of the Golden Age of Ceaușescu. In 1965 there were also expectations that the meetings would prove significant. They were heavily covered by Western journalists, who were allowed to attend most sessions[18] and who waited eagerly for announcements of internal de-Stalinization or for quarrels among the foreign delegates because the general secretaries of the Soviet and Chinese parties, Leonid Brezhnev and Deng Xiaoping, were present.[19] The congress was beautifully organized: seats reserved for each participant or observer, including the bourgeois journalists; the simultaneous translation quite good; the proceedings distributed in several languages; the buffet richly provisioned; and politeness and efficiency in evidence throughout.[20] Bucharest was draped with flags and signs with slogans oriented toward patriotism and economic development, but no pictures of the Romanian leaders were hanging on public buildings.[21] This would never be true again, for at subsequent congresses RCP leaders, and eventually Ceaușescu alone, would be pictured all over the city, often on banners several stories high. In 1965, however, the leadership portrayed itself as both collective and modest, and foreign reporters were disappointed when only a few public ripples disturbed the surface calm and harmony. The Romanians were quite successful in preventing any sensational rifts or protocol disputes among foreign delegates, and no radical changes occurred in domestic affairs either. In short, unity and continuity were preserved.

Ceaușescu opened the proceedings on 19 July,[22] dispensed with some business (including a moment of silence in memory of Gheorghiu-Dej), and then took the rest of the morning to present the report of the Central Committee. The congress returned to the more traditional and prestigious name, Romanian Communist Party, and the main picture of the leaders, which appeared on the front page of *Scînteia* on 21 July, showed them interspersed with a number of old Party members so that no single individual was the focus of attention and reverence. The speakers referred to prominent figures in Romanian history, often patriots rather than communists, but also cited foreign Marxist theorists who had made positive comments about Romania.[23]

The agenda of the congress contained no major surprises. Ceauşescu presented the report of the CC, Maurer explained the economic plan for 1966–1970, and Chivu Stoica spoke on the long-range plan for power and electrification. One small sign of potential conflict appeared, however: The report on changes in the Party statutes, usually the responsibility of the CC secretary for organizations and cadres, was given by Gheorghe Apostol. In some respects he had greater seniority in the Party than did Ceauşescu; Apostol had been one of Gheorghiu-Dej's closest colleagues and had assumed his duties as first secretary of the Romanian Workers' Party in 1954–1955 when Moscow demanded collective leadership. But Apostol had not held a Party post since 1955, except for his membership in the Political Bureau; instead, he had headed the trade unions from 1955 to 1962 and then continued in the Council of Ministers as first vice-president. Thus his selection to report on the Party statutes indicated his great influence within the new leadership—and his potential as a rival to Ceauşescu. But Apostol's place on the program was a minor event, of little significance to outside observers at the time. One journalist reported that the only speaker who "in personal style . . . trod a somewhat individualist path" was Chivu Stoica, and his individualism consisted in a rather "dogmatic style . . . in contrast to the flat realism of most other talks."[24] A more devastating comment on the speeches would be hard to find.

There were also no great surprises in the Party statutes as proposed by Apostol. The top Party office was renamed "general" secretary rather than the "first" secretary that Moscow had insisted upon after Stalin's death. As Apostol explained it, this return to the traditional name "more accurately expresses the significance and real content of the powers implied in the office."[25] In other words, Ceauşescu was not to be the "first," or most important secretary, but the one with "general" responsibilities. (Brezhnev, of course, would do the same in 1966.) The supreme RCP body officially remained the congress, to meet every four years, and between congresses the Central Committee, elected by the congress, was required to hold a plenum at least every four months to "debate and resolve" important questions. The CC was also to elect the general secretary, the Secretariat, the Executive Committee, and the Presidium.

The last two bodies, the Executive Committee (EC) and the Presidium, were not mentioned until the end of the congress. Ceauşescu, not Apostol, reported their creation, explaining that the Political Bureau was to be replaced by a somewhat larger Executive Committee—fifteen full members and ten candidate members—and a smaller Presidium, whose members would be from the EC. The increased size of the Party and the CC, he argued, required a larger executive organ for making decisions between sessions of the Central Committee.[26] Furthermore, some problems required resolution on a daily basis, and such decisions could only be made by a small collective group, the new Presidium. "Until now," he explained, such decisions have been made "through consultations with a number of comrades. Such a practice is deficient, since it makes it possible for such decisions to emanate not from a statutory Party organ, but from a single person [unul singur]."[27]

This important change in the statutes cast further light on Apostol's role in the 1965 leadership. Apostol's report on the new statutes, given the morning of 21 July, specifically mentioned the election of a Political Bureau, not a Presidium.[28] Only with the report of the Editing Commission on 23 July was the change to Presidium publicized, and Ceauşescu was the one to speak in defense of the new wording. The decision must have been made between 21 and 23 July. Ceauşescu, in contrast to Apostol, did not use the term Political Bureau in his report to the congress on 19 July, although he discussed many changes in the statutes. He probably knew what was coming—indeed, he is likely to have planned it—but Apostol either did not know or opposed the change. This difference between them, resolved during the congress, was the first public split in the collective leadership.

Ceauşescu's explanation of the changes to the congress was ingenious. By portraying the Presidium as new and different—not just a renamed Political Bureau but a small group that could prevent concentration of executive decisions in any one individual's hands[29]—he associated the change with collective leadership. Anyone arguing against it would have been rejecting that basic principle of the succession period. Almost half of those on the 25-member Editing Commission[30] that produced the new wording were immediately made members of the two new bodies, most of the rest were soon promoted by Ceauşescu, and all had an interest in the continuation of collective decisionmaking. No one could object. Yet the results were highly favorable to Ceauşescu: Within a year he would have a majority in the Presidium, and the EC would eventually be dominated by his supporters.

Meanwhile, the personnel changes made at the congress promised to strengthen collective decisionmaking. There was not even implied criticism of the individuals involved, and no major demotions occurred. Despite Ceauşescu's call for a statutory organ much smaller than the Political Bureau, seven of its nine members joined the new Presidium: Ceauşescu, Chivu Stoica, Maurer, Apostol, Bîrlădeanu, Bodnaraş, and Drăghici. Only Petre Borilă and Alexandru Moghioroş were excluded—and they were not dropped altogether, but became full members of the EC and remained in that body until December 1968. Both were rumored in 1965 to be ill[31] (Moghioroş died in 1969, and Borilă in 1973) and neither had appeared frequently during the preceding year, so the failure to include them in the Presidium was not unexpected.[32] All candidate members of the former Political Bureau were elected to the EC, including Leonte Răutu, the CC secretary for propaganda and culture, Leonte Sălăjan, the defense minister, and Ştefan Voitec, president of the GNA. For most members of the RWP leadership, the Ninth Congress seemed to mean continuity.

A major change in Article 13(b) of the Party statutes did force a number of high officials to shift jobs and in the long run had crucial implications for the relative power of individual leaders. The wording was clear: "A member of the Party may hold only one position of political leadership which necessitates full-time activity, whether it is in the Party organs or the state organs."[33] The effect was to prevent one person from being CC secretary, for example, and as such responsible for implementing Party decisions, and at the same time holding a position on the Council of Ministers. However, membership in one of the Party policymaking bodies, the Presidium or EC, was not full-time activity because no administrative responsibility was involved.

Ceaușescu described the new statute as an expression of collective leadership and internal Party democracy and as a means to assure "efficient control of state activity by the Party organs."[34] However, the general secretary's approval in 1965 probably was expedient rather than wholehearted: The statute would be eliminated in late 1967 to allow Ceaușescu to become head of state as well as head of Party, and in fact he would unite the Party and state hierarchies at the county and local levels as well. In contrast, Apostol in 1965 stressed the provision's "exceptional importance in avoiding a situation where, through the holding of more than one office, the relationship between the controlled [state] organ and the controlling Party organ could be altered." He continued: "The precise definition of responsibilities tied to the exercise of various functions in the Party and state line guarantees a real Party control, not influenced by incompatible dependence."[35] But he gave no specific example of such "incompatible dependence," and neither Apostol nor Ceaușescu lost a position as a result of the change. Of those directly affected, only Chivu Stoica and Drăghici spoke at the congress, and neither mentioned 13(b).[36]

Evidently the crucial individuals during this succession period were the seven members of the Presidium, and their consensus on the need for collective leadership must have extended to Article 13(b). Ceaușescu, Chivu Stoica, and Maurer were limited to their current posts (the top three) by the article and were always treated with formal equality, although alphabetical order put Ceaușescu in first place. Three other members of the Presidium were now first vice-presidents of the Council of Ministers; Apostol had been joined at this level by Bîrlădeanu and Bodnaraș, both mere vice-presidents up until now. Bîrlădeanu had overseen foreign trade and so was closely involved in planning and economic policies. Bodnaraș controlled relations with foreign communist parties, focusing on military and defense issues as well as cultural and educational matters. Apostol had given up his post as head of the trade unions just before the congress, but he continued to oversee them and also began to include agriculture among his concerns, probably as a troubleshooter in a sector causing great anxiety to the leadership.[37] The positions of these three men implied continuity, but Apostol was weakened in relation to the other two because Article 13(b) prevented him from acquiring any new positions.

The seventh member of the Presidium, and the only CC secretary other than Ceauşescu to be a member, was Alexandru Drăghici. To comply with 13(b), Drăghici gave up the Ministry of Internal Affairs[38] (which he had controlled since May 1952) and his vice-presidency of the Council of Ministers in order to join the Party Secretariat. Apparently he expected to continue overseeing the security sector from the Party, and his subsequent public activities indicated that he shared responsibility in the Secretariat for military and security affairs with Vasile Patilineţ and for cadre and organizational matters with Virgil Trofin. Drăghici's speech at the ninth Congress reflected his concern with defense and internal security, and his discussion of foreign policy resembled the statements of military officers rather than of other Party officials. He stressed the "danger of war" and warned against "complacency" or "weakening of revolutionary vigilance."[39] His responsibilities for cadres and organizations were revealed by his detailed report on promotion criteria to the CC plenum in April 1966.[40] Relinquishing the Ministry of Internal Affairs would prove disastrous for Drăghici; he was cut off from his base of support, and Ceauşescu would be able to denounce him and eject him from the Party leadership in April 1968.

Partly as a result of Article 13(b), the composition of the CC Secretariat changed much more than that of the Political Bureau/Presidium. Although the total number of secretaries increased from six to nine, two men lost positions: Chivu Stoica and Ilie Verdeţ, who had become, respectively, president of the Council of State and vice-president of the Council of Ministers. The Verdeţ shift was surprising—he had just been made CC secretary along with Niculescu-Mizil after Gheorghiu-Dej's death. Formerly deputy chief of the CC organizational section, Verdeţ also had experience as a regional Party first secretary and had received a medal for his efforts in the collectivization drive of the early 1960s. His move to the Council of Ministers appeared to be a demotion, but it later became clear that he was Ceauşescu's man in the government. Eventually Verdeţ remained as the only first vice-president, for many years serving as Maurer's heir apparent, and finally he became prime minister himself.

Four men—Ceauşescu, Dalea, Răutu, and Niculescu-Mizil—continued as CC secretaries. Dalea gave up the presidency of the Higher Agricultural Council to remain on the Secretariat. Răutu was secretary for propaganda and culture, and Niculescu-Mizil, who became a secretary in March 1965, had been Răutu's assistant since 1958 as head of the CC propaganda section. One of the new secretaries, Manea Mănescu, had been Răutu's other deputy in the CC apparatus since 1961 as head of the science and culture section. Joining the four holdovers were five new secretaries, including Drăghici and Mănescu.

The third, Alexandru Moghioroş, yielded his post as vice-president of the Council of Ministers to move to the Secretariat, but his failure to move from the Political Bureau to the Presidium marked him as on his way out, either from ill health or disgrace. The fourth new secretary, Patilineţ, was a former regional first secretary who had been involved in military and defense issues at least since 1961. The last, Virgil Trofin, had been in charge of the Party youth organization until June 1964, when he evidently moved into the CC apparatus. As CC secretary, he became involved in agricultural problems, but he eventually wrested cadre and organizational responsibilities from Drăghici and served as second secretary until after the Tenth Party Congress in 1969.[41]

The Secretariat after the Ninth Party Congress therefore was a rather junior body that Ceauşescu came to dominate rather quickly. Only he and Drăghici served on both the Secretariat and the Presidium, and the other secretaries were not significant rivals. Ceauşescu may not have had full support from Dalea, Moghioroş, and Răutu, and certainly did not from Drăghici. However, the remaining four secretaries—Mănescu, Niculescu-Mizil, Patilineţ, and Trofin—had moved up from the CC apparatus controlled by Ceauşescu, and they would become prominent members of his leadership group. As a result, the general secretary's influence was much greater in the top Party administrative body than in the top policymaking organ, the Presidium, where the six other members had all belonged to the Gheorghiu-Dej group and so could rival Ceauşescu in prestige, seniority, and ambition.

The new EC presented a more complicated picture, and it was clear that Ceauşescu could not yet dominate the meetings. Twelve of the fifteen full members had been either full or candidate members of the Political Bureau. The remaining three were Niculescu-Mizil, Gheorghe Rădulescu (vice-president of the Council of Ministers since 1963, specializing in Comecon trade), and Constantin Drăgan, who replaced Apostol as head of the trade unions after serving as his deputy for a year and who had long-term connections to Ceauşescu in regional Party bodies. Eight EC members were on the Council of Ministers, two held other state positions, and five had full-time Party posts. The EC was clearly dominated by those with state responsibilities, and all but two full members had been prewar Party members. Both younger men, Niculescu-Mizil and Drăgan, had spend most of their careers in Party work and were close to Ceauşescu; he was beginning to bring in his own supporters.

Because the EC's full members came largely from Gheorghiu-Dej's Political Bureau, we must look to the candidate members to discern any pattern among new entrants into the leadership. Here the promotion of Party administrators is quite clear. Nine of the ten candidate EC members had been extensively involved in Party work. The one exception was Mihai Gere, head of the People's Council of the Mureş-Maghiar Autonomous region until his election in August 1965 as vice-president of the Council of Ministers. Dumitru Coliu had been president of the Party Control Commission; Petre

Lupu had been chief of the CC organizational section since 1961; and János Fazekas, also elected vice-president of the Council of Ministers in August 1965, had been a CC secretary from 1955 to 1961, when he became minister of food. The remaining six had all been or were in 1965 regional first secretaries.[42]

The predominance of Party work did not hold for their occupations after the GNA met in August 1965. Five of the ten became vice-presidents, four of the Council of Ministers and one of the Council of State. Of the remaining five, four would move into the Council of Ministers during the next two years. Party administrators thus were moving into the highest state positions, a trend that would continue for at least four years. In addition, seven of the ten belonged to ethnic minorities.[43] This trend and the continuing efforts to recruit minorities to Party membership persuaded some members of the smaller ethnic groups that their status might improve as Ceauşescu established his authority. Finally, the stress of recruiting intellectuals had an added dimension (beyond promises of greater cultural autonomy): The trade unions—and therefore the workers—whose influence in the Party was being reduced, were Apostol's base of support; if their preponderance in the Party was weakened, so was Apostol, and Ceauşescu was strengthened accordingly.

The period from Gheorghiu-Dej's death through the Ninth Party Congress was perhaps most remarkable for the stability and continuity of political leadership in Romania. The former leader's offices were divided between Ceauşescu and Chivu Stoica, and the collective leadership then proceeded to enhance the power of the Party in society and (less deliberately) the power of Ceauşescu within the Party. The Political Bureau was replaced by a Presidium and an Executive Committee, but most of the members of the older body merely moved to the Presidium. The pattern followed in personnel shifts seemed to be promotions, not demotions, as the size of most Party organs was increased to receive new entrants and few officials lost their jobs. This was true also of the Central Committee. All but ten full and thirteen candidate members of the CC were re-elected in 1965, and the overall size rose from 100 to 196. The Secretariat was most radically altered, its size increased, and four of its nine members promoted from Ceauşescu's CC apparatus. What few newcomers did appear on the national scene tended to be Party officials, brought in by the general secretary. Finally, although Ceauşescu was clearly the most prominent individual before and during the congress,[44] the new RCP leadership in these first months was very much a collective and unified group. The one difference of opinion that did become visible between Apostol and Ceauşescu on the creation of the EC and Presidium was resolved in Ceauşescu's favor. The Ninth Party Congress, like the months immediately preceding it, demonstrated the reality of collective leadership in Romania—but it also foreshadowed the eventual dominance of Nicolae Ceauşescu.

4

Preparations:
The Early Years, 1965-1967

The first months after the death of Gheorghe Gheorghiu-Dej had established a collective leadership at the top of the Romanian Communist Party with Nicolae Ceauşescu as the most prominent individual. For the next several years, the Romanian political process was marked by public unity and cooperation among the new leaders while Ceauşescu gradually brought a number of his supporters into the top Party organs. Not until the end of 1967 did he initiate the major organizational and personnel changes that would allow him to consolidate his personal control over the Romanian political system by 1969. His personnel strategy is analyzed more fully in Chapter 8, but now we need to focus on the policies and political techniques that emerged in these early years as Ceauşescu and his colleagues tried to win acceptance from specific groups inside Romania and from the population as a whole.

Most political leaders, Ceauşescu included, seek to rule by right rather than by coercion alone. That is, they prefer to justify coercion, to legitimize it, to turn power into authority and have it accepted by those over whom the power is exercised. Such acceptance becomes particularly important during a transition in political leadership, when the regime is temporarily weakened, but it is also necessary when the leaders wish to accomplish certain goals of economic and social development that require cooperation from society and not merely obedience. The search for legitimacy is complex and difficult for any ruler—but particularly so for leaders of revolutionary parties. If we use Max Weber's categories of legitimacy, we can see the problems immediately.[1]

According to Weber, legitimacy may be (1) rational-legal, (2) traditional, or (3) charismatic. In other words, people may accept the right of an individual, a party, or a government to rule on the basis of legality and reason, tradition, or the charisma of the leader. A revolutionary party cannot appeal to legality, however—the legal government has just been overthrown. Nevertheless, that party should have a series of specific goals, an ideology perhaps, that provides a rational basis for rule. If the population accepts that ideology, it may accept the new ruler and party as long as they appear to be implementing that ideology. But the party must constantly prove itself; obedience is not given without question. Weber's second category, tradition, certainly is not an effective base on which to rest a new regime that has had no time to establish any continuity. Thus the most effective source of legitimacy for a revolutionary regime—until it can produce concrete achievements—often turns out to be Weber's third type. Charisma may help to consolidate a post-revolutionary government, but it is, of course, difficult to pass on because it is by definition based on the personal attributes of an individual. This is one reason Leninist parties have difficulties with succession.

The new Romanian collective leadership, with Ceauşescu as its spokesman, tried to enhance its legitimacy in the eyes of the Romanian population in a variety of ways in order to maintain support. During the 1970s Ceauşescu would turn to charisma; not so in the late 1960s. Although there were dramatic episodes of personal leadership, such as Ceauşescu's speech protesting the 1968 intervention in Czechoslovakia, the attempts by the regime to achieve legitimacy were based mainly on rationality and legality—policies and procedures promised by Ceauşescu in the name of the collective leadership—and also on tradition, especially Romanian history and nationalism.

Ceauşescu made the most of his position as spokesman. His statements were masterpieces of ambiguity, creating hopes on the part of very different groups—from artists to the secret police—that the Party leadership and especially he, Ceauşescu, shared their goals and would satisfy their specific needs within Romanian society. To the population at large he promised higher living standards, respect for legality and institutionalized processes, and continuity in the two fundamental goals established by Gheorghiu-Dej: industrialization and national independence. He also introduced a number of populist political techniques during these early years to encourage support for the regime. Many of these techniques and goals would form the basic framework of Ceauşescu's methods and policies for more than two decades.

Ceauşescu and his colleagues could not, of course, rely exclusively on promises and persuasion; they simultaneously took steps to maintain their power and implement their policies through coercion if necessary. They needed to exercise oversight throughout society by means of the Party and so had to maintain Party unity. They also needed two traditional levers of coercion, the army and the secret police. During 1967 Ceauşescu would advocate some changes in internal Party life, in the armed forces, and in the Ministry of Internal Affairs, developments that were part of his preparations for the events of 1968 and 1969. Therefore, after we analyze the policy ambiguity and populist political techniques, we shall consider the relations between the Party leadership and these organizations—Party, army, and police. Of course, the major issue that concerns us continues to be the role of

Ceauşescu himself, and the chapter ends with an analysis of his status in the collective leadership from 1965 to 1967.

Policy Ambiguity

Ceauşescu's speech to the Ninth Party Congress established the basic outlines of regime policy for the next several years. In the name of the collective leadership, he reasserted the two basic priorities: industrial development and national autonomy. His defense of industrialization illustrates the appeal of the new leaders to every possible base of support and is one of the earliest examples of Ceauşescu's political skill. He quoted first a nineteenth-century Romanian historian, A. D. Xenopol, next the Romanian Social-Democrat Constantin Dobrogeanu-Gherea, and finally his own predecessor. Xenopol had written that "to remain only agricultural is to condemn ourselves to the production of raw materials . . . to make ourselves for all time the slaves of foreigners." Gherea had insisted that "we must develop all the resources of our country and become an industrialized state." Finally, Ceauşescu cited Gheorghiu-Dej at the October 1945 Party conference: "The development of heavy . . . industry opens the widest possibilities for utilizing the entire labor force of our people and for creating the wealth necessary to rebuild the country."[2] In a few minutes Ceauşescu managed to demonstrate the Romanian national origins of the RCP's emphasis on industrialization, point to the deep roots of socialism in Romania as shown by Gherea, and reassure any worriers in the Party that the goals and methods of Gheorghiu-Dej would not be totally abandoned. Indeed, the economic policies of Gheorghiu-Dej so reminiscent of Stalin were continued in 1965: Whereas the accumulation fund in 1961–1965 had averaged 24.3 percent of national income per year, in 1966–1970 it would rise to 28.8 percent; in addition, the share of industry in investment would increase from 46.5 percent to 50.0 percent, while that of agriculture would drop from 19.4 percent to 16.0 percent.[3]

Actually, the most controversial economic issue in 1965 involved the powers and responsibilities of the central ministries and planning institutions as compared with those of the enterprises. Ceauşescu neatly sidestepped this problem at the congress by declaring that it was possible to enlarge the roles of the ministries and planners and also of enterprise managers. The only speaker who elaborated on the issue was Alexandru Bîrlădeanu, but even he was ambiguous except on the issue of economic sovereignty—an "inalienable" and "indivisible" right of each country.[4] He did hint that measures to increase the operational independence of managers were being considered. This theme was then picked up in December 1966 by Maxim Berghianu, head of the State Planning Committee, and by Ceauşescu in a major article on the Party published in May 1967, in which he promised that new measures were begin worked out to give greater responsibilities to enterprises and to include the best experts as well as the masses in solving economic problems. In the summer of 1967 an experiment in "new forms of planning, credits, and material incentives" was introduced under which a number of enterprises were given some flexibility for the rest of the year in organization, hiring labor, and adjusting wages.[5] Finally, more than two years after the 1965 congress, the October 1967 CC plenum advanced proposals for nationwide change; these were adopted as part of the general reorganization approved by the December 1967 Party conference.

In contrast to the postponement of reforms in the industrial sector, agriculture received immediate public attention. At the Ninth Congress, Ceauşescu had criticized the management of agriculture and called for a new legal organization for the cooperatives to ensure increases in their production by making them more democratic and improving the reimbursement of the peasants.[6] In his report to the November 1965 CC plenum, he called again for material incentives to "stimulate" the efforts of the peasants.[7] The following March the founding congress of the Union of Agricultural Cooperatives opened in Bucharest in order to ensure the broad discussions appropriate for socialist democracy.[8]

The new union was described as the instrument of the peasants because a general assembly in each cooperative would elect representatives to district and regional unions (whose constituent conferences had already been held in February[9]). These bodies in turn sent representatives to the national congress in March, but the election, of course, remained under the close supervision of the Party. It became clear that the union's purpose was to help the cooperatives solve any economic and social problems that might arise,[10] whereas the Higher Agricultural Council, which had replaced the Ministry of Agriculture in 1962, would continue to "establish the level and rate of development of all agricultural sectors . . . in close collaboration with the State Planning Committee, the National Union . . . and other [state bodies]."[11] In other words, the union would try to alleviate any difficulties caused by the continued centralization of agricultural planning. The congress did pass new statutes for the cooperatives, requiring a participatory democratic structure, a pension system, wages based on the quantity and quality of work and production achieved, and additional payments allocated by the cooperatives, as Ceauşescu had suggested in November 1965.[12] The overall emphasis at the congress was not on radical departures in agriculture but— and this is particularly clear in Maurer's speech—on the codification of agricultural practices made possible by the achievement of fully cooperativized agriculture back in 1962.[13]

Perhaps the most radical aspect of the congress was that it was held at all. The first of its kind in Eastern Europe since the war,[14] it was held in the modern, glass-domed exhibition hall in Bucharest in front of thousands of peasants—many in their colorful regional costumes—and representatives of all the ruling communist parties were present.[15] A foreign journalist reported that Ceauşescu was "the star of the show," which was "marked by long speeches . . . and efficient and disciplined cheering."[16] In addition, the various Romanian speakers began to use some phrases praising the general secretary that later became routine. Maurer in particular stressed Ceauşescu's important personal contribution to the measures proposed and adopted by the congress. Already in 1966 Ceauşescu was accorded considerable respect and was demonstrating his flair for drama.

The Party leader spoke for over two hours the first day,[17] using the opportunity to extol the history of the Romanian peasantry. He spoke of Dacian agriculture, of the tradition of peasant uprisings, of the important role played by the peasants in the armies of Romanian heroes such as Decebal, Michael the Brave, and Tudor Vladimirescu. He bemoaned the "chains of the feudal system" and denounced the "bourgeois-landowner regime." It had failed to help the peasants in part because of the country's "dependence on the great imperialist powers . . . which had transformed Romania into a supplier of raw materials and agricultural produce." At last, he continued, thanks to the leadership of the communists, the peasants have become "masters of their destiny." He managed to combine class struggle and national struggle in Romanian history and even included the Hungarian and German peasants and the peasants of other nationalities as "defenders of the homeland . . . shoulder to shoulder . . . [with] the Romanian peasants." The entire extravaganza was perhaps the first example of Ceauşescu's participatory and populist techniques: a new pyramid of general assemblies electing representatives to a grandiose forum that would bring thousands of Romanians into personal contact with Ceauşescu himself.

The three-day show demonstrated the growing influence of the general secretary, but it brought no significant shift of resources toward agriculture; at the June 1966 CC plenum, Ceauşescu announced "big investments" providing an increase of 6 to 12 percent over the 20 percent rise in agricultural production envisaged at the Ninth Congress for 1966–1970, but industrial production was revised upward by 8 percent at the same time.[18] Although the new decisions increased material incentives to some extent and called for discussion and participation by the collective peasants, they left untouched the centralized planning mechanisms and the priority of industry.

Scientific training and research also received public attention from the leadership. The same radical change as had been brought to party education— the shift from theoretical orientation to a concern for concrete professional problems—was advocated for scientific research as well. At the congress Ceauşescu had insisted that science must contribute actively to economic and social development and that research should focus on the technical sciences. At the same time, he insisted that research required a "broad exchange of opinions, . . . [an] open confrontation of viewpoints . . . [including] collaboration with scientists . . . from other countries, . . . [and access to] all that is best in world science and technology."[19] Again hopes were raised among the scientists by these comments. However, Ceauşescu wanted a guarantee of correct results in research; insisting that they must "concentrate cadres and material resources . . . more efficiently," he proposed the creation of a National Council of Scientific Research to work out a national research program. Established at the CC Plenum of 8–10 December 1965, the council was composed of 80 to 90 members, including Ceauşescu's wife, Elena. His subsequent pronouncements on research were quite consistent with these early statements: "Whether applied or fundamental, scientific investigation must serve society and the latter's advance."[20] Again Ceauşescu had produced expectations of change, but simultaneously he moved to centralize the process and appointed his wife for the first time to a prestigious position.

Educational policy also emphasized pragmatism and the needs of society. Here his patriotism began to emerge, for students were to study not only the classics of Marxism but also "the glorious traditions of our Party."[21] Although technical education had to be emphasized because of production needs, the humanities and social sciences should not be slighted. Indeed, "political economy, history, and philosophy" must be studied, but with a focus on "the policy of the RCP."[22]

No overall educational reform was instituted until April 1968, although some piecemeal changes came earlier. Scînteia announced a reform of social science teaching on 8 April 1966, and in June the Higher Party School was renamed the Ştefan Gheorghiu Academy of Social and Political Sciences, attached to the CC of the RCP.[23] In February 1967 Ceauşescu criticized the Ministry of Education and those involved in higher education for not improving curriculums, courses, and teaching, and in May he called on the Party bodies to help "do away with ossified and stereotyped forms of theoretical activity."[24] Then on 20 July 1967 Scînteia published a major study on higher education and called for a basic reorganization. The main features of the new proposals were a reduction in required courses in Marxism-Leninism, whose concepts should have been "assimilated in secondary school," and a return to the more decentralized administrative system used in prewar Romania. The essence of the new reforms had been expressed by Ceauşescu in May: "Knowledge . . . is not measured by the number of memorized quotations, . . . but by the correctness of the answer . . . in the process of social development."[25]

This instrumental view, combined with the dialectical method—progress through conflict or, in Ceauşescu's frequently used phrase, "exchange of opinions"—characterized the new leaders' attitudes toward writers and artists as well. In February 1965 the Writers' Union had replaced its conservative president, Mihai Beniuc, with the aging and therefore transitional figure, Demostene Botez.[26] In February 1966 Botez was in turn replaced by Zaharia Stancu, widely regarded as an opportunist but probably the power behind Botez. As such, Stancu had allowed extensive access to Western literature, diversity of styles, and relatively open discussions in literary journals.[27] Ceaușescu confirmed the new tone in an interview with a group of Italian journalists in mid-1966:

> We challenge the men of letters and art to place their talent at the service of socialist construction. . . . But we allow them to decide how to write, how to paint, how to compose, we leave it to them to find the most suitable forms. . . . We meet with them not in order to tell them how and what to write, but to make them understand the priorities of our Party and our people, which they should try to express, each according to his talents and abilities.[28]

While promises of intellectual diversity were being made to elite groups in Romanian society, various steps were also being taken to improve the standard of living and the supply of consumer goods to the general population.[29] Wages were increased in September 1965 and again in June 1967; a new pension system was instituted by the October 1966 CC Plenum; housing facilities were improved by the offer of state support for private apartment construction; prices were reduced on certain types of consumer goods such as refrigerators and radios; and private restaurants, boarding houses, and artisans' shops were allowed to operate. The revised 1966–1970 plan promised a 25 percent increase in real wages and a 65 percent rise in consumer goods production.[30] By the spring of 1967 a London *Times* correspondent in Bucharest commented on the steady improvement in living standards during the preceding year:

> Shop windows are better filled, [and] there is a greater variety of imported goods, more attention to satisfying public demand, [and] more concern for the consumer. . . . The number of private cars . . . has risen considerably, and whereas a year ago black . . . prevailed in what was still a trafficless city, there is now a fair sprinkling of colour and variety of French and Italian makes that give Bucharest an air of greater prosperity.[31]

Measures were also introduced, especially by the trade unions, to improve working conditions, and the GNA passed a new law on labor protection in December 1965. In his explanation of the new provisions,[32] Apostol pointed out that deficiencies in supply and bad management in production and labor had often led to "unrhythmical plan fulfillment and abusive supplementary hours," which hurt both the workers and the quality of the goods produced. He cited a case in a coal mine in Valea Jiului where the directors did not respect rational norms or the safety of the miners, but tolerated dangerous working conditions. The Party leadership, he reported, had been forced to intervene directly, sending a commission of specialists led by Drăghici to eliminate the deficiencies. (Evidently the miners' discontent was not permanently alleviated, for it would be strikes in the Valea Jiului mines that would cause a major crisis in 1977.)

Signs of potential conflict with the population were already visible in the new regime's puritanical attitude—widely attributed to Ceauşescu himself—toward certain types of social behavior such as abortion, divorce, or smoking. The first two issues were related to demographic policies: By 1965 the annual rate of population increase in Romania had dropped to a postwar low, and the country faced a potential labor shortage that threatened the Party's long-term plans for economic development. In an effort to raise the birth rate, the regime in October 1966 made abortions and divorces almost impossible to obtain and increased taxes on childless adults. An intense press campaign also encouraged people to have more children. The new laws had an immediate effect—the population growth rate almost doubled during the next year—but Romanians soon developed ways to avoid the unpopular new measures. After the initial jump, the birth rate declined again; similar attempts to raise it would recur in the 1970s and 1980s. A campaign against smoking was part of a general drive against long hair, beards, miniskirts, and other signs of Western decadence and was also closely associated in the minds of most Romanians with the person of Ceauşescu.[33] These campaigns, in contrast to other policies, did nothing to endear the new leader to the Romanian people.

In these early months, therefore, the RCP and Ceauşescu continued the basic emphasis on industrialization established by Gheorghiu-Dej, but promised improvements in the lives of those working in agriculture, promises emphasized by a grandiose celebration of the Romanian peasantry. Ceauşescu also raised the hopes of intellectuals that a new era in cultural life was beginning, marked by diversity and pragmatism. In addition, the Party leaders introduced a number of concrete improvements to bring an immediate rise in the general living standards of many Romanians and to cement popular support for the regime. The puritanical streak it demonstrated was not popular, but many citizens could find ways of avoiding the most onerous of the new policies. In general, life seemed to be improving, and there was sufficient ambiguity in Ceauşescu's pronouncements for citizens to hope that the future without Gheorghiu-Dej would be better than the past.

Populist Techniques

In addition to promising everything to everyone, the new leaders used a variety of political techniques to encourage popular acceptance of the regime. Many of the measures emphasized the legality and representative nature of the political system. For example, during the Ninth Congress Ceauşescu called on the Grand National assembly and the People's Councils to be major forums for discussion and participation. The constitution adopted in August 1965 gave the GNA new responsibilities and made important state organs— the Council of State, the Council of Ministers, the Supreme Court, and the Procurator General—responsible to the legislature. Commissions such as the one created to oversee the constitutionality of laws were required to report to the assembly regularly, and articles on these groups began to appear frequently in the press. Thus, the entire legislative process was to be institutionalized, and individual deputies were to have a sense of participation in the drafting and preparation of legislation.[34]

At the same time, Ceauşescu insisted that the county People's Councils ensure broader participation in resolving public problems. The stress on these local organs of state power, as the People's Councils were defined, and on the "permanent and active participation of the working masses in the solution of state problems" had begun under Gheorghiu-Dej,[35] but was intensified after his death. Then, in late December 1965, a state committee was created to oversee the councils because of the "increased tasks" assigned to them by the Ninth Congress. As in the case of industry and agriculture, the regime was apparently unwilling to allow institutionalized procedures and participatory government to jeopardize centralized control.

Another political technique to increase the citizens' sense of participation in policy formulation was the regular publication of letters to newspapers from readers, both complaints and suggestions. At the Ninth Congress, Ceauşescu had mentioned the thousands of letters received by the Central Committee and regional Party organizations and he called for better handling of them. He emphasized that the letters expressed unanimous support for the basic policies of the Party, but they included useful suggestions of improving production in various sectors and revealed cases of "bureaucratism" or "failures of socialist discipline."[36] He singled out certain Party committees for their excellent response, but criticized others, such as Iaşi region or Bucharest city, where in 1964 only 65 percent of the letters had been dealt with successfully. He then urged the press to pay increased attention to readers' letters; in the next year, Romanian newspapers carried such a large quantity of them that even the *New York Times* commented, describing the volume of complaints about shortages or the poor condition of public transport facilities and roads.[37]

At the April 1966 CC plenum, Manea Mănescu reported that over a million citizens had written during 1965. In July 1966 the Council of State set general rules for handling letters: time limits on resolving the matter, investigations by higher bodies or administrators, and open discussion of the difficulties at meetings with employees. A year later the GNA passed a law providing remedies against illegal administrative acts. The law excluded such areas as defense, security, public order, and planning and provided that only individual, arbitrary acts—not the norms established by administrative bodies—could be appealed. But the courts could summon individual officials and set daily fines for delays, and many Romanians must have hoped that the new requirements would bring positive results.[38]

Yet another strategy to enhance Romanians' sense of participation was the initiation of huge national conferences for workers in various economic sectors, with extensive preparation in local meetings and in the press. This type of event would become characteristic of the entire Ceauşescu era; the agricultural congress in March 1966 was only the first example. As he pointed out at that time, the purpose of consulting the masses was to strengthen "the unity of the people around the Party and the government."[39] In other words, he hoped to increase popular support for the regime, not popular influence on policy. Thus workers in construction, retail trade, and machine-building met with Party leaders at various levels in that first year, and women also had their own conference.[40]

Finally, Ceauşescu made a series of visits to localities outside Bucharest to emphasize the Party's desire to consult all the people. Between July 1965 and January 1973, for example, he made 147 tours; most took two to three days and included several different places.[41] The events were by no means spontaneous—they were carefully arranged to indicate the overwhelming support of the population for the leaders, the interest and concern of the Bucharest officials for the development of the particular region, and the contribution of the area to the nation's history and economy. In 1966 and 1967 the press coverage always stated that "Party and state leaders" visited a given area, although Ceauşescu was mentioned much more frequently than other individuals: *Scînteia* referred to him over fifty times during the four days of stories on the trip to Crişana and the Banat in February 1966, to Maurer about fifteen times, and to the other two participants, Bîrlădeanu and Banc, once or twice a day.[42]

The staging of the visits was very dramatic, with motorcades in flower-draped cars,[43] ovations, balcony appearances, and the traditional Romanian greeting of bread and salt upon arrival. Oradea, near the Hungarian border, provided an example:

> The appearance on the balcony of the Party and state leaders was hailed with an ovation and prolonged cheers. Addressing the crowd, Nicolae Ceauşescu conveyed . . . a warm salute on behalf of the RCP Central Committee. . . . Referring to the prospects for Crişana region, Nicolae Ceauşescu said that further construction of industrial projects is planned under the new five-year plan. . . . They will raise the region's economic strength and further increase the contribution made by the working people of Oradea town and Crişana region to the blossoming of our socialist homeland.
>
> The square resounded with cheers for the Party and its leadership. Leaving the regional Party committee the motorcade traveled the streets of Oradea, heading for the aluminum factory. The people lined up along the route applauded warmly, greeting the leaders. Large

groups of Oradea residents waved red and tricolored scarves and offered flowers.[44]

Visits were then paid to important factories where "Nicolae Ceauşescu inquired about . . . the mechanization process" and "gave advice on the most judicious use of production space," while Alexandru Bîrlădeanu "pointed out the necessity of . . . high quality production . . . and the assimilation of new world techniques," and Ion Gheorghe Maurer "recommended the stimulation of creative effort as advised by the Party and state." The personalities of the leaders are revealed by these brief statements: the self-confident Ceauşescu giving advice on any topic, Bîrlădeanu focusing on international trade and therefore the quality of goods produced, and Maurer recognizing the need to stimulate efforts, presumably by material rewards.

Once economic production had been given first priority, it was time to address housing:

> The motorcade made its way to the new district where the workers of these enterprises and their families will live. No less than 5,625 apartments will be built here. . . . Nicolae Ceauşescu inquired about the cost of an apartment, whether the tenants were satisfied with the units. . . . The latter question was put to the thousands of tenants in the square. Enthusiastic applause was the response. It was an expression of gratitude of the working people for the care shown by the Party and state to improve their living conditions.[45]

It was nothing of the sort, of course, but it did reveal that housing was an area of concern and that the Party could mobilize the appropriate responses from thousands of citizens.

Next, the local area was lauded during each stop. For example, in Timişoara Ceauşescu described the city as a "powerful cultural and scientific center of our homeland," in Maramureş he stressed the "old and rich revolutionary tradition" of the region, and in Galaţi he visited monuments at "places that evoke the glorious past, the heroism and ardent patriotism which animated the struggle of the Romanian people for national and social liberation."[46]

A final aspect of these visits worth noting is their role in Romanian nationality policies. Early tours were to areas having large minority populations. The first, in November 1965, was to Cluj and Maramureş, areas close to the Soviet and Hungarian borders. On the next trip, three months later, the leaders visited Crişana and the Banat, bordering on Hungary and Yugoslavia. The third trip was also to a border region, Suceava and Iaşi, in Bucovina and northern Moldavia, near the USSR. During all of these tours the speaker emphasized the cooperation of the various nationality groups in building socialism in Romania. A typical statement was made by Ceauşescu during his speech to the Cluj Party activists in November 1965:

It is known, comrades, that for centuries Romanians, Hungarians and working people of other nationalities have been living together in the Cluj region. Throughout history they have created together all the material and spiritual wealth . . . achieved by their united endeavor, in spite of the exploiting classes' efforts to sow discord. History is full of examples of heroic struggles waged in common by the Romanians, Hungarians and working people of other nationalities against exploitation. . . . The very victory over fascism . . . and the building of socialism in Romania are the fruit of the united struggle. . . . Cluj region is a living example of the relationship of harmony and brotherhood . . . of different nationalities. . . . The Romanian and Hungarian working people work with enthusiasm, fraternally united, making their contribution to the struggle to . . . complete socialist construction in Romania. . . . Socialism . . . ensures fully equal rights . . . in the country's social life of all citizens, irrespective of nationality.[47]

The nationality themes were always present in Ceauşescu's speeches: the past cooperation of the various national groups in progressive political and social movements; the wisdom of current RCP nationality policy in ensuring equality of opportunity for all nationalities; the need for continued cooperation in building a better future. During the Cluj visit, Ceauşescu went out of his way to accept petitions handed to him on the streets, and evidently some concrete steps were taken soon afterward to improve living conditions and professional status of Hungarians in the city of Cluj.[48]

This effort to include the various nationality groups in the social fabric of the country was but one aspect of the regime's broad appeal to all groups for popular support. Ceauşescu and his colleagues hoped that promises to effect desired changes—especially higher standards of living, legalized procedures, and participatory processes—would induce specific groups and also the general population to accept their authority. If successful, then the Party's right to rule, its legitimacy, would be based on legality and rationality, the first category among Weber's sources of legitimacy. But that first category would not be sufficient in Ceauşescu's view, and he would also appeal for legitimacy on the basis of tradition; in this case, it would be the traditions of Romanian history and Romanian nationalism that would prove most successful in gaining popular support.

Historical Tradition

The emphasis on history, so clearly visible during the regional trips, was a constant theme in these years. Not only were "progressive" (socialist) movements from Romania's past honored, but also feudal princes such as Michael the Brave, who for a brief period in 1600 was the ruler of all three Romanian principalities—Wallachia, Moldavia, and Transylvania—"thus achieving the first political unification of the entire country," as Ceauşescu put it. He went on: "By honoring the outstanding deeds of our forerunners, we make the new history of our socialist homeland."[49] Even Carol I, Romania's first king, became acceptable. The red curtain that had covered a fresco of him in the Athenaeum, a concert hall and major Bucharest landmark, was removed in early 1967. As a Bucharest editor remarked, "Our anti-monarchic period is over. After all, Carol is a piece of history which you cannot pass over if you want to study our past thoroughly."[50]

To this embracing of tradition Ceauşescu in speeches from 1965 to 1967 added a particular stress on the history of the Romanian Communist Party, expressed so as to establish the Party as the rightful successor to previous regimes. In his report to the Ninth Congress Ceauşescu called for publication of a *History of the RCP*, which would "from the very beginnings of the workers' movement in Romania, present the whole path of the working-class struggle of the RCP." He then referred indirectly to the negative effects of the Comintern on the Romanian Party during the interwar years:

> In evaluating Party activity during the years of illegality, we must remember the difficult conditions under which it had to operate, the influence exercised by certain elements in its leadership which were opportunistic, sectarian, and foreign to the working class and our people, as well as the effect of certain negative phenomena in the international communist and workers' movement of that time. We must analyze critically the decisions of the congresses and other Party documents from that period . . . which contain incorrect ideas on important aspects of Party tactics and strategy, on agrarian, national and other problems.[51]

One other speaker at the congress, Gheorghe Stoica, repeated Ceauşescu's description of the "negative phenomena" and then denounced the Comintern attempt "to establish from outside the political line, organizational forms, methods of activity, and even the leaders of each Party."[52] Ceauşescu would not be so specific until May 1966, but already implicit in these remarks was a warning to the Soviets not to interfere in Romania or to try to influence the RCP's choice of leaders.

Soon after the July 1965 congress, a special commission was set up to edit a new *History of the RCP*, a task whose extraordinary importance was reflected in the choice of members: the entire Presidium and the three CC secretaries involved in culture and propaganda. The commission was mandated to do exactly what had been proposed by Ceauşescu and Gheorghe Stoica: "analyze in a critical spirit the decisions of the congresses and other Party documents . . . [while remembering] the difficult conditions" under which the Party had been forced to work.[53] The first task of the commission during 1966 was to prepare an outline of Party history on which researchers at various institutes would collaborate. The authoritative history that was to appear in 1967 was never published, but a series of monographs was based on the conclusions of the outline—studies of important moments in Party history such as the 1907 peasant revolt, the 1920 general strike, or the August 1944 insurrection.[54] The following spring, at the April 1966 CC plenum, the Institute of Party History was renamed the Institute of Historical and Social-Political Studies, still attached to the Central Committee,[55] and in May a new Museum of Party History opened in Bucharest.

The occasion for the museum opening was the forty-fifth anniversary of the founding of the RCP, and Ceauşescu's speech that day laid out in much greater detail than ever before his own version of RCP history.[56] He started by connecting the foundation of the Party in 1921 to Romania's struggle for "social and national liberation" and described the RCP as "the continuer of the centuries-old struggle of the Romanian people for the country's independence, for the formation of the Romanian nation and of the unitary national State, for the acceleration of social progress." Thus, national independence received more emphasis than the class struggle. He then went on to make a dramatic and direct denunciation of Comintern policy,[57] specifically rejecting the assertion that Romania was "a typical multi-national state" that must give the nationalities the right to "self-determination" and secession. These ideas were imposed on the Party at its congresses in 1924, 1928, and 1932, he explained, but were corrected when the leaders took a strong stand in 1938–1939 "in defense of national unity . . . independence and sovereignty."[58] He reminded his listeners that the Romanian principalities had suffered for centuries under foreign rule, and criticized the Comintern again for centuries under foreign rule, and criticized the Comintern again for rejecting the RCP's slogan "defense of the frontiers," devised in 1940 when Hungary took northern Transylvania (and shortly after the USSR seized Bessarabia). Although he made no specific reference to Bessarabia, many of his listeners heard it between the lines of his remarks. Bessarabia was soon mentioned in the Party theoretical journal, *Lupta de clasă*, and other indictments of Comintern interference in the interwar period were published during 1966.[59] The clear lesson in Ceauşescu's interpretation of Party history was the harm foreigners cause by interfering in the domestic affairs of a communist party when they do not understand the local conditions and needs. Thus, the Soviets were warned off—though indirectly because only the interwar years were the subject of specific complaints—and most Romanians, Party members and non-members, welcomed the remarks.

Nationalism and Foreign Policy

This rejection of foreign interference—whether by the Comintern, feudal princes, or bourgeois capitalists—had a double emotional appeal to Romanians because it made use of both tradition and nationalism. Indeed, the most effective source of legitimacy for the RCP and its leaders was Romanian nationalism and the post-1960 foreign policy that derived from and also contributed to it. Even the fundamental goal of economic development has usually been defined by Ceauşescu as a means to the end of national independence and sovereignty. The RCP's prompt reassurances to the Romanian population that the foreign policy established by Gheorghiu-Dej would continue were accompanied by pledges to the Soviets that Romania would remain loyal to the Warsaw Pact and maintain close ties with the other socialist countries.

The first official visit Romanian leaders made abroad after the Ninth Congress was to Moscow.[60] On 4 September 1965 *Scînteia* reported the departure of Ceauşescu, Maurer, Apostol, Bîrlădeanu, the two new CC secretaries (Manea Mănescu and Niculescu-Mizil), and the foreign minister (Corneliu Mănescu). Except for the July 1963 Comecon conference, the last high-level delegation to Moscow had been in August 1961, to the Twenty-second Congress of the CPSU. The composition of the 1965 delegation suggests that economic relations were a prominent topic during the talks, and the visit received heavy coverage in the Romanian press, which reported stops in Moscow, Volgograd, and Leningrad. Ceauşescu's toast at the end of the visit was quite cordial, and though he intoned the usual Romanian phrases about sovereignty and equality between socialist states, his attitude toward his hosts was warmer than on his arrival.[61]

This trip was evidently one of the high points in Soviet-Romanian relations during the 1960s. This is not the place to detail the deteriorating situation between the two allies leading up to and following the Warsaw Pact invasion of Czechoslovakia,[62] but one set of examples will quickly illustrate the tension. During the spring of 1966, Tito, Brezhnev, and Zhou Enlai visited Bucharest on separate occasions, and the public treatment accorded the three leaders was strikingly different. On 17 April, the day before Tito's arrival, *Scînteia* appeared with a huge picture and biography of the Yugoslav leader on page one, and for seven more days Tito completely dominated the front page. When he arrived, he was greeted by a city draped in bright colors and flowers, huge portraits of himself and Ceauşescu, and bilingual signs of welcome; the entire Presidium, Executive Committee, and Secretariat met him at the airport.[63]

Zhou Enlai's visit in June received almost as much coverage, this time for nine days. As head of state, he was met by Maurer rather than Ceauşescu, but was then received immediately by the entire Presidium. After several days of talks, he and Ceauşescu went to the seashore together before resuming the formal discussions. There were other trips within Romania, gala evenings, and mass meetings with workers' groups, all portrayed in the press with many photographs, and usually the entire Presidium participating in a "cordial, comradely atmosphere of warm friendship."[64]

In stark contrast to the other two visits, *Scînteia* announced on 14 May that Brezhnev had been in Romania from 10–13 May for "friendly" talks. This was just after Ceauşescu's speech in which he had criticized the

Comintern. He and Brezhnev were reported to have "exchanged opinions on problems of continued development of cooperation," and Ceauşescu had then given a dinner in a "warm, friendly atmosphere." This was the extent of the coverage given to Brezhnev's visit. Shortly thereafter, during a speech in Argeş on 12 June, Ceauşescu repeated his earlier suggestion that both NATO and the Warsaw Pact be abolished "to create security throughout the world." Brezhnev returned to Bucharest in July with Kosygin and other Soviet leaders for a meeting the Political Consultative Committee of the Warsaw Treaty Organization, which itself then called for the elimination of both alliance systems. Even so, although the various delegations received extensive coverage in *Scînteia*, the accompanying text was formal, not enthusiastic, and no mention was made of subsequent Soviet proposals to strengthen the Warsaw Pact.[65]

During the rest of 1966 there were few high-level contacts with the other socialist states. Ceauşescu spent some time vacationing in Bulgaria, and the Polish leader, Władisław Gomułka, did likewise in Romania.[66] In addition, Ceauşescu made a trip to Moscow with Maurer and Ioniţă, the defense minister, which received little attention in the Romanian press.[67] In contrast to the Romanians' visit to the USSR a year earlier, the issues this time were clearly military. The following year contacts with their allies picked up only slightly. Signs for WTO cooperation were not promising: Romania had broken ranks with its allies by establishing diplomatic relations with the Federal Republic of Germany in January 1967 during the first phase of Bonn's new *Ostpolitik*. Ceauşescu did travel to Moscow and Budapest and received Todor Zhivkov in Bucharest,[68] but in June the Romanians took the unprecedented step of refusing to side with the other socialist states against Israel and break diplomatic relations with Tel Aviv during the war in the Middle East—a major departure from bloc unity. Ceauşescu again made a quick trip to Moscow, this time with Maurer.[69] He did not attend the Budapest summit meeting in mid-July, and during the rest of the summer the Romanian leader continued to sit on the fence between Bonn and Moscow, receiving Willy Brandt in Bucharest in August, but at the end of the month allowing Romanian troops to take part in WTO troop maneuvers on Bulgarian territory with Soviet and Bulgarian troops and observers from other Pact countries.[70]

Thus, relations with the Soviet Union deteriorated from cordial agreement on economic issues in the fall of 1965 to covert hostility on military matters in 1967. But as before there was neither a complete break nor capitulation by the Romanians. The tension with Moscow and the symbolic gestures of neutrality in foreign policy were popular within Romania and brought the country and Ceauşescu himself a great deal of international publicity. The regime was beginning to convince some Romanians that its intentions were in the best interests of the nation. This appeal to Romanian nationalism, bolstered by policy ambiguity and populist techniques promising legality and broad participation in decisionmaking, provided the RCP with an opportunity for the first time to gain a measure of legitimacy within the country.

Preparations: Party, Army, Police

The new Party leaders did not, of course, depend only upon persuasion and appeals for popular support in order to maintain their control of Romania. Ceauşescu in particular wished to expand the power of the Party and his own influence within that crucial organization. His objective was to keep the Party united in support of his policies. In 1965 the themes most frequently expressed by Party leaders about the internal processes of the RCP had included "collective leadership" and "Party democracy." By 1967, as Ceauşescu extended his control into the higher Party bodies, "Party unity" and "democratic centralism" gradually came to dominate.

In his May 1966 speech on the forty-fifth anniversary of the RCP, Ceauşescu had criticized the Party's errors before World War II. A year later, at the 1967 celebrations of the RCP's founding, he published an article in *Scînteia* that by implication criticized current Party deliberations. He continued to occupy the policy center by warning against both dogmatism and reformism, but demanded that Party members practice self-criticism, a term reminiscent of Stalin and Gheorgiu-Dej. Ceauşescu called for "open recognition of shortcomings and mistakes" within the Party to prevent errors, and the method he proposed to accomplish this was democratic centralism: open discussions within Party meetings until a decision was made, and then total unity in applying that decision.[71]

Democratic centralism, Ceauşescu explained, would resolve the opposing needs of Party harmony and dialectical struggle, the contradiction between "monolithic unity" and "free confrontation of opinions." As he put it:

> Party policy presupposes free debate within its framework of all the problems of social development. Without free confrontation of opinions . . . neither the elaboration of a correct political line, nor the ensuring of a strong unity in the Party are possible. . . . Democratic centralism—the basic organizational principle of the Party—ensures the wide discussion of Party questions, creates conditions for each Party member to speak his mind on all the problems of Party policy, to take an active part in shaping its line.[72]

He went on to demand "inner-Party democracy," defining its essential principle as the "active participation of the Party members in the elaboration of decisions in all the Party bodies and organizations." There was nothing new in this demand; what was new in the 1967 article was the sudden shift in emphasis to Party unity and discipline:

> Discussions must proceed in an organized manner, within the framework of Party bodies . . . and not outside the Party. . . . An intense inner Party life has . . . nothing in common with anarchic concepts which would turn the Party into a club of endless discussions. . . . Once the political line has been established and decisions have been endorsed with a majority of votes, the decisions become binding for all the Party members. . . . Each Party member is answerable to the Party for the way in which he fulfills his tasks. . . . Can a Party member be allowed to consider himself freed . . . from the obligation to respect the standards of Party discipline on the ground that he has a different opinion? No. Nobody can be allowed this! No Party member has the right to evade the responsibilities devolving upon him under Party membership, to violate the Party rules and discipline. Party discipline is one for all Party members— both for the rank and file and for the executives of the Party. Moreover, a greater responsibility in work is required for a top Party worker, as his transgressions . . . have far more serious repercussions.[73]

Thus discussions could be open and frank only inside the Party, and each member had to abide by whatever decision was reached. Ceauşescu made a special point of binding high Party officials by Party discipline, and then continued with a scathing criticism of factionalism, past or present:

> Unity is one of the basic conditions of the fulfillment of the historic tasks facing the Communist Party. Our Party knows from its own experience how great are the injuries caused by factionalism. . . . The division of our Party . . . in 1929 . . . brought the Party to the brink of dissolution. Our Party suffered as a result of . . . factional elements also in other periods. Fortunately, each time the Party found inner resources to cope with these situations in order to strengthen the unity . . . of its ranks. . . . Today our Party is stronger than ever; it acts closely united around the Central Committee.

The need for unity had been a constant theme of Romanian Party statements for years, with the unspoken assumption since the early 1960s that unity enabled the leadership to withstand Soviet pressure and maintain flexibility in foreign policy. The publication of such a severe warning against factionalism, combined with the warning about "dogmatic" and "reformist" tendencies within the Party, implied that collective leadership permitted disagreement to exist among Party members to such an extent that factions were forming within the RCP. Even worse, Ceauşescu also seemed to suggest that these factions actually were in touch with other communist parties:

> The problem has been raised whether it is permissible for a Party member to establish, without approval and over the head of the Party

leadership, relations with representatives of another Party, whom he would inform as to the activity in the ranks of the Party to which he belongs, and so participate in actions against the political line of his own Party. The answer to this can be but one: it is not permissible. . . . Any support given by a Party . . . to members or groups of another Party signifies an interference in the latter's internal affairs.[74]

At the time, Ceaușescu's words were interpreted by Western observers to be a warning against interference by other communist parties, particularly that of the Soviet Union, either overtly or through individual Romanian officials. In reality, the Romanian leader was speaking to Romanians as well, and equating any breach of Party discipline with betrayal of the Romanian nation. This was a tactic that Ceaușescu would use repeatedly: To disagree with him was to be a traitor to Romania. His implication made it very difficult for anyone to oppose Ceaușescu, although a number of individuals in the Party leadership could have profited from factional activity as four members of the Presidium were removed in the next two years.

One issue on which the Romanian leaders must have compromised among themselves was the pending reinterpretation of postwar Party history and the rehabilitations already begun of individuals who had been removed from office in disgrace. For example, Miron Constantinescu, dropped from the Political Bureau for anti-Party activity in 1957 and severely criticized (by Ceaușescu, among others) at the December 1961 Central Committee plenum, was made deputy minister of education in late 1965. Constantin Doncea, involved in the Grivița railroad strike in 1933, a veteran of the Spanish civil war, and former deputy defense minister and mayor of Bucharest (where he was renowned for his use of tanks to raze old housing in the capital), became president of the State Committee for the Development of Agricultural Production. Constantin Pârvulescu, Party general secretary in 1944 but reproached in 1961 for his "insufficient" criticisms of Constantinescu in 1957, delivered the report of the Central Revisory Commission at the Ninth Congress and was elected its president.[75] All of these men had been prominent in the prewar RCP and then incurred the enmity of Gheorghiu-Dej.[76]

No public explanation was given for their reappearances, although it was announced at the April 1966 CC plenum that party sanctions had been erased against some members.[77] These individuals had considerable prestige within the Party, and although they differed greatly among themselves in background and policy tendencies, their rehabilitation could only have enhanced Ceaușescu's image as a moderate and compromiser and even as a reformer. Simply restoring them to public life was an affirmation of socialist legality, to use Ceaușescu's term; the return of Constantinescu and Pârvulescu, in particular, signaled that the RCP under Ceaușescu might be moving toward the kinds of reform that Gheorghiu-Dej had rejected in the 1950s.

An even more spectacular rehabilitation, although posthumous and therefore symbolic, was of Lucrețiu Pătrășcanu, the prominent RCP leader arrested in 1948 and executed in 1954. He was mentioned in an April 1967 article as representing the RCP in 1943 in talks to establish the United Labor Front. The reference occurred in *Magazin istoric*, a new popular history journal aimed at familiarizing a wide audience with Romanian history.[78] Then the July issue of *Lupta de clasă* mentioned Pătrășcanu along with other members of the Union of Communist Youth studying *Das Kapital* in the early 1920s.[79] Again the rehabilitation was accomplished indirectly, by allowing his name to appear; the explicit acknowledgment of errors in his case would come only in 1968.

The Armed Forces

Ceaușescu implemented many of the same strategies toward the armed forces that he used to gain support within the Party and the population as a whole. Appointments of his own supporters to positions of power, material rewards, promises of new weapons and modern technology, and appeals to national unity and loyalty were important components of his policies in the military sector.[80]

The first major change came with the August 1966 death of Leonte Sălăjan, defense minister since 1955. His young successor was Ion Ioniță, who had joined the Party in 1945 and the army in 1948 and by 1966 was deputy defense minister and head of the air force.

Ioniță was was promoted over more senior officers who were also deputy ministers because there were few career officers in Romania old enough to have served in World War II who were not politically suspect on some basis. The Romanian officer corps had been extensively purged during the early years of Soviet occupation, and those professional officers who remained tended to be veterans of the Tudor Vladimirescu Division, a military unit composed primarily of Romanian prisoners of war in the USSR who had been persuaded to fight with the Soviet army against the Germans. Officers in this unit always had the taint of opportunism about them because many had come over to the Soviet side only after they were prisoners of war. Party leaders wondered whether they were loyal communists, and other Romanians questioned their patriotism. For example, one of the deputy ministers in 1966 was Iacob Teclu, an older career officer who had been in the Romanian army since 1916. Teclu had completed the Higher School of War in 1935 and in 1942 was captured in the USSR, where he eventually became chief of staff of the Tudor Vladimirescu Division.[81] Another deputy minister of defense and veteran of military service in the USSR was Mihai Burcă. He, however, had served in the Spanish civil war and then had not been allowed to return to Romania; instead, he went to the USSR voluntarily and in 1943 was one of the founders of the Tudor Vladimirescu Division. Commander of the air force by 1955, he remained deputy minister until 1972, when he became president of the Romanian Red Cross.[82] Burcă, undoubtedly a communist, nevertheless became vulnerable in the nationalistic atmosphere after 1964: Was he really a patriotic Romanian?

Both Teclu and Burcă remained prominent in the mid-1960s, but two relative youngsters were becoming the most visible officers (after Ioniță) in the defense ministry: Ion Gheorghe and Ion Coman. Both had been elected members of the Central Committee in July 1965, when Gheorghe became chief of staff and Coman was made secretary of the Higher Political Council of the armed forces. Gheorghe had been a CC member from 1955 to 1960, when he was also political director of the army, and speculation in the West asserted that he was a friend of Ceaușescu.[83] His subsequent career success certainly supports that contention. At any rate, the death of Sălăjan brought to the top of the armed forces officers educated in the period after the war, whose loyalty to the RCP and/or Romania was not automatically suspect.

Ioniță moved quickly to demonstrate his political acumen: At the October 1966 plenum, while explaining that pensions for military men who had retired before 1949 would be increased by over 35 percent in appreciation for their participation in the anti-fascist war, he praised Ceaușescu by name, unlike most of the speakers, and affirmed the support of the army for the Party.[84]

The next year brought more dramatic developments in military policy. Tension grew in military relations with the USSR, and in June 1967 Ceaușescu called for improved domestic production of armaments, new types of weapons, and computers and asserted the need of each socialist country for a well-organized, powerful army with "its own command."[85] These hints were spelled out more clearly in the speeches by Ioniță and Teclu at the Grand National Assembly session in July. Teclu called for a general rethinking of defense policy: "Taking into account the colossal confrontation of forces in war, and the geographical areas which could be involved, the defense capacity of Romania must be considered . . . on a broader basis than heretofore."[86] Ioniță stressed that Romania should perfect the weapons now produced within the country, develop new types of military technology to be used domestically, and import only what could not possibly or rationally be produced in Romania.[87] This was both a call to save on foreign exchange and a plea for more self-sufficiency in national defense.

In late August 1967 Romanian troops cooperated in WTO maneuvers in Bulgaria, but in October national military exercises and tactical operations were held inside Romania to demonstrate the "combat techniques" and the "research and innovation" of the military cadres. The importance attached to these matters was underlined by the participation of Ceaușescu, Chivu Stoica, and Maurer, as well as three CC secretaries and seven members of the Council of Ministers.[88] The Romanians were beginning to extend the autarkic economic policies they had advocated in Comecon into the defense sector—with the justification that the more each socialist country took care of its own defense capacity and armed forces, the greater would be its contribution to its Warsaw Pact obligations. Ceauşescu was taking steps to end the dependency of the Romanian military on Soviet supplies and so ensure its loyalty to him and the Romanian Communist Party.[89] In return, Ioniţă consistently reassured the RCP and its leader that the armed forces did indeed support the policies of the Party and Ceauşescu personally.

The Ministry of Internal Affairs

Ceauşescu's assessment of the Ministry of Internal Affairs (MIA) was quite different from his cordial alliance with the military. The contrast was emphasized by his speeches to the Party activists of both ministries just six weeks apart in the summer of 1967. To the armed forces in early June he expressed the "full satisfaction of the Party and state leadership," but at the MIA in mid-July he focused on the serious problems in the ministry's activity and the need for improvement.[90] His attack was not aimed at the current minister, Cornel Onescu (who had replaced Drăghici in 1965 and would remain in office until 1972); instead, it was aimed at Drăghici himself, who was weakened but still influential in 1967. Therefore, Ceauşescu was rather cautious in his criticism, and in speaking to the MIA he claimed to be simply reporting on the decisions of a Central Committee plenum held at the end of June when Vasile Patilineţ, CC secretary for military and security affairs, had made an unpublished speech about the ministry.[91]

In his own remarks to the MIA officials, Ceauşescu began by asserting the leading role of the Party—"The Party knows how to put right the mistakes made"—and praised the ministry for its accomplishments.[92] He then went on to focus his remarks on the past errors of the MIA. Some people in the ministry, he reported, had not been able to distinguish between behavior truly hostile to socialism and that resulting from retrograde or mistaken ideas. The latter cases, he implied, could have been resolved through educational activity; instead, "abuses" of socialist legality had occurred. Even worse, Ceauşescu continued, the MIA had interfered in Party affairs:

> There were also cases of abuses against some Party and state activists who . . . had different views on some aspects of the political line, or made mistakes in their activity. Instead of such problems being solved by Party discussions, they were sometimes referred to the security bodies, creating conditions for the latters' interference in Party life, gravely injuring the authority and leading role of the Party.[93]

Speakers at the CC plenum had evidently criticized the MIA for resisting Party complaints about such actions and rejecting Party oversight as inappropriate interference. Ceauşescu again attacked: "There is no kind of secret or matter of a conspiratorial character that . . . can be a reason for an organ to avoid Party oversight, especially a security organ which, due to the specific nature of its work . . . must always be under the guidance . . . of Party bodies."[94] The way to prevent future abuses, he asserted, was to make sure that "the Party bodies exercise ever broader control on the activity of the security bodies."[95]

The Ministry of Internal Affairs, Ceauşescu explained, was charged by the Party with preserving socialist legality, but in doing so the ministry had to ensure that no citizen could be arrested without just cause and that no RCP member could be investigated or arrested without the approval of the Party.[96] In other words, he insisted that the constitutional rights of all citizens had to be observed—and equally for all, regardless of nationality—but he implied that Party members were to be treated with special care and that they were immune to investigation or arrest unless the Party agreed. Ceauşescu defined a second task of the ministry as the defense of state security, but emphasized that attention should be paid to foreign espionage rather than to internal enemies. The security forces, he repeated, must "distinguish between harmful activity and justified and correct criticism" and act only against those "hostile to socialist construction."[97]

The June 1967 CC plenum had also set up a Council of State Security to ensure that measures would no longer be taken by "a single person," but would result from "collective judgment." The language used was identical to that in which Ceauşescu had explained the need for the Presidium to make daily decisions for the Party Executive Committee. The council was to remain within the ministry, but it would be directly responsible to both Party and government, presumably the Central Committee and the Council of Ministers.[98] Its president would simultaneously hold the rank of minister and the position of first deputy minister of internal affairs. This rather strange combination and the separation of the council from the ministry less than a year later suggest that a temporary compromise was worked out under which an outside body with direct access to higher organs was injected into the ministry to help establish Ceauşescu's control and prepare for the ouster of Drăghici.

By the fall of 1967, the two ministries—armed forces and internal affairs—presented an unusual comparison. In both the leadership had changed, apparently smoothly, as Sălăjan died and Drăghici moved to the CC Secretariat. The new ministers, Ion Ioniţă and Cornel Onescu, seemed firmly in office (and indeed were to hold their positions into the 1970s). At the same time, the ministries were under a great deal of pressure—the armed forces from their Warsaw Pact allies, and the Romanian security forces from their own Party—and the next year would see major crises in both relationships.

The Party Leaders

In the two years following the Ninth Congress, Ceauşescu's prestige increased dramatically in comparison with that of the other RCP leaders. The process began immediately during the transition period following Gheorghiu-Dej's death in March 1965 and continued at the July 1965 congress, where Ceauşescu was mentioned by most of the speakers. However, prominence was only to be expected of the RCP general secretary, and the references were to "the report of the Central Committee, delivered by Comrade Nicolae Ceauşescu," rather than to Ceauşescu himself.[99] Indeed, the triumvirate of Nicolae Ceauşescu, Chivu Stoica, and Ion Gheorghe Maurer formally continued to function until the end of 1967.

Chivu Stoica's role quickly became that of the symbolic head of state, but Maurer almost rivaled Ceauşescu in his activity, particularly in foreign affairs, as he continued to conduct negotiations with non-communist states and with government (not party) delegations from the socialist bloc. His trips abroad were covered extensively in the Romanian press,[100] and he gained considerable prestige in the West for his diplomatic abilities. In 1967, for example, he spoke at the United Nations, met with President Lyndon Johnson, and was reported to have made a secret trip to Beijing to convey a message on Vietnam from Johnson to Mao Zedong.[101] He delivered major speeches in Romania as well, but his principal area of responsibility was clearly foreign policy.[102]

Despite Maurer's prominence, Ceauşescu was by far the most visible of the Party leaders during this entire period. He gave the main report at plenums in November and December 1965 and presented the new five-year plan in June 1966. In October 1966 he began delivering the closing speech at each Central Committee plenum. The heavy coverage given to Ceauşescu by the Party newspaper during 1966, however, exaggerated his actual status within the leadership.[103] Speakers at the various meetings and conferences where texts were printed in *Scînteia* usually did not mention his name. For example, on the first two days of the agricultural congress in February, only 9 of 38 speakers referred to him, most only once. In the general discussions at the Grand National Assembly meetings in June–July, only 23 of 52 participants named Ceauşescu, and eight mentioned Maurer. A year later it still was not obligatory to refer to Ceauşescu in a GNA speech, although nearly everyone did; for example, on the first day of the July 1967 GNA sessions, 12 of the 13 speakers mentioned him, 7 of them three times, and 4 of them twice. He was not yet the object of worship—there was no "cult"— but his position was certainly powerful.

Ceauşescu's shrewdness at staging news events was made clear as early as the September 1965 visit of the Romanian leaders to the USSR. The group included Ceauşescu and Maurer, Gheorghe Apostol, and the two new CC secretaries, Manea Mănescu and Paul Niculescu-Mizil. During the visit,

Ceauşescu was mentioned four to five times as often as Maurer, who received the second heaviest coverage.[104] The Romanian delegation visited a number of places, including Moscow, Leningrad, and Volgograd (formerly Stalingrad). Usually Ceauşescu spoke for his colleagues, as in Leningrad where he gave the main address and briefly praised the anti-fascist struggle of the citizens during World War II. At Volgograd, however, the scene of Romanian humiliation and defeat as Germany's ally in 1943, Ceauşescu remained silent and his rival Apostol delivered the obligatory speech stressing at some length the anti-fascist heroics of the Soviet citizens and army. Ceauşescu realized everyone at home reading the news would remember that many Romanian soldiers had been killed at the Battle of Stalingrad fighting against the Soviet army that Apostol was praising so highly. In contrast to his prominence during the rest of the trip, the patriotic Ceauşescu managed to remain silent in Volgograd on what must have been a painful occasion. Surely observers in Romania noted and silently cheered his reticence.

The new members of the top leadership who were included in that delegation to the Soviet Union, Paul Niculescu-Mizil and Manea Mănescu, became increasingly prominent over the next several years. As CC secretary, Niculescu-Mizil was involved in ideological problems and foreign policy, especially relations with other communist parties, and he headed the Grand National Assembly Commission for Culture and Education.[105] Mănescu, like Niculescu-Mizil, had been involved in the culture and propaganda section at the Central Committee, but as CC secretary he was apparently assigned to make use of his training in economics, and at the October 1966 CC plenum he spoke on changes in the pension system and in June 1967 reported on salary increases. He was president of the Center for Economic Calculation and Cybernetics in Bucharest and frequently attended academic and educational gatherings. He also chaired the GNA Commission on Economics and Finance.[106] Mănescu and Niculescu-Mizil, along with Trofin (gradually taking over Drăghici's responsibilities in the Secretariat) and Verdeţ (soon to be the only first vice-president of the Council of Ministers and already in July 1967 fulfilling Maurer's duties in his absence[107]), formed the core of Ceauşescu's new leadership. Indeed, Niculescu-Mizil and Verdeţ were added to the Presidium in June 1966 where they, with the cooperation presumably of Maurer and Bodnaraş, gave Ceauşescu a majority.

In contrast to the rise of the new guard, the visibility and influence of a number of the older members of the leadership were lessening during 1966 and 1967. Apostol, for example, who had gone to the Soviet Union with Ceauşescu in September 1965 and made three major speeches in the next six months[108] rarely appeared after the middle of 1966, except on occasions when the entire Presidium was present as a group. The decline of Drăghici was more gradual. He was quite active in 1965 and 1966, making a number of speeches, traveling with Ceauşescu to various regions in Romania (only Maurer was a more frequent companion), and dealing with foreign communist parties.[109] He was not included on Ceauşescu's trips to the Soviet Union, however, and despite his past connections with the Ministry of Armed Forces and the Ministry of Internal Affairs, he was absent when Ceauşescu met with their Party activists in summer 1967. Indeed, the criticism of the MIA was an indirect attack on Drăghici and a reminder to him that any breach of Party discipline would be regarded as betrayal of the RCP and treason against the Romanian nation.

One final trend in the RCP leadership must be mentioned here because of its subsequent significance. In July 1966 Elena Ceauşescu and the wives of the other leaders began to appear in press reports of the events in which they participated. After Elena Ceauşescu was elected to the Executive Committee in June 1973, she was included in official events and press reports due to her new status; spouses who lacked formal credentials were once more excluded from media coverage.[110]

In summary, the period from 1965 to October 1967 was one of caution and preparation rather than of concrete achievement or startling innovation. The new leaders, and Ceauşescu in particular, sought to enhance their popularity with policy ambiguity and promises. They introduced new political techniques and economic improvements to increase popular support for the regime and to stimulate citizen participation in political and economic processes. They took steps to separate Romania militarily, as well as economically, from its socialist allies. Ceauşescu publicly committed himself again and again to socialist legality, participatory democracy, Romanian nationalism (combined with equal treatment for the ethnic minorities), and moderate reform. But he also promoted a number of his supporters into positions of power,[111] identified Party unity with loyalty to the Romanian nation, and ensured his personal influence over the military and the security forces. Ceauşescu's stature within the collective leadership grew tremendously in relation to the other individuals, but collective leadership remained the accepted method of rule. There were signs of impending changes in policy; however, major departures from past policies were merely discussed rather than introduced or implemented. In the fall of 1967, the changes were about to begin.

5

Change and Crisis: October 1967-April 1968

By October 1967 the long period of preparation was over. During the rest of the year, at three Central Committee plenums and a national Party conference, Ceauşescu would announce a series of political and economic reorganizations and several shifts in personnel. Three more plenums in early 1968 would bring still other changes against a menacing international background. The problems in foreign policy would culminate in the Warsaw Pact intervention in Czechoslovakia in August 1968, but the crisis for internal Romanian politics would come earlier, in April, with Ceauşescu's denunciation of Gheorghe Gheorghiu-Dej and the ouster of Alexandru Drăghici from the Party leadership. Many of the important organizational and policy changes, however, were already outlined by the end of 1967. Because Ceauşescu remained spokesman for a collective leadership, his pronouncements still did not necessarily reflect his personal views. But those views were beginning to emerge more clearly as he gained support and prepared to move against his rivals.

Preliminaries

When the Central Committee of the RCP met in plenary session on 5–6 October 1967, there were five items on the agenda.[1] First, a new set of economic directives was passed unanimously and referred to a special national Party conference to be held in December after countrywide debates on the issue in the press and at regional Party conferences. The discussions first mentioned by Bîrlădeanu back in 1965 had produced at last a series of new laws. The RCP leaders faced the same dilemma that confronted other East European parties: how to increase economic efficiency, quality, and flexibility without relinquishing the power to centralize priorities according to a national plan. The October plenum claimed that the new directives retained the central role of the plan but gave broad powers to economic enterprises and to the People's Councils; Ceauşescu would elaborate further at the December conference.

The second item was also important enough to be referred to the upcoming conference: an administrative reorganization of the entire country. In 1950 Romania had introduced the Soviet pattern of two administrative layers—regions and districts—between Bucharest and the local Party and state organs. The new proposal would restore the pre-communist single-layer structure of counties, and even the old name, *judeţ*, was to be used once again.

The remaining items of the October plenum were passed immediately and unanimously. Third, a general wage increase was approved, an average of 12.3 percent per year, with incentives for quality, initiative, and efficiency. Fourth, new provisions on housing established much higher rents, differentiated according to income, but also gave enterprises and cooperatives the right to build their own housing and offered state support to individual citizens to build private dwellings for their own use. At the Party conference, Ceaușescu would justify the rent increase on the basis of changes in the administration of housing: The introduction of "economic self-management" would bring self-sufficiency and make impossible the previous system—low rents offset by state subsidies. The new rents, he asserted, would allow "the expansion and maintenance of housing in good repair," and the salary increase would more than offset the higher costs to citizens.[2] The theory sounded promising. In reality, more new housing did become available, but it was never enough to satisfy demand and the quality was low. In addition, costs rose much more than did wages in the name of "self-sufficiency." Similar laws would be passed again and again under Ceaușescu.

The fifth and final agenda item involved plans for the national Party conference to be held in December. One delegate for every 1,500 Party members would be elected at conferences of the regional Party organizations in November.

Yet another CC plenum intervened between the October meeting and the national conference. At this time, four more Ceaușescu protégés joined the Executive Committee, two as full and two as candidate members,[3] but most of this meeting was evidently devoted to the youth question. The plenum called for greater coordination of activities involving school, family, army, and the Union of Communist Youth (UCY) and recommended that the first secretary of the CC of the UCY should henceforth be minister for youth problems as well. Thus the first step was taken toward uniting Party and state responsibility for a particular sector in one individual, an organizational strategy that would almost immediately be replicated throughout the political system. The next day, a UCY plenum replaced the longtime first secretary, Petre Enache, with Ion Iliescu, a former high official of the UCY who had been in the RCP Central Committee apparatus with Ceaușescu since 1960.[4] So far the changes—in wages, housing, and political organization—were typical of what would come to be known as the Ceaușescu era.

The National Party Conference

When the Party conference opened on 6 December, there were 1,150 delegates: 28 percent workers, 15 percent peasants, and 57 percent professionals (engineers, technicians, professors, scientists, artists, Party activists).[5] The main order of business was the discussion and approval of the economic changes and the administrative-territorial reform, and Ceauşescu mentioned both in his report of the CC on the first day. The public explanations by Ceauşescu and the other conference speakers seemed to imply some economic decentralization and, simultaneously, a tightening of political control.

The Economic Reform

The new economic program was evidently the product of major compromises within the collective leadership; it did not reflect the priorities that would later be characteristic of Ceauşescu himself. Yet, most of Ceauşescu's report was devoted to economic issues.[6] He began by setting forth the basic principles of the Romanian economy that could never be abandoned: the "unitary" national plan, socialist ownership of the means of production, and guidance by the Marxist-Leninist Party. He assured his listeners that these principles (which did reflect his personal beliefs) were not obstacles to change and development, but would allow constant renewal and improvement of economic management. He pointed out that renewal was now taking place in Romania before any "negative phenomena" had a chance to develop (reminiscent of Gheorghiu-Dej's claim that Romania had de-Stalinized before the Soviet Union). The Romanians, he asserted, were taking these steps without the pressure of economic difficulties, and so their reform resulted from a long period of study and could be applied after considerable experimentation and without undue haste.[7]

Ceauşescu formulated the main difficulty as being to "harmonize individual interests with the general interests linked to the flourishing of socialist property."[8] The solution in 1967 was to continue centralized planning, but also to increase reliance on economic levers such as credits, profits, and prices. Ceauşescu insisted that this did not mean that "the socialist economy should spontaneously regulate itself on the basis of fluctuations in the free market." But these levers would increase efficiency, decentralize decisionmaking, and reduce organizational duplication without giving up one of socialism's most important advantages: the plan.[9] Need for change did not spell failure for the socialist economy, he insisted, because its "form" must be constantly renewed.[10] This renewal apparently would shift the locus of decisions downward: Enterprises would be responsible for organizing both production and labor; they would retain more profits for investment, modernization, or labor incentives; and they would be judged by quality indices as well as by quantitative goals. A new level of administration was to be created—industrial "centrals"—by joining a number of enterprises that were in a particular sector or were involved in the manufacture of a finished product. The centrals would stress cooperation among enterprises in such areas as technical-material supply, modernization of production, assimilation of new products, and analyses of domestic and foreign markets. They would even have the right to deal directly with foreign organizations. In theory, these reforms would relieve the ministries of operational details so they could focus only on major problems.[11]

The Council of Ministers also would be affected because that body would be responsible only for coordination and long-range planning rather than for immediate issues.[12] There would henceforth be a functional division of labor between Party and state, with the economic sections of the Central Committee apparatus eliminated and their functions moved to the Council of Ministers.[13] The implications of the December 1967 decisions for the government were therefore rather ambiguous, but it seemed that the vice-presidents of the Council of Ministers would benefit because Ceauşescu suggested that they be given the right to decide current problems in the sectors for which they were responsible rather than bringing them to the full body.[14]

Within each enterprise, collective management bodies—composed of managers, specialists and researchers, delegates elected by the workers, and trade union representatives—were to be established. Ceauşescu insisted that they must be deliberative, working bodies, not just "representative, formal ones," and that their decisions should be legally valid on all economic issues.[15] There would also be a general assembly of employees, an organ of collective leadership, receiving regular reports from the management committees. This body would eliminate arbitrary decisions, he promised, and take advantage of the experience of both specialists and workers. According to Ceauşescu, the principle of "unipersonal management" was out of date: "A single man, however competent he may be, cannot cope by himself with the highly complex problems raised by . . . leadership of an enterprise, central or ministry."[16] As a result, collective decisionmaking was to be adopted at all levels, but this had to be combined with individual responsibility. Officials were to be held responsible not only for their individual decisions, but also for those of any collective body in which they took part, whether or not they agreed with the particular steps taken. Conversely, every collective body was to be held responsible for the individual decisions of each member of that body.[17] How this blending of responsibilities would be implemented was not clear, but the new rules did not imply greater security for members of decisionmaking bodies.

The one area of economic decisionmaking that would in no way be decentralized was the overall plan, including the balance between accumulation and consumption funds. Ceauşescu listed the improvements in the consumer sector since the Ninth Congress in 1965—the increases in salaries, pensions, retail sales, housing, bonuses—but he left no doubt as to his emphasis: "The maintenance of a high rate of accumulation . . . [is] an absolutely vital first-rate imperative."[18]

In retrospect, we can see some elements of compromise among the RCP leaders in these 1967 economic directives, with Ceauşescu insisting on centralized planning, accountability, and high rates of accumulation, while others were stressing the efficiency of decisionmaking at the enterprise level. The 1967 directives, even as explained by Ceauşescu, must have given hope to those who wished for major reforms, as well as to those who favored centralization. The outcome would be clear only in the implementation.

Administrative-Territorial Change

The second major proposal to be approved by the Party conference was the administrative-territorial reorganization. The elimination of one level of administration by substituting about 40 counties (*judeţe*) for the 16 regions (*regiune*) and 150 districts (*raione*) was aimed at reducing "parallelisms" and "overlapping powers." According to Ceauşescu, "The essential positive result . . . is that the central leadership will be closer to the basic units, to the place where the Party and state decisions are directly implemented."[19] An intermediate layer was thus eliminated from the political structure just as an extra link, the central, was added to the economic hierarchy.

The exact divisions of the new counties had not yet been worked out. Instead, a Party and state commission would draft proposals demarcating their boundaries, a map would be published for discussion, and the final plan would be submitted to the Grand National Assembly for approval. Ceauşescu explained that the commission would try to make each county an optimal size for economic organization and at the same time try to alleviate another chronic problem, uneven regional development. More rapid growth of insufficiently developed areas would be easier to administer because every commune would be relatively close to a county capital, providing cultural and educational opportunities.[20] This step foreshadowed the systematization program of the 1970s and 1980s.

The use of the county as the basic unit of territorial organization was a return to prewar terminology. Mihai Gere, president of a new Committee for Problems of Local Administration felt compelled to assert that the reform was not simply blind imitation of the old system, but that the new counties would reflect the changes of socialist construction. Nevertheless, whenever possible the counties should be given their traditional names; the aim was to have the counties "correspond to the political, economic, and social realities of our country and to reflect at the same time the historic traditions of the Romanian people."[21]

The selection of Mihai Gere to head the new committee indicated the importance of nationality issues in the territorial reorganization. Gere and János Fazekas were the two Hungarians in the top leadership, and both concentrated on the territorial reform and nationality questions in their speeches to the conference. Any change in territorial boundaries was immediately regarded by the minorities, especially the Hungarians, as an attempt to eradicate what autonomy they had, and indeed the new provisions did eliminate the Maghiar-Mureş Autonomous Region. Fazekas stressed that "full equality of rights for all citizens . . . regardless of nationality . . . would continue," and there would be "even broader participation of the working people of all nationalities in . . . civic affairs."[22] Gere also promised that "the Party will ensure . . . the free use of the mother tongue in state administration, in education of all grades, in cultural institutions, and in editing books, magazines, and newspapers."[23]

These reassurances probably meant little to the Hungarian population, however. What was important to them was the proposal made by Fazekas for the creation of a "strong county" composed of five districts with mostly Hungarian inhabitants. The autonomous republic had been diluted in 1960 by the loss of two Hungarian districts and the addition of three districts with mainly Romanian populations. Fazedas now proposed to reverse this decision by placing the three Romanian districts in another county and reuniting the Hungarian areas.[24] Eventually, after much public debate, it was decided to make the three Romanian districts into a county and to divide the Hungarian population into two counties, each of which would be more equal to the other thirty-seven counties in population and economic potential. The final result was indeed the promised concentration of Hungarians, for each of the two new counties had a large Hungarian majority.[25] The fulfillment of this promise was undoubtedly more reassuring to the minority nationality than were either the frequent slogans about the fraternal friendship of the cohabiting nationalities or Fazekas's references to the "vigor" with which "Lenin fought against the manifestations of national nihilism."[26]

Political Organization: The Party and the State

The Party conference also dealt with some crucial changes in political organization announced by Ceauşescu and other speakers. First was the elimination of Article 13(b) of the Party statutes, which had been introduced in July 1965 at the Ninth Congress to prevent one person from holding a full-time job in both Party and state at the same time. Apostol and Ceauşescu then had defended the separation of offices as a guarantee of Party control, although Ceauşescu later hinted in a May 1967 article that "parallel forces are wasted on carrying out the selfsame tasks."[27] But it was not until the December conference that Ceauşescu totally reversed his 1965 position, declaring it a "deficiency" to have several comrades of the Executive Committee responsible for the same field of activity.[28] Instead, he went on, the Party must simplify the decisionmaking and "enhance responsibility" by having "one single comrade" deal with a particular sector in both Party and state. Virgil Trofin, in his report on Party organization and cadres, stated that Article 13(b) had led to "parallelism and overlapping" and proposed that the conference "eliminate" it from the statutes.[29]

The most notable result of this change was Chivu Stoica's suggestion that henceforth the Party general secretary serve also as president of the Council of State.[30] The proposal was seconded by most subsequent speakers, and it soon became clear that not only was Ceauşescu to hold both offices, but also that the first secretary of each county was to be president of the county People's Council. This "unitary leadership" would be carried down to the local level, as each city would have its own *primarul*, the prewar term for major, who would combine Party and state leadership in one person. Thus the parallel hierarchies of Party and state were to be tied together at key points from top to bottom.

At the same time, Ceauşescu announced a functional division of labor between Party and state. Foreign policy problems would be handled by the Party Presidium, and the Central Committee would guide ideological, scientific, and cultural institutions as well as the armed forces, state security, and cadres policy. On the other hand, "the apparatus required for solving economic problems shall function [henceforth] at the Council of Ministers,"[31] and the economic sections at the Central Committee would presumably cease to exist. This would hold true at county and local levels as well. In addition, however, a new Economic Council, a joint Party and state body, was created to oversee the implementation of economic decisions and establish direct links with economic commissions in each county. Exactly how the Economic Council would exercise its oversight was unclear, as was the distinction between its functions and those of the defunct CC economic sections. Neither Ilie Verdeţ, who discussed the other economic changes, nor Manea Mǎnescu, the president of the Economic Council, added to Ceauşescu's explanation. But Trofin did reveal that each county commission would be attached to the county Party committee, so the new economic organs could in theory play the role originally filled by the Party economic apparatus. The implications of the reforms for the functions and relations of the Party and state hierarchies were ambiguous, to say the least.

Personnel implications of the changes were somewhat more revealing. Manea Mǎnescu, who had been overseeing economic problems in the Secretariat, was not substantially affected because he retained authority over the Economic Council. However, the new Party secretary who might have been expected to deal with economic problems—Chivu Stoica—moved into the Secretariat without a staff beneath him. In addition, the elimination of the CC economic sections provided a reason for moving Drǎghici out of the Secretariat and back to the Council of Ministers. His speech to the conference concentrated on economic problems,[32] so he clearly had been replaced by

Trofin as the CC secretary for cadres and organizational problems. Thus both Drăghici and Chivu Stoica were considerably weakened by the reorganization.

Ceauşescu's report to the conference also criticized the Council of State as it had operated under Chivu Stoica, when it had issued decrees as laws and only afterward submitted them to the GNA for discussion. Proposed laws, he insisted, should be scrutinized by the standing commissions of the GNA, which should play a larger role in drafting laws and should hear reports from ministers on their implementation. To accomplish this, the GNA would have to hold longer sessions and, as the role of the GNA increased, the Council of State would also exercise "a more active control" over the national and local state bodies, the Procurator, and the Supreme Court.[33] Ceauşescu was advocating a greater role for the Council of State as he took over that body; he was also continuing his emphasis on the legality, or institutionalization, of the legislative process.

December 1967: An Assessment

Policies

Apparently, the decisions of December 1967 were the product of compromise within a collective leadership in which Ceauşescu was the most powerful individual but could not impose his will unchecked. The main thrust of the economic directives appeared to be a major reform of the Romanian economy. It was never called a reform, however, but a "perfecting" of the economic process, and although the RCP leaders were able to agree on the need to make enterprises more efficient, they could not agree on effective measures to reduce the power of the planners in Bucharest. As one analyst has observed, "The crucial inconsistency in the Directives was the unwillingness to give up detailed centralized control while simultaneously proposing greater autonomy for economic units to stimulate production efficiency."[34] Other socialist states have had the same problem.

As a result, there was a delay in implementation, some further experimentation, a partial implementation from 1969 to 1972, and then what appeared to be a reversion to ministerial control after 1972.[35] As early as 1973 it was apparent that the 1967 directives were unlikely to improve the system of planning and management in significant ways.[36] Separate studies based on interviews in Romania in 1970 and 1977 concluded that economic decisions in Romania were still made by ministries, not by enterprises.[37] If we take a longer view, however, we can interpret another set of economic changes announced in 1978—the New Economic and Financial Mechanism (NEFM)—as a reaffirmation of some of the 1967 proposals, another attempt to make enterprises more efficient with financial levers, profitability requirements, and material incentives (although trouble again would develop in the implementation, this time by 1980).[38]

Repeatedly during the 1970s and later, Ceauşescu expressed intense hostility toward any genuine decentralization of economic or political processes. Nevertheless, he seemed to support the modest goals of the 1967 directives at the time, and in the years immediately following he often voiced frustration that they were not being implemented. It was clear both in 1967 and thereafter that attitudes toward economic change cut across Party and state lines. Much of the strongest opposition to any decentralization, for example, came from state officials within the ministries or the planning bodies. Ceauşescu, despite his own instinct to tighten control and his determination to centralize basic priorities in an overall plan, did not support the ministries in their desire to retain their prerogatives. In 1971 and 1972, for example, he protested that the centrals were simply carrying out the ministries' programs rather than exercising the powers assigned to them.[39] He evidently accepted the idea of the centrals back in 1967 because he viewed them as a means of moving the responsible decisionmakers closer to the production process, thus increasing the efficiency of the process. He wanted the centrals to become large-scale production units, not just an extra administrative layer—indeed, he claimed in 1971 that his original support for their creation had been based on that expectation—and he vehemently criticized the managers of some centrals in 1974 for "taking over the old working methods" and using "circular letters" rather than "direct and concrete guidance, on-the-spot solutions."[40]

There were, of course, other features of the 1967 directives that Ceauşescu could be expected to favor. To the extent that the changes were successfully implemented, they increased participation by individuals other than enterprise managers in the decisionmaking process by including technicians, workers, and trade union representatives in new collective management bodies responsible to the workers' general assemblies. Ceauşescu never saw these new participatory bodies as affecting policy, but rather as improving the implementation of the plan; likewise, he probably did not view the 1967 directives primarily as a means of increasing the prerogatives of managers, whom he instinctively mistrusted as educated technocrats, but instead saw the limits that would be placed on them by these new consultative groups. Evidently, Romanian enterprise managers until 1971 were able to keep these collective bodies "at bay . . . but between 1971 and 1977 they served as a constraint on the director to limit any excessive display of authority."[41]

In addition, unlike elsewhere in Eastern Europe, the economic changes of 1967 did not aim to ease centralization, but rather to tighten the process because the Romanian plan targets had been less demanding from 1965 to 1967 than thereafter.[42] It is therefore likely that, as Maurer stressed in his speech at the conference, Ceauşescu's "personal role" in initiating and working out the details of the changes had been considerable.[43]

The administrative-territorial reform was undoubtedly Ceauşescu's work. Economic considerations were important in terms of the organization, provision, and redistribution of production,[44] and there were also historical and patriotic grounds for the return to the prewar structure. Most important, however, the reform totally reorganized the political system. For example, a regional first secretary usually became the head of a county, but as one of forty, not one of sixteen, certainly a reduction in power and prestige. This was offset, but only partially, by direct control over the People's Council.[45] Equally important, over twenty new positions were created, to be filled presumably by Ceauşescu with the help of Trofin. The possibility existed for a complete reshuffling of personnel, an infusion of new individuals into the political network and the retirement of many others, in the process of eliminating an entire layer of administration. All of these changes could be used to enhance Ceauşescu's control.

The third set of reforms, the political restructuring, also had broad implications for the future administration of Romania. Ceauşescu's announced intention was to eliminate excess personnel and the duality of responsibility that he termed "parallelism" by uniting the Party and state hierarchies at key points from top to bottom. This complete reversal of his 1965 position—total separation of Party and state—suggests that his motivation on one or both of those occasions derived to a large extent from personal career motives. Because he has maintained the organization adopted in 1967 for over two decades, it is likely that this creation of Article 13(b) in 1965 was designed to weaken some of his rivals, as it did, and that he abandoned it as soon as he was strong enough to take over the Council of State himself.

The announced intention of the unification of Party and state in 1967 was, strangely enough, the functional separation of their responsibilities. The Party temporarily gave up its direct supervision of the economy with the closing of the economic sections at the Central Committee, but the RCP's authority over ideology, education, science, culture, military and security matters, and cadre policy was strengthened and these sectors were attached directly to the CC. In reality, however, the Party continued to supervise the economy through Mănescu and the Economic Council, and the intended functional separation never became operational.

The Collective Leadership

The conference speeches of the individuals within the top leadership contained no major surprises. Ion Gheorghe Maurer, who remained president of the Council of Ministers, stressed even more than the other speakers Ceauşescu's personal role in formulating the decisions and seconded the general secretary's interpretation of almost every change. Although Ceauşescu and Maurer would have serious (but covert) disagreements after 1969, they apparently managed to reach a genuine compromise on most issues in 1967. Both could find aspects of the economic reforms to support, and they had a number of major goals in common: industrial development and efficiency, foreign policy autonomy, and the continued unity and stability of the Romanian Communist Party.

Seen in retrospect, the 1967 conference contained hints of the future disagreements between Maurer and Ceauşescu. Maurer evidently expected to direct the economy from the Council of Ministers, and he emphasized its increased responsibility as the "supreme organ of state administration,"[46] whereas the thrust of Ceauşescu's remarks indicated that his Council of State would play a new and more important role. Their views also seemed to diverge on scientific research: Maurer spoke of developing research in the various ministries and eventually in enterprises, implying a decentralized effort closely related to production.[47] Ceauşescu, in contrast, emphasized the need for coordination of research and called for an end to "the present smothering of research activity, the division of scientific forces among the Academy, ministries, and educational establishments."[48] He went on to praise Romanian scientists, urging that "by joining their efforts they will be able to solve at a higher speed all the problems that are tackled now by three or four institutes or researchers separately." Ceauşescu would wage a running battle over this issue for the rest of his rule, trying to impose coordination in science, culture, and education—although seeing it avoided or resisted whenever possible.

No other major disagreements emerged in the conference speeches.[49] It was apparent from their remarks that other holdovers from the Gheorghiu-Dej leadership—Chivu Stoica, Gheorghe Apostol, Emil Bodnaraş, and Alexandru Drăghici—were facing reduced responsibilities, and most would be out within two years. Alexandru Bîrlădeanu, the architect of Romania's autonomous economic policies in Comecon under Gheorghiu-Dej, elaborated in great detail on the economic directives, explaining in an economist's phrases the changes he had hinted at in 1965. Yet he would retire within a year, ostensibly for reasons of health but more likely because of disagreements with Ceauşescu over economic policy. His apparent replacement, the only first vice-president of the Council of Ministers to continue as such after the conference, was Ilie Verdeţ, who spoke on the economic changes, but in the words of a Party organizer, not as an economist. Bîrlădeanu's departure did not bode well for the Romanian economy. The two remaining members of the Presidium, Paul Niculescu-Mizil and Virgil Trofin, had been promoted under Ceauşescu. The former spoke on his sector of responsibility, ideology, whereas Trofin, by now clearly established as the CC secretary for cadres and organizations, proposed the elimination of Article 13(b) to allow Ceauşescu to become head of state.

The December 1967 Party conference did not give Ceauşescu all of the policy outcomes he might have desired, but it made him head of state and greatly strengthened his influence in the top Party bodies. He was now ready to move against Drăghici and to set the stage for his final consolidation of power at the Tenth Party Congress in 1969.

Mounting Tension: January–April 1968

The months preceding the April 1968 Central Committee plenum were a time of increasing turmoil within Romania. The December 1967 measures affected most of the population in some way: After all, the Party conference had reorganized the entire political and economic structure of the country, altered criteria for planning and production, and shifted internal territorial boundaries. Simultaneously, the Romanian Party leaders were facing serious difficulties in their relations with foreign communist parties, both in the world communist movement and in the Warsaw Treaty Organization. The Soviets still wished to maintain a unified community of communist parties that would act in concert on foreign policy issues, a stance the Romanians had always rejected—especially the possibility that one party could judge another or interfere in its policies. They preferred a loosely organized grouping of independent parties rather than a tightly disciplined alliance of parties in total compliance with Soviet policies.[50] Inside the Warsaw Pact, Alexander Dubcek—who had become head of the Czechoslovak communist party—and his colleagues were embarked on what would become known as the "Prague Spring," a period of internal reforms that the Soviets eventually concluded were a threat to Marxism as defined in Moscow. Ceauşescu was not an enthusiastic supporter of the new policies in Czechoslovakia, but he did not criticize the Prague leadership (as he later did the Solidarity movement in Poland), and in 1968 he defiantly asserted the right of the Czechoslovak party to decide what was best for its own country.

Czechoslovak reforms and Soviet threats formed a backdrop to developments within the Romanian Communist Party during 1968 as Ceauşescu and the Romanian press conveyed to citizens a picture of rising tension among communist parties and particularly between Bucharest and Moscow. Such reports helped to create inside Romania an atmosphere of hostility, frustration, and fear and strengthened the perception of most Romanians that political unity and popular quiescence were necessary to keep Soviet troops out of their country.

Foreign Policy

The difficulties within the world communist movement in early 1968 can be gauged by the intensity of inter-Party relations during January and February. Thirteen major non-ruling communist parties sent delegations to Bucharest,[51] and there were high-level contacts with half a dozen more. Relations with the ruling parties were also intense, and the travel schedule of Romanian leaders was significant: The mavericks, Czechoslovakia and Yugoslavia, were singled out for special attention, but the most frequent and prolonged contacts were with the Soviet Union.

During February, for example, Ceauşescu and Niculescu-Mizil, the CC secretary for relations with foreign communist parties, received Boris Ponomarev, Niculescu-Mizil's Soviet counterpart, in a "warm" and "comradely" discussion that produced no agreement but merely an "exchange of views."[52] Soon after, Ceaușescu went to Prague for the twentieth anniversary of the "workers' victory" of 1948 and spoke warmly of the Czechoslovak party and of Dubcek.[53] Then, at the end of the month, Niculescu-Mizil represented Romania at an international meeting of communist parties in Budapest, where he insisted that decisions at international meetings required unanimity, not a mere majority, because the principle of democratic centralism was not applicable in relations among communist parties. According to a Romanian CC communiqué, published in *Scînteia* on 1 March , the Syrian delegate attacked the RCP on the first day of the sessions. When the other parties did not support Niculescu-Mizil, he withdrew from the conference and returned to Bucharest on the instructions of the RCP Executive Committee. The Romanians thereafter refused to take part in any preparations for a conference of communist parties unless there was "public agreement" in advance that "fraternal parties will not be attacked and criticized."[54] To Romanian citizens, their country seemed surrounded by enemies, and the RCP leaders were defending its sovereignty and independence.

Within a few days a disagreement surfaced within the Warsaw Treaty Organization. All the top leaders gathered in Sofia on 6 March 1968, and Ceaușescu refused to sign a joint statement affirming their intention to sign the nuclear non-proliferation treaty recently worked out by the Soviet Union and the United States and presented to the United Nations, where it would be signed by most states in midsummer. The others approved the declaration anyway,[55] demonstrating bloc support for the treaty, but the Romanians remained apart, emphasizing their membership in the UN rather than their adherence to a particular bloc. This was apparently the first time a document issued from a Warsaw Pact meeting had not been unanimous.[56]

At least at Sofia the Romanians had been invited to sign. When the other six Warsaw Pact countries met later in March at Dresden to discuss developments in Czechoslovakia, the Romanians did not attend, and Ceaușescu later revealed that they had been excluded from the talks.[57] The Dresden meeting was not an official gathering of the Pact, but problems of Comecon and the military alliance were discussed,[58] and Ceaușescu later protested that such questions should not have been considered in the absence of Romania, a member of both organizations.[59] Meanwhile, the Romanian press was silent following the Sofia meeting, ignored the Dresden gathering, and for an entire month let it remain unclear whether Romania had been excluded or had chosen not to participate at Dresden. The population was, of course, aware of these developments from foreign radio broadcasts, so the level of tension inside the country rose. (Ceaușescu finally confirmed Romanian's exclusion from the Dresden meeting at the April plenum.[60])

The Kremlin leaders were undoubtedly nervous during this period about a possible Little Entente of Yugoslavia, Romania, and Czechoslovakia. Diplomatic contacts among the three were quite frequent in 1968, and the Czechoslovak delegate to the Budapest meeting supported some of the Romanian positions and criticized documents of earlier communist meetings as "out of date on the issue of Yugoslavia."[61] Moscow's fears must have been heightened by Ceaușescu's separate meetings with Czechoslovak and Yugoslav representatives on 20 and 23 March, just at the time of the Dresden conference. Then on 3 April Romania reached an agreement with Czechoslovakia calling for a 10 percent increase in trade in 1969–1970 over and above the increase planned in their long-term trade agreement.[62]

Nothing had been resolved by the time of the RCP Central Committee plenum in April. Thus, at a moment of high tension inside Romania, the Romanians simultaneously faced a crisis in the Warsaw Pact. Having been excluded from meetings of their allies, they could not be sure what had been decided in the discussions of military and economic policy, although they did know the internal affairs of Czechoslovakia had been considered. This was just the type of interference that the Romanians for so long had refused to permit at international meetings of communist parties or states. Romanian-Soviet relations were at a postwar low in April 1968, and the bases of inter-Party relations that Romania had carefully established over such a long period of time—sovereignty, equality, and mutual non-interference—were seriously threatened.

Internal Restructuring

During these weeks of tension in foreign policy, the Romanian press and most top-level Party meetings focused on the internal changes approved in December. Several themes were by now characteristic of political rhetoric under Ceaușescu. The problem of "bureaucratism," for example—the "rigid" adherence to "routine" rather than flexibility in achieving goals—was frequently attacked in the press with glaring examples of abuses. But perhaps the theme most often expressed was that of participation, a concept Ceaușescu was beginning to explain more clearly. Democracy, he insisted, should be understood as participation and not, as it had come to connote in Western democracies, representative government: "We do not understand democracy in its bourgeois meaning—of babbling, lack of discipline, anarchy. We understand democracy as the active participation of the citizens in formulating and implementing the Party's policy."[63] Not yet clear was whether his concept of participation was limited to the "mobilized" participation traditional in Leninist parties, or included the assumptions of efficiency, voluntarism, and regime responsiveness attached to the concept in pluralist political systems: He explicitly rejected "bourgeois" democracy, but accepted citizens' participation in "formulating" as well as "implementing" policy.[64] The ambiguity would be resolved only in the 1970s (see Chapter 9); meanwhile, citizens were skeptical, but in 1968 many nevertheless saw Ceauşescu as the only hope for improvement.

Indeed there were signs that the nature of participation in Romania was to change—it was to take place at all levels and in all bodies. In the Grand National Assembly, for example, the role of deputies and commissions was to be increased, which would require longer and open sessions.[65] The new collective bodies would ensure participation, as would the conferences held to discuss issues and make suggestions before the final drafting of important decisions. The entire process the preceding fall had been an example of Ceauşescu's version of democracy within the Party: Proposals were presented at the October 1967 plenum, discussed at regional Party conferences in November, and approved at the national party conference in December. The parameters for discussion were set in advance and the final results determined by the RCP leadership, but Party members had opportunities to state their views. So far, this was what Ceauşescu meant by "participatory socialist democracy."

Similar discussions occurred in early 1968 as the administrative-territorial reorganization was implemented. Details of the proposed changes, including a map, were published on 14 January. During the following month *Scînteia* was crowded with academic studies, comments, questions, and suggestions, including a special feature on each of the new counties. Then the Central Committee ended the process by holding a plenum that examined and approved proposals by Ceauşescu on the "definitive" form of county organization, now ready for submission to the Grand National Assembly. Trofin, as cadres secretary, reported on the structure of the new local Party organizations, indicating that the unification of the regional and district organizations would proceed slowly and that elections would be held by the end of the year.[66]

On 15 February the Grand National Assembly opened a special session to enact the recommendations of the Party conference into law. The major agenda items—constitutional amendments, the territorial reorganization, and measures to create temporary local governments—were all interrelated and so considered together. After Ceauşescu's address came a joint report from the GNA Juridical and Administrative Commissions on the constitutional amendments and another report from the Administrative Commission on the territorial changes. A general discussion followed, and the texts of the speeches were printed. The following day the three items were approved by secret ballot with only some minor amendments on details such as names or time deadlines.

Worth noting were the careful observance of parliamentary procedures (at least in the published reports); the role of the commissions in drafting, explaining, and defending the legislation; and the weak role of the GNA as a body. Proposals made in the month preceding the GNA session had evidently been considered seriously, because substantive changes had been made after mid-January. But these were accomplished before the GNA session and were incorporated in Ceauşescu's address at the start of the meetings.[67] In fact, on 16 February, the very day on which the GNA approved the final boundaries, regional meetings were already being held to elect provisional officials for each county within the region. The entire process was yet another example of Ceauşescu's concept of participation.

In his speech to the assembly, Ceauşescu explained that suggestions made since the original proposals deemed it advisable to establish four additional counties, making a total of 39 plus the municipality of Bucharest. In areas where these changes were proposed, "large civic rallies" had been organized, and the modifications made were "based on these consultations, [and] on a multi-faceted study of the proposals."[68] Various reasons were given for creation of the new counties: Mehedinţi would provide "easier links" to the county seat; Sălaj, an extremely poor area in terms of industry, would develop more quickly as a separate county; and the industrial power of Brăila town justified Brăila as a separate county.

The creation of the fourth county was linked to the nationality question. The original plan had included a single large county with an overwhelming majority of Hungarians; the new proposals divided that area into two counties, Covasna and Harghita. The Hungarians would achieve their goal of overwhelming majorities in both counties, but as two units, each would conform more closely in size and economic potential to the other thirty-seven. In addition, Ceauşescu named both of these counties among the nine he singled out as "marked . . . for faster industrial advance" under the current five-year plan.[69] Both counties were less developed than the average, but they were not among the least industrialized, nor were they mentioned as being among the worst in any particular sector such as education or health.[70] Their economic growth from 1965 to 1967 had not been particularly rapid, but other counties with large Hungarian populations had registered a high growth rate.[71] Naming Covasna and Harghita among the counties to expect high investments was a signal to the Hungarians that the abolition of the autonomous region did not reflect an intention to make their lives more difficult, and elsewhere in his speech Ceauşescu spelled out in detail the cultural rights of the minorities with statistics on their schools, publications, and theaters.[72]

In late March 1968 a conference at Central Committee headquarters in Bucharest brought the county first secretaries and the first deputies of the People's Councils together with members of the CC and top Party and state officials to evaluate the steps already taken.[73] Ceauşescu's comments were positive, especially with regard to combining the top Party and state offices in each county in one person. He admitted that it was "premature to draw conclusions from one month's experience," but claimed that the measure was highly regarded by the first secretaries, some of whom reported at the conference that they could now "not only give guidance and advice but also act directly to fulfill Party and state decisions."[74] At the same time, he reported that the Party and government apparatus had been reduced by over 30 percent, but that most people already had new jobs.

There must have been considerable worry and resentment on the part of local officials about jobs, and Ceauşescu's statements during this period tried to reassure the affected groups. In February he promised the "comrades" who have to go to "other jobs" that they would find employment and, if their new wages should be lower, that they would continue to receive the higher salary for three months. If they should need "refresher" courses, their previous salary would continue for six months, and after graduation they would be paid "according to the training acquired."[75] Ceauşescu took special pains to express his respect for experienced cadres. For example, during a visit to Tulcea, a new county center, he praised the "youth" of his audience, but then said: "I do not in any way want to anger older comrades. As a matter of fact, I do not know in what category I should place myself, the elderly or the young. I am over 50 now, but I still place myself in the ranks of youth."[76] He went on to stress that "youth" was not so much age as a state of mind; he praised "experience" and criticized only "political aging, reduced receptivity to what is new."

There were also attempts to reassure the Party workers. Constantin Dăscălescu, the first secretary of the new Galaţi County and later president of the Council of Ministers, wrote in a front-page *Scînteia* article on 10 March: "It is not true that Party organs no longer have responsibility for important problems such as investment and other economic questions. . . . Now that they do not have technical, administrative duties, they can pay more attention to their own work."

Because problems in Romania are often discovered by reading proposed solutions and reassurances given in the press, we can conclude that officials throughout the political process feared for their futures and had questions about their new duties. Nevertheless, the outlines of administrative-territorial change had been accomplished by the time of the April plenum. Most of the new county organs had been set up, the top cadres selected, and some of the administrative chaos was over. Within the Party and state bureaucracies, however, most individuals were preoccupied in trying to keep their old jobs, finding new ones, or learning to cope with new responsibilities. In a period of confusion and insecurity in domestic politics and of tension and fear in foreign policy, Ceauşescu would have an excellent opportunity to move against his most formidable rival, Alexandru Drăghici.

Popular Support

In this period of internal and external upheaval, the Party leadership appealed to various groups inside Romania for support. Some appeals were general and unstated, such as to nationalism in foreign policy and to Romanian traditions in the territorial restructuring. Other moves for support were more concrete: For example, on 11 April a 25 to 30 percent rise in student stipends was announced, effective May 1. Then on 21 April *Scînteia* announced price reductions on a huge variety of consumer goods, such as refrigerators and radios (15–25 percent); textile products, including stockings, shoes, and vinyl products (11–22 percent); plastic articles (21–29 percent); and certain foods such as margarine (12.5 percent). A special effort was made to attract youth, not only with the student stipends and the price reductions, but also by criticism of the Union of Communist Youth, whose meetings, Ceauşescu complained, were excessively long and boring and had thus become an "obstacle" to useful activity.[77]

Ceauşescu received the heads of all the religious groups on 29 February with a conciliatory speech promising that all persons who contributed to the country's social and economic development—"irrespective of nationality . . . religious belief and philosophical concept"—would be given "fully equal rights" as citizens of Romania.[78] This symbolic acceptance of religious believers paralleled and reinforced his overtures to the minority nationalities because in Romania, as elsewhere in Eastern Europe, nationality and religion are closely linked.

Another group given special attention in early 1968 was the Union of Creative Artists and, by implication, intellectuals in general. At a country-wide conference of the union, Ceauşescu's statements were somewhat ambiguous but surprisingly hard-line. Ceauşescu aroused the hopes of the artists by promising that Party policy would "encourage the unhampered development of the personality of all artists . . . [and] a great diversity of styles and manners . . . to broaden the palette of contemporary art." Then came the "but": "The common denominator of our socialist art is the Marxist-Leninist ideal . . . of the lofty social responsibility of the socialist artist." History, he went on, the only judge of true art, shows the lasting value of works focusing on reality. It also demonstrates the ephemeral worth of artists "who have ignored reality or . . . shut themselves up in an 'ivory tower,' " who succumb to bourgeois ideology and "create only for a handful of 'elect' people." Thus, the social responsibility of the artist and the demand that art reflect reality turned out to be his major themes, despite his initial call for diversity of forms.[79] His personal attitudes toward art were beginning to emerge.

Ceauşescu's attitudes toward literary and artistic criticism expressed in the same speech were rather dogmatic. The mass media and specialized publications were to promote "advanced principles" and criticize "unsound tendencies." He did make some friendly gestures: He asked for the participation of older, experienced artists as well as the younger generation and praised the contributions of Romanian, Hungarian, German, and other artists to "the country's spiritual treasury." He also talked about substantial improvement in the "material basis" of cultural and artistic life, indicating that the economic benefits evident in the 1967 reforms would include, and perhaps especially favor, artists and writers.[80] As in 1965, he was promising diversity of forms and material rewards, but demanding realism and social responsibility. A decade later, Romanian intellectuals would look back on this period with nostalgia, but those positive memories were based more on the hopes of the late 1960s then on any significant relaxation. Romanian culture had been derussified, but it had not been freed from party oversight.

Another measure introduced in early 1968 was a new penal code, published in draft form in early April. The debate in *Scînteia* began with an editorial on 6 April calling for public discussion of the proposals and pointing out that the previous code of 1937 had been amended many times but had never been systematically rewritten. The new version had been presented by the Council of Ministers to the RCP Executive Committee, accepted there, and would next be submitted by the EC to the Central Committee for debate. Then it would be discussed at mass meetings before presentation to the Grand National Assembly. The most important new feature, the editorial argued, was the return to the principle "no punishment without crime," which would eliminate "abuses" and "arbitrariness" and create the "security . . . indispensable for a civilized society."

Ceauşescu himself declared the new penal code second in importance only to the constitution. His explanation of its meaning picked up some of the themes for which the Ministry of Internal Affairs had been criticized the preceding summer and foreshadowed events at the upcoming April 1968 CC plenum:

> It is no secret for anybody that certain outrages have been committed over the years. . . . The Penal Code must ensure the strict observance of socialist legality, so that nobody may infringe upon it in any way or commit abuses. . . . The main responsibility for the application of the laws devolves on our Party, on its executive, on the Party and state activists. They must set an example in observing legality. . . . It is only by carefully observing the law that we can make our society the most equitable in the world.[81]

This theme—strict observance of the law by all—had become characteristic of the Ceauşescu era. In 1968 the references to past abuses provided justification not only for a new penal code but also for the removal of Drăghici at the April plenum. Although the new code, like many of Ceauşescu's reforms, streamlined the penal system and eliminated contradictions and confusions that had evolved over the years, it did nothing to solve the basic problem in Romanian law: the absence of an independent judiciary to which violations could be appealed.

On 3 April 1968 a further reorganization of the Ministry of Internal Affairs and the Council on State Security (CSS) took place[82]: The Council of State, presided over now by Ceauşescu, separated the CSS from the ministry and charged it with the defense of state security, including elimination of conspiracies, protection of state secrets, and "verification" of cadre policy in social organizations. Emphasis was placed on the need for legality in all actions. In addition, the Council of State passed a special decree explaining and limiting the conditions under which the homes of citizens could be entered without the authorization of a procurator. Like the new penal code, these were all indications that a new era of legality was about to begin. Unfortunately, once Ceauşescu consolidated his control of the RCP, there would be no way to hold him to his promises.

Romania in April 1968 was in turmoil: Complete territorial reorganization, change in the economic decisionmaking process, and radical restructuring of Party-state relationships all contributed to the confusion. Ceauşescu was continuing and intensifying his rhetorical commitment to participatory processes and appealing to a variety of economic, social, ethnic, and religious groups for support. At the same time, tension in foreign affairs was instilling uneasiness in the entire population as Romania faced the disapproval and hostility of its Warsaw Pact allies and communist parties throughout the world. It was in this chaotic atmosphere that the Central Committee of the Romanian Communist Party began one of the most important sessions in its history.

The April Plenum

The Central Committee of the Romanian Communist Party opened its plenum on 22 April 1968 with a crowded agenda. In addition to the usual spring reports on Party composition and structure and on the way officials were handling letters and suggestions from citizens, the CC was to consider a major educational reform; the preparation, equipment, and tactics of the armed forces; the recent problems in foreign policy; and the rehabilitation of certain party activists. The final item, minor though it seemed, turned out to be the dramatic focus of the meeting, for it involved the posthumous rehabilitation of Lucreţiu Pătrăşcanu, the denunciation of Gheorghe Gheorghiu-Dej, and the ouster of Alexandru Drăghici from all of his Party offices.

The Preliminaries

The first five topics for discussion produced no major surprises. The educational reform took up the first two days. Hinted at by Ceauşescu as early as 1965, the general reorganization of the entire educational system extended basic education to ten years, diversified vocational-technical institutions, and provided some increased autonomy for universities within a system that remained highly centralized. These changes attempted to provide the higher level of training and greater specialization necessary in a more diversified and industrialized society,[83] but they did not yet have the focus on technical training, to the total exclusion of less pragmatic subjects, that would be typical of education under Ceauşescu.

The report on Party composition called on party members to "set a high moral example in their social and family life"[84]; it echoed the laws against abortion and divorce, the anti-smoking campaign, and the other attempts made since 1965 to influence personal ethics, but it was also reminiscent of the attack on the Ministry of Internal Affairs the previous summer and foreshadowed the denunciations of Gheorghiu-Dej and Drăghici soon to follow. The report on responses to letters and complaints of citizens was strident in its complaints that "some leading cadres" still did not understand that they were required to solve these problems[85]; this was another demand for higher ethical standards, but in professional rather than personal activities, and it was already a frequent theme of the period after Gheorghiu-Dej.

The fourth topic for discussion was the report delivered by Ion Ioniţă, minister of the armed forces, who continued his public friendship with Ceauşescu by expressing his satisfaction with Romania's military readiness and endorsing the policy established a year earlier to intensify domestic production of some armaments in order to import more advanced military technology.[86] Ceauşescu, speaking several days later, announced that measures had already been taken for Romania to produce more of its own military equipment and to import only that which could not be produced at home.[87] Although both men recognized the advantages of domestic production, Ceauşescu emphasized the self-suffiency that would result, whereas Ioniţă saw the military possibilities of limiting imports to more advanced weapons. The seeds of future disagreements were planted, but the atmosphere was quite friendly. Ion Coman, deputy defense minister and head of the armed forces political directorate, even pointed out that this was the first time the Central Committee had discussed the armed forces in a plenary session, and he thanked the Party and Ceauşescu personally for "the measures taken to give the army weapons and modern technology."[88] The entire discussion was a signal of defiance to the Warsaw Treaty Organization; at the same time, it helped Ceauşescu to gain the support—or at least the neutrality—of the military officers in his pending move against Drăghici.

The penultimate report then addressed the dramatic developments in foreign policy over the past several months; the plenum approved the decisions of the Party Executive Committee and explicitly rejected the right of any international group to impose policies on an individual party.[89]

Rehabilitations

The final topic discussed at the April 1968 plenum was the crucial one; the contents of the report of the Party Commission on the Rehabilitation of Some RCP Activists came as a surprise to most CC members. The plenum decision based on this report[90] continued the re-evaluation of Romanian and RCP history that had begun just after the 1965 congress with the creation of the Commission on Party History and with the quiet return to public life of individuals removed by Gheorghiu-Dej. In addition, Ceauşescu (in the name of the collective leadership) had reinterpreted Party history in 1966 and 1967 to blame past mistakes on the difficult conditions of underground work, on inexperience during the early days of Party rule, or on outside interference— not on the RCP cadres themselves. There had been a growing emphasis on socialist legality, accompanied in 1967 by the criticism and reorganization of the Ministry of Internal Affairs and most recently by the publication of the new penal code. This report on rehabilitations was thus the culmination of a long process.

The original Commission on Party History had included the entire Presidium among its members, but the plenum decision explained that the Executive Committee had set up a smaller group of prewar Party members[91] to look into abuses against Party activists. They had been investigating since November 1965, and their report had gone to the Presidium and Executive Committee and now was before the Central Committee. Most of the published decision concerned the case of Lucreţiu Pătrăşcanu because the commission had been asked to investigate the circumstances surrounding his arrest, trial, and execution and to consider whether the accusations against him had been well founded and the methods used against him correct.

Once one of the most prestigious members of the Romanian Communist Party, Pătrăşcanu—the plenum now revealed—had been arrested on 28 April 1948 and was investigated for seventeen months by a commission that included Gheorghiu-Dej and Drăghici. Eventually he was turned over to the security organs of the Ministry of Internal Affairs, but still by the spring of 1952 no reliable evidence against him had been discovered. Meanwhile, Gheorghiu-Dej had already denounced Pătrăşcanu at a Cominform meeting in December 1949 as an agent of Anglo-American espionage. In May 1952, when Pauker and Luca were ousted from the Party leadership, Teohari Georgescu was removed as minister of internal affairs, rebuked by Gheorghiu-Dej for "not having carried through the investigation on the counterrevolutionary and spying activities of Pătrăşcanu." Drăghici, Georgescu's replacement, set up a special team under his direct leadership "to get at any cost evidence to justify the assertion that Lucreţiu Pătrăşcanu had allegedly been an agent of the *Siguranţa* [the pre-communist secret police] and an Anglo-American spy." The 1968 plenum decision continued:

On 18 March 1954, based on the information presented by Alexandru Drăghici, the Political Bureau of the CC of the RWP decided "to proceed to the trial of the group of spies headed by Pătrășcanu." The trial took place 6 to 13 April 1954, in violation of the most elementary procedural guarantees. The death sentence was pronounced on 14 April and on the night of 16–17 April 1954 Lucrețiu Pătrășcanu was executed at the Jilava prison.

Nicolae Ceaușescu, not a candidate member of the Political Bureau or secretary of the Central Committee until two days later, could credibly claim not to have taken part in the decision to execute Pătrășcanu, but the revelations were disastrous for Drăghici.

The 1968 plenum added other details in its criticisms of Gheorghiu-Dej and Drăghici. The party leader had intervened directly in the Pătrășcanu inquiry, indicating the direction it should take, what testimony should be obtained, and what additional arrests should be made. Drăghici had then "brought false conclusions to the Political Bureau" that led its members to place Pătrășcanu on trial. The 1968 plenum also pointed out that Pătrășcanu's original arrest had occurred at a time when "differences of views on policy . . . [resulted in] criminal investigations of party cadres. . . [instead of] political solutions"; in other words, this happened while Stalin was still alive. But Pătrășcanu's execution was another matter entirely. As the decision pointed out: "The judicial repression against Lucrețiu Pătrășcanu took place precisely in a period when, after the death of J.V. Stalin . . . in the USSR and other socialist countries there started a course toward the rehabilitation of some persons sentenced without justification." Thus Pătrășcanu's execution could not even be excused on the basis of Stalin's interference.

Gheorghiu-Dej and Drăghici were able to do all this, the plenum concluded, because "the Ministry of Internal Affairs did not act under the guidance of the collective executive bodies of the Central Committee, and the Minister of Internal Affairs evaded the control of these collective bodies." The major cause of the abuses was that "inner-Party democracy and the principles of collective work and collective leadership were not observed." As a result, "great harm" was done to the Party, and many activists who had done nothing wrong were expelled from the RCP and sentenced to prison. In view of these findings, the 1968 plenum decided on the "posthumous political rehabilitation of Lucrețiu Pătrășcanu" and recommended revision of his sentence to the appropriate judicial bodies.

Yet another rehabilitation was immediately considered by the plenum: the case of Ștefan Foriș. Like Pătrășcanu a founding member of the RCP, Foriș had been removed as general secretary at the legendary prison infirmary meeting in 1944 involving Gheorghiu-Dej, Bodnaraș, Chivu Stoica, and others (see Chapter 2). The 1968 decision did not question his removal as Party leader, which it asserted had been necessary due to "grave" but unspecified "shortcomings" in his work; what the 1968 report found unacceptable was the later accusation that he had been an informer for Antonescu's secret police, resulting in Foriş's arrest after 23 August 1944 and his execution in the summer of 1946 "on the basis of a decision taken by Gheorghe Gheorghiu-Dej, Teohari Georgescu, Ana Pauker, and Vasile Luca." Consequently, the plenum granted "posthumous political rehabilitation" for Foriş also.

The 1968 decision also rehabilitated a number of Romanian communists who died in the USSR from 1936 to 1938 during Stalin's purges, among them Marcel Pauker, the husband of Ana Pauker. Several party members who had been removed more recently, and who therefore were still alive, were restored to the full rights of Party membership, including Miron Constantinescu. The Central Committee then empowered the Executive Committee to investigate similar cases and take "suitable measures." The final step was to oust Drăghici: Because of his "particular and direct responsibility" in the "impermissible" actions against Pătrăşcanu, his "misleading the organs of Party leadership" in this case, his repressive measures against other Party activists, and finally his stand during the 1968 meetings of the Presidium, the Executive Committee, and the Central Committee,[92] the plenum removed Alexandru Drăghici from the three top Party bodies and recommended his dismissal as vice-president of the Council of Ministers.[93]

Not surprisingly, the major conclusions drawn by the Central Committee from these discoveries were both themes of Ceauşescu: the need to strengthen (1) the role of the Party in society and (2) the role of the Central Committee in the Party. Respect for collective leadership and "thorough discussions within the framework of the Party organs" were other familiar themes repeated in the plenum decision. Predictably, the plenum advocated a greater role for the Grand National Assembly and the Council of Ministers, a recommendation "foreshadowed by the National Conference of the RCP in December 1967." The Ministry of Internal Affairs and the Council on State Security were warned to observe strict legality and to carry out all their activities in "close and direct liaison with Party organs."

A final aspect of the plenum's decision—rather ominous for some members of the Presidium—was the repetition of the theme of collective and personal responsibility: "Each activist is personally responsible both for his own activity and for the activity of the Party organ to which he belongs." Thus, the plenum warned: "A significant responsibility for the decision taken in committing Lucreţiu Pătrăşcanu to trial, since they never ascertained the basis of the accusations brought by the investigating bodies, falls on the members of the Political Bureau at that time." This implicated not only Drăghici, but Apostol, Bodnaraş, and Chivu Stoica (and, incidentally, the newly rehabilitated Constantinescu), but not Maurer, who had been dropped from the Political Bureau from 1952 to 1960, or Ceauşescu, who joined the Party leadership just at the right time in 1954.

The last action taken by the 1968 plenum sealed Drăghici's dismissal: Virgin Trofin was elected a full member of the Executive Committee and a member of the Presidium, placing him on all three top party bodies along with Ceaușescu and Niculescu-Mizil. In addition, Emil Drăgănescu and Dumitru Popescu became candidate members of the EC, and Ion Iliescu moved from candidate to full member of the Central Committee. They would all be important members of Ceaușescu's leadership group during the 1970s.

Ceaușescu's Speech to the Bucharest Party Activists

The day after the plenum closed, Ceaușescu gave his major public explanation of it in a speech to the Bucharest Party organization.[94] His remarks paralleled those of Khrushchev and other leaders of Leninist parties who have found it expedient to denounce their predecessors. In addition, we can infer what Drăghici said in his own defense at the plenum from Ceaușescu's criticisms of his remarks—an example of how an older generation might seek to justify itself.

Ceaușescu began his speech by focusing on the details of the "crime" against Pătrășcanu, the motives of Gheorghiu-Dej and Drăghici, and the stand taken by Drăghici at the April 1968 meetings. Ceaușescu's language was much more colorful than that of the plenum decision: He called the Pătrășcanu case a "foul frame-up" and a "dastard[ly] assassination" and revealed that Pătrășcanu had been executed two days after his trial by "shooting him in the back." Although Drăghici had been the "organizer and executor" of the crimes, Gheorghiu-Dej had "initiated and sponsored" them because "he had a grudge against Pătrășcanu." Gheorghiu-Dej directed the inquiry personally, reading the witnesses' statements, annotating them, and giving instructions as to further statements to be obtained. Ceaușescu admitted that Gheorghiu-Dej had had indisputable virtues, but "no merits . . . can excuse his abuses and responsibility in the assassination."[95]

One of Ceaușescu's major complaints about Drăghici was that he had tried to defend himself before the Central Committee. According to the general secretary, Drăghici "regretted" that he had not found sufficient proof to justify the condemnation of Pătrășcanu, but he blamed this on the "poor work" of his subordinates, implying that Pătrășcanu had indeed been guilty. Then he tried to shift the burden of proof by suggesting that it was up to the commission in 1968 to "demonstrate the baselessness of the accusations" against Pătrășcanu.[96] He also attempted to justify his subordinates' methods by pointing out that the "bourgeois-landlord" police had "acted in the same way toward communists," a remark that Ceaușescu of course called an "insult to our security organs" because "resorting to forgeries, frame-ups, and imagination is not in line with the ethics of communists." A man who acted in accordance with bourgeois practices, Ceaușescu asserted, had no right to head the Romanian security forces.[97]

Drăghici also must have justified his actions by referring to the fight his ministry had waged against counterrevolutionary elements, and this gave Ceauşescu the chance for a long discourse on one of his favorite themes: the role of Party and security forces in society. He rejected the idea that the security organs bore the main responsibility for the struggle against "the enemy." "Already in 1956," he asserted, "we criticized this idea, emphasizing that it was not the *Securitate*, but the Party, that organized and led the fight." The defeat of the reactionary classes had not been due to "repressive measures," but to "successes in socialist construction . . . under the leadership of the RCP." He attacked Drăghici for "hiding behind the screen of struggle against the enemy," pointing out that the Party activists arrested were not enemies but "comrades-in-arms" and sources of pride. Ceauşescu said he had known Pătrăşcanu slightly both before and after the war and described him as "one of the outstanding activists and leaders of the Party and of the Romanian people." He was "a man of vast erudition and Marxist-Leninist culture, a remarkable Party leader." If Drăghici had been looking for enemies, Ceauşescu remarked, then he should not have been looking among such people within the Party.

Evidently Drăghici also claimed that he personally had not given orders for any abuses, but Ceauşescu pointed to the evidence to the contrary that had been amassed by the commission.[98] Then Drăghici stated that he had merely carried out the Party line in his ministry, but Ceauşescu noted, "Such an allegation . . . slanders the Party . . . [for] the abuses and illegalities committed do in no way represent the line of our Party.[99]

Of course, the record is one-sided because it is primarily Ceauşescu's version of events that is known. But it is clear that Drăghici's downfall was inevitable, once the abuses had been acknowledged, in order to maintain the infallibility of the Party. His final defense that he had merely followed Party instructions was politically suicidal; by blaming the Party and the entire political structure for events, he abandoned the only forgivable view (the same view expressed by Khrushchev about Stalinism)—that the abuses had been aberrations in the system caused by exceptional conditions and specific individuals. Drăghici must have concluded that he would not be allowed to keep his positions on any account, and so he decided to defend himself. We do not know what the other plenum speakers said,[100] but it is likely that the failure to publish the 1968 remarks reveals that some debate did take place.

In addition to refuting Drăghici's statements, Ceauşescu tried to answer three questions: (1) How could such events occur? (2) Why should the crimes be made public in 1968? (3) What should be done to prevent future abuses? His arguments, though couched to serve his own personal advantage, were in a number of ways remarkably similar to those of Khrushchev in 1956.

First, in explaining how such things could happen in a socialist state, he referred to other speakers who had blamed "the general climate of suspicion and mistrust" and the "trials and sentences during those years in a number of socialist countries." Ceauşescu admitted the poisonous effect of the political atmosphere, but as the decision of the plenum had pointed out, the execution of Pătrăşcanu took place in 1954—"when in other socialist countries, in the Soviet Union, a course was starting to disclose such illegalities and to rehabilitate the victims." Besides, he went on, "We cannot explain what has happened in Romania only by references to what happened in other countries." So the answer to how abuses could have occurred had to be found also in the internal conditions prevailing in Romania.

Two factors were singled out by Ceauşescu as especially important: First was the "harsh, factionalist struggle" through which the RCP had passed prior to and during World War II. This struggle had continued after 23 August, "and Pătrăşcanu was one of the victims." The other contributory factor was the "personal character" of Gheorghiu-Dej and Drăghici. Ceauşescu then went on to explain very carefully that the abuses revealed were "not an inevitable companion of socialism—as some are trying to explain—but . . . phenomena outside socialism. . . . Such practices stem from the concepts of the bourgeoisie, of reactionaries . . . the retrograde mentality of those who committed these abuses. . . . They spring from ignorance and violation of our Party's principles."[101] The blame, therefore, was to be placed not on the system or the party but upon factions and individuals.

The next question Ceauşescu tried to answer concerned the reasons for public revelation in 1968 of the crimes. His answers here fell into three categories.[102] First, the Party leaders had certain responsibilities as communists—to history, to the Party, to the people. As communists, he said, "We have a moral and political obligation to re-establish objective truth." History would of course eventually be just, but we "cannot leave it to history and time to bring clarification." Second, full disclosure would "strengthen even more the authority and prestige of our Party before the people." The Party was strong "precisely because it is capable of analyzing its activity critically and self-critically." Third—and the most frequently repeated reason later—the revelations would have a deterrent effect. Never mentioned was the advantage the denunciations gave Ceauşescu personally in his struggle to control the Party.

The final question Ceauşescu addressed was how to prevent similar abuses. Here he gave four answers. First, the role of the Party must be strengthened, especially in its control and guidance over the security forces. Second, the role of the Central Committee within the Party should be enhanced; it should take part in formulating policy, not just approving it. Third, participation in every Party and state body must be increased, in observance of the "principle of collective work." Party members must speak their minds openly, Central Committee members must help to work out decisions, and their participation must include the implementation of decisions. As Ceauşescu had said so frequently over the past several years, "All decisions must be the product of a broad, principled, and thorough debate in the Party bodies."[103] Finally, he called for an increase in socialist legality, which involved reciprocal demands: Laws must be observed by both citizens and officials. Not only must citizens be intolerant of "petty abuses," but arbitrary actions on the part of officials must cease: "We must ensure that never again should any citizen of this country, whether minister, Party official, or just an ordinary worker, fear that on going to his work place he may not return home—as happened during the period to which we refer and which we have fortunately left behind long since."[104]

All of these solutions were themes that Ceauşescu and others had been repeating since the Ninth Congress in 1965. What was new about the April 1968 plenum was the admission that Party leaders had made mistakes. But in this speech, as in the plenum decision, the blame was placed on aberrations in the system and the personalities of individuals, including the members of the Political Bureau, who did not ask for "firm proofs" as they should have.[105]

One last point to be made about Ceauşescu's talk to the Bucharest Party organization concerns a revelation he made about his own role in the April 1956 Political Bureau meeting. Ceauşescu claimed to have criticized Drǎghici then and to have supported measures to limit the power of the security organs. He quoted his own 1956 remarks as follows:

> As far as the Ministry of Internal Affairs is concerned, Party spirit remains as thin as Party control. Comrade Drǎghici thinks that he can do anything, because he has relations with Gheorghiu-Dej and is not accountable to anybody else. The unwholesome manifestations at the Ministry of Internal Affairs are largely due to the influence and the attitude of Comrade Drǎghici. Comrade Drǎghici does not work with the cadres: He does not consider people, and a large number of Party members are being dismissed from the security machinery under various pretexts. In 1954 alone some 900 Party members were dismissed. For three years now, that is, since Drǎghici has been there, the Ministry of Internal Affairs has not had a united executive. This is the result of Drǎghici's stand on the question of cadres. He likes to be surrounded by toadies. He poorly guides the security work.[106]

There clearly had been a long-standing rivalry between Ceauşescu and Drǎghici, but it is doubtful that Ceauşescu could have gone quite this far in 1956. Nevertheless, there is no doubt that in 1968 Ceauşescu wanted to be viewed as a critic of the Ministry of Internal Affairs—and as a champion of the Party, the Central Committee, inner-Party democracy, and socialist legality for all members of society. The April plenum allowed him to foster this image.

Reactions: The Presidium, the Police, and the Army

Although Ceauşescu's interpretation of the April plenum decisions received the most attention, the other members of the Presidium had the chance to express their own views to the Party organizations of the various counties. These speeches are the only public record of the other leaders' reactions.[107] The speakers followed Ceauşescu's lead in certain respects: All pointed out that Gheorghiu-Dej's acknowledged merits could not excuse the discovered abuses. All criticized Drăghici for not practicing self-criticism at the plenum. All pointed to the factional struggle within the Party and the failure to work collectively as major causes of the abuses. Finally, all criticized the Ministry of Internal Affairs for evading Party control.

Despite these similarities, there were significant variations among the speeches that reflected the different backgrounds and positions of the individuals. Bodnaraş practiced the most complete self-criticism, with Apostol a close second. Both praised Ceauşescu for his personal initiative in bringing about the revelations, with Apostol crediting Ceauşescu for suggesting that the Presidium and the Executive Committee set up the commission to investigate the cases of Pătrăşcanu and Foriş. Bodnaraş went even further, saying that Ceauşescu had initiated many attempts to bring the Ministry of Internal Affairs more closely under Party control while Drăghici was in charge before 1965. (This supported Ceauşescu's self-laudatory version of the 1956 Political Bureau meeting, although Bodnaraş was the only speaker to refer even indirectly to Ceauşescu's claim.) In addition, both Bodnaraş and Apostol explicitly accepted their responsibility for the death of Pătrăşcanu because they had been members of the 1954 Political Bureau. Chivu Stoica did not acknowledge any error on his own part. Instead, like Khrushchev in 1956, he excused himself by stressing that the Political Bureau had not functioned as a collective group. Both Bodnaraş and Apostol mentioned this as an extenuating circumstance. As Apostol put it, "The powers of the Central Committee and Political Bureau were monopolized by the First Secretary and several members of the Political Bureau." Bodnaraş emphasized the Political Bureau's ignorance of the actions: "No matter how strange it might seem, the fact remains that not one of us who are today in the Party leadership—I am thinking of the entire Central Committee and of its constituted organs—had full knowledge of what the inquiry commission was able to reveal." Maurer managed to avoid the issue of personal responsibility; he noted the faults and merits of both Gheorghiu-Dej and Pătrăşcanu and focused on the need for collective leadership and socialist legality. He could afford to be vague in his remarks—he had not been a member of the Political Bureau in 1954.

The younger Presidium members did not feel the need to point to the incorrect decisionmaking processes of the Political Bureau in order to exonerate themselves. Another generational difference appeared in the speakers' attitudes toward the Party's relationship with the population: In discussing the reasons for the revelations, most speakers stressed the need to prevent a repetition of such abuses. But only Ceauşescu, Niculescu-Mizil, and Verdeţ thought to highlight the need to maintain the authority of the Party in the eyes of the people. They viewed the April plenum as a step toward the legitimization of Party rule, recognizing that it could affect relations between Party and people, not just internal Party politics.[108]

Many of the speeches by local officials were also published. They were by no means unanimous in denouncing Drăghici by name, although they of course expressed support for the plenum. Whereas the security officers criticized Drăghici harshly and repeated many details of his crimes, the army officers tended to ignore Drăghici, support the plenum in general terms, and express their gratitude for "the Party's concern with defense capacity."[109] This contrast continued in the separate meetings of the Council on State Security and the armed forces in May 1968. The CSS letter to the Central Committee denounced Drăghici and expressed "indignation" at the crimes of which he and "a small group of investigators under him" were guilty.[110] The defense minister, Ioniţă, did support "the political measures taken against Alexandru Drăghici," but the letter to the Central Committee merely approved the decisions and expressed "satisfaction with the measures for intensified production of armaments and battle technology."[111] Clearly the security forces were anxious to dissociate themselves from their former minister, but the military was eager for more weapons and budget allocations during a time of crisis in the Warsaw Pact.

Rumors swirled in Bucharest for years afterward that some army officers had walked out of the plenum rather than vote against Drăghici, and the speeches after the plenum are not incompatible with that possibility. More active opposition from the military would have been quite difficult at this time of extreme hostility in Romanian-Soviet relations. The professional officers would always be on the horns of a dilemma with respect to Ceauşescu: During the next two decades he would consistently reduce their budgets, cut off their access to modern weapons and military technology, give them and their troops non-military duties, emphasize the development of "patriotic guards" rather than traditional military units, and change Romania's strategic military doctrine to that of a people's guerrilla war, similar to that of Yugoslavia. On the other hand, he always stressed Romanian nationalism and independence, so how could the military act against him either in 1968 or later?[112]

Ceauşescu's Rationale

The drastic revisions of Party history made in the April 1968 plenum brought surprisingly little public reaction inside Romania. Lightning had struck—but the loudest rumbles came from the Soviet Union and its Warsaw Pact allies. Articles did appear praising Pătrăşcanu,[113] and on 5 June *Scînteia* published the decision of the Supreme Court officially reversing the verdicts against him and several dozen other activists. Drăghici's punishment was much less severe than what he had applied to others; Ceauşescu kept the promise inherent in his speech on education at the beginning of the April plenum: "When they [Party activists] make mistakes, we take them to task, but that does not mean that we harm them."[114] Drăghici lost his top Party positions and many privileges, but he became a factory director in Bucharest.

The question remains why Ceauşescu chose this method to rid himself of a major rival. Not before or since has he staged such a dramatic confrontation. Certainly one motive in the entire process must have been the excuse to rehabilitate many of the old Party members who had been demoted under Gheorghiu-Dej. Men such as Constantin Doncea, who had served the Party with Ceauşescu in the 1930s and who later worked with him in the Ministry of Defense in the early 1950s, were old comrades who would presumably be loyal to the general secretary if he were to return them to public life. They would give him another source of support in addition to the younger officials he was promoting.

Second, and probably most important, the crimes of which Drăghici was accused could also be attributed to—and thus weaken—Ceauşescu's potential rivals in the Presidium who had been members of the 1954 Political Bureau. In contrast, Ceauşescu emerged unscathed because he had joined the Party leadership after Pătrăşcanu's execution and had evidently developed a reputation as an opponent of Drăghici starting as early as 1956. In addition, the attack on Drăghici was an attack on the Ministry of Internal Affairs, which had frequently evaded Party control in the past and which could thus form a base of resistance to Ceauşescu and the RCP in 1968. This institutional rivalry between the Party and the MIA, according to Bodnaraş and Ceauşescu, went back at least to 1956.

The denunciation of Drăghici also involved a diminution of Gheorghiu-Dej's role in Party history and thus enhanced the Ceauşescu image. The new Party leader had from the beginning chosen not to stress his position as heir to Gheorghiu-Dej, whose contributions had been stressed only in the first panicky days following his death. Instead, it was to the Ninth Congress in 1965 that Ceauşescu and other speakers and articles repeatedly referred. Romanian officials did not yet praise Ceauşescu's personal contributions as a matter of course or speak glowingly of the "Ceauşescu era," as they would in the 1980s, but they no longer referred to decisions made under Gheorghiu-Dej. The April plenum merely hastened this process of diminution.

Finally, the method chosen to eliminate Drăghici was intended to bolster Party legitimacy. According to the new interpretation, it had been infractions of Party rules and of the concept of collective leadership and work that had caused the abuses. Once the correct procedures were reintroduced (as they had been in 1965, it was implied), the Party had demonstrated its ability to admit and correct its mistakes. So the immediate threat to Party infallibility was transformed into proof of its infallibility in the long run.

It was this unique combination of factors that enabled Ceauşescu to dispose of his rival so successfully. Nevertheless, a great deal of skepticism remained in Romania regarding any fundamental difference between the rule of Ceauşescu and that of Gheorghiu-Dej. This skepticism would be put aside temporarily in the rush of national feeling during the summer and fall of 1968 as a result of Ceauşescu's resistance to the intervention in Czechoslovakia, and enthusiasm for the Party leader would last through the Tenth Party Congress the following summer. But thereafter it would be up to Ceauşescu and his new colleagues to prove to the average citizen that there was, as a number of speakers reportedly declared at the April 1968 plenum, a "new wind blowing . . . within the ranks of the Party."[115]

6

Aftermath:
Intervention and Consolidation,
1968-1969

The period between the April 1968 Central Committee plenum and the Tenth Party Congress in August 1969 brought no major policy or structural innovations inside Romania. Instead, Ceauşescu and his colleagues attempted to deal with the changes approved in December 1967 and April 1968. One important event did occur: the August 1968 military intervention by the other Warsaw Pact states in Czechoslovakia. Even though Romania was not directly involved, the occupation of Czechoslovakia by the armies of the Warsaw Pact helped to consolidate Nicolae Ceauşescu's political power and therefore had a profound impact on Soviet-Romanian relations and Romanian internal politics. The Romanian leader became a national hero by denouncing the violation of Czechoslovak sovereignty and asserting publicly that Romania would fight rather than submit to occupation by foreigners. In the months following the intervention, Ceauşescu drew increasing praise from Romanian officials, and he in turn began to reveal his own personality more clearly in his public statements. Nevertheless, just as policy content and administrative structure were marked by continuity rather than new departures during this period, so too did collective leadership continue to be a formal feature of Romanian politics—at least until the Tenth Party Congress.

The Intervention in Czechoslovakia

Romanian support for the Czechoslovak experiment gradually grew during 1968 as Bucharest strongly asserted the right of the Prague leaders to determine policy within their own party and state. The RCP leaders stressed Romania's military strength and preparedness and their determination to defend the homeland against external enemies, and in May they held special meetings of the Party organizations at the Council of State Security and in the armed forces to reiterate these points.[1] That same month President de Gaulle of France visited Bucharest with great pomp and ceremony, and soon afterward Ceauşescu went to Belgrade and was equally well received by Tito.

These high-level visits overshadowed contacts with Moscow, which were maintained in public only by Ceaușescu's reception of the Soviet ambassador.[2] During these visits Ceaușescu made no public comments on the Czechoslovak situation, instead focusing on general issues and the usual Romanian intonations of sovereignty, equality, mutual non-interference, and the inviolability of frontiers.[3]

Then, on a mid-July visit to an iron and steel combine in Galați, Ceaușescu made the first in a series of strong statements supporting the Czechoslovak party: "The Romanian Communist Party does not share the view of those who are alarmed over what is happening in Czechoslovakia and who consider that there has to be an intervention. . . . We have full confidence in the Communist Party of Czechoslovakia."[4] This sudden vocal defense of the Czechoslovak position may have been prompted by the East European allies who had just met in Warsaw and issued an ultimatum that included a rationale for invasion.[5] They then seemed to back off as agreements with the Czechoslovaks were reached at Cierna and Bratislava, and Ceaușescu on 11 August reacted with "satisfaction" to the "acceptable solutions . . . [reached by] patient discussions."[6]

Nevertheless, he continued to signal both the Soviets and the Romanian population that the RCP was prepared to defend its country. On 14 August he made a great occasion of the graduation exercises for officers' schools in the Ministry of Armed Forces, the Ministry of Internal Affairs, and the State Security Council,[7] stressing the training and competence of the military forces, the new types of weapons available, and the recent increases in domestic production of military hardware. He also praised the courage and patriotism of the young graduates and their resolve to defend their homeland. He warned that command of the armed forces was "a sovereign attribute of the leadership of our Party and state" and that military cooperation of socialist countries could only be directed against imperialist aggression from outside: "There can be no justification for admitting in any way the use of armed forces for intervention in the internal affairs of any of the Warsaw Treaty socialist member countries." At the same time, he emphasized Romania's obligations within the Warsaw Pact and claimed that his country's armed forces were "ready at any moment to fulfill their duties." The RCP, he implied, by raising the fighting potential of its armed forces, was fulfilling a supreme internationalist duty.

Two days later he was in Prague signing a Treaty of Friendship, Cooperation and Mutual Assistance.[8] During the visit Ceaușescu's major themes were his confidence in his hosts—despite certain temporary difficulties—and the need to solve differences of opinion by comradely discussions. He described the new treaty as evidence of a joint decision to cooperate in defending the independence and territorial integrity of the two states "against the aggressive policy of imperialist circles" (although it was difficult to see how Romania's "territorial integrity" could be threatened by

Western imperialists because the country, unlike Czechoslovakia, had no common border with a NATO power). At a press conference Ceauşescu was pressed on whether he had noticed anti-socialist activities during his visit; his reply was typical of Romanian diplomacy and of Ceauşescu: "I think you [Czechoslovaks] know better the situation in Czechoslovakia." He did admit that Dubcek had referred in their talks to the existence of some problems, but Ceauşescu was confident that these could not "endanger the socialist conquests of the Czechoslovak people." Questions about the recent difficulties within the Warsaw Pact were also avoided with typical Romanian tact. When asked why Romania had not been invited to the Dresden and Warsaw meetings, Ceauşescu merely suggested that the question be put to those who had participated in those conferences. At no point during the visit did he criticize the Warsaw Treaty Organization publicly; instead, he concentrated on demonstrating his support for the Czechoslovak party and urging caution on everyone.

After returning to Romania, he continued to express confidence in the Dubcek leadership. As late as 20 August, in a speech at the Piteşti automobile factory, he declared "full satisfaction" with developments in Czechoslovakia and reported on his recent visit: "We were profoundly impressed. . . . The destinies of the Czechoslovak people are in safe hands, in the hands of the Communist Party. . . . In the Czechoslovak people we have a wonderful friend in the joint struggle for socialism."[9]

The next day, when the other members of the Warsaw Treaty Organization sent their armies into Czechoslovakia, Ceauşescu for the first time combined his support for Czechoslovak sovereignty with explicit criticism of the other socialist states. At popular rally held on the Palace Square in Bucharest, Ceauşescu spoke briefly, first of the desire of the Romanian people to ensure "the peaceful construction of socialism in our homeland."[10] He then declared that the "penetration" of the troops of the five socialist countries (the USSR, Bulgaria, East Germany, Hungary, and Poland) into Czechoslovakia was "a great mistake and a grave danger to peace in Europe, to the fate of socialism in the world" and "a shameful moment in the history of the revolutionary movement." He went on: "There is no justification whatsoever . . . [for] military intervention in the affairs of a fraternal socialist state. . . . The problem of choosing the roads of socialist construction is a problem of the respective Party. . . . Nobody can pose as advisor."

He announced that Romania's revolutionary gains would be defended by the immediate formation of "armed patriotic detachments of workers, peasants, and intellectuals, defenders of the independence of our socialist homeland." This time he defiantly explained the need for such militia units not in terms of the "imperialist" threat, but to defend against an action in Romania similar to that taken in Czechoslavakia:

It was said that in Czechoslovakia there was a danger of counter-revolution; maybe tomorrow there will be some who say that here, too, at this rally, counter-revolutionary tendencies were manifest. We answer all of them: the entire Romanian people will not allow anybody to violate the territory of our homeland. . . . We are communists and anti-fascists who faced prisons and death, but we have never betrayed the interests of the working class, of our people. Be sure, comrades, be sure, citizens of Romania, that we shall never betray our homeland, we shall never betray the interests of our people.

Ceauşescu was speaking both to the Soviets and to Romanians, expressing his determination to preserve socialism in Romania but also to resist with force an incursion by any foreigners, socialist or "imperialist."[11]

The rally in Bucharest was followed by spontaneous rallies throughout the country and visits by RCP leaders to many localities where they were greeted for once with genuine enthusiasm by the crowds.[12] Units of "patriotic guards" were organized, and citizens began mass training in the tactics of guerrilla warfare. Never again would Romanian military service and doctrine rest only on professional units of officers and draftees.

Meanwhile, Ceauşescu continued to assert that the invasion had been a terrible mistake, but he very quickly began to emphasize the friendly relations that must exist between Romania and the USSR. For example, in Braşov on August 26, he stated: "Nothing can hinder the good cooperation and friendship between Romania and the Soviet Union. . . . There is no problem that could be a reason for disagreement between our peoples."[13] He went on to stress Romania's long-standing friendly relationships with Hungary, Bulgaria, and Yugoslavia, and also with the Czechs and Slovaks. He mentioned each of the other socialist countries by name, called for the development of cooperation with them, and recognized the need for Romania "to participate actively in the international division of labor." He also repeated that Romania would fulfill its obligations under the Warsaw Treaty "if imperialism attacks a socialist state."[14] He therefore made it quite clear that his country would continue its alliance with the USSR despite these recent difficulties over Czechoslovakia.

Ceauşescu also asserted his country's right to internal diversity, however, and the right of each party to determine its own path to socialism:

These differences cannot and must never . . . weaken the unity of the socialist countries. . . . Why should it be wrong if in one country enterprise management is resolved in one way, and in another in a different way? If in Romania there are managing committees in enterprises? What is wrong if in our country the first secretary of the county Party committee is also president of the county People's Council and in another country it is not like that? . . . Can this harm the interests of socialism? Is it not our people and ourselves who must judge and see whether things proceed well or not?[15]

Implicit in his argument was the assumption not only that each country must decide for itself how best to carry out socialist development, but also that the only way to strengthen socialism throughout the world must be to strengthen each individual socialist state. Nevertheless, Ceaușescu had become more circumspect in his statements on relations within the socialist bloc: While stressing mutual non-interference, he also began to acknowledge the need for "international division of labor"—the slogan from the early 1960s that implied greater cooperation in Comecon.

Whether Ceaușescu's actions had any effect in Moscow is questionable. The Soviet leaders probably had no intention of using military force against Romania in 1968, but Ceaușescu's commitment to fight certainly raised the potential cost of such an operation, even though Romanian resistance could hardly have been effective for very long. Ceaușescu's emotional speech in Bucharest seemed inflammatory when he gave it, but he evidently had been issuing private warnings against a move into Czechoslovakia for weeks. They had not been heeded, and Ceaușescu was determined to prevent military intervention in Romania—his personal power would have been unlikely to survive occupation. His vehement public stance made the threat to fight more credible and enhanced whatever deterrent effect that threat might have had.

Ceaușescu's reactions had dramatic effect on his own fate: He became a national hero, and his popularity would allow him to complete his consolidation of personal power in Romania. At last there was an issue on which the Party and the entire Romanian population were on the same side. Although outsiders may question whether the Soviets actually intended to invade, most Romanians in 1968 felt an invasion was imminent—and Ceaușescu received personal credit for preventing it. He stood up to the Soviets, publicly denounced their action, and called on his fellow citizens to form armed units in the national defense. The response was overwhelming enthusiasm: His defiant speech gained him in one day the personal popularity that no conceivable set of economic achievements or diplomatic successes could have achieved.

The impact of the Czechoslovak intervention on Ceaușescu and on Romania therefore cannot be overemphasized. In the early 1970s, Romanians disillusioned with other aspects of Ceaușescu's policy would still point to the events in Czechoslovakia as the major reason for supporting him and the Romanian Communist Party. August 1968 turned any opposition to Ceaușescu into betrayal of the Romanian nation. Unfortunately for the Soviets, their military action in Czechoslovakia contributed to the personal power of this most nationalistic and anti-Soviet of East European leaders. Two major events of 1968—the removal of Alexandru Drăghici from the RCP leadership by the April plenum and the Warsaw Pact intervention in

Czechoslovakia—rendered Ceauşescu's position unassailable for years to come.

Internal Policy Developments

In these months following the April 1968 plenum, Ceauşescu's growing power and prestige encouraged him to reveal his personal priorities more forcefully than he previously had been willing to do. His emphasis on "revolutionary morality" intensified—hard work, "equitable" remuneration, equality, and a stable family life. He increased his demands for socialist legality and democracy and combined this with rhetorical overtures toward the national minorities. His conservative tendencies in cultural policy became more overt, but were tempered by an apparent reluctance to intervene directly in the quarrels of academic specialists. Nevertheless, most of the policies announced in 1968 and 1969 simply reinforced tendencies that had emerged in the period after Gheorghiu-Dej's death.

In economic policy, the push to link remuneration closely to production was furthered by measures adopted in 1968. "Payment according to the quantity and quality of work done," as Ceauşescu put it, was a major feature of the salary and economic directives approved by the Central Committee plenum in June.[16] These not only differentiated wages according to workers' quality, initiative, and promptness, but also eliminated lifetime annuities for holders of honorary titles (such as Member of the Academy, People's Artist, or Master of Sports) and introduced different levels of reward for "artistic, creative and performing work."[17] Simultaneously came promises of greater economic equality: The minimum wage was slated to rise, complemented by a progressive income tax and a measure prohibiting multiple salaries for persons holding more than one job. Ceauşescu complained that a lack of skilled personnel had allowed some individuals to hold "a plurality of paid jobs," resulting in extremely high incomes that "do not comply with their effective contribution." "No one," he continued, "can fulfill several offices with the same intensity and proficiency."[18] This rule would prove difficult to implement, however, and similar measures would be passed repeatedly during the next two decades.

Both of these apparently contradictory goals—remuneration according to production and equalization of income—were related to one of Ceauşescu's personal priorities that was gradually becoming more obvious in his statements: the "moral purification of social life." In his opinion, the sole source of income should be work, and excessively high incomes produce "negative phenomena." Incomes would remain stratified, but the range of inequality would be reduced. Illicit activities required special attention, and he called on citizens to report such matters: "Those who cannot justify the sources of the sums they spend will have to pay the state a tax representing

90 percent of the sum, and those who are proved to have cheated the state will be referred to justice."[19]

Ceauşescu's beliefs found tangible expression in his own life, even after he consolidated his control of the political system: In contrast to frequent rumors about other Romanian communist leaders, particularly in the Gheorghiu-Dej period, Ceauşescu was regarded as somewhat of a moralist throughout the 1960s and 1970s, and his long working hours were well known in Romania. "Social equity" in the distribution of goods—defined not as equality but as "the material reward of every citizen for his or her contribution to the national wealth"—became a constant theme.[20] Again, it would be difficult to translate rhetoric into reality, and corruption and bribery would increase rapidly as citizens tried to avoid these unpleasant new rules.

Socialist Legality and Democracy

The demands of the April 1968 plenum for socialist legality brought more rehabilitations of former Party officials. In September the Romanian Supreme Court reversed the convictions of fourteen men accused in 1952 and 1954, including Vasile Luca and a group of managers and engineers convicted of sabotage on the Black Sea–Danube Canal, the notorious labor camp project of the early 1950s (resumed and completed in the 1980s), and a few days later the sentences of some army officers were also reversed.[21] Even so, on the twentieth anniversary of the creation of the security forces, 29 August 1968, Ceauşescu took care to praise them highly, apparently to reassure them that the April discussion of past abuses had closed the matter.

Ceauşescu's emphasis on participatory democracy produced several new political structures in the fall of 1968, the broadest of which was the Socialist Unity Front (SUF), an organization for the Romanian Communist Party and all other mass, civic, and professional groups. The SUF was to coordinate the activities of all these organizations, ensure the participation of these groups in fulfilling Party policies, and nominate candidates and organize the elections to the Grand National Assembly and the People's Councils. When the SUF was set up on 19 November, Nicolae Ceauşescu was elected president, and he explained that the SUF National Council also would debate major problems of domestic and foreign policy. The SUF was but another example of how Ceauşescu would impose his vision of participation.

Not long before, at the Central Committee plenum of 24–25 October 1968, Ceauşescu had announced the formation of a Council of Hungarian Workers and a Council of German Workers, as well as county councils for other nationality groups, such as the Serbs, in areas where they were concentrated. The councils were to contribute to political and educational activities carried on by the Party among the national groups and "stimulate scientific, artistic and literary production among the cohabiting nationalities in their mother tongue."[22] This implicit appeal for support among the minorities was by now characteristic of Ceauşescu's political rhetoric, and he rarely missed an opportunity to speak of the various national groups working together to build socialism in Romania.

The Hungarians were particularly sensitive because of the RCP's wholehearted support of Soviet suppression of the 1956 Hungarian revolution. In 1968, therefore, almost immediately after Warsaw Pact troops moved into Czechoslovakia, Ceauşescu went to Transylvania to preempt any possible recurrence of unrest. He spoke in Braşov and in the two new Hungarian counties, and on 30 August he was in Cluj, the old capital of Transylvania, for a "Great People's Rally" and a meeting with the city's intellectuals. In Harghita he admitted that some Hungarian areas of Romania remained among the most backward industrially, and although socialism had brought some improvement, "we must honestly say that not too much has been done." That would be changed: Ten important enterprises were to be built in the Hungarian counties during the current five-year plan, for "there can be no true equality of rights, the national question cannot be considered solved, if material conditions are not ensured." His speech in Odorheiul Secuiesc was built around the same theme. In both of these talks, once he had emphasized the measures under way to improve economic conditions in the Hungarian areas, he went on to appeal for support in the face of the difficult international situation.[23] His listeners were meant to read between the lines of his remarks the fear that unrest among the population of Romania would provide foreign troops with an excuse to intervene.

This special attention paid Transylvania was given to other outlying areas during the rest of the year. In late September, Ceauşescu visited the counties of Caraş-Severin, Timiş, and Arad, bordering Yugoslavia and Hungary and including considerable minority populations.[24] His next major trip was in mid-October to Bucovina and northern Moldavia, the counties of Botoşani and Iaşi on the Soviet border. Whether Ceauşescu's travels made any difference is questionable, but according to one observer, mutual fear of the Soviets after events in Czechoslovakia helped to improve Romanian-Hungarian relations in Transylvania.[25] Of course, the situation in 1968 was completely different from that in 1956: Neither nationality could have been expected to sympathize with the Warsaw Pact move against Czechoslovakia, whereas in 1956 the Romanians had actually helped the Soviets against the Hungarians in Budapest. But in 1968 Ceauşescu clearly was making an effort to satisfy any ethnic grievances and prevent potential trouble.

Cultural Policy

One final area of concern to the Party and its leadership in 1968 and 1969 was literature and the arts. Since 1965, Ceauşescu had shown ambiguity in his attitude toward cultural policy. He had called for exchanges of opinions and diversity of forms—his concept of creative freedom—and he had implied that Western and Romanian literature and art should replace the previous Soviet models. Yet he had also stressed the need for ideological militance and expressed his own instrumental view of creative activity: that each artist has a responsibility to contribute to society and socialist development.

This ambiguity in cultural policy produced a struggle between conservative and radical writers during 1968, culminating in a session of the General Assembly of Romanian Writers in November 1968.[26] This meeting was significant in a number of respects: For example, genuine debate took place over the type of literature that should be published; when no new statutes for the writers' union could be agreed upon, a committee composed of various factions within the union was delegated to work out a final text. In addition, the General Assembly set up local writers' organizations in the various regional centers and established a number of publishing houses with different specialties, both in the capital and in other cultural centers such as Cluj and Iaşi. This decentralization reversed a reorganization of the State Committee on Culture and Art the previous December that had reduced the size of the bureaucracy and centralized policy coordination.[27] The measures were evidently a reaction to the protests of writers from outlying areas regarding the dominance of Bucharest residents in the writers' union and in publishing activity throughout Romania, and especially to complaints of Hungarian and German writers, who could play a more important role in certain regions than in the capital.[28]

The November meeting culminated a series of debates that had been going on in the specialized cultural press during 1968. A number of young writers had published avant-garde and anti-realist works that had drawn attacks from more conservative defenders of socialist realism. These press debates were significant in Romanian cultural life, which previously had been known for its conservative content and lack of creative controversy. Ceauşescu had been advocating an exchange of opinions since 1965, and in 1968 his calls had finally been answered positively—now he would find it necessary to issue warnings as to the limits.[29]

His position was helped at this time by a reluctance on the part of even the most radical young writers to provide the Soviet leaders with a perceived need to intervene in Romania, as they had in Czechoslovakia, on the pretext of danger from counterrevolutionary forces. All participants in the Romanian cultural debates—conservative and radical writers, and the Party as referee—preferred to find a compromise acceptable to all through quiet discussion. So, for example, they delegated the sensitive task of new statutes to a committee.

When Ceauşescu spoke at the 1968 meeting, he did not take a clear position in the debates. He praised the young writers, but warned that the correct path for them was "not the loud contestation of the achievements of others, but diligent work."[30] There were proposals made at the conference to set up a program of visits abroad for the young, but although he did stress the need for contacts with the West, the general impact of his statements was nationalistic and narrow: "This wish [to go abroad] is understandable. . . . Of course, acquaintance with international culture is an imperative to any intellectual, but our country offers today broad possibilities. . . . We hope that ideas will also come forward for the drawing up of a program of visits by the young writers in [outlying regions of] our country."[31]

This conservative position on literature and art echoed the remarks Ceauşescu had made on education at the April 1968 plenum. Since 1965 he had consistently maintained that the writer had a social duty to contribute to the general enlightenment of society, but in 1968 he chose to emphasize this duty. He seemed particularly annoyed by the arrogance of the younger generation, and at the writers' meeting he used a parable about a young poet to make his point. The young man—Ceauşescu called him "Prince Charming"—was still in his teens, but he had come to believe in his own superiority as a poet. He read his poems to passersby from a high tower— "clay or ivory"—and became very angry and rude if anyone dared ask him what his poems meant. The lesson in the parable was clear: Artists have a responsibility to create for the society in which they live. The arrogance of the young poet was childish and irresponsible and did not lead to publication. Fortunately, Ceauşescu concluded, "almost all our writers write for the people in whose midst they are living, for them to understand."[32] Passages from this parable later became shorthand formulations in Romania of incorrect approaches to literary and artistic creativity.

Yet another principle emerged from Ceauşescu's speech, a principle on which there could be no ambiguity or compromise—the role of the Party in cultural activity: "The leadership and guidance given by our Party to the arts is an imperative necessity [and] is meant to ensure that the arts and literature in our country serve the cause of socialism and progress."[33] Hence the diversity of forms and exchange of opinions must always take place within limits established by the Party. True, in November 1968 the Party chose to allow discussion and to establish regional publishing houses that might be expected to foster divergent points of view and reduce centralized censorship. Nevertheless, the Party reserved the right to intercede with more restrictive limits in the future. In a sense, Ceauşescu was urging the writers to discipline themselves and so make it unnecessary for the Party to exercise its prerogatives.

The End of Collective Leadership

In the months leading up to the Tenth Party Congress there were no major surprises. Ceauşescu continued to demonstrate his populism and the participatory democracy of Party rule with a number of personal visits to outlying areas of Romania, several mass meetings (another in agriculture, for example), and general elections to the Grand National Assembly in March. He proudly reinterpreted great occasions in Romanian history on his travels and on the anniversaries of the events themselves. His foreign policy reflected reduced tensions in relations among members of the socialist bloc as he took part in an international conference of communist parties in June 1969 on the promise that the delegates would not attack absent parties or each other. The results were mixed, but at least he was back in the socialist community. He also strengthened ties with the West, where his great triumph was the visit of President Richard Nixon to Bucharest in early August. Nixon had been given royal treatment in Bucharest when he was a mere ex-vice-president; he now reciprocated by singling out Romania for a personal tour. Ceauşescu by mid-1969 had undoubtedly established his personal control over the Romanian political process, but it would be the Tenth Party Congress that would give final sanction to his authority.

The congress opened on 6 August 1969, just three days after President Nixon left Bucharest. As one correspondent put it, "The American flags which bordered the avenues of Bucharest for the visit of Nixon have yielded to red flags with sickle and hammer, the emblem of the RCP."[34] Sessions were held in the huge Congress Hall, the platform decorated with "red bunting and large bas reliefs of Marx, Engels, and Lenin."[35] There were 1,915 delegates, and 66 foreign communist parties sent representatives. In contrast to the Ninth Congress, when both the Soviet and the Chinese party leaders were present, the Chinese refused to come; the Soviets sent party secretary Konstantin Katushev.[36] Katushev was given the place of honor among the foreign delegations, but even so he walked out when a telegram of greeting was read from the Chinese party wishing the RCP success in its "defense of national independence."[37] His nineteen-minute speech[38] was critical enough to raise chuckles from Romanians in the foyers, as they reportedly commented, "He's angry with us, isn't he?"[39] but he ended on a friendly (and condescending) note by presenting them with a huge statue of Lenin.[40]

The congress as a whole was marked by "work, calm, and seriousness."[41] Ceauşescu spoke for five and a half hours, and during the "marathon" his "delivery was a brisk monotone," interrupted only by pauses "to gulp a glass of water brought to him every half hour by a waiter in a white jacket."[42] His praise for the Soviet army in World War II was greeted only by "polite applause."[43] Reports on the congress in the foreign communist press were mixed. The East German, Polish, and Bulgarian papers gave only scanty coverage. Hungarian coverage was substantial, even printing those parts of Ceauşescu's speech that revealed disagreements with other parties, and the Yugoslav and West European communist papers carried "intensive" coverage.[44] It was quite clear from the foreign coverage and the charged atmosphere that Romania's reputation as independent troublemaker within the bloc remained unchanged. Also, Katushev's sharp criticism of Romanian "bridge-building," following Nixon's visit as closely as it did, revealed continuing Soviet concern about the country's relations with the United States and Western Europe. In short, Romania's status as a maverick member of the socialist bloc had not been affected by its stand against the Czechoslovak intervention.

Policy Developments

No dramatic policy changes were introduced at the Tenth Party Congress; those had been accomplished in December 1967 and April 1968. In foreign policy, Ceauşescu's report to the congress continued his cautious but stubbornly independent line, but he did initiate a major departure from Soviet doctrine by elaborating a theory of nationalism that denied that "the nation's role and mission cease after the proletarian revolution." Instead, he argued, "The transition from capitalism to socialism represents the nation's rise to a higher qualitative stage," with the Romanian nation a particularly apt example of this thesis because its formation had been especially difficult due to foreign domination. Only under socialism could "the energies and creative abilities of our nation . . . [be] fully released." In Romania, then, socialism did not imply the sacrifice of national interests, but rather provided the context for their full assertion.[45] In Ceauşescu's view, the nation would flourish under socialism as it never had before.

Domestic policies intensified rather than reversed previous trends. Rapid industrialization was to continue: Although annual growth under the new five-year plan would average a mere 8.5–9.5 percent as compared with 12.3 percent during the first three years of the 1966–1970 plan, the starting point would be 75 percent higher than in 1966.[46] The high rate of accumulation would also continue—28–30 percent of national income—and the priority given to heavy industry would be unchanged.[47] Ceauşescu spent quite a bit of time justifying this in terms of future consumption funds, so he must have been aware that the announcement would bring disappointment, perhaps discontent. Flexibility in the consumer sector was to rise gradually, as real wages would increase by 23 percent over five years; by 1975 over a half million new apartments would be completed, half of them privately owned. As before, the distributive emphasis was to be on equity as Ceauşescu defined it: income closely tied to quantity, quality, and initiative in production.

Still another emphasis visible as early as the Ninth Party Congress was reiterated in 1969: socialist legality. Ceauşescu repeated many of the statements he had made at the April 1968 plenum regarding the positive and negative contributions of Gheorghiu-Dej (without mentioning Drăghici) and stressed the need for Party control over the security forces to prevent the errors that "cost the lives of some outstanding Party activists, including Lucreţiu Pătrăşcanu" and to ensure that "nobody should ever be sentenced or punished without a justifiable reason in our society."[48] His discussion of the judicial system also stressed the need for Party supervision: "One must do away with the bourgeois concept according to which the law is beyond any control and the judge is only accountable to his own conscience. The judge guides himself by the law, and by the socialist conscience; he must . . . answer to the people for the way in which he carries out his assignment."[49] The ultimate arbiter of socialist legality, then, would not be the courts but the Party.

A final recurring theme was the emphasis on mass participation in policy formulation. Since the invasion of Czechoslovakia, he had called for mass participation in national defense, and he elaborated on this in great detail at the congress. After briefly mentioning Romania's intention to cooperate with members of the Warsaw Treaty Organization and to "fulfill its obligations in case of an imperialist attack," he continued:

> The defense of the country is the duty of every citizen. . . . Not only the army, but all the citizens must be ready to fight for the defense of the . . . homeland . . . [strong, prolonged applause]. A war of defense cannot be but a popular war, and victory will be won not only at the battle front, but through the general fight of the whole people [lively applause]. This is the meaning of the measures taken by the Party and government for the formation of patriotic detachments and for the military training of the youth—measures prescribed in the classics of Marxism-Leninism on arming the whole people for the revolution.[50]

Direct attack by an imperialist NATO enemy would have been highly unlikely, so the type of defensive warfare envisaged by the formation of militia units could only have been aimed at confronting an invasion like that in Czechoslovakia. Thus Ceauşescu's elaboration on this theme was another warning to the Soviets not to attempt any military action on Romanian soil. Whether he seriously believed such a warning was necessary is questionable, but his statement was very effective with his primary audience, the population of Romania.

Party Organizational Changes

In contrast to the continuity in policies, some major changes were made in the Party statutes, the stated goal being to increase "inner-Party democracy."[51] The democratic rhetoric had become so prevalent in the statements of Party leaders that one Western newspaper was moved to comment: "It has always been Ceauşescu's aspiration to weaken the elite character of the party, to seek contact with wider circles in the land, to establish the Party as a national mass organization."[52] Although the size of the Party had greatly increased since 1965 (see Table 2.1), the objective was not to turn it into a "national mass organization." The goals of the 1969 changes as Virgil Trofin described them[53] were not new: to strengthen the leading role of the Party in society, to enlarge the powers and responsibilities of its organs and organizations, to strengthen internal democracy and Party discipline, and to stimulate more active participation on the part of each communist in formulating and applying Party policies. Only some of the methods introduced to achieve these goals were new.

First, the period of time between congresses and conferences was to be lengthened.[54] Party congresses would be held every five years instead of four; Trofin explained that a national Party conference could always be called if necessary. The time between county Party conferences would be extended from two to four years, and that between municipal, city, communal, and base organization conferences from one to two years. The leading bodies elected by these sessions would have longer tenure and more experience and so in theory could solve problems more effectively.

Trofin connected the rest of the changes in the Party statutes directly to internal Party democracy. Two innovations affected the Party congress. First, as in the Soviet party under Brezhnev, the congress would elect the general secretary, which would not only add to the formal powers of the congress, but also would give Ceauşescu more prestige and security: He could no longer be removed by the Central Committee. When Trofin announced that the county Party conferences held just before the congress had all unanimously supported Ceauşescu's re-election, the news was greeted by "stormy, prolonged applause," a long-standing ovation, and the rhythmic cheer "PCR, Ceauşescu, PCR, Ceauşescu."[55] Election of the general secretary by the congress did not seem in practice to be evidence of an increase in Party democracy, but it certainly demonstrated Ceauşescu's ascendancy in the Party.

The second innovation affecting the Party congress was the creation of sections for various policy areas, which would presumably allow the delegates to participate more actively in the discussions of the section to which each belonged. Such sections were unknown in other socialist states except Yugoslavia, where they had only just been introduced at the most recent meeting of the League of Communists.[56] These new sections therefore symbolized Romania's close ties with a socialist state outside the Warsaw Treaty Organization.

Other measures were adopted with the stated goal of increasing internal democracy at intermediate levels of the Party. The requirement that the executive organs of Party committees report regularly to their respective committees was spelled out in more detail, and each committee was in turn to report to those who had elected it.[57] In addition, each Party organization was to discuss and propose candidates for election by its conference to the next higher Party organ. At the conference, candidates would be discussed, and the delegates could elect them to the respective Party committee. Trofin explained that this would make the officials better known to their constituents because they would be discussed at lower-level Party meetings, increasing their sense of responsibility to "the members of the Party and the entire people."[58]

Actually, this measure had already been put into effect. The county Party conferences had not only elected delegates to the Party congress, but also had nominated candidates for "higher Party bodies"—the Central Committee and the Central Revisory Commission. The Party congress was then to discuss these candidates and elect the new CC by secret ballot.[59] A total of 360 candidates were proposed by the county conferences; only 35 were not elected, among them Gheorghe Apostol and Chivu Stoica. Although it was possible to be elected without nomination by a county, only two candidate CC members and three Revisory Commission members had not received this prior endorsement.

Other changes in the Party statutes were directed at rights and responsibilities of individuals. Trofin emphasized several times "the unlimited right of communists to express their opinions on all problems of Party policy in organized meetings" (but not outside official forums). It was not enough for this right to be written in the Party statutes, but a "favorable climate of creative debate" had to be established in each Party body so that differences of opinion would be treated with correct "Party spirit."[60] Ceauşescu had reiterated this need since 1965—its repetition in 1969 indicated that "Party spirit" had not yet been achieved.

In order to reinforce this freedom of speech for Party members, the revised statutes would allow anyone to appeal to the immediately higher Party committee if the individual disagreed with a majority decision and to explain the objections. Nevertheless, the member had to support the decision until the higher group had reached its conclusions; the right of appeal was thus tempered by Party discipline.

Both Ceauşescu and Trofin were careful to stress that there were limits to this freedom of speech: "Internal Party democracy has nothing in common with anarchic concepts, according to which the Party would become a club of endless discussions." Decisions did not have to be unanimous, but once a decision had been reached, it was "absolutely obligatory . . . for the minority to submit unconditionally to the will of the majority."[61] The vehemence of these references to Party discipline and democratic centralism not only set the limits of debate and appeal, but also implied that these new measures actually were intended to be used. In the first place, if the right of appeal was not to be taken seriously, then why the need to stress the limits to such appeals or the obligation of the applicant to obey the original decision pending the eventual outcome? Likewise, if there was no intention to allow real debate within the Party bodies, then why the need to define the limits of such debate? These new provisions in practice turned out to be completely meaningless in Ceauşescu's Romania, but in 1969 the optimists took hope, although the skeptics remained unmoved.

Two other minor changes in the Party statutes indicated that the new provisions were to be taken seriously. First, it would henceforth be slightly more difficult to expel an individual from the Party. The phrase "or any other act inconsistent with the privilege of Party member" was reworded to read "or any other act which contravenes the provisions of the statutes."[62] To justify expulsion thus would require finding that a specific rule was broken, rather than relying on subjective interpretations of "inconsistent." If effective in practice, this new wording could give Party members more security. A less favorable change from the viewpoint of a Party member was the addition of Article 13(f), which made each member responsible for collective decisions whether or not the person had agreed with them. This provision tried to encourage Party members to take an active interest in the discussions because they would be held responsible and to appeal if they disagreed with a decision. Again, both provisions proved meaningless, but that was not clear in 1969.

Other alterations in the statutes reflected such Ceauşescu themes as the rights of the national minorities, personal ethics and morality, and concrete problems of social development. Party organs were reminded to report to their constituents regularly on Party policies and decisions. Some of the revisions were also intended to inform the higher Party organs about lower-level Party activity so that important decisions could be based on a more accurate picture of problems related to the production process. But all of these organizational changes were officially explained as attempts to increase internal Party democracy. Ceauşescu was attempting democracy by fiat.

This insistence on Party democracy did not begin with Ceauşescu. In fact, Gheorghiu-Dej at the Third Congress of the Romanian Workers' Party in June 1960 had called for strict observance of Leninist principles, democratic centralism, inner-party democracy, and collective leadership. Likewise, he had advocated the active participation of Party members in discussions, the development of criticism and self-criticism, and "especially criticism from below aimed at revealing shortcomings and mistakes."[63] The words used by Nicolae Ceauşescu and Gheorghe Gheorghiu-Dej were the same—the issue was whether the new procedures would lead to changes in practice.

The Leadership

If the December 1967 Party conference marked the beginning of the end of collective leadership in Romania, the Tenth Party Congress in 1969 brought its final demise. Neither Chivu Stoica nor Gheorghe Apostol was re-elected to the Central Committee, although they had both been nominated by county Party conferences. Chivu Stoica was made president of the Central Revisory Commission and so retired with honor. Apostol, on the other hand, was removed from his post as head of the trade unions "for inappropriate activity, for grave violations of communist ethics and the ethical principles of our socialist society."[64] Chivu Stoica still appeared in the press from time to time; Apostol did not, although he was appointed to oversee the General Directorate of State Reserves,[65] rather a mild punishment.

With the demotions of Chivu Stoica and Apostol, only three of the nine Presidium members remained from the Gheorghiu-Dej Political Bureau: Nicolae Ceauşescu, Ion Gheorghe Maurer, and Emil Bodnaraş. Two members of the Executive Committee had been candidate members of the Political Bureau in March 1965, Leonte Răutu and Ştefan Voitec, so that five out of twenty-one on this Party organ remained from the pre-Ceauşescu leadership. Only Ceauşescu himself had been on the Secretariat before Gheorghiu-Dej's death. The composition of the three highest Party bodies had almost completely changed during Ceauşescu's tenure as Party leader.

The supremacy of Ceauşescu within this new leadership was made quite clear at the Tenth Party Congress. Speakers felt compelled to begin and end their remarks by praising the Party leader. Many, especially Party workers, referred to him in almost every paragraph, crediting him personally with the great economic achievements since 1965. The period before he became general secretary was scarcely mentioned; it was as if socialist development in Romania had begun only with the Ninth Party Congress.

In the speeches to the Tenth Congress, individuals within the leadership concentrated on their areas of expertise. Ceauşescu delivered the main address, the report of the Central Committee. Maurer gave the other major report, the plans for economic development for 1971–1975 and 1976–1980, and presided over the section on international relations. Bodnaraş was sick and did not attend. Two individual speeches were worthy of note. First, Ion Ioniţă, the defense minister, spoke very positively of Party policy toward the armed forces. However, unlike Ceauşescu, who spent some time describing the need for the "whole people" to participate in the defense of the homeland and praised the formation of the "patriotic detachments" of militia, Ioniţă almost ignored these paramilitary guard units. He mentioned them only once; in discussing military education, he promised full support for "the activities of the patriotic guards and the preparation of the youth for the defense of the homeland."[66] Perhaps the military officers were not quite so enthusiastic as the Party leaders about these defense forces outside of the regular channels of military command.

The second significant speech was that by Dumitru Popescu, former editor of Scînteia, who spoke mainly about cultural policy. He claimed that fifty years of growth had been accomplished in the preceding four years. In that short period, he said, Romania had abandoned all that was "rudimentary" in socialism—rigid, simplistic views—and had substituted "a spirit of clarity, realism, rationality." He went on to explain that "socialist humanism . . . [had] left the pages of the textbooks and been introduced into life." One result of this change was the elimination from the Party of "suspicion—that corrosive element in social relations." Each person must "think for himself

. . . be himself, and, by this means, be together with all of society, of the country."[67]

Popescu drew two important conclusions about the political situation within Romania. First, he declared proudly:

> Never has the Romanian people so fully merged its destiny with that of the communist party. The people's choice in favor of socialism is definitive and unanimous. . . . Whoever penetrates to the hearts of our people, whoever takes the pulse of this nation, understands fully the loyalty to communism and internationalism of these 20 million builders of the new order in Romania.

For the first time, this was probably true—but not because of the introduction of socialist humanism into Romania. Certainly the new emphasis on socialist legality had helped; some of the suspicion and uncertainty had been eliminated, and citizens did feel more secure in their beds from arbitrary actions by the security forces. But the major reason for the new loyalty to the RCP was the stand the Party had taken in the face of the Warsaw Pact intervention in Czechoslovakia. The very force that had once made the Romanian Communist Party so unpopular within its own country—the people's antagonism toward the Soviet Union—in 1968 caused the Romanian population to "merge its destiny fully with that of the communist party." The RCP had established a measure of internal legitimacy because Ceaușescu had dissociated himself from the Soviet Union. As a result, the RCP was emancipated from the Soviet Union for the first time in the eyes of many Romanians.

The other conclusion that Popescu drew from the changes since 1965 had more direct relevance to his own cultural sphere: He asserted that literary and artistic creativity and Party *agitprop* (agitation and propaganda) were extremely inadequate. He criticized the press for "dilettantism" and "platitudes" and television for resembling "an illustrated magazine, remaining almost motionless in the face of the great social and spiritual concerns of our society." The State Committee for Culture and Art, "the rightful coordinator of all artistic life," and its organs "suffocate each other in administrative acts and protocol festivities." Art was "submediocre" and "puerile." He stressed that "we communists who work in the fragile sphere of spiritual creation must . . . work more energetically for the ideas in which we believe . . . [but this must be done] without imposing our will by administrative fiat where it is a question of taste, of personal originality." He was careful to place limits on cultural life—dialectical materialism and social responsibility—but, unlike Ceaușescu, he did not criticize younger writers.

Popescu himself was only 41, one of the youngest members of the Party leadership. He had been a candidate member of the Executive Committee only since the April 1968 plenum and in December 1968 had become a CC secretary. Not until the Tenth Congress did he join the EC as a full member.

During this time of real debate over cultural policy, this speech from the CC secretary for culture was quite significant. Popescu's remarks were a definite contrast to Ceauşescu's "clay or ivory tower" speech of the year before and the general secretary's stress on realism at the congress. Popescu did not contradict Ceauşescu or align himself with the poet in his tower, but he did severely criticize prevailing cultural policy, which could only have been a positive sign for hopeful young writers and artists.

The major result of the Tenth Congress, however, was the supremacy of Ceauşescu as leader of Party and state. Maurer remained president of the Council of Ministers, the head of government, but it was Ceauşescu who was venerated by the speakers during the congress. The Council of State had been gaining in importance ever since Ceauşescu became its president in December 1967; at the March 1969 CC plenum, for example, control over the Economic Council, the People's Councils, and the commissions of the Grand National Assembly had been transferred from the Council of Ministers to the Council of State.[68]

By August 1969, just a little more than four years after the death of Gheorghiu-Dej, Ceauşescu had achieved a radical turnover in personnel in the top organs of the Romanian Communist Party. He had become the undisputed leader of the Party and state and had established himself as the fount of all knowledge within Romania. In addition, his popularity and the legitimacy of his Party's rule were at an all-time high in the aftermath of the intervention in Czechoslovakia. The Romanian leader's problems, however, were not over. He had raised the expectations of the population with respect to personal security and the standard of living, and he had wooed the intellectuals with promises of creative freedom. Now that his personal rule had been consolidated and the immediate danger of Soviet intervention had receded, Ceauşescu's difficulties were only beginning.

7

From Revolutionary to Idol:
The Emergence of the
Leadership Cult

In the five years between the 1969 Tenth Congress and the 1974 Eleventh Congress, Nicolae Ceauşescu became the omnipotent and omniscient ruler of his country and the object of a leadership cult surpassing even that of Stalin in its intensity. Any observer of Romania in the Ceauşescu era is immediately confronted by this extreme adulation of the ruler, which has the characteristics of a religious cult with (1) an iconography, (2) inspired scriptures, (3) an infallible leader, and (4) rituals of mass worship. Icons of Ceauşescu are found in most public places and private offices (but not in most homes). The "scriptures" of the Romanian Communist Party—about thirty volumes of his collected speeches—have been published in Bucharest in many languages, and there is even a concordance to his words—not merely an index, but a series of volumes recording his pronouncements on specific topics such as culture, socialist democracy, agriculture, and national defense. The Romanian leader is infallible in his own country: Successes are attributed to him, failures to organizations or individuals that have not correctly carried out his suggestions. In addition, when Ceauşescu appears in public, his speeches are frequently accompanied by many voices rhythmically chanting "Ceauşescu, PCR" [Partidul Comunist Roman, the Romanian Communist Party] or "Ceauşescu şi poporul" [Ceauşescu and the people] or a variety of other ritualistic slogans.[1]

Although Ceauşescu clearly dominated the Tenth Party Congress, he was not yet the object of a leadership cult, which evolved over the next five years, emerging fully in March 1974 when the position of president of the Republic was created especially for him. He was sworn into office wearing a sash and carrying a mace, both suggestive of royal supremacy rather than revolutionary leadership. The intensity of the Ceauşescu cult is astonishing to all who encounter it firsthand: Reminiscent of the cults of Stalin and Mao, indeed it offends many observers both inside and outside Romania. Nevertheless, Ceauşescu has remained the absolute ruler of his country for over two decades, and the cult has been a prominent characteristic of Romanian politics since the early 1970s.

In a recent study of leadership cults in Leninist regimes, Jeremy Paltiel observed that the cult is not "simply leader-worship or hero-worship" but also "the establishment of personal authority . . . [instead of] the institutionalized authority of the party."[2] The current worship of Ceauşescu meets both of these criteria—not only is he worshiped, but he has personalized political power and authority in himself in a variety of ways. First, he holds the top offices in Party and state. Second, his personal decisions and preferences have determined policy directives and cadre appointments since 1969. Third, he has appointed members of his family to high posts: cousins, brothers, sisters, in-laws, one of his sons, Nicu (during the early 1980s minister of youth and head of the Party youth organization and in 1987 appointed to head Sibiu County), and especially his wife, Elena. She holds high offices in Party and state, appears with her husband on most official occasions, and even enjoys a birthday celebration second only to that of the president himself as a day of national rejoicing.[3] Finally, Ceauşescu has personal authority as well as power: No one in Romania can make a speech or write an article without crediting Ceauşescu as the source of inspiration and guidance.

At least three factors combined fortuitously to produce a cult of such intensity: Ceauşescu's strategies for domestic economic development, his independent foreign policy, and his personality. In addition, the specific features of the cult were shaped by the political environment of Romania, which has been receptive to this type of rule. In this chapter we shall analyze first the causes of leadership cults, especially the search for legitimacy and national independence on the part of communist parties, and the personal attributes of the ruler—in this case Ceauşescu. Next we shall describe the specific features of the Ceauşescu cult as its exists in Romania, including the images of the leader projected to different audiences throughout the country. Then we shall examine in some detail the evolution of the cult and Ceauşescu's leadership in the early years of his dominance. The last part of the chapter focuses on the propagators of the cult, the journalists of the mass press, as a case study to demonstrate Ceauşescu's skill in coercing and co-opting the loyalty of one professional group within Romania. This chapter will demonstrate that the *creation* of any leadership cult results from the search for legitimacy on the part of the regime and the ruler as well as the ruler's personal attributes. The *specific features* of the cult and the image it portrays depend largely on whose adulation is being sought—in this case, the Romanian Communist Party and the Romanian people.

The Sources of Leadership Cults

Contemporary Romania is not, of course, the only political system to produce a leadership cult. Other political regimes have found it expedient to deify their rulers, living or dead. The political systems in which deification has occurred seem quite diverse at first glance, including as they do ancient civilizations as well as post-revolutionary regimes of the twentieth century, but the underlying causes of this leader worship are quite similar. Indeed, all of these cults seem to stem from the need to establish the legitimacy of a new regime or new ruler. In ancient Rome, for example, the first emperors needed a justification for empire instead of republic. Modern revolutionaries who find ideology alone insufficient for legitimacy turn to glorification of the leader (rationality reinforced by charisma, to use Max Weber's categories).[4] As Nina Tumarkin has pointed out: "[R]evolutionary cults were generated by political imperatives. . . . In all cases, new political rituals evolved to mobilize popular loyalty and demonstrate the legitimacy of regimes that claimed to represent a hitherto oppressed populace."[5]

Communist Parties

The need for political legitimacy is obvious in a political system that has just undergone a change in the basic rationale of rule, but it extends also to systems in which leadership depends upon informal relationships within a party instead of institutionalized procedures.[6] Ruling communist parties therefore may face crises of legitimacy not only in the initial period after the revolution, but also during any subsequent years when the leader feels the need of charisma, real or artificial, to solidify his position. This would be particularly true if the general population does not endorse the individual's policies—Ceaușescu's strategies for rapid industrialization based on hard work and low rewards, for example. When rationality fails, the leader looks to charisma.

Charismatic leadership (either genuine charisma or charisma manufactured by the propaganda resources of the state) has been used repeatedly in communist parties, whose leaders have a special source of guidance in formulating their policies. Unlike religious leaders (charismatic in the original sense of the word) these communist leaders derive their infallibility not from divine guidance but rather from a "scientific" belief, Marx's philosophy of history. If the term "charismatic" is extended to include a "call" based on such a "science," then these men might be deemed "charismatic" leaders.[7]

But charisma also implies a close personal relationship between leaders and followers that enables the leader to inspire the followers. Here the charismatic nature certainly of Stalin's leadership can be questioned. Stalin's relationship with the masses was never direct and personal; in fact, he created an image of himself that was so idealized, so far from reality, that he shrank from direct and spontaneous contact with large groups. He became an idol, and "idolized leaders" cannot be "authentic leaders," if we accept James MacGregor Burns's definition of leadership, because there is no "true relationship . . . characterized by deeply held motives, shared goals" between idol and followers. Rather, the followers become mere "spectators."[8] Indeed, neither Lenin's nor Stalin's cult could be termed charismatic if charisma is an "authentic" form of leadership involving a "true relationship" between leader and followers. The followers of the Lenin and Stalin cults may have been inspired, but they were inspired by a false image rather than by the actual personality of the leader. This is not to say that Lenin was not a charismatic figure; he did in fact achieve a charismatic relationship with his followers in the Bolshevik party. But his authentic leadership of the party was not a cult aimed at the masses, and while alive he was not a cult object. Lenin's Bolshevik colleagues in the Politburo created the cult after his death, turning the worship of him to their own purposes.[9]

The creation of a cult does not preclude authentic leadership. Mao Zedong, for example, was both a cult figure and an authentic leader. Such a leader must, however, resolve two major difficulties in order to maintain a "true relationship" with his followers. First, he must be certain that his own motives and goals continue to be shared by his followers; if he senses a difference—that his own perception of needed change differs from theirs—he must be able to instill in them beliefs similar to his own. He must be able to mobilize them, persuade them, and woo them by the force of his own personality—not by projecting a false image of himself or by claiming special anointment by his predecessor. He must lead the masses, but not fool them. Second, the leader must retain a realistic picture of his own strengths and weaknesses. This permits an accurate estimate of the limits (as well as the possibilities) of his leadership.

An authentic leader must also have a dual sense of confidence: in himself, and in the intelligence of his followers to understand his goals and be persuaded by his arguments. Stalin had neither. He absorbed Lenin's elitism—his distrust of mass spontaneity—rather than Mao's confidence in the capacity of the masses to effect needed change. Hence the cults that Stalin and his colleagues established (Lenin's and later his own) were intended to dupe the masses by setting up an idol to be obeyed. Stalin also lacked faith in his own abilities. He did not have available to him one essential source of self-confidence possessed by leaders such as Mao, Tito, and Castro: Stalin had not led a successful revolution. Stalin's road to leadership had never necessitated the establishment of an authentic relationship between himself and the masses, and therefore he had no confidence in his ability to do so. He found the position of an idol demanding obedience more comfortable than that of a role model eliciting imitation.[10] By contrast, Mao's cult as well as his Cultural Revolution—kicked off by his famous swim in the river—appealed to the best instincts of the population by setting an example to be imitated.

A distinction can be made between first- and second-generation leaders of revolutionary parties—between those who actually participated in a revolutionary movement and those who gained power through post-revolutionary political competition. These two types of individuals have contrasting qualities, both personal and professional. But the second generation of leaders is less likely to have that requisite dual sense of confidence that can be produced in the crucible of revolution and that can promote authentic leadership.

Where, then, does Nicolae Ceauşescu fit into this picture? He is a first-generation revolutionary, but does he have that dual sense of confidence? He is clearly the object of a cult, but is he, like Mao, an authentic leader or, like Stalin, an idolized leader? Is he an example to be imitated or an idol to be obeyed? It has been argued that Mao's cult began as an authentic relationship between him and his followers, but that he deteriorated into an idol in the last years of his life as his intellect weakened and his ability to influence their motives and goals declined. Ceauşescu shows some parallels: In 1968 he had the opportunity to become an authentic leader and base his rule on the goals of his followers, shaped and guided by his own beliefs to the extent that he was able to persuade citizens to accept them. For a number of reasons—the tremendous gap between his goals and those of other Romanians, his abilities and personality, the political environment in which he operated—Ceauşescu did not become for most Romanians an authentic leader with genuine charisma, an example to be followed. Instead, he became an idol.

One factor clearly contributing to the formation of leadership cults in Romania and elsewhere has been the discrepancy between the policies formulated by the leader and those desired by the population; the cult has therefore been an attempt to substitute charismatic legitimacy for rational legitimacy. But still another factor seems crucial in the creation of these cults: national independence. Leadership cults have appeared in the Soviet Union, Romania, Albania, Yugoslavia, Korea, and China; all of these states have also attempted to establish the independence, or at least the autonomy, of the local communist party. On the other hand, many ruling communist parties have not created leadership cults; they have not appeared in loyal Moscow allies (except for the cult of Dimitrov in Bulgaria, and it can be interpreted as a supportive imitation of the Stalin cult). The correlation between cults and national autonomy can be explained at least in part by the inability of an autonomous communist party to rely on external (Soviet) support. Instead the party seeks local support, the acceptance of the regime by its own population—in effect, domestic legitimacy. Nationalism is often the original factor stimulating such acceptance, but the local regime will be further strengthened if it can produce a national hero on whom to focus the newly established—and often anti-Soviet—allegiance. Yet even the creation of mass loyalty is not sufficient; in addition, the local party must replace the ideological authority of Moscow among its own members with a national interpreter of Marxism.[11] A charismatic leader with revolutionary credentials can serve this function for Party loyalists.

Thus the absence of a cult may be as significant as its presence. The distinction among socialist states between loyal Moscow allies and regimes seeking autonomy helps to explain the presence of a cult in Romania and elsewhere. The absence of a cult in a communist state may mean that legitimacy is not a problem for the local party, which can mobilize internal support on the basis of rational policies without charismatic leadership. More often in Eastern Europe, however, the absence of a cult has meant that legitimacy was not an option for the local party because its reliance on outside (usually Soviet) support had produced popular hostility and therefore had precluded legitimacy.

Ceaușescu's Attributes

In addition to the quests for internal legitimacy and external independence, a third set of factors has contributed to the emergence of leadership cults in Romania and elsewhere: the abilities, priorities, and personality of the ruler. In Romania, for example, starting in 1969 Ceaușescu needed to influence public opinion, to persuade the masses by the force of his personality to accept his policies. Here he ran into difficulties. Ceaușescu's interpersonal skills are not those of a Trotsky or a Mao or a Castro. He evidently has been able to gain the respect of many with whom he works on an individual basis, but he does not move crowds spontaneously by his oratorical abilities. He can appear impressive on television during a crisis, issuing directives to local officials as they deal with floods or earthquakes, but he is managing small groups and making quick decisions then. Whenever Ceaușescu faces a large crowd, he becomes awkward and retreats into formality, reading speeches in a monotone and underlining crucial phrases by ineffective fist-pounding, with the stress all too often falling on the wrong word. He may have total faith in his own abilities and his own decisions, but he does not have the ease and confidence in his relationship with the masses that is a prerequisite for authentic mass leadership. Like Stalin, he may be a first-generation revolutionary, but his Party and people never followed him to revolution. As a result, he would not be able to persuade Romanians to accept his policies: He would have to accede to their wishes and moderate his goals, or use coercion and abandon his attempt at genuine leadership.

As Ceaușescu's background indicates, he is a dedicated Marxist-Leninist-Stalinist who, like Marx, defines progress in terms of industrialization. He adopted Lenin's elitism and Stalin's economic views, insisting on the political monopoly of the Romanian Communist Party and the rapid growth of heavy industry rather than of consumer goods and services. Since a very early age, his life has revolved around the collective experience of revolutionary and post-revolutionary activity within the Romanian

Communist Party. It is no wonder that his policies all reflect one goal, the rapid development of socialist Romania.

After 1969 it became increasingly clear that Ceauşescu would accept any reform or any organizational change only if he viewed it as a means toward economic development. He permitted economic reform measures only if they did not interfere with centralized planning and high rates of accumulation. He encouraged material rewards only when directly related to improved production, but he kept investment in the consumer sector too low to provide incentives. He approved contacts with the West only if they aided the development of Romanian scientific and technical expertise at minimal cost to Romania. But none of these changes could be allowed to threaten the primacy of the RCP in the political system or the personal control of Ceauşescu. Measures vital to large-scale industrial projects received priority, and policies in every sector were subordinated to the needs of the nation as defined by Ceauşescu.

As a first-generation revolutionary, Ceauşescu is an impatient activist, willing to use force to achieve his goals. At the beginning of his rule Ceauşescu, like Khrushchev and Mao, had great faith in the possibilities of education and propaganda to move the masses, and he was just as confident that the masses themselves could move mountains if correctly motivated. In fact, he tried to bridge the gap with the Romanian population through his "Little Cultural Revolution" of 1971: Romanians would be taught what was best for them. Ideological activism was expected to overcome all obstacles, and education was to be pragmatic and closely tied to the workplace. But the campaign intensified passive resistance to his plans, temporarily frustrating his attempt to motivate Romanians and lead them toward his perception of a higher moral goal.

As Romanians refused to be persuaded by his plans, Ceauşescu gradually abandoned genuine leadership for the cult. During the early 1970s the cult itself grew more and more extreme in its flattery, and Ceauşescu became isolated from the masses. He lost his sense of reality—of what was actually happening in Romania as well as of his own strengths and weakness—so that he could not longer assess with any accuracy the possibilities and limits of his economic strategies. He cut himself off from the people, and he chose to surround himself with sycophants selected for their personal loyalty rather than for their honesty and competence. He turned a deaf ear to critics, gradually removing them from the RCP leadership, and after the mid-1970s came to rely heavily on family members whom he trusted. When his economic strategies fell apart after 1979, he gradually became frustrated, then resentful, and finally vindictive, blaming the Romanian citizens for failing to fulfill their responsibilities, which he believed he had clearly and rationally articulated.

Ceauşescu's rejection of criticism and expert advice can be explained in part by his background. Not formally educated, he is suspicious of those who have had that opportunity. He has no patience with individuals who wish to devote themselves to personal creativity. Culture must serve the masses: Economists, engineers, artists, and writers should all work together to raise the educational level of the workers and peasants so that everyone contributes more effectively to the socialist development of Romania. A fist-pounding reminder to intellectuals in November 1974 was to "place all creative capacities . . . at the service of the people." No one should become complacent or assume adequate knowledge: "Today's intellectuals must be educated in order to educate others."[12] Yet he does not fully understand the creative process. His calls for a diversity of views are based on a simplistic concept of the dialectical process in which contradictions produce synthesis. There is enough of Lenin's mistrust of spontaneity within Ceauşescu's Marxism to convince him that the Party must determine the correct content of any synthesis.

Another aspect of Ceauşescu's personality is his strong emphasis on personal integrity and a strict attitude toward family life—condemnation of divorce, abortion, adultery, or any other acts he considers detrimental to the nuclear family. Yet this emphasis on personal morality is pragmatic: his stress on honesty, the work ethic, and protection of state property is directly connected to increased economic efficiency, and his defense of the nuclear family is part of an attempt to increase population growth. Nevertheless, his failure to understand human motivations—or more accurately his unwillingness to accept the desires of individuals for higher living standards or greater privacy and to design his policies to take advantage of these goals—has been detrimental to his plans, which have proven both unrealistic and impractical. Ceauşescu's unwillingness to "transact" in domestic politics—to engage in bargaining, compromise, and mutually advantageous political agreement (just the type of foreign policy negotiation at which he excelled in the 1960s and 1970s)—eventually destroyed his ability to "transform" Romania, that is, to move the country gradually toward the implementation of his goals.[13]

In summary, Ceauşescu is a Marxist-Leninist-Stalinist and a first-generation revolutionary, impatient to achieve rapid industrialization, demanding heavy sacrifices from all citizens toward that goal, puritanical in his personal life, mistrustful of experts and intellectuals, unwilling to compromise, vengeful if opposed, and yet confident that he knows best how to bring Romania to a truly socialist society. Both his policies and his personality have contributed to the formation of a leadership cult, but so too has his nationalism. Ceauşescu aims at the independence of the Romanian nation, and he insists all citizens must contribute to this goal. Economic development must be accomplished independently of outside aid whenever possible, whether from East or West. Ironically, this means that Romania has followed the Soviet model: rapid industrialization gained not by external borrowing but by suppressing the internal standard of living. This is not a policy likely to endear Ceauşescu to many people in his own country—perhaps to the Party elite, whose special privileges cushion them from the worst hardships, but not to ordinary Romanians. This quest for independence in turn coincides with a need for internal authority, a national hero, a cult of the leader. Thus a combination of factors—Ceauşescu's personal attributes, his political and economic priorities, and his nationalism—have all contributed to the creation of Ceauşescu the idol.

The Features of the Cult

Although a leadership cult usually arises because the leader's policies and personal attributes preclude support founded on rational legitimacy or genuine charisma, the specific features of the cult and the image it creates of the ruler depend on those who direct the cult—Ceauşescu and his propaganda apparatus—and those at whom the cult is directed, in this case the Romanian Communist Party and the Romanian people. The image of Ceauşescu created by the Romanian media has a number of features, not all of them compatible with each other. Ceauşescu, like Lenin and Stalin, is portrayed as an individual who despite lowly peasant origins rose to become a national leader through hard work, courage, and intellectual ability—the socialist equivalent of a Horatio Alger hero. "As the son of a peasant," he has written, "I experienced the landlords' oppression and, after the age of eleven, capitalist exploitation."[14] He is portrayed as overcoming these disadvantages through the same means that he would like all Romanians now to use in overcoming their economic difficulties: hard work, stamina, cooperation with others in working for the common good, and dedication to the cause of the Romanian Communist Party. In short, Romanian peasants and workers are encouraged to identify with his sufferings, take heart from his successes, and follow in his footsteps.

Reminiscences (many obviously biased and thus idealized) by those who knew him reinforce this image of rags to riches and also reveal a second facet of the cult: Ceauşescu's admirable personal qualities[15]—diligence, good humor, self-discipline—all qualities worthy of admiration and emulation. In addition, however, is his innate intelligence, apparently demonstrated so convincingly at a tender age, which if real would justify his position as president and Party leader and help to shape an additional facet of his image: the revolutionary. In addition to the masses, after all, Ceauşescu must attract the support of his colleagues in the RCP. So the image created by the Romanian media, at Ceauşescu's urging, emphasizes not only his lowly origins, his admirable personality, and his capacity for hard work, but also his revolutionary credentials and brilliance that supposedly enable him to understand and interpret the dialectical process in history and thus make him the authoritative interpreter of Marxism in Romania. Ceauşescu's credentials as a prewar Party member are of course impeccable. Although he was not a major architect of the RCP's seizure or consolidation of power, he was deeply involved in its activities before, during, and after World War II—which is more than can be said for his second-generation colleagues in the RCP leadership. Ceauşescu does have the revolutionary credentials to lead the Romanian Communist Party, but does he really have the intellectual ability?

According to the Romanian media, the answer is a clear yes. As proof of his intelligence, he has received honorary doctorates from dozens of universities, not just in Romania but all over the world, beginning with the University of Bucharest on his fifty-fifth birthday in 1973. On his sixtieth birthday in 1978, he received doctorates in political science and economics from the Party Academy and the Academy of Economic Studies in Bucharest. Messages to the Romanian president on that occasion praised his "theoretical and practical contribution to the development and enrichment of political science" and credited him with the "decisive role" in developing the Romanian economy "at a rate that has aroused admiration in the whole world." At the 1978 ceremonies Ceauşescu was also given credit for Romania's foreign and defense policies, the broadened "participation of numerous groups in the political process," and "strengthening socialist legality in all fields of activity."[16] The foreign policy successes and rapid economic growth of the 1970s helped to make these claims credible, although the honorary degrees from Europe, North and South America, Africa, and Asia were regarded with justifiable skepticism throughout Romania. Needless to say, the economic difficulties after 1979 were blamed on events beyond his control, such as the crisis of world capitalism or the mistakes of lower officials. Nevertheless, in Romania Ceauşescu's public image continues to be that of brilliant initiator and administrator of all policy as the RCP follows its scientifically determined path to developed socialism.

Therefore, perhaps the major lesson implied by the Romanian media (a lesson constantly repeated, as though repetition would make it true) is that Ceauşescu has the personal qualifications necessary to rule Romania, qualities admired by the Romanian masses and by his colleagues in the RCP. In addition, however, the media try to show that a more general lesson for all Romanians can be found in Ceauşescu's life: His sufferings—poverty, arrests, imprisonment—were all rewarded in the end; thus loyalty to the Party brings its reward in the long run. The Romanian people should not give up on the economic improvement promised by their political leaders, in particular Nicolae Ceauşescu. This lesson may have convinced some Romanians in the 1960s, and it continued to be credible during the 1970s, but by the 1980s it had lost its persuasive power, as indeed had the cult itself.

The Royal Couple

So far, the major features of the Ceauşescu cult described here have not differed greatly from the images of Lenin and Stalin created in the Soviet Union. Some of its aspects, however, do not resemble the cults of other communist leaders. Ceauşescu and his wife, for example, are portrayed not only as former revolutionaries who fought and suffered for the RCP; they have also become royal symbols of the Romanian nation. In March 1974, for example, when Ceauşescu was sworn in as president, *Scînteia* described the occasion as follows:

> March 28, 1974, will remain engraved in the history of the homeland, in the consciousness of our people. On this memorable day, fulfilling the will of the entire nation, the Grand National Assembly . . . proclaimed Comrade Nicolae Ceauşescu President. . . . This most brilliant son of the Romanian nation, the leader who crowns a succession of great statesmen of our lineage, is [our] first President.

Ceauşescu was then presented with "the symbols of worth and prestige, of state power," as a sash in the national colors was placed across his chest and he was handed the mace symbolic of his new status. He took the oath of office, and those assembled sang the national anthem. "The solemn session . . . was transmitted directly by Romanian radio and television; thus the entire country witnessed this historic act."[17] Ceauşescu was inducted into his new office with all the pomp and circumstance accorded any bourgeois president or feudal monarch.

He has also been given a monarch's niche in history. As Romanian rhetoric has become increasingly nationalistic, personalities from the country's pre-communist past have been cited more frequently and praised for their achievements. Gradually over the two decades of Ceauşescu's rule, these heroes have come to include not only revolutionaries, reformers, and leftist politicians, but also any individuals who are seen as having contributed to Romanian independence and national unity. Ceauşescu now traces Romanian political continuity back to Burebista and the pre-Roman Dacian heritage and mentions as national heroes a number of "feudal" monarchs such as Michael the Brave and Stephen the Great. Today, praise of Ceauşescu compares him with these past kings, describing him as one more star in Romania's crown.[18]

Even his daily routine reinforces this symbolic royalty. He travels in a fleet of Mercedes, for which all traffic is stopped, or by helicopter, an innovation of the mid-1970s. He and his wife have acquired a variety of residences, including a number of former royal palaces—thus cutting off ordinary Romanian citizens from access not only to their president but also to these "museums of royalty" that in the 1950s and 1960s were open to the public as recreation areas to emphasize the egalitarian nature of communist rule. The leaders of other communist states also live well, but not in the palaces of former monarchs, and the luxury surrounding the communist elites is hidden from the population whenever possible. In Romania, however, the royalty of the environment surrounding the Ceauşescus—furnishings, silver, crystal, furs—is emphasized every day by photographs in the mass media as part of the homage paid to him. This symbolic royalty presents a strange contrast to other aspects of the Ceauşescu image: Ceauşescu the monarch is not compatible with Ceauşescu the puritanical, hardworking revolutionary, devoted to the egalitarian goals of Marxism.

Included in this image of royalty is Ceauşescu's wife, Elena. She is her husband's constant companion on official and unofficial occasions. She presides with him at Party and state ceremonies, travels with him inside the country and abroad, and even holds formal positions directly below him in the political hierarchy. She became a public figure in 1971 and rose quickly to the top of the political hierarchy, receiving promotions rapidly: to the Central Committee in 1972, to the Political Executive Committee in 1973 and its Bureau in 1977, and to the Council of Ministers first, in 1979, as president of the National Council for Science and Technology and then, in 1980, as first vice-president.

In the late 1970s the worship paid her by the Romanian press almost came to equal that given her husband. On her sixtieth birthday, in January 1979, she was praised for forty years of revolutionary activity, and *Scînteia* devoted two days to the celebrations. Two years later the Party newspaper greeted the occasion with a drawing of the First Lady smilingly receiving dozens of bouquets of flowers from a crowd of children. Underneath was a poem entitled "Homage," ending as follows:

> To the first woman of the country, the homage of the entire country,
> As star stands beside star in the eternal arch of heaven,
> Beside the Great Man (*Marele Bărbat*) she watches over
> Romania's path to glory.

On International Women's Day in 1982, reports of the celebrations rejoiced in the presence of "comrade academician doctor engineer Elena Ceauşescu, outstanding activist of Party and state, eminent personage of Romanian and international science." Even her birthplace—the village of Petreşti in Dîmboviţa County—has reportedly yielded archaeological evidence demonstrating that human habitation dates to the Paleolithic era. Petreşti has received special seeds, fertilizers, and Austrian breeding cows unavailable to most Romanian cooperatives, and at least five industrial enterprises producing consumer goods and processed foods have located in or are planning to establish branches in Petreşti. Like her husband, Elena Ceauşescu has brought prosperity to her native village.[19]

Despite the praise heaped upon her by the Romanian press, Elena Ceaușescu is not a popular personality in most of the country. She does not project the practical competence and concern of an Eleanor Roosevelt or the mystical charm and beauty of an Eva Peron. Although Nicolae Ceaușescu's image has become extremely ostentatious and lacking in credibility, it remains more palatable then hers; at least, Romanians say, he *earned* his high office, rising to the pinnacle of power through hard work and political skill. She, on the other hand, is usually regarded as the undeserving beneficiary of his generosity. She does have revolutionary credentials as a textile worker and communist activist in the 1930s, but those activities are not as documented as her extravagant use of furs and designer fashions in the 1970s and 1980s. The somewhat contradictory image of king and revolutionary projected for Nicolae Ceaușescu is roughly paralleled by his wife's dual roles of queen and scientist. However, these is less balance in her case and therefore, if possible, even greater resentment against her in Romania.

Unique Aspects of the Romanian Cult

The symbolic royalty of Ceaușescu and his wife and the widespread political nepotism distinguish the Ceaușescu cult from cults in other communist systems.[20] Why, then, is this public image presented to the Romanian population such a contradictory one of king and revolutionary? And why has Ceaușescu placed so many family members in important positions throughout the political system and included his wife in the required adulation?

One important advantage of personality cults in conveying legitimacy is their flexibility. By focusing political loyalty on an individual and giving that person a variety of characteristics, a regime can simultaneously attract different segments of the population to the various faces of the image. The religious and royal aspects of the Ceaușescu cult, it can be argued, have been designed to appeal to the peasant origins of the majority of Romanians, strongly influenced by the religious traditions of Orthodox Christianity with its icons, scriptures, and saints. Indeed, Romanian officials in the mid-1970s, embarrassed by the then relatively moderate manifestations of the cult, often attributed the excessive reverence shown for Ceaușescu to the low political and educational level of the Romanian population. The peasants were regarded as particularly backward due to their intense religious beliefs—Orthodox saints continue to be displayed on the walls of peasant homes—and the Romanian church had always reinforced the political authority of its head, the king. Thus Ceaușescu's royal trappings by implication gave him religious as well as secular authority, facilitated by the regime's continued domination of the church.

The Ceaușescu cult sought also to appeal to the political elite, that crucial minority of the population that is politically active. In a Leninist regime this means the members of the revolutionary party and other supporters of the revolution. The Romanian leadership cult therefore had to create loyalty based on Marxist ideology as well as on the religious nationalism of Romanian peasants. Thus the media had to project to Party members the image of Ceaușescu as the hardworking, ascetic revolutionary and brilliant interpreter of Marxism-Leninism while at the same time providing a royal figure for the people to worship—hence the blurred double image of Ceaușescu as both king and revolutionary.

The dual image that distinguishes the Ceaușescu cult from other Leninist cults can therefore be explained at least partially by the social structure and political culture of Romania, especially the peasant origins and nationalism of most of the population. But the other distinctive feature of the Romanian leadership cult is less easy to analyze. Why have the members of Ceaușescu's family, especially his wife, become so prominent? Here again we find part of the answer in Romanian political tradition, for families have often played important roles in the policymaking process. This tradition began with princely dynasties, continued in the great aristocratic and landowning families, and remained important throughout the nineteenth and twentieth centuries when members of powerful families with names such as Cantacuzino, Catargiu, Ghica, Bibescu, Sturdze, Golescu, and Rosetti repeatedly appeared on rosters of government officials and political activists. In the 1920s, for example, the politics of the ruling Liberal Party were dominated by the Brătianu family.[21] To some extent, then, the Ceaușescu family is simply following in a long line of politically prominent Romanian families, although the political environment and the path to power have clearly changed. Thus the importance of the Ceaușescu family is exceptional in the context of communist regimes, but not in the context of the Romanian political process.

What is unique, however, both in Romania and among communist parties, is the political adulation paid to Elena Ceaușescu. Indeed it is impossible to explain this homage without putting it into the context of RCP policies toward all Romanian women. Before World War II women played no direct role in Romanian politics. Their influence was felt only through men, not as political officials in their own right. Since the RCP came to power, however, women not only have been granted legal equality and joined the paid labor force in huge numbers, but also have participated directly in the political process in a variety of ways. The outstanding example was Ana Pauker, described by a colleagues as the "real leader" of the Party in the years from 1944 to 1950.[22] She was the exception at the top, however, for the overall participation of women has followed a pattern all too familiar to students of comparative politics: The proportion of women varies inversely with the power of the political body or position; women are concentrated in certain sectors where they are assumed to have special competence, such as health, education, light industry, and consumer goods;

and, finally, women are regarded as a separate group that needs special protection, treatment that at times prevents full participation and therefore full equality.[23]

At a national conference of women in June 1966, Ceauşescu praised women for their contributions to revolutionary and economic activity and demanded that they receive jobs "corresponding to their abilities." In the same speech, he promised to develop the "production of household appliances and utensils, and ready-cooked foods" to facilitate housework and create "better conditions" for women's "participation in the social-political life of the country."[24] But these promises were quickly forgotten. In 1966 the Romanian economy faced a potential labor shortage that the Party leaders apparently blamed on a falling birth rate and their lack of success (compared with most East European regimes) in drawing women into the labor force, particularly in urban areas.[25] Ceauşescu's April speech sounded like the beginning of a campaign to provide greater incentives for women to work, but later that year a new emphasis appeared. In October 1966 abortions were made illegal, and divorces and contraceptives almost impossible to obtain. These harsh pronatalist measures were accompanied by few positive incentives to have children. In Romania, cash payments for giving birth are "quite low," maternity leave is "the shortest of any country in Central or Eastern Europe," and as late as 1974 kindergarten places for children aged 3–6 were available to "only about 42 percent of eligible children." Although the population growth rate almost doubled during 1967 following the new requirements, Romanians soon adjusted to the changes. Live births per thousand inhabitants jumped from 14.3 in 1966 to 27.4 in 1967, but were down to 18.5 by 1973.[26]

In 1966 Ceauşescu chose to increase the future labor force rather than the current labor force, but that choice did not produce the long-term dramatic results that he had anticipated. As as result, in 1973 he began a new campaign to entice women into the labor market by promising them promotions and full equality with men. Because the most obvious result of the 1973 campaign was the promotion of Elena Ceauşescu to the RCP Executive Committee, it seemed that his goal was not really the promotion of women but of one particular woman. Indeed, the campaign did fade after 1973, but it began again in 1979 with more vehemence and some startling results. Women's share in Central Committee membership jumped from 33 to 100 (9 percent to 25 percent—apparently a quota was established), and two women joined what had been the exclusively male group of forty county first secretaries (those crucial posts equivalent to the Soviet *obkom* first secretaries). In the general elections of 1980, women increased their share of Grand National Assembly seats from 50 to 120 (14.3 percent to 32.5 percent). The emphasis on promoting women continued in the 1980s, as the 1984 Central Committee contained 126 women (28 percent), and more women were made county first secretaries and members of the Council of

Ministers. Of course, the GNA by then barely pretended to be an important body, and to fulfill the quotas women were often promoted to the CC sooner than their specific Party or state post could justify, placing them among those least likely to be re-elected to a body that saw extensive turnover starting in 1979. In some ways, therefore, the rapid promotion would not prove advantageous to those promoted. In addition, several times during the 1980s the pronatalist campaigns against abortions were reinstated, with harsh penalties for anyone involved in terminating a pregnancy and intrusive measures to ensure a high birth rate.[27]

It is within this general context of public policy toward women—forcing them to have more children and simultaneously requiring their full participation in the labor force—that we need to examine the inclusion of Elena Ceauşescu in the leadership cult. Of course, the personal vanity of both Nicolae and Elena Ceauşescu must be considered the major cause of her prominence. But other factors are also involved. In her own life Elena Ceauşescu embodies two major goals of the RCP: She is the mother of three children, and she holds full-time positions outside the home. Hence, she sets a positive example for all Romanian women, making it not only possible but compulsory for each of them to aspire to such success. This distinctive feature of the Ceauşescu cult—the inclusion of his wife—can therefore be justified by the mass media and by other defenders of the regime in terms of Party policy.

One of the earliest expressions of the cult, a massive volume entitled *Homage (Omagiu)*, issued on Ceauşescu's fifty-fifth birthday in 1973, illustrates this point. Near the end of a biographical introduction, under a picture of Nicolae Ceauşescu, his parents, and Elena, the text observes:

> We gaze with esteem, with respect, at the harmony of his family life. We attach special ethical significance to the fact that his life— together with that of his life comrade, the former textile worker and UCY militant, member of the Party since the days of illegality, today Hero of Socialist Labor, scientist, member of the Central Committee of the RCP, comrade Elena Ceauşescu—offers an exemplary image of the destinies of two communists. [The three children are then described: Valentin, a physicist; Zoe, a mathematician; and Nicu, a physics student.] . . . And we should know that the three children of the President work, like any of us, following the example of their parents, to bring socialism to Romania. All this attests clearly to the truth that work and personal example are obligations in the Ceauşescu family.

Here the Ceauşescu family—husband, wife, children—are portrayed as examples to be imitated.

Gradually, as the emphasis in the Romanian media shifted from motherhood in the 1960s and 1970s to the promotion of women into positions of authority in the 1980s, Elena Ceauşescu's image has separated to some extent from the family and she has become "comrade academician doctor engineer Elena Ceauşescu, brilliant politician and patriotic scholar of broad international renown."[28] She is still pictured with dozens of smiling children paying homage to her, but her image has become that of a famous scientist, who brings credit to Romania for her scientific achievements, as well as by caring for her family. As Party priorities have shifted, the image of Elena Ceauşescu has changed as well; thus the adulation paid to her has roots in regime policy as well as her own personal vanity.

The Beginnings of the Cult

A number of policy developments in the years immediately following the Tenth Party Congress quickly revealed the gap between Ceauşescu's priorities and those of various groups within the population, but by now he was ready to insist on his own way. There would still be opposition, but that would be effective only temporarily. Ceauşescu's determination to centralize decisionmaking in his own hands, to strengthen Party oversight throughout the political process, and to impose discipline in production became obvious as early as 1970. In culture and education, for example, a new Academy of Social and Political Sciences was founded in February 1970 and attached directly to the Party Central Committee, in part to exert greater control over the various Romanian research institutes in the social sciences and history, and in part as an alternative to the prestigious Romanian Academy, which would remain for many years resistant to political influence. This move foreshadowed a general tightening of cultural policy that would be introduced with a vengeance in mid-1971.[29]

The trade unions were the next focus of attention. A Central Committee plenum in March 1970 passed a number of measures to strengthen labor discipline, but in the same month several high officials were removed as public examples of corruption. Thus the Party leadership attempted to demonstrate its evenhandedness. A year later, after the December 1970 labor unrest in Poland and the removal of Władisław Gomułka as party leader, the RCP announced further changes within the Romanian trade unions at a CC plenum in February 1971.[30] Labor discipline was to be tightened yet again, and the unions were to assure broad participation by workers in management and enforce safety regulations to protect workers—another combination of measures to preempt any possible complaints. At the same time, Virgil Trofin was moved from his position as CC secretary for cadres and organizations to become head of the trade unions in what was portrayed as a horizontal move, not a demotion. Of course, it was also convenient for Ceauşescu to remove from the Secretariat this individual who was rather popular with colleagues. In fact, Ceauşescu was always careful to keep anyone from serving too long in that crucial second position in the Secretariat, where he could build up considerable support within the Party just as Ceaușescu himself had done under Gheorghiu-Dej. Trofin, however, would turn out to be a special challenge to Ceaușescu's authority; after having served in a variety of positions, he finally refused to engage in self-criticism in 1981 and apparently committed suicide several years later.

The Economy

Economic policy—the crucial area of disagreement within the RCP leadership and between Ceaușescu and the Romanian population—also saw intensified pressure soon after 1969. By now, however, it was too late to disagree with Ceaușescu; he and his supporters were able to override any direct opposition, although some of his initiatives would be delayed to some extent. Growth in 1966–1970 had averaged about 6 percent per year, which according to Marvin Jackson was a "substantial achievement by world standards, one that would have pleased most developing countries."[31] Romania in 1970 appeared to be "in transition from a phase of extensive growth to a phase of intensive growth," and success in making the change would demand quality of products, efficiency of production, and successful marketing techniques, needs apparently addressed by the December 1967 economic measures. Given the difficulty of such a transition, the "modest" increases envisaged in the 1971–1975 plan approved by the Tenth Party Congress seemed reasonable to Jackson. Instead, he concluded, "what was to come was a very ambitious remobilization of the economy."[32]

During 1971 the targets for the five-year plan were raised considerably until, at the July 1972 Party conference, many Party organizations at Ceaușescu's urging pledged to fulfill the original plan in four and a half years. Thus Romanian goals for agricultural and industrial production and for national income would be roughly twice those of the other Comecon states.[33] Evidently in response to criticism, Ceaușescu in his closing speech to the 1972 conference insisted that the upward revisions in the plan would not be accomplished by increased investment but by more efficient use of previously planned investment; despite this promise, the conference determined that investment would have to average 32 to 34 percent rather than the 28 to 30 percent predicted at the Tenth Party Congress.[34] As it turned out, poor results in agriculture for several years prevented the RCP from fulfilling the overall plan in four and half years. Nevertheless, it was completed two months ahead of schedule,[35] and so the early 1970s were years of high growth in Romanian industry.

Achievements in agriculture, though less successful, were impressive. The original five-year plan for 1971–1975 as set forth in 1969 included much higher investment in irrigation, fertilizer, and agricultural machinery than had the 1966–1970 plan. The investment tended to focus, however, on grandiose projects and huge new factories rather than on incentives for the labor force to increase productivity. Then in May 1970 devastating floods in Transylvania and eastern Moldavia prevented plan fulfillment in agriculture for 1970 and 1971. There was one positive result: The extensive flood damage prompted measures to improve the daily standards of living of agricultural workers. Despite the natural disasters—serious floods hit again in 1975—the decade of the 1970s saw substantial increases in agricultural production at the same time that agricultural employment was declining rapidly, from 50 percent to 30 percent of the labor force in the ten years following 1970.[36] Clearly, Ceauşescu was making considerable demands on the Romanian population, and it is only in light of these demands—and simultaneous disagreements with the Soviet Union—that we can understand the evolution of the cult.

Events of 1971

The crucial year was 1971. Much of what came later was foreshadowed by events in those twelve months, and the entire year must be viewed against a background of exceedingly strained relations with the Soviet Union. Back in July 1970 a new Romanian-Soviet Treaty of Friendship, Cooperation, and Mutual Assistance had been signed, but at the last minute Kosygin had replaced Brezhnev as head of the Soviet delegation to the signing ceremonies in Bucharest, ostensibly because the Soviet leader had a cold. However, he managed to attend a soccer game in Moscow, so the cold was evidently diplomatic rather than viral, probably caused by Soviet displeasure with some of the details of the treaty.[37] Relations were not improved by Ceauşescu's speech at the Soviet party's Twenty-fourth Congress on 1 April 1971, where he repeated his rejection of interference in the internal affairs of other parties and asserted not only the right but the duty of each communist party to develop socialism independently in its own country.

Meanwhile, Ceauşescu was also strengthening relations with Moscow's enemies. He had visited the United States in October 1970, and in June 1971 he made a long trip to China amid speculation in the Western press that he was mediating between Peking and Washington. The ideological aspects of the Soviet-Romanian quarrel also had economic ramifications because the Romanians were attempting to diversify their trade whereas the Soviets were again pushing for greater integration in Comecon. Indeed, China and the United States had given considerably more aid to Romania than had the USSR to help rebuild after the 1970 floods, so the economic benefits of associating with Soviet rivals were already being realized.

Relations with Moscow continued to deteriorate during 1971. A Comecon summit meeting in Bucharest at the end of July endorsed a thirty-year program of economic cooperation, but Ceauşescu immediately began to state publicly a number of his own interpretations of the agreement in which he preempted any supranational planning agencies, and he did not attend a meeting of East European leaders in the Crimea on 2 August. Later in August, at a great public rally in Bucharest celebrating both the 150-year anniversary of the Tudor Vladimirescu uprising and the graduation of a new class of Army cadets, Ceauşescu insisted that "the communist movement can no longer be led from any center; . . . it is necessary for each party to act independently."[38] (Tudor Vladimirescu had led an unsuccessful rebellion against the Turks in 1821, counting on Russian support, but he was betrayed by the Russian tsar and executed by his Romanian enemies. The result had been Russian occupation and a Russian protectorate, a lesson not lost on the Romanian population of 1971.)

But Romanians were not only reminded of the long history of interference from the East: Friction with Hungary also emerged in this crucial year. A long article by Paul Niculescu-Mizil, still CC secretary in charge of relations with other communist parties, appeared in *Scînteia* on 9 July, charging Hungary with "flagrant" contradictions in reporting on Ceauşescu's visit to China and urging the Hungarians to refrain from harmful "invectives" and criticism of Romanian policies. Until this point, Ceauşescu had been careful to include the national minorities in his Romanian patriotism (although they reacted with skepticism). And this first overt criticism of Hungary boded ill for Hungarians inside Romania.[39]

Ceauşescu needed support from the Romanian population in order to resist pressure from his socialist allies, and yet he was unwilling to compromise on his ambitious economic goals. Indeed, it was these very strategies of economic development that provoked opposition to him both at home and abroad. The events of 1971 began to show how he would resolve his dilemma. His basic strategies involved the mobilization of all educational and cultural facilities to induce Romanians to accept his goals, while he simultaneously ensured his control of the Party and the Party's control of society.

The first sign of impending change came in a speech to a meeting of cultural organizations on 10 February, when Ceauşescu's strong criticism of the State Committee on Culture and Art hinted at events to come later in the year. The Central Committee also opened on 10 February a two-day session during which it approved the proposed changes in the trade union leadership and outlined an ambitious new plan for educating and re-educating state and Party officials. In addition, Ceauşescu introduced his new cadre policy of circulating officials from Bucharest to the counties and back, which would later be crucial to him in maintaining his power but which he portrayed at the time as a deepening of socialist democracy because the policy would "strengthen the ties between the leading organs and the masses" and "combat excessive centralism."[40]

Nicolae and Elena Ceauşescu spent June traveling in China, North Korea, North Vietnam, and Mongolia, with a brief stop at the Moscow airport on the return. Given the state of Soviet-Romanian relations, it was again Kosygin rather than Brezhnev who met with Ceauşescu. The Asian trip evidently had a considerable impact on Ceauşescu, who must have studied Chinese techniques of political and ideological mobilization as well as the extensive personality cult of Kim Il-song already in operation. At the time, however, the main effect of the visits seemed to be the continued deterioration of Soviet-Romanian relations, and the Asian trip was quickly overshadowed by events in Bucharest.

On 6 July Ceauşescu presented to the RCP Executive Committee a series of proposals to "improve the political-ideological activity, the Marxist-Leninist education" of Party members and of all Romanians. These proposals served as the basis for his own "cultural revolution,"[41] Ceauşescu's attempt to lead Romania toward a socialist transformation and create a new society inhabited by citizens who conformed to his expectations. Several days later a conference of Party officials involved in culture and education met to discuss his ideas and prepare for a special CC plenum in November. His proposals[42] rested essentially on three legs: (1) centralized control of culture, education, and the mass media, to be exercised by the Party and its officials; (2) expansion of agitation and propaganda among the masses, especially the youth, including "patriotic" work and large-scale cultural festivals (both ostensibly voluntary) and a required system of periodic re-education; (3) Ceauşescu's own synthesis of Marxism-Leninism and Romanian nationalism, which would provide content for the propaganda and cultural activities. In his speech Ceauşescu also criticized Ion Iliescu, CC secretary for culture, and Ilie Rădulescu, head of the CC propaganda section. Both were removed from their posts on 15 July by the RCP Executive Committee.

The most obvious result of the new ideological campaign in the short term was a temporary halt to rock music concerts and a reduction in Bucharest nightlife. Ceauşescu had instructed the media to emphasize Romanian productions rather than imported foreign films, music, or plays, and for the time being there was an effort to do just that. Many people did not take the new campaign seriously, however, considering it an unfortunate inconvenience that would soon run its course. For example, a number of Romanian diplomats and intellectuals interviewed by a *New York Times* reporter did not seem alarmed, assessing Ceauşescu's proposals as merely "the reinforcement of things that had been said mildly before."[43]

By November, however, after the CC plenum on ideology and education, Romanian writers, artists, and other intellectuals were taking the situation more seriously and viewing developments with some dismay. At that meeting, although most of the speakers endorsed Ceauşescu's proposals for cultural mobilization, there was little enthusiasm. Some speakers, even the poet Eugen Jebeleanu who had reported so favorably on Ceauşescu at his trial in 1936, were ambiguous in their statements.[44] Resistance to Ceauşescu was consolidating, and the next year would see him postpone some of his demands as Bucharest partially regained its cosmopolitan atmosphere, and Romanian intellectuals once more became optimistic about the future.

One other development of importance for Ceaușescu's leadership occurred during 1971: the emergence of Elena Ceaușescu as an individual in her own right. Until that year she had appeared in public only as an appendage of her husband, on occasions when the Romanian leaders were hosting foreign dignitaries and their wives in Bucharest or returning such visits abroad. However, on the trip to Asia in June 1971 Elena Ceaușescu was much more prominently featured in photographs than had been customary for the Romanian press. She was still defined as his wife (*soție*), and she wore a cloth coat and rather shapeless suits and bulky shoes. But her hair was carefully styled during the trip, and she was beginning to be aware of photographers and to prepare for them.

In the 9 July issue of *Scînteia* she began to achieve a separate political identity. At a meeting of a national commission on economic forecasting, the Party newspaper showed her seated among the other members and listed her alphabetically, with the title "doctor-engineer, and Director of the Central Institute of Chemical Research." Later that month she broke precedent by publicly accompanying her husband on a working tour to the Constanța shipyards. By then she was a completely different women, stylishly dressed and elegantly coiffed. In August she reviewed the fleet with him at Mangalia and took part in several other visits inside the country.[45] So far, in all joint appearances she was described as his "wife."

A new development occurred on the Romanian national holiday, 23 August 1971, when Elena Ceaușescu appeared on the reviewing stand for the first time, the only woman, beside her husband and at the center of attention. Then the 4 October issue of *Scînteia* raised her status still further: At a mass meeting on Harvest Day in the Piața Obor in Bucharest, Nicolae Ceaușescu was accompanied by "Comrade Elena Ceaușescu"—at last a comrade (*tovarășa*) rather than a wife.[46]

Aftermath

During 1972 Ceaușescu carried out a number of personnel changes, most of them at the 18 April CC plenum or the 11 October Executive Committee session, and twenty new members including Elena Ceaușescu were added to the Central Committee at the July 1972 Party conference on șescu's suggestion. These shifts would eventually strengthen him considerably, but meanwhile he was forced to compromise. In his conference speech, for example, he promised higher wages, a shorter work week, better pensions, and more consumer goods, and he was also quite conciliatory toward the national minorities. Nevertheless, Ceaușescu was not able to get the conference formally to adopt the proposal to fulfill the 1971–1975 plan in four and a half years. A number of speakers endorsed the idea and the rate of investment was raised, but the conference resolution referred merely to completion "ahead of the plan" (*înainte de termen*). Indeed, the conference itself was postponed for several days, prompting speculation as to disagreement in the leadership; Maurer was conspicuously silent, hinting at his own opposition to changes in the plan.[47] Despite these difficulties, the adulation of Ceauşescu at the conference and in Romania prompted the *New York Times* to run its report from Bucharest on 23 July 1972 under the caption "A Ceauşescu Cult Emerges in Rumania."

By the middle of 1972 the worship of Ceauşescu had become a prominent feature of Romanian public life, and his wife was beginning to join in his prominence. He could not yet impose his will arbitrarily on all sectors of society, but he was now expressing his opinions openly because he was no longer the spokesman for the collective leadership, as in the 1960s, but leader in his own right. A number of organizational and personnel changes in 1973 and 1974 would enhance his power still further, especially Maurer's retirement and Ceauşescu's election as president, both in March 1974. However, the cult itself would be propagated by the journalists of the mass press and guaranteed by a new press law that would codify control over the media by the Party—and therefore by Ceauşescu. The journalists provide an example of Ceauşescu's techniques in coercing and co-opting an entire profession into his service. What he did to them was repeated many times in other sectors of the economy and the society.

Romanian Journalists and the Cult

In order to understand how Ceauşescu gained control of the Romanian mass media during the 1970s, we need to go back to the first years after the death of Gheorghiu-Dej, when some professional autonomy was enjoyed by editors and journalists. The evolution of *Presa noastră*, the official organ of the Union of Journalists, is illustrative: The lead article in January 1967 explained carefully that the Romanian Communist Party did not dictate the editorial policies of newspapers. Party officials were expected to help, to criticize, to explain Party decisions, or to ensure a serious attitude, but they were not to exert direct control. Although we must regard this assertion with skepticism, there is no doubt that the twin themes of the journal in 1967 were professional independence and national pride. Each issue contained at least one article on the "glorious traditions" of Romanian journalism, which was portrayed as playing a "revolutionary" role before 1944 and later as an important "instrument of the Party to found a new order, consolidate the Romanian nation as a free nation, and focus its energies on building socialism."[48] Journalists were expected to serve the cause of the party, but they were also encouraged to be "detached" and "objective" in the tradition of Voltaire, Matthew Arnold, or Dickens.[49] Within a short time, the journal's claim of independence would no longer be possible.

Shortly after the Tenth Party Congress, Ceauşescu's attitudes toward the media began to emerge more clearly. On 25 September 1969, the twenty-fifth anniversary of the first legal issue of *Scînteia*, he outlined his expectations, repeatedly demanding "the press must . . ." and listing a variety of current Party priorities that it had to explain and defend.[50] He then went on to leave no doubts among his listeners as to his own interpretation of freedom of the press:

> It must be understood that in our society the whole press . . . must consistently and firmly promote the political line of the Party and only the line of our Communist Party. . . . It cannot be permitted for any reason that works or opinions be published . . . that contravene the ideology of our Party, the concepts of our society. . . . It is therefore necessary that the executive committees of all reviews and publications should include only those people who are determined to . . . promote with passion and determination the policy of the Party in the sphere of culture and art, in all spheres of activity.

Nevertheless, in January 1970 *Presa noastră* was still able to insist that "respect for the truth" was the first crucial attribute of any journalist,[51] and the periodical throughout that year continued to function as the organ of a professional elite. Articles tried to raise professional pride and to improve journalistic skills as well to inform readers on recent interpretations of Party policies. The end to professional autonomy in journalism, as in the entire cultural sector, began in 1971. In March Ceauşescu created a National Council on Romanian Radio and Television and placed it directly under CC secretary Dumitru Popescu.[52] At the July 1971 conference of Party officials, Ceauşescu complained:

> We have slackened our concern in the training of communist journalists. Some thought that if a young person comes with a diploma from one or another faculty, he automatically has become a journalist. . . . [But] the journalist must be a communist militant, must be a Party activist. . . . For the training of new journalists—and for the improvement of the existing ones—we must re-open the political schools of journalism for all domains of activity.[53]

Thereafter, the training of journalists would be centralized in the Ştefan Gheorghiu Party Academy, rather than at the University of Bucharest under the state Ministry of Education, and would follow the lines of other Party specialties in cultural, managerial, or Party administration. There would be an undergraduate program of three years, a one-year postgraduate course (often for specialists in other areas who wished to become journalists), and a center for periodic retraining of experienced journalists.

In August 1971 one union was established for all workers in the media (although it was not actually formed until 1976). In October 1971 the State Committee on Culture and Art was replaced by a new body, the Council on Socialist Culture and Education, under the direct supervision of the Party Central Committee. Party control of culture and the mass media would thereafter be difficult to challenge except by delay or diversion. By the end of 1971 it was clear that Ceauşescu intended the media to be a "unitary system of publishing, radio, and television . . . a press of the Party."[54] But Party control would not be complete until the new press law in 1974.

The 1974 Press Law

The new law was enacted at the same session of the Grand National Assembly that elected Ceauşescu president of the Republic with such pomp and circumstance in March 1974—just after Maurer's retirement. The preface stated explicitly that the mission of the Romanian press was to fulfill the policies of the Romanian Communist Party, and the press was defined to include all means of communication—written, oral, visual—destined for a broad audience.[55]

The law spelled out the obligations and organization of the press in great detail, as well as the political and professional qualifications of journalists. Although they were expected to be investigators, to search out and reveal incompetence, and although officials and ordinary citizens were required to cooperate with them, the law also listed a series of limits on the press that might make a crusading reporter somewhat timid. Forbidden under Article 67, for example, were attacks against Party policy, slander against Party or government leaders, false or alarming information that disturbed public order, chauvinistic propaganda, or offenses against good manners or ethics. Both the chief editor of a publication and the individual journalist were responsible for observing these broad and ambiguous limits.

Another reform affecting journalists came in May, when the CC Secretariat, ostensibly because of an international paper shortage, reduced the number, size, frequency, and circulation of Romanian newspapers and journals.[56] The decision asserted that there were some inadequacies and redundancies in the newspapers and periodicals then being published and that excessive amounts of paper were wasting forestry resources and hard currency imports. Therefore a number of steps were being taken to reduce waste, but a side benefit would be to improve the content and enhance the combativeness of the press in fulfilling the Party's ideological program.

Henceforth, for example, Scînteia would appear six times a week instead of seven and have fewer pages. The national dailies Romania libera and

Scînteia tineretului would also be shorter, and two others—*Muncă* and *Satul socialist*—would become weeklies. Only eight of twenty-nine county papers were to continue as dailies; the rest would become weeklies, and all would have fewer pages and smaller formats. The cultural weekly *Contemporanul*, published by the Council of Socialist Culture and Education, would be reduced in size and also turn into a political journal with the stated goal of "fighting to instill in the masses the concepts of Marxism-Leninism, of our Party's materialist-dialectical views of life and society." As Anneli Ute Gabanyi observed: "Control of printing runs and of paper allocation to publishing houses and reviews is one of the simplest means of exercising censorship,"[57] and censorship in Romania was to be much more complete after 1974.

Not only external censorship would prove easier to enforce. Journalists had also been warned to be more vigilant in exercising internal censorship. With the reductions in publications, fewer journalists would be needed, and so job security was in question from the moment the new decision appeared. Indeed, 160 journalists in Bucharest alone reportedly lost their jobs in the first few weeks.[58] Those who managed to keep their positions undoubtedly employed strict self-censorship to avoid the newly enlarged ranks of professionally unemployed.

As if the 1974 press law and paper shortage were not enough, a third blow soon fell on Romanian journalists. In May 1975 a decree of the Council of State created a new Committee for Press and Printing directly subordinated to the Central Committee and the Council of Ministers.[59] The stated goal of the new group was to enforce Party and government policy throughout the various mass media, and it was empowered to prevent publication or distribution of any materials it deemed illegal. In addition, this new committee would register and enforce the permit of any publication to publish; attest to the professional qualifications of all journalists; authorize any unregistered printing; control access to all machines for printing, typing, or copying; control the export and import of printed, visual, or audio materials; oversee the finances of publishing; and develop publishing plans. The committee would have 45 to 55 members—chief editors, heads of professional and creative unions, relevant ministers, and others involved in press and culture—with individual and collective responsibility for all the mass media.

After 1968 there had been a brief decentralization of book and journal publishing, which had temporarily given young writers access to the media and produced a wide variety of styles and opinions in the press. Ceaușescu's criticisms of 1971 had apparently been intended to reverse that process, but he was not very successful at that time. By 1974, however, after the intervening personnel changes and reorganizations, he was strong enough to impose his own rules; whether they would be observed in practice still remained open to question. But one disappointed observer concluded in June

1975 that the preceding year could be "compared only with the gloomy one of 1948, when the legal and administrative foundations were laid for a new order in Rumanian culture."[60]

Education and Mass Culture, 1976–1977

Ceaușescu did not rely exclusively upon coercion and fear to gain the cooperation of journalists. His strategies also provided for the education of new members of the profession who would achieve upward mobility and owe him and the Party allegiance. In 1976, for example, the entrance examinations to the journalism faculty at the Ştefan Gheorghiu Academy could be taken by secondary school graduates, factory workers, or technicians.[61] The first group was presumably quite young, attempting to gain admission immediately upon graduation, whereas the workers or technicians probably were in their middle or late 20s, having worked for some years and come to the attention of the Party secretary at their workplace because of their written or verbal skills. A recommendation from that secretary was undoubtedly required for admission.

One of the main thrusts of Ceaușescu's educational policies for everyone has been an attempt to link education more closely to production—and even to require a year or two of manual labor between secondary school and university. Future journalists were to be no exception, and a number of places in the journalism classes likely were reserved for workers returning to acquire a higher education. Such individuals would be less inclined to demand professional insulation from Party directives when they became journalists; they would, after all, have the Party and Ceaușescu to thank for the opportunity to improve their status.

Ceaușescu's control over the entire sphere of culture was reinforced during 1976 when the first Congress on Political Education and Socialist Culture was held in Bucharest in early June. This meeting brought together over 6,600 individuals involved in "science, culture, art, eduction, and mass communications."[62] The participants were a *Who's Who* of prominent Romanian intellectuals as well as Party officials responsible for culture and ideology. The congress returned to the basic cultural themes laid out by Ceaușescu back in 1971, and obvious in every speech was adulation of Ceaușescu as the Romanian authority on questions of culture. All speakers thanked him for his inspiration and example, and his speech was adopted as the program to be followed in the cultural sector. Then in July he was placed in charge of the CC Commission on Ideology.[63] Ceaușescu was not only omnipotent, he now seemed omniscient and infallible.

Two major themes of Ceaușescu's cultural policy during the 1970s were closely related: nationalism and "mass culture." The Romanian nation and Romanian patriotism had been raised to an ideological status equivalent to (and usually referred to more often than) Marxism-Leninism. Appeals to patriotic pride gained a positive response from many Romanians, drawing them into group activities. In 1976, for example, Ceauşescu initiated a grandiose series of pageants entitled "Hymn to Romania," which would be celebrated annually over the following years by pageants, musicales, and sports events, eliciting the maximum participation from the population by celebrating the glories that socialist development had brought to the Romanian nation. In literature, "mass culture" implied simple, realistic styles of writing on topics approved for mass readership. In music and theater, it meant amateur contests and performances, and professional performers traveling to the provinces to produce shows with local talent. Needless to say, this "Hymn to Romania" met with scorn from many writers and from professionals in music or theater. Professional journalists, however, saw in it more activity and more jobs for the mass media. Ceauşescu's "mass culture" has therefore been less unpopular with the journalists than with other intellectuals.

Other aspects of Ceauşescu's policies did, however, threaten the professional autonomy of journalists directly. During 1976 the Union of Journalists was finally merged into a Union of Workers in Press, Printing, and Publishing, with 40,000 members, a reorganization first attempted in 1971.[64] A Council of Journalists within the union was formed immediately, but members of the press had to be very careful that their writing conformed to Party policy, and they were given examples of what could happen when they incurred the displeasure of the president.

In the fall of 1976, for example, there were a number of changes made in the foreign press agency Agerpres, and about thirty foreign correspondents were recalled to Bucharest in December.[65] Threatening job security by making examples of a small number of people is another technique often used by Ceauşescu, and it served him well in controlling the press. Journalists have cooperated with outward enthusiasm in explaining his policies and creating the aura of infallibility around him that is part of the leadership cult.

One surprise in cultural policy occurred in December 1977; Ceauşescu declared an end to censorship and abolished the Press and Printing Committee. Poland had tried a similar experiment in 1973, and the result had been self-censorship by editors.[66] In Romania the responsibility assigned to editors and writers for observing the provisions of Article 67 of the 1974 press law made both groups very effective censors. In fact, the major results of "ending" censorship in Romania was to make it easier to control printed matter: The editor and censor could no longer hide behind each other. As a result, there was no more diversity in the Romanian media after 1977 than before.

Conclusions: Ceauşescu, the Mass Media, and the Cult

The techniques used by Nicolae Ceauşescu in gaining power over the mass media were remarkably similar to those he used in the Party: control of the personnel process, including hiring, retention, and promotion; rewards for loyalty; and commitment to certain basic themes and policies that enhance the followers' professional prestige and remuneration without giving them greater autonomy. Indeed, in much of what follows, the term "Party member" or "Party official" could be substituted for "journalist" or "mass media."

In order to remain infallible, Ceauşescu has exercised meticulous control over the mass media and enlisted the cooperation of the professionals who work there. This situation is not necessarily disadvantageous to those involved in such an important sector. In fact, because the press is so crucial in protecting Ceauşescu's image and because he values its didactic role so highly, journalists and the mass press are guaranteed substantial support as long as they manage to satisfy the Romanian president. They need only portray an image, after all; they can largely ignore reality, and so they find it easier to please Ceauşescu than do most professionals.

It is not hard to see why journalists have assisted in propagating the leadership cult. If a Romanian journalist does not wish to make independent judgments, the profession is an extremely attractive one with important fringe benefits unavailable to most Romanians: the opportunity to travel, even within the county; access to libraries and communication facilities, including typewriters and copying machines;[67] and a certain amount of power over officials whose activities are under inspection by the press.[68] The last, reflecting the ombudsman function of journalists, provides extensive opportunity for trading favors in an economy where favors are crucial to minimal daily comfort. For those who choose to support the regime, there is also a considerable amount of job security. In a highly ideological environment such as journalism, the major pressure on anyone is political. Failure to graduate, or loss of a job after graduation, will usually result from political mistakes rather than from professional inadequacy. Membership in the Council of Journalists does not guarantee professional autonomy, but instead is a prerequisite to professional activity because Party disapproval could revoke a journalist's certification.[69] In Ceauşescu's Romania, political loyalty rather than assertive inquiry is the crucial criterion for gaining and keeping a position as a journalist. Thus there are a number of advantages for journalists in contributing to the worship of Ceauşescu: status, privilege, and security.

The charismatic aura of authority created around the ruler by his colleagues and the press emerged as the Party and Ceauşescu himself sought to implement regime policies and maintain national autonomy. The need for charisma had been felt in other ruling communist parties, but was particularly acute in Romania because Ceauşescu's personal priorities led him to choose domestic policies—especially in the economic and cultural spheres—that were incompatible with rational legitimacy and therefore required a charismatic figure to attract support. The gap between Ceauşescu's goals and those of most Romanians was clear to him by 1971, and in that year he initiated a number of policy and organizational shifts to enhance his coercive power as well as his authority. His personal skills were not those of a genuinely charismatic leader, however, and all he could muster was a kind of false charisma in which he became an idol to be obeyed. As the leadership cult evolved, its specific features were shaped by those who were supposed to worship the leader—the Romanian population and the RCP—hence the dual image of king and revolutionary. Other anomalies of the cult such as its nepotism and the inclusion of Elena Ceauşescu in the adulation can be explained in part by Romanian traditions and regime policies toward women—as well as the personal vanity of the two objects of worship. By idolizing Nicolae and Elena Ceauşescu, the cult—maintained by Party and government officials and by the press—has assured external conformity. More questionable is the success of the cult in creating any genuine support for the ruler, his Party, and his policies—that search for legitimacy that prompted the cult initially.

8

From Promotion to Circulation: The Party and Its Organs

Now that we have a sense of the policy priorities and political style that emerged in the first decade of Ceauşescu's rule, it is time to examine the most important methods by which Ceauşescu was able to gain and maintain power within the Romanian political system: his manipulation of personnel and of organizational responsibilities. Ceauşescu first learned from Gheorghiu-Dej, and then decided for himself, that he would need to make the Romanian Communist Party into an organization staffed by individuals loyal to him, a Party that would accept and enforce his policies throughout Romania and enable him not only to rule but also to accomplish his revolutionary goals. He began to create such an organization when he served as CC secretary for cadres in the decade before Gheorghiu-Dej's death, and he then continued these organizational efforts in the early years of his rule, when compromise, ambiguity, legality, and participation were his political themes.

Ceauşescu's rejection of policy compromise during the 1970s—especially his insistence on high rates of economic investment at the expense of living standards—weakened the persuasive power of his populist methods, and his techniques of rule in the 1970s differed considerably from those he had used to consolidate his power. The most obvious change was the leadership cult, but his personnel strategies were also transformed after 1971. Later, the economic difficulties of the 1980s would bring still new methods to maintain his control in the face of internal economic crisis and foreign hostility.

From 1965 to 1968 Ceauşescu's appointments to high Party bodies, to regional posts, to the Central Committee, and even to membership in the Party itself can be characterized by one word: promotions. He added new members to the Party and its bodies and promoted many of its officials to positions of power, thus consolidating his basis of support in that organization. In 1968 and 1969 he continued this process (and moved his own people into state positions as well), but he began to remove any rivals who remained from the Gheorghiu-Dej Political Bureau and any of their supporters who refused to cooperate wholeheartedly in the new order. Top-level demotions took place at plenums of the CC and at the Tenth Party Congress, while the administrative-territorial reform permitted Ceauşescu and Trofin to restructure and restaff the lower Party and state organs.

Then, in the early 1970s, Ceauşescu's personnel strategy changed from the promotion of his supporters to their circulation from office to office and place to place: No individual was allowed to remain in one position long enough to establish a fiefdom independent of direction from the Party leader. He also began to ignore some of the formal structures and procedures he himself had created to demonstrate the legality and institutionalization of the political process. Yet during most of that decade any changes that occurred preserved high status and living standards for loyal Ceauşescu followers if they accepted their new duties and continued to praise and support Ceauşescu. Beginning as early as 1978, however, as Ceauşescu intensified his efforts to mobilize the Party and the entire population in the face of mounting economic difficulties, he speeded up his circulation of cadres. In addition, for the first time some of his loyal supporters began to fall off the merry-go-round. By the early 1980s loyalty and deference—which had become the best means of career advancement—no longer guaranteed continued high status.

Despite the economic troubles of the 1980s, Ceauşescu was able to maintain his tight personal control of the Romanian political system. Hence his personnel strategies provide an excellent model for the successful consolidation and preservation of power in a ruling communist party. Four groups were crucial in the process: the entire Party membership; the Central Committee; regional and county Party officials; and the highest RCP bodies, including the Political Bureau or Presidium, the (Political) Executive Committee, and the Secretariat.[1] This chapter will examine the changing composition of these groups and compare Ceauşescu's techniques toward each of them before 1969, during the 1970s, and in the 1980s to see what methods enabled him to establish such complete personal power and then to keep it despite continuing hostility from the Soviet Union and, after 1979, severe economic difficulties at home.

The Party

Since World War II, changes in the size of the Romanian Communist Party have been influenced by conscious policy on the part of its leaders, as they saw a need for growth or decline in membership and took the appropriate steps, and also by the perceptions of citizens, as they were attracted or repelled by RCP policies or by the benefits or costs of membership for the individual. Likewise, the social composition of the Party has shifted as the leaders adopted new priorities and recruited from particular social categories, or as specific groups saw advantages in membership.

In the early postwar years it was clearly advantageous for citizens to join the RCP. The Party provided an avenue of rapid promotion and a protective shelter for its members in the period of reconstruction and insecurity following the war. At the same time, the small number of pre-1945 members impelled Party leaders to accept almost anyone willing to support the Party, and so growth was quite rapid (see Table 2.1). Then, as we have seen, membership actually dropped between 1948 and 1955, in part because the leaders consciously decided to reduce the Party's size and in part because membership was not longer so beneficial. During the late Stalin era the organization still provided an avenue of upward mobility, but it had ceased to be a haven for its members. In fact, during those years Party status could be more disadvantageous than political anonymity. This would never be true under Ceauşescu.

After Stalin's death the situation changed. Party membership was safer, and the Party needed more members to help implement its economic priorities. In 1955 Gheorghiu-Dj initiated a dramatic increase in membership: 40 percent by the 1960 congress (see Table 2.2). However, the most rapid increase (except for the 1940s) occurred during the dispute in Comecon between April 1962 and December 1964: In less then three years, Party membership rose by 50 percent because the RCP leadership was bidding for domestic support and the population was responding positively to the shift in foreign policy and the internal derussification measures.

From 1965 to 1969 the annual percentage growth remained high, averaging 8 percent a year between the Ninth and Tenth Congresses (see Table 2.2), and then gradually tapered off to about 2 percent a year by 1987. However, the lower increase was in part because the entire Party was growing; in absolute numbers, the annual increase in membership has averaged roughly 100,000 throughout the Ceauşescu era, though annual variations are considerable (see Table 8.1). As a result, Ceauşescu has made the RCP the largest communist party in Eastern Europe both in absolute terms and as a proportion of the population: By the end of 1987, the Party had 3.7 million members, representing approximately 23 percent of the adult population and 33 percent of the working population.[2]

Trends in the Party's social composition have been more erratic than those in membership, resulting partly from redefinitions of occupational categories which have been so frequent that the published data can be almost meaningless except as an indicator of regime priorities. These priorities have shifted over the decades following World War II, from workers to peasants to intellectuals and back again to workers under Ceauşescu. The basic dilemma is, of course, the contradiction between the Party as an organization of the working class (which would require recruitment primarily among workers) and the Party as the leader of economic and social development and interpreter of the dialectics of history (which would require that new members come from the educated elites). The Party, like Ceauşescu himself, is expected to be both revolutionary and ruling, egalitarian and elitist, mobilized and mobilizing.

Table 8.1. RCP Annual Growth, 1974–1987

Date[a]	Total Party Membership	Absolute Growth	Percentage Growth	New Members
1974	2,500,000	113,181	4.7	
1975	2,577,434	77,434	3.1	
1976	2,650,000	72,566	2.8	
1977	2,747,110	97,110	3.7	
1978	2,842,064	94,954	3.5	
1979	2,930,000	87,936	3.1	
1980	3,044,336	114,336	3.9	132,000
1981	3,150,812	106,476	3.5	141,460
1982	3,262,125	111,313	3.5	143,748
1983	3,370,343	108,218	3.3	145,260
1984	3,465,069	94,726	2.8	132,001
1985	3,557,205	92,138	2.7	132,000
1986	3,639,344	82,137	2.3	123,284
1987	3,709,735	70,391	1.9	116,041

Sources: Computed from data in Table 2.1.

[a]December figures except for 1979 (November).

Until 1962, Gheorghiu-Dej had stressed the need to recruit the most reliable (in Marxist terms) social group, the workers. The proportion of members classified as workers had peaked in October 1945 at 54 percent, but the Party was then quite small. The share of workers dropped steadily to a postwar low of 37 percent in 1950, reflecting the recruitment of other social groups and substantiating the criticism later directed against Ana Pauker that she had encouraged unreliable individuals to join. By 1955, however, the continued drop in membership had raised the proportion of workers (see Table 2.1). Nevertheless, workers were emphasized in Gheorghiu-Dej's 1955 recruiting campaign, and by 1960 they once again made up over 50 percent of Party members.

In the 1960s two new priorities appeared. First, after the collectivization of agriculture was completed in 1962, the stress in recruiting moved to peasants in an attempt to alleviate the scarcity of rural members. The number of peasant members more than doubled from 1962 to 1964,[3] but thereafter their share gradually declined, leveling off at about 16 percent in the 1980s. The second and most striking shift was the effort to attract intellectuals. Gheorghiu-Dej recognized the new priority as early as the April 1962 CC plenum, and in July 1965 the number of intellectuals in the RCP was given as 145,000, double the 1960 figure but only 10 percent of all members. In the next five months, although total membership increased by only 68,000, the number of intellectuals reportedly rose by 185,000 to 22 percent of Party members (see Table 2.1). This huge rise could only have been accomplished by shifting certain groups from one classification to another, but the change in itself reflects the desire of the new Party leadership to encourage membership among the educated. Reports on Party composition at CC plenums began to stress the need "to recruit those with prestige and authority."[4] At the time, Ceauşescu presumably favored this emphasis, which would strengthen the governing role of the Party, weaken his rival Gheorghe Apostol, whose basis of support was in the trade unions, and help the Party to meet its goals of modernizing the economy by raising membership among the economic elites.

As early as March 1969, however, a Central Committee plenum warned that the Party must maintain a preponderance of workers among its members.[5] Thereafter, statements about Party recruitment stressed the need for workers and those working directly in production, as well as the "most advanced" cadres in all sectors. The result was a steady increase in the proportion of workers in the Party, from 43 percent in 1969 to 55 percent by the end of 1981 and thereafter (see Table 2.1). As early as the Eleventh Party Congress in November 1974, Ceauşescu could proclaim proudly that 71 percent of Party members worked directly in material production.[6]

Such statements were characteristic of the 1970s. For example, in the spring of 1977, the Central Committee reported that 83.5 percent of new members the preceding year had been workers and peasants and only 16.5 percent intellectuals and functionaries. The report insisted that those working in "key sectors of the national economy" continue to receive priority in admissions and also that 80 percent of new members be workers and peasants. Then in March 1979 the categories were redefined to understate the proportion of intellectuals (now defined as "those working in health, education, science, art and culture," a group that made up only 7.9 percent of the Party) and overstate peasant membership ("those involved in agriculture," a larger group that could be described as 25 percent of Party members). At the same time, the Central Committee announced a renewed emphasis on recruiting workers and peasants, perhaps a response to events in 1977 and 1978: a negative reaction to the protests of intellectuals such as Paul Goma and Vlad Georgescu and an attempt to bring in more workers in the aftermath of the miners' strikes. By November 1979, however, in Ceauşescu's report to the Twelfth Congress, the worker and peasant categories (54 and 18 percent) were apparently back to their previous definitions, and everyone else was considered an intellectual: 29 percent of the Party.[7] In the late 1970s, therefore, published data were again erratic with respect to specific social groups; what was consistent was the priority given to recruiting workers and peasants and also those from key productive sectors.

During the early 1980s both of these emphases continued. When Ceauşescu revealed the Party's social composition at the Thirteenth Congress in November 1984, he seemed quite satisfied, boasting that those who had joined since the last congress had been almost 80 percent workers.[8] Thereafter the pressure to attract workers seemed to ease a bit, and from 1984 through 1987 (see Table 8.2) the social categories of new members stabilized at levels that the March 1988 Central Committee plenum recommended for the future: 55–65 percent workers and 15–25 percent peasants. The remainder presumably would be intellectuals, a range of 10–30 percent.[9] Ceauşescu, if published data are reliable, has chosen to preserve the Party as an organization of workers, but even such stringent recruitment priorities as those from 1979 to 1984 cannot ensure this goal: Many of those who enter from a worker background are promoted into occupations with greater influence, prestige, and remuneration. They are, however, dependent on the RCP for their upward mobility, and this produces quiescence and support for the Party leader.

Many Party members also have the Party—and indirectly Ceauşescu—to thank for their education. In February 1971 a Central Committee plenum initiated an ambitious program to improve the professional preparation of Romanians at all levels and in all sectors.[10] Special emphasis was placed on the need for training (*pregătire*) and improvement (*perfecţionare*) of cadres, and the Ştefan Gheorghiu Party Academy in Bucharest was reorganized and facilities set up in ten cities throughout the country in order to accomplish these tasks. A large new complex of classrooms and dormitories was completed in Bucharest during 1976 to house the various programs, which included (1) undergraduate institutes to train future Party activists, journalists, trade union and youth leaders, presidents of agricultural cooperatives, and officials in economic and state administration and foreign relations; and (2) improvement programs for continuing education in most of these and other specialties.[11]

Table 8.2. Social Background of New RCP Members, 1974–1987
(by percent of total)

	Total	Workers	Peasants	Intellectuals	Women	UCY
1974–1979		85[a]				
1979–1984		80			46	75
1980	132,000	71	13		43	70
1981	141,460	71	15	14	46	71
1982	143,748	72	15	7	49	76
1983	145,260	68	16	16	50	70
1984	132,001	65	16	19	51	77
1985	132,000	66	16	18		
1986	123,284	65	15	20	50	79
1987	116,041	66	14	19	41	

Sources: Congresul al XII-lea, p. 59; Scînteia, 28 March 1981; 1 April 1982; 31 March 1983; 27 March 1984; 20 November 1984; 3 April 1985; 8–9 April 1986; 28 March 1987, 1–2 April 1988.

[a]Data was given only for the total of both categories.

The undergraduate programs were full-time for three to four years and usually took individuals who had been working for several years and who were recommended by their local Party organizations. These future Party officials and activists would later thank Ceauşescu for their education and reward him with their loyalty. The "improvement" program, on the other hand, was to be a continuous process involving all members of the labor force throughout their careers. Each position—from minister to worker, from Central Committee official to local Party secretary—was to have a particular type of continuing education attached to it. Some programs would take place locally for brief periods, others in Bucharest for a longer time, but everyone would be required to take part at set intervals in what came to be called "recycling" (*reciclare*) program. These courses were often regarded with annoyance, especially by those who had to catch up on their regular work at night or when they returned from Bucharest. Others treated the opportunity as a vacation, or at least a change of pace, whereas a minority were actually enthusiastic about the chance to theorize about their jobs and learn about the problems and solutions of others in similar positions. A number of Party activists were educated or "recycled" at the Party academy in the early 1970s, and after the new building complex was completed in 1975, about 10,000–11,000 students completed courses each year.[12]

The recycling program was only part of the overall change in educational policy that extended also to secondary school pupils. At that same Central Committee plenum in February 1971, Ceauşescu called for workshops in schools to establish links two years before graduation between pupils and the factories where they would work so that when students graduated they would already be experienced workers. The proposal aroused tremendous opposition among parents, pupils, enterprise managers, and workers (manifested covertly, of course, through delay in working out the details), but it was finally approved by a CC plenum in June 1977.[13]

That there was a serious need for further education of Party members was made clear in 1975: Because there were "too many functionaries without a higher education," the primary Party organizations were directed to "accept more such members only in special cases, when the county, municipal, or city organization considers it absolutely necessary." In addition, Party officials were required to ensure that younger Party members "complete their studies, at least to 8th grade level."[14] Two years later the directive was repeated, and the efforts continued in 1979 as the Central Committee promised to support Party members under age 50 to complete secondary education. In the next two years, 300,000 Party members completed the eighth grade, and 107,000 more were taking correspondence courses to finish.[15]

Data published in 1981 on the education of those in the Party revealed some differences between Party members and the population as a whole (see Table 8.3). Party members were much more likely to have a higher education

Table 8.3. Educational Levels Completed: Romanian Socialist Republic
(RSR) and Romanian Communist Party (RCP) (by percent)

	Primary	General Schools	Professional or Technical	Higher
RSR 1966	75	11	14	2
RSR 1977	48	27	21	4
RCP 1980	47	15	26	11

Sources: *Recensămîntul popula͵tiei ͷi locuin͵telor din 15 martie 1966*, vol. 1, *Resultate
generale*, pt. 1, *Popula͵tie* (Bucharest: Direc͵tia centrală de statistică, 1969), p. 189;
Recensămîntul popula͵tiei ͷi al locuin͵telor din 5 ianuarie 1977, vol. 1, *Popula͵tie—Structura
demografică* (Bucharest: Direc͵tia centrală de statistică, 1980), pp. 622–623; *Scînteia*, 28
March 1981.

and somewhat more likely to have completed professional or technical
training (although in the latter case the time difference between 1977 and
1980 may be responsible for much of the gap). What was discouraging,
however, was that despite Party efforts during the 1970s, about 47 percent of
the membership had not yet completed secondary or professional education.
Figures on the educational level of Party members since 1980 are
incomplete, but partial data produce an estimate at the end of 1986: 13
percent with higher education, 21 percent with secondary education, and 27
percent with technical or professional training, leaving 39 percent of RCP
members without educational qualifications beyond the primary level.[16] If
accurate, this would certainly be an improvement, but it would still leave
Romania far behind the Soviet Union, for example, where a mere 8 percent
of party members possessed only a primary education in 1986.[17]

Whatever the current educational levels, Ceauşescu is not publicizing
them—instead he boasts about the high proportion of workers among new
members. The undergraduate program at Ştefan Gheorghiu Academy provides
an opportunity for a small number of younger Party members to receive an
education, but with 130,000 new members each year, a significant proportion
of them would have to enter the Party with an education in order to improve
the current situation. Ceauşescu's priorities over the last decade have been
ideological rather than pragmatic: to admit uneducated workers in order to
maintain the working-class basis of the Romanian Communist Party and to
raise the educational level of its membership by the necessarily slow process
of educating workers rather than by attracting the educated to join the Party.

In addition to the need to improve the educational level of Party
members, a second difficulty has faced Ceauşescu: His revolutionary Party
has tended to grow old along with him (see Table 8.4). The influx of new
members between 1962 and 1965 lowered the proportion of Party members
over 40 years of age from 41 to 36 percent, but the addition of "those with
prestige and authority" between 1965 and 1969 brought the age structure back
almost to the 1962 figure. This was still considerably younger on the average
than in other ruling communist parties such as that of the Soviet

Table 8.4.   Age Levels in the RCP, 1962–1985 (by percent)

	1962	1965	1969	1973	1980	1984	1985
Over age 40	41	36	40	44			50
Under age 40	59	64	60	56			50
Under age 30	25				24	23	
Age 30–50					52	51	
Age 50–60					16		
Over age 50						26	
Over age 60					8		

Sources: 1962: Scînteia, 17 May 1962; 1965: Congresul al IX-lea, p. 72; 1969: Congresul al X-lea, p. 128; 1973: King, History, p. 83; 1980, 1984, 1985: Scînteia, 28 March 1981, 3 April 1985, 8–9 April 1986.

Note: Blanks indicate no data available.

Union,[18] but the aging process continued at exactly the same rate over the next several years.

An open discussion of the difficulty took place at the Eleventh Congress in 1974, when several speakers repeated the need for renewal (înnoire) in the Party—to attract young people to its ranks and to promote young people to higher positions. Near the end of the Congress, while Gheorghe Pană, the CC secretary for cadres and organizations, was presenting the revised Party statutes for approval by the delegates, the proceedings were interrupted rather dramatically from the back of the hall by a county first secretary, Petre Blajovici. His motion—clearly not expected by most of the delegates, who began to whisper excitedly among themselves—asked that a mandatory retirement age be established for Party leadership positions from top to bottom, including the Central Committee. Ceauşescu quickly rejected the idea by pointing out that different individuals have different capabilities and that political and physical capacities are more important than age. He headed off any further discussion by suggesting that the Central Committee be empowered to work out changes in the statutes, and several paragraphs indeed were added to Article 14(a) recognizing the need for renewal but referring to individuals' capacities instead of setting a specific age limit.[19]

At the time, the major item of interest to many observers was the proposal by the Bucharest Party organization that Ceauşescu be elected general secretary for life, a proposal he himself had appeared to reject (although rather ambiguously) earlier in the proceedings, and speculation immediately began that Blajovici was trying to prevent the issue from being raised again. Ceauşescu had been made president just eight months earlier, and the leadership cult had already grown to what then seemed to be extravagant dimensions, but there did not seem to be a great deal of enthusiasm for lifetime tenure for the Party leader among the delegates or in the capital. It was, after all, in direct conflict with Ceauşescu's rhetorical advocacy of democracy and legality—presidents are elected for terms, not for life, some Romanians pointed out privately, and the Party leader should be no exception. It will probably never be known whether it was a serious proposal that just did not gain support, or whether Ceauşescu had it proposed so that he could magnanimously turn it down, as he did. In any case, his refusal of the honor could be used to encourage the retirement of older members of the Party leadership, and one of the congress speakers, Miu Dobrescu, made that very suggestion.[20]

The issue of renewal was a sensitive one in 1974, for on 30 July *Scînteia* had published a list of criteria for election to central and local party organs in preparation for the November congress. One requirement provided that at least one-third of the members of each body (including the Central Committee) not have served during the preceding term. This would have institutionalized turnover in all the Party bodies, but the top position at each level would not have to change; only Blajovici's suggested age limit would have accomplished that. However, even the proposed turnover was softened in the new Party statutes into the suggestion that renewal be "considered" in nominating candidates for Party offices. It is quite possible that Ceauşescu was attempting to institutionalize rotation in the party bodies in 1974 and, when he failed, put the best possible face on the situation by making himself the champion of renewal and refusing lifetime tenure. He then could reassure the older cadres by blocking Blajovici's suggestion, thus making himself simultaneously the protector of both generations.

Throughout the rest of his tenure, Ceauşescu would frequently stress the need to bring younger members into the Party to "assure a harmonious combination of experience and maturity of older communists with the elan and revolutionary enthusiasm of the young."[21] When an exchange of Party cards—essentially a re-evaluation of all members' credentials and a potential purge—was announced in the spring of 1979, to take place during 1980, it was unclear whether the process would resemble the harsh verification campaign in Romania back in 1948 or the mild Brezhnev version introduced in the Soviet party in the early 1970s. At it turned out, the report in March 1981 indicated that only 30,210 members had not retained their membership—scarcely enough turnover to bring significant renewal and more lenient even than the exchange of cards under Brezhnev.[22] Nevertheless, one of the major requirements in accepting new members during the 1980s was that a large number come from the Union of Communist Youth. The proportion of new members from the UCY crept up steadily from 70 percent in 1980 to 79 percent in 1986; in 1987 it was announced that 75–80 percent of new members thereafter should come from the youth organization. By 1985 Ceauşescu was able to announce with pride that half the Party membership was under age 40. The median age must have been somewhat higher during the early 1980s, and that is confirmed by the figures he was willing to give in 1980 and 1984 (see Table 8.4).

One notable departure from previous practice during the 1980s was the publication of these detailed figures on Party composition and structure, although Ceauşescu had regularized procedures to some extent in the mid-1970s by having the spring CC plenum each year publish and evaluate some membership data. Even so, the frequent changes in categories mean the data are not always useful for analyzing change in the RCP. Instead, their main importance is what they reveal about Ceauşescu's priorities, which in the 1970s and 1980s have been the recruitment of workers and peasants into a Party that already includes one-third of the entire work force.

The Romanian Communist Party under Ceauşescu is meant to be an elite group only in the sense that—as he repeats over and over—membership is limited to "the best" in each category. In fact, the RCP has become a mass party, whose members are intended to replicate the entire society from top to bottom, including all occupational groups, with emphasis on certain sectors according to current economic needs. The Party is the organization through which Ceauşescu still hopes to accomplish his goals for Romania; in order to do this, he wants workers, peasants, and young people to feel that the Party can be their path to success in socialist Romania—membership not only is possible, but it also is the means by which they can achieve their personal goals. The entire Party has become part of Ceauşescu's participatory populism: Those outside the Party are encouraged to join, and those in the Party are required to take part in Party discussions and then accept Party discipline in fulfilling the decisions that result.

The Central Committee

Membership in the Central Committee of the Romanian Communist Party does not attempt, as does Party membership, to represent all levels of society. The CC is broadly based—the various economic sectors are indeed included—but its members are for the most part top-level Party and state administrators. Perhaps the most striking change over the years has been the CC's increase in size (see Table 2.3), which Ceauşescu has attributed to the rise in total Party membership, a reasonable explanation for the period from 1960 to 1974 when the entire Party membership rose by 72 percent, roughly parallel to the 84 percent increase in the Central Committee. Indeed, the greatest proportional growth of the CC did occur at the 1965 congress, just after a period of rapid Party growth, but the second highest increase came in 1955, when Party membership was at a post-1946 low.

In fact, the pattern of Central Committee growth differs significantly from the pattern of Party growth, which is closely tied to the Party's bid for popular support. By contrast, Central Committee growth is more closely related to the needs of the general secretary in his personal bid for support within the Party. Whereas Party membership jumped in the 1940s and

1960s, the greatest increases in the CC took place at the Party congresses of 1955 and 1965, following shifts in the top Party leadership. Presumably the general secretary in each case—Gheorghiu-Dej and Ceauşescu—used the congress to add supporters to the Central Committee.

There is, however, an important difference between these two congresses: retention (see Tables 2.4, 2.5, 2.6). The 1965 congress had the highest retention rate (84 percent of the previous CC members were re-elected) and the 1955 congress the lowest (only 61 percent) of all RWP or RCP congresses before 1979. Of course, there were important reasons for the low retention in 1955: The First and Second RWP Congresses (1948 and 1955) were separated by eight years instead of the usual four or five, and those years had seen the ouster of the Pauker-Luca group, the verification campaign, and a 44 percent drop in Party membership. In addition, Gheorghiu-Dej had essentially gained control of the Party in May 1952 and thus had more than three years to prepare for the Second Congress. As a result, many of his rivals and their supporters had already been weakened or removed, and a low retention rate was only to be expected from 1948 to 1955.

In contrast, Ceauşescu in 1965 did not yet control the top levels of the RCP, nor did he dominate the Central Committee. Consequently, he was not yet strong enough to remove his rivals or their supporters and had to content himself with simply increasing the size of the CC by an unprecedented 78 percent. The CC has tended to be a rather stable body, with a retention rate of over 60 percent (until the late Ceauşescu period), but the retention in 1965 of 84 percent of the former CC was also unprecedented—and a significant contrast to what later occurred. Ceauşescu's strategy with the Central Committee in 1965 illustrates his personnel policy for the next several years: the retention of officeholders to assure stability and to prevent disaffection and the promotion of new individuals into the top Party organs. Not until 1968 did some demotions begin, as Ceauşescu then started to move against his rivals from the Gheorghiu-Dej era and to form his own leadership group.

This process accelerated in 1969, when the proportion of Central Committee members not re-elected was almost double the 1965 figure, though still not very high (31 percent)—and even then over two-thirds of the previous committee (and three-fourths of its full members) were re-elected. However, another large increase in the size of the body—45 percent—would mean that in both 1965 and 1969, exactly 48 percent of the new committee would have served previously, and 52 percent would be new.

The Central Committee continued to be relatively stable in 1974, when 65 percent of the previous body was re-elected and much of the turnover occurred, as in the past, among the candidate rather than the full members. For example, 81 percent of the full members in 1974 had served in the previous committee, whereas 78 percent of the candidate members were being elected for the first time. That high turnover among candidates would continue throughout Ceauşescu's rule because he apparently used the candidate stage for two purposes: (1) a probationary period, after which about one-fifth of the candidates would be raised to full membership, and (2) a chance for a number of individuals prominent in their professions to circulate in and out of the CC and briefly experience such high status.

The rather high retention rate among full members in 1974 was somewhat unexpected, for Ceauşescu had already begun to circulate offices at the regional level as early as 1971 as part of his emerging campaign for change and renewal in the Party. As it turned out, the 27 percent increase in the CC's size and the high turnover among candidate members were sufficient to ensure that 45 percent of all members were newly elected in 1974. This was well above the one-third required by the directives published in July, but the 1974 CC had a lower proportion of new members than any Central Committee before or after except for the body chosen in 1960, when Gheorghiu-Dej continued in power and emphasized stability and continuity. This acceptance of stability in the top Party organs would not be shared by Ceauşescu, who did not allow the security of CC members to continue unchallenged after the 1974 congress. He had used his influence at lower levels of the Party and in the Central Committee to gain control in the 1960s; in the 1970s he began to weaken the CC by continuing to enlarge it (making membership consequently less prestigious) and increasing the turnover.

Despite Ceauşescu's penchant for personnel circulation, the Eleventh Party Congress merely produced hints of future turnover in the CC rather than accomplishing a radical renewal.[23] At age 56 Ceauşescu was presenting himself as a compromise between renewal and stagnation—as the hope of both older and younger colleagues—and he was just beginning the process of shifting individuals from post to post, which in any case did not affect Central Committee membership because that status could be retained when someone moved to a new job. CC members must have felt some insecurity in 1974, but it would not be until the later congresses of 1979 and 1984 that turnover in the CC would come close to 50 percent.

Lists of Central Committee members are published at every Party congress, and so turnover can be easily calculated. Other information on the composition of the membership is much more difficult to obtain. Data on the members' age and education are not consistently available. Seniority in the Party is often unknown, although beginning in 1974 new CC members had to have twelve years seniority in the party and six years experience at the county, municipal, or city level.[24] Nationalities usually have been represented in the Central Committee, as in the Party, in close conformity to their proportions in the entire population, although the CC elected in 1984 did underrepresent the minorities to an ominous degree.On the other hand, women, who had been woefully neglected in elections to the CC, have seen their numbers jump toward more respectable levels since 1974. This might be regarded as a positive development for Romanian women; however, given the patterns of political participation in Romania and the experience of other countries with rapid and forced promotion of disadvantaged groups beyond their experience and qualifications, this campaign is more likely a sign of the weakening of the power and prestige of the Central Committee in comparison with that of Ceauşescu and his personal supporters.[25]

The occupations of CC members have shifted to some extent during Ceauşescu's rule—in predictable directions, given what is known of his priorities. In 1969 about 80 percent of the full members were Party or state officials, mostly at the county level or above. About 15 percent were individuals involved in science, education, culture, or the arts, and another 3 percent were military or security officers. That left only about 2 percent of the full members directly involved in production, although about 16 percent of the candidate members could be placed in that category. By 1974 those directly involved in production made up 9 percent of the full members and over 20 percent of the candidate members; their share was still higher in 1979 and 1984. Military and security officers rose to about 5 percent and remained steady, but cultural figures dropped to 11 percent in 1974, 10 percent in 1979, and less than 5 percent of full members by 1984.[26]

In summary, at the five congresses over which Ceauşescu has presided, his policies toward the Central Committee have shifted from promotion and stability to circulation and insecurity for its members: The congresses in 1965 and 1969 saw large increases in the CC's size and high rates of retention; 1974 was a transitional session; and the congresses of 1979 and 1984 brought much lower growth and retention rates. The priorities of the Party leaders are visible in the occupational structure of this elite group, for the proportion of members working in science, culture, and education has fallen, and the members who are not political officials tend to be involved directly in economic production. They are, however, mostly directors, managers, or presidents of agricultural cooperatives, rather than workers or peasants, because the Central Committee, unlike the Party, is not meant to reflect all levels of society among its members. Ceauşescu may have diluted the elite status of CC members by enlarging the body, and he may have weakened it as a potential forum for opposition to himself by increasing the insecurity of its members (arbitrary turnover rather than terror). Nevertheless, its members hold the top economic and political positions in Romania; if *they* cannot oppose him successfully, then resistance within the Romanian political elite is highly unlikely. Ceauşescu's success in dominating the CC has been as great as his ability to control the Romanian Communist Party as a whole.

Regional and County Party Organs

The same shift visible in Ceauşescu's strategies toward the Central Committee took place in his appointments of lower-level Party officials.

From the retention and promotion that characterized the careers of regional secretaries in the 1960s, he shifted to a circulation of individuals in the 1970s, a merry-go-round that speeded up considerably in the late 1970s and 1980s. Initially these regional Party secretaries were promoted by Ceauşescu into high positions throughout the political system so they could provide the extended support he needed to consolidate his personal control of the Party and then the government. Of course, the regional first secretaries were not Ceauşescu's only power base within the political system—he had worked in the Central Committee apparatus in Bucharest for eleven years and promoted a number of individuals from its CC staff—but local Party officials would form the most numerous group from which he would make appointments.

The December 1967 administrative-territorial reform, which replaced the two tiers of 16 regions and 150 districts with a single tier of 40 counties, provided him with an opportunity to restructure the entire administrative system and to move his personal supporters into the state hierarchy. His efforts were aided when the December 1967 Party conference lifted the prohibition against one person's holding a full-time position in both Party and state and even placed the same person in charge of both Party and state administrative structures at various points throughout the system, which allowed one individual henceforth to be both first secretary and president of the People's Council. Even before the 1967 reform occurred, however, Ceauşescu began to make use of the regional first secretaries: By December 1967 eight of the sixteen in office in 1965 had been promoted to Bucharest, and three more would make the move by 1969.

The change in status of current or previous regional first secretaries during Ceauşescu's consolidation of power casts some light on his position as Central Committee secretary under Gheorghiu-Dej. Ceauşescu must have influenced appointments at the regional level before 1965; the extent of that influence over time can be roughly estimated if we compare the date on which these regional first secretaries were appointed with their status change after Ceauşescu became Party leader. In other words, given their post in 1965 (which by then may not have been regional first secretary), did their status rise, fall, or remain comparable over the next four years?[27] Presumably, if Ceauşescu had been responsible for their original appointment and had established a positive working relationship with them before 1965, he would be more likely to promote them in 1965–1969.

Table 8.5 groups the data according to three time periods in the years from 1952 to 1964, and the most striking finding is that 8 of the 12 demoted between 1965 and 1969 were appointed before 1957, whereas 20 of the 26 promoted gained their regional posts after 1957. These dates confirm what we know of intra-Party rivalry in the 1950s: Iosif Chişinevschi and Miron Constantinescu may very well have influenced cadre appointments before 1957, and individuals appointed in that period may have been less favored by (and favorable to) Ceauşescu. Of course, we cannot conclude that Ceauşescu

Table 8.5. Regional First Secretaries: Status Change Under Ceauşescu

Year Appointed	New Posts in 1965–1969			Total Appointed
	Higher	Lower	Comparable	
1952–1956	6	8	2	16
1957	0	0	0	0
1958–1960	5	2	1	8
1961–1964	7	0	1	8
1965–1967	8	2	2	12
Total	26	12	6	44

Sources: Personnel files compiled from Scînteia.

controlled the original appointments of certain people merely because he later promoted them. However, he must at least have developed a favorable relationship with those individuals so that he and they cooperated to their mutual advantage in the years to come.

The administrative-territorial reorganization in February 1968, which disrupted other Party organs, did not adversely affect the regional first secretaries: Twelve of the 16 were put in charge of counties, and at least 3 of the remaining 4 were promoted to Bucharest. Of course, the change from regional to county first secretary—from being one of 16 to one of 40—could in itself be considered a demotion; however, each first secretary at the same time became president of the county People's Council and so in some ways had his power enhanced.

Of the 40 county first secretaries elected in 1968, 33 remained in office after the Tenth Party Congress in August 1969 and were also elected full members of the Central Committee. Four of the 7 changes involved promotions, 1 in December 1968 and 3 in August 1969, but the remaining 3 individuals were summarily removed from office in December 1968 and dropped out of sight. The position of county first secretary therefore was not completely secure. Significantly, the 4 who were promoted had been regional first secretaries, while the 3 demoted had been only regional secretaries prior to the reorganization and may simply have proven ineffective in their new duties.

Thus personnel trends at the regional and county level in these early years of Ceauşescu's rule were definitely upward: Many officials moved into positions as first secretary of a county, and others moved into positions in Bucharest, either in the CC apparatus or in high posts in the Party and the government. Unfortunately, we know little about personnel change at lower levels. There evidently was a greater rate of demotions in local organizations than was visible in higher circles. A hint of this was given in a June 1967 editorial in Lupta de clasă, which announced that during the preceding year 85 secretaries of district and city Party committees had been removed because they could not fulfill their duties or had frequently violated Party discipline and morality. Also, over 240 directors, chief-engineers, and chief-accountants of major enterprises had lost their jobs. Either they had proven themselves incapable of "leading and organizing economic activity" or they had committed abuses such as "breaches of financial discipline" or "misinforming Party and state organs on the state of affairs in their sector of responsibility"—in other words, they had covered up errors or failures.[28] The editorial was part of the dual campaign to improve professional education and to establish high ethical standards and socialist morality, but the results were not apparent at the regional or county levels.

The stability at the level of county first secretary continued until February 1971. Out of a total of 59 individuals who held the post of regional or county first secretary between 1965 and 1971, only 4 were demoted, and 15 went on to higher positions. The rest remained in office. Then the same CC plenum that had initiated the reforms and retraining in professional education called for a movement of cadres from the central organs to the counties, closer to the "concrete leadership of the economy and social life." This shifting of personnel was intended to "strengthen the ties between the leading organs and the masses" and to "combat excessive centralism." In accordance with this decision, 2 members of the Party Executive Committee and a CC section chief "expressed the wish to be sent to work in local Party organs," and they subsequently were elected county first secretaries.[29] The 3 incumbent first secretaries were sent to fulfill "other duties."

The changes were not necessarily demotions because the Executive Committee members were sent to Brașov and Constanța, two of the most important counties outside of Bucharest, and they remained members of the EC.[30] However, their "election" did demonstrate that the choice of county first secretary was made in Bucharest and not in the respective county: The CC plenum had been held on 10–11 February; already on 16 and 17 February the three county committees "decided to coopt as members" the three officials and "elected" each first secretary. A member of the Presidium "participated" in each of the county meetings.[31]

Three other changes among county first secretaries soon occurred, two of which involved circulation between Bucharest and the counties, bringing the total turnover for 1971 to six. The sixth change, not announced until April 1972, was the ouster of the first secretary of Caraș-Severin from the Central Committee for "breaches of communist ethics and serious negligence in work."[32] At the same time, two other changes were announced for 1972: The first secretary of Bucharest, Dumitru Popa, was removed for "serious short-comings," and the first secretary of Covasna, Károly Király, resigned for "personal reasons." (It later became public that Király was protesting Party policies toward the Hungarian minority.) One final change during 1972 again involved circulation between Bucharest and the counties. Thus, six of the nine changes in these two years involved circulation, but four of the six were moves out of Bucharest and could be interpreted as demotions; of the three remaining changes, two officials were publicly removed in disgrace; and one resigned. These were the years when Ceauşescu was trying to impose his cultural revolution and fulfill the five-year plan in four and a half years. Clearly, he was signaling Party officials that their security depended on him and him alone.

Suddenly in 1973 eleven changes were made in county first secretaries, more than the total since 1969, and at least eight involved circulation between the central and county administrations, four in each direction. By now the process involved top state positions as well as Party posts, as two high state officials became county first secretaries and three county first secretaries moved to the Council of Ministers. Just as Ceauşescu had used the regional and county Party officials as a pool from which to promote new faces to the capital from 1965 to 1971, so now he was using the top posts in outlying counties to circulate personnel between and within the Party and state bureaucracies.

This circulation would continue throughout the 1970s and 1980s. In the sixteen years between 1968 and 1984, the counties averaged just over 4 first secretaries each (See Table 8.6), and most individuals served between three and four years in one place. The number of changes tended to be higher in years of Party congresses or conferences, with 1979 having the most with 24, followed by 1984 with 17 (see Table 8.7). However, the changes usually came during the spring and summer preceding the meeting, thus weakening the power base of many delegates and reminding them of their dependence on Ceauşescu.

No general explanation of the various shifts emerges. Circulation between Bucharest and the outlying counties was frequently involved, but determining whether a particular move was in the long run a promotion or demotion for an individual was often not possible. Most changes were not even announced; a new first secretary would simply appear in a county and the predecessor would eventually turn up somewhere else—or drop permanently from sight. Major features of the process included (1) the high number of shifts, (2) their clustering in advance of the major Party meetings, (3) the adulation rendered Ceauşescu by those who left office as well as those who remained in place, and (4) Ceauşescu's use of the position of county first secretary as a test of ability: At least twenty individuals who moved into these positions during the 1970s and early 1980s were eventually promoted to top posts in Bucharest.

The Top Party Leadership

That pattern of promotion and then circulation of personnel found in the Central Committee and at the regional and county level also characterized the top Party bodies. Between July 1965 and December 1967, for example, the three top organs—the Presidium, the Executive Committee (EC), and the

Table 8.6. Turnover of County First Secretaries, 1968–1984 (by county)

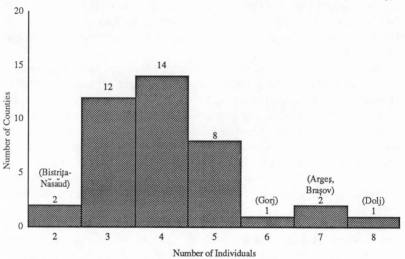

Sources: Compiled from appearances in *Scînteia*.

Table 8.7. Turnover of County First Party Secretaries, 1968–1984 (by year)

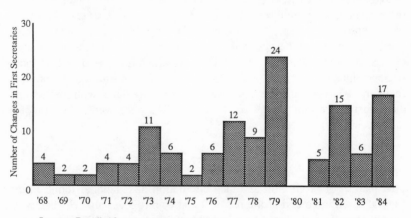

Sources: Compiled from appearances in *Scînteia*.
Note: There were no changes in 1980.

Secretariat—did not lose a single member.[33] Each body simply increased in size during those early years, evidently to give Ceauşescu a majority of supporters in all three. Two members were added to both the Presidium and the Secretariat, five candidate members of the EC became full members, and four new candidates were elected. The demotions began only after the Party conference of December 1967, but by the Tenth Congress in August 1969, over half of the Presidium members and almost half of the Secretariat and Executive Committee had resigned or been excluded in disgrace. During that eighteen months, a new Party leadership formed around Ceauşescu.

Although membership stability in the top Party bodies need not coincide with stability in high government positions in Romania, during the 1965–1967 period the Council of Ministers was a relatively stable body. There were a few exceptions: In December 1965 Maxim Berghianu, a former regional first secretary in both Braşov and Cluj, replaced Roman Moldovan at the State Planning Committee, but Moldovan received other high posts to soften the blow. In late May 1966 a bad railroad crash killed thirty-eight people, prompting Ceauşescu to rush to the scene and immediately remove the minister of railroads in a dramatic gesture[34]; his replacement was Florian Dănălache, until then first secretary of Bucharest. The defense minister, Leonte Sălăjan, died on 29 August 1966 following a "serious digestive hemorrhage" and was replaced by one of his deputies, Ion Ioniţă. The day before his death, the Minister of Health and Social Services was abruptly replaced, evidently due to "grave deficiencies" in the treatment of Sălăjan.[35] These last two were fortuitous disasters, presumably, which Ceauşescu used to his advantage. Then Ilie Verdeţ was promoted to first vice-president of the Council of Ministers in January 1967.

More changes began to occur at the Party conference in December 1967. The RCP Executive Committee was enlarged slightly, and Ceauşescu replaced Chivu Stoica as president of the Council of State. The latter then moved to the Secretariat, Drăghici left that body for the Council of Ministers, and Bodnaraş completed the circle by going to the Council of State. Of the original members of the Presidium, all except Ceauşescu and Maurer were weakened by the changes, but no one was excluded from the leading organs in 1967.[36] Ceauşescu was demonstrating exceptional skill in neutralizing his rivals and preventing them from forging successful alliances among themselves.

The demotions began in 1968, the year of Drăghici's disgrace and the Czechoslovak intervention. Usually the Central Committee held three or four sessions a year. In 1965 the number had jumped to eight with the death of Gheorghiu-Dej and the Ninth Congress, but 1968 brought ten CC plenums. Not only was Drăghici excluded from all of his positions in April, but in December three members of the old guard—Bîrlădeanu, Borilă, and Moghioroş—submitted their resignations, all ostensibly for reasons of health.[37] Meanwhile new members were joining the Executive Committee, and several government shifts in March 1969[38] left Maurer and Gheorghe Rădulescu as the only two (of nine) government officials with the rank of vice-president or above who had held the same office before the death of Gheorghiu-Dej.

The turnover in Party leadership was completed at the Tenth Party Congress in August 1969. Apostol, Chivu Stoica, and Mihai Dalea were dropped; the Presidium gained three new members, and the EC four full and seven candidate members. The CC Secretariat by now consisted of only seven secretaries, four remaining from 1965 (of whom Ceauşescu was by far the most senior), and three added since then. Six secretaries had lost their positions over the four years, five of whom had been important members of the Gheorghiu-Dej leadership group. The new members of the Presidium included Gheorghe Pană, former first secretary of the Braşov region, who was made a CC secretary at the same time. His rise was spectacular: Before the congress he had not even been a member of the Central Committee; afterward he was one of four men (with Ceauşescu, Niculescu-Mizil, and Trofin) to belong to all three leading Party organs, and he would eventually replace Trofin as CC secretary for cadres and organizations. The new candidate members of the Executive Committee were indicative of future developments: Five of the seven had been regional or county first secretaries, the only exceptions being Ion Ioniţă, the defense minister, and Ion Iliescu, from the CC apparatus.

The personnel turnover that replaced the Gheorghiu-Dej Political Bureau with Ceauşescu's supporters can be grasped more easily if we divide the EC into three groups—those elected before, during, and after 1965—and show the varying size of each over time. As Table 8.8 shows, the periods of radical change were the years of the Party congresses: 1965, 1968–1969, and 1974. Aside from these years, the composition of the EC was quite stable. The "retirement" of the members of the former Political Bureau came in 1968 and 1969; 13 of the 15 in the Gheorghiu-Dej group were elected to the EC in 1965, but only 5 (including Ceauşescu) remained after August 1969.[39] Twelve new faces appeared in 1965, and the same 12 continued in office until 1974. In fact, out of 27 new members elected between 1965 and 1969, not one was demoted until April 1972.[40] Ceauşescu had brought in a new group of leaders who continued to serve with him for an extended period. The composition of that stable group of 12 is significant: 7 had been regional first secretaries, and 3 had spent many years in the CC apparatus in Bucharest. Apparently only 1 of the 12, who moved in laterally from the government, had a formal higher education in technical subjects.[41]

1969 to 1974

The first four years of Ceauşescu's rule had been characterized by promotions that enlarged the size of the top Party bodies, but the pattern of personnel

Table 8.8. RCP Executive Committee Membership, 1965–1987

Year[a]	Pre-1965 Leaders	Elected 1965	Elected After 1965	Total Membership[b]
1965	13	12	0	25
1966	12	12	2	26
1967	12	12	4	28
1968	8	12	6	26
1969	5	12	15	32
1970	6	12	15	33
1971	6	12	19	37
1972	6	12	20	38
1973	6	12	23	41
1974	6	8	22	36
1975	5	8	22	35
1976	4	7	27	38
1977	4	7	27	38
1978	4	7	29	40
1979	3	7	35	45
1980	3	7	35	45
1981	2	7	38	47
1982	2	6	32	40
1983	2	6	34	42
1984	1	5	41	47
1985	1	5	41	47
1986	1	4	43	48
1987	1	3	44	48

Source: Personnel files compiled from Scînteia.

[a]Figures given are for the end of each year except for 1969 (August) and 1976 (July).
[b]Includes full and candidate members of the Executive Committee.

change would be quite different in the years following the Tenth Party Congress. Between 1969 and 1974, membership in the Presidium and Executive Committee remained almost stable. These policymaking bodies contained those individuals with high status within the Party; changes in their specific area of responsibility—the personnel circulation that soon began—affected the Secretariat and Council of Ministers, but not the EC or the Presidium.

There were some new faces promoted into these bodies including the election of CC secretary Manea Mănescu to the Presidium in early 1971[42]— the only change in that organ until its elimination in March 1974—and the move of Gheorghe Cioară onto the EC in 1972 when he became the first secretary of Bucharest, one of the few high state officials to move horizontally into a top Party post. The only other changes among full EC members occurred in June 1973 and were justified as part of an attempt to increase the role of women in Romanian political life: Elena Ceaușescu and Lina Ciobanu were elected to the Executive Committee.[43] Eleven new candidate members were added to the EC during these years, and 3 were removed, so by 1974 the total had increased by 8, to 19.

Changes in the Secretariat and the Council of Ministers were much more extensive, reflecting the shifting responsibilities of their members. For example, only Ceaușescu, Gheorghe Pană, and Dumitru Popescu remained on the Secretariat from 1969 to 1974, although a total of 16 secretaries served in those five years. Over half of these individuals also spent time on the Council of Ministers, reflecting the extensive interchange between the top Party and state administrative bodies, and the latter saw even more change during this period than the Secretariat. In both 1969 and 1974, for example, there were 23 ministries, but in the five intervening years 10 were extensively reorganized to include different sectors of responsibility. Of the 23 ministers and 10 other officials with ministerial rank in 1969, only 5 remained unchanged in 1974, and about a third of the offices had changed hands more than once.

The careers of several important officials illustrate clearly this exchange at the highest levels of Party and state. Ilie Verdeț, for example, was made a CC secretary in March 1965, four months later moved to the Council of Ministers, and in 1974 returned to the Secretariat. Virgil Trofin, a CC secretary from 1965 to 1971, became head of the trade unions in 1971, vice-president of the Council of Ministers and minister of internal trade in 1972, and returned to Party work in 1974 as first secretary of Brașov County. From 1969 to 1974, Miron Constantinescu was successively minister of education, rector of the Ștefan Gheorghiu Party Academy, president of the Academy of Social and Political Sciences, president of the Economic Council, CC secretary, vice-president of the Council of State, president of the Council of Workers' Control of Economic and Social Activity, and finally, in March 1974, president of the Grand National Assembly. Manea Mănescu moved from head of the CC Section for Science and Culture and president of the GNA Commission on Economics and Finance in the early 1960s to CC secretary and president of the Economic Council, then vice-president of the Council of State, eventually vice-president of the Council of Ministers and president of the State Planning Committee, and finally president of the Council of Ministers, replacing Ion Gheorghe Maurer when he retired in March 1974.

This situation of "change but no change" ended in 1974 when Maurer retired from his offices in March and could no longer moderate Ceaușescu's influence. Maurer apparently opposed some of Ceaușescu's more extreme demands in culture and the economy in the early 1970s (although in public he did so more by silence than by overt criticism), and his resignation and Ceaușescu's election as president were devastating blows to any who wished to check the Party leader. Then the Eleventh Party Congress in November failed to re-elect 9 of the full and candidate members of the EC to the new Political Executive Committee (PEC), including 4 of that stable group of 12 who had served with Ceauşescu since 1965.[44] In addition, the congress reorganized the top Party bodies, changes implied the preceding March when the plenum, pending ratification by the congress, had abolished the Presidium and substituted a Permanent Bureau of the Executive Committee, responsible to this smaller body rather than to the CC as a whole. As described in March, the new bureau was to have about 15 *ex officio* members, plus others chosen by the EC[45]; hence it would have been much too large to fulfill its charge: the "operational coordination" of Party and state activity. Its role was clarified to some extent after the Eleventh Party Congress that fall when only five individuals were actually included: Ceauşescu, Manea Mănescu, and three newcomers just elected to the new PEC at the same congress—Gheorghe Oprea, Ion Pățan, and Ştefan Andrei.

At that congress, the new name for the EC was justified as a means of emphasizing its role in setting policy, whereas the new Permanent Bureau was portrayed as merely an administrative organ to coordinate policy. Nevertheless, the PEC was a large and unwieldy group, meeting on the average about twice a month, and its agenda and decisions were now being reported publicly in *Scînteia*. It did not appear to be an effective forum for discussing policy alternatives, but evidently ratified decisions made elsewhere. The Permanent Bureau might have served as a small "collective" body, such as Ceauşescu had advocated in 1965, to run the Party between PEC meetings and propose policies and solutions for the approval of the larger body. However, the Permanent Bureau was not designed to be powerful; its members were responsible to the PEC, not to the Central Committee, and they were identified in press reports of their activities only as members of the PEC, the group with high public status. In addition, and most important, the other four members of the new body were junior members of the RCP leadership. As a result, the new organ presented less of a potential challenge to Ceauşescu's authority than had the Presidium, whose members were beginning to achieve senior status in the Party in their own right, independent of Ceauşescu.

In summary, during 1974 the Party Presidium was eliminated, and the new Permanent Bureau turned out to be a small council of advisers to Ceauşescu rather than an organ with any independent stature.[46] These changes in Party organization thus reinforced Ceauşescu's personal power, which was enhanced considerably in the state hierarchy by the creation of the office of president of the Republic especially for him. Thereafter, he could use a variety of groups to advise him or, more realistically, to listen to him and devise ways of carrying out his policies. The Permanent Bureau, the CC Secretariat, the Council of State, and the Council of Ministers were all statutory bodies now dominated by Ceauşescu. In addition, his election as president led him to appoint around himself a number of "presidential counselors," individuals who had somehow gained his ear and whose services he wanted available on a permanent basis, but who served completely at his pleasure. Thus, the changes of 1973–1974 initiated a period of personalized rule in Romania that would soon contradict Ceauşescu's original promises of legality and constitutionality.

RCP Leadership Groups: 1965, 1974, 1984

After November 1974 only two important figures remained from the 1965 Political Bureau—Ceauşescu himself, and Emil Bodnaraş, who would die in 1976.[47] Ceauşescu had created, and was already beginning to restructure, a new leadership group within the RCP. A comparison of the 15 full and candidate members of the Gheorghiu-Dej Political Bureau just before his death in 1965 with the 23 full members of the Political Executive Committee (PEC) elected at the Party congresses in 1974 and 1984 reveals some significant continuities and contrasts among the three groups (see Table 8.9).

The two dominant characteristics of the Gheorghiu-Dej leadership—longevity in office and prewar Party activity—were no longer typical of the PEC in 1974. However, 10 individuals, including Ceauşescu and Bodnaraş, had been at least candidate members of the PEC since its formation in 1965, indicating that the new group was establishing its own tradition of longevity. Aside from Ceauşescu and Bodnaraş, only 7 apparently had been RCP members before the war,[48] and most had not become full members of the Central Committee until the 1960s (see Tables 8.10 and 8.11). Another bond had, however, appeared within the group: ethnicity. Seventeen of the 23 were ethnically Romanian, and only one person (aside from Bodnaraş) had lived for any extensive period in the USSR.

There were also age and educational differences between the Gheorghiu-Dej and Ceauşescu groups. Ceauşescu, born in 1918, had been the youngest member of the 1965 Political Bureau; by 1974 he was one of the oldest on the PEC (see Table 8.12). The educational backgrounds of the leaders reportedly had improved, although the quality of the education was open to question.[49] Only about a third of the 1965 group had had some post-secondary studies, but in 1974 it seemed that 16 of the 23 had completed a higher education and the rest, including Ceauşescu, had risen in the Party apparatus after the war and studied at Party schools during their careers. By 1974, then, the RCP leadership was composed predominantly of ethnic Romanians who had joined the Party after the war and lived all their lives in Romania, and some of them had received a higher education.

The generational change in the RCP leadership between 1965 and 1974 did not have an equivalent over the next decade. The 10-year gap in median birth date between the 1965 and 1974 groups fell to six years between the two later groups, and the overwhelming majority of individuals in both Ceauşescu groups were born between 1916 and 1930. By 1984 individuals of Ceauşescu's age or older had died, retired, or moved to titular positions, but as in 1974 the core members of his leadership group were born in the 1920s.

Table 8.9. RCP Leadership Groups: 1965, 1974, 1984

1965	1974	1984
G. Gheorghiu-Dej	N. Ceauşescu	N. Ceauşescu
G. Apostol	E. Bobu	I. Banc
E. Bodnaraş	E. Bodnaraş	E. Bobu
P. Borilă	C. Burtică	V. Cazacu
N. Ceauşescu	E. Ceauşescu	E. Ceauşescu
C. Stoica	G. Cioară	L. Ciobanu
A. Drăghici	L. Ciobanu	I. Coman
I. G. Maurer	E. Drăgănescu	N. Constantin
A. Moghioroş	J. Fazekas	C. Dăscălescu
A. Bîrlădeanu	P. Lupu	I. Dincă
D. Coliu	M. Mănescu	M. Dobrescu
L. Răutu	P. Niculescu	J. Fazekas
L. Sălăjan	G. Oprea	A. Găinuşe
S. Voitec	G. Pană	P. Niculescu
M. Dalea	I. Păţan	C. Olteanu
	D. Popescu	G. Oprea
	G. Rădulescu	G. Pană
	L. Răutu	I. Păţan
	V. Trofing	D. Popescu
	I. Uglar	G. Rădulescu
	I. Verdeţ	I. Verdeţ
	V. Vîlcu	Ş. Voitec
	S. Voitec	

Sources: Congresul al IX-lea: Congresul al XI-lea; Scînteia, 23 November 1984.

Fourteen of the 23 remained from 1974, so the Ceauşescu group had indeed established its own pattern of longevity. Moreover, the 9 newcomers resembled the holdovers not only in age but also in Party seniority, ethnicity, and career pattern. Hence the 1984 group, like that of 1974, was composed mostly of postwar communists, promoted to the Central Committee in the early 1960s, with careers in Party administration, production technology, or the political supervision of culture (see Table 8.13).

In 1974, despite the homogeneity in background of the PEC as compared with the Gheorghiu-Dej Political Bureau, several different groups could be distinguished among its members according to education and career pattern. First, there were the Party administrators, who had little or no formal education, who tended to be generalists rather than specialists, and who had moved up through the local Party apparatus or the Union of Communist Youth; Gheorghe Pană, Virgil Trofin, Iosif Uglar, and Ceauşescu himself can be considered representatives of this pattern. Then there were the better-educated technical specialists, who often began their careers in the state hierarchy, moving laterally into high Party positions after demonstrating their expertise in industrial or financial administration; Emil Drăgănescu,

Table 8.10. Party Seniority of RCP Leadership Groups by Date of Joining the Party

	Before 1939	1940–1944	After 1944	Total
1965	13	1	1	15
1974	9	2	12	23
1984	5	1	17	23

Sources: Personnel files compiled from *Scînteia* and the archives of Radio Free Europe in Munich.

Table 8.11. CC Membership of RCP Leadership Groups by Date of First Election (Full or Candidate Member)

	By 1948	1954–1958	1960	1965	1969–1972	1974–1979
1965	14	1	0	0	0	0
1974	4	6	4	7	2	0
1984	2	3	4	9	2	3

Sources: Same as for Table 8.10.

Table 8.12. Birthdates of RCP Leadership Groups

	1900–1905	1906–1910	1911–1915	1916–1919	1920–1925	1926–1930	1931–1935	Median
1965	4	4	5	2	0	0	0	1910
1974	2	2	1	4	6	7	1	1920
1984	1	0	1	3	5	11	2	1926

Sources: Same as for Table 8.10.

Table 8.13. Career Patterns in the RCP Leadership

	Party Generalists	Economic Specialists	Culture/ Agitprop	Military	Mixed
1974	10	6	6	1	3
1984	12	4	3	2	2

Sources: Same as for Table 8.10.

Gheorghe Oprea, and Ion Pățan exemplify this route to the top. Finally, there were the more broadly educated cultural specialists such as Paul Niculescu (formerly Niculescu-Mizil) or Dumitru Popescu, who had held the position of CC secretary for culture, education, and/or propaganda. The same three groups were present in 1984, but the shares of each had changed. Contrary to what might have been expected, there was no rise in the proportion of highly educated economic specialists. Instead, it was the Party generalists who had increased in number.

The similarities between the 1974 and 1984 groups should not obscure the differences. Most obvious was the presence of three women in the later group: Elena Ceaușescu, wife of the president; Lina Ciobanu, who made her career in Party work and light industry; and Alexandrina Găinușe, one of the first women ever to serve as a county first secretary. The promotion of women was a major theme of Party pronouncements after 1979 as a means of enticing them into the work force, and in the 1980s women appeared more and more frequently in prominent political and economic posts. One disadvantaged group—women—had joined the Party leadership, but others— the ethnic minorities—had almost disappeared. Only two Hungarians, Banc and Fazekas, were exceptions to the ethnic homogeneity of the Romanian leadership in 1984.[50]

Other differences between the 1974 and 1984 leadership groups related to age and education. The number of leaders born after 1927 had increased slightly, and these individuals tended to be better educated because they were less likely to have had their education interrupted by World War II. This may in fact help to explain why more Party administrators formed part of the 1984 leadership: The younger Party officials by then had some education, and so Ceaușescu could find individuals with higher degrees in the Party apparatus rather than bringing them over from the state ministries. Vlad Georgescu, who criticized Party education as political rather than technical in its criteria for advancement, regarded this development as a disadvantage for contemporary Romania. He attributed some of the successes of the Gheorghiu-Dej elite to "the ability with which they had been able to coopt a large number of technocrats and intellectuals belonging to the old regime." In Georgescu's view, "the present elite is anti-intellectual, xenophobic, isolationist, anti-technocratic, and hostile to change."[51] Whether this typifies the entire elite under Ceaușescu is questionable, but with the exception of the last phrase, Ceaușescu himself has certainly exhibited these qualities at times during the 1980s— and he is even "hostile to change" not initiated by himself. In any case, the differences between the RCP leaders of 1974 and 1984 were far outweighed by the similarities, and this is not surprising when we recognize the influence that one man—Nicolae Ceaușescu—had in their selection.

Personnel Change, 1974–1988

The pattern of personnel change established by Ceauşescu in the top Party and state bodies from 1969 to 1974 continued and intensified over the next decade. Membership in the major policymaking organ—the Political Executive Committee—remained rather stable from one Party congress to the next, whereas the composition of the top administrative bodies—the Party Secretariat and the Council of Ministers—changed rapidly when individuals circulated from one post to another, rotated out to a county, or, as happened with increasing frequency over the years, simply were demoted into obscurity. Seventeen of the 23 full members of the PEC elected in 1974 were re-elected in 1979, and 20 of the 27 elected in 1979 were re-elected in 1984 (74 percent retention at both congresses). However, only 3 of the 6 changes in the earlier period were demotions, whereas all 7 of those in the next five years appeared to result from Ceauşescu's dissatisfaction with the individual involved (although several were ostensibly retirements). Thus, turnover in the PEC was low, but growing with time. In contrast, turnover in the Secretariat was quite high; only 1 CC secretary in 1974 in addition to Ceauşescu was re-elected in 1979, and a total of 17 individuals filled the 7 to 10 posts in the Secretariat during those five years. This pattern continued among the secretaries elected in 1979; again only Ceauşescu and one other secretary were re-elected at the next congress, and the turnover intensified: A total of 21 individuals served as CC secretaries from 1979 to 1984. Turnover in the Council of Ministers was just as high: In both periods, only about 10 of the more than 50 posts remained unchanged, and many shifted hands several times. What was different after 1979 was not only that the circulation intensified, but also that it was no longer upward or horizontal—loyal Ceauşescu protégés could now be removed in disgrace.

In 1981 three of Ceauşescu's supporters who had served under him since he succeeded Gheorghiu-Dej—Virgil Trofin, Paul Niculescu, and Dumitru Popescu—moved out of the top leadership. The last two remained members of the PEC, but Niculescu was put in charge of a Union of Cooperatives (Centrocoop) and Popescu became rector of the Ştefan Gheorghiu Party Academy. In contrast, Trofin was summarily removed from his position in charge of the energy sector in September and expelled from the Central Committee when he refused to engage in self-criticism at the November 1981 plenum. The following year his suicide was announced in May on the day that another close colleague of Ceauşescu from the 1960s, Ilie Verdeţ, was removed as prime minister amid serious criticism. A younger protégé of Ceauşescu, Cornel Burtică, was dismissed at the same time as minister of foreign trade. To have Trofin, Verdeţ, and Burtică all in disgrace must have given many Ceauşescu supporters nightmares about their own security, although Verdeţ remained in the PEC and was elected to the CC Secretariat in October.[52]

Constantin Dăscălescu was moved from the Secretariat to replace Verdeţ as prime minister, and Emil Bobu, already in the Secretariat, moved from agriculture to cadres. Ceauşescu must have put a great deal of trust in both these individuals, for they still held the same positions seven years later. Nevertheless, he evidently felt the need in 1982 to have beside him some of his colleagues from earlier times, and in November Manea Mănescu was persuaded to come out of retirement to the Council of State and eventually to the PEC and its Permanent Bureau. Other major shifts in the mid-1980s included Verdeţ to minister of mines and eventually out of the CC and PEC altogether, kicked upstairs to head the Central Revisory Commission; Ştefan Andrei from minister of foreign affairs to CC secretary; and Gheorghe Pană from head of the Bucharest Party to minister of the food industry and farm products acquisitions.[53]

Some other members of the PEC had served there for many years—such as Gheorghe Rădulescu, Elena Ceauşescu, Gheorghe Oprea, Lina Ciobanu, Ion Dincă, and Ion Coman—but still more had been promoted in the 1980s. Indeed, the general pattern for the top Party bodies was for them gradually to increase in size in the 1970s and then shrink considerably in the 1980s. The Permanent Bureau, for example, grew steadily from it original 5 members in 1974 to 15 in 1979; it thereafter remained the same size (except for the removal of Burtică in 1982) until the 1984 Party congress reduced it to 8 members. The PEC increased in full membership from 23 in 1974 to 27 in 1979, but had dropped to 22 when the 1984 congress opened and by the Party conference in 1987 was down to 19. Candidate membership, in contrast, grew steadily from 13 in 1974 to 29 in 1987. Ceauşescu was using that position to bring new individuals into the leadership and then either to promote or to remove them, just as he used candidate membership in the Central Committee. For example, 18 candidate members of the PEC were elected in 1979, with 9 more added before the next congress. Of those 27, 2 were eventually promoted to full membership, 8 were dropped, and 17 were re-elected in 1984, joined by 8 new candidates.

Several factors about personnel manipulation under Ceauşescu are important to note. First, changes often seem arbitrary. Individuals in the circulating elite tend to be generalists—Party activists who may focus on a particular sector such as agriculture, culture, or foreign trade but who are just as likely to shift from one sector to another. They are presumably valuable to Ceauşescu for their personal loyalty and their ability to mobilize and motivate others, rather than for their technical expertise.

Second, changes are frequent. They occur in spurts, and the frequency and intensity of change have increased over time. Two to four years seems to be the usual length of service in one office, insufficient time for anyone to build a power base from which to challenge Ceauşescu. This has been particularly true of the CC Secretariat and the position of secretary for organizations and cadres, which went from Trofin to Pană to Bobu to Dăscălescu and back to Bobu. He must be an especially trusted supporter, because his return to the job and his retention of its functions from 1982 into 1989 were unprecedented.

Yet another characteristic of Ceauşescu's circulation of his colleagues in the top leadership has been the emergence of a new position for training and testing cadres: the post of presidential counselor. At first a small group of individual advisers from a variety of sectors and backgrounds, the counselors were identified more and more frequently by that title during the 1970s, and by the 1980s several had moved directly from that job into the Secretariat or Council of Ministers or out to a county.[54]

This leads us to a final feature of Ceauşescu's personnel policies: Personal loyalty to Ceauşescu is usually rewarded in the long run. If we total the number of changes that have occurred, we find that very few top officials have been permanently removed—like Trofin and Burtică—in disgrace. More often top leaders who lose their positions are quietly retired to a comfortable position, sometimes even remain CC members, and live out their days in comfort, if not luxury. At intermediate and lower levels of both Party and state the situation is somewhat different, but even there the primary punishment seems to be loss of the job (and, of course, its vital perquisites in an economy of scarcity).

In short, the arbitrary and rapid shifts in personnel contribute to the personal power of Ceauşescu. He uses both his presidential advisers and the Party apparatus as sources of new appointees, and local Party posts serve the additional function of warehousing officials who hope to be recalled to Bucharest. Their hopes are fulfilled often enough to deter overt opposition.

Policy Formulation

Ceauşescu's manipulation of top-level personnel has had important effects on decisionmaking. Just as he has centralized promotion and retention in his own hands so has he maintained personal control over the details of policy. Neither of the top Party bodies is an effective forum for making decisions. The PEC is unwieldy; its meetings, reported in print, were originally held every two weeks, but within several years were down to an average of sixteen per year. The sessions often include guests and presumably are formal, and it is difficult to imagine that much frank discussion takes place. The Permanent Bureau has probably served as a decisionmaking body from time to time, but when it started it was composed of individuals with little experience in the Party leadership; as it approached the size of Gheorghiu-Dej's old Political Bureau, it became more cumbersome. Cut to eight members in 1984, it probably has been the center of decisionmaking since, containing as it does both Ceauşescus, Dăscălescu and Bobu, Manea Mănescu, Verdeţ, Gheorghe Rădulescu, and Oprea. From the outside, it seems that Ceauşescu carries the day whenever he wishes, and that most decisions of the PEC and the Permanent Bureau involve ways to implement his suggestions.[55]

During the 1970s, decrees appeared more and more often from the president himself rather than from the Council of State and were issued without having the implications worked out and solutions to obvious problems provided in advance. The presidential answer to almost any problem was a new decree or perhaps a major new campaign, often so extreme as to produce complications that had to be resolved by yet another campaign. For example, in the fall of 1974 a decree required all foreigners to reside in hotels, not Romanian homes, creating extensive confusion for foreign students, researchers, diplomats, and relatives visiting Romanians from abroad. Some exceptions were worked out temporarily, but in the long run very few foreign visitors were ever again able to stay with Romanians in their homes either as guests or by paying rent. Then in the summer of 1979 hundreds of East European tourists were stranded throughout Romania when foreigners were suddenly required to pay for gasoline in hard currency. Relations with the other East European governments became quite strained because the Romanians for some time refused to make concessions sufficient to allow the tourists to get home, forcing many to camp at their embassies in Bucharest. This was the beginning of the end for foreign tourism in Romania as new rules and regulations combined with the economic scarcity of the 1980s deterred many visitors.

Not only foreigners were affected by arbitrary decrees: Regulations proliferated, invading all economic sectors and the personal lives of citizens. The severe floods of 1975 led to greater centralization of water policy and a campaign to regulate all waterways, but a later campaign to increase irrigation soon required emergency measures to provide drainage for the newly irrigated fields.[56] Attempts to improve livestock production led to a national animal census that even included chickens and rabbits. A campaign to estimate and protect the national heritage required a declaration of all historical (pre1945) items in the possession of individual citizens; any property not declared was subject to confiscation.[57] Of course, many Romanians believed that declared objects would be seized, so they were afraid to comply or not to comply, creating insecurity and intensifying the suspicion of the political authorities already so prominent in their political culture. All employed persons were affected by Ceauşescu's comprehensive training and retraining regulations associated with jobs. Ceauşescu responded to any need with coercion—issuing regulations and imposing penalties for non-compliance instead of providing incentives to carry out the new laws. Nevertheless, for many years his responses were successful: Throughout the 1970s Romania maintained by far the highest economic growth rate in Eastern Europe (and among the highest in the world).

Summary: Ceauşescu and the Party

Nicolae Ceauşescu's political techniques have been quite successful—he has maintained his control over the Romanian political process—but since 1979 he has not been able to achieve his major economic priority: rapid and sustained development of industrial production at levels competitive on the international market. His strategies toward the Romanian Communist Party and its officials are crucial in explaining these successes and failures.

First, his policies toward the Party as a whole have made it the largest of any European communist party as a proportion of the population. A third of the working population belongs to the RCP, which contributes to Romanians' quiescence because Party members expect to have special privileges and upward mobility. However, the increased size has weakened the boundaries between Party members and the rest of the society and made the organization less effective as an agent of mobilization and control. In addition, recruitment of new members has focused on workers rather than on those with an education. This emphasis has enabled the Party to remain proletarian in its overall social composition and to be perceived as a means of advancement from blue-collar to white-collar status, but it has hurt the Party's capacity to manage economic development—a capacity that might have been furthered more rapidly had the standards for recruitment and promotion given priority to those with education and expertise. Ceauşescu's ideological prejudices and pursuit of personal power have taken precedence over his need to develop the Party as a ruling political organization composed of the new economic elites.

The Central Committee already consisted of top political and economic officials when Ceauşescu inherited the Party leadership. Indeed, he used many of these individuals—especially those in the Party apparatus—to gain and then maintain his personal control of the country. As a body, the Central Committee was able to some extent to resist Ceauşescu's demands for revolutionary renewal through circulation and change in CC membership, but when turnover in this once powerful body increased to almost 50 percent in 1979 and 1984, the result was not more efficient and effective economic policies. Quite the contrary: Higher turnover (and therefore insecurity) in the Central Committee has been accompanied by economic deterioration.

One of Ceauşescu's most important political techniques has been the promotion of regional and county Party first secretaries into high positions. Their loyalty to him has been extremely important in maintaining his control, but they are for the most part Party generalists, skillful in organizing and mobilizing for extensive development, where growth depends on increasing inputs. They are not economic or technical specialists, who would be sophisticated analysts of production and distribution and who would have a better chance of moving the Romanian economy toward intensive development, where growth depends on quality, efficiency, and productivity. In addition, they themselves have been circulated more and more rapidly in recent years, again promoting Ceauşescu's political domination at the expense of economic efficiency and rationality.

This rapid circulation has also been a feature of the top political elite in the late 1970s and 1980s, with the insecurity introduced at the county and Central Committee levels also reaching the leading bodies of the RCP hierarchy. Nevertheless, the various groups have not been affected in the same way. Indeed, we can see a hierarcy of insecurity: Although cadres are rotated rapidly at all levels, the higher the level, the fewer individuals removed in disgrace.

These strategies of Ceauşescu toward the Romanian Communist Party and its officials have enabled him to retain power but not to accomplish many of the goals of a ruling Party. In his closing speech to the Twelfth Party Congress in 1979, he announced with great pride: "I must confess, comrades, that if I had not known the comrades who have spoken—and I'm sure we could all say the same—it would have been difficult to tell the president of a[n agricultural] cooperative from the academician. Indeed, our entire Party has risen to a high ideological and political level."[58] What Ceauşescu meant as high praise for the state of the Party we can interpret in another way: The Party had been leveled to such an extent that experts were reduced to mouthing platitudes and masking their knowledge. Of course, his statement was an exaggeration—a populist appeal to the rank and file Party members who attended the congress. But it does indicate the priority he gives to ideology rather than to expertise in promoting and retaining cadres.

As a result, Romania under Ceauşescu has become an example of arrested political development in which the political system has not developed the capacity to improve the economic situation. Instead, we see the deterioration of the economy as Ceauşescu has chosen to maintain his own priorities rather than listen to the advice of others and to promote those who are politically loyal rather than expert. Ironically, his attempts to preserve revolutionary spirit—to keep the Party a proletarian organization run by party loyalists—have preserved his own rule, but have precluded sustained movement toward the goals of the revolution.

9

From Hope to Despair: The Distortion of Participatory Democracy, National Equality, and Economic Growth

Two of the major features of Ceauşescu's rule in the 1970s and 1980s have been his personalization of power in the leadership cult (Chapter 7) and the rapid, often arbitrary, circulation of officials (Chapter 8). But during his first years as Party leader, he frequently called for open discussion and reform, the broad participation of citizens in decisionmaking, and the institutionalization of the political process (Chapter 4). Indeed, just as his general policy goals have always been rapid industrial growth and national independence, so has his rhetoric always emphasized the need to achieve these goals by legalized processes based on equity, efficiency, and participatory democracy.[1]

Chapter 6 demonstrated that by the end of the Tenth Party Congress in 1969, Ceauşescu had become the undisputed leader of Party and state. He enjoyed broad public support, based mainly on Romanian nationalism but also on popular expectations raised by his promises of personal security, higher living standards, and democratic reforms. At that time, he had the opportunity to give his authority a rational basis by implementing the promises and introducing balanced economic policies that compromised between his own goals of rapid development and the desires of most Romanians for higher living standards. Indeed, such policies would have been pragmatic, and Ceauşescu prides himself on his pragmatism. Instead, he adopted personnel techniques the success of which left him unchallenged (and unadvised), and he chose economic strategies that precluded widespread support. He attempted to paper over the gap between his policies and the hopes of the population with the false charisma of the leadership cult and also to manufacture a type of legal, if not rational, legitimacy by promoting his version of participatory democracy. Even when his participatory techniques became formalized and burdensome, evoking resentment and cynicism rather than support from the population, he continued to assert the legitimacy of his regime, but he abandoned any serious attempt to base his rule on popular support.

Ceauşescu's combined strategies proved disastrous for his relations with most of the population, but especially intense was the hostility of the ethnic minorities, unimpressed by his foreign policy successes. Ever suspicious of his intentions because of his role under Gheorghiu-Dej and his intense nationalism, these groups by the early 1970s were convinced (with considerable justification) that Ceauşescu was deliberately destroying their communities by political reorganizations, economic development policies, and educational reforms—and later, in the 1980s, with bulldozers. When the 1980s brought general economic disaster, the failure of his long-term economic strategies became clear to everyone except, seemingly, to Ceauşescu himself.

This chapter will examine the implementation of Ceauşescu's populist techniques of participatory democracy during the 1970s to see what happened to the promises that had raised such hopes in his first years as general secretary. In addition, we shall look at Ceauşescu's policies toward the national minorities as a measure of his commitment to equality and an example of his reactions to opposition. Finally, we shall discuss the economic difficulties that developed after 1979 and their impact on Romanian politics and Ceauşescu's techniques of rule.

Equity and Efficiency

Ceauşescu's search for authority in the 1960s included demands for legal processes based on equity and efficiency. This rhetoric continued throughout the next two decades of his rule, but the way most of these demands evolved in practice did not contribute to his popularity. For example, legality as used by Ceauşescu seemed at first to imply Party control over the Ministry of Internal Affairs (achieved in 1968), a result personally beneficial to the Party leader and also one that most Romanians applauded. But legality also seemed to mean institutionalized politics, based on parliamentary processes and broad participation of citizens in policy formation and implementation. These goals were always incompatible with Ceauşescu's personal power and his concept of Party rule, and thus these frequently repeated promises were not put into practice. In addition, however, by legality Ceauşescu also meant codifying procedures in dozens of sectors, such as cooperative agriculture, the trade unions, criminal justice procedures, the activity of the press, cultural affairs, and education. Changes took place, but in many cases the new legislation merely multiplied the rules regulating the behavior and invading the privacy of Romanian citizens, reducing rather than improving efficiency and leading many people to ignore them in practice.

Ceauşescu has also tried to tie remuneration closely to production, using equity as his justification but again with the goal of efficiency. However, because the links between work and reward have usually taken the form of penalties for failing to fulfill the plan (instead of rewards for satisfactory achievement) and because failure to fulfill production targets is often the fault of planners or suppliers rather than of the managers and workers who are held responsible, the penalties have neither improved efficiency or labor productivity nor been regarded as equitable.

Ceauşescu the self-styled pragmatist has again and again chosen impractical methods of implementation. His educational reforms, for example, have required "practical" economic applications for all courses of study and also for research; he has tried to tie both closely to the workplace, often by requiring apprenticeships for students, a method not appropriate for all types of education or production and not popular with pupils or the workers who must supervise them. In the name of equity, he has insisted that all secondary school graduates work for several years before admission to higher institutions of learning; neither the young people nor their parents have embraced the idea. He has provoked deep resentment in higher education as well by attempts to reduce "inefficiencies"—the elimination of overlap in faculties between the University of Bucharest and the Polytechnic Institute, for example—and although his plans have sometimes been diverted or delayed,[2] he has usually had his way in the end.

He has also used the stated goal of efficiency to justify unification of Party and state offices in one individual at many levels within the political structure, a far-reaching reorganization quite unusual within the socialist bloc. Ceauşescu once favored the opposite, of course—it worked in 1965 to force Drăghici from his post as minister of the interior—but he implemented the unification policy in 1967 and thereafter the top administrator at the level of county, city, town, or commune combined Party and state leadership in one person.[3] Ties between Party and state were extended further at the November 1972 Central Committee plenum, which announced that the Party secretary responsible for economic matters was to be elected vice-president of the People's Council and placed in charge of socioeconomic activity, including economic planning. The transfer of economic supervision from the Central Committee to Maurer's Council of Ministers mandated back in 1967 had been circumvented by the creation of the Economic Council under Manea Manescu, and in 1972 the economy was explicitly recognized as an area for joint Party-state control. Also in November 1972 it was announced that propaganda secretaries were to become vice-presidents of the People's Councils and would directly administer culture and education. Even the secretaries for labor problems were given state functions.[4] The major goals of the 1972 unification were described as simplification of procedures, improved coordination, and more effective leadership.[5] But it was also emphasized that "control of internal Party activity"—the selection of new members, verification of cadres, and the "custody and release of Party documents"—was to "remain the exclusive prerogative of the Party organs and apparatus."[6] None of Ceauşescu's plans for reorganization ever questioned the primacy of Party officials in the political process.

The desire for "improved coordination" and the "elimination of parallelism"—in short, the goal of efficiency—resulted in the creation of a large number of Party-state organs, including the Supreme Council of Economic and Social Development, the Defense Council, the Council of Socialist Culture and Education, and the National Council for Science and Technology, most of them presided over by Ceauşescu himself.[7] The unification of Party and state at specific points from top to bottom has been one of the most significant reorganizations to emerge in Romania under Ceauşescu because it has facilitated centralized control of all social and economic sectors. In addition, it has allowed the Party leader and president to reproduce himself at the county level in the county first secretaries and to exert his personal control through them.

Participatory Democracy

Before discussing Ceauşescu's participatory techniques, we must define what he does and does not mean by this term "participation" that he uses so often. Ceauşescu's concept places him squarely in the tradition of other Marxist-Leninist rulers, for "communist systems tend to be highly participatory,"[8] mobilizing citizens to take part and behave correctly in many types of activities, from the overtly political (voting) to what might be non-political in other systems (social clubs, or workers' councils, or even the family—the decision to have children). High levels of mobilized participation to engender and demonstrate loyalty to the regime and to improve policy implementation certainly have characterized Romania under Ceauşescu. In terms of the quality of participation, however, the situation is less clear. As used in the West, participation usually implies "efficacy, voluntarism, and responsiveness,"[9] and participation in communist systems often lacks these characteristics. However, as some analysts have argued persuasively, many types of participation by citizens in communist systems are indeed voluntary and do bring positive results for those individuals and also for the system.[10]

There are, of course, different types of participation, different degrees of voluntarism, and different measures of efficacy and regime responsiveness within any system at one time—and the situation can change considerably over time. Ceauşescu resembles any revolutionary leader, Marxist or non-Marxist, for whom "mass participation becomes . . . a technique for promoting rapid socioeconomic development, and a process of socialization through which citizens learn and internalize the norms of the future communist society."[11] This was indeed what he expected from the type of participation he was encouraging in the 1960s and 1970s. As modernization advances, however, what Donald Schulz has called the "participation crisis" occurs: "Previously, citizen involvement had been defined predominantly in terms of mobilization for the purpose of policy intelligence and implementation and political socialization and recruitment. Now, however, issues of autonomy, interest articulation, and even elite selection and accountability [arise]."[12] In other words, the nature and function of participation change as the system moves from the "mobilization" stage to the "inclusion" stage—in the words of Kenneth Jowitt, when "manipulation rather than domination becomes the defining relationship between regime and society."[13]

Certainly during the 1960s the Romanian regime under Ceauşescu and the collective leadership seemed to be shifting toward inclusion. As the term implies, the shift should bring participation of "previously excluded, distrusted sectors of the population" and "the admission of a wide range of social elites to consultative status in sociopolitical activities."[14] By 1971, however, Ceauşescu was becoming disillusioned with specialists because they told him what he did not want to hear about the economy and other issues. The functions that Ceauşescu wanted participation to fulfill remained policy implementation and political socialization. He wanted to encourage the specialized elites and other groups in society to help find ways to implement regime policies (and in doing so to develop a commitment to those policies), but he did not want voluntary and effective participation that could easily become "antisystemic or elite challenging" and begin to serve "policy input functions."[15]

As a result, Ceauşescu began to change his strategies of rule beginning in 1971, and thereafter his calls for participation—ambiguous in their content until then—were more clearly limited to the types of mobilized participation he had just seen in China and Korea. Indeed, his June 1971 Asian trip seems to have made several contributions to his concept of leadership. Although we cannot know for certain what happened, on his return he initiated his ideological campaign, intensified the cult, included his wife in his major public appearances, and began to retreat from inclusion back to mobilization[16]—from manipulation to coercion. His rhetorical commitment to participatory democracy would continue throughout his rule, but the implementation of that concept in Romania would bear little resemblance to the usual meaning of the term.

With these reservations in mind, we will now consider Ceauşescu's calls for greater participation from the Romanian population. His participatory reforms include at least three general categories: (1) increased "consultation" with interested groups at all levels but mostly in local decisionmaking; (2) a more important role for the Grand National Assembly and its committees in the formulation of legislation; and (3) the introduction of multi-candidate elections for the GNA and other legislative bodies.

Consultations

The term "consultation" is Ceauşescu's; like "participation," it connotes a concept intended to serve the functions of policy implementation and political socialization. One type of consultation, has been the holding of regular national conferences for workers in various sectors; these are usually preceded by extensive local discussions at meetings and in the press preparing for the huge congresses. At one of the first of these national meetings in 1966, Ceauşescu declared emphatically to construction workers that "the discussions . . . are part of our Party's current practice of conferring with the broad masses. . . . The participation of the masses in the solution of public matters . . . guarantees the strength of our system."[17]

Still other types of consultation were introduced. For example, Ceauşescu himself made hundreds of whistle-stop tours throughout the country, during which he always made a point of talking with ordinary citizens on the street as well as with local officials.[18] Romanian television instituted a regular program in which citizens' complaints were investigated and the official who had failed to pave a street or make repairs on a building was brought before the camera to explain his negligence; follow-ups several months later reported on what had or had not been accomplished, and officials were at times removed as a result of the inquiries.[19] Citizens' complaints and suggestions were published frequently in the press, and a statutory limit was placed on the length of time that any public organ could take to respond. The deadlines were not always observed, as Ceauşescu often complained, but each spring's Central Committee plenum began to receive a regular report on the ways in which citizens' grievances had or had not been resolved.

The consultative process was intended to involve political and economic policies at the local level as well. On political questions, the People's Councils were instructed to make extensive use of committees in order to involve citizens in political decisions; these committees could be standing committees on perennial problems such as housing construction, road maintenance, or beautification, or they could be *ad hoc* committees set up to deal with a specific new project such as a city hall or stadium.[20] On economic issues, committees were set up in enterprises with representatives from management, the Party, and the trade unions, as well as supervisors, specialists, and workers. Extensive consultation did occur at this level, but again the questions asked seemed to be limited to the ways by which the plan could be fulfilled.[21] Apparently these groups had no input into the plan itself, except as part of a formal report upward to the relevant bodies for consideration in formulating future requirements.

This, in fact, reflects the basic difficulty with these consultative procedures: As implemented, they rarely gave citizens that sense of efficacy and regime responsiveness that would make the effort of participation worthwhile. The huge congresses provided an opportunity for people to travel into Bucharest, eat well for a few days, and buy some scarce goods in the city. But the sessions were not forums for genuine discussion and participation; rather, they were opportunities for the ritualized worship of Ceauşescu as a manifestation of the new leadership cult. Ceauşescu's trips around the country became more of the same: He gradually insulated himself from any spontaneous contact with Romanian citizens and instead held mass meetings at which he could be cheered and worshiped. As a result, these forms of consultation ceased to be voluntary. Instead, they became coerced and formalized and produced cynicism and boredom.[22]

Legislative Activity: The Grand National Assembly

The second category of participatory reforms involved legislative activity, specifically by the Grand National Assembly. The constitution adopted in August 1965 had implied increased responsibility for the GNA.[23] Important state organs—the Council of State, the Council of Ministers, the Supreme Court, and the prosecutor general—were thereafter required to submit to it reports on their activity. A new Constitutional Commission was to be elected to "control the constitutionality of laws," presenting reports to the Assembly "at its own initiative" or at the request of other GNA bodies. Other standing commissions or "temporary commissions for any problem" were to be elected to report on bills or other matters, and reports on the work of these groups began to appear frequently in the press. Thus, this representative body was to be more important within the government, and individual deputies were to have a sense of participation in the drafting and preparation of legislation.

At the December 1967 Party conference, Ceauşescu called for still greater activity by the GNA. He indirectly criticized the Council of State by insisting that its practice of passing decrees as laws and only later submitting them to the Assembly for discussion must stop. "As a rule," he went on, "important normative acts [should be] passed as laws and discussed as such by the GNA." This would involve examination and discussion of proposed laws by the GNA's standing commissions, which not only should play a larger role in drafting laws but also should "hear reports presented by ministers . . . on the way laws are put into operation." To accomplish this, the Assembly would have to hold "open sessions of longer duration."[24]

In 1965 Ceauşescu had described the GNA as a major forum for discussion and participation.[25] His choice of words was significant: Policy formulation—the setting of political priorities—was to remain a Party function, highly centralized within a highly centralized hierarchy. The role of the GNA was limited to discussing the form of new legislation. Nevertheless, such legislation was henceforth to be enacted into law according to a constitutional, codified procedure rather than through the previous informal and arbitrary process, which had operated without regard to the constitution.

This emphasis on legality and the GNA was a constant feature of Ceauşescu's first decade as Party leader. In 1975 Ion Ceterchi, then president of the GNA Legislative Council and later minister of justice, singled out two significant changes that had occurred under Ceauşescu.[26] First was an increase in direct (as opposed to representative) democracy: As Ceterchi explained it, this meant the direct participation of the citizen in the political process, not the mere expression of satisfaction or dissatisfaction through a vote. He went on to mention as examples some of the "consultative" measures outlined in the previous section. The second change was a reversal in the relationship between the executive and legislative branches of government: In his opinion, the previous supremacy of the executive over the legislature was being reversed, and the GNA was becoming the superior organ. This was, of course, the official viewpoint in 1975 of someone working at the GNA, and over the next decade his optimistic predictions turned out to be totally wrong. Nevertheless, in 1975 he openly acknowledged that the GNA had previously functioned largely as rubber stamp of executive authority, and he seemed genuinely enthusiastic and hopeful that the status of the legislature was improving.

To show that the Grand National Assembly indeed was becoming a more powerful body, Ceterchi pointed first to the very existence of the Legislative Council, a GNA body that was created in November 1971 and started work in March 1972. Its role was mainly to advise on drafts of all normative laws (GNA) or decrees of the Council of State (which had to be approved by the GNA) to be sure there were no ambiguities or conflicts with existing law. In addition, the Legislative Council was to conduct studies of its own in order to modernize or eliminate contradictions in existing legislation and to point out the need for new laws. He also mentioned the various GNA commissions, whose meetings were frequently being reported in *Scînteia*. The most important of these was the Juridical-Constitutional Commission, formed in March 1975 out of two previous bodies. This group analyzed all proposed legislation, whereas the other commissions dealt only with legislation within their particular sectors.

His evidence was not very convincing, however. GNA sessions had not lengthened substantially by 1975 (and became even shorter thereafter), despite Ceauşescu's 1965 suggestion. The size of the body was reduced in 1975 from 465 to 349 (by 1985 it was 369) with the stated goal of increased discussion,[27] but at the GNA's July 1975 meeting, just after its membership had been reduced, the proceedings were even more of a formality than the Eleventh Party Congress had been the preceding fall. Motions were put and carried in rapid succession, with no time allowed for voices to be raised in opposition or abstention (although at least the questions were formally put to the floor). It is true that this was a time of extreme emergency in Romania, just after the peak of the 1975 floods, but a Central Committee meeting several days before had dealt at length with the recent catastrophe. The floods were not discussed by the Grand National Assembly at all.

During the GNA sessions the floods were mentioned, but it was explained that the CC proposals had not been available in time for analysis at this meeting. The floods were indeed discussed by the assembly in the fall, but clearly the GNA was expected merely to ratify decisions and actions taken elsewhere. Even in 1975, therefore, when the legislature was being encouraged to play a more important role in the political process, the response to the 1975 floods revealed the continuing precedence of the CC over the GNA, a superiority also reflected in terms of personal prestige: Membership in the Central Committee has always carried much greater honor and many more privileges than has election to the GNA.[28] Still another indicator of the lower status of GNA delegates has been their high turnover rate. Only 129 of the 349 delegates were re-elected from the previous legislature (37 percent), and 104 of these were important national figures whose prestige in no way depended upon GNA membership.

If, as seemed to be the case, the full meetings of the GNA in 1975 were still completely formal, with no discussion, then the formulation of legislation was being done elsewhere in advance of Assembly sessions. At the time, the process for proposing laws differed according to the initiator of the legislation, which could be any of the following: Party Central Committee; the Socialist Unity Front; the Bureau of the GNA; any group of 35 delegates (usually a commission); the Council of State; and the Council of Ministers. According to Ceterchi, legislation was most often initiated by the Council of Ministers, and the process had reportedly been much simplified in recent years. Previously, a law was first worked out by a group in a particular ministry; once signed there, it would be circulated to all other ministries for their approval or suggestions, which could take two to three months. After being rewritten and recirculated until all disagreements had been worked out, it would then be presented by the originating minister to the Council of Ministers, and any remaining disputes would be resolved at that level. By 1975, however, the original draft was worked out by a group in which all ministries and the GNA Legislative Council were represented, and the approval of those representatives was taken to signify approval of the ministry. Then it was presented to the Council of Ministers. All ministries still collaborated on the draft, but the cooperation was immediate and direct rather than written. Once the Council of Ministers approved the draft, it was submitted to the GNA, or to the Council of State if immediate action was necessary. In effect, this new procedure streamlined the process in accordance with Ceauşescu's often expressed desire, but it reduced the power of ministries to delay and even to block a piece of legislation.

If a body other than the Council of Ministers initiated a piece of legislation, the law was prepared by a group of specialists, then passed by the initiating body, and finally submitted to the Council of State or the GNA. Presumably this would be the procedure followed by the Party Central Committee or, as happened more frequently after 1975, by Ceauşescu and his presidential counselors. According to Romanian legislators in 1975, the Party was kept informed throughout the process, and it was always possible that the Party organ at the relevant level would change, approve, or disapprove specific legislation to ensure that it complied with Party policy. No outsider is privy to information on unpublished Party decisions, of course, and the relationship between the Party and the state is one aspect of the political process on which no Romanian will comment officially. But it was clear even in 1975 that the Party and often Ceaușescu remained the most important initiators of legislation. In fact, major departures from previous policies were usually initiated by Ceaușescu himself in a well-publicized speech, and legislation was often enacted without any apparent consideration given to its implications, implying that it had not emerged from a ministry or been carefully studied by legislators or a group of ministerial representatives. Indeed, legislation after the mid-1970s often appeared as a presidential decree, and only later was it approved by the Council of State and, eventually, the GNA. By the mid-1980s presidential decrees were a regular and frequent source of Romanian laws.[29]

Even so, the legislative process under Ceaușescu has put a number of important laws to public debate before enacting them in final form. Debate in newspapers and journals (articles, editorials, letters), on radio and television, and at public meetings produces suggested changes frequently incorporated into the final legislation. One early example of this method was the administrative-territorial reform of 1968, which was approved in preliminary form by the December 1967 Party conference, discussed throughout the country in January and February, and then passed with several adjustments based on those discussions. Of course, it is difficult to judge just how much of the discussion is spontaneous, but suggestions do not go unheeded. Again, the unspoken rule seems to be that discussion is allowed as long as the speaker expresses support for and gratitude to Ceaușescu and his wisdom and care in working out the new policy—and then proceeds to offer a suggestion as to how best to implement it.

Multi-Candidate Elections

Still another effort during the 1970s to demonstrate the democratic nature of the Romanian political process was the introduction of multi-candidate elections to the Grand National Assembly. In previous elections to state organs in Romania—the GNA and the People's Councils—the candidate for each district was nominated by the Socialist Unity Front and then elected by about 99 percent of the voters. In February 1971, however, Ceaușescu indicated that the electoral procedures should be improved to ensure "heightened responsibility" of candidates toward the masses. The first national elections after he made this suggestion were held in March 1975, and indeed almost 40 percent of GNA candidates and 76 percent of all candidates were opposed.[30] The somewhat limited information available on these 1975 elections includes the names and occupations of all candidates, press accounts of their nominations and of the electoral meetings held prior to the elections, the winner for each district, the total number of votes cast, the total number of votes for and against the list of candidates, and the number of null votes. Unfortunately, there are no totals available for each candidate, nor is there any way to determine how geographical or social groups within a district cast their ballots.

In 1975 there were 488 candidates for 349 seats in the GNA; members of the RCP Political Executive Committee were unopposed, and all were nominated and elected.[31] Of the 361 full and candidate members of the Central Committee, 173 were candidates for election to the GNA; 16 (about 9 percent) of these were opposed, and 6 of the 16 were defeated (only two by non-members, however, and only one of these seemed related to political grievances).[32] Hence comparatively few important political officials had to compete for re-election.

The Candidates. Nominations took place during a ten-day period beginning 3 February, just a month before the 9 March elections. Individuals were nominated by the Socialist Unity Front at public meetings in each electoral district. The candidates can be divided into three general groups: First were the officials holding important posts in the central Party and state organs (about 30 percent of those elected); at least one such candidate was nominated in each county, often with little or no formal connection to that county. (Indeed, many of the Central Committee members were elected to the CC from one county, and to the GNA from another.) These top officials were almost always unopposed and usually nominated first, along with the first secretary of the county Party organization. The county first secretaries were part of the second major group of candidates: those holding an important post in the county political structure, making up about 20 percent of the Assembly. These individuals did have important ties to their constituents, were among the first to be nominated in the county, and were usually not opposed by other candidates.

It is within the third group of candidates, just over 40 percent of the delegates, that the term "multi-candidate" election is applicable. These were local residents working in industry, agriculture, education, and other sectors of the economy. They tended to be nominated later than the others, and frequently two candidates ran for the same seat. When this happened, however, the two candidates usually came from the same occupational category—both were presidents of agricultural cooperatives, for example, or teachers, researchers, local Party or trade union secretaries, or directors or deputy directors in a particular sector of the economy such as machine building, petroleum products, or wood processing. Thus, a balanced composition was ensured for the GNA by opposing candidates with similar responsibilities. In fact, 96 of the 139 races—almost 70 percent—included candidates with exactly the same backgrounds in terms of economic sector, professional expertise, and level of responsibility. Even the proper ethnic and gender balance among the elected delegates was guaranteed: Candidates with Hungarian (or Romanian, or German) names ran against each other, and there seemed to be only three races in which a man and a woman were opponents. About 55 women were elected, and about 38 (almost 70 percent) ran against other candidates.[33]

The Elections. In the weeks between nomination and election, public meetings were held in the electoral districts. Usually both candidates appeared at the same meeting and spoke to their constituents to solicit votes. Because the candidates had been nominated by the Socialist Unity Front, both were considered fit to hold office: They had in some way made a major contribution to society and so were worthy of election. Consequently, both candidates supported the same platform, and the voters' decision was not meant to be based on issues but on personalities. As Romanian election officials explained,[34] "subjective" factors were decisive: Which candidate had the personal qualities to become a public figure and represent constituents in the parliament? This in fact was their explanation as to why top political leaders were not opposed—it would be "inappropriate" to nominate a candidate to oppose a major official. All candidates, they explained, were nominated locally, and usually the local officials decided that the candidate was so outstanding that no opponent was necessary. The same would be true for the first secretary in each county. It would not be appropriate, they argued, to nominate a candidate to run against such an eminent person. Who would wish to make such a nomination, and who would wish to run?

In electoral meetings, according to reports in the local press, all candidates tried to impress the voters with their sincerity and their ability to represent them effectively. The election officials asserted that because the "same program and means" were available to both candidates, the voters had to "sense tiny differences in nuance, in decisiveness, for example," and too often victory went to the person who was better known. In some cases, they said, this was "regrettable, but inevitable," probably a reference to the defeat of CC member and director of the national theater, classical actor Radu Beligan. Although well known, Beligan was opposed by Octavian Cotescu, a professor at the Institute of Theater and Cinematography, who had been involved in many movie and television comedies and therefore was more widely recognized and more popular.[35]

Skeptical Romanians had privately recognized this "regrettable" possibility in the summer of 1974 when the announcement was made that the following spring "more candidates will run for one seat [in the GNA], the citizens thus being afforded the possibility to elect those who demonstrate more competency, resourcefulness, energy, ardor and managerial skills, more firmness and responsibility in the implementation of Party policy."[36] Some citizens had asserted then that the quality of government would not be improved by multi-candidate elections because most voters would know neither of the individuals nominated and, even if they did, would favor one or the other for the wrong reasons. The Beligan case seemed to support the skeptics, but another result of the voting was much more significant in demonstrating voter apathy: Many people simply did not exercise their right to choose between the candidates, but merely turned in a ballot endorsing both.

Ceaușescu had an explanation for the voters' behavior. Soon after the elections he announced that "in *most* cases, the citizens preferred to vote for *both* candidates." His own public interpretation was that the voters "considered both candidates to have the necessary qualifications."[37] Romanian election officials in the summer of 1975 suggested an alternative interpretation—"disinterest"—noting that the failure to choose could result from either satisfaction or indifference, and it is impossible to distinguish between the two. (Even Ceaușescu apparently complained privately about "indecisiveness" after the election.) This failure to decide could indeed have resulted from the ignorance predicted before the elections; it could also have been a form of protest against the absence of choice based on concrete issues; or it could have resulted in part from the electoral procedures themselves.

When Romanian citizens appeared to vote, their names were checked off on the registration list, and they received ballots. They could then, as in the past, merely register a favorable vote by dropping the ballot into the ballot box. This constituted a vote in favor of both candidates; according to Ceaușescu, this is what most voters chose to do. But if they wished to vote against one candidate or the other (or for one or the other), they had to go into the voting booth, pull the curtain, and then cross out one name. Habit dies hard; going into the voting booth in previous years gave a clear signal—the voter was voting against the Party's candidate—and invited retribution. In this election, when citizens were encouraged to enter the booth to vote privately, the number of votes against all regime candidates jumped from 0.23 percent of the voters (30,748) in the previous elections of March 1969 to 1.2 percent (178,053) in 1975, not a serious opposition movement by any measure, but still almost a sixfold increase. Clearly, more voters felt free to vote against the regime under the new procedures, and this was regarded by Romanian officials as a serious problem. By 1985 the problem had not yet been solved, for in that year 2.27 percent of the vote went against Party candidates, a total of 356,573 voters.[38] Nevertheless, most voters still followed the previous routine of dropping their ballot openly into the box without marking it; they thus guarded against any suspicion that they had voted against the official candidates, but they also failed to exercise their right to choose.

The Implications. What can we learn from those first multi-candidate elections in Romania in the Ceaușescu era? First, they were not—and were not intended to be—multi-candidate elections in the Western sense; there was no difference between the candidates on substantive issues. Of course, some argue that this is frequently characteristic of elections in the United States, but that is because both candidates try to attract the political center, not because both are running on the same platform. In Romania, all candidates were nominated by the Socialist Unity Front with the approval of the RCP, and so their statements assumed support for official policies. In most cases, major political officials ran unopposed; thus citizens had no way to register discontent with the top leadership except by voting against all candidates. Often there was no real connection between the candidates and their constituents, although even major candidates were required at least to put in an appearance in their electoral district between nomination and election. Finally, the composition of the GNA was predetermined by the selection of candidates and their opponents within categories of occupation, ethnicity, and gender. The overall outcome of the elections was therefore assured by the carefully organized nomination process.

But there was a purpose for holding these elections. As in other Leninist parties, elections in Romania have certain unstated functions from the regime's point of view: training Party cadres in techniques of political mobilization, for example, educating them in the problems of their localities, and testing their ability to elicit certain types of behavior from citizens. The elections were thus intended to serve the traditional functions of mobilized participation by enhancing the loyalty of citizens to the regime and improving policy implementation. If the citizens could be convinced that they had gained real input into the political system or that the quality of political officials was improved by multi-candidate elections, or if the delegates felt a heightened sense of responsibility to their constituents, then the elections would have served a valuable function. However, Ceauşescu did not really expect such results. The nomination procedures allowed controlled discussion but no real choice for the electorate. The result was a high number of unmarked ballots, revealing the legacy of suspicion on the part of voters from previous elections and their boredom and resentment at the new system. Most people did not overtly defy the regime by refusing to vote or by voting against the official candidates; citizens turned out in overwhelming numbers, demonstrating the Party's ability to elicit obedience, and although protests tripled, the total number was miniscule. Nevertheless, the population did show indifference by refusing to choose between candidates who essentially represented no choice.

The widespread apathy shown at the polls in 1975, had another source, however: the general sense of disenchantment that was already making itself felt in Romania. The summer of 1974 had been a time of relatively high optimism, perhaps the highest since the late 1960s. Romanians were hoping for a major reorientation in political and economic priorities at the Eleventh Party Congress in November. Not only were the multi-candidate elections announced, but there were also promises of increased incomes and shorter working hours. The proposed rotation of CC members, under which at least one-third would be newly elected at each Party congress, excited even some of the usual skeptics. But the congress never voted on this last proposal; most devastating, the long-range economic directives passed by the congress made it clear that a shift in economic priorities would not occur. Disillusionment set in.

A number of other reforms negatively affected the status of particular groups within the society. The 1974 press law was followed by the paper crisis. Writers were no longer allowed to live on their royalties, but were required to meet annual publication quotas. Work norms were increased in some industries to impossible levels, in effect reducing the minimum wage that had officially been raised. At the same time, a number of laws were passed (many of them initially introduced as presidential decrees) restricting contact with foreigners. A variety of events therefore combined to dishearten Romanian voters just before those first multi-candidate elections and lessened any positive impact they might have had.

Romanian political scientists often complained in the 1970s about the low level of political responsibility in their country, explaining that because Romanian citizens still had to be educated into democracy, the leadership cult and the carefully controlled electoral process were necessary. Romanian political culture certainly has been an important element in the failure of multi-candidate elections in Romania: Not only does no strong tradition of active political participation exist, but citizens harbor resentment of political authority and a cynicism about electoral processes. Ceauşescu has emerged from this political culture as well, yet he and his colleagues chose procedures that helped to reinforce rather than overcome these tendencies. Like the forms of consultation, which gradually became routinized and formalized, the elections—even with more than one candidate for some seats—failed to give citizens the promised role in "elite selection and accountability" characteristic of post-mobilization participation. Although many had remained skeptical throughout, the hopes of others were raised and then dashed, and they responded with renewed doubt and indifference. Ceauşescu had avoided the "participation crisis" by turning back the clock; he continued to advocate participation—but only in the very limited sense characteristic of mobilization regimes.[39]

Growing Tension, 1975–1980: National Inequality

If it was difficult by the late 1970s to convince many ethnic Romanians that support for Ceauşescu and his policies was justified in the name of equity, efficiency, or participatory democracy, it was impossible to convince the ethnic minorities. Many did not regard equality with Romanians as equitable;

indeed previously advantaged groups such as the Hungarians felt Ceauşescu's stress on national equality was camouflage for persecution. They saw him in the name of efficiency reducing and even eliminating facilities linked to their special linguistic needs, and they ridiculed his participatory democracy, regarded as a sham even by ethnic Romanians. The major area of success for Ceauşescu had always been foreign policy. His overtures to the United States and Western Europe, his activism in the Third World, and his maverick status within the socialist bloc had all contributed to the national pride of Romanians and enhanced his personal stature at home. But national pride did nothing for Romanian citizens who did not define themselves as Romanian.

The disaffection had not always been so strong. A major feature of the first years of his rule had been his overtures to the other nationalities to join in bringing a better life to all citizens of socialist Romania. Beginning in 1975, however, a number of circumstances combined to exacerbate the underlying tension between the regime and the non-Romanian ethnic groups just as many ethnic Romanians were becoming disillusioned with Ceauşescu. The Helsinki agreements of 1975 that linked economic credits and trade to observance of human rights raised hopes throughout Eastern Europe and in the West that the socialist governments would ease restrictions on emigration, communication, and visits, raise living standards, and allow more intellectual freedom. These hopes were quickly dashed in the case of Romania, although the government did ease emigration for the German and Jewish minorities (in return for payments by the West German and Israeli governments). Meanwhile, the Hungarian government had produced considerably higher living standards for its population, in part through economic reforms and Soviet subsidies; for the first time Hungary, like West Germany and Israel, could attract the envy of co-nationals inside Romania. Hungarians in Romania thus began to feel a sense of relative deprivation; they compared themselves with their kin across the border in Hungary, not with other Romanian citizens, and the comparison left them intensely dissatisfied. As a result, the late 1970s saw increasingly open resentment among the Hungarians and other minorities in Romania.

Ceauşescu faced a number of internal challenges in the late 1970s, though none of them seriously threatened his continued control of the political system. A small number of Romanian intellectuals criticized the regime and were imprisoned during 1977, including the writer Paul Goma and the historian Vlad Georgescu, both of whom eventually emigrated to the West. A severe earthquake in March brought economic dislocation in Bucharest and elsewhere, and the intensified pace of the 1976–1980 plan drove 35,000 miners to strike in the Jiu Valley in August. In early 1978 protests by an ethnic Hungarian became public: Károly Király, who had resigned as a candidate member of the RCP Executive Committee and head of Covasna County in 1972 for "personal reasons," revealed that he had actually resigned in order to protest regime policies discriminating against ethnic

Hungarians. He had written a number of letters to high Romanian officials, and finally some of his letters had reached the West.[40] There were also several religious protests in 1978 and 1979, sometimes associated with ethnic groups because religion and nationality in Romania are closely linked. Then in 1979 several thousand workers in Bucharest and elsewhere tried to form an independent trade union movement. As Vlad Georgescu described the situation: "The period from the Helsinki Accords in 1975 until 1980 seems to have been rich in outspoken protests and attempts at creating an institutionalized human rights movement. But the different individuals or groups—workers, intellectuals, minorities, and religious activists—acted separately, and with no attempt to create a united front." He perhaps exaggerates the extent and frequency of any overt protests, but is quite accurate in assessing the responses: The police therefore had no difficulty in suppressing "one by one, with a mixture of diplomacy and toughness, these isolated attempts to challenge the established order."[41]

There was even some direct criticism of Ceauşescu at the Twelfth Party Congress in November 1979. Constantin Pârvulescu, the founding member of the RCP who had preceded Gheorghiu-Dej as general secretary, was given the floor by Ceauşescu near the end of the congress when he complained he had not received permission to speak. At age 84, Pârvulescu then delivered the first open attack against Ceauşescu at an RCP congress. His speech was not included in published reports of the proceedings, but according to foreign observers and sequences shown on West German television, he "accused the secretary-general of putting his personal interests before those of the country, attacked the congress as passing over the country's problems while devoting its energies to promoting Ceauşescu's re-election, and declared that he would not vote for the secretary-general." Evidently there were attempts to drown him out with pro-Ceauşescu chants, and he was accused of not understanding the situation in Romania because he had spent so much time "abroad"—meaning, of course, in the USSR. Ceauşescu picked up this theme and accused Pârvulescu of wanting to return to the days when Romania's fate was decided "abroad." His credentials as a delegate were then revoked so that Ceauşescu could be re-elected unanimously.[42]

The interference of foreigners was not a new theme. Ceauşescu had been using the widespread anti-Soviet feeling in Romania as a support for his rule since 1965 and in 1971 had even warned the Hungarian government not to interfere in Romanian affairs. But after the Király incident in 1978 and the Pârvulescu embarrassment in 1979, the theme of foreign governments using traitors inside Romania appeared in Ceauşescu's rhetoric more and more frequently. It was, of course, a way of denying that genuine cause for protest existed in Romania; those who complained were themselves traitors sowing discontent. As economic conditions deteriorated in the 1980s, many members of the ethnic minorities, particularly the Hungarians, blamed the Romanian government (and Romanians in general) and interpreted the deterioration in their status as deliberate discrimination. The events of the late 1970s and early 1980s, instead of uniting the various ethnic groups in joint antipathy toward Ceauşescu and his policies, intensified their hostility toward each other, as all Romanian citizens vied among themselves for scarce resources.

The polarity also has spread abroad. Hungarian groups in Western Europe and the United States have accused the Bucharest government of systematic persecution of ethnic Hungarians and violations of their human rights and have testified repeatedly in Washington against Romania's most-favored-nation trade status. In contrast, Romanians in the West have risen to the defense of Ceauşescu's nationality policy, regardless of their attitude toward his other strategies.

In the early years of his rule, Ceauşescu's nationalism did not seem to contradict equality among the nationalities in Romania. As Kenneth Jowitt has observed: "Under Ceauşescu there has been an ideological acceptance of the nation as opposed to a simple political manipulation of it."[43] The problem has been that Ceauşescu does not recognize the minorities as belonging to other nations; instead he claims that because a nation is created by centuries of "living together," the Hungarians, Germans, Serbs, and other groups are actually part of the Romanian nation. Thus he sees no potential contradiction between Romanian nationalism and the needs of the nationalities.

According to Ceauşescu, the nation is a "necessary and obligatory" form of human community at a certain "stage in the evolution of all peoples," and dozens of nations still have a "long road to full development."[44] His emphasis on international recognition of Romania as a "developing" country during the 1970s was motivated not only by the economic benefits (aid and credits) to be gained but also by the ideological justification for nationalism and national independence, which are "obligatory" at this stage of development. Throughout the Ceauşescu era, Romanian theorists have examined the international system from the viewpoint of the class struggle and the dialectic, but their analyses differ radically from those of most theorists in the Soviet bloc. For example, Aurel Brucan postulates the existence of two "essential forms of human aggregation"—classes and ethnic communities—and asserts that modern history has been distinguished by a dialectic higher than the class struggle, "the seesaw of class and national motive forces in international politics." Classes, nations, and states, he argues, will "eventually disappear," but he does not anticipate global integration until "a very distant future (perhaps the late twenty-first century)."[45]

Such theories justify Ceauşescu's overall stress on the importance of the nation; they also support a number of his specific initiatives in foreign policy, including his call for the dissolution of all military blocs, his rejection of further regional integration, and his insistence on ideological diversity among nations. But he has never been willing to extend ideological diversity to domestic Romanian politics. The RCP's monopoly of power and Ceauşescu's periodic tendencies to lapse into xenophobia have always made the national minorities in Romania somewhat uneasy about his real intentions toward them, no matter what his rhetoric. Only nations, in Ceauşescu's view, have the right to sovereignty and independence. Nevertheless, he does recognize a nationality as a historical form of human community with national characteristics: The 1974 Party program stated that the nationalities in Romania would "continue to exist for a long time, both in the period of socialist construction and in that of communist construction."[46]

RCP Nationality Policies Before 1970

According to Romanian sources, national minorities make up less than 11 percent of the population.[47] The various groups are geographically dispersed and diverse in socioeconomic background, reflecting the complex history of the region. Their dispersed locations for the most part preclude territorial autonomy as an effective strategy,[48] and the possibility of cultural autonomy is preempted by the RCP demand for a monopoly in cultural affairs. The two largest linguistic groups, the Hungarians and the Germans, were for centuries granted special privileges by the Austro-Hungarian empire, and as late as 1966 had a higher average level of urbanization and education than did the ethnic Romanian population.[49] However, other minorities such as the Serbs and Ukrainians have not enjoyed such favored status, and even many Hungarians live in less-industrialized sections of the country, such as the counties of Sălaj and Covasna.[50]

When the RCP came to power after World War II, its first attempt to deal with the Hungarian minority was modeled on Soviet practice; an autonomous region was established, and officials "from Bucharest, Moscow and Budapest allegedly poured into the . . . region . . . to make it a kind of show-piece."[51] Unrest among the Hungarians in Transylvania during the 1956 Budapest uprising evidently indicated to the Bucharest regime that autonomy had not succeeded in gaining the loyalty of this group, and during the late 1950s assimilationist tendencies appeared in directives from Bucharest. For example, the Romanian and Hungarian universities in Cluj were merged in 1959—at a meeting over which Ceauşescu himself presided.[52] Although the Hungarians did retain the right to study in their own special sections within each faculty and classes and exams were conducted in Hungarian, losing the separate institution came as a blow (and its rector eventually committed suicide as a result). Fears intensified still further in 1960 when boundary changes increased the proportion of Romanians in the Hungarian Autonomous Region—in a territorial reorganization presided over by Ceauşescu.[53]

Of course, the years from 1958 to 1961 reflected a general tightening of the political situation in Romania that affected the entire population, and not just the minority groups. In 1958, for example, the Party began its attempt at rapid industrialization, and the final campaign to collectivize agriculture was completed in 1960 and 1961. In 1962 the situation began to ease as the RCP made a concerted effort to increase domestic support. The attempts at ethnic assimilation continued throughout the 1960s—but characterized by inducement rather than by coercion.

The new constitution in 1965 listed the Hungarian Autonomous Region (along with the other regions) with no special provisions for its autonomy, but continued to guarantee to the minorities education in their mother tongue and use of their language in political organs and cultural institutions. At the same time, the new Party statutes encouraged minorities to join the RCP.[54] Thus in the first months after Ceauşescu became Party leader, steps were taken to lessen the legal separation between the Hungarian and Romanian ethnic groups.

This policy of induced participation continued in 1967 and 1968 as Ceauşescu's rhetorical concern for the nationalities became more pronounced. The administrative-territorial reform discussed at the December 1967 Party conference aroused some uneasiness within the minority communities; the Hungarians managed to effect some changes that reversed the boundary shifts of 1960 and created two Hungarian counties, Harghita and Covasna. At the same time, Ceauşescu named both of these counties among those he singled out for higher investment under the current five-year plan.[55] Radio and television news broadcasts inevitably noted the friendship and cooperation of the Romanians, Hungarians, and other ethnic groups in the development of their common homeland, the Romanian Socialist Republic. And in his visits to outlying regions, Ceauşescu gave priority to areas of minority concentration.[56]

Conciliation of the minorities continued to be a major theme in 1968. In contrast to the 1956 intervention in Hungary, the Warsaw Pact move into Czechoslovakia tended to reduce tension among ethnic groups inside Romania as they all faced a common threat: the Soviet Union. Nevertheless, Ceauşescu took no chances, going immediately to major centers of the nationalities, responding publicly to unstated complaints, and promising major economic projects to improve living standards.[57] Soon after, the nationality councils were created,[58] and assigned two specific tasks: (1) the "cultivation of socialist patriotism" for every inhabitant of the RSR, regardless of nationality; and (2) resolving the specific problems of each nationality. Each council was to operate under the direct supervision of the Central Committee Secretariat, and its operating funds would come out of the CC budget.[59] Thus the councils, in no way autonomous, were charged with promoting the unity of the RSR as well as minority culture. As was the case with Ceauşescu's other participatory techniques, their functions were to be policy implementation and political socialization. Conciliation did not mean capitulation.

The 1970s and After

Ceauşescu's rhetorical concern for the nationalities has continued, but their status gradually deteriorated in the 1970s.[60] Their formal participation in Party and state bodies remained roughly proportional to their share in the total population until the 1980s, but their share in the CC dropped in 1984 and Ceauşescu has stopped giving the figures on Party membership. They were heavily represented in the Gheorghiu-Dej Political Bureau, and the Political Executive Committee had a number of minority members until the mid-1980s, by which time their representation had largely disappeared. Of course, participation in political organs does not guarantee ability to influence policy (as ethnic Romanians have discovered), and nationality does not necessarily indicate an individual's policy priorities: Hungarians need not speak for the interests of their own ethnic group. But at least during the 1970s Ceauşescu insisted on their presence. Their gradual elimination from public life and Party leadership does not bode well for their future under him.

The economic position of the nationalities in Romania is less clear than their political status. No income data are available by nationality, so comparison of county statistics in regions of Romanian and minority habitation must suffice. Although Hungarians form a large portion of the population in some less developed areas, the poorest counties are inhabited mostly by ethnic Romanians. In the late 1960s the national minorities clearly were concentrated in the more advanced areas of the country, whether defined in economic or sociocultural terms.[61] In the decade from 1965 to 1975, the Hungarian counties did not appear to be deprived economically; all showed above average growth in gross industrial production and most were above average in investment and per capita sales. By contrast, 1976 to 1979 investment figures—given the context of Ceauşescu's systematization campaign to distribute production more equally throughout Romania—gave cause for justified Hungarian alarm; not one of the major Hungarian counties was above the RSR average in per capita investment.[62] Instead, the big recipients of investment were the port facilities along the Danube and their related industries, the mineral areas of the Jiu Valley, and the traditional industrial regions of Bucharest and the Prahova Valley, including Braşov. (The Danube and Jiu Valley are areas of mixed nationality, but not mainly Hungarian.) Although the economic picture remains ambiguous—the poorest Romanian counties also ranked low, along with the Hungarian regions—only one county (Maramureş) of the ten counties singled out in the 1981—1985 plan for special efforts in economic and social development had a significant Hungarian population. In Romania, as in Yugoslavia, ethnic tensions are heightened by resentment over economic allocations, and the hostility is intensified when a smaller ethnic group believes that its very existence is being threatened by regime policies.

Cultural and educational policies also create difficulties on all sides.[63] The nationalities still have the constitutional right to education in their own languages, but enjoying this right is difficult outside areas of minority concentration. Also, there has been strong pressure to learn Romanian for purposes of upward mobility. In fact, the Romanians define bilingualism as a characteristic of the nationalities and require the study of Romanian as a second language. The merger of minority institutions with their Romanian counterparts, such as the universities in Cluj, has caused intense resentment. However, it has been possible for members of the national minorities to receive education in their own languages if they lived where there was sufficient demand for elementary and secondary school classes (and the minimum number of students has increased significantly over time), and if they could make a career in the special cultural facilities provided to these groups, as teachers of language or literature, for example, or as journalists or actors. The numbers of places provided in the universities for such specialties is not large, however, and the financial rewards not high.

Members of a national minority who live outside an area of minority concentration, who fail to gain entrance to specialized institutes, or who choose careers in the prestigious and high-paying natural sciences or engineering find it essential to become fluent in Romanian. Ceauşescu himself argued that "we cannot set up special institutes of physics, chemistry, or other specialities for young people who do not know Romanian." Persons who fail to learn Romanian will be "in a position of inequality compared to Romanian young people" because they will not have "free access to all the forms of higher education." He then insisted that "Romanian is not a foreign language to any youth living in Romania! It is the language of our socialist society and it must be learned by all Romanian citizens."[64]

Although Romanian census data may be of questionable accuracy, the general pattern between the 1966 census and that of 1977 was an increase in the Romanian population and a decrease in minorities in every county, in both real and proportional terms.[65] The major exception was an increase in the number of Hungarians in Covasna, Harghita, and Mureş, but even in these counties the Romanian population rose more than the Hungarian, both absolutely and proportionately.[66] Emigration accounts for much of the decrease in the German and Jewish minorities and for some of the change in other groups, but a major role was played by assimilation, a process due in part to the overwhelming numerical superiority of ethnic Romanians in the population, but also to regime reinforcement of trends inherent in the economic development process.

For example, all university graduates were assigned to jobs where they had to remain for several years after graduation. The assignments were usually made without regard to ethnicity (or, at least in some cases, were deliberately manipulated[67]), so minority graduates were sent to Romanian areas at a time when they were likely to marry (or, more likely, to intermarry). A similar process occurred when a specialist was transferred from one enterprise to another: A Hungarian engineer in Transylvania might be offered a job in another part of the country and given sufficient economic inducements to go;[68] the attempt to equalize the level of industrialization throughout the country tended to disperse ethnic groups and result in assimilation. Another factor encouraging assimilation during the 1970s was the prestige and economic reward of careers in science, which demanded fluent Romanian and international skills such as mathematics, not linked to language. Thus, compliance with Party policy for whatever reason reduced the vitality and cohesion of the smaller ethnic communities within Romania as the professional skills of young people drew them away from their separate communities and weakened their ethnic identity.

This process of assimilation provoked little overt resistance as long as the Romanian economy continued to perform well. There was no doubt that the nationalities had grievances. They were inevitably at a disadvantage compared with those whose first language was Romanian. As one thoughtful Hungarian citizen of Romania explained sadly: "No member of a national minority can ever be 'equal' to someone whose mother tongue is the dominant language."[69] After all, even if 20 percent of the titles in Romania were published in Hungarian, ethnic Romanians would have four times the number of books available in their mother tongue than the Hungarians. This, of course, made Ceauşescu's policies of cultural isolation in the 1980s much harder on the minorities than on the ethnic Romanians. Official policies demanding equality could do little to prevent discrimination by impatient sales personnel or petty government employees. And humiliating symbols remained of the Romanians' triumph at the end of World War I, when they finally achieved control of Transylvania; the Romanian theater in Cluj, for example, was established in the elegant old edifice that was the Hungarian theater until 1920, whereas the Hungarians were given an ugly modern structure. These grievances stayed in the background, however, as long as the overall economic picture seemed positive.

The deterioration of living standards, which never fully recovered from the 1977 earthquake and dropped sharply after 1979, evidently increased the resentment of many ethnic Romanians—who with Ceauşescu's encouragement saw the minorities either as traitors or as potential scapegoats—and intensified the hostility of the minorities, who saw themselves as persecuted and excluded even from the president's rhetorical commitment to participation and equality. Ceauşescu's retreat into economic isolation after 1980 would reinforce his own xenophobic tendencies and make him less dependent on the good will of those foreign governments that might have persuaded him to moderate his policies toward their co-nationals inside Romania.

Ceauşescu's Views of Equality

Ceauşescu's policies toward the nationalities reflect a combination of egalitarianism and elitism, idealism and pragmatism, in ways that have characterized communist leaders since Lenin. As an old revolutionary from the illegal prewar days, Ceauşescu has egalitarian tendencies, at least in the way *he* defines equality. As a Party organizer from the late 1940s, he also believes in the need for an elite and highly centralized organization to bring about the socialist development of Romania. He may alternate his distributive emphasis between equality and reward for performance (usually he calls the latter equity and implies that equity and equality are compatible), but he is consistent in his view that all individuals must cooperate fully in furthering the economic strategies of the RCP.

He repeatedly points out in his speeches that it is the duty of all Romanian citizens, regardless of gender, occupation, or nationality, to contribute to the economy. Women must work full time outside the home, but also must accept the double burden of their special function: bearing and rearing children. Intellectuals must not only do their own work, but also must educate and inspire other Romanians to improve their contribution to society. The double burden of the nationalities is to become bilingual so that they can participate in the fulfillment of Party and state goals. Individuals have the duty to contribute equally—that is, as much as their full effort can produce. If they do so, he has been willing to allow for their special economic and cultural needs as long as the cost does not detract too much from his development funds. Just as his priorities precluded the cost of facilities to lighten women's double burden by producing sufficient consumer items and childcare facilities, so too did his objectives bar sufficient cultural and educational opportunities in minority languages to attract the loyalty of the smaller ethnic groups. In Ceauşescu's view, these sacrifices were necessary in the name of socialist Romania.[70] Not many Romanian citizens, regardless of ethnic origins, would agree with him.

Still another consideration in defining national equality involves the distinction between individual equality and group equality. One unfortunate aspect of the current situation is that the group rights to political and cultural autonomy now sought by the Hungarian minority from the Romanian government are precisely the rights Budapest refused to grant to Romanians in Transylvania a century ago. In each case the existing government offered full legal equality to all individuals as citizens of the larger political entity, Hungary before 1918 or the Romanian Socialist Republic today. In both cases it was the group right of nationality that the non-ruling group perceived to be threatened. In 1869 a group of Romanian intellectuals voted to boycott the upcoming elections to the Hungarian parliament; they were permitted to vote as individuals, but were guaranteed no rights as a nation. One Romanian argued that the Hungarians "offered civil liberties as the price of nationality."[71] This distinction between individual and group rights is crucial when nationality is at issue, for language, culture, and often religion are involved, and all require unrestricted activity within a group or community. Individual members of that group regard autonomy—insulation from the outside world to preserve the special interaction of the group—as a prerequisite to individual rights.

Today an individual Hungarian, like any citizen of the RSR, enjoys formal legal rights under the RSR constitution. Of course, such rights mean very little in contemporary Romania under the personal rule of Ceauşescu and the political monopoly of the Romanian Communist Party. This situation threatens the individual rights of all Romanian citizens, regardless of ethnic background, but by refusing to accept the need for group autonomy, Ceauşescu and the RCP present a special threat to the group rights of the nationalities. "Nationality rights . . . are essentially collective rights, and do not exist in any other way, because the nationality is a form of communal existence. The restriction of these collective rights to individual rights meant practically the deprivation of the nationalities of any rights."[72] This lament of a Hungarian in Transylvania describing the 1950s could as well be a Romanian complaint from the preceding century. In both cases the stress on individual rights seems eminently fair to the rulers—and totally unacceptable to the ruled. National autonomy, the minority would argue, is a prerequisite for national and individual equality, but Ceauşescu would never accept such freedom for nationalities in Romania.

After 1980 Ceauşescu's suspicion of foreigners and their intentions grew dramatically. Simultaneously, his commitment to expenditures for cultural and educational facilities for the nationalities declined, as did his willingness to include them in the political process or in the rewards of the economy. Signs of these tendencies had appeared during the 1970s, but it was only in the 1980s that his change in attitude became clear. As economic conditions in Romania deteriorated, what had begun in the 1970s as complaints by Hungarians inside Romania (picked up and publicized by Hungarians and human rights groups in the West) emerged during the early 1980s as protests by cultural figures inside Hungary, especially over the destruction and resettlement of villages involved in the systematization campaign to redistribute economic resources more "equally" throughout the country. Hungarian government officials, in contrast, remained publicly silent on the issue, evidently in the name of bloc solidarity, and tried to improve the situation for the Transylvanian Hungarians through quiet diplomacy. They had had little success when, in December 1986, the Hungarian Academy published a three-volume history of Transylvania that drew angry responses from Romanians because it denied the continuity of the Romanian presence in Transylvania and therefore the legitimacy of Romanian possession of the area. When Gorbachev visited Romania in May 1987, he lectured Ceauşescu on the need for a "Leninist" policy toward nationalities, and during June the

Soviets attempted unsuccessfully to find a solution acceptable to both Bucharest and Budapest. By early 1988, in the wake of anti-Romanian demonstrations in Budapest, Warsaw, and Prague, as well as Hungarian leniency toward Romanian tourists who overstayed their visas and/or requested asylum, Romania rejected proposals from Hungary to resolve the dispute. By May the Hungarian press was publicly accusing Romania of trying to erase the Hungarian heritage in Transylvania by the razing of villages. Finally, in August the new Hungarian leader, Károly Grosz, met with Ceauşescu in Arad, Romania, near the Hungarian border, but his inability to extract any compromises from the Romanian leader on major issues produced temporary difficulties for his own government.[73]

Ceauşescu, of course, implied that the entire series of events was a Soviet conspiracy to use Hungarian traitors as an excuse to interfere in Romania, and he therefore refused any compromises on what he insisted were internal affairs. His concept of equality provided little help for Hungarians in Romania who considered group rights a prerequisite to equal treatment, and his reaction to the criticism and opposition of his neighbors was anger and a hardening of his position. This was not unusual behavior for Ceauşescu by this time: During the 1980s he had become increasingly frustrated with ethnic Romanians for failing to fulfill his goals for Romania. He had turned hostile toward foreign governments and banks for daring to make suggestions about Romania's economic strategies. He had grown angry with women for failing to have enough children and so pushed the campaign against abortions to extreme measures. And he had allowed his hostility toward the ethnic minorities to develop into overt xenophobia. What had happened to Romania to offset the successes of the 1960s and 1970s and produce such a disastrous situation?

Deterioration and Stalemate: The 1980s

After 1979 Romania entered a period of severe economic difficulties. Although the underlying causes were much deeper, the initial sign of crisis was a shortage of hard currency resulting apparently from structural imbalances in the international petroleum market.[74] Because of their oil resources, the Romanians had long specialized in petroleum-related products and had developed a major refining capacity. As the needs of their domestic industries grew, they began in the late 1960s to import larger and larger quantities of oil. The 1973–1974 rise in international oil prices was not disastrous because the price of Romanian exports—refined products—also went up. The Romanians failed to protect themselves from further increases, however, and in 1978, when the price of crude oil jumped again, the value of refined products did not. The Romanians were caught in a price squeeze. Then their supply problems were worsened first by the Iranian revolution (Ceauşescu had worked out a favorable barter arrangement with the Shah) and later by the Iran-Iraq war. By the 1980s the Romanians were buying oil even from the Soviet Union, though evidently they have had to pay in hard currency or equivalents.

By 1981 the previously rather self-sufficient Romanian economy was seriously in debt to Western banks. Although initially stimulated by the unfavorable balance in oil trade,[75] this debt also had roots in unwise investment decisions of the 1960s and 1970s. Indeed, two crucial economic decisions—to invest heavily in petroleum and petro-chemical products and to minimize cooperation in Comecon—increased the country's dependency on hard currency imports of technology and raw materials, and the cost of these imports together reached unprecedented levels about 1980. As Marvin Jackson has demonstrated, the "serious deterioration" of Romanian economic indicators did not begin until that year. In 1980 Romania's debt-service ratio was better than that of Hungary or Bulgaria, its ratio of convertible currency debts to convertible currency exports was lower than that of Hungary, the GDR, or Yugoslavia, and its debts per capita were a third less than in any of those three countries.[76]

Then in 1981 Poland's potential default (for somewhat different reasons—the Poles in contrast to the Romanians had borrowed heavily in the early 1970s) created among Western bankers a crisis of confidence in all the East European economies. Romania was particularly affected; the country found it much more difficult to obtain extensions on its loans than did neighbors such as Hungary or Yugoslavia—perhaps, as Marvin Jackson suggests, because the banks lacked confidence in the Romanians due to their excessive secrecy, restrictions on contacts with foreigners, and erratic leadership.[77] Ceauşescu at this time seemed unable to call on his usual negotiating skills to help the crisis, in part because the policies now causing difficulty were so closely associated with him personally. Unable to accept any blame himself, he began to blame the international environment—greedy foreign banks, capitalists, and other enemies—and to seek internal scapegoats. His responses did not inspire confidence in Western financial circles.

Simultaneously, Romanian agriculture, which had in the past been a source of exports and so might have helped the balance of payments, was falling short of its production goals, the result partly of several years of bad weather and partly of long-term structural problems that reached crisis proportions only after 1979. Romanian agriculture had been long neglected in favor of industry, but the country's rich soil, favorable climate, and large (though inefficient) agricultural labor force nevertheless had continued to feed the population and produce a surplus for export. However, the economy was structured to encourage labor to move into industry and left little incentive for the ever-shrinking agricultural work force to raise productivity. Those who remained in villages tended to be old, less qualified, or tied to their homes by children. Although after 1970 investment in agriculture increased substantially, it was too rapid to be efficiently utilized, and 1979 brought major shortfalls in planned production for internal and external markets.[78]

The international structure of oil prices improved in 1981 and 1982 and eased the hard currency crisis somewhat for the Romanians, but for the most part, Ceauşescu evened the balance of payments in the same way that he found investment funds: by reducing imports, depressing the domestic standard of living still further, and exporting consumer goods and agricultural products.[79] There were reports of food shortages throughout 1981, and by 1982 Romanians in Bucharest were complaining that food supplies were scarcer than they had been since World War II. Prices of available foods seemed to have tripled in just over a year.[80] Restaurants were empty because what little food was available was not worth the price. Even the peasant markets with supplies from private plots were often empty. Bread, sugar, and oil were rationed, eggs would disappear for weeks at a time, and meat was usually not available. Gasoline for private cars was strictly rationed, and driving was easy (for those with hard currency to buy fuel) because there were few cars on the road.[81] Ceauşescu was able to impose such stringent controls on imports and consumption that the trade balance showed a slight surplus in 1982 and improved steadily over the next few years.

The short-term balance-of-payments crisis did ease, but the fundamental challenge facing the Romanian economy was the need to shift from methods appropriate for extensive growth—adding inputs such as land, labor, and capital—to those that would promote intensive growth—more efficient use of inputs and production of higher quality goods for the world market. This shift would require a number of important changes in the Romanian economy, such as close links between effort and reward—a concept Ceauşescu had always supported with words but not money. Instead, he has relied mainly on regulations and coercion to create motivation, not a very effective strategy. Other requirements for intensive growth usually include a price structure closely aligned to the costs of inputs and outputs; flexibility in decisionmaking so that responses reflect and adjust to demand; and a long learning process on the part of both labor and management. There would be a number of decrees and campaigns to link labor and income more closely in the 1980s, but they would stress penalties (not incentives), tighten labor discipline, and impose more regulations.[82] Ceauşescu reluctantly introduced some price reforms demanded by the International Monetary Fund,[83] but he has rejected any major concessions that might threaten centralized control.

Before Romania's economic difficulties began, there had been two reorganizations that showed some possibility of improved performance. One was the establishment in 1979 of "unified agro-industrial councils" to help the agricultural cooperatives, the weakest part of the sector. The other reorganization had much broader implications, including as it did a series of changes announced in March 1978 under the title of New Economic and

Financial Mechanism (NEFM).[84] Some of the major features of the NEFM, as Alan Smith points out, had been approved in December 1967, but had not been implemented successfully except for the creation of the intermediate level of "centrals" between the ministry and the enterprise.[85]

The basic themes of the 1978 NEFM centered on the "self-financing" (*autofinanciare*) and "workers' self-management" (*autoconducerea muncitorească*) of enterprises. According to Smith, the first concept substituted net output for gross output as the vital performance indicator and required each enterprise to calculate costs as well as to meet production targets and to finance bonuses and social and cultural expenditures out of profits. Under the 1978 directives, enterprises would still have little autonomy because most investment was still determined in Bucharest, and both centrals and enterprises still received detailed instructions in the plan. What autonomy had evolved was apparently limited to questions of production efficiency. The second theme, worker's self-management, should not, Smith warns, "be confused with workers' self-management on Yugoslav lines" because in Romania "the function of Workers' Councils appears to be largely to act as a transmission belt for the discussion of centrally determined decisions."[86] This, then, was a continuation of the mobilization techniques of the 1960s and 1970s.

The directives of 1978 did not try to decentralize decisionmaking in the Romanian economy, nor did they introduce market mechanisms. Rather, the NEFM aimed at greater efficiency in production and more accurate fulfillment of plan requirements. Hence the number of centrally determined indicators was increased to include some of the desired improvements in efficiency, quality, and productivity. On the other hand, Smith argues, the NEFM should not be considered "purely a cosmetic or political operation" because each economic unit was now expected to cover its costs.[87] In a sense, the Romanians were experimenting with reforms similar to those introduced elsewhere in the Soviet Union and Eastern Europe during the 1960s without major results—tinkering with success indicators within a central plan—but the Romanians were also withholding the security net typical of such systems by requiring that each enterprise pay its own way.

Subsequently, however, the economic difficulties of the 1980s seemed to distract Romanian managers from both organizational innovations—the agro-industrial complexes and the NEFM—and reinforced the centralization of the economy.[88] The announcement of the NEFM, followed by the hard currency crisis, brought Party and enterprise officials tremendous insecurities; when these were compounded by Ceauşescu's intensified circulation of personnel, most officials retreated to the previous system that they knew well. As early as May 1980 Ceauşescu complained bitterly that the provisions of the NEFM were not understood and were not being implemented.[89]

Not only the Party and managerial elites had reason to fear organizational innovation, however: The army also had dilemmas to face. Many professional soldiers were feeling some displeasure with military doctrine and the role of the armed forces in Ceauşescu's Romania. They were (and still are) restricted to a defensive doctrine of guerrilla rather than conventional war, forced to train alongside the non-professional Patriotic Guards, and required to fulfill duties unrelated to the military role, particularly in construction. In late January 1983 rumors circulated in Bucharest that a military coup had been attempted, and Ceauşescu immediately began to pay considerable attention to the military. For example, he met with leading cadres of the Ministries of Armed Forces and Internal Affairs on 4 March and justified at great length the low levels of military spending, which was not to increase through 1985—surely a source of grievance for military officers. Yet Ceauşescu has kept Romanian soil free of Soviet soldiers, ended the country's previously subservient role in the Warsaw Treaty Organization, prevented Soviet officers from interfering in Romanian personnel decisions, and made Romanian nationalism the cornerstone of his internal and external policies. The officers must still have been torn between approval of his foreign policy and disappointment in his defense strategies. Whether their discontent was sufficient to produce an organized attempt to seize power is unclear[90]; in any case it was unsuccessful. Ceauşescu's own background in the armed forces, his support in the Party, and his political techniques kept him in power with scarcely a ripple to break the surface of political continuity.

The 1980s also brought a new sense of insecurity to Romanian workers. The major innovation of the decade was a system of remuneration introduced in 1983, the *acord global*, which provided that "remuneration per person is to be a function of output in physical units per person, *without lower or upper limits*"—in effect abolishing the minimum wage. Also, there were incentives for managers to increase wages by reducing the number of workers, and it seemed possible that entire units would be closed and employees assigned to other jobs. Thus workers faced unemployment, and managers found their salaries tied to plan fulfillment with no minimum guarantee. By the October 1987 CC plenum, Ceauşescu was demanding revisions in the *acord* and complaining vigorously that goods were being produced irrationally for plan fulfillment rather than for sale.[91]

Romanian peasants have not escaped the general insecurity of the 1980s. A plan for the villages that Ceauşescu has termed "systematization" (*sistematizarea*) was hinted at in the 1960s, most notably in connection with the 1968 administrative-territorial reform. The goal was to distribute industrial development more equally throughout the country and to bring industry, higher standards of living, and cultural facilities to outlying and previously disadvantaged counties. In the 1980s systematization has become a scheme to reorganize the entire Romanian countryside by concentrating the rural population in selected villages with high-rise apartments built on sites from which single-family houses have been razed. These new towns would help to shape a new, urbanized Romanian citizen, who would work nearby in agriculture or in newly established factories. Villages not selected for such treatment would simply be destroyed and their residents moved to apartments in one of the new towns. The original idea had promise—to distribute the jobs and social amenities of economic development more evenly—but it has become distorted into a revolutionary scheme to transform the entire country in accordance with Ceauşescu's wishes.[92]

Needless to say, there is tremendous hostility to the obliteration of villages and the relocation of rural families into apartment houses. The traditional social fabric of the countryside is being destroyed and families torn apart as the extended family structure becomes impossible to maintain. In addition, families already separated by the urbanization process are now unable to reunite: Romanians in the labor force have for some time been forbidden to leave villages and move into a city without a job already waiting for them, but now even retired citizens are not allowed to move to an urban area to live with their children and grandchildren in their old age. This total restructuring of private life has aroused the resistance of a large number of previously apolitical rural Romanians.

Other grandiose projects introduced by Ceauşescu also provoked strong opposition, but were adopted nonetheless. The Danube–Black Sea Canal, associated in the minds of Romanians with the Stalinist era, political prisoners, and thousands of deaths, was started again in the 1970s; after huge investments of labor and materials, it finally opened in 1984 with great pomp but little economic success. The razing of the southern part of old Bucharest to build gigantic government buildings is another dramatic scheme forced through by Ceauşescu at great cost, in this case not only in current economic inputs but also in the permanent loss of historic buildings, churches, and homes. Many of Ceauşescu's plans began with great promise in the late 1960s or early 1970s, but were altered in the 1980s into caricatures of their original form.

Indeed, in responding to the crisis of the 1980s, Ceauşescu has not returned to the rhetoric of collective leadership, legality, and participatory democracy characteristic of the late 1960s when he was attempting to consolidate his position at the top of the Romanian Communist Party. Instead, the leadership cult is stronger than ever. Ceauşescu remains infallible and omniscient, and mistakes are the fault of officials who have not followed Party policy or who do not understand the directives. Even so, he has continued to promise change in many sectors and has appeared to take steps to back up his rhetoric. When the *acord global* was first announced, for example, the description made it seem possible that this could provide an effective incentive system that could increase efficiency and productivity. Once again Ceauşescu created hopes for change by introducing the policy ambiguity that was so successful for him in the 1960s.[93]

Nevertheless, it soon became clear that what was in the offing was further insecurity from top to bottom in both the economic and the political systems. Although high officials remained somewhat secure in their elite status (though not in their particular job), more of them have been removed in disgrace in the 1980s than in any other period of Ceauşescu's rule except 1968–1969. The Party Secretariat and the Council of Ministers have seen rapid rotation, as have county first secretaries.[94] The ministries suffering most have been in the sectors of mining and petroleum, agriculture, and foreign trade, but changes have been made in other areas as well. At the same time, criticism has not always brought demotion, and so the personnel circulation has become more unpredictable and more arbitrary with time and has seemed to depend totally upon Ceauşescu's personal whims. Hence he has abandoned any pretense of institutionalizing the political process, but rather has increased its personalization. An individual's security and promotion clearly depend on placating Ceauşescu rather than on job performance. Not even for Ceauşescu's family and close friends has there been complete security.[95]

On the other hand, since 1979 Ceauşescu has continued to use the participatory populism introduced in the 1960s. There have been periodic national conferences in almost every economic sector, preceded in each case by local and county conferences that keep citizens and officials occupied. As if that were not enough, he introduced a "beautification" campaign to maintain order and discipline, keep up morale, and incidentally to ensure that citizens had no spare time to convert private grumbling into action. Ceauşescu's personal schedule has been more hectic than before 1979, except for much of 1985, when he apparently was ill. He visits several counties at a time, criticizing local officials and appealing over their heads to the population. For example, on a visit to the Bucharest markets in October 1982 at the height of the food shortages, he dismissed three officials on the spot for failing to supply the population with adequate food.[96]

He has also continued his activism in foreign policy, catering to Romanian national pride by his visits abroad and his apparent prestige with foreign leaders that is conveyed at home through the press. His attitudes and Romanian policies remain covertly anti-Soviet, but they have become more overtly anti-West as well, particularly on disarmament and Third World issues. In 1981, for example, he staged giant demonstrations against both superpowers for engaging in a nuclear arms race, pointing out his own rejection of military alliances. In 1986 he held a referendum on nuclear disarmament, in which over 99 percent of eligible Romanians voted to support his call for military budget cuts throughout the world. Such demonstrations surely served his domestic and foreign policy goals by demonstrating both his ability to mobilize the Romanian population to specific actions and his independence of both blocs.[97]

In general, Ceauşescu's nationalism has become more xenophobic in the 1980s. He has been stressing Romania's need to be self-sufficient and to find methods of continuing development and growth in many economic sectors (energy, shipping, agriculture) by utilizing internal resources. He is also firmer than ever in rejecting outside efforts to influence his human rights policies. In 1982 he introduced fees to be charged Romanian émigrés for education received in Romania—and then proceeded to mobilize Third World support for this violation of the Helsinki agreements by portraying the fees as part of the fight against the "brain drain" to the industrialized countries.[98] In 1988 he unilaterally rejected most-favored-nation status from the United States because it was conditioned on his complying with emigration and human rights provisions imposed by Congress.[99]

Ceauşescu has shifted his techniques of rule to some extent since 1979, but not by returning to the strategies of the 1965–1969 period of collective leadership. Instead, he has intensified the methods used during the 1970s: the mobilized participation and populist rhetoric; the dramatic gestures in domestic and foreign policy; the circulation of personnel; the almost frenzied round of activities at home and abroad; the centralization and personalization of political power; and the leadership cult. Ceauşescu has not accomplished his social and economic goals for Romania, nor has he moved toward long-term solutions to the fundamental economic problems facing his country. However, he has kept himself firmly in control of the levers of power and the policies adopted, and he has managed to prevent successful opposition to his rule. In Romania the 1980s under Ceauşescu have been years of scarcity and stalemate.

10

Conclusions

Nicolae Ceauşescu has shaped public policy in Romania for over two decades. He has in some ways continued the policies of his predecessors—communist and non-communist—but he also has imposed his personal priorities on politics and society. Romania after Ceauşescu will not be the same as it was before his rule. Among the distinctive features that have characterized Romania in the Ceauşescu era we must list the following as the most significant:

• *Personalized power, including nepotism and the leadership cult.*
Extensive praise is heaped upon Ceauşescu as the ruler of the nation. He is publicly portrayed throughout Romania as the brilliant interpreter of Marxism-Leninism, the hardworking communist who rose from poverty to Party leadership, and the stately symbol of Romanian sovereignty in dealing with foreign heads of state, royal or revolutionary. The adulation of him is indeed reminiscent of a religious cult, although the actual commitment and fervor of his worshipers is highly questionable.

His personal and often arbitrary decisions and preferences determine policy directions and personnel appointments. Since the early 1970s, after he had established his supremacy in the Romanian Communist Party, he has been the source of all major policy initiatives—announcing them, explaining them, and blaming others if problems develop. Promoting his supporters enabled him to consolidate his power, and rotating them in and out of different offices kept them off balance. Only rarely did anyone stay in one post more than four years, and moves usually occurred much more frequently. Rather than institutionalizing governmental power, Ceauşescu made it more and more personal, increasingly ignoring constitutional requirements for legislation and for appointing personnel.

Ceauşescu elevated his family to prominence: His wife Elena, his son Nicu, and a number of brothers, sisters, cousins, nephews, and in-laws have been placed throughout various ministries, the armed forces, and the police. Ceauşescu has not merely carried on Gheorghiu-Dej's tradition of personalized political power and decisionmaking; rather, he has intensified the personalization of the political process into a leadership cult and has made his family a crucial part of his support network.

• *Nationalism, including autonomy in foreign and military affairs and pride in the history and accomplishments of Romania.* Before World War II, nationalism was a prominent feature of Romanian politics. Soviet occupation following the war temporarily substituted Marxist internationalism, or loyalty to the USSR, but after the withdrawal of Soviet troops in 1958, the RCP leadership began to reassert an autonomous and eventually nationalistic line in foreign policy. Initiated by Gheorghiu-Dej, this new foreign policy was continued even more vigorously by his successor.

Ceauşescu's nationalism in international affairs has had several components, the most significant being his efforts to distance Romanian policies from those of the Soviet Union whenever feasible, not only in arenas of peripheral importance to Moscow such as the United Nations or the Middle East but also in the Warsaw Pact and Comecon. Simultaneously, the Romanian leader has established political and economic relations with as many different countries as possible, including Third World countries and NATO members, in order to reduce his dependence on any one state or alliance system. Ceauşescu has also criticized both the Soviet Union and the United States on issues such as development aid or disarmament, which divide the superpowers from the less wealthy and less powerful states throughout the world and from their own allies.

Ceauşescu's approach to autonomy affects the country's military doctrine. Unlike the other Warsaw Pact states, Romania has been able to reduce military expenditures because its doctrine focuses on a relatively inexpensive and defensive guerrilla war, which also allows the country more self-sufficiency in weapons production than would otherwise be the case. This war would be carried on against a foreign invader within Romanian borders by units of "patriotic guards." But because Romania is surrounded by allies (except for neutral Yugoslavia), it is difficult to see how its armed forces could support that alliance or be directed against NATO. In fact, Ceauşescu's guerrilla doctrine is directed against his allies, whom he sees as potential invaders. He has refused to cooperate in joint WTO maneuvers except on paper, and so his insistence on national autonomy has weakened the Soviet alliance system.

• *Rapid industrialization of the economy at the expense of improved living standards.* Ceauşescu defines himself as a Marxist, and he views economic progress in terms of industrialization at the cost of broadening or even maintaining a solid agricultural base. More specifically, he insists on the Stalinist model of economic development: the rapid growth of heavy industry financed largely by internal resources, which thus requires postponement of adequate supplies of consumer goods and services. During the 1970s, for example, the investment rate in Romania averaged one-third of national income, and the country's debt-service ratio at the end of 1979 was the lowest in Eastern Europe.[1] Despite these high rates of investment, economic growth was sufficient to provide modest improvements in living standards. The 1980s then brought a sudden rise in the foreign debt, much lower rates of growth and investment, and a drastic fall in living standards. Even so, Ceaușescu blamed the problems largely on the international economic environment and never abandoned his commitment to the fastest growth possible. Indeed, he has insisted that high rates of investment be resumed, again from internal resources whenever possible—with minimal help and no interference from foreigners.

• *Centralized political and economic control.* Ceaușescu is also a Leninist, a believer in a highly centralized political process. For Ceaușescu, as for Lenin, the Party is the vehicle that must monopolize politics and direct economic and social policy. Like Lenin, Ceaușescu is a first-generation revolutionary, a supremely self-confident activist who dominates his Party; impatient with slow processes of development, he is willing to speed the course of history by force when necessary. Unlike Lenin, however, Ceaușescu is unwilling to compromise. He rejects any reforms reminiscent of Lenin's New Economic Policy of the 1920s, with its balance between heavy and light industry and its tolerance of private agriculture and small-scale private enterprise. Instead, Ceaușescu insists that any change in policy or organization must bring even more rapid economic development. Economic reform measures are permissible only if they do not interfere with centralized planning, high rates of accumulation, and socialized property and economic activity. Productivity is stimulated by increasing requirements and penalties rather than by offering incentives—the stick rather than the carrot. Ceaușescu's response to the economic problems of the 1980s has been to tighten central control under his personal aegis and impose still heavier burdens on the population.

Ceaușescu's Rule

These characteristics of Ceaușescu's rule reveal much about the man. First, for most of the years Ceaușescu has held the top position, he has ruled as well as reigned—but he has not been the leader of Romania. Leadership is a reciprocal relationship between leader and followers. As James MacGregor Burns has pointed out, "authentic leaders" rest their authority on a "true relationship" with their followers "characterized by deeply held motives [and] shared goals."[2] Measured by this standard, Ceaușescu was on his way to establishing himself as an authentic leader in 1968 partly through his criticism of Gheorghiu-Dej, Drăghici, and the security forces, but mainly as a result of his opposition to the Warsaw Pact intervention in Czechoslovakia.

Romanians approved of Ceauşescu's defiance of the Soviet Union when he defended the Prague government and refused to send Romanian troops into Czechoslovakia. Although unwittingly, the Soviet Union helped to solidify Ceauşescu's popularity—for a while—with the Romanian people. Ceauşescu must have thought it would last forever.

His popularity in the late 1960s was also rooted in promises of legalized and participatory politics, higher standards of living, and greater social and cultural diversity. Except for modest improvements in living standards during most of the 1970s, however, these promises were never kept. As a result, Ceauşescu's "followers" quickly ceased to share his goals, and he was forced to manufacture a bogus legitimacy based not on Weber's three criteria (tradition, charisma, and legality-rationality[3]) but on his own distorted concepts of Romanian traditions (both history and nationalism), the false charisma of the cult, and the formalized political processes that he defined as "participatory."[4] Only his appeal to Romanian nationalism was genuinely successful at engendering widespread support, but even that wore thin by the 1980s. Starting in 1971 he gradually increased his coercive techniques and personnel circulation and eventually abandoned his search for legitimacy. He became a ruler, not a leader.

Second, just as Ceauşescu has had a tremendous impact on his country, so too has Romania shaped his goals and his perspectives on the political process. His strategies and choices cannot be attributed exclusively to Romanian political culture, but they nevertheless echo Romania's past, particularly the frustrated desires for successful industrialization and national independence, the lack of institutionalized constitutional procedures, and the reliance on personal leadership and family ties in reaching and implementing political decisions and maintaining political control.

In addition, Romanian society has not placed significant limits on his choices. Both Michael Shafir and Steven Sampson have provided extensive and perceptive analyses of political quiescence in Romania.[5] In brief, there are no strong independent structures or groups in the country that might offer an alternative to collective loyalty to the state or that might resist political co-option with some effectiveness. The Romanian Orthodox Church, for example, does not play that role, and other churches are usually associated with ethnic minorities. Some of the characteristics of Romanian society discussed in Chapter 1 that mitigated against RCP support in the interwar years—for example, the absence of a strong, independent trade union tradition, or the strength of Romanian nationalism in seeking national unity—now in fact contribute to the Party's power. Most Romanian intellectuals have been co-opted, or at least neutralized, by their nationalism and by their reluctance to sacrifice themselves by what they conclude would be ineffective protest. Romanians traditionally tend to choose individual, indirect, and non-confrontational methods to avoid, rather than oppose, government demands. Honor in Romanian culture comes from success in achieving personal goals, however indirectly, or even from patient suffering and acceptance of one's fate.[6] In any case, Ceauşescu himself emerged from this same culture. He understands it and makes use of it in his political strategies of manipulation and coercion.

Third, the history and ideology of the Marxist revolutionary movement have been crucial in the formation of Nicolae Ceauşescu as a political leader. The revolutionary Ceauşescu probably was regarded by many of his contemporaries as a juvenile delinquent—impatient with authority, determined to overcome all obstacles, and willing to condone whatever violence seemed necessary to bring communism to Romania. He recognized the need to direct mass action, and displayed deep disappointment with the tendency of most Romanians to focus on their own personal needs and desires rather than to cooperate collectively in his gigantic projects to develop socialist Romania.

Ceauşescu's experiences in the Romanian Communist Party between the wars shaped his world outlook, giving him a rather simplistic view of history and economics but underscoring his belief in his own and his Party's infallibility and solidifying his dogmatic ideology. Having seen the Party torn by factionalism and weakened by Comintern demands, he thereafter was intolerant of disagreement within and fearful of interference from outside. These views were reinforced by his experiences under Gheorghiu-Dej in the first two decades of Party rule, when Ceauşescu evidently placed loyalty to the Party leader above his own interests and followed the wavering Party line without reservation. Later, when Ceauşescu had come to dominate the Party, he refused to hear dissent from his colleagues and rejected the suggestions of foreigners from East or West with a vehemence that bordered on xenophobia.

The pragmatic rejection of Soviet guidance begun by Gheorghiu-Dej mutated into a passionate embrace of national independence, history, and Romanian culture, concepts that Ceauşescu not only revered but redefined. By the 1980s independence had become isolation, lest interaction and interdependence become interference. History was a glorious succession of heroes fighting to defend their country against evil foreigners and tracing their roots to prehistoric times. Culture was mass culture, shaped to appeal to the broadest possible audience, derived from the memories of his own peasant childhood, and exhibited in huge rallies and amateur singing, dancing, and theatrics. Ceauşescu was no sophisticated intellectual in his approach to politics or culture; had he been, he would never have reached the pinnacle of power in the Romanian Communist Party.

Therein lies a fourth facet of Ceauşescu that we need to recognize: his shrewd use of a variety of techniques of political control. He first gained the top RCP position in 1965 in part because he did not seem to pose a threat to any of his colleagues. He had also demonstrated his devotion to the Party first by years in prison and then by decades of hard work and loyalty to Gheorghiu-Dej. He had extensive influence at lower levels of the apparatus from his years as CC secretary, and he moved quickly in 1965 to gain control of the Central Committee by enlarging it with his supporters. Ceauşescu soon created a new Executive Committee packed with loyalists, carefully using the CC and the Party apparatus to gain a majority in the EC and the new Presidium. Once he controlled the Party, Ceauşescu used it to extend his control over the state apparatus and established a whole new system of joint Party-state positions and organs to ensure his personal domination of the political system. All these changes were justified on grounds of collective leadership and inner-Party democracy.

While Ceauşescu was consolidating his power within the political system through personnel manipulation, he also was using policy moderation and compromise to enhance his support—promising all things to all people. Different sectors of the Party and state apparatus, intellectuals, the military, peasants, and workers—all groups were encouraged to look to Ceauşescu as their champion within the RCP leadership. He also promised consultation and mass participation in the political process, a newly institutionalized process that would respect legality and democratic procedures. His personal priorities were all evident in this early period, but his ambiguity and calls for openness and discussion encouraged many to hope that he would change regime goals and procedures to the advantage of many different groups in society.

Ceauşescu did his best to cater to these hopes as he searched for popular support to enhance his authority. But the galvanizing event that temporarily legitimized his rule and that of his Party was the Warsaw Pact intervention in Czechoslovakia in 1968. His vehement denunciation of Soviet interference in another socialist state convinced many Romanians, even those who were skeptical about his intentions in domestic affairs, that Ceauşescu's foreign policy justified his rule. The Tenth Party Congress in 1969 brought an end to collective leadership and signaled Ceauşescu's victory in establishing himself as the dominant political force in Romania. Thereafter he became explicit in expressing his own goals and priorities. The gap between him and most Romanians widened into a chasm by the mid-1970s as he intensified his demands for rapid industrial development and cultural conformity.

The crucial year was 1971. He initiated reorganizations in culture and education and demanded revisions in the five-year plan to bring even more rapid growth. On his return from his Asian trip, he instituted his own cultural revolution, intensified the leadership cult, and began to include his wife in the power structure. To mute any resistance, he used the false charisma of the cult and mobilization measures (characterized as participatory) to demonstrate popular support for his plans and coerce any non-believers into accepting his omniscience. Indeed, by 1974 further personnel changes and control of the press had made him omnipotent, and his omniscience became less relevant, though no less widely touted.

The cult continued and intensified, propelled by its own momentum as well as its original impulse. The weakening of rational legitimacy based on common policy goals widened the gulf between the regime and the population and increased the need for traditional appeals for support to supplement coercion. The creation of a charismatic halo around Ceauşescu fitted into this process. A variety of factors are important in the formation of a leadership cult in a Leninist party: policy choices by individual leaders in their search for acceptance; systemic factors (tradition, social structure, and political culture), which encourage or resist a cult and help to define its features; and bilateral relations with Moscow, which may require or forbid the substitution of local authority for Soviet support. All have played a role in the emergence of the Ceauşescu cult, but as it evolved and grew, ironically genuine support for Ceauşescu declined. Charisma proved to be elusive. The halo kept slipping off.

As the conflict between regime priorities and popular expectations became clear during the 1970s, Ceauşescu intensified the methods of control that had emerged in earlier years. His promotion of elites became circulation, and the rotation became more and more rapid as the years passed. He intensified his participatory and populist rhetoric and his use of dramatic gestures in domestic and foreign policy. His busy schedule became frenzied as trips and conferences multiplied both at home and abroad. But most of the promises made in the 1960s were never fulfilled. Mass participation did not affect policy choices, and the political process became totally personalized rather than institutionalized. Yet Ceauşescu's skill at manipulation and coercion allowed him to continue in power without forcing him to compromise in his relations with the population.

What, then, has been Ceauşescu's effect on Romania? He did fulfill one of his promises from the early days of the collective leadership in 1965: He continued the autonomous foreign policy begun by Gheorghiu-Dej. He also contributed significantly to Romania's international prestige in the 1960s and 1970s, and he kept Soviet troops out of the country. These are not insignificant accomplishments in the eyes of most Romanians, and Ceauşescu's success in achieving these goals must be recognized. In contrast, his plans for economic development failed miserably, and his reactions to those failures have brought worse disasters, including severe energy and food shortages, and total disaffection to most Romanians. In retrospect, the ultimate irony for Romanians is the doubtful economic viability of the entire plan for multilateral industrialization, a plan first associated with Gheorghiu-Dej's resistance to Comecon integration and then with Ceauşescu's nationalism.[7]

This plan as it evolved under Ceauşescu in the 1970s was essentially a continuation of the emphasis on heavy industry and large-scale extensive development projects associated with the early 1950s, a strategy Khrushchev tried to persuade the RCP leadership to change in the 1960s. Its adoption in Romania both facilitated and symbolized the country's autonomy from the USSR. The high economic growth rates throughout the 1970s helped to justify Ceauşescu's rule, but his development strategy has proven economically inefficient in a number of ways, primarily because of the need to import large quantities of raw materials and the neglect of the agricultural sector. In addition, the one area in which the Party chose to specialize— petroleum rigging and drilling equipment and petroleum-dependent industries such as petro-chemicals—proved disastrous because of changes in the international petroleum market and events in the Middle East.

Ceauşescu the skillful politician has gained and maintained control of Romania despite internal and external hostility. However, as a Leninist-Stalinist—a firm believer in centralized power and coercive economic solutions to his problems—he so far has rejected economic changes that would increase efficiency, flexibility, and productivity. His skills have been effective in creating personal power, but he has not demonstrated the understanding necessary for complex economic planning, nor is he willing to listen to the advice of experts.

The leadership cult resulted in part from an attempt to bridge the gap between his economic goals and those of most Romanians. The widening of that gap during the economic difficulties of the 1980s merely intensified Ceauşescu's need for the cult. Ceauşescu has cut ties to the USSR, but at the same time has forced Romania to follow the Soviet development model more closely than any other East European state. Ironically, Romanian isolationism has been accompanied by low levels of consumption and tight political control that have made Romania a replica of the Soviet system forty years ago. Most of the successes and hopes of the first years of Ceauşescu's rule have evaporated; only national autonomy has been maintained at great economic cost to the Romanian population. Nationalism and personalized power have become a mutually dependent combination of political strategies employed by Nicolae Ceauşescu in the pursuit of power and the ever-receding utopia of communist Romania.

The Transition to New Leadership

Predictions in politics are both risky and futile. Not even Ceauşescu can be certain about the future—which policies might prove successful, what challenge to his power might occur, who might succeed him—and he knows more about the Romanian political system than anyone. Nevertheless, there are some probabilities to consider.

It is unlikely that Ceauşescu himself will change his strategies of political control or economic development. If Romania's severe economic difficulties and strained international relations have not yet moderated his views, there seems little chance that external realities will move this doctrinaire ruler to compromise his beliefs.

It is of course possible that Ceauşescu will be removed from office by colleagues within the political elite—any observer who remembers the ouster of Khrushchev would be foolhardy to ignore the possibility. There are some signs that Ceauşescu not only has failed to generate significant support for his policies, but also that he has generated considerable opposition. But Ceauşescu's technique of shifting personnel has been so successful that it is hard to see how any elite coalition might form in opposition. Even so, we can speculate that a group within the Party leadership, perhaps with the cooperation of some military or security officers, could carry out a successful coup. If that should occur, we might—but only in retrospect—find signs of Ceauşescu's impending doom. There would be no more advance warning than is visible today—delays in important Party meetings, his complaints that policies are not being implemented correctly, or the frequent rotation of officials in order to preempt opposition. If any indications of danger were visible, Ceauşescu, his family, and his loyalists would surely recognize them before any outside observers and take steps to thwart a successful challenge.

The June 1987 CC plenum, for example, provided some hints that there was resistance to his policies and that he was unhappy with his colleagues. These signs continued in the fall, when a number of individuals were again rotated in the counties and in top positions. Then in December 1987, as had occurred in 1972, the Party conference had to be postponed several times; when it finally met, nothing new happened. Despite the *sub rosa* discontent that appears to be present, the surface of Romanian politics and the media adulation of Ceauşescu continue undisturbed, testimony to his personal power.

Rumors of an attempted military coup did produce ripples in early 1983. A coup may indeed have been planned because a number of middle-level officers were later removed, but Ceauşescu was evidently able to abort it in its early stages. He has ruled successfully by means of the Party apparatus for over twenty years, and in doing so he has eliminated or co-opted the other hierarchies of power, including the military and the police. He has weakened the military as a profession by blurring the distinction between officers and civilians—downplaying investment in sophisticated weapons, turning soldiers into construction workers, and creating citizens' units of patriotic guards—thus mitigating against any challenge to Ceauşescu from the officer corps. The police, in contrast, have been among the few beneficiaries of Ceauşescu's rule (at least since the ouster of Drăghici), and they know they have a great deal to lose should he leave the scene. There is today no Jaruzelski or Beria in Bucharest, and although there are precedents in Romania for both military and police threats to civilian control—Ion Antonescu during World War II, for example, or Alexandru Drăghici in the 1960s—neither officer corps seems to pose a serious challenge to Party control today.[8]

A successful revolution against Ceauşescu from below also seems unlikely. Communist Romania has never had the cooperation between workers and intellectuals—apparently a prerequisite for mass revolt in Eastern Europe—that occurred in Hungary in 1956 or in Poland after 1970. Whenever isolated strikes and demonstrations have occurred in Romania, Ceauşescu has dealt successfully with them, promising and delivering material concessions to end the disturbances and only later rescinding the concessions, arresting the leaders one by one, and sending them to prison for long terms. The immediate crisis was always resolved rather quickly, and potential rebels were usually deterred by the outcome. The failure of the 1977 strikes in the Jiu Valley and the 1987 demonstrations in Braşov, for example, produced a sense of impotence on the part of the population that mitigated against other similar actions. This does not mean, of course, that future actions could not topple Ceauşescu; the sheer weight of deprivation in a country with such a low standard of living and already suffering from considerably more disaffection than a decade ago could be the trigger. Or an unexpected incident could stimulate mass revolt: A natural disaster, for example, could create widespread confusion and weaken the power structure, or a mistake in judgment by a policeman or soldier could ignite a hungry and resentful crowd in a marketplace. Even such events, however, more likely would bring an effective response from the police and the Party, cooperating as before to restore their mutual authority.

In addition, we must recognize that after 1965 Ceauşescu managed to identify himself and his rule with Romanian national interests in the eyes of many citizens. They saw him as responsible for keeping Soviet troops out of Romania and preventing Soviet political interference and economic exploitation. As a result, many Romanians—workers, peasants, intellectuals, Party and non-Party—feared that open opposition to RCP control would bring Soviet interference. This fear contributed to political passivity as individuals and groups, paralyzed by nationalism, failed to challenge the Party.

In the 1980s, however, more and more Romanians have begun to question the high cost of their autonomy, as exploitation by Bucharest appears worse than any that might emanate from Moscow. Another irony of Ceauşescu's continued domination has been the shift in Romanian perceptions of the USSR: By the time Gorbachev came to Bucharest in May 1987, he was regarded with some hope by Romanians who wished that Soviet *glasnost* and *perestroika* might spread to their country. Ceauşescu has therefore accomplished what none of his predecessors in the RCP leadership was ever able to do: create a positive image of the Soviet Union in Romania!

Whether Ceauşescu dies in office or is removed by a group of his colleagues within the Party leadership, the most probable outcome would be a collective leadership and a transition similar in some ways to the one that followed Gheorghiu-Dej's death—although the USSR under Gorbachev probably would seek a more active role in influencing events. The new collective leadership would quickly introduce a major reorientation in economic policies, including slower growth rates, incentives for agricultural production, and immediate improvements in the standard of living (aided by some credits from abroad, probably from the Soviet Union as well as the West). Personnel policies would be characterized by Party unity to preserve stability, with only a few immediate demotions from the Party leadership. Members of Ceauşescu's family, however, would be abruptly removed if he were forcibly ousted—more slowly if he died of natural causes. There would be an immediate emphasis on legality and institutionalized procedures rather than on presidential decrees, and indeed the post of president might even be eliminated in the interests of collective leadership. Some populist policies might continue, but there would be attempts to dissociate the new regime from the Ceauşescu era. The huge rallies or flag-waving parades would be eliminated, except on national holidays or other occasions when it would seem appropriate to stress nationalism, the only truly successful populist appeal in Romania. This transitional period would presumably last until a new individual consolidated power; in Ceauşescu's case, it was about four years, but it could be much less for his successor.

This post-Ceauşescu transition might bear resemblance to the 1960s in part because the three sources of support unavailable to Ceauşescu then— revolutionary prestige, outright terror, and foreign support—will also be of little use to his successors. Apart from the president himself, there is no individual in Romania with any significant prestige, and Ceauşescu's failures in recent years make highly improbable any handing on of his mantle to family members or to any other designated heir. Extensive use of terror is also unlikely. Civilian successors to Ceauşescu would certainly not hesitate to use whatever military or police coercion would be needed to maintain Party control, and the threat of such force would be constantly in the background, but the new civilian leaders would probably prefer to try less drastic measures first, if only to prevent the military and security forces from gaining too much influence on the political scene. In addition, these measures would stand a good chance of success because there is so much room for improvement in both political and economic life.

Strong Soviet support for the new regime, the third possibility, might be offered. Most likely, however, any economic aid would come with strings, and given Gorbachev's economic priorities at home, the cost to the Soviet Union would have to be minimal. The RCP in its turn would not accept many strings. A genuine and permanent rapprochement with Moscow would be unlikely for Romanian leaders who had risen to the top under Ceauşescu, particularly because the departure of the Romanian president would probably bring past anti-Soviet grievances to the fore once again and reduce the internal viability of any Bucharest regime that seemed too enthusiastic about friendship with Moscow.

The new Romanian leadership would probably try to present the Soviets with a *fait accompli* as in 1965, the quick election of new officials. They would appeal to the population for unity and support, subtly fueling the fear that disorder might lead to Soviet intervention. The weakened Party thus would continue to placate both the Soviet leaders and the Romanian population, reassuring Moscow about its intentions toward the Warsaw Pact and Comecon but also implying indirectly to its own population its determination to maintain national independence. The RCP also would try to walk the foreign policy fence between East and West to take advantage of foreign credits, but would be likely to introduce conciliatory policies toward the national minorities and reach a compromise with the Hungarian government. Recalcitrance from Romania's socialist neighbor, however, or disturbances in Hungarian regions of Transylvania could provoke just the opposite: continued hostility and extreme repression. In fact, any of these predictions are extremely tentative, and could be preempted by unexpected developments inside or outside Romania.

If the post-Ceauşescu transition is decided within the Romanian Communist Party, who would be the major figures in the new leadership? A dynastic succession is improbable, although not impossible, especially for a brief period. Ceauşescu has promoted family members because he is assured of their loyalty, but they themselves fear that their political power will not long survive him. As yet, neither Elena Ceauşescu nor Nicu Ceauşescu seems to have the personal attributes or the independent base of power to take control for any length of time, although both are apparently attempting to gain internal allies. She, for example, gave the major address at the 23 August celebrations in 1988, a significant honor. Most important to them in any bid for power would be her influence over cadre selection and Nicu Ceauşescu's 1987 appointment as county first secretary in Sibiu. The longer Nicolae Ceauşescu remains healthy, the better their chances. If Nicu should somehow make a success of himself in Sibiu, he might return in triumph to a high Bucharest post in 1990 or so. He has yet to demonstrate such competence, however, and any such "triumph" would probably be as manufactured as his father's cult. Ceauşescu has established a tradition of quiet retirement for Party leaders; he likes to send even those who have been publicly disgraced to distant corners of the world as ambassadors or to remote corners of Romania as enterprise directors. Therefore, it is likely that Nicu Ceauşescu and his mother will both be gradually retired after Nicolae's death. If he is forcibly removed, or if they prove unwilling to go quietly, a less comfortable retirement could await them.

If we restrict candidates for succession to the Party leadership and eliminate Ceauşescu's immediate family, who remains? To answer this question, we need to remember that during the 1970s Ceauşescu changed his personnel strategy from promotion to circulation of cadres. Individuals moved back and forth between Party and state or to a mixed Party-state organ, and also geographically from Bucharest to county posts or the reverse. The horizontal circulation of top officials enabled a relatively stable group to remain on the Political Executive Committee, while the Secretariat and Council of Ministers saw frequent turnover. The geographical type of elite circulation has emphasized the importance of certain posts in the Party apparatus, especially that of county first secretary. There are just over forty of these individuals at any one time, and each is a "little" Ceauşescu directly administering both Party and state hierarchies at the county level. Ceauşescu uses the posts to train and test people on their way up and also to move others away from the center temporarily. This exile is not necessarily a demotion—Ceauşescu may be entrusting a crucial region to a competent subordinate.

This group of past and present county first secretaries is most likely to produce Ceauşescu's successor. These individuals have proven themselves competent to rule at the county level, as general administrators implementing Party policy. Other positions are important under Ceauşescu—in the CC apparatus or as presidential counselor—but those who have been effective as county first secretaries are most likely to have the political skills to propel them to the top. They will also have acquired a number of supporters from the counties in which they have served, and some of these individuals will already have been promoted to other posts throughout the political system. We must see Nicu Ceauşescu's move to Sibiu as county first secretary in this light: His parents are clearly grooming him for higher positions, and they see the position of county first secretary as crucial to his future in Romanian politics. Setting aside Nicu Ceauşescu as a potential successor, however, we should look to the members of the Political Executive Committee who have served as county first secretary, who are (or have been recently) on the Secretariat, the top policymaking organ, and who also are members of the Permanent Bureau, the top administrative body. During the mid-1980s this made Emil Bobu the top candidate to replace Ceauşescu on his death, but his chances recede as Ceauşescu continues to hold power.[9]

Romania after Ceauşescu

What aspects of the Ceauşescu era will remain as permanent features of Romanian politics under a new leader? First, although the commitments to Marxism and the Soviet alliance are departures from pre-1945 traditions, no change in either is likely without a basic restructuring of the overall international environment. Romania will remain a Soviet ally and a member of the Warsaw Pact and Comecon. Second, nationalism is likely to remain a feature of Romanian politics. This is not to say that a transitional leadership in Bucharest will not reach an immediate accommodation with Moscow that would include mutually beneficial trade. But the Soviets accepted the autonomy achieved by Gheorghiu-Dej and Ceauşescu and are unlikely to pay the economic and military price of forcing permanent conformity on the

Romanians. If Moscow does not take steps to try to eliminate nationalism from Romanian politics, the RCP is unlikely to abandon it voluntarily. The regime needs every shred of legitimacy it can muster. Nationalism, a feature of Romanian politics for over a century, is likely to outlive Ceauşescu. Third, personalized power centered around one individual has been just as frequent as nationalism and is also likely to continue—though it need not include nepotism or a cult. In fact, the post-Ceauşescu era in Romania is likely to have less nepotism and no cult—at least during the transition period, when the new leaders should emphasize legality and institutionalized political processes and try to dissociate themselves from the unpopular aspects of Ceauşescu's rule. They should move immediately to alleviate economic grievances, but on other issues the break with the past may be more gradual. Eventually the dissociation from Ceauşescu will probably turn into a denunciation of him, reminiscent of his criticism of Gheorghiu-Dej.

After the transition period, regime policies will depend on the priorities of the new leader who emerges from the process. That individual will face a set of circumstances similar to those that shaped the rule of Ceauşescu: the political environment of Romania, including its geographical proximity to the Soviet Union; the ideology and political organization of a Marxist-Leninist Party; and the personal experiences and capacities of the new general secretary. The leader may eventually initiate a new cult, or he may find more institutionalized methods acceptable to himself, the party, and the population. That leader may also choose new methods of economic management that will enable Romania to achieve the transition to intensive development strategies. Policies may be more balanced and moderate because the new leader will not be a first-generation revolutionary and will probably have a better education than Ceauşescu. Finally, the new leader should have learned from Ceauşescu's mistakes. But we must remember that this individual will have spent many years in Ceauşescu's Romania and will probably have gained the top position through success in applying Ceauşescu's methods. The possibilities for change in Romania after Ceauşescu are therefore not unlimited.

Notes

Introduction

1. The Romanian Communist Party was called the Romanian Workers' Party from the time of its unification with the Socialist Party in 1948 until the Party congress of July 1965.

2. *Scînteia*, 22 August 1968.

3. See, for example, his speech to the Ninth Party Congress in July 1965; *Congresul al IX-lea*, pp. 61, 93.

4. See, for example, Bucur, *Ceaușescu of Romania*, or *Nicolae Ceaușescu: Builder of Modern Romania*.

5. Pacepa, *Red Horizons*.

6. See Shafir, *Romania*; King, *History*; Jowitt, *Revolutionary Breakthroughs*; Fischer-Galati, *The New Rumania* and *Twentieth Century Romania*; and Ionescu, *Communism*.

7. For examples, see the works cited in the bibliography by Braun, Farlow, Floyd, Linden, and Weiner.

8. See the Ceaușescu entries in the bibliography.

Chapter 1

1. For a perceptive survey of the literature on "political culture," see Archie Brown's introduction to Brown and Gray, *Political Culture and Political Change*. See his definition of political culture on p. 1, and his distinction on p. 8 between the official political culture (which the regime promotes) and the dominant political culture (which dominates the minds of the citizens). This is useful in analyzing Romania, where both official and dominant political culture coincide on issues of nationalism and pragmatic elitism. Kenneth Jowitt, in "An Organizational Approach to the Study of Political Culture in Marxist-Leninist Systems," p. 1173, views political culture as a "set of adaptive postures—behavioral and attitudinal—that emerge in response to . . . ideological, policy, and institutional [definitions]," and he distinguishes among elite, regime, and community political cultures. A more recent survey of the issue is Brown, ed., *Political Culture and Communist Studies*.

2. A number of excellent studies of the Romanian political environment and the early development of Marxism have been published; see

Shafir, *Romania*, chs. 1–3; King, *History*, ch. 1; Fischer-Galati, *Twentieth Century Rumania*, chs. 1–4; and Ionescu, *Communism*, ch. 1.

3. Fischer-Galati, *Twentieth Century Rumania*, p. 9. For a brief but excellent survey of Romanian politics in the interwar period that emphasizes the role of nationalism, see the chapter on Romania in Rothschild, *East Central Europe*.

4. See the essays in Jowitt, ed., *Social Change*, especially Montias, "Notes on the Romanian Debate on Sheltered Industrialization"; and Chirot, "Neoliberal and Social Democratic Theories of Development." On the National Peasants see Roberts, *Rumania*, ch. VII; quote is from p. 165. For an excellent conceptualization and bibliography, see Michelson, "Romanian Perspectives on Romanian National Development."

5. Janos makes the point about Codreanu in his "Modernization and Decay," p. 11.

6. Lampe and Jackson, *Balkan Economic History*, pp. 428, 339.

7. Lampe and Jackson, *Balkan Economic History*, p. 593.

8. On disparity of ownership and the extent of the reform, see Rothschild, *East Central Europe*, pp. 290–293. The best analysis focusing on the politics of agriculture in interwar Romania remains Roberts, *Rumania*. A comparative study with excellent data on the Romanian peasantry is Jackson, *Comintern and Peasant*. On 1907, see Eidelberg, *The Great Rumanian Peasant Revolt of 1907*. The most detailed study of the land reform remains Mitrany, *The Land and the Peasant in Rumania*.

9. Lampe and Jackson, *Balkan Economic History*, p. 352. See also Jelavich, *History of the Balkans*, vol. 2, pp. 161–163.

10. On *pays légal* and pays *réel*, see Shafir, *Romania*, pp. 5–6; the "gap" is Jowitt's term in "The Sociocultural Bases of National Dependency in Peasant Countries," in Jowitt, *Social Change*, p. 1, where he quotes Constantin Dobrogeanu-Gherea, *Neoiobăgia* (Bucharest: Ed. Librariei SOCEC & Comp., 1910), p. 5, on the "abyss," and Rothschild, *East Central Europe*, p. 321, on the "chasm." See also Janos, "Modernization and Decay," pp. 72–116.

11. Rothschild, *East Central Europe*, p. 296. The major exception to electoral corruption was the "genuinely free" general election of December 1928, which produced a National Peasant majority; Rothschild, p. 301.

12. Rothschild, *East Central Europe*, p. 295.

13. See Lampe and Jackson, *Balkan Economic History*, pp. 502–504. On the relationship between education and stability, see Janos, "Modernization and Decay," pp. 95–101.

14. On Romanian fascism, see the following: Weber, "Romania," "The Men of the Archangel," and *Varieties of Fascism*; Turczynski, "The Background of Romanian Fascism"; Fischer-Galati, "Fascism in Romania"; and Nagy-Talavera, *The Green Shirts and the Others*.

15. Shapiro takes exception to the general interpretation of interwar Romanian politics as a series of failures in "Romania's Past as Challenge for the Future." His thesis that Romania was indeed developing a viable multi-party system is intriguing, but the process, if it was taking place, was interrupted too early to have any lasting effect.

16. Despite promises made by Ceauşescu at the Ninth Party Congress in 1965, no official history of the RCP has appeared to date. *Lecţii în ajutorul celor care studiază istoria PMR* and *În slujba cercetării marxiste a istoriei PCR* provide useful surveys of the historiography of the Gheorghiu-Dej and early Ceauşescu periods respectively. For general treatments by Western scholars,

see Shafir, *Romania*; King, *History*; Ionescu, *Communism*; Jackson, *Comintern and Peasant*; Roberts, *Rumania*; Fischer-Galati, *Twentieth Century Rumania* and *The New Rumania*.

17. Jackson, *Comintern and Peasant*, p. 245; King, *History*, p. 19; Shafir, *Romania*, p. 28.

18. In 1930, 130,433 of 140,948 industrial enterprises in Romania employed fewer than six persons; King, *History*, p. 20.

19. King, *History*, p. 20.

20. The Comintern source was the Sixth Plenum of the Comintern Executive Committee (1925), cited by Jackson, *Comintern and Peasant*, p. 254.

21. Jackson, *Comintern and Peasant*, pp. 247–265.

22. Jackson, *Comintern and Peasant*, p. 247.

23. Shafir, *Romania*, p. 26.

24. *Lecţii în ajutorul celor care studiază istoria PMR*, p. 233.

25. Burks, *The Dynamics of Communism in Eastern Europe*, pp. 195–196.

26. Rakovsky was put on trial by Stalin in 1938 for his close association with Trotsky, and he died in prison in 1941. On both Gherea and Rakovsky, see Shafir, *Romania*, chs. 2–3, and the sources cited. See also his "'Romania's Marx'" and his "Sociology of Knowledge."

27. Shafir, *Romania*, pp. 10–11, 17–19; Ionescu, *Communism*, p. 4.

28. Shafir, *Romania*, pp. 18–20. See also Ionescu, *Communism*, pp. 4–8.

29. On factional struggles in the Bulgarian party, for example, see Rothschild, *The Communist Party of Bulgaria*, esp. pp. 11–45.

30. Shafir, *Romania*, p. 15.

31. Shafir, *Romania*, p. 10.

32. On the struggles between the RCP and the Comintern over agrarian policy, see King, *History*, pp. 23–25; Jackson, *Comintern and Peasant*, pp. 247–265; Roberts, *Rumania*, pp. 274–292.

33. Ionescu, *Communism*, p. 6.

34. A description of the November 1920 meeting is given in Ionescu, *Communism*, pp. 15–17, citing the German edition of *Kommunistische international*, no. 16, 1921.

35. Shafir, *Romania*, p. 22.

36. The circumstances of the meeting and the vote taken are matters of dispute, but the outcome is not. See Shafir, *Romania*, pp. 22–23; King, *History*, p. 17; and Ceauşescu's speech on the forty-fifth anniversary of the Party, *Scînteia*, 8 May 1966, reprinted in Ceauşescu, 1: 315–390, esp. 332–333.

37. See Jackson, *Comintern and Peasant*, p. 250, and the sources cited. Romanian sources claim 100,000 members for the Party by 1920; see, for example, Pascu, *Istoria României*, p. 370.

38. The Comintern resolution is quoted in Roberts, *Rumania*, p. 252.

39. *Lecţii în ajutorul celor care studiază istoria PMR*, p. 233.

40. Roberts, *Rumania*, pp. 255–256.

41. Ceauşescu quoted from the 1940 directives in the Archives of the RCP Central Committee in May 1966; see Ceauşescu, 1: 351.

42. Shafir, *Romania*, p. 20.

43. *Scînteia*, 8 May 1966, or Ceauşescu, 1: 332, 336–340.

44. For details, see Shafir, *Romania*, pp. 24–25.

45. Ceauşescu, 1: 339.

46. Nedelcu, "Concepţia tactică şi experienţa de luptă a PCR 1933–35," p. 284.

47. Ceauşescu, 1: 351–352. On the thirty-fifth anniversary of the Vienna *Diktat, Era socialista* (no. 17, 1975) carried an article praising the RCP for leading the "mass demonstrations" against Hitler's decree.

48. *Scînteia*, 27 March 1948, pp. 1, 3. This was the biography printed to elicit votes for him in the elections to the Grand National Assembly.

49. See *Scînteia*, 27 March 1948, and Chivu Stoica, *Eroicele lupte ale muncitorilor ceferişti ,si petrolişti din 1933*, pp. 95–96. According to Chivu Stoica, the real battle took place the day after Gheorghiu-Dej was arrested, 15 February.

50. For descriptions of Doftana, see Sălăjan, "Doftana," and *Muzeul Doftana*. For Ceauşescu's use of the Doftana myth, see the reports of his visit there; Scînteia, 26 September 1986.

51. Early examples include Hamelet, *Nicolae Ceauşescu*; Catchlove, *Romania's Ceauşescu*; and Siegert, *Ceauşescu*. Hamelet was granted interviews and given access to documents, and many of his quotations have been repeatedly used by subsequent authors. The Catchlove biography is a good presentation of the Ceauşescu mythology in English; it exemplifies the hopes that many observers had for Romania in the early Ceauşescu era. More recently, see *Nicolae Ceauşescu: Builder of Modern Romania*, which reflects the extremism of the mythology in the later years of Ceauşescu's rule. Official biographical sources of Ceauşescu worth consulting include *Dicţionar enciclopedic român*; *Mic dicţionar enciclopedic*; and *Omagiu Tovara ,sului Nicolae Ceauşescu*, pp. 10–13.

52. The Cunliffe quotation is from his *George Washington, Man and Monument*, p. 190; chapters I and V elaborate on the origins, content, and intent of the Washington legends.

53. Myths serve similar functions in other societies. For example, was Abraham Lincoln really born in a log cabin? Did George Washington chop down the cherry tree or throw a coin across the Potomac? It is not the historical accuracy of these events that is important, but rather the lessons they are intended to convey about upward mobility, honesty, and hard work in American society. On Washington, see Schwartz, *George Washington: The Making of an American Symbol*.

54. See Hamelet, *Nicolae Ceauşescu*, p. 9. Unless otherwise indicated, the quotations that follow are from Hamelet's interviews of July 1970; I have translated from the French edition, pp. 8–10. For similar quotations, see Catchlove, *Romania's Ceauşescu*, pp. 40–44. The descriptions of Scorniceşti are Hamelet's from 1970, and my own from 1975 and 1982.

55. On the 1985 status of Olt County as a model, see, for example, the speeches of Barbulescu, Nicolae Mihalache, and Gheorghe David to the Central Committee plenum, *Scînteia*, 15–16 November 1985. The discovery of ancient human remnants in Oltenia (Bugiuleşti is now the village of Tetoiu in Vîlcea County) was pointed out by Georgescu in *Politică ,si istorie*, p. 66; he cites Mihnea Gheorghiu, president of the Academy of Social and Political Sciences, in an introduction to *Thraco-Dacica* (Bucharest, 1976), p. 7.

56. On Ceauşescu's siblings, see Hamelet, *Nicolae Ceauşescu*, p. 11, and Catchlove, *Romania's Ceauşescu*, p. 44. Of the three girls, Nicolina, the oldest, became a worker in a shoe factory and like Nicolae was involved in communist activities before and during the war; Elena became a history teacher in the Scorniceşti high school; and Maria was for some years a factory worker in Bucharest and married an engineer. Of the seven boys, one died young; Ilie

gained a doctorate in history and became a professor at the Military Academy; Ion earned a doctorate in agriculture; Florea became a journalist at *Scînteia*; Marin became an official involved in foreign trade; the first Nicolae became president; and the youngest child, a second Nicolae (villagers told Hamelet that the parents ran out of names), became a police officer in Bucharest. All the brothers were in top positions in their respective ministries by the early 1980s.

57. Hamelet, *Nicolae Ceauşescu*, p. 13. The scholars were Iorgu Iordan and Petre Constantinescu-Iaşi. On Ceauşescu's illegal activities during the 1930s, see Hamelet, pp. 11–34; Catchlove, *Romania's Ceauşescu*, pp. 46–73; *Nicolae Ceauşescu: Builder of Modern Romania*, pp. 25–40.

58. These family contacts are described by Catchlove, *Romania's Ceauşescu*, p. 56.

59. Hamelet describes the trial on pp. 19–22, *Nicolae Ceauşescu*.

60. In *Cuvînt liber*, 6 June 1936; I have seen an original issue. Strains between Jebeleanu and Ceauşescu were apparent by the early 1980s; see the poet's speech at the *Plenara CC al PCR, 3–5 noiembrie 1971*, pp. 237–242.

61. See above, esp. note 50, and the accompanying text.

62. Quoted in *Nicolae Ceauşescu: Builder of Modern Romania*, p. 34.

63. Hamelet describes these events from police files, pp. 31–34, *Nicolae Ceauşescu*.

64. On the Doftana guards and the final quotation, see *Nicolae Ceauşescu: Builder of Modern Romania*, pp. 31 and 37; on "pollyanna," see Catchlove, *Romania's Ceauşescu*, p. 69.

65. Hamelet, *Nicolae Ceauşescu*, pp. 39–42; Catchlove, *Romania's Ceauşescu*, pp. 72–73.

66. Hamelet, *Nicolae Ceauşescu*, p. 41.

67. Stern, *Ulbricht*, pp. 15–17.

68. As paraphrased by Stern in *Ulbricht*, p. 17.

69. Stern, *Ulbricht*, p. 17.

Chapter 2

1. On the general pattern of takeovers, see Seton-Watson, *The East European Revolution*, pp. 167–171; and Gati, *Hungary and the Soviet Bloc*, ch. 1. On Romania, see Shafir, *Romania*, ch. 4; King, *History*, ch. 2; and Fischer-Galati, "The Communist Takeover of Rumania."

2. There was some partisan activity in Romania. See, for example, Ionescu, *Communism*, p. 81, or King, *History*, p. 162, note 13.

3. Ionescu, *Communism*, p. 119; Fischer-Galati, *Twentieth Century Rumania*, p. 78; or Jowitt, *Revolutionary Breakthroughs*, p. 78.

4. Jowitt calls this period "one of reformism—of the partial though significant restructuring of the political system" (*Revolutionary Breakthroughs*, p. 92) and then terms the years from 1948 to 1955 the "breakthrough." For more information on these early years, see Ionescu, *Communism*; Shafir, *Romania*; King, *History*; and the works in the bibliography by Fischer-Galati, Cretzianu, and Markham.

5. Even sources hostile to the RCP acknowledge its cooperation in the coup; see, for example, Markham, *Rumania Under the Soviet Yoke*, pp. 181–182.

6. On the functions of history in communist states, see Heer, *Politics*

and History in the Soviet Union. King applies her categories in the Romanian context in *History*, ch. 1. On historiography in Romania, see Georgescu, *Politică şi istorie.*

7. Several different versions of the meeting have appeared in print; for example, a biography of Bodnaraş in *Scînteia*, 28 October 1946, puts him and Gheorghiu-Dej in adjoining beds in the Tîrgu Jiu Civil Hospital in March and July 1944, with Gheorghiu-Dej giving instructions for the coup of 23 August. For the more frequently cited version, see the speeches by Ceauşescu, Ion Vinte, and Maurer at the CC plenum in December 1961, *Scînteia*, 13, 16, 14 December 1961; Vinte, "PCR în fruntea"; and Roşianu, "Cum a fost organizată."

8. Zaharescu describes these steps in "Întărirea partidului," pp. 216–223.

9. Romanian sources frequently use the term *în frunte cu* (headed by) to describe the Party's relationship to Gheorghiu-Dej in 1944, but he was not general secretary. *Scînteia* referred to Pârvulescu as general secretary on 22 September and 12 October 1944, and the treatment of Pârvulescu by the Party daily for the next year indicates he probably retained that position until he was elected president of the Central Control Commission at the Party conference in October 1945. On the broader implications of the Foriş episode, see the discussion in Shafir, "Socialist Republic of Romania," pp. 595–596, and Shafir, *Romania*, pp. 34–35.

10. Pîrvulescu (Pârvulescu), "Unitatea de actiune a clasei muncitoare." As Shafir has pointed out, the decisions of 4 April may have had anti-Soviet implications, but they were not primarily anti-Soviet in their motivations. In fact, just the reverse was true. The USSR was at war with Germany, and the immediate result of the infirmary meeting was for the RCP to help that war effort by cooperating with all political groups willing to remove Antonescu and end the war against the Soviet Union. Gheorghiu-Dej himself pointed that out in 1951 (*Scînteia*, 11 May 1951) when he was removing Ana Pauker and Vasile Luca from the RCP leadership, and the parallel with the Foriş episode was implicit in his remarks; of course, in 1951 he had to reassure Stalin that his actions were not anti-Soviet. The Foriş episode was used again as a weapon in intra-Party rivalry in 1961, when several speakers at the December CC plenum criticized Pauker for daring to question the removal of Foriş when she arrived in Romania in 1944; this renewal of criticism against her threatened those still in the leadership in 1961 who had been close to her. See especially the speeches of Moisescu, Vinte, and Bodnaraş, *Scînteia* 10, 16 and 17 December 1961.

11. Just after the April 1968 CC plenum; *Scînteia*, 28 April 1968, or Ceauşescu, 3: 173.

12. For excellent surveys of the historiography of the coup both inside and outside Romania, see King, *History*, pp. 40–46, and Shafir, *Romania*, ch. 4.

13. On the 1945 celebrations, see *Scînteia*, 23–24 August; the four communist leaders whose photographs appeared on page 1 were Bodnaraş, Pârvulescu, Rangheţ, and Pătrăşcanu—the provisional leadership chosen on 4 April 1944—plus Pătrăşcanu, Gheorghiu-Dej's major rival among the home communists. On 1948, see the article by Brucan, "August 23, 1944," *Scînteia*, 22 August 1948. On Ceauşescu, see *Scînteia*, 23 August 1985.

14. According to a biography published in *Scînteia*, 13 November 1946, p. 3, Pârvulescu was born in 1895, one of seven children in a Romanian peasant home. When he was 14, he went to Bucharest to find work and was

involved in socialist activities by age 17. He joined the communist party in 1920 and in 1929 was elected to its Central Committee. Arrested and imprisoned in the 1930s, he became a member of the RCP Political Bureau in 1935 and spent the war underground in Romania. He was appointed to the Party Secretariat at the April 1944 meeting in the prison infirmary and "with Pătrăşcanu, Bodnaraş, and Rangheţ" played a "decisive role" in preparing for 23 August. He would have a rather erratic career: general secretary in 1944–1945, then president of the Party Control Commission, severely criticized during the 1950s, partially rehabilitated in the early 1960s, and honored by Ceauşescu in the late 1960s and 1970s. Finally, he would commit political suicide by openly attacking Ceauşescu and his leadership cult at the Twelfth Party Congress in 1979.

15. A brief autobiography accompanied the 1925 publication of Pătrăşcanu's doctoral thesis, "Reforma agrară în România Mare şi urmările ei," in his *Studii economice şi social-politice*, p. 9. Compare this with the biography that appeared in *Scînteia*, 10 November 1946. His most important works include *Sub trei dictaturi* and *Problemele de bază ale României*.

16. See their memoirs: Lee, *Special Duties*, pp. 245–246, and Ileana, Princess of Romania, *I Live Again*, pp. 191, 285–286. Lee described Pătrăşcanu as "astute, capable and not unfriendly" and spoke French with him and English with his "handsome, vivacious wife." Princess Ileana also commented particularly upon his wife, whom she called "beautiful, talented . . . the only smartly dressed woman present" at a party in Bodnaraş's home for the entire RCP leadership and special guests, including the Princess.

17. For Pătrăşcanu, see, for example, *Scînteia*, 23, 27, and 28 September; for Gheorghiu-Dej, 21, 26, and 27 September.

18. Ceauşescu appeared in *Scînteia* on 22 September, 3, 11, and 14 October. For Constantinescu, see 2, 4, 8, and 20 November; for Drăghici, 10 November.

19. The description is from Hamelet, *Nicolae Ceauşescu*, p. 49. See also the picture of them as a young couple on the beach at Constanţa in 1946; *Omagiu Tovarăşului Nicolae Ceauşescu*, p. 14.

20. According to a biography in *Scînteia*, 17 March 1948; on Ploieşti, see his statement to Tito on a joint visit to the plant, *Scînteia*, 26 June 1956.

21. A biography of Apostol appeared in *Scînteia* on 18 March 1948. Drăghici (born 1913) would serve as minister of the interior from 1952 until 1965. Like Ceauşescu, he would become a full member of the Political Bureau in 1955, and he would be Ceauşescu's major rival after the death of Gheorghiu-Dej.

22. Compare the biographies in Ionescu, *Communism*, pp. 353, 355, with those in *Scînteia*, 14 and 17 November 1946 and 25 and 26 March 1948.

23. *Scînteia*, 10 November 1944.

24. Both in *Scînteia*, Ceauşescu on 13 December 1961, and Bodnaraş on 17 December 1961.

25. See *Scînteia*, 18, 20, and 21 January 1945.

26. Official biographies appeared in *Scînteia*, 28 October 1946 and 15 March 1948; see also *Dicţionar enciclopedic romîn*, and *Mic dicţionar enciclopedic*. The last states unequivocally that he was interned in Romania from 1934 to 1942. Another source, *Muzeul Doftana* (1960), places Bodnaraş in Doftana during the 1940 earthquake.

27. See, for example, Ionescu, *Communism*, p. 79; Fischer-Galati, *The*

New Rumania, pp. 18-19; and Tomasic, "The Rumanian Communist Leadership," p. 486.

28. Georgescu-Cosmovici, in *Au Commencement Était la Fin*, p. 295, states that he deserted to the USSR in the 1930s, attended school in Moscow, and then was sent on a mission to Bulgaria. He was recognized in transit through Romania, arrested, and imprisoned there for eight years until he escaped shortly before the Soviets entered the country. Pool, *Satellite Generals*, p. 87, is ambiguous about where Bodnaraş spent the war, but both he and Georgescu-Cosmovici agree that Bodnaraş spent time in the Soviet Union and had special ties to the Soviet intelligence service.

29. According to Markham, *Rumania Under the Soviet Yoke*, pp. 181-182.

30. *Scînteia*, 18 March 1945.

31. *Scînteia*, 23 October 1945.

32. Teohari Georgescu, minister of the interior from November 1944 until he was removed with Pauker and Luca in 1952, was a member of the RCP Central Committee by 1939. Official biographies appeared in *Scînteia* on 4 November 1946 and 24 March 1948; neither mentions that he spent any time in the USSR, but most Western sources agree that he was there during the war. He appeared in Bucharest at the same time as Pauker and Luca and presumably returned with them and the Soviet army. He was almost prominent enough in the 1945-1947 period to turn the ruling trio into a quartet.

33. See *Scînteia*, 8 October 1945 and 18 November 1946. Ceauşescu's memories were paraphrased in Hamelet, *Nicolae Ceauşescu*, p. 49.

34. See Ceauşescu's criticism of her in *Scînteia*, 13 December 1961. The Party paper began to print lists of members excluded for "violations of Party ethics" as early as April 1947; see the issues of 6, 11, 28 April, 4 and 19 May for examples.

35. The unification had been foreshadowed by a joint meeting of their leaderships reported in *Scînteia*, 29 September 1947.

36. The new name had been originally announced as the United Workers' Party (Partidul Unic Muncitoresc); *Scînteia*, 8 February 1948.

37. For the proceedings of the congress, see *Scînteia*, 22 February 1948, and the days following.

38. See Ionescu, *Communism*, pp. 151-156, and *Scînteia*, 21 June 1948.

39. *Scînteia* 3 March and 26 July 1949.

40. Ceauşescu described the "verification" in *Scînteia*, 13 December 1961. See also King, *History*, pp. 60, 72-77.

41. *Scînteia*, 7 September 1950 and 23 December 1960.

42. Pauker did remain a member of the Orgburo for a short time. See the discussion of these changes in Ionescu, *Communism*, pp. 208-215.

43. See the discussion in Pool, *Satellite Generals*, pp. 87-89.

44. *Scînteia*, 29 May 1952. King discusses the Orgburo in *History*, pp. 74-75, 93.

45. After Stalin's death the trio would be criticized for *left* deviations. For examples of Ceauşescu's activities, see *Scînteia*, 23-24 February, 18 April, 8 and 10 May, 4 June, 2, 15, and 23 August, 25 September, 1 and 10 October, 5 and 29 November 1952.

46. *Scînteia* reported such trials on 10 October and 1 November 1953.

47. Details were given by the CC plenum that posthumously rehabilitated Pătrăşcanu and denounced Gheorghiu-Dej and Drăghici for his arrest and execution; *Scînteia*, 26 April 1968.

48. *Scînteia*, 20 April 1954. See the discussion in Wolff, *The Balkans*, pp. 469ff.

49. According to Wolff, *The Balkans*, p. 517.

50. Coverage of the congress began in *Scînteia* on 24 December 1955, and Gheorghiu-Dej's report was printed in full that day.

51. Ceauşescu's report appeared in *Scînteia* on 29 December 1955.

52. The assumption that these 1948 candidate members were later supporters of Gheorghiu-Dej is not based merely on their re-election or promotion in 1955, but also on the backgrounds and subsequent careers of individuals within that group. Turnover in Central Committees elected under Ceauşescu would be somewhat different.

53. These last years of Gheorghiu-Dej's rule have been extensively analyzed by sources already cited. See especially the works by Fischer-Galati, Ghita Ionescu, Jowitt, King, Montias, and Shafir.

54. For details, and an excellent analysis of literary politics in Romania from 1945 to 1974, see Gabanyi, *Partei und Literatur*.

55. The GNA proceedings appeared in *Scînteia* 28–30 March 1956 along with summaries of the new laws. On the judicial reforms, see the report by G. Diaconescu (minister of justice), *Scînteia*, 31 March, and the speeches printed April 1. On Lenin's birthday, see *Scînteia*, 22 and 24 April.

56. This 1956 Political Bureau decision was revealed only in 1968, when Ceauşescu denounced both Gheorghiu-Dej and Alexandru Drăghici, the 1956 minister of internal affairs; see *Scînteia*, 26 April 1968, and Ceauşescu's speech to the Bucharest Party organization, *Scînteia*, 28 April 1968. See also Ceauşescu, 3: 179.

57. On the events of 1956 in Romania, see Ionescu, *Communism*, ch. 12; *East Europe* 6 (January 1957): 45–46, and 6 (February 1957): 50; King, *Minorities Under Communism*, pp. 82–85, and the sources cited; Urban, *The Nineteen Days*; and Fischer-Galati, *The New Rumania*, pp. 62–63. Gheorghiu-Dej re-established his personal precedence even earlier than the fall: *Scînteia* accorded him first place during Tito's visit (June 25) and at the 23 August celebrations, and by September the old order seemed to be back in place.

58. *Scînteia*, 9 July 1957.

59. The 1961 plenum speeches appeared in *Scînteia* as follows: Gheorghiu-Dej, 7 December; Ceauşescu, 13 December; Drăghici, 15 December; Borilă, 10 December.

60. Pârvulescu's complicity was not revealed until the December 1961 plenum, but he was removed from the RWP leadership at the Third Congress in 1960.

61. Biographies of Chişinevschi and Constantinescu appeared in *Scînteia*, 19 and 20 March 1948.

62. Brown, *The New Eastern Europe*, p. 67.

63. The Romanian CC plenum met 28–29 June and 1–3 July. On 4 July *Scînteia* reported that Chişinevschi and Constantinescu had been removed from the Political Bureau and also printed the decision of the 22–29 June Soviet CC plenum that had expelled the Moscow "anti-Party" group.

64. See works already cited by Fischer-Galati, Jowitt, and Shafir. The best description of the economic issues remains Montias, *Economic Development*; the most detailed chronological account is Floyd, *Rumania: Russia's Dissident Ally*. See the survey of Western sources on the dispute in Linden, *Bear and Foxes*, note 21, pp. 260–263.

65. Included are the nine full members of the Political Bureau, the five candidate members, and the one CC secretary not on the Political Bureau:

Gheorghiu-Dej, Apostol, Bodnaraş, Borilă, Ceauşescu, Chivu Stoica, Drăghici, Maurer, Alexandru Moghioroş; Alexandru Bîrlădeanu, Dumitru Coliu, Leonte Răutu, Leonte Sălăjan, Ştefan Voitec; Mihai Dalea.

66. Jowitt discusses the Romanians' emulation of the Soviet model in *Revolutionary Breakthroughs*, pp. 100–102, 178–182.

67. On protectionism in the Romanian past, see Montias, *Economic Development*, pp. 195–196, and the essays in Jowitt, *Social Change*.

68. Marx, *Însemnări despre Români*. See the discussion in Shafir, *Romania*, p. 50. For the other developments, see Ionescu, *Communism*, p. 343, and *East Europe* 13 (December 1964): 54.

69. For more details, see the sources cited in note 64.

70. *Scînteia*, 26 April 1964.

Chapter 3

1. See, for example, his speech on the fifteenth anniversary of the Romanian-Soviet Friendship Treaty, *Scînteia*, 4 February 1963, in which he praises the alliance with the USSR as a guarantee of "independence" and speaks of the need to raise industrial and agricultural production more rapidly "in each country" of the socialist bloc. The Soviet leaders could not have been happy listening to these remarks; they were advocating economic specialization by country, but Ceauşescu was merely expressing the Romanian line at the time, and the major theme of his speech was, after all, the close friendship between Romania and the USSR. Likewise, when Ceauşescu was the main speaker at the 23 August celebrations that year (*Scînteia*, 23 August 1963), he advocated the dissolution of all military blocs; but that also was the Romanian line at the time.

2. For a recent survey of political succession in communist systems, see McCauley and Carter, *Leadership and Succession*, and the sources cited. See especially Shafir's chapter on Romania, pp. 114–135.

3. George Breslauer has compared the political strategies of Khrushchev and Brezhnev to demonstrate that the leaders of Leninist parties do have alternatives in attempting to establish their authority over the Party. They may, as Khrushchev did, follow a "populist" strategy and appeal to the lower levels of the Party over the heads of the intervening elites. Or, like Brezhnev, they may rule by ensuring the security of those elites and attempt to implement policies with their help. See his *Khrushchev and Brezhnev as Leaders*. Ceauşescu would use both strategies at different periods in his rule, but such strategies are used by Party leaders who have already consolidated their power and are trying to implement policies. During the succession stage their alternatives are much more limited, and they cannot afford to alienate groups within the Party unless they are assured that the Political Bureau is united behind them.

4. The president of the Council of State was the titular head of state, but the president of the Council of Ministers was the actual head of government.

5. Bucharest Domestic Service in Romanian, 1609 and 2049 GMT, 19 March 1965. Information in this section is from *Scînteia* unless otherwise cited. The Party leadership is listed herein in Chapter 2, note 65; the others present were Gheorghe Gaston-Marin, Gheorghe Rădulescu, and Gheorghe Rădoi. The funeral commission was reported at the same time: Chivu Stoica, president; and Bodnaraş, Drăghici, Sălăjan, and Voitec. It was appropriate that

Gheorghiu-Dej's closest friend should be head, but the exclusion of Ceauşescu seemed to signal weakness on his part. In retrospect, we can speculate that it might have been considered purely a state function, and of course he held no state position.

6. *Times* (London), 25 March 1965. For the funeral orations, see *Scînteia*, 25 March 1965.

7. The proposed statutes appeared in *Scînteia*, 6 June 1965.

8. The CC plenum was reported in *Scînteia*, 17 April 1965. These changes in Party recruitment were clearly planned under Gheorghiu-Dej because they were foreshadowed by the elections to the GNA just before his death, when the intellectuals in that body rose from 28 percent to 40 percent; see Radio Free Europe Research (RFER), Situation Report (SR), 19 March 1965, p. 3.

9. See the analysis in *Neue Zürcher Zeitung*, 10 June 1965.

10. Compare 1965 articles on education in *Scînteia*, 1 and 21 April, and 4 May.

11. For his speech to scientists, see *Scînteia*, 9 May 1965, and to writers and artists, 20 May 1965.

12. *Scînteia*, 13 June 1965.

13. *Scînteia*, 29 June 1965.

14. *Scînteia*, 23 June 1965.

15. See, for example, an interview with Dr. Erich Appel, deputy premier of the GDR, in *Lumea*, 18 February 1965; an agreement with Czechoslovakia was reported in *Scînteia*, 17 February, and with Poland, 19 March.

16. *Scînteia*, 29 March and 25 June 1965.

17. For a sampling of these other speeches, see *Scînteia* on the following dates: Maurer, 16 June; Chivu Stoica, 10 and 15 June; Apostol, 26 May, 28 June; Bîrlădeanu, 18 June; Bodnaraş, 17 and 25 June; Drăghici, 2 May, 19 June.

18. *Neue Zürcher Zeitung* commented that this was "rare" for communist party congresses; 20 July 1965. *Le Monde* characterized it as "without precedent"; 23 July 1965.

19. The Romanians were extremely careful to preserve neutrality and treat the Soviets and Chinese equally throughout the congress. The two delegations, for example, entered the congress hall at the same time by different doors; *Neue Zürcher Zeitung*, 22 July 1965.

20. *Le Monde*, 21 July 1965.

21. *Neue Zürcher Zeitung*, 20 July 1965; *New York Times*, 21 July 1965.

22. For the proceedings of the congress, see *Congresul al IX-lea*.

23. For example, Ceauşescu himself quoted a bourgeois Romanian historian, A. D. Xenopol; a Romanian Social-Democrat, C. Dobrogeanu-Gherea; and Engels—all in praise of Romanian socialism. See *Congresul al IX-lea*, pp. 35, 36, 74.

24. *Neue Zürcher Zeitung*, 25 July 1965.

25. *Congresul al IX-lea*, p. 345. The final version of the statutes is on pp. 797–818. See esp. pp. 805–807. The proposed statutes were printed in *Scînteia*, 6 June 1965.

26. See Ceauşescu's explanation, *Congresul al IX-lea*, pp. 731–732. On 1960, see Gheorghiu-Dej's speech in *Scînteia*, 21 June 1960, and the CC list, *Scînteia*, 26 June 1960.

27. *Congresul al IX-lea*, p. 732.

28. *Congresul al IX-lea*, p. 345.

29. *Congresul al IX-lea*, p. 732.

30. The members of the Editing Commission were Ceauşescu, Chivu Stoica, Maurer, Apostol, Bîrlădeanu, Bodnaraş, Drăghici, Răutu, Niculescu-Mizil, Iosif Banc, Ion Cozma, Constantin Daicoviciu, Gaston-Marin, Nicolae Giosan, Nicolae Hudiţeanu, H. Hulubei, Petre Lupu, Manea Mănescu, Gheorghe Mihoc, Roman Moldovan, Dumitru Popescu, Titus Popovici, Gheorghe Rădulescu, Ludovic Takăcs, and S. Tripşa; *Congresul al IX-lea*, pp. 111–112.

31. See the *Frankfurter Allgemeine Zeitung*, 26 July 1965; *Le Monde*, 21 July 1965; and *New York Times*, 26 July 1965.

32. Neither was an ethnic Romanian; their removal meant that the only non-Romanians left in the Presidium were Maurer and Bodnaraş.

33. *Congresul al IX-lea*, p. 803.

34. *Congresul al IX-lea*, p. 79.

35. *Congresul al IX-lea*, pp. 343–344.

36. Five men did lose positions: Chivu Stoica and Ilie Verdeţ in the CC Secretariat; Dalea, Drăghici, and Moghioroş on the Council of Ministers. See the following discussion of the Secretariat for details.

37. Apostol had been minister of agriculture in 1953–1954. In September 1965 he gave the opening address at the International Congress on Water Resources in Bucharest and was the main speaker reporting on the decisions of the November CC plenum to the Higher Agricultural Council; *Scînteia*, 27 August, 1 September, and 17 November 1965.

38. Drăghici was replaced by his deputy, Cornel Onescu, who remained minister until 1972, when he moved into the CC apparatus.

39. *Congresul al IX-lea*, pp. 426–427.

40. *Scînteia*, 16 April 1966.

41. For Trofin's participation in agricultural conferences, see *Scînteia* of 8 August, 17 September, 12–13 October, 17 November, 12 December 1965; 2 and 9–10 February, 24 March, 18 June 1966; etc. For his growing organizational responsibilities, see his speech at the April 1966 CC plenum, *Scînteia*, 14 April; his article, "The Rules of the RCP," *World Marxist Review* 9 (July 1966): 71–76; his frequent contacts with Drăghici at meetings dealing with organizational matters or foreign parties (*Scînteia*, 26 September, 12 October 1965; 22 January, 19 June, 1 and 20 August 1966; etc.); and his reports on organizational problems at CC plenums (*Scînteia*, 15 February, 20 June and 25 October 1968). Finally, at the next Party congress in August 1969, it was Trofin who reported on changes in the Party statutes.

42. Banc in the Hungarian Autonomous Region, Berghianu in Cluj, Blajovici in the Banat, Dănălache in Bucharest, Verdeţ in Hunedoara, and Vîlcu in the Dobrogea.

43. Banc, Fazekas, and Gere were Hungarian; Vîlcu and Coliu were Bulgarian; Lupu was Jewish; and Blajovici was of Serbian origin.

44. Ceauşescu was mentioned at least once during most speeches at the congress, but usually in direct connection with the report of the Central Committee. Other individual leaders were mentioned very rarely by name.

Chapter 4

1. For Weber's categories, see his *Economy and Society*, vol. 1, p. 215, and the discussion following. "Legitimacy" is used here in its simplest sense: popular acceptance of the right to rule. The literature on this topic is extensive. See, for example, Meyer, "Legitimacy of Power," or

Rigby and Feher, *Political Legitimation*, esp. Rigby's introduction and sources cited.

2. Ceauşescu's comments on the need for industrialization are from *Congresul al IX-lea*, pp. 35–37. Citations for his quotations are given in the translation, Ceauşescu, 1: 23–25, as follows: A. D. Xenopol, *Opere economice* (Bucharest: Academy Publishing House, 1967), pp. 180, 247; C. Dobrogeanu-Gherea, *Neoiobăgia* (Bucharest: 1910), pp. 488–489; and Gheorghe Gheorghiu-Dej, *Articole şi cuvîntări* (Bucharest: Publishing House for Political Literature, 4th ed., 1956), p. 64. The reference by Ceauşescu was one of the few times during the congress that Gheorghiu-Dej was mentioned, except for the moment of silence in his memory the opening day.

3. Tsantis and Pepper, *Romania*, pp. 82, 85.

4. *Congresul al IX-lea*; for Ceauşescu, see p. 65; for Bîrlădeanu, pp. 578–584.

5. *Scînteia*, 27 December 1966, 7 May 1967, or Ceauşescu, 2: 245. Bucharest, Agerpres International Service in English, 1925 GMT, 15 July 1967.

6. *Congresul al IX-lea*, pp. 51–52.

7. *Scînteia*, 13 November 1965.

8. According to Ceauşescu in his opening speech to the Congress; *Scînteia*, 8 March 1966, or Ceauşescu, 1: 257.

9. See *Scînteia*, 25 February 1966, for details.

10. According to Vasile Vîlcu, the new president of the union; *Scînteia*, 8 March 1966, p. 5.

11. According to Maurer, *Scînteia*, 10 March 1966.

12. For these provisions, see Ceauşscu's speeches in *Scînteia*, 8 March 1966 and 13 November 1965, and Eugen Alexe's report, *Scînteia*, 9 March 1966.

13. *Scînteia*, 10 March 1966.

14. According to Michel Tatu in *Le Monde*, 9 March 1966. See his eyewitness account and that of Henry Kamm in the *New York Times*, 13 March 1966.

15. Except for Yugoslavia where, as Tatu put it, "agricultural cooperatives are not the order of the day."

16. In the words of Henry Kamm.

17. *Scînteia*, 8 March 1966.

18. *Scînteia*, 29 June 1966.

19. *Congresul al IX-lea*, pp. 59–61.

20. For the creation of the council, see *Scînteia*, 11 December 1965. Later comments by Ceauşescu on the topic appeared in *Scînteia*, 15 July, 27 September, and 4 October 1966, trans. in Ceauşescu, 1: 514–518 and 2: 23–33, 34–44. The quote is from 1: 516.

21. *Congresul al IX-lea*, p. 89.

22. *Scînteia*, 4 October 1966, or Ceauşescu, 2: 39.

23. *Scînteia*, 3 June 1966. The new academy would have three faculties, in philosophy and political science, labor history, and economics. Courses would be offered to activists of Party, state, and mass organizations; ideological workers; and graduates of secondary schools recommended by the Party organizations. The normal program would last four years, and each faculty would also offer a doctoral program. For a discussion of educational policy in Romania during the 1960s, see Braham, *Education in Romania*.

24. *Scînteia*, 21 February and 7 May 1967.

25. *Scînteia*, 7 May 1967

26. *Scînteia*, 25–26 February 1965. For evaluations of the Writers' Union conference, see *Le Monde*, 13 March 1965, and *East Europe*, 14 (April 1965): 47.

27. See RFER-Rumania, 22 February 1966, pp. 1—2 (on Stancu), and 23 March 1967, pp. 1–11 (on cultural life). See also Gabanyi, *Partei und Literatur*, chs. V and VI.

28. *Scînteia*, 18 June 1966.

29. See, for example, the descriptions in the *Christian Science Monitor*, 26 January 1966.

30. These steps were all reported in *Scînteia*; on the 1966–1970 plan, see Ceauşescu's speech in *Scînteia*, 29 June 1966, or Ceauşescu, 1: 491, 487.

31. Dessa Trevisan in the *Times* (London), 29 May 1967.

32. *Scînteia*, 23 December 1965.

33. On population policies, see Chapter 7 herein; for popular attitudes toward the puritanical campaigns, see reports in the London *Times*, 23 and 29 May 1967, and *New York Times*, 23 May 1967.

34. For Ceauşescu's comments, see *Congresul al IX-lea*, p. 70. The relevant constitutional articles were 69, 75, 99, 108, 53, and 52. This emphasis on the Grand National Assembly would last throughout the next decade; see, for example, Ionescu, ed., *The Grand National Assembly*.

35. See, for example, a review of a new book entitled *People's Councils: Local Organs of State Power*, in *Scînteia*, 19 February 1965.

36. *Congresul al IX-lea*, p. 109.

37. *New York Times*, 15 March 1966.

38. *Scînteia*, 14 April 1966; Radio Bucharest, 12 July 1966; *Scînteia*, 27 July 1967; the law appears on p. 11 and the speech by the minister of justice on p. 9. See the discussion in Jacobini, *Romanian Public Law*, pp. 81–90.

39. *Scînteia*, 8 March 1966.

40. For the conferences, see *Scînteia*, 27 February, 15 April, 31 May, 24 June 1966.

41. See *Omagiu Tovarăşului Nicolae Ceauşescu*, p. 20.

42. *Scînteia*, 19–22 February 1966.

43. See, for example, *Scînteia*, 11 June 1966, in Argeş; this is only one of many such photos.

44. *Scînteia*, 19 February 1966. The Party color is red, and the Romanian state flag is tricolored—red, blue, and yellow.

45. *Scînteia*, 19 February 1966.

46. *Scînteia*, 22 February 1966, 9 November 1965, 17 September 1966.

47. *Scînteia*, 7 November 1965.

48. See the report by David Binder in the *New York Times*, 5 February 1966, "Rumania is Lifting Restrictions on Hungarians in Transylvania."

49. In his speech to the Party activists in Hunedoara, *Scînteia*, 10 October 1966; Ceauşescu, 2: 53–54.

50. As reported in the *New York Times*, 23 May 1967.

51. *Congresul al IX-lea*, p. 92.

52. *Congresul al IX-lea*, pp. 161–162.

53. The Executive Committee decision establishing the commission appeared in *Scînteia*, 28 October 1965. Members were Ceauşescu (president), Chivu Stoica, Maurer, Apostol, Bîrlădeanu, Bodnaraş, Drăghici, Niculescu-Mizil, Răutu, M. Mănescu.

54. Many such monographs and collaborative volumes have appeared;

for an overview of publications in the 1960s, see Crăciun, et al., *Bibliografia istorică a României.*

55. *Scînteia*, 14 April 1966.

56. See *Scînteia*, 7–8 May 1966; Ceaușescu, 1: 315–390.

57. See the discussion in Chapter 1, notes 43–47, and the related text.

58. *Scînteia*, 8 May 1966; Ceaușescu, 1: 351–353. All criticisms of the Comintern and of RCP policies were deleted from the version of his speech published in *Pravda*, 8 May 1966.

59. Voicu, "Pagini de lupta," p. 78. See, for example, Stoica and Cruceanu, "Momente din perioada Congresului I al PCR."

60. Except for a brief trip to Varna to meet with Zhivkov by Ceaușescu, Maurer, Drăghici, and Vîlcu; *Scînteia*, 16 August 1965.

61. Compare *Scînteia*, 4 and 10–11 September 1965.

62. For such a background, see Remington, *The Warsaw Pact*, esp. pp. 80–93. See also the works cited by Braun, Farlow, Fischer-Galati, and Linden.

63. This was an unprecedented turnout of the top leaders. Only Gheorghe Rădulescu, Alexandru Moghioroș, and Mihai Gere were missing. *Scînteia* described the arrival on 19 April.

64. *Scînteia*, .17–25 April 1966.

65. For Ceaușescu's remarks in Argeș, see Ceaușescu, 1: 439. On the WTO meetings, see *Scînteia*, 3–9 July 1966; for background, see Remington, *The Warsaw Pact*, p. 87.

66. *Scînteia*, 5–10 and 16–17 August 1966.

67. *Scînteia*, 18 and 22 October 1966.

68. *Scînteia*, 18–19 March; 25–27 May; 18–22 April 1967.

69. *Scînteia*, 10–11 June 1967.

70. *Scînteia*, 4–8 and 28 August 1967.

71. *Scînteia*, 7 May 1967; Ceaușescu, 2: 232–277, esp, 258–262. Ceaușescu did not refer to Lenin in connection with democratic centralism (he did not, as had Khrushchev in 1956, advocate a return to Leninist norms of Party activity), but he did cite Lenin on the need for creativity in applying Marxist doctrines; see p. 260.

72. Ceaușescu, 2: 260–261.

73. Ceaușescu, 2: 261–262.

74. Ceaușescu, 2: 269. For Western reports, see the London *Times*, 8–9 May 1967.

75. On Doncea, see Pool, *Satellite Generals*, p. 152, and *Scînteia*, 3 February 1966. (Ironically, Ceaușescu began to follow Doncea's example in the early 1980s and raze the older sections of Bucharest to make way for grandiose new government buildings.) On Pârvulescu, see *Scînteia*, 10 December 1961, and *Congresul al IX-lea*, pp. 105–111, 738, 740.

76. Victims of more obviously arbitrary action on the part of Gheorghiu-Dej also returned to public life. Marcel Popescu, a former security captain, had married the daughter of the Party leader and served as minister of foreign trade in the 1950s before his divorce and subsequent obscurity; he became vice-president of the Chamber of Commerce in early 1966; *Scînteia*, 3 March 1966, and RFER-Rumania, 9 March 1966, p. 2. Radu Dulgheru, reportedly dismissed as first secretary of Cluj for attending the church wedding of his son, also received a new position; he was dropped from the CC from 1960 to 1965; see RFER-Rumania, 29 April 1966, p. 4

77. *Scînteia*, 14 April 1966; the item was not included in the agenda, but was mentioned at the end of the communiqué without names or details.

78. "How the United Workers' Front Was Set up," based on an interview

with Pârvulescu and Ştefan Voitec. A year earlier Ştefan Voitec had written an article on the same topic for *Scînteia*, 6 May 1966, in which he did not mention Pătrăşcanu.

79. Lucaciu, "'Capitalul' în gîndirea românească," esp. p. 52.

80. Alexiev, "The Romanian Army"; Bacon, "The Military and the Party in Romania"; Bacon, "Civil-Military Relations"; Pool, *Satellite Generals*.

81. *Scînteia* found it necessary to defend Teclu's decision when it printed his biography as a candidate for election to the Grand National Assembly on 13 March 1948:

> In 1942 . . . he was captured on the Don [River]. He became acquainted with Soviet reality and was made to realize that the only regime which could free his country was the USSR and the only way to help the Russians was to fight against Germany. So Lieutenant-Colonel Teclu, not forgetting his country, decided on a new life. Together with other soldiers . . . and officers—moved by the same desire for liberty—he formed a unit of Romanian volunteers to fight alongside the glorious Soviet army against the hordes of hitlerist invaders. On 15 November 1943 they formed the Tudor Vladimirescu Division. Lt.-Col. Teclu was Chief of the General Staff. He led the division bravely and was gravely wounded in the battle for Oradea. With the wound not completely healed, he returned to his post at the front and remained until the defeat of Germany. He then returned to his country and worked to democratize the army. . . . In 1948 he was named a general secretary in the Ministry of Internal Affairs.

82. For this description, see the election biography in *Scînteia*, 18 March 1948.

83. See, for example, the analysis in the *Christian Science Monitor*, 26 July 1965, and RFER-Rumania 13 May, 1966, p. 4, and 31 August 1966, pp. 1–2.

84. *Scînteia*, 15 October 1966.

85. In his speech to the Party organization in the armed forces, *Scînteia*, 1 June 1967; Ceauşescu, 2: 299–309, esp. 308; and his talk to the Braşov regional Party organization, *Scînteia*, 19 June 1967; Ceauşescu, 2: 310–326, esp. 325.

86. *Scînteia*, 27 July 1967.

87. *Scînteia*, 26 July 1967.

88. *Scînteia*, 14 October 1967; participants were Ceauşescu, Chivu Stoica, Maurer, Drăghici, Niculescu-Mizil, Verdeţ, Patilineţ, Ioniţă; the ministers of internal affairs, chemistry, machine building, and metallurgy; and the president of the Council of State Security, Ion Stănescu.

89. On the dangers of military dependency, see Bacon, "Civil-Military Relations," pp. 247–248; see also pp. 245–246 on the army's loyalty to the RCP.

90. *Scînteia*, 1 June 1967; Ceauşescu 2: 299–300, 307; and *Scînteia*, 19 July 1967; Ceauşescu, 2: 369–386. For a discussion of the MIA, see Bacon, "Romanian Secret Police."

91. *Scînteia*, 27–28 June 1967.

92. Ceauşescu, 2: 373–374.

93. Ceauşescu, 2: 375.

94. Ceauşescu, 2: 376.

95. Ceauşescu, 2: 376–377.

96. Ceauşescu, 2: 377, 385.

97. Ceauşescu, 2: 380–381, 377–378.

98. Ceauşescu, 2: 383.

99. *Congresul al IX-lea*, passim.

100. See, for example, Maurer's trips to Iran, *Scînteia*, 13–17 July 1966;

Turkey, 26 July–1 August 1966; Denmark, 16–21 August 1966; Greece, 1–6 September 1966; the United States, 19–28 June 1967; the Netherlands, 18–22 July 1967.

101. See the rumors about Maurer's role as messenger between President Johnson and Mao Zedong in the *Baltimore Sun*, 24 and 26 July 1967.

102. *Scînteia*, 11 and 22 December 1965; 30 June and 10 March 1966; 9 May 1967; 25 February and 29 February-10 March 1966; 18–19 March and 8– 11 June 1967.

103. The editor of *Scînteia*, Dumitru Popescu, was to move into the top Party leadership in 1968 and become the RCP's chief ideologist.

104. *Scînteia*, 4–12 September 1965.

105. For Niculescu-Mizil's meetings with foreign parties, see *Scînteia*, 12 April, 8 and 18 June, 14 and 25 October, 2, 5, and 12 November 1966; 19 July and 31 October 1967. For the Commission on Culture and Education, see *Scînteia*, 29 June 1966, 17 September and 23 December 1967.

106. *Scînteia*, 15 October 1966; 26–27 June 1967. On the cybernetics center, see 14 February 1966 and 21 October 1967. For academic gatherings, see 18 March, 22, 25, and 27 September 1966; 3 February, 22 April, 3 and 21 October 1967. On the GNA commission, see 20 March, 17 April, 22, 25, 27, 29–30, June, 26 November, 20, 22, 24–25 December 1966; 26 March, 16 and 23 April, 16 and 20 December 1967.

107. A law published in late July provided that "on the proposal of the president, the Council of Ministers permanently designates a first vice-president to fulfill, under the guidance of the president, some of his assignments. If the president is absent, the first vice-president so designated fulfills all assignments." See *Buletinul oficial al RSR*, 29 July 1967, as quoted in RFER-Rumania, 8 September 1967, p. 2.

108. *Scînteia*, 17 November and 22 December 1965, 16 April 1966.

109. For examples of Drăghici's major appearances, see *Scînteia*, 25 November 1965; 15 January, 14 April, 10 June 1966; 6 and 27 July 1967; for trips with Ceauşescu, see 11–12 June, 13–15 June, 13–15 August, 8–10 October 1966; for trips abroad, see 26 September–12 October 1965; 29 March–10 April 1966; 7–14 April, 25 May and 21 August 1967.

110. See Chapter 7.

111. For details, see Chapter 8.

Chapter 5

1. The press reports on the October plenum are in *Scînteia*, 6–7 October 1967. The decision regarding the national Party conference is in 7 October. Texts of the other decisions were printed as follows: economic directives, 8 October; territorial organization, 11 October; salaries, 13 October; housing, 15 October.

2. *Scînteia*, 7 December 1967; Ceauşescu, 2: 540.

3. The communiqué of the 29 November–1 December plenum appeared in *Scînteia*, 2 December 1967. The decision on youth was published the next day. The following promotions to the Executive Committee took place: Florian Dănălache and János Fazekas as full members, and Gheorghe Stoica and Virgil Trofin as candidate members.

4. For Ceauşescu's explanation of youth problems, see Ceauşescu, 2: 564–565. The UCY plenum was reported in *Scînteia*, 12 December 1967.

Enache was released to "take up other duties," and he eventually became a CC secretary. Iliescu, by education an electro-technical engineer, was a former UCY secretary and president of the student association, but since 1960 had been in the CC apparatus of the RCP, eventually deputy chief of the education and health section, and after 1965 chief of the section for agitation and propaganda. Both high officials taking part in the UCY plenum were Ceauşescu protégés: Niculescu-Mizil, Iliescu's immediate superior in his old and new positions, and Trofin, CC secretary for organizations and cadres, who had been UCY first secretary with Iliescu under him.

5. In addition to the delegates, 1,633 invited observers attended the proceedings; *Scînteia*, 7 December 1967.

6. *Scînteia*, 7 December 1967; translated in Ceauşescu, 2: 471–571.

7. Ceauşescu, 2: 487.

8. Ceauşescu, 2: 492.

9. Ceauşescu, 2: 499–500.

10. Ceauşescu, 2: 488.

11. Ceauşescu, 2: 502–505.

12. Ceauşescu, 2: 559–560.

13. Ceauşescu, 2: 554, 561.

14. Ceauşescu, 2: 559.

15. Ceauşescu, 2: 506.

16. This at the time that Party and state functions at various levels were to be combined in one person; Ceauşescu, 2: 505.

17. Ceauşescu, 2: 505–506.

18. Ceauşescu, 2: 535.

19. Ceauşescu, 2: 546.

20. Ceauşescu, 2: 543–549.

21. *Scînteia*, 9 December 1967.

22. *Scînteia*, 8 December 1967.

23. *Scînteia*, 9 December 1967.

24. *Scînteia*, 8 December 1967.

25. The two new counties were Harghita, always in a predominately Hungarian region as befitted its 88.1 percent Hungarian majority, and Covasna, separated despite its 79.4 percent Hungarian population from the Autonomous Region in 1960 and added to Braşov region, but made an independent county in 1968. Data are from the 1966 census, as reported in *Judeţele României Socialiste*. For the division into two separate counties, see Ceauşescu's speech in *Scînteia*, 16 February 1968, or Ceauşescu, 3: 13.

26. *Scînteia*, 8 December 1967.

27. Ceauşescu, 2: 274.

28. Ceauşescu, 2: 553.

29. *Scînteia*, 8 December 1967.

30. *Scînteia*, 8 December 1967.

31. Ceauşescu, 2: 554.

32. *Scînteia*, 8 December 1967.

33. Ceauşescu, 2: 557–558.

34. Smith, "Romanian Economic Reforms," p. 39. This provides an excellent and detailed analysis of the economic provisions of the 1967 directives and the stages of implementation through 1979. See also Shafir, *Romania*, pp. 120–125.

35. Kaser and Spigler, "Economic Reform in the 1970s," pp. 254–255.

36. Spigler, *Economic Reform in Rumanian Industry*, p. 166.

37. Granick, *Enterprise Guidance*, and Tsantis and Pepper, *Romania*.

38. See, for example, Smith, "Romanian Economic Reforms," p. 48; Smith, "The Romanian Industrial Enterprise," p. 64. Kaser and Spigler treat the reforms of 1967 and 1978 separately, rather than seeing the second as an extension of the first.

39. See his speeches to the managers of industrial centrals, *Scînteia*, 25 February 1971 (Ceauşescu, 5: 540); to the 1972 Party conference, *Scînteia*, 20 July 1972 (Ceauşescu, 7: 467); and to the conference of Party and state activists of industrial centrals, *Scînteia*, 3 July 1974 (Ceauşescu, 10: 408–409).

40. Ceauşescu, 10: 408–409.

41. Kaser and Spigler, "Economic Reform in the 1970s," p. 261.

42. Kaser and Spigler, "Economic Reform in the 1970s," p. 255.

43. *Scînteia*, 8 December 1967.

44. For a discussion of the reorganization of the territorial distribution of economic resources, see Turnock, "Romania," pp. 229–273.

45. As it turned out, many former presidents of People's Councils became first vice-presidents of the *Judeţ* People's Council. Also, only four of the regional first secretaries did not become county first secretaries, and at least three of these four received positions of equal or higher status.

46. *Scînteia*, 8 December 1967.

47. *Scînteia*, 8 December 1967.

48. Ceauşescu, 2: 522–523.

49. All the conference speeches appeared in *Scînteia* on 8 or 9 December 1967.

50. See, for example, the discussion on permeability of bloc boundaries in Zimmerman, "Hierarchical Regional Systems," and Lévesque, *Le conflict sino-soviétique*. See also the sources cited by Braun and Linden.

51. Those of France, Italy, Mexico, Portugal, Spain, Norway, Belgium, Israel, Morocco, Finland, Denmark, Austria, and Japan.

52. *Scînteia*, 18 February 1968.

53. *Scînteia*, 23 February 1968, or Ceauşescu, 3: 76–77.

54. According to a subsequent description by Ceauşescu; see his speech to the Bucharest Party organization, *Scînteia*, 28 April 1968; or Ceauşescu, 3: 189.

55. *Scînteia*, 28 April 1968; Ceauşescu, 3: 186.

56. According to Michel Tatu, *Le Monde*, 7 March 1968; see also Remington, *The Warsaw Pact*, p. 95.

57. *Scînteia*, 26 April 1968; see also *Scînteia*, 28 April 1968, and Ceauşescu, 3: 187. The six bloc members that attended were Bulgaria, Czechoslovakia, the German Democratic Republic, Hungary, Poland, and the USSR.

58. For the communiqué, see *Pravda*, 25 March 1968.

59. *Scînteia*, 28 April 1968; Ceauşescu, 3: 187.

60. *Scînteia*, 26 April 1968.

61. Remington, *The Warsaw Pact*, pp. 96–97.

62. *Scînteia*, 4 April 1968.

63. On "bureaucratism," see the absurd runaround criticized by *Scînteia* on 10 January 1968, p. 1, or its editorial on socialist democracy on 14 March. The Ceauşescu quote on democracy is from his speech to the Constanţa Party organization, *Scînteia*, 14 April 1968; Ceauşescu, 3: 115–116.

64. See the discussion in Sharlet, "Concept Formation"; Schulz and Adams, *Political Participation*, and the sources cited; and Chapter 9 herein.

65. *Scînteia* editorial, 14 March 1968.

66. *Scînteia*, 15 February 1968.

67. For reports of the sessions, see *Scînteia*, 15–17 February 1968. Ceauşescu's speech appeared on 16 February; see also Ceauşescu, 3: 9–35.

68. Ceauşescu, 3: 12.

69. Ceauşescu, 3: 16.

70. Ceauşescu elaborated on the new counties at length in this talk, giving comparisons on sectors such as area, population, economy, education, health, and cultural services.

71. Sălaj and Satu Mare, for example. See *Judeţele României Socialiste*, which has detailed information on each county. Of course, the growth rates were in percentages, and because Sălaj and Satu Mare were among the least industrialized, their high rates of growth were not so impressive.

72. Ceauşescu, 3: 20–21.

73. The conference was reported in *Scînteia* on 23 March, and Ceauşescu's speech appeared the same day; Ceauşescu, 3: 84–111.

74. Ceauşescu, 3: 97–98.

75. *Scînteia*, 18 February 1968; Ceauşescu, 3: 66.

76. *Scînteia*, 14 April 1968; Ceauşescu, 3: 122.

77. This was at the countrywide UCY conference, *Scînteia*, 10–11 February 1968. For Ceauşescu's speech, see 11 February, or Ceauşescu, 3: 42–55, esp. 50 and 52–53.

78. *Scînteia*, 1 March 1968.

79. *Scînteia*, 20 April 1968; Ceauşescu, 3: 137–139.

80. Ceauşescu, 3: 142, 133, 137.

81. In a speech in Tulcea; *Scînteia*, 14 April; Ceauşescu, 3: 117.

82. The Council of State passed the decree on 3 April, and a summary of its provisions was published in *Scînteia* on 4 April.

83. For a discussion of this reform, see Braham, *Education in Romania*, esp. pp. 13–17.

84. *Scînteia*, 25 April 1968.

85. *Scînteia*, 25 April 1968.

86. *Scînteia*, 25 April 1968.

87. *Scînteia*, 28 April 1968; Ceauşescu, 3: 169.

88. *Scînteia*, 27 April 1968. Both Ceauşescu and Coman were speaking to the Bucharest municipal Party organization.

89. *Scînteia*, 26 April 1968. A more detailed explanation by Ceauşescu may be found in his speech to the Bucharest Party organization, *Scînteia*, 28 April 1968; Ceauşescu, 3: 185–189.

90. The report itself was not published, but the decision of the plenum appeared in *Scînteia*, 26 April 1968, where all subsequent quotations from the decision may be found.

91. The members of this smaller group were Gheorghe Stoica, a founding member of the RCP; Vasile Patilineţ, CC secretary for security affairs; Nicolae Guină, a CC section head and former Soviet prisoner of war; and Ion Popescu-Puţuri, a prominent interwar Party member and director of the Institute of Party History.

92. Drăghici evidently tried to justify himself during these 1968 meetings.

93. The Council of Ministers acted the next day; *Scînteia*, 27 April 1968.

94. *Scînteia*, 28 April 1968; Ceauşescu, 3: 163–190.

95. Ceauşescu, 3: 172–173, 177–178.

96. Ceauşescu, 3: 174.

97. Ceauşescu, 3: 174.

98. Ceauşescu, 3: 175, 180, 177.

99. Ceauşescu, 3: 180.

100. We do not know who spoke; see *Scînteia*, 26 April 1968. By contrast, speeches criticizing Constantinescu and Chişinevschi in December 1961 appeared in *Scînteia*.

101. Ceauşescu, 3: 181–182.

102. Ceauşescu, 3: 170–171.

103. Ceauşescu, 3: 183.

104. Ceauşescu, 3: 184.

105. Ceauşescu, 3: 178.

106. Ceauşescu, 3: 179.

107. The texts of these speeches may be found in *Scînteia* as follows: Maurer (Cluj), 28 April; Apostol (Braşov), 29 April; Bodnaraş (Galaţi), 30 April; Chivu Stoica (Prahova), 28 April; Niculescu-Mizil (Timiş), 30 April; Trofin (Satu Mare), 29 April; Verdeţ (Hunedoara), 30 April. Other leaders spoke in the remaining counties, but the texts were not published in *Scînteia*.

108. Jowitt discusses this attempt under Ceauşescu "to build the Party's authority." See his *Revolutionary Breakthroughs*, pp. 273ff., esp. p. 280. The difference in attitude between the Gheorghiu-Dej and Ceauşescu groups on this issue is striking in the post-plenum speeches.

109. See the speech of Lt. General N. Militaru in Cluj, *Scînteia*, 28 April 1968.

110. *Scînteia*, 6 May 1968.

111. *Scînteia*, 11 May 1968.

112. See the works cited by Bacon and Alexiev.

113. See, for example, the article by George Ivascu in *Contemporanul*, 3 May 1968, pp. 1–2, and that by Mihnea Gheorghiu in *Luceafărul*, 17 April 1968, pp. 1, 7.

114. *Scînteia*, 25 April 1968; Ceauşescu, 3: 160.

115. As described by Maurer in *Scînteia*, 28 April 1968.

Chapter 6

1. *Scînteia*, 6 and 11 May 1968.

2. *Scînteia*, 15–19 May, 28 May–2 June, and 22 May 1968.

3. See, for example, his speech at the official dinner given by Tito, *Scînteia*, 30 May 1968.

4. *Scînteia*, 16 July 1968; Ceauşescu, 3: 301.

5. *Pravda*, 18 July 1968. See Remington, *The Warsaw Pact*, p. 102.

6. In a speech celebrating "Miners' Day," *Scînteia*, 12 August 1968; Ceauşescu, 3: 325.

7. *Scînteia*, 15 August 1968; Ceauşescu, 3: 328–351, 330–332, 335–336, and 349.

8. His remarks in Prague are found in *Scînteia*, 17 August 1968; Ceauşescu, 3: 352–372, esp. 354, 362, 365, and 367.

9. *Scînteia*, 21 August 1968; Ceauşescu, 3: 379–380.

10. *Scînteia*, 22 August 1968; Ceauşescu, 3: 382–385.

11. At the time, there were rumors throughout Romania of shots fired by Soviet troops across the Soviet-Romanian border. According to the story, the shots were returned, and there was no further trouble. In the early 1970s, many

in Romania believed that the Soviets would have invaded had the Romanians not returned the fire. The suggestion that the rumor was manufactured by the RCP to increase its own domestic support was dismissed with incredulity and amusement even by Romanians who were quite cynical toward the RCP on other issues.

12. For example, Ceauşescu himself spoke in Braşov, the two Hungarian counties, and Cluj; Maurer went to Tîrnăveni and Tîrgu Mureş; and Chivu Stoica to Craiova and Turnu Severin. Apostol spoke in Brăila; Bodnaraş in Iaşi; Niculescu-Mizil in Timiş, Arad, and Bihor; Trofin in Suceava and Botoşani; and Verdeţ in Hunedoara. See Scînteia, 27 August–2 September 1968. All speeches mentioned here were printed.

13. Scînteia, 27 August 1968; Ceauşescu, 3: 394–395.

14. See his speeches in Harghita, Scînteia, 27–28 August 1968; Ceauşescu, 3: 411.

15. In his speech in Covasna, Scînteia, 27 August 1968; Ceauşescu, 3: 400–401.

16. See Scînteia, 20 June 1968, or Ceauşescu, 3: 231–255, esp. 234.

17. Ceauşescu, 3: 234–235, 238–239.

18. Ceauşescu, 3: 237; excluding himself, of course.

19. Ceauşescu, 3: 241–243.

20. See, for example, his speech on the 120th anniversary of the 1848 revolution, Scînteia, 30 June 1968; Ceauşescu, 3: 277.

21. Scînteia, 18 and 21 September 1968.

22. See Ceauşescu's speech in Scînteia, 25 October 1968; Ceauşescu, 3: 590. For the creation of the councils, see Scînteia, 16 November 1968.

23. Scînteia, 27–28 August 1968; Ceauşescu, 3: 405, 414–415.

24. Timiş, for example, was 18 percent German, 12.5 percent Hungarian, and 7.3 percent Serb; see Judeţele României Socialiste, p. 527.

25. Philippe Ben in Le Monde, 1 October 1968.

26. The meeting of writers was held 14–16 November. For Ceauşescu's speech, see Scînteia, 17 November, or Ceauşescu, 3: 606–630.

27. See the report by SCCA President, Pompiliu Macovei, to the Grand National Assembly, Scînteia, 29 December 1967.

28. See Gabanyi, Partei und Literatur, pp. 156–161. As she indicates, the new statutes finally appeared in România literară in April 1969.

29. Gabanyi, Partei und Literatur, pp. 141–156.

30. Ceauşescu, 3: 620–621.

31. Ceauşescu, 3: 620.

32. Ceauşescu, 3: 615–617.

33. Ceauşescu, 3: 622.

34. Le Monde, 6 August 1969. In fact, the opening of the congress was postponed from 4 to 6 August so that arriving delegations would not interfere with the Nixon visit; Scînteia, 29 July 1969.

35. Washington Post, 7 August 1969.

36. Evidently the Romanians had requested no polemics, and the Chinese had been unwilling to come as mere spectators; Le Monde, 6 August 1969.

37. He did not stay away long, but returned for the next speaker. See New York Times, 8 August 1969, and Neue Zürcher Zeitung, 9 August 1969.

38. Neue Zürcher Zeitung, 9 August 1969.

39. Christ und Welt, 15 August 1969.

40. Le Monde, 8 August 1969.

41. All the Western press reports give this impression; the words are from Le Monde, 7 August 1969.

42. *New York Times*, 7 August 1969; *Washington Post*, 7 August 1969.

43. *Christian Science Monitor*, 7 August 1969.

44. Stolte, "The Romanian Party Congress," pp. 31–35.

45. *Congresul al X-lea*, pp. 59–60.

46. *Congresul al X-lea*, p. 26.

47. *Congresul al X-lea*, pp. 37–38, 27, 33.

48. *Congresul al X-lea*, pp. 66–67.

49. *Congresul al X-lea*, p. 56.

50. *Congresul al X-lea*, p. 55.

51. The revised statutes are printed in *Congresul al X-lea*, pp. 717–735.

52. *Neue Zürcher Zeitung*, 8 August 1969.

53. In his report to the congress on the Party statutes; *Congresul al X-lea*, pp. 126–138.

54. Articles 17 and 27. For Trofin's comments, see *Congresul al X-lea*, p. 132.

55. *Congresul al X-lea*, pp. 136–137. The new article was 18(d).

56. According to RFER, Romanian Situation Report (SR)/71, 14 August 1969, p. 4. For the composition of the Romanian sections, see *Congresul al X-lea*, pp. 16–17.

57. Articles 13(c), 30, and 32.

58. Article 13(b); this statement was greeted with "lively applause"; *Congresul al X-lea*, p. 135.

59. *Congresul al X-lea*, p. 135. See also Ceauşescu's speech to the Cluj Party conference, *Scînteia*, 13 July 1969; Ceauşescu, 4: 138.

60. Article 13(g) of the revised statutes required all Party organs to ensure the participation of members in decisionmaking; Trofin's remarks appeared in *Congresul al X-lea*, pp. 134, 136, 137.

61. *Congresul al X-lea*, p. 136. The quote is from Trofin's speech. For Ceauşescu's remarks, see pp. 61, 66.

62. The change is in Article 10. The earlier version appears in *Congresul al IX-lea*, p. 801; the 1969 revision in *Congresul al X-lea*, p. 721.

63. See Gheorghiu-Dej, *Articles and Speeches*, pp. 68–69.

64. *Scînteia*, 15 August 1969. Apostol had divorced his wife, a Party activist, to marry a popular singer; see RFER, Romanian SR/72, 18 August 1969, pp. 1–2.

65. RFER, Romanian SR/90, 16 October 1969, pp. 1–2.

66. *Congresul al X-lea*, p. 413.

67. These quotes and those that follow from Popescu's speech are found in *Congresul al X-lea*, pp. 493–496.

68. See Ceauşescu's speech, *Scînteia*, 12 March 1969; Ceauşescu, 3: 860–862.

Chapter 7

1. The terms "iconography" and "Bible" as well as "Gospel" and "shrine" have been applied to the Lenin cult by Nina Tumarkin; see her *Lenin Lives!* A series of what are essentially concordances to Ceauşescu's collected works has been published as "Documente ale Partidului Comunist Român." On ritual, see Bacon, "The Liturgics of Ceauşescuism," pp. 7–9. For an earlier discussion of the Ceauşescu cult, see my "Idol or Leader?"

2. Paltiel, "The Cult of Personality," pp. 49–50.

3. On the "Elena cult," see my "Women in Romanian Politics."

4. Weber, *Economy and Society*, vol. 1, pp. 215ff. "Legitimacy" here again means popular acceptance of the right to rule; see Chapter 4, note 1.

5. Tumarkin, *Lenin Lives!* pp. 1–2. Of course, as she also observed, "The deification of Greek and Roman rulers was rooted in earlier conceptions of power and divinity," but it was still "stimulated by current needs of state"; p. 1.

6. On the structural aspects of the Soviet system that foster a leadership cult, see Gill, "The Soviet Leader Cult."

7. Under this condition, even Carl J. Friedrich reluctantly granted charismatic status to Lenin; "The Theory of Political Leadership," p. 22.

8. Burns, *Leadership*, p. 248.

9. See Tumarkin, *Lenin Lives!*

10. Burns implies this contrast in his discussion of the two men; see *Leadership*, esp. pp. 248–254. Bialer also comments on Stalin's lack of interpersonal skills in the context of the cult; see his *Stalin's Successors*, p. 31.

11. Paltiel, "The Cult of Personality," p. 56.

12. *Congresul al XI-lea*, p. 78. I witnessed the speech as an observer at the congress.

13. See Burns's discussion of transactional and transforming leaders in *Leadership*.

14. *Scînteia*, 26 January 1978.

15. The reminiscences are quoted in Hamelet, *Nicolae Ceauşescu*, p. 10.

16. See *Scînteia*, 25 January 1978, for the awards; and 26 January 1978 for the joint message of the Central Committee, Council of State, and Council of Ministers. Certainly the honorary degrees granted him outside Romania are testimony of his skills in foreign policy, if not his academic achievements.

17. The ceremony was printed in *Scînteia*, 29 March 1974, with photographs.

18. For examples, see the celebrations of his birthday as reported in *Scînteia* for the last decade. The day itself is January 26, but the ceremonies and adulation begin before and continue after. For a highly critical evaluation of current Romanian historiography and its relationship to the Ceauşescu cult, see Georgescu, *Politică și istorie*.

19. See *Scînteia*, 6 January 1979, 7 January 1981, and 9 March 1982; and my "Women in Romanian Politics." On Petreşti, see *Tribuna Romåniei*, 15 May 1987, pp. 7–9, and RFER Romanian SR/9, 3 September 1987, pp. 19–21.

20. Only in Albania and North Korea does nepotism seem to be a prominent feature of another Leninist party. There have been isolated instances in other countries—Liudmila Zhivkova in Bulgaria, for example—but nowhere else has there been the extensive use of family members in key political positions.

21. In the mid-1980s Ion C. Brătianu, an engineer, carried on the family tradition by writing a series of open letters to the CC and the government, calling for political reforms. He had spent more than a decade in prisons and labor camps and died in the summer of 1987. See Vladimir Socor "Dissent in Romania," and RFER, SR/10, 21 September 1987, pp. 7–9.

22. Emil Bodnaraş, a member of the RCP leadership from 1944 until his death in 1976, described her as such in a speech printed in *Scînteia*, 17 December 1961, pp. 3–4.

23. For more details, see my "Women in Romanian Politics."

24. *Scînteia*, 24 June 1966; Ceauşescu, 1: 473–474, 476–477.

25. On the labor shortage, see Jackson, "Industrialization, Trade, and Mobilization," p. 932. On women in Eastern Europe, see Wolchik, "Ideology and Equality," esp. Table 3, pp. 452, 465.

26. Demographic data are from *Anuarul demografic al RSR, 1974*, pp. 132–133. The assessments of Romanian demographic policies are from David and McIntyre, *Reproductive Behavior*, esp. pp. 176–197. Quotations are from pp. 183, 193.

27. *Scînteia*, 20 June 1973; 3, 6, and 8 March 1984; see also my "Women in Romanian Politics." Supervisors in each workplace were made responsible for preventing women working for them from obtaining abortions, and many reacted by ordering monthly gynecological examinations to ensure that any pregnancies were brought to term.

28. *Scînteia*, 7 January 1988. The long description of the Ceauşescu family appeared in *Omagiu Tovarăşulvi Nicolae Ceauşescu*, p. 24.

29. See, for example, Gabanyi, *Partei und Literatur*, ch. vii.

30. For the plenums, see *Scînteia*, 19–20 March 1970, and 11–12 February 1971. On corruption, see *Scînteia* on 1, 4, and 5 March, the *Scînteia* editorial on 24 March, and *România liberă* on 15 March.

31. Jackson, "Industrialization, Trade, and Mobilization," p. 894. These growth figures are given in GNP; Ceauşescu would have used net material product, 7.7 percent.

32. Jackson, "Industrialization, Trade, and Mobilization," pp. 894–895.

33. Jackson, "Industrialization, Trade, and Mobilization," p. 897.

34. *Conferinţa naţională a PCR, 19–21 iulie 1972*, pp. 18, 541–542, and passim; Jackson, "Industrialization, Trade, and Mobilization," p. 897; *Congresul al X-lea*, p. 38.

35. Jackson, "Industrialization, Trade, and Mobilization," pp. 897–898.

36. On living standards in agriculture, see the two CC plenums later in 1970; *Scînteia*, 10 July and 17 December 1970. The decline in the agricultural labor force is cited by Hunya, "New Developments," p. 255. See also Gilberg, "Romanian Agricultural Policy."

37. See the reports in Western newspapers; for example, the *Baltimore Sun*, 7 July 1970. On the significance of 1971–1972, see Jowitt, "Political Innovation."

38. *Scînteia*, 21 August 1971; Ceauşescu, 6: 328.

39. By 1978 tension between the two small allies would rise to the point where Ceauşescu would declare with considerable hostility that he would not allow outsiders to use nationality problems to interfere in Romania: *Scînteia*, 16 March 1978; Ceauşescu, 15: esp. 512–515. See Chapter 9 herein.

40. The speech on culture appeared in *Scînteia* on 11 February, and the plenum was reported on 11–12 February. The new cadre policy was explained in *Scînteia* on 18 February.

41. For an early description of the campaign, see Gilberg, "Ceauşescu 'Kleine Kulturrevolution' in Rumänien." On the events themselves and the broader implications for Romanian culture, see Gabanyi, *Partei und Literatur*.

42. *Scînteia*, 7 July 1971; Ceauşescu, 6: 173–182.

43. *New York Times*, 25 July 1971.

44. *Plenara CC al PCR, 3–4 noiembrie 1971*, pp. 237–242.

45. *Scînteia*, 24 July 1971. The August visits were to the seaside, to Tulcea, to a Bucharest market, and to Harghita; *Scînteia*, 5, 6, 13, and 16 August 1971.

46. The contradictory nature of her image began almost immediately: on

6 January 1972 *Scînteia* pictured her wearing a full-length leopard coat on a "working visit" to Braşov with her husband.

47. *Conferinţă naţională a PCR, 19–21 iulie 1972*; for Ceauşescu, see pp. 13–107; for the resolutions, pp. 443–453. Maurer did preside at the first session when Ceauşescu spoke.

48. Constantin Mitea, "Ziarul—Factor dinamic în viaţa socială," pp. 1–4.

49. Sergiu Fărcăsan, "Jurnalistul ca om al meşteşugului literar," p. 24.

50. *Scînteia*, 25 September 1969.

51. Mircea Manea, "Prestigiul ziaristului," p. 1.

52. *Scînteia*, 9 March 1971.

53. Ceauşescu, 6: 230.

54. Alexandru Ionescu, "Principii politice şi organizatorice ale presei noastre," p. 25.

55. For the law itself, see *Scînteia*, 29–30 March 1974. The original version and explanation appeared in *Buletinul oficial al RSR*, 10, part 2, no. 2 (4 January 1974): 20–28. For a detailed analysis of the law, see Gabanyi, "Rumania's New Press Law."

56. Published in *Scînteia*, 7 May 1974, p. 2. It was very unusual for the CC Secretariat to issue a decision; decisionmaking bodies were usually the Political Executive Committee, the Council of State, the Council of Ministers, or the Grand National Assembly. More and more often after March 1974, however, laws began to appear initially as presidential decrees.

57. Gabanyi, "The Writer in Rumania," p. 55. The first quotation is from the decision as published in *Scînteia*, 7 May 1974, p. 2. For further analysis, see RFER, Romanian SR/16, 15 May 1974, pp. 14–17, and SR/17, 24 May 1974, pp. 1–2.

58. According to RFER Romanian SR/17, 24 May 1974, pp. 1–2.

59. *Buletinul oficial al RSR*, 10, part 1, no. 51 (30 May 1975): 1–3.

60. Gabanyi, "The Writer in Rumania," p. 51. For further comments on the Committee on Press and Printing, see RFER, Romanian SR/24, 26 June 1975, pp. 2–7.

61. "Preselecţie la facultatea de ziaristică," p. 36.

62. The proceedings were printed in *Congresul educaţiei politice şi al culturii socialiste, 2–4 iunie 1976*. See p. 5 for a description of the participants. See also the discussion by Maier, "The Romanian Congress on Political Education and Socialist Culture."

63. *Scînteia*, 15 July 1976; see also RFER, BR/167, 29 July 1976, pp. 1–9.

64. See *Presa noastră*, no. 4 (239), 1976, p. 2, and *Scînteia*, 28 March 1976, p. 5.

65. For further analysis, see RFER, Romanian SR/45, 17 December 1976, pp. 8–10.

66. See RFER, Romanian SR/2, 30 January 1978, pp. 8–9. On Poland, see, for example, Shanor, "Poland's Press and Broadcasting."

67. Among the restrictions imposed on Romanian citizens by the early 1980s would be limits on travel and residence, registration of typewriters, and strict monitoring of any copying facilities.

68. Article 49 of the 1974 press law, for example, gives Romanian journalists the right to "the facilities and priorities of transport and telecommunications, housing while away on business, access to cultural and sport events, procurement of special professional equipment," and to "receive support from relevant bodies"; *Scînteia*, 30 March 1974.

69. Article 57 of the 1974 press law specifies that "grave or repeated infringement by any journalist of professional duties or ethics leads to temporary or permanent withdrawal of the journalist's card and a shift to other duties"; *Scînteia*, 30 March 1974.

Chapter 8

1. The Executive Committee was renamed the Political Executive Committee at the Eleventh Congress in 1974. Another vital group is the Central Committee apparatus, but there is simply not enough information to analyze these individuals effectively.

2. *Scînteia*, 2 April 1988; the percentages are from the preceding year, *Scînteia*, 28 March 1987.

3. According to *Scînteia*, 17 April 1965.

4. See, for example, *Scînteia*, 14 April 1966.

5. *Scînteia*, 12 March 1969.

6. *Congresul al XI-lea*, p. 69.

7. *Scînteia*, 7 April 1977, 30 March 1979; *Congresul al XII-lea*, p. 60.

8. *Scînteia*, 20 November 1984.

9. *Scînteia*, 2 April 1988.

10. The plenum decision and the proposed law were printed in *Scînteia*, 17 February 1971, and the final version of the new law appeared a month later. See "Lege privînd perfecţionarea pregătirii profesionale," pp. 224–230.

11. See *Academia "Ştefan Gheorghiu"* and *The "Ştefan Gheorghiu" Academy*; both are pamphlets with no publisher given. I was able to interview professors at the academy in 1974–1975 and sat in on several retraining courses in 1978. Figures not otherwise cited were made available to me at the academy.

12. We know that of 10,623 individuals who went through retraining programs in Bucharest from 1971 to 1975, 4,208 were activists from the Party and mass organizations. The number jumped in 1975–1976 when the new complex was finished, and about 10,000 students attended in the one year. In that academic year alone, 4,510 Party activists were "recycled": 273 CC activists, 345 Party secretaries and heads of sections at the county level, 54 first secretaries of municipal Party committees, 760 other Party activists, 1,960 editors from the press, publishing, radio, and television, and 1,118 activists from mass organizations. A decade later the total number of students was similar: 11,000 in 1985. These figures for the 1970s were posted publicly at Ştefan Gheorghiu Academy in 1978. On 1985, see *Scînteia*, 9 April 1986.

13. For Ceauşescu's remarks, see Ceauşescu 5: 471. For the program in secondary schools, see *Scînteia*, 29 June 1977. The various programs were discussed extensively at the Ştefan Gheorghiu Academy in 1978,

14. *Scînteia*, 25 July 1975.

15. *Scînteia*, 7 April 1977. The efforts and results from 1977 to 1981 were described in the decision of the March 1981 CC plenum; *Scînteia*, 28 March 1981.

16. *Scînteia*, 28 March 1981 and 3 April 1985. The March 1985 Central Committee plenum reported increases in the number of Party members who had completed each of the educational levels during 1984, and they were quite similar to increases reported for 1980. The estimate assumes similar increases for the years after 1980, optimistic because figures were perhaps revealed only in better years.

17. Hill and Frank, *The Soviet Communist Party*, p. 41.

18. In 1973, for example, almost 56 percent of the Soviet party was over 40; see Rigby, "Soviet Communist Party Membership Under Brezhnev," p. 324.

19. The interruption, Ceauşescu's response, and the changes in the new statutes appeared in *Congresul al XI-lea*, pp. 580–582 and 589–590. I was able to observe the reactions of Ceauşescu and the delegates from one of the balconies.

20. *Congresul al XI-lea*, p. 440. Ceauşescu's refusal is on pp. 291–292.

21. See, for example, *Scînteia*, 28 March 1981, p. 2.

22. *Scînteia*, 30 March 1979, 31 March 1981. On the Brezhnev example, see Rigby, "Soviet Communist Party Membership Under Brezhnev," pp. 320–322.

23. See note 19 above and the accompanying text.

24. According to Article 14(b) of the Party statutes, *Congresul al XI-lea*, p. 591.

25. See my "Women in Romanian Politics."

26. For more details, see my "Romanian Communist Party and Its Central Committee," pp. 19–20 and Table 7. On cultural figures in 1984, see DeFlers and Socor, "The RCP's New Central Committee," p. 6.

27. If anyone was appointed first secretary in 1966 or 1967, that year rather than 1965 is taken as the starting point. Unfortunately, the data before 1958 are incomplete, but promotions are more likely to be known than demotions, thus strengthening the correlation. A move to the CC apparatus or a high state position in Bucharest was considered a promotion; continuing in the region as county first secretary or being appointed to a minor state position in Bucharest was considered comparable; and officials who were relegated to a minor local position, who were removed in disgrace, or who simply dropped out of public office were considered demoted. For annual status changes, see my "Political Leadership and Personnel Policy," Table 5, p. 223.

28. "Omul potrivit la locul potrivit," p. 5.

29. Constantin Drăgan, Vasile Vîlcu, and Andrei Cervencovici; *Scînteia*, 18 February 1971.

30. This was a return to the past for Vîlcu, who had been first secretary of the Dobrogea region, with Constanţa as his administrative center, for over ten years before moving to Bucharest in November 1965.

31. As described in *Scînteia*, 18 February 1971.

32. *Scînteia*, 19 April 1972.

33. Leonte Sălăjan, the defense minister who died in 1966 of a stomach ailment, was the only exception.

34. *Scînteia*, 1 June 1966. This was one of his first dramatic scenes; they would become more frequent as the years passed. The minister of railroads, Dumitru Simulescu, may very well have had close ties to Apostol.

35. *Scînteia*, 25, 29, 30 August 1966.

36. *Scînteia*, 8–9 December 1967. Another change worth noting involved Petre Blajovici, a former regional first secretary who had helped plan the administrative-territorial reform from the CC apparatus under Ceauşescu and Trofin: He moved to head the new Ministry of Labor, a post that would become vital in controlling personnel appointments, and where Ceauşescu could use him to challenge Apostol (once again heading the trade unions). By 1974 Blajovici would be a county first secretary and would intervene dramatically at the Party congress suggesting an age limit for Party

officials; the subsequent decline of his career suggests that Ceauşescu did not approve the intervention.

37. *Scînteia*, 26–27 April 1968 and 18 December 1968.

38. *Scînteia*, 14 March 1969.

39. The two not elected in 1965 were Gheorghiu-Dej and Mihai Dalea, who did continue as CC secretary and finally was elected a candidate member of the EC in 1970. The five remaining after 1969 were Ceauşescu, Maurer, Bodnaraş, Răutu, and Voitec.

40. Dumitru Popa was removed for "serious shortcomings" as first secretary of Bucharest; *Scînteia*, 19 April 1972.

41. This was Gheorghe Rădulescu, reportedly educated at the Tashkent Planning Institute. Other EC members did have higher educations—Niculescu-Mizil and Lupu, for example—and Berghianu had received advanced Party training in economics. Nevertheless, the educational background of this group presents a sharp contrast to the subsequent promotion of technical specialists such as Mănescu, Oprea, and Păţan.

42. Mănescu had been dropped from the Secretariat at the Tenth Party Congress, but was reappointed in December 1969. Reasons for the temporary demotion are not clear.

43. At the same time, two women—Aurelia Dănilă and Magdalena Filipaş—were elected candidate EC members.

44. The four were Maxim Berghianu, Petre Blajovici, Florea Dănălache, and Constantin Drăgan, all former regional first secretaries. The other five were Constantin Băbălău, Aurelia Dănilă, Magdalena Filipaş, Ion Stănescu, and Gheorghe Stoica.

45. According to *Scînteia*, 27 March 1974, the Permanent Bureau would consist of the general secretary and all CC secretaries; the president of the Republic and president of the Council of State; those vice-presidents of the Council of State who "assure the permanent activity" of this body; the president of the Council of Ministers; the first vice-president and one or two vice-presidents of the Council of Ministers; the president of the Central Council of Workers' Control of Economic and Social Activity; the president of the State Planning Committee; the head of the trade unions; and others chosen by the Executive Committee.

46. In subsequent years, the Permanent Bureau would become the equivalent of the former Presidium.

47. Bodnaraş's obituary appeared in *Scînteia* on 25 January 1976.

48. These included Elena Ceauşescu, Petre Lupu, Manea Mănescu, Paul Niculescu-Mizil, Gheorghe Rădulescu, Leonte Răutu, and Vasile Vîlcu.

49. On the question of education, see the comments by Georgescu in "Romania in the 1980s," pp. 81–82.

50. In 1974, six full members of the PEC were members of the ethnic minorities: Bodnaraş, Fazekas, Lupu, Răutu, Uglar, and Vîlcu.

51. Georgescu, "Romania in the 1980s," pp. 81–82.

52. *Scînteia*, 27 March, 8 September, 27 November 1981; 21–22 May and 9 October 1982.

53. *Scînteia*, 22 May 1982, 14 November 1985, 25 June 1986, 18 December 1985.

54. Presidential counselors appointed to high office have included Ştefan Bîrlea, Emilian Dobrescu, Marin Enache, Petre Gigea, and Vasile Pungan.

55. A similar relationship existed between the enterprise director and the joint worker-management body I was allowed to observe in 1978; the director

explained the policies (in this case sent down to him from above) and asked for advice on how to fulfill them.

56. *Scînteia*, 26 July 1979; 8 July, 16 October, 27 December 1975; 12 October 1977; 18 January 1975; 15 July 1976; 6 October 1982.

57. *Scînteia*, 19 March 1982; 2 September, 1 November, 18 December 1978; and 25 November 1979.

58. *Congresul al XII-lea*, pp. 903–904.

Chapter 9

1. For an earlier analysis of Ceaușescu's participatory reforms and the 1975 elections, see my "Participatory Reforms."

2. See, for example, Ceaușescu's speeches to the Central Committee, 18–19 June 1973, and to a conference of cadres in higher education, 13 September 1974; Ceaușescu, 8: 586–600; 10: 645, 668. Not a lot had changed a decade later; see *Scînteia*, 13–17 and 20 September 1986; 18 September 1987; and 16 September 1988.

3. *Congresul al IX-lea*, p. 79; *Scînteia*, 8 December 1967.

4. The decision appeared in *Scînteia*, 23 November 1972; the plenum proceedings, including Ceaușescu's speech, on 21 November. A number of personnel changes had preceded the decision; see *Scînteia*, 12 October.

5. *Scînteia*, 12 October 1972.

6. *Scînteia*, 23 November 1972.

7. Other examples are the Council of Economic-Social Organization, the Central Council of Worker's Control of Economic and Social Activity, and the Committee for the Problems of People's Councils. See *Organizațiile obștești în sistemul organizării politice din RSR*, p. 24. On these questions, see also Tontsch, *Das Verhältnis von Partei und Staat in Rumänien*.

8. Schulz, "Political Participation," p. 3.

9. Schulz, "Political Participation," p. 7. See his distinction between quantitative and qualitative dimensions of participation. See also Sharlet, "Concept Formation."

10. See, for example, Little, "Mass Political Participation," and his "Bureaucracy and Participation." See also the articles and sources cited in Schulz and Adams, eds., *Political Participation*; Hahn, *Soviet Grassroots*, esp. Chap. 2; and the sources cited.

11. Schulz, "On the Nature and Function of Participation," p. 29.

12. Schulz, "On the Nature and Function of Participation," p. 30.

13. Jowitt, "Inclusion and Mobilization," p. 99.

14. Jowitt, "Inclusion and Mobilization," p. 96.

15. Schulz, "On the Nature and Function of Participation," p. 67.

16. Jowitt also dates the beginning of this retreat as June 1971; "Inclusion and Mobilization," p. 110. See also his "Political Innovation" for the significance of the Asian trip.

17. *Scînteia*, 27 February 1966.

18. Between July 1965 and January 1973 he made 147 such tours, usually of more than one day each. For details, see *Omagiu Tovarășului Nicolae Ceaușescu*, p. 20.

19. This is the ombudsman role of the press discussed in Chapter 7. In the 1980s, however, television was cut drastically, down to two hours per day, and much of the two hours was taken up in reporting Ceaușescu's daily schedule.

20. During 1975 I was able to interview several city and county Party

officials who told me with great enthusiasm about these new processes introduced under Ceauşescu.

21. During the summer of 1978 I was able to attend one such meeting. See also the comments by Smith, "The Romanian Industrial Enterprise," pp. 64, 80.

22. See also the findings of Nelson in his "Development and Participation."

23. See especially Articles 69, 75, 99, 108, 53, 52 of the constitution; and Chapter 4 herein, note 34.

24. Ceauşescu, 2: 557–558.

25. *Congresul al IX-lea*, p. 70.

26. In an interview with me in the summer of 1975. Ceterchi served as minister of justice from 1980 to 1982, when he was removed "for reasons of health." In 1984 he was named ambassador to Sweden; *Scînteia*, 24 January 1982, 5 July 1984. My own observations did not give much basis for optimism that the GNA was becoming more powerful.

27. When the announcement of the impending reduction was made in the summer of 1974, many Romanians skeptically concluded that the real motive was financial savings.

28. Romanians themselves are unofficially very skeptical about the role of their parliament; most people were simply unable to understand why I even wanted to attend the session.

29. See, for example, the series of decrees in *Scînteia*, 2, 4, 12, 13, 30 September and 1 October 1987.

30. In his speech to the February CC plenum; *Scînteia*, 12 February 1971, or Ceauşescu, 5: 468. For the elections, see *Scînteia*, 11 March 1975. I was permitted to study the local press reports for the 1975 elections, and so I have the published data on each candidate. For 1980 and 1985 I have seen only the totals in *Scînteia*, but the process does not seem to have changed significantly. For an earlier report on the 1975 elections, see my "Participatory Reforms." See also Nelson, "Development and Participation," especially the commune results in 1977 on pp. 248–249.

31. The only exception was Chivu Stoica, still a candidate member of the PEC, but he did not run for re-election.

32. This was Suzana Gâdea, a candidate CC member and perceived to be close to Elena Ceauşescu. Defeated in 1975, she was elected the following year in a by-election; *Scînteia*, 5 November 1976. See the text accompanying note 35 below for the non-political case.

33. In Romanian, as in English, it is not always possible to determine gender by name; hence these figures may be off by one or two.

34. The explanations that follow are from interviews with Romanian election officials during the summer of 1975.

35. This was the one case in which a full CC member was defeated by a non-member. The interpretation given here of his defeat was current in Bucharest in July 1975.

36. See the draft *Programme of the RCP* (Bucharest: Agerpres, 1974), p. 109. The final form of the program (Meridiane, 1975) omitted all the above qualifications except "managerial skills" and "firmness and responsibility." See pp. 137–138.

37. Italics added. See his speech to the joint plenum of the CC and the Socialist Unity Front, *Scînteia*, 18 March 1975.

38. The election results appeared in *Scînteia* on 4 March 1969, 11 March 1975, 19 March 1985.

39. Schulz, "On the Nature and Function of Participation," p. 30.

40. The resignation of Király was reported in *Scînteia*, 19 April 1972. On his actions in 1978, see *Christian Science Monitor*, 8 February, 2 May, and 25 May 1978; RFER, SR/4, 5, 6, 7 (16 and 25 February, 9 and 17 March 1978); and a report by Amnesty International entitled *Romania* (1978). The letters appeared in *Witnesses to Cultural Genocide*, pp. 162–178.

41. Georgescu, "Romania in the 1980s," pp. 88–89. See also the sources cited there on the Romanian dissident movement, especially his own "Romanian Dissent."

42. Moore, "The Romanian Communist Party's 12th Congress," p. 10. For a brief biography of Pârvulescu, see Chapter 2 herein, note 14.

43. Jowitt, *Revolutionary Breakthroughs*, p. 273. See here his excellent discussion of the RCP and the nation, ch. 18.

44. *Scînteia*, 8 May 1966. A collection of such statements is found in *Documente ale PCR: Naţiunea socialistă*.

45. Brucan, *The Dialectic of World Politics*, pp. ix–x, 21–22. See also Vlad, *Essays on Nation*; Florea, *Naţiunea Română şi Socialismul*; or *Naţiunea şi problema naţională*.

46. *Programme* of the RCP (draft), p. 122.

47. *Recensămîntul . . . 1977*. Hungarian estimates are usually about 15 percent; for a discussion of the Romanian inaccuracies, see Shafir, *Romania*, pp. 164–165; see his discussion of the nationalities, pp. 158–168. For my own more detailed treatments of the subject, see my "Nation and Nationality" and "National Inequality in Romania," and the sources cited.

48. Except in the counties of Covasna and Harghita, where Hungarians make up about 79 and 88 percent of the population.

49. *Recensămîntul . . . 1966*. This may have been true in 1977 as well, but urbanization and education by nationality were not included in the published 1977 data.

50. For a brief but perceptive analysis of the historical complexities, see Rothschild's chapter on Romania in *East Central Europe*.

51. Wolff, *The Balkans*, pp. 453–454.

52. See Shafir, *Romania*, p. 160.

53. *Scînteia*, 24 December 1960.

54. *Scînteia*, 29 and 6 June 1965.

55. *Scînteia*, 16 February 1968.

56. See, for example, pp. 93–94 herein.

57. *Scînteia*, 27–28 August 1968. See also Chapter 6 herein.

58. *Scînteia*, 25 October 1968.

59. See Colceriu-Leiss, "Consiliile oamenilor muncii aparţinînd naţionalităţilor conlocuitoare," in *Organizaţiile obşteşti în sistemul organizării politice din RSR*, pp. 165–173.

60. For much more detailed analyses, see the sources cited in note 47 above.

61. See my "National Inequality in Romania," esp. Table 8.5, p. 209.

62. See my "National Inequality in Romania," pp. 209–211.

63. Again, for more details, see my "Nation and Nationality" and "National Inequality in Romania," and the sources cited.

64. *Scînteia*, 20 June 1973.

65. *Recensămîntul . . . 1966* and *Recensămîntul . . . 1977*. There were minor exceptions: The entire population of Botoşani, including Romanians, declined because of high emigration rates. The Gypsies showed a widespread

increase, perhaps in part because of better counting methods; and the Turkish population rose in Constanţa and Bucharest.

66. Again, these official Romanian statistics are subject to doubt.

67. There are a number of indications that the assimilation was covertly coerced rather than induced; see Shafir, *Romania*, p. 163, and the sources cited.

68. Again, the engineer may have had little real choice in the matter.

69. In private conversation.

70. Ceauşescu's combined egalitarianism and elitism are discussed more fully in my "Idol or Leader," and his views on women in my "Women in Romanian Politics." For his arguments on the costs of nationality education, see my "Nation and Nationality," esp. p. 511.

71. Hitchins, *Orthodoxy and Nationality*, p. 170.

72. *Witnesses to Cultural Genocide*, p. 98.

73. See, for example, Schopflin, "Gorbachev, Romania, and 'Leninist Nationalities Policy,'" RFER, SR/2, 28 January 1988, pp. 15–19; *New York Times*, 7, 15, and 21 February, 29 May, 1 and 4 September 1988.

74. The causes are of course much more complex. Probably the best single treatment is Jackson, "Romania's Debt Crisis."

75. For example, in 1979 Romania would have had a positive balance were it not for large deficits with Iran, Iraq, Libya, and Nigeria. See RFER, SR/4, 5 March 1981, pp. 20–21.

76. Jackson, "Romania's Debt Crisis," p. 494.

77. Jackson, "Romania's Debt Crisis," pp. 491–492.

78. Hudson, "Romania's Economic Performance Flawed," pp 5–6. See also Jackson, "Romania's Economy," and his "Perspectives on Romania's Economic Development."

79. Again, the picture is much more complicated, as Jackson demonstrates; see "Romania's Debt Crisis," pp. 526–534.

80. In reality, official retail prices in 1982, for example, rose an average of 17 percent, and retail prices of agricultural goods were up by about 35 percent; Jackson, "Romania's Debt Crisis," p. 527.

81. The descriptions are from my own observations in 1982.

82. See, for example, the summaries of PEC meetings in *Scînteia*, 24 June 1981 and 23 January 1982.

83. See the PEC meetings in *Scînteia* as follows: 3 December 1980; 11 March, 24 June, and 16 December 1981; 8 February, 1 June, 23 June, and 21 November 1982.

84. Smith, "The Romanian Industrial Enterprise," and Jackson, "Romania's Debt Crisis," pp. 534–538.

85. Smith, "Romanian Economic Reforms"; see also Smith, "The Romanian Industrial Enterprise," pp. 64–65.

86. Smith, "The Romanian Industrial Enterprise," pp. 64, 80; this agrees with my own observations.

87. Smith, "The Romanian Industrial Enterprise," p. 80. The agro-industrial enterprises would become part of the "systematization" campaign in the 1980s.

88. Jackson, "Romania's Debt Crisis," p. 493.

89. In a speech to a CC working conference, *Scînteia*, 1 June 1980; Ceauşescu, 20: 68–103.

90. On the attempted coup, see, for example, RFER, SR/3, 19 February 1983, pp. 8–12.

91. On the *acord global*, see Jackson, "Romania's Debt Crisis," p. 536

(italics mine); on 1987, see *Scînteia*, 6 October 1987, and RFER, SR/12, 6 November 1987, pp. 6–7.

92. For early descriptions of the "systematization" plans, see *Scînteia*, 4 August 1974, or Ion, "Perfecţionarea repartizării pe teritoriu." For more recent evaluations, see Shafir, "The Historical Background to Rural Resettlement"; Ionescu, "Bucharest's Hinterland"; and Turnock, "Romania."

93. For another promise to make major changes, see the discussion of agriculture by the PEC, *Scînteia*, 23 January 1982.

94. See the game of musical chairs in September 1987; *Scînteia*, 2, 4, 12, 13, 14 September; for background, see RFER, SR/11, 15 October 1987, pp. 15–17.

95. For examples of high officials removed in disgrace, see *Scînteia*, 27 November 1981 (Trofin and Gavrilescu) and 22 May 1982 (Burtică and Verdeţ).

96. *Scînteia*, 5 October 1982.

97. *Scînteia*, 21 November 1981 and 22–25 November 1986.

98. For the stress on self-sufficiency, see reports of PEC meetings in *Scînteia*, 15 October 1980; 29 April, 4 July, 20 October and 21 November 1981; 9 April, 1 June, and 21 November 1982; etc. The decree instituting the educational tax was published in *Scînteia* on 6 November 1982; an editorial on "human rights as a pretext for stealing brain power" appeared 5 December 1982; reports of activity at the UN were published on 10 November and 16 December.

99. For an evaluation, see RFER, SR/4, 4 March 1988, pp. 3–4.

Chapter 10

1. On the debt-service ratio, see U.S. Department of Commerce, "U.S.-Romanian Trade Trends," p. 2.

2. Burns, *Leadership*, p. 248. See also Chapter 7 herein, note 8, and the accompanying text.

3. Weber, *Economy and Society*, vol. 1, pp. 215ff. See also herein Chapter 4, note 1, and Chapter 7, note 4, and the accompanying text.

4. On Ceauşescu's concepts of participation, see Chapter 9, especially notes 8–16, and the accompanying text.

5. See Shafir, *Romania*, ch. 9; his "Political Culture, Intellectual Dissent, and Intellectual Consent"; and works by Sampson in the bibliography.

6. As in the legend of *Mioriţa*, in which a Romanian peasant submits passively to his death at the hands of strangers. Another illustration of this tendency in Romanian culture is the proverb repeated to me in Romania numerous times: "A bowed head is not cut off by the sword."

7. Montias questioned the long-term efficiency of this policy over 20 years ago; see his *Economic Development*, pp. 244–247.

8. Wojciech Jaruzelski is the professional military officer who became defense minister, then premier, and eventually head of the Polish party in 1981; Lavrenti Beria was head of the Soviet secret police until he was executed by his Politburo colleagues after Stalin's death—apparently because they feared he might try to seize power. For a recent evaluation of the military and police, see Crowther, " 'Ceauşescuism' and Civil-Military Relations in Romania."

9. Bobu has already been heir apparent longer than any of his predecessors, however, so a change here would not be surprising. In addition, the position of heir apparent is not always advantageous during a succession struggle in a Leninist party.

Bibliography

Academia " Ştefan Gheorghiu." Bucharest: N. p., 1975.

Alexiev, Alex. "Party-Military Relations in Eastern Europe: The Case of Romania." In Roman Kolkowicz and A. Korbonski, eds., *Soldiers, Peasants, and Bureaucrats: Civil–Military Relations in Communist and Modernizing Societies,* pp. 199–227. Boston: George Allen and Unwin, 1982.

———. "The Romanian Army." In Jonathan R. Adelman, *Communist Armies in Politics,* pp. 149–166. Boulder, Colo.: Westview, 1982.

Anuarul demografic al RSR, 1974. Bucharest: Direcţia centrală de statistică, 1974.

Bacon, Walter M., Jr. "Civil-Military Relations in Romania: Value Transformations in the Romanian Military." *Studies in Comparative Communism* 11 (Autumn 1978): 237–249.

———. "The Liturgics of Ceauşescuism." Paper presented at the AAASS meetings, Boston, November 1987.

———. "The Military and the Party in Romania." In Dale R. Herspring and Ivan Volgyes, eds., *Civil-Military Relations in Communist Systems,* pp. 165–180. Boulder, Colo.: Westview, 1978.

———. "Romanian Secret Police." In Jonathan R. Adelman, ed., *Terror and Communist Politics,* pp. 135–154. Boulder, Colo.: Westview, 1984.

Bialer, Seweryn. *Stalin's Successors: Leadership, Stability, and Change in the Soviet Union.* Cambridge: Cambridge University Press, 1980.

Binder, David. "Rumania Is Lifting Restrictions on Hungarians in Transylvania." *New York Times,* 5 February 1966.

Braham, Randolph L. *Education in Romania: A Decade of Change.* U.S. Department of Health, Education and Welfare, Office of Education. Washington, D.C.: U.S. Government Printing Office, 1972.

Braun, Aurel. *Romanian Foreign Policy Since 1965: The Political and Military Limits of Autonomy.* New York: Praeger, 1978.

Breslauer, George. *Khrushchev and Brezhnev as Leaders: Building Authority in Soviet Politics.* Boston: George Allen and Unwin, 1982.

Brown, Archie, ed. *Political Culture and Communist Studies.* Armonk, N.Y.: M. E. Sharpe, 1985.

Brown, Archie, and Jack Gray, eds. *Political Culture and Political Change in Communist States.* 2nd ed. New York: Holmes and Meier, 1979.

Brown, J. F. *The New Eastern Europe.* New York: Praeger, 1966.

Brucan, Aurel. *The Dialectic of World Politics.* New York: Free Press, 1978.

Brucan, Silviu. "August 23, 1944." *Scînteia,* 22 August 1948.

Bucur, Nicholas A. *Ceauşescu of Romania: Champion of Peace.* Cleveland, Ohio: Quills and Scrolls Publishing Co., 1981.

Buletinul oficial al RSR.

Burks, Richard V. *The Dynamics of Communism in Eastern Europe.* Princeton, N.J.: Princeton University Press, 1961.

Burns, James MacGregor. *Leadership.* New York: Harper, 1978.

Catchlove, Donald. *Romania's Ceauşescu.* London: Abacus, 1972.

305

Ceauşescu, Nicolae. *Romania on the Way of Building Up the Multilaterally Developed Socialist Society: Reports, Speeches, Articles*. Vols. 4– (about 30 to date). Bucharest: Meridiane, 1970–. Cited as Ceauşescu with volume and page.

———. *Romania on the Way of Completing Socialist Construction: Reports, Speeches, Articles*. Vols. 1–3. Bucharest: Meridiane, 1969. Cited as Ceauşescu with volume and page.

Chirot, Daniel. "Neoliberal and Social Democratic Theories of Development: The Zeletin-Voinea Debate Concerning Romania's Prospects in the 1920s." In Kenneth Jowitt, ed., *Social Change in Romania, 1860–1940: A Debate on Development in a European Nation*, pp. 31–52. Berkeley: Institute of International Studies, University of California, 1978.

Christ und Welt.

Christian Science Monitor.

Colceriu-Leiss, Maria. "Consiliile oamenilor muncii aparţînind naţionalităţilor conlocuitoare." In *Organizaţiile obşteşti în sistemul organizării politice din RSR*, pp. 165–173. Bucharest: Ed. Academiei, 1973.

Conferinţa naţională a PCR, 19–21 iulie 1972. Bucharest: Ed. politică, 1972.

Congresul al IX-lea al PCR, 19–25 iulie 1965. Bucharest: Ed. politică, 1966.

Congresul al IX-lea al PCR, 6–12 august 1969. Bucharest: Ed. politică, 1969.

Congresul al XI-lea al PCR, 25–28 no jembrie 1974. Bucharest: Ed. politică, 1975.

Congresul al XII-lea al PCR, 19–23 noiembrie 1979. Bucharest: Ed. politică, 1981.

Congresul educaţiei politice şi al culturii socialiste, 2–4 iunie 1976. Bucharest: Ed. politică, 1976.

Contemporanul.

Crăciun, Ioachim, et al. *Bibliografia istorică a României*. (Academie de Ştiinţe sociale şi politice a RSR, Institutul de istorie şi arheologie Cluj). Bucharest: Ed. Academiei RSR, 1970.

Cretzianu, Alexandre, ed. *Captive Rumania*. New York: Praeger, 1956.

Crowther, William, " 'Ceauşescuism' and Civil-Military Relations in Romania," *Armed Forces and Society* 15 (Winter 1989): 207–225.

Cunliffe, Marcus. *George Washington, Man and Monument*. Boston: Little, Brown, 1958.

Cuvînt liber, 6 June 1936.

David, Henry P., and Robert J. McIntyre. *Reproductive Behavior: Central and East European Experience*. New York: Springer, 1981.

DeFlers, R. A., and V. Socor. "The RCP's New Central Committee." RFER, BR/6, 11 January 1985, pp. 1–9.

Dicţionar enciclopedic romîn. Bucharest: Ed. politică, 1972.

Documente ale PCR: Naţiunea socialistă. Bucharest: Ed. politică, 1972.

East Europe.

Eidelberg, Philip G. *The Great Rumanian Peasant Revolt of 1907*. Leiden: E. J. Brill, 1974.

Era socialistă.

Fărcăşan, Sergiu. "Jurnalistul ca om al meşteşugului literar." *Presa noastră* 12 (September 1967): 24–28.

Farlow, Robert H. "Romanian Foreign Policy: A Case of Partial Alignment." *Problems of Communism* 20 (November–December 1971): 93–113.

Fischer, Mary Ellen. "Idol or Leader? The Origins and Future of the Ceauşescu Cult." In Daniel N. Nelson, ed., *Romania in the 1980s*, pp. 117–141. Boulder, Colo.: Westview, 1981.

_____. "Nation and Nationality in Romania." In George W. Simmonds, ed., *Nationalism in the USSR and Eastern Europe in the Era of Brezhnev and Kosygin*, pp. 504–521. Detroit, Mich.: University of Detroit Press, 1977.

_____. "Participatory Reforms and Political Development in Romania." In Jan F. Triska and Paul M. Cocks, eds., *Political Development in Eastern Europe*, pp. 217–237. New York: Praeger, 1977.

_____. "Political Leadership and Personnel Policy in Romania, 1965–1976." In Steven Rosefielde, ed., *World Communism at the Crossroads*, pp. 210–233. The Hague: Nijhoff, 1980.

_____. "Political Leadership in Rumania Under the Communists." *International Journal of Rumanian Studies* 5, no. 1 (1987): 7–31.

_____. "The Politics of National Inequality in Romania." In Daniel N. Nelson, ed., *Communism and the Politics of Inequality*, pp. 189–220. Lexington, Mass.: Lexington Books, 1983.

_____. "The Romanian Communist Party and Its Central Committee: Patterns of Growth and Change." *Southeastern Europe* 6, pt. 1 (1979): 1–28.

_____. "Women in Romanian Politics: Elena Ceauşescu, Pronatalism, and the Promotion of Women." In Sharon L. Wolchik and Alfred G. Meyer, eds., *Women, State and Party in Eastern Europe*, pp. 121–137, 388–393. Durham, N.C.: Duke University Press, 1985.

Fischer-Galati, Stephen. "The Communist Takeover of Rumania: A Function of Soviet Power." In Thomas T. Hammond, ed., *The Anatomy of Communist Takeovers*, pp. 310–320. New Haven: Yale University Press, 1975.

_____. "Fascism in Romania." In Peter F. Sugar, ed., *Native Fascism in the Successor States, 1918–1945*, pp. 112–121. Santa Barbara, Calif.: ABC-Clio, 1971.

_____. *The New Rumania*. Cambridge: MIT Press, 1967.

_____. *Twentieth Century Rumania*. New York: Columbia University Press, 1970.

_____, ed. *Romania*. New York: Praeger, 1957.

Florea, Elena. *Naţiunea Română şi Socialismul*. Bucharest: Ed. Academiei, 1974.

Floyd, David. *Rumania: Russia's Dissident Ally*. New York: Praeger, 1965.

Frankfurter Allgemeine Zeitung.

Friedrich, Carl J. "The Theory of Political Leadership and the Issue of Totalitarianism." In R. Barry Farrell, ed., *Political Leadership in Eastern Europe and the Soviet Union*, pp. 17–27. Chicago: Aldine, 1970.

Gabanyi, Anneli Ute. *Partei und Literatur in Rumänien seit 1945*. Munich: R. Oldenbourg, 1975.

_____. "Romania's New Press Law." *Index on Censorship* 3 (Autumn 1974): 65–71.

_____. "The Writer in Rumania." *Index on Censorship* 4 (Autumn 1975): 51–55.

Gati, Charles. *Hungary and the Soviet Bloc*. Durham, N.C.: Duke University Press, 1986.

Georgescu, Vlad. *Politică şi istorie: cazul comuniştilor români 1944–1977*. Munich: Ion Dumitru Verlag, 1981.

_____. "Romania in the 1980s: The Legacy of Dynastic Socialism." *East European Politics and Societies* 2 (Winter 1988): 69–93.

_____. "Romanian Dissent: Its Ideas." In Jane L. Curry, ed., *Dissent in Eastern Europe*, pp. 182–194. New York: Praeger, 1983.

Georgescu-Cosmovici, Adriana. *Au Commencement Était la Fin: La Dictature Rouge à Bucarest*. Paris: Hachette, 1951.

Gheorghiu-Dej, Gheorghe. *Articles and Speeches, June 1960–December 1961*. Bucharest: Meridiane, 1963.

Gilberg, Trond. "Ceauşescus 'Kleine Kulturrevolution' in Rumänien." *Osteuropa* 22 (October 1972): 717–728.

———. *Modernization in Romania Since World War II*. New York: Praeger, 1975.

———. "Political Socialization in Romania: Prospects and Performance." In Daniel N. Nelson, ed., *Romania in the 1980s*, pp. 142–173. Boulder, Colo.: Westview, 1981.

———. "Romanian Agricultural Policy: Persisting Problems." In Karl-Eugen Wädekin, ed., *Current Trends in the Soviet and East European Food Economy*, pp. 239–272. Berlin: Duncker and Humblot, 1982.

Gill, Graeme. "The Soviet Leader Cult: Reflections on the Structure of Leadership in the Soviet Union." *British Journal of Political Science* 10 (April 1980): 167–186.

Giurescu, Dinu C. *Illustrated History of the Romanian People*. Bucharest: Ed. Sport-Turism, 1981.

Granick, David. *Enterprise Guidance in Eastern Europe*. Princeton, N.J.: Princeton University Press, 1975.

Hahn, Jeffrey W. *Soviet Grassroots: Citizen Participation in Local Soviet Government*. London: Tauris, 1988.

Hamelet, Michel-P. *Nicolae Ceauşescu*. Paris: Seghers, 1971 (French language version); Bucharest: Ed. politică, 1971 (Romanian language version).

Heer, Nancy W. *Politics and History in the Soviet Union*. Cambridge: MIT Press, 1971.

Hill, Ronald J., and Peter Frank. *The Soviet Communist Party*. 3rd ed. Boston: Allen and Unwin, 1986.

Hitchins, Keith. *Orthodoxy and Nationality: Andreiu Şaguna and the Rumanians of Transylvania, 1846–1873*. Cambridge: Harvard University Press, 1977.

"How the United Workers' Front Was Set Up." *Magazin Istoric*, no. 1 (April 1967).

Hudson, Cam. "Romania's Economic Performance Flawed." RFER, BR/173, 18 June 1981, pp. 1–7.

Hunya, Gabor. "New Developments in Romanian Agriculture." *East European Politics and Societies* 1 (Spring 1987): 255–276.

Ileana, Princess of Romania. *I Live Again*. New York: Rinehart, 1952.

În slujba cercetării marxiste a istoriei PCR. Bucharest: Institutul de studii istorice şi social-politice de pe lîngă CC al PCR, 1971.

Ion, Ion Şt. "Perfecţionarea repartizării pe teritoriu a forţelor de producţie." In *Perfecţionarea organizării şi conducerii vieţii economice de stat şi sociale*, pp. 208–228. Bucharest: Ed. Academiei, 1972.

Ionescu, Alexandru, ed. *The Grand National Assembly of the Socialist Republic of Romania*. Bucharest: Casa Scînteii, 1974.

Ionescu, Alexandru. "Principii politice şi organizatorice ale presei noastre." *Presa noastră* 16 (October–November 1971): 25–33.

Ionescu, Dan. "Bucharest's Hinterland: A Test Ground for Rural Resettlement." RFER, Romanian SR/10, 23 August 1988, pp. 9–15.

Ionescu, Ghita. *Communism in Rumania, 1944–1962*. New York: Oxford University Press, 1964.

Jackson, George D. *Comintern and Peasant in Eastern Europe 1919–1930*. New York: Columbia University Press, 1966.

Jackson, Marvin R. "Industrialization, Trade, and Mobilization in Romania's

Drive for Economic Independence." In U.S. Congress, Joint Economic Committee, *East European Economies Post-Helsinki*, pp. 886–940. 95th Congress, 1st sess., 1977.

————. "Perspectives on Romania's Economic Development in the 1980s." In Daniel N. Nelson, ed., *Romania in the 1980s*, pp. 254–305. Boulder, Colo.: Westview, 1981.

————. "Romania's Debt Crisis: Its Causes and Consequences." In U.S. Congress, Joint Economic Committee, *East European Economies: Slow Growth in the 1980s*. Vol. 3, *Country Studies on Eastern Europe and Yugoslavia*, pp. 489–542. 99th Congress, 1st sess., 1986.

————. "Romania's Economy at the End of the 1970s: Turning the Corner on Intensive Developments." In U.S. Congress, Joint Economic Committee, *East European Economic Assessment, Part I, Country Studies, 1980*, pp. 231–297. 97th Congress, 1st sess., 1981.

Jacobini, H. B. *Romanian Public Law*. Boulder, Colo.: East European Monographs, 1987.

Janos, Andrew C. "Modernization and Decay in Historical Perspective: The Case of Romania." In Kenneth Jowitt, ed., *Social Change in Romania, 1860–1940: A Debate on Development in a European Nation*, pp. 72–116. Berkeley: Institute of International Studies, University of California, 1978.

Jelavich, Barbara. *History of the Balkans*. Vol. 2. New York: Cambridge University Press, 1983.

Jones, Christopher D. *Soviet Influence in Eastern Europe: Political Autonomy and the Warsaw Pact*. New York: Praeger, 1981.

Jowitt, Kenneth. "Inclusion and Mobilization in European Leninist Regimes." In Jan F. Triska and Paul M. Cocks, eds., *Political Development in Eastern Europe*, pp. 93–118. New York: Praeger, 1977.

————. *The Leninist Response to National Dependency*. Berkeley: Institute of International Studies, University of California, 1978.

————. "An Organizational Approach to the Study of Political Culture in Marxist-Leninist Systems." *American Political Science Review* 61 (1974): 1171–1191.

————. "Political Innovation in Rumania." *Survey* 20, no. 4 (1974): 132–151.

————. *Revolutionary Breakthroughs and National Development: The Case of Romania, 1944–1965*. Berkeley: University of California Press, 1971.

————. "The Sociocultural Bases of National Dependency in Peasant Countries." In Jowitt, *Social Change*, pp. 1–30.

————, ed. *Social Change in Romania, 1860–1940: A Debate on Development in a European Nation*. Berkeley: Institute of International Studies, University of California, 1978.

Județele României Socialiste. Bucharest: Ed. politică, 1969.

Kaser, Michael, and Iancu Spigler. "Economic Reform in Romania in the 1970s." In Alec Nove, H. Hohmann, and G. Seidenstecker, eds., *The East European Economies in the 1970s*, pp. 253–279. Boston: Butterworths, 1982.

King, Robert R. *History of the Romanian Communist Party*. Stanford, Calif.: Hoover Institution, 1980.

————. *Minorities Under Communism: Nationalities as a Source of Tension Among Balkan Communist States*. Cambridge: Harvard University Press, 1973.

Lampe, John R., and Marvin R. Jackson. *Balkan Economic History, 1550–1950*. Bloomington: Indiana University Press, 1982.

Le Monde.

Lecţii în ajutorul celor care studiază istoria PMR. Bucharest: Ed. politică, 1961.

Lee, Arthur S. Gould. *Special Duties: Reminiscences of a Royal Air Force Staff Officer.* London: Sampson, Low, Marston, & Co., 1946.

"Lege privînd perfecţionarea pregătirii profesionale a lucratorilor din unităţile socialiste." *Buletinul oficial*, pt. I, no. 34 (18 March 1971): 224–230.

Lévesque, Jacques. *Le Conflit sino-soviétique et l'Europe de l'Est: ses incidences sur les conflits soviéto-polonais et soviéto-roumain.* Montréal: Les Presses de l'Université de Montréal, 1970.

Linden, Ronald H. *Bear and Foxes: The International Relations of the East European States, 1965–1969.* Boulder, Colo.: East European Monographs, 1979.

———. *Communist States and International Change: Romania and Yugoslavia in Comparative Perspective.* Boston: Allen and Unwin, 1987.

Little, D. Richard. "Bureaucracy and Participation in the Soviet Union." In Donald E. Schulz and Jan S. Adams, eds., *Political Participation in Communist Systems*, pp. 79–107. New York: Pergamon, 1981.

———. "Mass Political Participation in the U.S. and the U.S.S.R.: A Conceptual Analysis." *Comparative Political Studies* 8 (January 1976): 483–460.

Lucaciu, Petre. "'Capitalul' în gîndirea românească dintre cele două războaie mondiale." *Lupta de clasă* 47 (July 1967): 51–65.

Luceafărul.

Lumea.

Lupta de clasă.

Magazin istoric.

Maier, Anneli. "The Romanian Congress on Political Education and Socialist Culture," RFER, BR/155, 7 July 1976, pp. 1–17.

Manea, Mircea. "Prestigiul ziaristului." *Presa noastră* 15 (January 1970): 1–2.

Markham, Reuben H. *Rumania Under the Soviet Yoke.* Boston: Meador, 1949.

Marx, Karl. *Insemnări despre Români.* Bucharest: Ed. Academiei RPR, 1964.

McCauley, Martin, and Stephen Carter, eds. *Leadership and Succession in the Soviet Union, Eastern Europe, and China.* Armonk, N.Y.: M. E. Sharpe, 1986.

Meyer, Alfred. "Legitimacy of Power in East Central Europe." In Sylvia Sinanian, Istvan Deak, and Peter C. Ludz, eds., *Eastern Europe in the 1970s*, pp. 45–68. New York: Praeger, 1972.

Mic dicţionar enciclopedic. Bucharest: Ed. enciclopedică romănă, 1972.

Michelson, Paul. "Romanian Perspectives on Romanian National Development." *Balkanistica* 7 (1981–1982): 92–120.

Mitea, Constantin. "Ziarul—Factor dinamic în viaţa socială." *Presa noastră* 12 (August 1967): 1–4.

Mitrany, David. *The Land and Peasant in Rumania.* London: Oxford University Press, 1930.

Montias, John Michael. "Background and Origins of the Rumanian Dispute with Comecon." *Soviet Studies* 16 (October 1974): 125–152.

———. *Economic Development in Communist Rumania.* Cambridge: MIT Press, 1967.

———. "Notes on the Romanian Debate on Sheltered Industrialization: 1860–1906." In Kenneth Jowitt, ed., *Social Change in Romania, 1860–*

1940: A Debate on Development in a European Nation, pp. 53–71. Berkeley: Institute of International Studies, University of California, 1978.

Moore, Patrick. "The Romanian Communist Party's 12th Congress." RFER, BR/263, 28 November 1979, pp. 1–16.

Muzeul Doftana. Bucharest: Ed. pentru turism, 1960.

Muzeul Doftana. Bucharest: Ed. pentru turism, 1974.

Nagy-Talavera, Nicholas M. *The Green Shirts and the Others*. Stanford: Hoover Institution, 1970.

Naţiunea ,si problema naţională: Antologia gîndirii social-politice, revoluţionare, şi democratice româneşti. Bucharest: Ed. politică, 1975.

Nedelcu, Florea. "Concepţia tactică şi experienţa de luptă a PCR în fruntea forţelor antifascist antifasciste în perioada 1933–1935." In *În slujba cercetării marxiste a istoriei PCR*, pp. 280–291. Bucharest: Institutul de studii istorice şi social-politice de pe lîngă CC al PCR, 1971.

Nelson, Daniel N. *Democratic Centralism in Romania: A Study of Local Communist Politics*. Boulder, Colo.: East European Monographs, 1980.

————. "Development and Participation in Communist Systems: The Case of Romania." In Donald E. Schulz and Jan S. Adams, eds., *Political Participation in Communist Systems*, pp. 234–253. New York: Pergamon, 1981.

————, ed. *Romania in the 1980s*. Boulder, Colo.: Westview, 1981.

Neue Zürcher Zeitung.

New York Times.

Nicolae Ceauşescu: Builder of Modern Romania, International Statesman. New York: Pergamon, 1983.

Omagiu Tovarăşului Nicolae Ceauşescu. Bucharest: Ed. politică, 1973.

"Omul potrivit la locul potrivit." *Lupta de clasă* 47 (June 1967): 3–13.

Organizaţiile obşteşti în sistemul organizării politice din RSR. Bucharest: Ed. Academiei RSR (Academia de Stiinte sociale şi politice a RSR), 1973.

Oţetea, Andrei, ed. *The History of the Romanian People*. New York: Twayne, 1970.

Pacepa, Ion Mihai. *Red Horizons: Chronicles of a Communist Spy Chief*. Washington, D.C.: Regnery Gateway, 1987.

Paltiel, Jeremy T. "The Cult of Personality: Some Comparative Reflections on Political Culture in Leninist Regimes." *Studies in Comparative Communism* 16 (Spring/Summer 1983): 49–64.

Pârvulescu. See Pîrvulescu.

Pascu, Stefan, ed. *Istoria României*. 3rd ed. Bucharest: Ed. didactică ,si pedagogică, 1974.

Pătrăşcanu, Lucreţiu. *Problemele de bază ale României*. 2nd ed. Bucharest: Ed. SOCEC & Co., 1945.

————. *Studii economice şi social-politice 1925–1945*. Bucharest: Ed. politică, 1978.

————. *Sub trei dictaturi*. 2nd ed. Bucharest: Ed. politică, 1970.

Pîrvulescu, Constantin. "Unitatea de acţiune a clasei muncitoare." *Scînteia*, 6 August 1964.

Plenara CC al PCR, 3–4 Noiembrie 1971. Bucharest: Ed. politică, 1971.

Pool, Ithiel de Sola. *Satellite Generals*. Stanford: Stanford University Press (Hoover Institution Studies), 1955.

Pravda, 8 May 1966.

Presa noastră.

"Preselecţie la facultatea de ziaristică." *Presa noastră*, no. 4 (239) 1976, p. 36.

Programme of the RCP. Bucharest: Agerpres, 1974 (draft); Meridiane, 1975 (final version).

Radio Free Europe Research.

Rausser, Vasile, ed. *Repartizarea teritorială a industrie.* Bucharest: Ed. Academiei RSR, 1977.

Recensămîntul populaţiei şi locuinţelor din 15 martie 1966. Vol. 1, *Resultate generale*, pt. 1, *Populaţie.* Bucharest: Direcţia centrală de statistică, 1969.

Recensămîntul populaţiei şi al locuinţelor din 5 ianuarie 1977. Vol. 1, *Populaţie—Structura demografică.* Bucharest: Directia centrală de statistică, 1980.

Remington, Robin A. *The Warsaw Pact.* Cambridge: MIT Press, 1971.

Rigby, T. H. "Soviet Communist Party Membership Under Brezhnev." *Soviet Studies* 28 (July 1976): 317–337.

Rigby, T. H., and Ferenc Feher. *Political Legitimation in Communist States.* New York: St. Martin's Press, 1982.

Roberts, Henry L. *Rumania: Political Problems of an Agrarian State.* New Haven: Yale University Press, 1951.

România. New York: Amnesty International, 1978.

Romania libera.

Roşianu, Mihail. "Cum a fost organizată evadarea tov. Gheorghe Gheorghiu-Dej din lagărul de la Tîrgu Jiu în August 1944." *Scînteia*, 18 August 1964.

Rothschild, Joseph. *The Communist Party of Bulgaria.* New York: Columbia University Press, 1959.

————. *East Central Europe Between the Two World Wars.* Seattle: University of Washington Press, 1974.

Sălăjan, Z. "Doftana—Bastion al luptei revoluţionare duse de militanţii comunişti şi antifascişti în anii ilegalităţi." *Anale de istorie* 16, no. 6 (1970): 30–42.

Sampson, Steven L. "Is Romania the Next Poland?" *Critique* (Glasgow) 16 (1983): 139–144.

————. "Muddling Through in Romania (Or Why the Mamaliga Doesn't Explode)." Paper presented at the Second International Conference of Romanian Studies, Avignon, October 1983.

————. "Regime and Society in Rumania." *International Journal of Rumanian Studies* 5, no. 1 (1987): 41–51.

Schopflin, George. "Gorbachev, Romania, and 'Leninist Nationalities Policy.'" RFER, BR/96, 12 June 1987, pp. 1–5.

Schulz, Donald E. "On the Nature and Function of Participation in Communist Systems: A Developmental Analysis." In Donald E. Schulz and Jan S. Adams, eds., *Political Participation in Communist Systems*, pp. 26–78. New York: Pergamon, 1981.

————. "Political Participation in Communist Systems: The Conceptual Frontier." In Donald E. Schulz and Jan S. Adams, *Political Participation in Communist Systems*, pp. 1–25. New York: Pergamon, 1981.

Schulz, Donald E., and Jan S. Adams, *Political Participation in Communist Systems.* New York: Pergamon, 1981.

Schwartz, Barry. *George Washington: The Making of an American Symbol.* New York: Free Press, 1987.

Scînteia, 21 September 1944.

Seton-Watson, Hugh. *The East European Revolution.* 3rd ed. New York: Praeger, 1956.

Shafir, Michael. "The Future of the Rumanian Leadership." *International Journal of Rumanian Studies* 5, no. 1 (1987): 33–40.

————. "The Historical Background to Rural Resettlement." RFER, Romanian SR/10, 23 August 1988, pp. 3–8.

————. "Political Culture, Intellectual Dissent, and Intellectual Consent: The Case of Romania." *Orbis* 27 (Summer 1983): 393–420.

————. "Romania." In Martin McCauley and Stephen Carter, eds., *Leadership and Succession in the Soviet Union, Eastern Europe, and China*, pp. 114–135. Armonk, N.Y.: M. E. Sharpe, 1986.

————. *Romania: Politics, Economics, and Society*. Boulder, Colo.: Lynne Rienner, 1985.

————. "'Romania's Marx' and the National Question: Constantin Dobrogeanu-Gherea." *History of Political Thought* 5 (Summer 1984): 295–314.

————. "Socialist Republic of Romania." In Bogdan Szajkowski, ed., *Marxist Governments: A World Survey*," vol. 3, pp. 589–639, London: Macmillan, 1983.

————. "Sociology of Knowledge in the Middle of Nowhere: Constantin Dobrogeanu-Gherea." *East European Quarterly* 19 (Fall 1985): 321–336.

Shanor, Donald R. "Poland's Press and Broadcasting Under the Gierek Regime." *Journalism Quarterly* 51 (Summer 1974): 271–277.

Shapiro, Paul. "Romania's Past as Challenge for the Future: A Developmental Approach to Interwar Politics." In Daniel N. Nelson, ed., *Romania in the 1980s*, pp. 17–67. Boulder, Colo.: Westview, 1981.

Sharlet, Robert S. "Concept Formation in Political Science and Communist Studies: Conceptualizing Political Participation." In Frederic J. Fleron, ed., *Communist Studies and the Social Sciences*, pp. 244–253. Chicago: Rand McNally, 1969.

Siegert, Heinz. *Ceau,sescu: Management für ein modernes Rumänien*. Munich: C. Bertelsmann Verlag, 1973.

Smith, Alan H. "Romanian Economic Reforms." In *Economic Reforms in Eastern Europe and Prospects for the 1980s* (NATO Colloquium, 16–18 April 1980, Brussels), pp. 35–57. New York: Pergamon, 1980.

————. "The Romanian Industrial Enterprise." In Ian Jeffries, ed., *The Industrial Enterprise in Eastern Europe*, pp. 63–83. New York: Praeger, 1981.

Socor, Vladimir. "Dissent in Romania." RFER, BR/94, 5 June 1987, pp. 1–7.

Spigler, Iancu. *Economic Reform in Rumanian Industry*. London: Oxford University Press, 1973.

The "Ştefan Gheorghiu" Academy. Bucharest: N. p., 1973.

Stern, Carola. *Ulbricht: A Political Biography*. New York: Praeger, 1965.

Stoica, Chivu. *Eroicele lupte ale muncitorilor ceferi,sti ,si petroli,sti din 1933*. 2nd revised ed. Bucharest: Ed. de stat pentru literatura politică, 1955.

Stoica, Gheorghe, and M. Cruceanu. "Momente din perioada Congresului I al PCR." *Scînteia*, 1 May 1966.

Stolte, Stefan C. "The Romanian Party Congress." *Bulletin* 16 (October 1969): 31–35.

Times (London).

Tomasic, D. A. "The Rumanian Communist Leadership." *Slavic Review* 20 (October 1961): 477–494.

Tontsch, Günther H. *Das Verhältnis von Partei und Staat in Rumänien: Kontinuität und Wandel 1944–1982*. Cologne: Wissenschaft und Politik, 1985.

Tribuna Romăniei.

Triska, Jan F., and Paul M. Cocks, eds., *Political Development in Eastern Europe*. New York: Praeger, 1977.

Trofin, Virgil. "The Rules of the RCP." *World Marxist Review* 9 (July 1966): 71–76.

Tsantis, Andreas C., and Roy Pepper. *Romania: The Industrialization of an Agrarian Economy under Socialist Planning.* Washington, D.C.: The World Bank, 1979.

Tumarkin, Nina. *Lenin Lives! The Lenin Cult in Soviet Russia.* Cambridge: Harvard University Press, 1983.

Turczynski, Emil. "The Background of Romanian Fascism." In Peter F. Sugar, ed., *Native Fascism in the Successor States, 1918–1945*, pp. 101–111. Santa Barbara, Calif.: ABC-Clio, 1971.

Turnock, David. *An Economic Geography of Romania.* London: G. Bell & Sons, 1974.

———. "Romania." In Andrew H. Dawson, ed., *Planning in Eastern Europe*, pp. 229–273. New York: St. Martin's Press, 1987.

———. *The Romanian Economy in the Twentieth Century.* London: Croom Helm, 1986.

U.S. Department of Commerce, International Trade Administration, Office of East-West Policy and Planning. "U.S. Romanian Trade Trends, January–June 1981" (October 1981).

Urban, George. *The Nineteen Days: A Broadcaster's Account of the Hungarian Revolution.* London: Heinemann, 1957.

Vinte, Ion. "PCR in fruntea luptei pentru răsturnarea dictaturii fasciste." *Scînteia*, 31 July 1964, pp. 2–3.

Vlad, Constantin. *Essays on Nation.* Bucharest: Meridiane, 1973.

Voicu, Ştefan. "Pagini de luptă a PCR impotriva fascismului, pentru independenţă şi suveranitate naţională (1934–1940). *Lupta de clasă* 4 6 (June 1966): 59–80.

Washington Post.

Weber, Eugen. "The Men of the Archangel." In George L. Mosse, ed., *International Fascism*, pp. 317–343. Beverly Hills, Calif.: Sage, 1979.

———. "Romania." In Hans Rogger and Eugen Weber, eds., *The European Right*, pp. 501–574. Berkeley: University of California Press, 1966.

———. *Varieties of Fascism.* New York: Van Nostrand Reinhold, 1964.

Weber, Max. *Economy and Society.* Ed. Günther Roth and Claus Wittich. Berkeley: University of California Press, 1978.

Weiner, Robert. *Romanian Foreign Policy and the United Nations.* New York: Praeger, 1984.

Witnesses to Cultural Genocide. New York: American Transylvania Federation, Inc., and Committee for Human Rights in Rumania, 1979.

Wolchik, Sharon L. "Ideology and Equality: The Status of Women in Eastern and Western Europe." *Comparative Political Studies* 13 (January 1981): 445–476.

Wolff, Robert L. *The Balkans in Our Time.* Cambridge: Harvard University Press, 1956.

Zaharescu, Vl. "Întărirea partidului şi a legăturilor lui cu masele—factor hotărîtor în lupta pentru organizarea şi înfăptuirea insurecţiei armate din august 1944." In *Din istoria contemporana a Romîniei*, pp. 201–223. Bucharest: Ed. ştiinţifică, 1965.

Zimmerman, William. "Hierarchical Regional Systems and the Politics of System Boundaries." *International Organization* 26 (Winter 1978): 18–36.

Index

About the Book
and the Author

Under the leadership of Nicolae Ceauşescu, Romania has repeatedly, without serious repercussions, failed to follow Soviet guidelines in Comecon and the Warsaw Pact, at the U.N., and in interbloc negotiations. In addition, Ceauşescu has been able to establish himself firmly in control of Romania's internal political system, and to create around himself and his family a leadership cult similar to those of Stalin and Mao. Despite this apparently total control of the Romanian political system, however, he has not been able to achieve a number of major policy objectives, most notably in the economic sphere.

Seeking the factors that account for Ceauşescu's remarkable abilities in foreign policy, his consummate skill in maintaining control of the political system, and his concurrent economic disasters, Professor Fischer examines in detail his personal background before World War II, his development as a party official, and particularly, his methods of rule since 1965.

This book demonstrates that two inseparable components of Ceauşescu's character—nationalism and Marxism-Leninism—have combined with his political skills to produce the disastrous failures, as well as the amazing successes, characteristic of his rule; ironically, his strengths have contributed to his weaknesses. Exacerbating his problems, his limited education has often rendered him incapable of accepting new economc policies, and his experience as a party organizer has made him reluctant to allow local initiatives in political and economic decisionmaking. The result is a political and economic stalemate in which Ceauşescu has abandoned his attempts at participatory populism and maintains tight control over an increasingly hostile population through traditional levers of coercion.

Mary Ellen Fischer received her A.B. from Wellesley College and her A.M. and Ph.D. in political science from Harvard University. At present, she is Joseph C. Palamountain Professor of Government and chair of the Government Department at Skidmore College. While completing this study in 1988-1989, she was a fellow at the Russian Research Center, Harvard University.

The Grasshopper King

by Elizabeth Boatwright Coker

Daughter of Strangers

The Day of the Peacock

India Allan

The Big Drum

La Belle

Lady Rich

The Bees

Blood Red Roses

The Grasshopper King

A STORY OF TWO CONFEDERATE EXILES
IN MEXICO DURING THE REIGN OF
MAXIMILIAN AND CARLOTA

Elizabeth Boatwright Coker

E. P. DUTTON   ✑   NEW YORK

This book is dedicated to
my constant friend Elliott Graham

For information contact:
Elsevier-Dutton Publishing Co., Inc.,
2 Park Avenue, New York, N.Y. 10016

Library of Congress Cataloging in Publication Data
Coker, Elizabeth Boatwright.
  The Grasshopper King.
  1. Mexico—History—European intervention,
1861"1867—Fiction. I. Title.
PS3505.0249G7   1981   813'.54   80-24974
ISBN: 0-525-10716-9

Published simultaneously in Canada by
Clarke, Irwin & Company Limited, Toronto and Vancouver

Designed by Kingsley Parker

10 9 8 7 6 5 4 3 2 1

First Edition

ACKNOWLEDGMENTS

I render hearty thanks

To Dr. Thomas L. Johnson of the Caroliniana Library at the University of South Carolina and Miss Harriet Oglesbee for locating and procuring the invaluable (to me) *My Diary In Mexico* by Prince Felix Salm-Salm with leaves from *The Diary of Agnes Princess Salm-Salm (Richard Bentley, New Burlington Street, Publisher in ordinary to Her Majesty, London, 1868) from the Evelyn family library in London.*

To my Mexican friends of all seasons who enabled me to see "through the looking glass" I acknowledge in particular, His Excellency Antonio Carillō Flores, Ambassador to the Soviet Union, and His Excellency Hugo Margain, Ambassador to the United States.

Also to Joan Haslip, for information and encouragement; Jonathan Daniels, Walter Spearman and Lynwood Brown for endless interest; Penelope Coker Hall for careful manuscript reading and pithy comments; Jeannine Lee for diverse reasons; and above all to my sweet friend, Sarah Grantham Brown, for keeping up with me all the way.

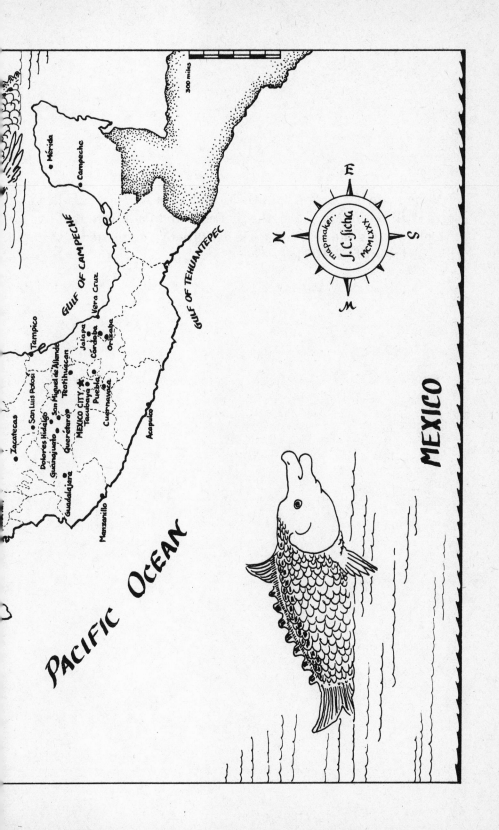

300 miles

Mérida

Campeche

GULF OF CAMPECHE

GULF OF TEHUANTEPEC

Tampico

San Luis Potosí

Zacatecas

Dolores Hidalgo

Guanajuato

San Miguel de Allende

Querétaro

Teotihuacan

Jalapa

Córdoba

Vera Cruz

Orizaba

MEXICO CITY

Tacubaya

Puebla

Cuernavaca

Guadalajara

Acapulco

Manzanillo

mapmaker·
J. C. Sicha·
MCMLXXX

N E S W

PACIFIC OCEAN

MEXICO

All the main characters with the exception of Angelica and Beau and Phillip, the Mirandas, the McLeods and Paco were real live people who did the heroic or wicked acts herein attributed to them during their life in Mexico.

PART I

The Exiles

APRIL 1865

The Heart of Heaven bound a bandage over their eyes which obscured them as when one breathes on the round moon of a looking glass. Their eyes were curtained so that they could see only what was close; and only what was close was clear to them.

POPOL VUH
RELIGIOUS BOOK
OF THE ANCIENT MAYA

1 🌿

It was an April day of soft sun following a morning of milky fog. The Yankee fleet was still anchored at the tip of Hilton Head Island, South Carolina, but many of the ships were readying to depart. Sails were unfurling and smokestacks sending up columns of heavy black to stain the blue-washed sky.

Gray Spanish moss swung raggedly among the live oaks of the avenue so quiet and deserted it seemed inseparable from the weed-choked family cemetery. Indeed so deep was the silence and so salt-fresh the air that when I listened closely I could hear the trumpeter swan's chicks hatching in the piney woods rimming the nearby creek.

Alone on the double front stairway, all that was left of the big mansion house, my husband was saying farewell to the ashes of his beloved homeplace. I remembered his standing on that exact top step when he brought me from Virginia to his Cotton Hall plantation gay with wedding guests—crinolined ladies and tall fine-faced gentlemen waving bonnie blue flags and singing the song of

Secession: "Hurrah Hurrah for Southern Rights, Hurrah—"

Beau had scooped me up as easily as if I were a feather and carried me over the threshold of the house I was to live in for the rest of my life.

But here I was, four and a half years later, in a shabby balmacaan traveling suit on my way to Charleston to board a steamer that would take me to a foreign country for what might well be the rest of my life.

The Civil War was over. General Lee had surrendered at Appomattox a week ago and Beau, among other unvanquished Confederates, had refused to sign the Oath of Allegiance to the United States. We were on our way to join a group of Confederate exiles bound for Brazil to start a new life.

The day was cool but perspiration was damp on my neck and my mouth felt dry. Funny! I was excited and eager to leave Hilton Head. Beau was anguished. I could tell by the way his head was bowed and his grand shoulders drooped that there was a cold emptiness and nausea at the pit of his stomach.

A six-oared barge, rowed by two ancient Negroes, bumped against the plantation dock. In it sat Stephen Elliott, returning to take us a ways upriver to the landing to meet the little steamer that went daily back and forth between Charleston and Savannah. From the twisting shadow of vines projected on the swirling water came his voice: "Damn all war to hell. And don't hit that turtle."

I could just make out the slim silhouette of the one-armed general stepping onto the dock.

"Where is my Cousin Beau? Has he run away?" he called.

I sat down on a bench and leaned my head against a pine trunk. A breeze like a ghost of rain rattled through the fronds of a palmetto thicket on the bank. I was glad of the needled shadows. Stephen might not detect my impatience to be off. For my life, here on the plantation, had vanished in the flames of war as surely as the house itself had gone up in smoke and fire.

"I wish you'd persuade Beau to change his mind about leaving the island," Stephen fretted, sitting down beside me, cradling the stump of his right arm with a trembling left hand. "I've known him longer than you. He won't like Brazil or anywhere but here."

"Beau has been planning to go ever since—"

"Ever since he rescued you from prison and the Yankees continued the hunt for you. I know, Angelica. But if Beau exiles himself from life as he knows it, he will crumble spiritually or he will go mad in defiance. The sanctuary of the familiar is as necessary to him as the air he breathes. It's in his blood."

4

"Well, I won't lose *my* mind. The years without him on this plantation, surviving behind Yankee lines, were the hard part. But not so hard as leaving Edward and Button. I know my baby is well looked after but it was hard to part with him. He is too young to make this long voyage." Tears I could not help ran down my cheeks.

Stephen threw a stick at a squirrel. "I wonder how many swan chicks have already hatched."

"It sounds like three. I'll flourish on the Amazon. Beau will too," I said, with forced cheerfulness.

"Oh, you could end up in a cave and be perfectly content as long as Beau was there to light your candle," Stephen laughed.

And I joined in because what Stephen said was true.

A jaybird began squawking overhead. Stephen stared up at the green leaf shadows. "Be sensible, Angelica. Nobody has come looking for you in the months you've been at our house on Parris Island; nor will they."

"Beau has made too many plans to change now. He sent a letter to Phillip in England before Christmas telling him to meet us in Havana with the cotton money he banked in London at the beginning of the war. If we aren't there to get it, Phillip will spend it. You know he will."

"Phillip was always Beau's least favorite brother. I'm surprised he wants him to go along to Brazil."

"He hasn't even considered that possibility. Once Phillip delivers the 1860 cotton money to the bank in Havana or to Beau, he will probably return to England. Certainly there's nothing for him here. He should arrive in Cuba about the same time we do."

Stephen reached in his pocket and took out a crumpled envelope. "Charlotte found this in a closet at the house in Beaufort. It's a page from Uncle Billy Elliott's diary. Read it when you leave Cuba for Brazil. Not before. It's about you."

"I'll read it now."

"No. Promise you'll wait. It will amuse you."

"Angelica, I see the steamer," Beau shouted. "Where are you?"

Beau's voice sounded jerky coming from the shaky steps. I could see him, Paladin among the ruins; a defeated soldier but higher-headed than any man I've ever known. His sharp green eyes must be wide and worried. He would not relax, he said, until we were safe on the ocean sea, safe so that no Yankee could ever find me. "*You're so beautifully different,*" he said, "*from any other woman in the world, I never know what might happen to you. A genie might jump from a bottle and lure you away from me—or a stranger—*"

A trumpet rang from the piney woods. A swan song.

"Stephen and I are on the dock, waiting for you." I tried to sound subdued but my voice refused. It sang with excited anticipation.

We watched Beau carefully descend the skeleton stairway. The minute his foot touched the ground the three slaves he'd loved the most emerged from where they had been standing behind a tree, watching him: Old Maum Hannah and the blind giant, Masai, and Cudjo Manigo. Cudjo was leading our white stallion, Teaser. I could hear Beau talking to them and also the swish and gurgle of the water as the rowers pulled closer to the dock.

Our scanty luggage was piled in the center of the barge. We would buy clothes and necessities in Havana. My body quivered in a fever of delight to be away from this place of too dark shadows and too bright sunlight.

I stood up and held out my hand to Beau. He lifted me down. His hands were cold and damp. Smiling rigidly he embraced the three former slaves. Then he stepped down into the barge.

"Get somebody to knock down those damn chimneys," he called to Cudjo Manigo as we pulled away. "They look like ghosts standing there by themselves with no house to hold onto."

"There's a golden eagle circling us," Stephen said, putting his hand on Beau's knee, forcing his attention away from the ruins.

Beau nodded, holding himself very still, then said, "You two must bear with me. I wanted to say goodbye to Cotton Hall by myself up there on the steps. I only hope I won't remember it as it looked today but as it did before the war."

Then he managed to get hold of himself and began talking about the wonders and opportunities waiting for us in South America.

2 🌿

It was hard to tell whether Beau was disappointed or relieved that Phillip hadn't showed up in Havana when our ship was ready to sail on from there to Rio de Janeiro. That same day, by chance, an alternate choice was given us. The United States Minister to Cuba, an amiable Baltimorean, who had taken an interest in all the Confederate expatriates, and in Beau especially, both being Harvard men, saw us in a box at the opera. On learning that we were not going to Brazil until a later passage, he invited us to accompany him and his wife the next afternoon to a four o'clock dinner at the home of the *intendente* of Havana.

Beau glanced from him to me and his expression changed from one of mere politeness to speculation, then back to politeness again as he turned once more to the Minister. It was the desperate look of a gambler holding three deuces. "You are kind, sir, but neither my wife nor I am bilingual in Spanish. I fear we would be *de trop*."

"French?"

"Fluent."

"Then you will find yourself quite at home. The *intendente*'s wife, the Marquesa Santovenia, is from Marseilles. Your lovely lady need only smile and permit the habaneros to admire her. Latins are not exacting, conversationally, with the opposite sex. The guest of honor is a Confederate exile like yourself, Commander Matthew Fontaine Maury."

"Maury! I thought he was still marooned in England."

"He was on his way back to Charleston to work on electric mines when the war ended and left him stranded here. Now he is headed for Mexico to establish a colony of Confederates at Córdoba for the Emperor Maximilian."

"Mrs. Maury is my aunt's best friend in Richmond!" I cried. "I'd love to meet him."

"I'll do what I can, Mrs. Berrien, to have you seated by him at dinner."

I date my present life from that invitation. When we arrived at the marble mansion of the *intendente*, I knew everything there was to know about the eccentric genius; or thought I did. Beau had patiently explained Commander Maury to me while I bounced up and down on an impossible elastic mattress and scratched mosquito bites in our filthy hotel room during the sweltering night after the opera.

Maury hadn't attended Annapolis but had attained high rank in the United States Navy when he was very young. He was *the* authority where oceans were concerned. He had scientifically noted the winds and currents and ocean floor encountered in the various regions he sailed and totally revised the sailing routes and wind and tide charts of the Atlantic, Pacific and Indian oceans. As a result an International Meteorological Congress was held in Brussels in 1853 and his system of recording oceanographic data was adopted for the naval vessels and merchant marine of the whole world. During the gold rush, his route shortened the sailing from New York to San Francisco by fifty days! And he cut over two weeks between New York and Rio! One of his pet projects before the war had been the opening of the Amazon Valley to free trade, hoping that this would draw slaves from the United States to Brazil.

"Then why isn't he going colonizing in Brazil? Why Mexico?"

"Mexico is nearer home than the Valley of the Amazon."

"Well?"

"Wait until we meet him. We may not want to have anything to do with him."

But the excited tremble in Beau's usually strong voice when he said "nearer home" gave him away.

We arrived with the Minister and his colorless wife at the *intendente*'s at four o'clock exactly, but the other guests were so long gathering that the Marquesa asked me if I could play either the piano or the harp. I answered, "Both."

This confused the Marquesa for a minute; then she ordered a Negro woman in white muslin and a huge white turban to bring a silver waiter piled with Mozart sonatas while a fat Negro man wearing nothing but full gold gauze trousers struggled up with an untuned harp.

I chose the piano and played Mozart for almost an hour while eighty or so guests and more than that many Negro waiters passed around the piano hissing and talking loudly. Finally the *intendente* signaled the Marquesa that dinner was ready. The Marquesa had the Minister tell me that if I would care to visit her until I sailed for Rio, she would teach me to speak Spanish if I would teach her to play just one Mozart sonata perfectly on the piano.

I looked over at Beau, who was fanning the Minister's wife with a lace fan, to see if he had heard. He had. We both nodded happily. I think I would have died if I'd had to stay longer in the hotel.

"Heaven smiles today," Beau said, squeezing my hand, as he led me to the endless table on the large gallery that went all around the house and looked down on a court bristling with *volantes* and mules and black men. The wind was blowing from all directions bringing odors of Havana to the feast—tobacco and oil and garlic and horse and flowers plus a strong flavor of Negro.

I was seated between Maury and the young Count of Santovenia, who spoke no English. Maury and I were free to get acquainted. I was relaxed for the first time in months, for I could hear Beau and the Marquesa talking animatedly in French. I could tell by his expression that everything pleased him, especially the prospect of living in all this luxury—if only for a little while.

Maury was somewhat tipsy. He leaned his big dome of a head against mine and his pink face shone as we giggled and traced our Virginia connections and made wicked comments about the food and the city and the perfumed company in our similar Tidewater tones.

After the main course of over 250 different *plats* everybody went into the salon where champagne and sweets and sherbets and cakes and meringues were spread out on long tables. An orchestra was playing and two flamenco dancers were whirling and tapping heels in the center of the room.

"They sound like skeletons dancing on tombstones," Maury said.

We walked arm in arm to a swing in the far end of the gallery. Maury was six inches shorter than I and very round but so cocksure of himself he made me feel small and almost delicate. I told him it was my fault we were leaving home. Beau's not taking the oath was mere excuse. My fault. Beau's little brother, Button, had shot a Yankee officer when he attacked me last November on the afternoon before my baby son was born, but it was I who had been accused by the Union Army.

"They suspected me not only of shooting Major Pierce but of having had his baby."

"You poor girl. The very idea sickens me."

"There was a terrible to-do. Yankee soldiers running round the house like hounds on a scent hunting the baby. Finally they got together a kangaroo court and tried me."

"And to think you were convicted!" Maury cried when he heard.

"Yes. Beau rescued me from the Yankee prison so I wasn't hung but since then our lives have been nothing but flight and hiding. We will be relieved to settle somewhere until our lawyer in Charleston takes the Oath of Allegiance and can practice law again. Mr. Pritchard is positive he can have my case thrown out of any proper court with no trouble at all since I *am* innocent and they'd never prosecute a twelve-year-old boy for accidentally pulling a trigger."

"Come to Mexico with me. You will find friends among the Confederates who are pledged to join me in Córdoba." A man with a high tenor voice was singing in the street below; his song came faintly to us, sweetening Maury's suggestion.

The air was tropically soft. A fresh evening breeze was blowing. The moon had risen so bright it appeared as the sun shining through silvery gauze. The bay was full of little boats and barks. A large ship, full sail, passed the Morro.

"There go General Gadsden and his colonists." Maury pointed a fragrant cigar bayward. "What good luck to have you here with me and not there with them. I have a promise from Major Berrien to permit me to visit him tomorrow and to listen to some plans I have in mind for you and him. You must exert all your most delightful woman ways and charm him into saying yes to joining me in my Mexican venture. I will pretend you are my wife and five daughters whom I have not seen in three years. I promise not to bore you with scientific musings."

I was tempted to tell him that I already loved him as if I were a daughter and nothing he could muse would ever bore me. But I felt no need to explain my feelings as I listened to his sentimental glimmers and all the time savored the roses in full bloom in a *jardinière* close by. I had a sure and secret strength, worn in my heart like a talisman, touched in a moment of danger, grasped firmly and surely. It was the belief that to know and to love one other human being as I did Beau was the root of all happiness. But this was not the hour for soul searchings so I told Maury a different truth, that I would like to drink a glass of champagne with him as a toast to our lives together in Mexico.

3

We reached Vera Cruz on a bright June dawn with lots of shooting sunrays. It was a still morning, very still, the stillness everywhere: on the glassy ocean; on the stifling hot steamer; on the sea birds, smooth as porcelain, winging past the tiny porthole.

Beau was asleep in the dawnlight, lying on his back in a canvas hammock after being tossed back and forth and up and down during the northeaster that had kept us away from Vera Cruz the past three days and nights. His naked white feet hung over the too-short hammock and his teeth were clenched against further hideous encounters of his backside with the wall. His mouth made a harsh jag in his wonderful young warrior face. A moment later when the ship made a slight pitch he almost rolled to the floor and the light struck him from a different angle. His mouth opened and he looked as if he were silently, desperately screaming.

What is he dreaming? I wondered. The past? What is to be? Or is he feigning sleep so I won't insist on his going on deck to actually face the reality of our exile?

I remembered the envelope from Uncle Billy that Stephen had given me to read "to amuse me." I'd never need amusement more than now. I knew exactly where it was in my hatbox. The light was dim but the handwriting bold in black ink:

Dec. 21, 1860

Yesterday was momentous:
1. *The Act of Secession was signed by the rulers of this poor misguided state.*
2. *My gigantic, hot-headed young kinsman Beau Baynard Berrien has brought a wife home to Cotton Hall.*

And what a wife! Even my old fingers twitched to unbutton the lace shirtwaist that she wore. She is the most beautiful lady I have ever seen. I adore her.

My wife's ninety-eight-year-old African nurse was among the first to drop a curtsy to Mistress Angelica. As we drove home I teased Maum Sarah into telling Angelica's fortune which I hereby translate from the Gullah so that Angelica's grandchildren can know they descended from a goddess. I will let her read it when she has safely turned twenty-seven.

Note from me to Angelica:
"There was none like thee among the dancers."
What follows is Maum Sarah's fortune for Angelica:
"Her hair is fine like black silk but her eyebrows are straight and thick. This is a sign of softness and strength entwined. Her spirit seems volatile and her dark blue eyes are round. This says she is full of enthusiasm. Her nose is straight. She will bear a first son. Her full lips are like red lilies. She has a passionate nature. Her voice is clear and deep; her laughter full of charm. She stands very tall, beautiful to watch, with footsteps swift and graceful as a doe running to the river.

Alas, a mole beneath the left corner of her mouth points to life in a faraway place. She will bring a wealth of loving to her husband but by the age of twenty-six she will caress another."

I could hear people suddenly running and calling and climbing the steep narrow stairs to the upper deck. Something exciting was happening up there. I kissed Beau's sweaty forehead and ran out.

When I was a child in Virginia, a gentleman who had recently returned from Egypt visited The Cedars. I remembered his describing the rising sun illuminating the faces of the statues of the Kings in the Nile Valley.

"That scene," he had said, "is without doubt the first wonder of the world."

It isn't. What I saw is.

Keeping my eyes lowered as I made my way through the passengers and sailors crowding the deck, completely unprepared, I looked up at a brilliant, crescending aureole of red and pink and flame on a snow-crowned mountain soaring up and up all the way to God's feet in heaven! O wonderful omen—thank you, Lord!

I tore up Uncle Billy's silly page and threw it into the sea. Then I flew down and forced Beau, grumbling sleepily, into his lightest-weight Confederate uniform and his shiniest boots. Maddeningly he took forever arranging the wide-brimmed panama hat he'd bought in Cuba at just the right angle to his big Norman nose.

"Oh, foot! It's too early in the day for you to sunburn."

"Red-haired people always sunburn in the tropics," he said.

I pulled his arm, "Please—before the grand glow is gone."

But it had already diminished and the sun had come fully out when Beau saw the dismal, reddish shoreline of Mexico, dominated by the snowcapped peak.

"Mount Orizaba is over eighteen thousand feet high." He turned his back to the mountain and began lighting a cigar. "We should have kept to our original plan: Brazil."

The pilot boat full of crow-faced officials was waiting below. He looked grimly down on them and frowned out at the black-walled, polygonal-shaped fort of San Juan de Ulua. I leaned against him and took his hand, sensing his melancholy, realizing that this approaching horizon was so different from the South Carolina coast he loved; so forlorn and disappointing; that is, if the snow-crowned Mount Orizaba were not there to glorify.

"It's too late now but look—"

A sailor had caught a dolphin about four feet long all gold and turquoise in the sun and thrown it on the deck, but in dying it was changing color, its glitter dulling. I hoped that, too, was not an omen. No; it couldn't be. I saw the mountain first.

The Marquesa Santovenia had kept her bargain and I mine. When we parted she could play the Mozart C-Major Sonata and never strike a wrong key and I could carry on a small conversation in Spanish with almost anybody.

To Beau's relief I easily found the head port official when we stepped ashore in Vera Cruz. He was a middle-aged *mestizo*, half-Mexican, half-Spanish, with loose black eyebrows and luxuriant mustaches. He was wearing a brand-new navy and white uniform with heavy gold epaulets that seemed to lift his shoulders with importance. Evidently he was dressed to greet someone very special.

"A moment, señora, a moment," he repeated irritably as I repeatedly requested his assistance in locating our baggage. "First I must complete stamping this crate of French hats to clear for delivery to the señoras of Mexico City in order for them to rival the Empress Carlota on the *paseo*."

"Where are the French soldiers, my good man? Commander Maury assured me that the French were in complete charge of the port of Vera Cruz. Angelica, ask him where the French soldiers are."

"Please, General, where are the French soldiers?"

"A minute, señora. Now, having stamped, I am occupied in seeking a señora of Scotland to whom I am to show unusual favors. The city is full of the black vomit fever. The French soldiers have fled to the mountains. The French ships have moved out beyond the rocks. The señora of Scotland must be removed from Vera Cruz in greatest haste. Oh, oh, where is the señora of Scotland?"

He started turning in circles like a bewildered rat.

I snatched the cue. "I know where the lady is, General, but you must attend me and speak more slowly or I will arrange not to understand you."

His attitude altered, became pleading. "The Virgin will bless you, señora, if you guide me to her immediately."

"Insist that he procure our baggage," Beau demanded. "We can't miss the train for Paso del Macho."

I caught Beau's arm and pinched it. "We must pretend to be cool and in control. Otherwise the official will do nothing."

"Señora—" the official was about to cry—"please aid me. It is of the supreme importance."

"And after I help you, will you also help me?" I gave him my most coquettish smile.

Disgusted, Beau marched away to forcibly locate our baggage while the official volubly assured me that nothing in this life could make him happier than to aid so beautiful and tall a doña as I. Nothing but—

Looking small and haughty, she was standing very near us with the three rough Cornishmen who trailed her everywhere. On board ship the pretty young Scotswoman had remained aloof from everyone. I approached her, saying pleasantly as if we were old friends, "I am Angelica Berrien of South Carolina. I know a little Spanish. Isn't this confusion awful?"

Unfriendly brown eyes appraised me. Then the mouth that had been a tight line began to tremble. "I am quite desolate, Mrs. Berrien. My husband was supposed to meet me. He isn't here. No one is. I am Flora McLeod of Edinburgh. I admired you on the ship and I need your help now."

"General!" Briskly I signaled the official, who stumbled on his toes in his eagerness to join us. "It is my pleasure to present to you the Señora McLeod."

The official who wasn't a general at all but who had enjoyed being called one was so relieved at having found the Señora McLeod that even his epaulets bounced up and down with joy.

He explained in detail why he, Manuel Lizarraga, and not the Señor McLeod, was present to welcome the señora and convey her in greatest safety away from this area of the fever and the bandits of Carabaje and the guerrillas of Porfirio Díaz and countless hidden Juaristi, all enemies of the Empire, into the safe and loving arms of the Señor McLeod, who was attending the Emperor in Puebla.

During this long pronouncement I was straining to see Beau, whose six feet six would make him easy to locate over the short Vera Cruzanos crowding the wharf. Fingering the gold epaulets on his shoulders to make sure they were still standing up, the official finally became silent and anxiously waited for the Scotswoman to speak.

I spotted Beau surrounded by sombreroed Mexicans, white-bloused Indians and Cuban sailors. My Beau who had stood in the middle of hundreds of howling, threatening black slaves and controlled them with a shout and a single wave of his cane, who had led one of the fiercest charges at Gettysburg, was now frantically shaking his cane this way, that way to the obvious merriment and heckling of the crowd.

"This North American is too big for his *pantalones*," one of them teased.

Beau's face was flushed and furious. If he struck one of them as he was about to do, they would mob him. Violence was certain. My toes clenched themselves together so hard I felt them almost dig through my shoes into the stones of the quay. I must play my cards with utmost care. The eyes of Flora McLeod and mine met. Restraining my impulses I let her make the first move.

"I didn't understand a word the official said. I have no idea what I should do. Will you help me?"

I swallowed the last vestige of my pride as she was swallowing hers. "The Emperor has detained your husband in Puebla. Señor Lizarraga has been ordered to show you every courtesy and escort you to the train for Paso del Macho where a coach is waiting to take you to Puebla. May I tell him that my husband and I are your traveling companions?"

"Of course. What a relief!"

Manuel Lizarraga was his most impressive official self as he scattered the hecklers and extricated Beau who, once rescued, behaved as if nothing had ever been out of order.

Manuel Lizarraga held a handkerchief over his mouth and nose and urged us to do the same as we hurried through the forlorn city that, with its melancholy backdrop of red sandhills, endless cracked walls and flat-roofed houses blackened by smoke and gunfire, resembled Jerusalem after the sack. The only signs of happy life were the buzzards with their glossy black feathers and gray heads lining themselves up along the walls and rooftops.

At first, none of us had much to say. The train, on the single-track railway, passed through first desert and marshland, then interesting plantings of coffee and tobacco, then reapers in golden fields of the yellowest and brightest barley I ever saw. Wheat was in golden beard and immense herds of cattle fed on the rich pastures spreading out miles away. And always there was the snowcapped Mount Orizaba looming grandly on the horizon. It held up my courage.

"This is Santa Anna country," Manuel Lizarraga explained as I translated Beau's interested questions. "The government owns it now."

"The Empire?" Beau leaned forward.

Manuel Lizarraga shrugged his shoulders and closed his eyes pretending sleep.

To our surprise, quite soon, the railway came to an end in a little Indian village not far from Paso del Macho. There was no coach waiting for Flora McLeod and the three Cornish miners; no Confederate soldier to meet us as Maury had promised. Apologizing profusely and sweating equally, Manuel Lizarraga led us through the picturesque village which was a cluster of tiny huts of bamboo thatched with palm leaves. Long-haired Indian women in white cotton *huipiles* stood in doorways with half-naked children beside them; their barefooted men, in baggy white cotton trousers, loaded and unloaded long-eared burros; goats grazed under palm trees. People from the train were of no interest to any of them.

Manuel led us to a sweet-smelling, palm-thatched pavilion. A soft light filtered down through the canes. A fat part-Chinese, part-Indian man, wearing a hat of woven grasses decorated with a red paper rose, served us gourds of warm new milk and passed bananas, pineapple, orange slices, goat cheese and shrimp on a gold-lacquered tray lined with cool, green vine leaves.

We were finishing this feast when the promised coach arrived in a noisy cloud of dust and sand accompanied by six fully armed, helmeted soldiers and eight sombreroed Mexican outriders. The coach was clumsy and old-fashioned. Its dust had barely begun to settle when a soldier in a faded Confederate uniform galloped out from a banana grove. This was Captain Mike O'Farrell from Maury's Carlota Colony near Orizaba in Córdoba. He announced that he had been cooling his heels in this primitive place for a week waiting for us and two Alabama families due to arrive from New Orleans, as well as a bunch of Confederates from Georgia who should have crossed the Rio Grande and been here days ago. He had wagons for our belongings in the banana grove. We'd just have to bite the stick and wait here with him.

An insect had stung Beau's hand in the pavilion. The hand was itching and swelling. The midday heat was sickening. Beau touched his hat lightly with his cane and told Captain O'Farrell that he'd be damned if he'd wait in the middle of hell for anybody. Especially anybody from Georgia or Alabama. It was high time to have a better understanding about his future with Commander Maury in Mexico City.

Flora McLeod was already in the coach but she had heard the conversation. She called from the window, inviting us to continue along to Puebla with her.

The English-speaking German driver of the coach said, "Yes, get inside. She'll rattle around like a dice in a cup without you folks to hold onto."

While our belongings were being gathered and loaded we settled ourselves quickly inside the coach. Beau was once more his charming self. He complimented our savior extravagantly on her forti-

tude in coming all this distance from the Firth of Forth without a
maid, looking as if she'd just stepped from a Paris hatbox.

"Remove your jackets and hats," Beau said kindly to the miners,
sweat-soaked in thick wool and tweed. "This climate will overcome
you if you aren't careful." .

I put my head out of the coach window. The soldiers remounted
their big horses, the outriders their lesser ones. The German driver
lashed up the ten sleek mules.

"*Vámanos a Mexico!*"

"Try not to get your arms broken or your teeth knocked out!"
Manuel Lizarraga ran alongside the coach for a few paces, waving
the handkerchief he'd held to his nose most of the way from Vera
Cruz.

"Whew!" Beau took off his hat and riffled his long fingers
through his thick red hair. "We really pulled off one hell of a fine
escape this time, didn't we, my sweet Angel?"

The wonderful thrill of touching him poured through me as the
coach jostled us against each other.

I caress another? Never!

5

Fragile Flora was by far the toughest occupant of the coach; perhaps there was just less of her to batter and bounce about. Her main
worry was digging a gnat out of each eye, refusing my help. The
wretched Cornishmen clung together in shocked misery. Between
scratching insect bites and rubbing bruises, Beau kept his hat
pulled down over his eyes, every hour or so peeping out and muttering, "Haven't we left that damned mountain yet?"

But I felt as if I had entered the enchanted garden of Beauty and
the Beast. Our rough, ascending way went through a succession of
tropical trees covered with flamboyant red and white and purple

blossoms, enlivened by hummingbirds, parakeets, squawking parrots and long-tailed jays. Orchids of every size and color and other exotic parasitical plants intertwined the dark branches. Blue convolvulus and pink, yellow and lavender trumpet-flowered vines turned round and round the trunks. Coconut palm, orange, lemon, chirimoya and banana trees loaded with fragrant fruits reached out to touch.

At a turning, in a green valley I saw an Indian girl lying under a shading tree by a running stream. A cascade of white foam leapt from the mountainside into the stream. There was a smell of fresh water. The girl's long black hair caressed her glistening copper body. One knee was lifted and the other, spread apart, nestled in a pile of creamy washing. Was the Beast nearby?

The leader of the outriders, he especially entrusted with the safety of Señora McLeod, was a swarthy, shifty-eyed Mexican named Francisco Dudas y Torres. His "little name" was Paco. He pointed his whip at Beauty and smacked his lips.

Paco was a picturesque figure in a short dark *charro* jacket, loosely held together in the middle with a cord strung between silver buttons on the lapels, showing a white cotton shirt and a wide red silk bow tie. Skintight dark trousers which buttoned all the way up the sides with silver buttons were belted in leather and buckled in heavy silver. His pointed black shoes had heavy silver spurs attached. But more shining than all that silver was Paco's white beaver sombrero, its immense rolled brim lined with glittery tissue. Strong and square, he sat erect in a high-pommeled, fancy saddle.

I didn't realize until we reached Plan del Rio that he thought *I* was Señora McLeod. He was always riding up beside the window, telling me to look at this and smell that. Sometimes he made his big brown horse rear and curvet. Flora said he was disgusting and smelled terrible. Beau blew cigar smoke in his face whenever Paco made one of his more flowery speeches.

To my delight Mount Orizaba traveled along with us no matter in which direction we twisted. At La Calear we had a distant sighting of the sea. Beau almost broke his neck looking back at it until a boulder in the road caused the coach to leap in the air and jam his head into the roof.

We changed mules every six leagues at stopping places in dusty little villages. As we drove off with a fresh team, I could imagine the unhitched mules heehawing in their shelter at the anguished shrieks they had managed to wrench from us inside the coach.

In late afternoon a diligence from Jalapa dashed into the courtyard of the inn in Plan del Rio at the same time as ours. A German musician, his wife and four children stumbled out, warning of the horrors we were in for at Puebla. Others of his orchestra had traveled ahead to Vera Cruz to board any ship sailing for anywhere. A scorpion had crawled far into the oboe, warm from being played. A bat had entangled itself in his oldest child's hair and bitten a hole in her scalp. Cockroaches and spiders covered the floors. The evil Archbishop of Puebla had refused what he'd promised to pay them to play at the Empress's Birthday Ball. Every innkeeper was a thief and every bootblack a rascal. He preferred starving in Bremen to feasting on goat and tortillas in Mexico. If we were wise we would turn back now before we went any farther from the coast.

Paco said no, we would sleep in Jalapa. He had bargained to present the tall, marvelously beautiful Scotswoman with shining black hair and wonderful eyes the color of blue morning glories to the esteemed manager of the rich Mon Real silver mine on the day after tomorrow in Puebla. He, Francisco Dudas, was famous all over Mexico for his deliverances.

"The food at this inn is good," Paco said, ignoring Flora and carefully helping me down first from the coach, holding my arm until I was steady enough to limp into the inn.

The Cornishmen turned up their snubby noses at everything, merely drinking a few sips of hot chocolate, complaining of head and back injuries. Beau discovered a skin of pulque and concentrated on it between mouthfuls of greasy vegetable soup, boiled fish, wild turkey smothered in *mole* sauce, fried beefsteak and piles of frijoles all saturated with garlic and oil.

Flora complained of her eyes hurting. Beau recommended that we try the pulque. The first taste was so dreadful and the smell so horrible we spat it out. The second gulp was awful, the third tolerable, the fourth drinkable and the fifth quite pleasant.

After supper Beau and I walked a ways to stretch our legs. We stopped at an impressive, arched stone bridge leading to a great highroad, once paved, now going to ruin, that Beau said the Spaniards had built probably three hundred years ago.

"Mexico fascinates me," I said.

"It repels me. Nothing reminds me of anything familiar. It's cruel and hard and dry. I haven't seen a single acre of good cotton land. I don't know what possessed me to listen to a man who thinks all the world is an ocean, ruled by inexorable tides. And Phillip will never find us, never; not that he'll care. Not with all our money in his pockets. Oh, my Angel, can you bear thinking of tomorrow and tomorrow and tomorrow?" he whispered, taking me in his arms and running his tongue around the inside of my ear.

I shivered. Passionate sensation? Foreboding? Homesickness? All three, I think. A night bird's cry came from nearby and a cold wind wailed from the mountains.

Beau gathered me closer. "Can you?"

The pulque had made me loose and comfortable and I was touching him all over. I could face anything.

"Can *you*?" I countered dreamily.

"I honestly don't think I can." He stopped short, looking skyward in the moonlight. "So far nothing in Mexico inspires me to do anything but run like hell away from it."

"Don't lose heart until we hear Maury's plans and see where we will live. And what of Maximilian? It will be exciting to meet an Emperor."

"Why would we ever meet the Emperor? If by chance we do, you know how I dislike foreigners."

Paco was shouting for us in a voice piercing as a child's.

"He won't come looking for us. Let's lie down on my cape and pretend we're on the beach at home. I'll name the stars for you."

I watched him take off his coat and I saw his hawklike profile abruptly silhouetted against the glow of a moonbeam. Then it vanished and he was lying beside me.

"Those little wisps of hair flying loose on your neck, those precious little wisps!" he said in a descending flight into grief.

I touched his throat with my forefinger. "Don't let's go rummaging in our souls tonight. There's no telling what secrets we may find if we do. What's past is past."

"But it's not past. Every few nights I dream of Cotton Hall burning in the night and every time it's the same heartbreaking shock and fear."

"It's nerves. It's because everything is new and strange."

"No. It's fear."

I felt the pulsing of his blood. His heart was beating so hard it seemed to shake the world. It was pounding with fear of our tomorrows of what was going to be when we reached the end of our journeying.

"How I wish I was not here. I agreed to come but I wish I was at Hilton Head." Suddenly his despairing homesickness changed to a despairing passion of physical desire. I was engulfed in his bigness; smothered by the intensity of his kisses, my neck, my breasts, my mouth.

Later while he lay relaxed at last in my arms, it was as though his despair had passed into me and I grieved that there was so much about him that I did not wholly understand, but I was grateful that his dark mood had passed and that in me he had found comfort.

The high moon was almost day-bright when we returned to the inn. The escort was mounted, the outriders ready. Paco said angrily, "The Señor McLeod will kill me if he discovers I have permitted the señora to walk off with a stranger into a night full of robbers and murderers."

Ignoring Paco, Beau presented each of the Cornish miners a cigar. They went to sleep with them in their mouths. First it was cool, then it grew cold. Flora and I bundled ourselves in cloaks and shawls. Beau pointed out nontropic oaks, black in the moonlight. We almost ran over one of the escort soldiers lying on the road asleep where he'd fallen off his horse.

As we went farther into the high country the road became pitted with washed-out gullies dammed at intervals with piles of rocks to turn off the water. The coach didn't just bounce and bound anymore. It leapt from dam to dam and rock to rock, sometimes at an angle of 45 degrees. The comforting effects of the pulque and of making love wore off. I clenched my mouth in a straight line against the jolts or screwed it into buttonholes of agony. Flora's faces were worse and the miners even more so. Once Beau gave a sharp cry and moaned in my ear, "I've just been gelded."

It grew colder and colder. Distantly I could make out Mount Orizaba with its white nightcap on and the Cofre de Perote glistening. The outriders in their serapes, especially Paco in his white sombrero, looked all silver in the moonlight. The feathers on the soldiers' helmets were flying like a flock of egrets and over everything was an odor of drenched roses as we clattered into the courtyard of a large clean inn in Jalapa at two o'clock in the morning.

Beau kicked out and ground his teeth the night through. I thought: When day breaks, if it ever does, I will agree to our going someplace else. He is right. He can bear any fate but this one. I think he will die if we continue on this nightmare journey in Mexico.

6 🌿

Blackbirds singing shrill-sweet songs in a fig tree outside the window waked me. Beau had vanished. I dallied getting into my rumpled Cuban traveling suit of gray linen and my rose silk shirtwaist. The depression that had overcome me in the night had lightened. It disappeared completely when I sat down at a table with Flora in the sweet-smelling courtyard. Roses were everywhere: covering the walls, set about in tubs, climbing up the oak and tallest palm trees.

A darling little old ginger-faced woman brought my breakfast. I had never tasted such fresh eggs, such sweet butter, crusty bread so hot from the oven, heavenly honey and fragrant coffee. Flora's eyes were red and stuck shut. She hadn't slept and wouldn't eat. She said she must have some soothing eye ointment or she would kill herself.

The outriders were gathered around the well in the center of the courtyard. Paco's sly glance met mine as I rose and approached the group. He had on a panama hat and was smoking a cigar. I recognized the hat and the cigar fragrance.

"Your very tall husband exchanged four of these fine Cuban cigars for an hour of my horse and my sombrero. He is inspecting this city of beautiful flowers as a proper caballero. The German driver has told that you two are from the United States. He laughed much at my error."

"I'm sorry you mistook me for Señora McLeod yesterday."

He ignored my apology. "I have a letter for the true señora which she is unable to read. You will read it to us. Is very necessary to know what it says."

The letter was a formal invitation from Don Carlos Miranda y Ruiz y Fagoagas, the Mayor of Jalapa, to the Señora McLeod. She was to call on the Miranda family at their home at ten o'clock this morning.

"I can't talk to strangers," Flora wailed, "and I won't. I am going blind."

I explained this to Paco who said the small woman's red and yellow eyes were unimportant. An invitation from Don Carlos was not truly an invitation but a command. Doña Teresa y Fagoagas

Miranda was of the wealthiest silver family in Mexico. Don Carlos had been great in the past government of Mexico, and was also great in the present one. It was much a puzzle.

Flora put her forehead down on the table as if the touch of the starched cotton cloth might cool the pain in her eyes. I was tempted to stroke her curly brown head but her touch-me-not quality dissuaded me.

"I'll go in your place," I said to her. "Come, Paco."

"Why not? You fooled me and I am a smart man. I will point out a few sights on the way, and I know where to buy eye medicine from a Mayan witch in the market for the true Señora McLeod."

The three of us walked up and down fascinating old streets of long low buildings with black iron grilles over the windows and iron-railed balconies. Roses clambered over the high walls and were massed in all the shops and open windows of the houses. There was a sound of music floating from doorways and under shading trees. Sitting between two little girls on a bench in a park a young man was playing a habanera on a mandolin. Everywhere I looked were shining mountains, flowers and white-washed walls tinged with celestial saffron from the morning sun.

Perhaps I could persuade Beau to choose a hacienda nearby. Surely his cotton seeds would flourish. Everything else seemed to. Deep inside I knew I could be happy here with him and the boys. I loved Mexico from that moment.

"Where will you live?" I asked Flora.

We had just passed a ruined, rose-covered convent, and were nearing the chiaroscuro cathedral.

"Wherever Their Majesties are in residence. These mountains remind me of Scotland. I wish I had never heard of Mexico. I know I am going to die here."

I said firmly to Paco, "We will enter the cathedral and rest for a few minutes."

"No. Never. It is not good inside the cathedral. Admire the outside—the bell tower—those carved arches, the magnificent double doors."

I longed to kneel down and close my eyes and tell God how much I missed my baby and beg Him to give me strength to continue on this pilgrimage if that was His will.

"I would like to say just one prayer, Paco."

"Go in then, but you will be sorry. No one goes inside churches anymore. Not even President Juárez."

"Do you follow Juárez or the Emperor?" I asked.

"Ah, Benito Juárez, that one!" Paco kissed his fingertips. "In his simple black carriage, riding alone throughout Mexico, he carries more hearts than the Emperor with all his white horses."

In contrast to the joyful town the filthy, ravaged interior of the dark, chilly cathedral was shocking. Stepping carefully, we tried unsuccessfully to avoid human and animal excrement and severed heads and parts of plaster saints.

Paco described the garments the saints had once worn—scarlet, blue, white and gold satin studded with precious stones. Paintings and banners of silk and velvet embroidered in gold threads had brightened the stone walls. A soaring arch of solid silver, worked in cherubim and garlands of fruits and flowers, had stood over the great marble altar that had gleamed with tall silver candlesticks and a massive golden cross on which had hung the dead silver Christ. But most beautiful had been the Holy Virgin who had sat on a white satin cloud high within the silver arch. Her flowing robes had been heavenly blue, her cheeks rosy and her hair the color of ripe wheat in the sun. What a sweet smile she had! In her arms was her baby, made of solid gold.

The infant Jesus had been the first object jerked down by the soldiers of Juárez and thrown into a pot to melt into money, Paco told us, money to buy bullets with which to kill the moderates of the Empire, and the wicked nuns and greedy priests. It proved the fact that there had never actually been a Holy Virgin. Had she been holy or even a virgin she would have jumped immediately from her white satin cloud and murdered the ones who stole her golden baby.

"I must get out of here at once. It is mean and ugly."

"What passes, Señora Angelica? You, yourself requested to enter here, not I. Why are you shocked? Nothing has altered since the conquistador Hernando Cortes obliterated the ancient city of Tenochtitlán, destroying the Aztec temples and murdering the gentle Emperor Montezuma. At that time the god of the Aztecs, Huitzilopochtli, retreated into the jungles and has been seen no more. This cathedral, at its greatest, was no more beautiful, no more holy, than the Indian temple that once stood on this exact spot! And where is Jesus the Christ? As Huitzilopochtli, is gone."

Paco and Flora left me with the mayor's frozen-faced majordomo, Joaquin, saying that as soon as the bugs in Señora McLeod's eyes were properly exorcised by the witch in the market they would return for me. If my visit had been finished, I must wait in the courtyard with Joaquin.

The extensive dwelling was built all the way around a cobbled square which was ornamented with flowers, statues, a fountain and talking birds in wicker cages hung in elaborately carved stone arches that outlined the shaded corridor.

As in the houses of Havana there was practically no furniture inside; mainly tall gold-leaf mirrors, dark religious paintings and heavy marble-topped mahogany tables holding wax flowers and colorful carved wooden saints under tall glass domes.

Joaquin showed me into a dim salon opening off the upstairs corridor where a little low wide lady overflowed a spindly cane settee. She couldn't have been more than thirty but her ill-made black crinoline and a snagged blond mantilla carelessly flung on fuzzy bronze hair smothered her youth. Two sallow-faced girls, with braided black hair and identical short white muslin dresses bordered with heavily embroidered flounces, sat on matching spindly chairs on either side of Doña Teresa. All three wore white silk stockings and red satin high-heeled slippers. The mother had on splendid diamond earrings, five diamond brooches, four diamond bracelets and on each finger a diamond as big as a pigeon egg. In their very early teens, the girls wore corals instead of diamonds and only four rings on each hand.

Doña Teresa ordered Joaquin to light all the silver-lustre lamps; then in halting English she said, "Pray be seated. Pass in front of me."

I sat on a cane bench facing her. The Marquesa had taught me a few of the unbreakable rules of making visits and the tiresome custom of compliments, but there was no reason for Doña Teresa to suffer needlessly. In Spanish I said, "It is a fine day, is it not so?"

"My husband was informed that you did not talk our language. What a charming error, Señora McLeod, for I talk no English. It took me many hours to learn that one sentence."

I was thankful my first mistake had been made before the mayor appeared, but I could have kicked myself. Now I would be forced to ask and answer questions.

At once Doña Teresa returned to proper etiquette. "How are you, Señora McLeod? Are you well?"

"A thousand thanks, Doña Teresa, and you?"

"Ever at your service."

"I am happy; what pretty girls!"

"To serve you, señora, without doubt," they said, about to burst with curiosity. "How do you like Mexico?"

Doña Teresa frowned. How must she apologize for her daughters' impetuousness? "The girls are twins, Ignacia and Maria. They have never seen a señora of Scotland before. I hope you have passed a pleasant night?"

Then came a dead silence and then Doña Teresa offered me a tiny cigar, called a cigarrillo, from a gold case with a ruby and emerald bird for a latch. The cigarrillo was very strong. The girls giggled when I started coughing. The ceremony of greeting over, Doña Teresa joined in as I puffed, complimenting everything in the room until I noticed two game chickens misbehaving under the round table in the center of the salon. Our eyes met—mine embarrassed, Doña Teresa's amused. Suddenly I was giggling too.

"Those two are my favorites," Doña Teresa said comfortably. "The only members of this household allowed to perform what they choose where they choose."

I was intrigued by an intricately carved mahogany openwork screen at the far end of the room. Wood spindles radiating from little wheels formed a striking design, of many small suns with flinging rays.

"Three hundred years ago the *cancela* separated the patio from the *zaguán*. My uncle moved it in here to make an alcove."

"May we show the señora what is behind the *cancela*?"

"Show," said Doña Teresa, puffing placidly.

Each girl took one of my hands and hurried me across the room and behind the *cancela* where sat an exquisitely carved life-sized medieval female figure. Her fall of human hair was yellow. Her smiling, serene features looked to have been designed and colored by Michelangelo. She was seated on a white satin covered stool. Her arms were empty but a fat yellow tomcat sprawled, sleeping, across her lap. She was wearing a simple gown of blue velvet. Her ruby and gold crown was on a smaller stool beside her.

My surprised enthusiasm delighted the twins who kept inter-rupting each other to explain that she, the Holy Virgin, had once sat above the silver altar in the cathedral but in the revolution when the soldiers came to take away the treasures, their mother's uncle, who had been a priest, had hidden himself in peon clothes and joined the looters. He was too late to save the golden baby Jesus but nobody had cared when he trundled away a mere wooden woman in a borrowed barrow. Later he had returned for the Virgin's clothes kept in an ancient chest behind the sacristy.

"She lives here now all the time. Once a year, on Shrove Tuesday, she is allowed to put on her gold and silver embroidered robes and is carried about the city for everyone to see and again on Good Friday," Doña Teresa said lazily.

"Next year you must come and see too," the twins said.

The mayor entered. All frivolity vanished.

Don Carlos was an aristocratic Creole, in his late thirties or early forties, it was impossible to tell. He was tall and lithe with a narrow, superior face the color of old ivory dominated by heavy-lidded brown eyes. His black hair was brushed close to his head with a thin line of sideburns that came together in a tiny pointed beard on his chin, making it look as if he were wearing a shiny black cap with a sharp V down the middle of his forehead. He was the opposite of his wife in all ways from his trim white merino frock coat and trousers, elegantly cut in the London fashion, to his quick graceful way of walking. It was obvious from his manner that his family wearied him and that he had not come here to be sociable but to perform a tedious duty.

"Señora McLeod talks Spanish," Doña Teresa said, touching her husband's arm.

Don Carlos looked up at the ceiling with a grimace that made his handsome face turn cruel. But as he bowed correctly to me, his hooded eyes showed unexpected interest.

"There now," he said, sitting down beside me, "I had planned to greet you and walk out at once. Instead I will take refreshments and we can have some conversation. I am eager to learn of Great Britain's reaction to the ending of the Civil War in the United States."

If only I were a genie able to sneak back in its safe bottle! Oh, why had I got myself in this trap? Dear God, I prayed, please don't let me say anything to ruin poor Mr. McLeod's image.

"Disraeli says that peace in the United States will make it possible for England to continue to collect her debts in Mexico," I ventured timidly, remembering a letter Phillip had written Beau.

Don Carlos opened his mouth to say something but his unobservant wife picked up a silver bell and rang it vigorously. Im-

27

mediately two barefooted, brown-skinned maids ran in with small
gilt tables which they placed in front of their mistress. Joaquin
followed with an enormous silver waiter holding a gold and white
French porcelain chocolate service and numerous silver sweet
baskets.

"Will you take chocolate, Señora McLeod?" Doña Teresa was
already eating a coconut cream patty-cake.

Don Carlos had been sitting stiffly erect, his eyes almost closed,
looking bored and sleepy. "I hate to hear anyone talk with their
mouth full." He snatched the delicate tall cup from her fat little
hands and gave it to me, after brushing off some coconut flakes that
clung to the rim of the saucer. Meanwhile Doña Teresa was fingering a banana tart with one hand while pouring him a cup with the
other. Taking it quickly he sat down beside me on the bench but in
the opposite direction, his back to his wife. When he talked his face
was very close to mine. He had excellent teeth and his breath
smelled of cloves.

I said, "Are you in favor of Napoleon's Grand Design for Latin
America?" How fortunate I had heard of this in Havana.

"You refer to Napoleon III's plan in which Mexico and the other
Spanish American Republics are to be 'regenerated into stable
prosperous monarchies putting an end to any further United
States expansion to the south and all operating within France's
orbit'?" he asked in a quiet, ironical tone.

"That's what I mean exactly. I understand the Emperor Maximilian is an enlightened man."

"Enlightened? Perhaps. Once before Mexico was blessed with an
enlightened Emperor. His name was Nezahualcoyotl. His emblem
was that of a hungry fox. A poet and a philosopher, he was an
Emperor who dreamed dreams of one all-powerful, merciful God
but who had the strength and wit to look the other way when the
Aztecs sacrificed to their old gods in their way of blood. Nezahualcoyotl was the builder of the most beautiful city in the three
kingdoms of Texcoco, Mexico and Tlacopán: Tezotzina, since razed
by the also enlightened Cortes. Maximilian resembles Nezahualcoyotl in his fantasies of building beautiful cities and gardens
but he lacks the hard core. He resembles more the descendant of
the Hungry Fox, the gentle Montezuma.

"The last thing we need in Mexico today is a Quixotic-minded
Emperor who travels around the country dressed in Mexican-style
riding clothes, treating the Indians as his equals and speaking too
loud of the rights of man and constitutional government. Poor
Maximilian, he thinks he can rule a Mexico by clemency that can
only be ruled by force, is it not so?"

Shocked, I rushed recklessly on. "Your President is an Indian. Don't you consider him your equal?"

Don Carlos's lips twitched in a mocking way. Doña Teresa put down two sugared dates and told the girls to pass the sweet baskets quickly, before an explosion came. Unable to reply, I stirred my chocolate clumsily with a stick of cinnamon.

"Your question is too naked, Señora McLeod. May I express it another way?" Don Carlos did not seem angry.

"Do, please!" I whispered gratefully.

"Is Benito Juárez, the Indian lawyer from Oaxaca, more qualified to govern Mexico than Maximilian, the Archduke from Austria? I will tell you a thing about the man Juárez, and you will be the judge. Juárez, though stripped at the moment of his powers as President of Mexico, nonetheless remains in Mexico gathering his forces while he sends his alter ego, also from Oaxaca, a brilliant young man who has twenty-three years, to Washington to influence President Lincoln, I mean President Johnson, and Secretary Seward *against* the monarchy. This young man, Matías Romero—"

"Was intelligent enough to marry a rich girl too, this one from Philadelphia. I think her name was Lucretia Allen," Doña Teresa interrupted, licking date sugar from her fingers.

Ignoring her Don Carlos spoke directly to me. "You in Great Britain probably are not aware that now that the North has won the Civil War, the United States will not tolerate a monarchy on its southern border. President Johnson has refused to recognize the Emperor's Consul while receiving Romero as the official Ambassador from Mexico. Johnson is also already sending massive quantities of arms and ammunition across the Rio Grande to Juárez. Had the South won the war I would say that Maximilian would have been safe for a time. It is amusing to us in official positions to watch the Confederate exiles pouring into our country to take part in another lost cause."

While he was speaking the yellow tomcat came out and leapt onto the bench and dug its yellow silk head into Don Carlos's half-closed right hand where he let it nestle like a lover in its beloved. Erectile and vibrant, the tomcat stretched itself to its breaking point, its eyes shiny green and hugely dilated, and went into a frantic moaning paroxysm writhing like a snake, covering Don Carlos's smooth wrists with yellow cat hairs.

I tried not to stare but to listen for I knew that I should remember what I heard not what I saw. Appearing oblivious of the cat, one of the girls spoke for the first time since Don Carlos had joined us. "But, Papa, why would the Confederates come into our country unless we invited them?"

"The Emperor Maximilian did invite us," I said too loudly.

"Us, Señora McLeod?" Don Carlos smiled.

"Them! I have trouble with my pronouns, Your Honor."

Don Carlos shook his head smilingly, as if surprised at my silly excuse.

"Have they a right to come, Papa?"

"No more right, Ignacia, than we would have galloping into South Carolina or Virginia and demanding the government to give us, free of charge, fine plantations and houses."

"I know so little of America," I murmured, frantic to remove myself from where I had no business being. To hide my mortification, I reached for a meringue. The girls giggled as the crisp confection crumbled on the marble floor where the two game chickens which had been roosting on the pedestal of the center table rushed forward and began picking up the shreds.

Don Carlos expertly placed another meringue on my plate with a pair of exquisite silver tongs. "My poor country. We have an Austrian Emperor, a French Army of Occupation, and foreign investors, colonists and concessionaires all trying to refashion Mexico in their composite image."

"I think Señora McLeod has heard enough of political talk for one day," Doña Teresa said tactfully. "*My* family has much respect for the Emperor and little for Juárez. *I* think the Emperor is very popular."

"How can the Emperor not be popular? There are thirty thousand French soldiers as well as Belgian and Austrian brigades in Mexico to guarantee it," Don Carlos said, flushing angrily but not changing his tone.

"Lacking the thirty thousand French soldiers, señor, would he still be popular?" I asked calming down.

"Prince Metternich said, 'It will take thirty thousand French soldiers to place the crown of Mexico on the Austrian Archduke's head,' but I say it will take many more than that to keep it there."

Doña Teresa leaned forward. She had a dimple in her left cheek when she smiled. "The Emperor loves flowers and butterflies. Recently, when he was here in Jalapa he was happy with everything in our city of flowers and butterflies. María, would you care to talk?"

"Papa, may I?"

Frowning, the head of the family agreed.

"The Emperor is in the city today. I saw him when I went with Joaquin to visit Tía Dolores Santos. People were out on their balconies throwing flowers and shouting *Viva!* Didn't you hear them?"

"Within these thick walls one hears little of the outside world," Don Carlos explained to me. "You are quite mistaken, María."

"No, Papa, he lifted his white sombrero with one hand and caught a rose with the other. The crowd adored him. He was beautiful. His face was very white and shining."

Prickles of suspicion invaded my toes and fingers. I wanted to die.

Ignacia requested permission to join the conversation. "The Emperor has little hair, that is why he wears the white sombrero when he rides in the sun," she explained to me.

Don Carlos delicately dusted some cat hairs from his sleeve. "The Emperor is a foreigner and fair-skinned. Our Mexican sun is his enemy. That is why he wears the white sombrero. The man on horseback was not the Emperor, for Joaquin said he had no beard and much hair of a fiery color on his head. The Emperor—" he turned to me—"has a fine blond beard."

The prickles attacked my throat. I swallowed hard and kept a straight face but didn't dare say a word.

"Surely," put in Doña Teresa, "if the Emperor wants to ride around Jalapa incognito, to remove his beard and put on a red wig would be the first step in a masquerade."

Don Carlos's studied control was giving way to irritability. He took a round gold watch from his waistcoat pocket. Not opening it, he swung it idly back and forth, back and forth on its gold chain. The now sleeping cat woke and dashed from the room. The girls and Doña Teresa stared at the shiny circle with sleepy eyes. My own eyelids began to droop. The trip was fatiguing me terribly. I was slipping away. I was— No I wasn't! Don Carlos was hypnotizing us! Forcing myself alert my startled eyes met his amused ones. Involuntarily I laughed. What an interesting man. In his own salon he was totally in control of three females! It would have been four except for my guardian angel warning me.

"What time did you say it was, Señor Mayor?"

"Did I say, señora?"

I'd caught him out. He didn't care. Strangely, neither did I. We both laughed as he snapped his fingers, opened the watch and said loudly, "Eleven o'clock, girls. Time for your lessons, isn't it?"

Time, too, for me to leave before I gave away my own wretched masquerade. I rose with the superior airs that only women six feet tall can put on, lifting my head as high as I ever did at a Hunt Ball in Virginia.

The girls jumped up and embraced me. They were slender like their father. "We hope you may pass a good day."

Doña Teresa struggled to her short fat feet and embraced me.

She looked better sitting down. "Señora McLeod, you know that my house is at your disposal. Command me in everything that you may desire."

"A thousand thanks, Doña Teresa. Mine is at yours." Mine? I had no house. Even the little foxes have their holes. . . .

Don Carlos escorted me along the gallery to the stairs. Midway he glanced at a monkey sitting on a table eating a banana. The monkey gave a panicked scream and leapt into its cage in two bounds, turned its back and put its hands over its eyes. There had been no animosity in Don Carlos's look, but it was a certain sort of look, indescribable. A shiver, in rhythm with the monkey's whimpering, trickled down my stiffened neck.

"Female monkeys are always an unpredictable challenge," he commented softly as he followed me to where Joaquin waited to show me out into the open court. Don Carlos lightly kissed my fingertips.

"Adiós, Señora McLeod, until soon, when my wife and I will have the pleasure of dining with you and the elusive Señor McLeod in Puebla at the birthday fiesta of the Empress Carlota."

8

A fresh escort of soldiers in smart navy blue and white uniforms and outriders in brown and tan serapes were gathered in the courtyard of the inn around the harnessed mules. Their dark, Arab-faced captain seemed relieved to see us and annoyed at our tardiness at the same time. "Quick, please," he called to the angry German driver who was shouting insulting things to Paco.

Paco explained that it was not he who was late, but the foreign señoras. One had insisted on calling on the Mayor of Jalapa and had emerged pale as a ghost and unable to make haste, while the other had sat too long on the stool of the Mayan witch in the marketplace. The Indian girls, those who had formerly woven flower garlands for the Holy Virgin but now wove them for themselves (what a joke!), had placed a garland of roses on the head of the quarreling señora to cheer her up as the powerful medicine was dropped into her eyes.

I pointed to the green-stained handkerchief Flora was holding against her temple. "Have we time to wash Señora McLeod's face before we start?"

The driver nodded courteously, saying that Herr Berrien had traveled ahead with a group of soldiers to make sure no bandits or guerrillas were hidden among the rocks, waiting to rob the coach. It was clear the driver admired me, but I caught the contemptuous glance he gave Paco as he tossed him a bundle of cigars. "Herr Berrien, the only sensible man present except me, myself, left these to pay for the use of your worthless horse and bids you take his place beside the ladies in the coach."

"Not so," Paco shrieked, turning to me. "Please, señora, it is necessary to discover your husband and force him to return my horse. It is not correct for the chief of the outriders to arrive in Puebla jolted out of his mind and body, riding inside the coach like a woman. I will not do so. No."

"Get in the coach, Paco, and shut your mouth," the driver yelled, cracking his whip.

The dear old crone who had served such a nice breakfast came running out with two bouquets of pink and red clove carnations and roses for Flora and me.

"Where are we going?" Flora asked dully, dropping her flowers on the floor as I settled her across from her faithful Cornish followers who had managed to purchase cotton blouses from a vendor and were almost merry in their relief at being cool and full of butter and eggs and milk.

Paco put his foot in the middle of Flora's flowers and complained furiously that Señora McLeod had been *muy estúpida* since swallowing a powder mixed with pulque from the witch's gourd to ease her pain.

Though I was dying to ask Beau if it had really been he whom the Jalapeños had mistaken for the Emperor, I was glad he wasn't beside me groaning and moaning, for I was still distraught from my own foolish impersonation.

But those long lonely war years behind enemy lines on Hilton Head had taught me not to let depression and guilt swallow me. Anyway, I thought, nobody but I would ever know how humiliating the visit was.

I would comfort myself with the magnificent mountain views, glorious flowers and blossoming trees. Flora slept with her head either on my shoulder or on Paco's, depending on the roll of the wheels, but the miners and I thoroughly enjoyed the first part of the day of spectacular scenery as we rattled through little villages and passed gutted churches and ruined convents and occasionally a white hacienda. And always there was Mount Orizaba on the horizon.

Gradually the tropical trees gave way to oak and somber pine and the air grew cold and colder. At San Miguel del Soldado we stopped for some food, to change horses and escorts and find our cloaks and shawls. The fresh escort said they had passed two soldiers and a horseman in an enormous white sombrero, riding a brown horse many miles ahead of us.

The innkeeper, who looked like a bandit himself, told of being robbed last night by ten strong men or maybe it was thirteen; he had been too shattered to count. They had eaten all of the food he had prepared for our diligence. We must content ourselves with roasted goat and mashed beans and tortillas which would taste very well with all the chili he had poured over them. Probably the bandits had murdered the tall man of the white sombrero who had eaten much goat earlier.

This statement settled it for me. We would proceed to Brazil as we first planned. Mexico was a blunder for Beau. He could never in a thousand years fit into an Empire made up of bandidos and Don Carloses and Pacos and Austrians.

As the coach ascended into the clouds over ground covered with lava and calcined rock, Paco pointed out faded garlands and crude crosses that marked either a murder or a fatal accident. Once as we almost turned over in a gully he muttered, "Keep a sharp eye. If you see a pile of rocks with a white sombrero upon it you will know who lies beneath."

I asked one of the Cornishmen to change places with me. I was beginning to loathe Paco. Everything he said and did infuriated me.

By the time we reached Perote, where we were to sleep, the sun had set and it was bitter cold. The inn was dirty and the food horrible. After supper, the landlady, a large, untidy, handsome Mexican woman with her hair in a thick plait and a mustache on her upper lip, showed Flora and me into the only private room, with one small bed. She told the miners to roll up in blankets on the floor near the fire in the kitchen.

I helped Flora undress and get into the bed, then hurried to look for Beau. "Have you seen a very tall señor in a gray uniform?"

The large woman was washing the soup bowls. "Yes," she chuckled, "he is much a man. Look—he gave me a cigar along with a fine embrace! He is sleeping out in the barn with the soldiers. But it is not permitted for you to go there. No women, not even I, or pretty boys, are permitted. So take your rest. I will wake you at two o'clock for breakfast. The new coach will take you away at three, the magic time between dark and light. You look as weary as I. Goodnight, señora."

I sat by the smoldering fire, drinking more pulque until she went to bed; then I went outside. The afterglow still lingered over the bleak, volcanic landscape. A little light filtered through a single window at the far end of the shelter lined with sisal hammocks full of snoring men wrapped in blankets. A white sombrero underneath a near hammock and a pair of dusty, booted feet hanging over the end indicated Beau.

"Wake up and come outside," I whispered in his ear.

"Hey, what's going on?" He would have fallen out of the hammock had I not caught it together and held him in. "For God's sake, Angelica, what the hell are you doing here?"

"I'm looking for you, that's what. You've been gone all day and not said a word to me. I've been crazy with worry."

"Here—give me your hand. It's freezing. Put it in here—no—down there."

"Beau, darling Beau, I've made up my mind. We will turn around and go back to Vera Cruz tomorrow. I've learned frightening things about Mexico today. There's a war going on here just like the one we fought through. Maury didn't tell you the whole truth."

"Maury has never been in Mexico before. I know as much about it as he."

"The Mexicans don't want us here. They don't want the Emperor either. Do you know that?"

"How wrong you are. You should have seen me in Jalapa this morning. The people thought *I* was the Emperor! They came out on their balconies and cried '*Viva! Viva!*' and threw flowers. It was the first time I've felt like myself since I left Hilton Head. I do wish you could have seen and heard."

"I didn't see but I heard. Now, Beau—"

"I'm listening. You're not cold?"

"Not standing close to you. Please let me talk to you tonight."

"What a precious one you are. Kiss me and then run back into your nice warm inn and climb into your nice warm soft bed. Nitey-bye."

The night was cold and damp. I was perplexed by the intensity of my feelings. I could not see the men in the other hammocks but heard the one in the next stirring.

"S-s-s-s," he hissed. "*Muchacha!* Do me next. I have much money."

I fled.

Flora was pacing agitatedly about the kitchen in her petticoat. Her hair was disheveled and her eyes wild. "You ran away from me. I had an awful dream about spiders and rocks falling on me and my feet are floating in air this minute. That old witch woman poisoned me this morning or was it last week? And there's blood on my chin. I saw it in the looking glass. A bat must have bitten me. No—I'm not going back in that room alone."

I wanted to drink another cup of pulque hoping it would make me sleepy but I lay down with her on the narrow bed in the damp chill room without undressing except to loosen my corsets. She put her arms around my neck and clung to me.

"Angus hurt me the night we were married. You don't know Angus, do you? Papa made me marry him because he has a brilliant future. A Mexican millionaire promised him a fortune to manage his silver mine."

"What Mexican?" I stroked her hair, knowing I shouldn't be asking her questions, but I was curious. She had never talked about herself before.

"Something Gutiérrez de Estrada. He lives in Paris and he's the one most responsible for the Archduke Maximilian of Austria being the Emperor of Mexico. Mother thought Maximilian would have refused the Mexican offer but Charlotte made him accept. Charlotte's brother, who is the heir to the Belgian throne, said, 'My ambitious little sister *will* have a crown, whatever the cost.' Mother said that even if having a crown meant living in a mud palace among the Zulus, Charlotte would have preferred that to being a mere Archduchess of Austria."

"I thought her name was Carlota."

"That's Spanish for Charlotte. My mother was Austrian and that's how I know all these things about the Emperor. She didn't want me to marry Angus, but Papa owed Angus's father a lot of money. Angus is common, but Papa is a laird who wants to be a duke. I was fifteen and we weren't married but a month when Angus went away. I think Mother arranged his going through her Austrian cousin who is married to de Estrada. That was three years ago. I prayed Angus would get the fever and die but he didn't; Mother did. Papa forced me to come here when Angus wrote saying he needed his European wife to show off at court. I *will* like being shown off at court. What a pity you won't ever see me all dressed up."

"Perhaps I will," I murmured in order to say something that might quiet her.

"Their Majesties would never receive you. My eye hurts worse."

"Will you try and sleep if I tell you about my little baby, Edward, and my precious little brother-in-law, Button, in Virginia? And there is another brother-in-law—a year younger than I. His name is Phillip. He is very handsome and opinionated. He ran away to England to keep from joining the Confederate Army. He is on his way from Liverpool to Cuba, bringing all the real money we have. It is the money from the 1860 cotton crop. We left word for him in Havana to follow us to Mexico. We were planning to buy a hacienda here with it, but now we're going to Brazil or back home. Phillip can stay in Mexico with Commander Maury in our place if he chooses."

Flora said she did not wish to hear any more about Phillip nor did she care what I did. Sighing, I asked her if she liked to dance. She became quite animated and chattered away about mazurkas and waltzes and cotillions. In the middle of a lively account of a ball at Schönbrunn she suddenly became silent and, as if the effects of the powdered drug had dissipated, she lay back down and sighed deeply.

"What in the world have I been saying? I hope nothing silly. Have I been talking nonsense?"

I did not reply. Five minutes later she was sound asleep.

It had just gotten black dark. With my hands behind my head I looked straight up at the ceiling raked by flickers of candlelight. A lizard was walking along a flicker as if the thin line of light was a tightrope. If only Beau were beside me I would fear nothing. What did I fear? The lizard? Becoming involved in another war? The thought of living in a foreign country that could never be *my* country? Perhaps all three. I tried to reflect on my childhood and girlhood in Virginia with my Aunt Dell and Uncle Jim and my little sister, but those days seemed far away and unreal as a fairy tale. Nothing had really mattered until five years ago on my eighteenth birthday when I saw Beau for the first time.

He was still all that mattered. His voice alone had the power to call me away from whatever I was thinking or doing or feeling—

"Angelica—it's two o'clock and I need you to help me."

"I'll be out in an instant."

Our roles of last night were reversed. Now it was he begging to talk to me. Hurriedly I hooked up my corsets and buttoned my shoes and, not waking Flora, went into the kitchen.

Beau, the Arab-faced captain of last night's escort, a lanky, sandy-haired stranger, and the landlady I'd met last night were eating breakfast around the center table by the light of one droopy candle. The landlady had piled her luxuriant black hair high and was wearing a faded, flounced red dress, cut low across imposing bosoms. She had powdered her mustache. It glistened whitely. Two sleepy Indian women with impassive faces and draggy black rebozos were serving fried eggs smothered in tomato and chili pepper sauce along with tortillas and delicious-smelling coffee.

The captain blushed and ducked his head when he saw me. He must have been the soldier in the hammock next to Beau last night! But I hadn't seen *his* face so it was easy for me to smile and say cheerfully, "Good morning, señors, or is it still good night?"

Beau looked up with a happy face. "You are beautiful in candlelight," he said warmly. "Don't worry, nobody here speaks English."

The sandy-haired stranger smiled and winked at me to let me know he was understanding every word spoken, be it French, Spanish or English.

Beau said he and the Mexican captain, who spoke French, had worked up a daring plan for today. However, since I had been upset over his absence yesterday, he had asked the captain to explain the strategy to me. The fresh escort of soldiers had not shown up, and yesterday's were too weary to continue. Everything was at a standstill.

The landlady wiped a drop of pepper sauce from her mustache. She regretted that she could not help in any way except to feed and sleep and urged everybody to go back to bed and rest comfortably as she planned to do, until the Lancers arrived, even if that should be tomorrow.

Paco refused to listen to this advice. He was sitting on a stool eating a rib of roast pig. He shook the rib at the landlady and said she was a meddling old whore but even so he realized that she was correct. However, today was the day he had sworn to deliver the Señora McLeod to Puebla, sixteen hours' hard traveling from here. Delay was unthinkable.

Nobody paid him any attention. The captain introduced me to the stranger, our new coachman. He was a blue-eyed Yankee from Bedford, Massachusetts, named Jake Smith. Jake said in English that he didn't mind a bit eating at the same table with a Johnnie Reb; then in Spanish that he would not take the mining company's brand-new, made-in-the-United States coach out on the road until the Lancers could accompany him. Mr. McLeod trusted Jake Smith, he did.

Paco said that the tall señor who insisted on wearing his sombrero and the Yankee coachman named Smith should ride on top of the coach side by side, fully armed. Seeing those two ugly faces, the robbers would gallop away as rapidly as the wind.

Beau laughed when I translated this.

The landlady told Paco he was a fool.

The captain wilted Paco with a glance, then turned to me (evidently satisfied I had not recognized him). "Your husband is a brave and daring man, Señora Berrien. He has the strength of ten men, is it not true? Me, I could not take the bad country today after the punishment of yesterday, even with—"

Beau interrupted excitedly, "Bandits are definitely in the area, guerrillas too. The landlady recognized eight guerrillas yesterday afternoon sitting on their horses on a peak watching the inn. She shouted to them and they melted away into the trees. The captain is convinced that Porfirio Díaz is aware of our important passenger and plans to waylay the coach and kidnap pretty Flora. Now while I would hate for that to happen, imagine how I would feel if, by mistake, they took the wrong lady—the one who was posing as Mrs. McLeod in Jalapa."

"And who were you posing as?"

We burst out laughing.

Puzzled, the captain stood up, sighing deeply. "Excuse me, señora. We must make a decision immediately. Your husband insists it shall be yours."

"Why would anyone kidnap poor little Señora McLeod?" I asked.

The captain said, "It is not she, Señora Berrien, whom they want. She is of no interest as you noticed yesterday in Jalapa. But her husband is the shrewdest manager of silver mines in Mexico, is it not true?"

"I still don't understand," I said trying to make myself care.

"It is simple. If General Díaz captures Señora McLeod it is possible that her husband will come over to the side of the Juaristi in exchange for his wife. He is known to be an opportunist. Now will you hear our plan?"

"Of course, Captain."

Rumors flew fast in Mexico, he declared. It was said by some that the Emperor himself had gone horse riding through the streets of Jalapa yesterday in his customary white sombrero and gray *charro* costume; by others that the Emperor had definitely been observed in a carriage with José Zorilla, the celebrated Spanish poet, on the road from Puebla to Oja de Agua or the other way around. Whichever, the fact was that Major Berrien in his gray uniform and wearing the white sombrero could easily be mistaken for the Emperor. Two such tall graceful caballeros were rarely seen in this country. Now, were robbers lurking (even Díaz's guerrillas) they would not dare attack a vehicle that followed after his Imperial Majesty riding a horse. The Empress Carlota herself might be inside the coach. And why would they not dare, those wild fierce ones? Because of all the Italians, Poles, Hungarians, even an English lord and an Irish dissenter, to say nothing of the great General Thun and his detachment of Austrian Hussars all ready to come galloping out of the woods waving their swords and rifles.

"So," Beau chimed in, his eyes sparkling, "if a major, late of the Confederate Army, could fool the wily Jalapeños—"

"Yes, but suppose neither the robbers nor Díaz's guerrillas are fooled?"

The captain lifted his hands and looked pleadingly at me. "If not fooled, señora, they will at least become confused and hesitate. The boldness of the major makes real danger small. When the new soldiers meet up with the coach, which will be soon I promise you, the travelers, the true foxes, can roll merrily on to Puebla while Díaz stalks the red fish across the hills, but not daring to attack."

I bit my lip. Everybody else clapped and cheered except Paco.

"Are you going alone?" I asked.

"No," Beau said, rising and buttoning his gray jacket. "Two of the soldiers who have sweethearts along the way will accompany me."

I followed him outside over a black mass of lava into a heavy mist, a white darkness so thick you could see nothing. The wind was howling among the rocks and cliffs.

"Please don't do this." I put out my hand and touched his wrist, sprinkled with fiery hairs and, as the first time, the thrill of him shot up my arm like glory.

"I feel it too," he murmured as if vexed. Then he sighed and took my hand and kissed it. "Do you love me?"

"Oh, yes, my darling."

"Then you must know how miserable I have been in this voluntary exile. There have been times that only by touching you have I held myself away from shooting myself. I hate this country. I miss Hilton Head and Cotton Hall and my slaves, especially Liney and Cudjo Manigo and Masai and Maum Hannah. I am lost without the plantation to run. I miss the boys, even wicked Phillip. I am the most homesick person in all the world. And I've been so damned bored. This is the first excitement that has come my way since Appomattox."

"Where will we meet?"

"I may be at any or all of the places where the change of horses and soldiers takes place. Certainly at Amozoc, which is the final stopping place before Puebla."

And he was gone.

We left the inn, unescorted, in freezing bright moonlight, the mist having temporarily swirled somewhere else. Swaying on his feet with fatigue, the captain refused to permit Paco to borrow or buy a horse, ordering him to continue inside the coach as protection for the ladies.

We were bouncing along in front of the ancient castle of San Carlos in the dismal, black-looking town of Perote when the Lancers finally came galloping up. The head officer of the Lancers made many excuses and apologies. He had brought a double number of soldiers, the next stage of our journey through the bad land being the most dangerous and difficult. Robbers and guerrillas, rattlesnakes and jaguars were hiding behind all those pine trees and craggy rocks out there, waiting for horsemen stupid enough to ride alone or in small groups.

As the sky lightened we passed over the very crater of a volcano. Had Beau fallen in? I made the coachman stop and let me look.

Everything was wild and grand, even the roadside crosses marking tragedies were iridescent in the shimmering half-lit gloom. The only signs of life were an occasional Indian village and a few small, plodding Indians in their baggy white trousers driving overloaded burros.

At dawn I excused myself and walked a ways from the group, stopping behind a big rock. I looked up at Mount Orizaba which seemed to have traveled forward and stood out in stark outline against a clove-pink and morning-glory-blue sky. I thought: Am I crazy? Dear God, what am I doing on top of this wild alien world— why am I here—how can I arrange our escape?

At every stop for a change of horses and escorts and food: Tepeyahualco, La Ventilla, Oja de Agua, Nopalucan, I inquired desperately for Beau. He had either just gone on or not been there at all. As the hours went by I lost all interest in the now fertile countryside and grew more and more miserable. After a torrent of rain almost swept us over a cliff I tried to explain my feelings to Flora and suddenly began to cry. Flora made no effort to be reassuring. The timid Cornishmen shook their heads and sighed. Paco took great pains to point out every cross and funeral wreath.

"If the señor is not at Amozoc," he said hopefully, "you can assume the worst. There is a trail first going up then going down, from Perote to Amozoc. It is familiar to the lecherous soldiers accompanying the señor. There are pretty Indian girls with rolling hips waiting along the way to trade mules for weary horses as well as selling other favors. So the señor is either dead beneath a pile of rocks or black and swelling from a rattlesnake bite or curled up in the arms of a lively whore. Believe me, señora, I know."

"He is dead. He has been murdered. I know it and I am wretched. But you all needn't worry. I will behave in a calm cool way when I see his body lying in the road."

No one spoke again until we clattered up to the inn at Amozoc.

"Look! Look!" Paco cried, pointing at a magnificent coal-black horse carrying a gigantic rider in full-dress Austrian uniform brillianted with gold braid and buttons and epaulets and belt and a silver helmet topped with flying feathers. "The Emperor! I have seen him before and I see him now."

To this day I can't remember how we came into each other's arms. Did Beau dismount and run to the coach? Did I jump out before the coach came to a halt? I do remember how lit up he was. He had been that exhilarated on Secession night, my first night on Hilton Head, when he had gone off with the Elliotts to celebrate, calling back, "Put a candle in every window, sweet Angel. Ours must be the most brightly illuminated house on the whole island!"

And I can still hear his wild laugh as he touched the silver helmet with a white gloved hand and shouted, "How do you like the Emperor's new clothes?"

That was one fairy tale I had hated. And I still see his bewitched face in the lustre mirror of that inn and his strange unnatural smile.

"Tell me every detail of what you did yesterday," I said, sipping orangeade and thanking the Lord that Beau was sitting beside me at breakfast.

"I would have told you last night but you distracted me in your own inimitable way."

"Not I. You slept the minute your head touched the pillow."

"I never, even in the war, spent such an exciting day. We took the wild way down to Amozoc. I intend to write down for our children and grandchildren a description of that perilous, marvelous journey. Orpheus's descent couldn't compare. If only I'd had Teaser under me to struggle up and down the precipitous cliffs and to leap over unimaginable chasms and waterfalls and fallen giant trees. Everything was bigger than life. There were blue jays with tails over a foot long, slinky animals that climbed to the tops of trees, and rattlesnakes coiled up two and three feet high."

"I'm glad I wasn't along. I prefer the evil Paco."

But Beau was back in the forest. He clenched and unclenched his fists as words leapt over each other in his eagerness to share his experience.

"It would rain suddenly; then rainbows would flash like meteors across the sky. I became separated from the two Mexican soldiers in a torrential downpour. Drenched and cold I was passing by an overhanging rock when my fourth mount of the day, a mean red mule, shied and began to buck as a detachment of Austrian Hussars galloped from behind the rock and surrounded me."

"Did you have your pistol?"

"It wouldn't have helped. The leader, bristling with blond sideburns and mustaches, lifted his sword and first in German then in French ordered me to identify myself.

"When I said, in French, 'Major Baynard Berrien, Confederate States of America,' he saluted: 'Major Alfons von Kodolitsch, Imperial Guard,' and asked if he could help me."

"What did you say next?" I was fascinated as much by Beau's happy face as by the events.

"I said I was lost and wet and would gratefully accept any aid he could give me. He lifted a gloved hand and crashed away through

the trees, I right behind him, and the Hussars all falling in beautifully. It was like the fairy tales Mother used to read aloud. Everything that happened after was straight out of one. She would have
adored it."

"Go on—don't stop."

"When we left the heavy forest we entered a lovely, deep-shaded
grove and, darling Angel, I wasn't in the least surprised at what I
saw: a group of gentlemen sitting in comfortable chairs around a
table covered with a white damask cloth laid with silver and
crystal. The ground was covered with Oriental rugs and masses of
flowers in jars were everywhere.

"The gentlemen were rising and bowing, lifting tall stemmed
hock glasses toward one who remained seated. He had on a white
merino frock coat. His aristocratic young face, sunburned, looked
like a golden mask.

" 'The Emperor!' they toasted.

"Von Kodolitsch gave the signal to halt. The Hussars raised
their swords.

" 'The Emperor!'

"I lifted my sodden white sombrero. 'The Emperor!'

"This gesture caught the attention of the man with the golden
face. Our eyes met and held. I felt as if I were looking in a cloudy
mirror. Then the mirror wasn't cloudy. We saw each other plainly.
A bond leapt between us. I want to be near him for the rest of my
life."

This was too much for me to take in all at once. I dropped my eyes
so he could not see my bewildered expression, and I held a napkin
over my chest lest the roar of my heartbeats deafen him; no, not
him; he was transported. His voice became unfamiliar.

"I was taken to a tent where a Captain Leopold most graciously
gave me a dress uniform, he, as I, being six feet six. When I took off
my draggled gray Confederate uniform and put on the scarlet
jacket, brightened with gold braid and buttons, and the tight white
trousers of the Palatine Guard, I felt like a snake shedding its
worn-out skin and growing a shinier new one. It was symbolic of
the enchantment of the day.

"Another chair was brought and a place set for me on the Emperor's right hand. The martinet majordomo, brought, they said,
from Maximilian's castle at Miramar, directed liveried servants in
the pouring of more wine. This time the glasses were raised to
Major Baynard Berrien! If only you had been there."

"Do you wish I had been?"

"To be truthful, no. It was a man's day. You understand."

There was no use to argue. I nodded.

"Little Tudos, the Emperor's Hungarian cook, frolicked around the table like a pleased puppy dog as caviar and lobster and stone crab and cold turkey and salads and sherbets disappeared. It was a treat to sit and smoke cigars and tell ribald stories and sing nostalgic songs. The Emperor enjoyed and entered in as if he, too, had missed such congenial fellowship."

Flies buzzed over my soggy eggs and bacon and tomatoes. Bees droned in the honeysuckle as Beau reveled in telling his adventure.

His Majesty was touring the eastern province in order to be seen and to meet his people. With him had been José Zorilla, the Spanish poet; old Dr. Billimek, the court naturalist (the Emperor being an intense nature lover); Count Thun, the Austrian Minister (stiff and formal); José Luis Blasio, the Emperor's new interpreter and secretary (a dear boy, twenty-two years old); and Don Ramon Bestiguis who had a rich hacienda nearby. Don Ramon had furnished the iced caviar and lobster.

In French they talked first of Commander Maury. The Emperor had known him by correspondence when he was Commander of the Austrian Navy and Maury was a Commander in the United States Navy. The Emperor said as a result of Commander Maury's genius, mail comes from Europe to Mexico weeks sooner. He doesn't feel so far away from home.

"The Emperor has grandiose plans for Maury's Confederate exiles. He considers us the most exceptional group of people to expatriate since the French Huguenots after the Revocation of the Edict of Nantes."

"Then what?"

"Then, the excellent hock mellowing and melding us, we spent two pleasant hours discussing Aztec and Mayan art, a new national theater under Zorilla's aegis, Dr. Billimek's butterfly collections, the cultivation of maguey, the breeding of bulls, the way the Cuban nightingale, Concha Mendez, sings 'La Paloma'—everything but politics.

"Oh!" His sudden sharp tone startled me from my semiattentive state.

"What? What?" I cried, thinking a lizard must have run up his sleeve.

"There was another Mexican gentleman—a Creole of course—most charming. Don Luis Escandon. His cousin died last summer and the widow returned to Spain. The cousin's hacienda is an ideal place for the experiment of growing long staple cotton and the quinine trees that Maury has ordered from India to introduce into Mexico."

"It sounds complicated."

"The hacienda is tastefully furnished and equipped with trained servants. It is not complicated at all. The peons on the land are hard-working. And the hacienda was for sale. It is named Miramontes."

"We must have a look at it sometime," I said, feeling quite tired. It had been an awfully long story, one I wasn't in.

"I bought it." Beau was pacing back and forth, waving his hands excitedly as if he couldn't wait to get them on Miramontes.

"You can't have bought a home without my at least looking at it. You just can't."

It was as if I hadn't spoken. The Emperor had encouraged him. The Emperor himself had chosen a *quinta* for himself—a retreat from Mexico City—in Cuernavaca near Miramontes. Their friendship would not end with the picnic.

"Why have you got that horrified look on your face?" Beau leaned down and stared in my eyes.

His expression unnerved me. "We probably can't afford the hacienda."

"More than." He resumed his restless pacing. "Phillip should be here within three weeks bringing many times that amount."

"I don't want a house I've never seen. Not even if it *is* named Mountainview."

He bumped into the table spilling coffee all over my traveling skirt. I had broken the magic spell. "You had no part in choosing Cotton Hall," he said curtly, "yet, unless I am mistaken, you were happy there. I've given my word as a gentleman. Your coachman has called his passengers. Didn't you hear? The exchange horses have come. Request a maid as soon as you reach the inn in Puebla. Have her unpack and freshen the ball gown I had made for you in Havana. We are invited to be the special guests of Their Majesties at the Birthday Ball for Empress Carlota in Puebla tomorrow night."

His spurs clanking harshly, he adjusted the embossed silver helmet on his high head and marched away to where the spirited black horse, a gift from the Emperor, was pawing the ground impatiently.

We were leaving the courtyard of the inn when Beau rode up to the coach window by which I was sitting. Removing the Hussar helmet he handed it in to me.

"This afternoon sun will blister my face if I don't have a hat."

Sitting across from me, Paco, though not understanding Beau's words, quite clearly comprehended his intentions. He reached up both hands to hold onto the Cuban panama. Beau was too strong for him. The hat came off the black head and went on the red one.

"Give him ten reales from your purse, Angel," he called back as he galloped ahead.

"That foreigner will pay more than this." Paco spat on the coins. He was quite beside himself. Snarling and rolling his eyes ferociously, he flung open the door of the coach and jumped out.

"Get back inside, you dummy," Jake yelled.

"Go to hell, foreigner," Paco shouted up at him. "Down with all foreigners. Down with the Señor Berrien, too big and too ugly. I will kill him when I catch him."

Cursing, he ran after the black horse, throwing the reales first, then sticks and stones and handfuls of dirt and dung.

"Don't worry, ladies," Jake called down to us. "Mr. McLeod knew I'd deliver you safely with or without Paco."

Sighing, I changed the way I was holding the silver helmet on my lap. The white feathers on top scraped against my throat. The helmet was hard and cold and heavy. Looking out the coach window I realized that Mount Orizaba had completely disappeared from the horizon.

11

With the isolated volcanic peak of Malinche looming like a gigantic backdrop, French taste and Mexican fantasy combined to stage a theatrical fiesta in the Spanish colonial city of Puebla. The bunting-draped houses, faced with colored tiles, were built in a festive style as if for the occasion. The flat roofs were packed with cheering flag- and flower-waving residents. All the doorways were decorated with palm branches or wreaths of leaves and flowers; even the poorest had falls of bright colored rags.

And the noise! Iron bells in churches, convents and the cathedral clanged and clanged and clanged. Firecrackers, *Vivas* and horns were deafening. There wasn't a chance of our coach crossing the Paseo Bravo. Police and army officers wielding clubs and sticks were pushing the crowd out of the wide flower-strewn street.

Jake found a place to leave the coach with two of the outriders and volunteered to escort Flora and me to watch the parade. "We must hurry if you ladies want to see the Emperor close up."

I could hardly wait to actually see the man who had so completely captivated Beau. Would he enchant me?

"I think I will die of excitement."

"I, too," Flora said, entirely awake. "Will you explain everything carefully, Mr. Smith?"

"Sure, but hold onto your purses and earrings. They'll even steal your gold teeth. Come on, let's push through to the edge of the street."

Ragged beggars clumped together in the shadows or flashed like minnows through the crowd, snatching at this and picking at that. The *poblanos* were in fiesta clothes; the men in *charro* or Indian style; the women in white muslin shifts trimmed with lace and embroidery, bordered with scarlet and black petticoats and soiled white satin shoes. Their hair was plaited and turned up, and often fastened together with a jeweled or flowered ring. Both men and women had on vests of yellow or black satin with silver cigar cases stuck in colored sashes.

We were stared at, mashed and, several times, purposely bumped and jabbed; but we were in the front row as the first military band came marching by under a great waving of French, Austrian and Mexican flags. Austrian Hussars, Belgian cavalry, detachments of Zouaves and Chasseurs d'Afrique filed by, each to its own special beat. The roaring chorus of "*Vivas!*" strengthened proudly as a mariachi band of cornets, all blowing shrill tenor notes, and many guitars and violins, preceded the Mexican Imperial Guard. They were led by a young officer with a strikingly beautiful face.

"That is Miguel López, one of the Emperor's pet monkeys," Jake said in answer to my query. "And here come Their Majesties. Stand in front of me, Mrs. McLeod, you being so tiny and all."

My throat tightened. I squeezed my hands tensely as a high, pale blue Viennese calèche covered in flowers, drawn by six purple-plumed white stallions at a prancing walk, brought the beautiful young stars on stage under a rain of roses and carnations.

The volatile *poblanos* went wild. "*Viva! Viva!*" I never heard such pandemonium. "*Viva* Empress Carlota on her twenty-fifth birthday! *Viva* Emperor Maximilian! *Viva Mama Carlota!*"

All male heads were bared. I heard myself shouting "*Viva! Viva!*" just because everybody else did. But all I really felt in my heart was a drowning wave of homesickness for our white stallion, Teaser, as the Lipizzaners arched their necks and kept perfect time to the Mexican national anthem.

Maximilian was in the full dress of a Mexican general, wearing the Grand Cross of the Order of Guadalupe and the jeweled collar of the Golden Fleece. He was as handsome and golden as Beau had described him but he had an even more elegant panache and was much more at ease with the people than the Empress.

Nestled in flounces of white organdy and Venice lace, Carlota had a blue satin band wound from one shoulder across her left breast and around her tiny waist. A jeweled crown was on her dark hair and she carried a tiny white lace parasol in one white gloved hand. Stiffly royal, she lifted the other, clutching a lace handkerchief, at precise intervals. What a pity she hadn't been trained to smile whether she felt like it or not.

On either side of the Imperial calèche rode the big French Marshall Achille Bazaine and the small Indian General Tomás Mejía holding up their unsheathed swords which reflected brilliantly in the late afternoon sun.

"You aren't as thrilled as I am!" Flora was jumping up and down and waving her reticule in the air. "What's the matter with you?"

Thrilled? Captivated? Enchanted? Puzzled, I shook my head, wondering why I only felt absolutely limp and worn-out.

"Don't miss this next carriage with the eye painted on the door." Jake pulled me closer to the edge of the street. "It's the wicked Labastida, Archbishop of Puebla. He's just returned from Rome where he ran when Juárez was elected President five years ago."

The archbishop was a floridly handsome man who held his head on one side and never stopped smiling. Leaning back on down cushions, he was dressed all in purple satin touched with fine point lace, with a large cross of diamonds and amethysts poised on his stomach. He also wore a cloak of purple satin lined with crimson and an immense amethyst ring. His smiling face dissolved into angles as he chewed a wad of tobacco and made sloppy signs of the cross to the onlookers who either ignored him or dropped hastily to their knees as he passed them by.

The people had started running after the Emperor's carriage which was headed for the cathedral. Jake said by the time we got back to the coach the way would be clear for us to go on.

An hour later, as our coach turned into the courtyard of the inn, the shapely figure of a fair-haired young man with clear gray eyes stepped from the entrance.

"That's him," Flora choked. "That's Mr. McLeod."

He came boldly to the coach as we halted.

"Mrs. McLeod," he said in a firm burry voice, "and Mrs. Berrien! Ye hae finally arrived, I trust in one piece."

I liked him at once and whispered so to Flora. She shrank back against me shaking her head. The smile in his eyes brightened his intelligent face. I pushed Flora out of the coach door.

"I'm verra glad to see ye," Angus welcomed his wife.

Saying nothing, Flora gave him a clenched hand to hold as she stumbled down the shaky steps. He kissed the tight little fist, then turned to me, still smiling. "She must be verra weary. If she needs anythin' may I come to ye, Mrs. Berrien? Major Berrien will be along quite soon now."

I wanted to ask this assured, positive young man how he was acquainted with Beau, who couldn't have reached Puebla more than a few hours ahead of us, but Angus McLeod would not be interrupted.

"The major and I hae been arranging a few matters of importance. He was requested to wait with the interpreter, José Luis Blasio, at the palace until Their Majesties return from the parade. And hae *ye* learned to talk Spanish, Mrs. McLeod?"

"French and German are quite all I will need at court."

"Pachuca is not 'at court,' Mrs. McLeod. Well, 'tis only a wee while to rest ye have before the ball at ten o'clock this evening. I'll take ye inside now, and then I'll reward Señor Paco for his excellent services. Jake! Where is your chief outrider?"

"The rascal ran off, Mr. McLeod. He's no good."

The inn was clean and cool, furnished with red wool carpets and heavy mahogany sofas and lustre mirrors. It was the most comfortable place I'd been since we left Charleston. After tea, I couldn't restrain myself from running ahead of the porter who was struggling under my trunk. As I ran I talked to myself:

I must send for a hairdresser and a maid. I can hardly wait for a tub of hot water to plunge my whole body into at one time. Oh, and suppose the bed is soft and smooth with fine linen sheets and down pillows! Tonight Beau will lie beside me and we will make love all night long! And, oh, I think I will die of happiness!

12

I was in the mood for being kissed and loved as we drove through an exploding galaxy of fireworks to the Bishop's Palace.

"They don't sleep together," Beau said, fidgeting with the lace ruffles at his wrist.

"The McLeods?"

"No. Maximilian and Carlota. Blasio told me this afternoon that when Bishop Labastida took the Emperor to inspect the apartment he'd had prepared for the Empress's reception, there was an enormous bed hung with lace and ribbons. Maximilian admired everything. When old Labastida went away Maximilian ordered his valet to find a room at another part of the house in which to put up his camp bed. Maximilian was cross and peremptory, very different from his usual affable self. The valet told Blasio that they never sleep together. This damned big silk cravat is choking me. I've got to untie it."

"Beau, are you all right?"

This was the first time he'd ever been unresponsive to me.

"I'm worried about your curtsy. I am anxious for you to make as good an impression on Carlota as I have on Maximilian." Fretfully he buttoned and unbuttoned his white velvet waistcoat worked in silver and gold threads.

"Mrs. Meriweather said I dropped a more graceful curtsy to the Master of the Hunt in Charlottesville than any of the Princesses or Duchesses did to Maximilian's aunt at Versailles. Look—I pulled these little curls of hair down on the back of my neck. Why does a silly curtsy mean so much anyway?"

"Maximilian's friendship excites me more than anything in Mexico."

"Even me?"

"Don't talk rubbish. I have a godawful stomachache. I never should have eaten seafood this far away from the coast. And I should have had you curtsying for the past hour."

I struck Beau's arm with my fan. "Stop the carriage at once. I'll get out and curtsy right here on the street corner for Your Highness's approval."

"Oh, God, Angelica," he groaned, "hand me your shawl, I'm going to throw up."

A crush of coaches and carriages were standing in front of the palace. We were among the last to arrive. Beau had somewhat recovered but I had to enter bare-shouldered.

The vast rooms were full. In the first were rich Creole aristocrats wearing diamonds all over themselves and heavy perfume in their hair. One old dowager was so smothered in emeralds the size of seagull's eggs she never rose from her high-backed chair all evening.

With neither shawl nor diamonds I felt naked.

In the second room were bearded generals and government and local officials loaded with all the medals they or their ancestors had earned or purchased. Their wives and daughters were as decorated as the women in the first room, with jewels in their hair and on their fingers, bosoms, wrists and ears. Their perfume was even stronger.

In both rooms there was a constant moving about and buzz of expectant voices as the women as well as the men smoked tiny cigars and strolled about.

The dressmaker in Havana had cut the square neck of my Empire yellow satin ball gown much too low. White kid gloves covered my arms but I fancied the ladies were looking at me and snickering behind their fans. I tried to keep out of sight behind Beau, who was head and shoulders taller than the French and Mexican nobles and officials. But anxious to be first to enter the ballroom he kept prodding me along, not caring whose toes I stepped on.

Angus had the same idea. He and Flora were standing against the closed, heavily carved double doors that opened into the ballroom. She wore her nose in the air, pointed toward where Their Majesties would make their grand entrance.

They were talking to the middle-aged, virilely handsome Marshall Bazaine, head of the French Army, and his sixteen-year-old Mexican fiancée, Josefina de Peina. Angus presented us. Bazaine had heard of the Confederate expatriates but immediately excused himself, saying he must present his fiancée to General Juan Almonte, "over there with Bishop Labastida."

Angus said, "Watch Bazaine show off his rank. They make a threesome, they do. Almonte is Commander of the Mexican Army, ruthless and so prochurch he fairly reeks of blood and incense. Bazaine, Almonte and Labastida: each secretly feels that *he* should wear the crown of Mexico."

Flora had been whispering to me how wonderful it was going to be when she danced with the Emperor. "How do you know so much?" she asked Angus, looking away from him to indicate she didn't like him any more in Mexico than she had in Scotland.

"Because," said cocky Angus, "I aim to become the richest mon in all Mexico so that I can return to Scotland and purchase Braemar Castle for my bairns to grow up in."

Even Beau laughed a little snort, though I could tell he didn't like Angus much either.

As Angus ceased speaking, I heard a familiar voice.

"Señor McLeod, you are he whom I seek."

"Good evening, Don Carlos. May I present Mrs. Angus McLeod."

"And which of the lovely señoras is the real Mrs. Angus McLeod? The one on your right or the one on your left?"

"Why, the prettier one, of course," Angus answered jauntily.

"Then you are a bigamist, Señor McLeod?"

The melancholy Mayor of Jalapa knew very well which of us was Angus's wife. As he kissed my hand first, Beau turned his back to him and walked over to an interesting-looking couple who had joined the people by the closed door.

"Is your wife with you, Señor Mayor? I was charmed by her and your attractive daughters."

"Doña Teresa is attending a cockfight in the patio. She brought two of her own along. She dislikes crowds and enjoys gambling. By the way, Señora Angelica, my name is Don Carlos, *not* Señor Mayor. When the dancing starts may I claim the first meringue?"

His whole personality was different from what it had been in Jalapa. He was playing cat and mouse with me. But I had spent the dreary days in Havana not only learning Spanish from the Marquesa but also the tango and the meringue and the habanera as well as the hat dance and the ribbon dance and other folk dances. I intended to win the game.

"It will be a pleasure, Don Carlos."

"I will find you easily because you rise above the other ladies."

"What are they saying, Mr. McLeod?" Flora was curious as to why I was blushing.

"Had ye studied your Spanish as I told ye, ye'd know."

"I don't really care," Flora sniffed.

"That's easy to see," Angus sighed.

As soon as Don Carlos left, Beau returned. "Mrs. Berrien and Mr. and Mrs. McLeod, I have the honor to present to you Her Highness, Princess Agnes Zu Salm Salm and the Austrian Minister, Count Thun. I met Count Thun at the picnic."

Count Thun clicked his heels and bowed. "I am happy," he said coldly in English. But his expression as he looked at the lady he was escorting left no doubt that this was a most unpleasant evening so far as he was concerned.

The Princess on the other hand was effusive and friendly. A

breezy beauty with a continuous laugh and masses of glossy brown side curls, she had on the most exaggerated crinoline I ever saw. She confided to me at once that she, too, was an American. We were the only American ladies at the ball.

"Is the Prince with you?" Angus asked the Princess, after bowing politely to Count Thun.

"No. He is in the United States in, of all places, Georgia! Let us push nearer the doors. I think they are about to open."

The Princess boldly grabbed Count Thun's stiff arm. Beau followed them but I lingered to hear what wicked Angus would tell Flora about the Princess.

"The Princess was a circus bareback rider from Ohio. The Prince discovered her in a circus tent in Pennsylvania," he tattled. "I met them both at a party in Washington two years ago. I wonder why she's turned up here without him?"

Beau motioned me to hurry. The rumbling noise of the doors rolling back sent us rushing into a long room with a vaulted cathedral ceiling, its beams gilded and painted light blue and red. A gallery for a choir and musicians was midway to the ceiling on one side. Black oak chairs and benches lined the rough white plaster walls hung with Gobelin tapestries and dark religious paintings. Bishop Labastida had entered through another door. In his voluminous purple robes and tall white mitre, his head on one side, he was smiling and drinking champagne, leaning against the longest, shiniest grand piano I've ever seen. My fingers twitched to touch it.

"The Emperor and the Empress!" Labastida announced in his resonant voice.

A door in the far center opened. The guests parted, leaving a wide path for the royal couple to walk through.

Maximilian, still in Mexican full dress uniform, covered with medals and orders and gold buttons, had one hand on his sword and the other lifted so that the Empress's white gloved hand could rest upon it. Carlota was again in white flounces, this time of rose-point lace embroidered with pearls. The Emperor was not wearing a crown, but she had on a diamond one. A wealth of Bourbon and Hapsburg jewels sparkled at her throat and on her breast.

I had not expected to be dazzled when we were presented, since I'd felt so little this afternoon. But I stepped awkwardly as I curtsied to Carlota and lost my balance. Catching it, I found myself staring straight into the saddest pair of brown eyes I have ever seen.

"Bow your head," Beau muttered.

I ducked quickly, realizing to my dismay that without my shawl my nipples were visible.

"You may rise, Mrs. Berrien." I looked up into Maximilian's amused blue eyes and distinctly heard his pleasantly human voice ask Beau, in English, "How do you feel, Major?"

"Terrible, and you, sir?"

"Ghastly."

Beau was so pleased with this little contretemps he didn't bother to criticize my wretched curtsy.

The McLeods found us soon after they were presented. Flora was in an ecstasy. Maximilian remembered her mother visiting Schönbrunn when he was a boy. He even recalled her name, Sophia Esterhazy!

"I'm in terrible trouble," Angus said, "the bishop hae put me in charge of locating a pianist among the guests. The German musicians hae run away. Every house in Mexico owns a piano but nary a soul studies music. A Mexican orchestra is in the gallery but they ne'er heard of a quadrille. The Emperor is programmed to start the dancing with a quadrille with the local prefect's wife."

"Angelica plays the piano," Beau said.

"Hush, Beau."

Angus continued, "The Emperor is perfectly agreeable to dancing a Spanish dance but the prefect stubbornly insists on a quadrille."

"Mrs. Berrien plays the—"

"I'll consult the Empress. She makes all the decisions anyway." Angus began to scurry off, but stopped short.

"He's a jackass," Beau moaned.

"What were ye saying, Major Berrien?"

"If you'd ever take the time to listen, by golly, you'd be better off. I said my wife is an accomplished pianist."

"No, Beau, I can't."

"Darling, you must. Once the Emperor has danced we will be free to leave."

"Yes!" crowed Angus. "I'll make much noise, Mrs. Berrien, in case ye miss the notes."

Beau escorted me to the piano. "I'll stand right behind you. This is a wonderful opportunity for you to make amends for your shabby curtsy. The Empress can't take her eyes off you. Don't fail me."

The piano hadn't been dusted in a long time. Certainly not since the German musicians were here. A sheaf of piano music was on the rack, open at a quadrille.

Angus pulled out the velvet-covered stool. It was the correct height. I put down my fan and tucked back the fingers of my white gloves. Memories of my first party at Cotton Hall when I had played and Beau had sung "I Know a Lady Sweet and Kind" flooded over me. Suppose I played that now. Would Beau sing to me?

"Go on. The Emperor is waiting." Beau nudged my bare shoulder impatiently.

It was an easy quadrille. The tone of the piano was magnificent. Everybody cheered as the beautiful sound filled the room.

The local prefect's young wife was nine months pregnant. No wonder the prefect refused to send her out to fly around in a meringue or be bent over in a tango. Knowing that Maximilian was suffering from the same dysentery as Beau, I made the quadrille as short as possible. When it was over, everybody crowded the piano making rapturous and enthusiastic demands.

"More! More!"

Princess Agnes pushed her way right up to me. "Don't stop now, honey. You've made a hit with the whole court. You're in the center ring. Keep playing."

I looked back to see what Beau wished.

He wasn't there!

I jumped up. Without him behind me it was as if all the candles in the room had gone out. Angus pushed me down on the stool. "He'll be right back. Dinna fret. Agnes is right, ye know. This is your act."

He'll be right back! He'll be right back! One two three, one two three, my heart sang as I leafed through the music, hesitating at the original Strauss score for *The Emperor's Waltz*. Why not? I mashed down hard on the sustaining pedal. My fingers crashed into the familiar Viennese waltz, expecting everyone to whirl onto the floor. Instead they drew back against the walls.

The Emperor was dancing with his wife. Young and beautiful and poised, they were what you always imagined a fairy tale Emperor and Empress were like. Carlota had a superb figure and was a skillful waltzer; Maximilian, grace itself.

His head on one side, Bishop Labastida stood at the far end of the piano smiling and waving a crystal goblet of brandy, calling out "*Glorioso*" and "*Magnificat*." I didn't need his encouragement or anyone's. I doubt I will ever be strung so high again in my life. I know I will never perform so brilliantly.

At the finale the dancers waltzed up to the piano. Maximilian impulsively caught my hand and pressed it to his lips. He was burning up with fever and there were tears on his cheeks. "You have carried me away from here, home to Vienna, danke schön," he murmured.

"You have made my Birthday Ball a success and I thank you, Mrs. Berrien," Carlota said in flawless English, tossing her pearl-embroidered lace shawl around my shoulders.

This time I curtsied gracefully and properly, having pulled the shawl safely across my pretty bosoms.

When everybody had finished telling me what a marvelous musician I was, I grabbed Angus's arm. "Where is Beau?"

"He left as soon as the Emperor did, right after the waltz. It was verra necessary. Two subalterns took him in a carriage. He insists that ye remain the evening, representing him at court. He is very proud of ye as is Angus McLeod himself. And I'll tell ye a secret: His Majesty whispered to Count Thun as he left that your resemblance to his sister-in-law, the beautiful Empress Elizabeth of Austria, startled him. He would hae told ye himself but 'twould hae upset the Empress, who is verra jealous. Now—will ye stay?"

"But naturally the lady will not depart until she fulfills her contract with me, is it not so?" The narrow interesting face of Don Carlos smiled into mine as from the musicians' gallery the orchestra struck up a lively meringue.

From time to time during the evening, as I was dancing Spanish dances with different partners, I looked over to the dais where, backed by a line of ladies-in-waiting, Carlota sat with a yawning but perpetually smiling Bishop Labastida. Her fixed expression never altered as she stared at the dancers and tore her lace handkerchief to pieces with her teeth.

13

Four days went by before Beau was able to travel on to Mexico City and then only with the aid of so much tincture of opium that he slept the entire fifteen hours of the journey in the clumsy, wide-bodied public coach. I clung to life and limb in fairly good spirits because of our fellow passenger, a wizened little earth-colored priest who talked constantly of the blood-soaked days of Mayan and Aztec and colonial empires.

When we stopped for a final change of horses at the last ascent, he and I walked along a wooded knoll looking at the breathtaking panorama of the Valley of Mexico. A bright light flooded the country below but still 7,000 feet higher than the sea, while the flaming spill of sunset reflected upon the whole landscape jeweled with small villages and glistened with lakes. The fiery glow brightened the fields of lordly maguey and touched with saffron the distant city's towers and baroque spires and flat roofs hanging motionless in the crystal-clear air, eventually spurting like blood on the snow-capped volcanoes of Popocatépetl and Ixtaccihuatl dominating the world beyond the city.

An Aztec girl named Malinche betrayed her people to the Spanish conquistadores. Without her their mission would have been impossible. Legend had it that Malinche's father, a tribal king, died, leaving Malinche his entire fortune so his wicked widow sold the child into slavery to a wandering tribe of Tabascan Indians. Malinche's owner rescued a shipwrecked Spanish sailor who taught Malinche his language before he shriveled up and died of a scorpion sting. This same Malinche, grown into a beautiful woman, was in the curious throng at what is now called Vera Cruz when the white men with their horses, which no one had ever seen, came ashore. Hearing the familiar Spanish words, Malinche stepped forth from the crowd and, dazzled by the conquistador Hernando Cortes, she willingly became his translator. Naturally she was much more than a go-between to this Cortes who changed her Indian name to a Spanish one—Marina. There were many statues in stone of them throughout Mexico, Doña Marina and Hernando Cortes, sitting hand in hand, equal in importance.

The priest described Montezuma's city, Tenochtitlán, as Cortes first saw it in 1519 from this exact hill.

" 'Of Spain's many diadems, the brightest,' Hernando Cortes said," the priest quoted sadly.

One word picture followed another as he described Tenochtitlán, built in the middle of five lakes upon lush, flower-covered islands, with thousands of boats gliding along its liquid streets between long lines of beautiful low houses and palaces rejoiced with a multitude of pyramids and temples. Canoes, flower-decked, filled with laughing youths and maidens, covered the mirror-clear lakes. Lofty trees, flowers and water and flying birds sparkled in the crystalline air braceleted with these same magnificent mountains and volcanoes.

As the Spanish soldiers, accompanied by hundreds of Indians, approached Tenochtitlán, there came Montezuma, the beautiful bronze-skinned young Emperor. Four of the most important caciques wearing mantles of bright feathers bore him high on their shoulders in a litter canopied with brilliant green feathers bordered with gold and silver and pearl embroidery.

Montezuma was covered with a mantle of bluebird feathers and a great crest of yellow bird feathers danced on his head. His sandals had gold soles and jeweled thongs. He brought with him the sacred masks of the four gods of the Aztecs. The turquoise mosaic mask of Quetzalcoatl was formed of a single snake, the folds of the snake's body forming the eyebrows; and the turquoise mask of the God of Fire, Tezcatlipoca, was crowned with rich orange feathers, and the turquoise mosaic mask of Tlalocantocutli with a mitre of tigerskins and tusklike teeth of silver, and there was another god whose name the priest had forgotten. Also Montezuma laid two great wheels of gold and one of silver, and two hundred pieces of fine cotton cloth and piles of valuable gold jewels wrought in various shapes, richly worked with feathers, at those iron Spanish feet, if the white men would turn around and go back to the coast and sail away from Mexico forever.

"Oh, gentle Emperor, beware," the old priest murmured.

"Are you speaking of Montezuma or Maximilian?"

But the storytelling was done. A clap of thunder and a black cloud of rain sent us flying back into the coach where Beau was struggling out of his drugged sleep, begging for a cup of water.

Later, everything became flat. On each side of us, where the lakes covered with gay canoes once surrounded the city, we now saw poorly drained marshy land darkened with great flights of wild ducks and geese.

At last we came to the gates of the city. It took an hour to find the suburbs of Buenavista where José Luis Blasio had told us Maury was staying in a house lent him by a rich Mexican.

Through the darkness and rain I caught an occasional dim lamp-lit glimpse of massive buildings, churches, tall gateways and plazas. The little priest got out at a church near Buenavista, inviting me to attend mass there next Sunday, he officiating. It was a tragedy I'd not seen the church before Independence, he said. It had been so full of gold and silver that its luster made it appear as if it were midday in the deep of night.

Just as I decided we would spend the rest of our lives in the coach we found the Del Campo house. When we were announced by a soldier standing at the gate, Maury himself came running out with a lantern and an umbrella to take us from the rain.

"Prince John and Jubilee are inside," Maury crowed excitedly to groggy Beau.

Making an heroic effort, Beau exuded a modicum of enthusiasm as Maury introduced us to the two Confederate generals who would be working with him in the Office of Immigration officially, as soon as the Emperor returned from Puebla.

"I hear you've bought the Escandon hacienda near Cuernavaca! I had counted on you to help put the Carlota Colony across."

"The offer was too good to turn down," Beau said. "Who told you?"

"Billy Gwin. You know, the former Senator from Mississippi. He was on his way back to Sonora where he has big get-rich-quick schemes. He heard it in Jalapa."

"I hope I made the proper decision."

Maury patted Beau's arm in a fatherly way. "Well, Angelica will be closer to me there than in Córdoba. I'll like that and I'll give you the first cinchona seeds that come from India. Also rumor has flown that you've become a friend of our patron, the Emperor. That should help our colony enormously. Oh, how glad I am to see you!"

The splendor of the Del Campo mansion was welcome. We quickly accepted Maury's invitation to stay with him until we were settled in our unseen hacienda. Relieved, Beau followed our host to the corridor to be shown our apartment, while I sank wearily on a down-filled, blue damask French sofa.

"I'll never get up from here," I moaned.

"We haven't eaten yet," General Jubal Early huffed while handsome General John Magruder delightfully bullied me into drinking a whole goblet of brandy before I had even unloosed my bonnet strings.

The brandy softened the pompous Early's resentment of a female entering the cozy male circle and forcing it to make small talk.

When Maury returned I had a little triumph which rallied me, for I distinctly heard Magruder whisper to him: "Jehosaphat, isn't she a beauty?"

"Indeed she is," Maury agreed, handing Beau a glass of brandy and saying, "Gentlemen, we'll drink to the third member of our Department of Immigration, Major Berrien."

"Hear, hear!" called General Early. "Well, let's start talking shop. I'm two days ahead of you in the city, Major Berrien."

"Do you like the Emperor?" I asked Maury who sat down beside me and clasped my hand.

"I haven't met him yet. My business so far has been done with the Empress while Maximilian has been on tour. Before then he was too busy designing wide tree-lined avenues, planting flowers in the plazas and transforming Chapultepec from a fortress into his own castle. And he is carried away with decorating the National Palace for General Bazaine's wedding and training the Mexicans in proper court etiquette, Viennese style. Always too busy to sit down and talk business with anyone. They call him the grasshopper the way he jumps from one pretty project to another to another. Rather that's what I've gathered in the short time I've been here."

"Well then, Commander Maury," Prince John said, "do you like the Empress?"

"Carlota has a fine, trained mind. As far as I can understand from what all these foreigners are saying, it's a pity she's not the ruler."

"Do you speak Spanish yet, Mr. Maury?" Already a bit giddy, I foolishly held out my empty goblet to my admirer, General Magruder.

"Not a word; a little French, a smattering of German, mostly scientific jargon. The Empress speaks excellent English," Maury said.

"Then how can you know what the Mexicans are thinking and feeling if you don't speak Spanish?"

"The French are in total control here, madame," Early said patronizingly. "I had no trouble whatsoever in Sonora."

"Did you meet the man Juárez? And did you sense the way the Mexican people are drawn to him?" I could see myself in a mirror across the room. My eyes were huge and deep navy blue. In the lamplight, I looked pale and obstinate and felt both.

"We are dealing exclusively with the Empire," Beau said in a harsh tone.

"What about Napoleon?"

"Oh, dust off that subject, Angelica."

"Well, it *is* important to speak the language of the country."

Maury jumped up, ran over and peered through some crimson velvet curtains. "Supper's almost ready. She's right, you know," he said, turning around, "about communication. You can be my interpreter, my Marina, Miss Angelica."

"But you mustn't be my Cortes."

As if removing himself from the conversation, Beau stared at a cruelly painful painting of Saint Sebastian, hands tied behind his back, pierced with hundreds of arrows.

Prince John came to my rescue, describing a shooting scrape he and General Kirby Smith had gotten into with some of Juárez's soldiers who had just picked up a pile of ammunition left by the United States patrol on the bank of the Rio Grande last week. He and Kirby Smith were coming out of a cantina at daybreak when . . .

The thick velvet curtains parted. A liveried servant, holding a seven-branched candlelabrum, called us to the dining room.

"If you will excuse me, gentlemen, I think I will retire," I said. "I've been up since last night." The room had got suddenly fuzzy despite the extra light.

Beau caught my arm as I bumped against him heading for the corridor. "Don't leave me. Please don't leave me. Not just yet. Stay . . ." His face was a smiling, unmoving mask.

What was happening behind that mask? Here he was with his own kind speaking his own language, knowing all the same things, having fought together in the same war and he wasn't enjoying himself. He was different somehow. Was it the aftereffects of the opium? I shuddered as he seated me on Maury's right. Did I have a premonition? Yes. Do I believe in such things? No.

"Bow your heads," chortled Maury. "The Lord make us thankful for what we are about to receive and make us needful of the minds of others."

"Mindful of the needs of others, my friend!" General Magruder laughed.

"No, Prince John, I need minds more than any other commodity in Mexico. There are too many soldiers gathered here already."

"I'm not sure I agree with that, Commander," General Early said frostily. "Present company excepted."

Maury's sharp eyes sparkled. He, at least, was having a good time.

An excellent supper was steaming on the black refectory table over which I fell into a sound sleep as the men droned on and on about the horn of plenty awaiting the Confederate expatriates in Mexico. Beau must have carried me to our room, for I waked in the night and knew without doubt that it was still raining outside and I was naked, snuggled between smooth linen sheets and that he, naked too, was lying beside me, one wonderful hand on my flat stomach and the other fastened in my thick tangle of hair. If only he'd taken off my cold wet shoes!

14 ❧

To:
Brigadier General Stephen Elliott
Hilton Head, South Carolina, U.S.A.

Dear Stephen,

I have an opportunity to put a letter along with two of Commander Maury's in the Emperor's mail sack which is being galloped by relays of couriers to Vera Cruz to catch a steamer bound for Europe. As it will be marked, my letter, will receive special attention in Havana, so I have hopes you and Charlotte will read this in less than two weeks.

I am trying to locate Phillip. He was due to arrive here four days ago. A French envoy who sailed from Marseilles with Phillip told José Luis Blasio, the Emperor's secretary, that he heard a telegram for Phillip Berrien called on the quay at Vera Cruz. Beau has the notion that Phillip foolishly overslept and remained aboard. The ship sailed on to New Orleans the same day it put in at Vera Cruz. After our own nightmare travel here from Vera Cruz I am afraid he has been captured or killed by robbers. Beau thinks not. He says Phillip is too big a rascal to be caught by Mexicans. Should Phillip turn up at Hilton Head you will be the first person he will visit. Please urge him to fly to Mexico at once, for Beau refuses to budge until the money Phillip is bringing from England to pay for Miramontes (the hacienda Beau has agreed to purchase) is here.

Anyway, Beau insists that is why he remains in Mexico City. Truthfully, I am concerned about him, not Phillip, who can always be relied on to look out for himself. If only you all would relent and join us in this venture I am convinced Beau would come back into himself. I had expected when we arrived at Commander Maury's house that all would be well. Instead, Beau avoids him and the generals, Early and Magruder, who are here along with us. I know Maury is disappointed in Beau though he has not said so.

Beau insists that the Confederate generals remind him constantly of the war, that being their only topic of conversation.

Beau is determined to forget the war because of all it took away from him.

He goes every day to the National Palace on the Zocalo with the Emperor who is redecorating the palace for the French Marshall Bazaine's wedding next week. Can you fancy our Beau spending his days deciding which shade of royal blue to paint the palace beams? When I remember the way he loved the hodge-podge of fat chairs and sofas, and collections of guns and stuffed birds and boot-worn carpets at Cotton Hall, I wonder if my ears hear correctly his enthusiastic accounts of happy hours rearranging delicate vases and matching up precious porcelain urns on proper pedestals and making sure the Gobelin tapestries that tell the story of the rape of Lucrece are hung in proper order!

Yesterday, after breakfast in the patio, he was teasing a parrot walking along the balustrade of the gallery when I gently reminded him that he had an appointment with Maury at the Office of Immigration. After imitating the parrot's squawk a few times he said he had decided to resign from the Commission.

I lost my temper and told him that he must be going mad, that decency and obligation and every proper instinct made his resignation from Maury's Commission impossible.

My vehemence surprised him. He sat down beside me and said that the altitude here is very high and the air unbelievably light and clear as glass, so different from the low-country salt air he grew up breathing that it confuses him. When he adjusts physically he might work with the Commission.

But he refuses to believe, as he rides out daily with the Emperor in a charro *costume and the Mexicanos cry* Viva! *and throw flowers from balconies on them equally, that he is leaving Maury already and with him leaving all the things he has ever known.*

That, dear Stephen, is why I am desperate to wrench him away from delusion and for him to take up the management of a plantation. You, who know him and understand him, will forgive the hopefully foolish fears of your

Angelica

P.S. Prod Joab Pritchard to work hard on my case. If I were cleared of the charge of murder (what a farce!) we could return to Hilton Head. It would make all the difference.

Dear Cousin Annie, I know you will not object to my promised account of my life in Mexico continuing on the same sheet of paper as Stephen's letter. My envelope must not be too heavy to be acceptable to travel in the Emperor's sack.

Yesterday I heard from Aunt Dell. Baby Edward has a tooth and smiles all the time. Maybelle and Israel are faithful to the trust we put in them as free people and take beautiful care of him. But little brother Button does not smile very much. He wishes to leave his school and come to us in Mexico. I live for the day both boys will be in my arms forever.

We are living temporarily with Matthew Fontaine Maury, a precious, brilliant man, much like your Billy. He and Maximilian became friends by writing letters to each other when Maury was a commodore in the U.S. Navy before the war.

Maury's connections, especially at court, have smoothed our path pleasantly. He escorted me to a tea party at Chapultepec Castle last Monday.

The Emperor forces the Empress to put on a velvet embroidered train and copy his mother's Kammerbälles at Schönbrunn, while he absents himself planting trees on the beautiful wide boulevards he has designed, and chasing butterflies under Montezuma's giant cypress trees. (Of course I exaggerate, but not much.)

Carlota looks much older than twenty-five. Uncle Jim would call her a "cold fish" but Maury seems fond of her. He declares she has a clear, well-ordered mind and political intuition inherited from her father, the King of Belgium, but he is completely at sea with volatile Maximilian. Maury and Beau argue constantly about their favorites. I leave them to it, for I have found a friend you would enjoy as much as I.

She is an American-born Prussian princess! A handsome, commanding middle-westerner with marvelous zest, Agnes has, in Aunt Dell's words, "taken me on." She is the wife of Prince Felix Zu Salm Salm, a professional soldier, the youngest son of the Prince of Anholt Castle. Ironically, he fought on the Union side in our war. He was a Colonel and Chief of the General Staff of the German Division and is now a Brigadier General and Military Governor of North Georgia under J.B. Steedman. You should get in touch with him. He might be able to help you. He has been recommended by twenty-six United States Senators for a position in the regular United States Army, but Agnes is horrified at the idea of living a dreary and idle life in some little garrison town out west among the Indians.

Prince Salm sent her to Mexico to discuss his future with the Emperor and to determine whether life here would be to her taste. She is convinced it will be and is attempting to persuade me to the same conviction.

For now she is staying with Herr Hube, the former Mexican Consul General of Hamburg. He lives in Tacubaya not far from Chapultepec but a long way from Maury's house in the city. Agnes plans to remain in Mexico only until she can arrange an

*audience with either Carlota or Maximilian but has been con-
stantly thwarted by the Austrian Ambassador, Count Thun.*

*Count Thun wants no Prussians in Mexico nor does he care
for Herr Hube's Liberal political leanings. In Mexico the Liberals and the Conservatives equal the Yankees and Confederates
back home.*

*I will be lost when Agnes returns to the United States to report
to Prince Salm. She is determined to see and know everything in
the city. We spend hours in the Mineria (all about
silver mines), the Botanic Garden, the Museum at the University, the Cathedrals, the Convents, the Alameda, etc., all of
which I find fascinating, but they leave a disagreeable impression since, without having the dignity of ruins, are fine buildings utterly neglected.*

*Soldiers are everywhere; mostly French. They are very con-
temptuous of the Mexicans. The bad feelings between them
fairly crackles in the air.*

*Ladies are supposed to remain inside their houses all day;
and never let their little fat feet touch the ground. One day I went
out walking in the Alameda though our gatekeeper warned me
that it was not safe to walk on the streets or in the parks. Three
dreadful men tried to steal my reticule, one even pinched me. A
little boy cut all the fringe off my best shawl. And a drunk
policeman arrested me for being a prostitute! Maury considered
my outrage a great joke but henceforth I will ride horseback
when I need exercise.*

*You would enjoy the fashionable paseos from four to six. They
resemble our summer afternoon promenades along the bay in
Beaufort. Here, however, everything is done according to etiquette and protocol. Everybody knows his place and keeps it.
Agnes came for me yesterday in the Prussian Minister's carroza, an elegant open carriage with glass side windows and a
liveried German coachman and footman. We drove out to the
Viga, a tree-lined paseo along a canal filled with gay canoes full
of Indians and flowers and fruits and vegetables headed for the
city market. The Indians wore poppy garlands and played
guitars and sang as they glided along, oblivious of the hordes of
gay ordinary folk selling dulces and flowers and strings of
beads, and the usual gathering of thieves and beggars, and the
double line of hundreds of equipages that ranged from fancy
English through heavy Mexican down to hackney carts and
country wagons.*

*The carriages dash up and down the shady drive and then
stop in a long line. The ladies, wearing silks and satin and
jewels, sit silently inside the carriages, smoking and fanning
and watching the gentlemen in fancy Mexican dress on fancy
saddles riding up and down and in and out between them.*

When the gentlemen come near a carriage of especially pretty ladies their horses suddenly become quite unmanageable, rearing and curveting to show off what fine horsemen the caballeros really are! Nobody speaks to anybody. It is the rule. If you see someone you especially wish to greet, you do it with a slight wink or an almost imperceptible flutter of your fan or finger.

The Countess Corbina rode by in a handsome gilded coach upholstered in crimson satin. She had on a vanilla velvet turban twisted with pearls and a cigar in her mouth. She lifted an old beringed forefinger toward Agnes. "She lives in Tacubaya near Herr Hube," Agnes explained. "She's promised to invite me to the theater with Their Majesties. Oh, look—there they are!"

Maximilian and Carlota were in a pale gray calèche drawn by spirited white stallions. Maximilian was smiling and waving. He had a precious little King Charles spaniel on his lap which barked excitedly as from every carriage dainty handkerchiefs fluttered like white doves and the gold-rolled sombreros of the gentlemen waved in the air like eagles. Their Majesties' reception at the paseo indicates that Maximilian and Carlota are very popular with the Mexican people.

As the royal calèche came abreast of our carroza Agnes raised her forefinger toward Carlota in the same gesture that Countess Corbina had greeted her. Carlota saw and turned away angrily. Agnes realized at once that she'd made a presumptuous error. I don't suppose she'll ever get to talk to the Emperor now. To quote her: "I put my foot through the hoop this time!"

Last night Beau and I attended a performance of The Barber of Seville *at the Theatre Principal. The building is basically grand—but oh the filth and smoke! Several times we could hardly make out the superb Italian singers through the dense haze. Everybody smokes—men and women, often the actors. A few nights ago Hamlet started his soliloquy thus: To be or not to be—puff-puff-puff-puff!!*

Please send me news of Maum Hannah and Masai and Cudjo Manigo at Cotton Hall. Does freedom agree with them? Do they miss us? Has anybody seen Teaser? If I thought Teaser had been hooked to a plow and imagined his proud Arab head hanging low, it would destroy me. But tell me anyway—with love—

Angelica

19 June, 1865

As I finished writing the letter I heard the courier at the gate. The dust of his horse's hoofs was still flying backward when I saw Beau riding up and heard him call to the porter as he dismounted.

"An escort is coming at four in the morning to take me and the señora to Cuernavaca. Will you have someone wake us ahead of time?"

Beau explained his sudden decision to, as he put it, take the bull by the horns and inspect his hacienda.

"The Escandons will be in the city next week to attend Bazaine's wedding. I will be forced to face Don Luis Escandon then, whether the money has arrived or not. So—you and I will be all by ourselves for five whole days and nights." He picked me up and whirled me around and around like old times. "Just think of the intoxicating bliss of going to bed in our own house once again."

Oh, why had I mailed that letter to Stephen Elliott? I ran to the gate but the courier's dust had settled.

Oh, dear, I thought, Beau will kill me if he ever finds out what I have written.

15 🌿

The *madrugada*, the beautiful name Mexicans give the predawn, was stilly cool under a low moon in a star-studded sky when I tied a heavy green veil around my panama hat and went out into the courtyard. Beau, four escort soldiers and a Mexican guide were grouped, laughing, among six restive horses and a mule. The animals were loaded with our two carpet bags and a saddlebag bulging with bread and cheese and pulque.

What a fool I've been, I thought. Why did I ever let myself imagine such awful things about Beau?

"Ah, there you are at last," he called.

Gathering up my voluminous calico riding skirt I ran toward him.

"You are quite different, your face all covered with Mexican moonlight." He slipped his arms around my waist, pressing me to him and shamelessly kissing me on my lips in front of everybody.

Angel—Beau—was all we could say to each other because magically it turned into almost the same kind of kiss as our first one, riding side by side through an apple orchard, when we both knew we had entered paradise.

"Then everything is all right," he whispered. "Sometimes, lately, I've felt you were far away from me."

"Oh, no, never that." I sprang lightly, he helping, into the wide sidesaddle the Mexican ladies prefer.

As I settled my knee over the horn, the guide yelled for the iron gate to be opened onto the boulevard. Giving my horse a smart cut with the whip I called gaily in Spanish, "We will gallop the whole eighteen leagues to Cuernavaca!"

"*Ole! Ole!*" cried the soldiers enthusiastically as we clattered through the sleeping city toward the powerfully looming, silvery volcanoes.

We stopped at San Augustin de las Cuevas for the first change of horses. It was a small village of mud huts with some fine old trees, a few very old ruined stone houses and a ruined church. There were traces of a long, low building that might have been an Aztec palace. We sat on soft green grass and ate tortillas that the horsekeeper's wife had just taken from hot stones. The majestic snowy cone of Popocatépetl, dominating the world on our left, was suddenly crimson-crowned with shooting rays of the rising sun behind it!

"It's almost as beautiful as Mount Orizaba."

The kiss in the courtyard was almost as good, the mountain was almost as wonderful, but Beau was more exciting!

"Popo is not as high as Ori." Beau smiled as he rubbed his knee against my thigh. He took a long drink from the pulque skin and motioned me to lean toward him. Then putting his lips against mine he squirted the warm liquid from his mouth into my mouth. Lights danced in his green eyes and I have never been more thrillingly pleasureful.

As we started on, I looked back at the vast picture of groves and flat dry fields to the timeless turrets of Mexico City shimmering in the distance. The dark pine-forested mountain of Ajusco frowned down on me but my world was back on its axis. The luminous shining volcanoes ahead responded to what was happening in my own exhilarated heart soaring forward into this new life of ours.

"Vámanos," shouted our guide.

The watch pinned on my dark dusty shirtwaist said exactly twelve o'clock when we came to a little Indian village called

Huitzilac, neatly filled with pretty cane cottages and flowery trees where we looked straight up at Popocatépetl and down on Cuernavaca.

One of the Mexican soldiers explained that Cuernavaca had been called Cuahunuac or Cow's Horn when it was the capital of the Tlahuica nation. It was a very fortunate place, defended on one side by great mountains and on the other by a precipitous ravine through which ran a beautiful little river. It had a delicious climate, abundance of the purest, sweetest water on earth, game to be shot, minerals to be dug or mined, fine trees and many lovely fruits and flowers. "All these you will discover at your hacienda also too, señora, is it not so?"

O glorious day! "How much farther to Miramontes?"

"Very near. A beautiful sugar hacienda is on the way. If you would care to refresh yourself there you would be welcomed; us too."

I translated this to Beau who ordered with sudden imperiousness, "Tell him to take us to the Borda Palace."

"No, we're not going to stop anywhere until we get home." Had I not been slightly ahead I would have seen his face stiffen.

"And pass up a luncheon with the Emperor? Foolish, my dear, very foolish." He was very agitated, his whole manner changed. "Maximilian bought the palace from the son of the rich silver miner, José de la Borda. Surely you remember. I told you all of this. I know I did. You should have worn a more becoming riding dress. I love to show you off. I didn't notice what you had on in the dark when we started out. Why are you shaking your head like a Chinaman?"

I didn't realize I was shaking my head. I knew I was feeling weak and he had stabbed. I was being cut to pieces inside with pangs of disappointment. It was the prospect of being with the Emperor that had fired him up last night and today. How could I keep from crying?

"You're going to have a mighty big red nose," Beau said calmly, heading his horse toward the palace. "You can come with me or you can proceed to Miramontes. The escort will accompany you. I will join you there before dark. And by the way—"

As Beau disappeared through a heavy wooden gate into the courtyard of the Borda Palace I drooped wretchedly on my horse under a wide fig tree.

Almost immediately the wooden gate opened again.

"Be sensible," Beau said miserably, clutching at my hand. "Pull yourself together and enjoy the party. I intended to amuse and astonish, not upset you. You look all right, really you do, even if your riding skirt *is* so torn your drawers show. Are you listening to me?"

"My skirt caught on a giant maguey spike," I said in a tremulous voice, loving him so much that my knee went weak on the saddle horn.

Five minutes later, hand in hand, we were stepping around a wrought-iron screen into an overgrown tangle that must have been a spectacular garden when it was created. Now the stone arcades and columns were crumbling, the gilded statues and marble fountains clambered by roses, the lily pools choked with sticky weeds and the mango and orange groves neglected ruins of sweetness.

"What a romantic retreat," I cried.

And it *was* the very essence of romance. Ladies in pale pink, lavender and green muslins with matching, flower-crowned horsehair hats were draped in chairs or strolling among beds of sweet peas, roses and dahlias or playing croquet with tall Teutonic gentlemen in white frock coats and wide panama hats. Everybody looked young and beautiful. Not a cloud was in the blue summer sky. Preceded by a frolicky little King Charles spaniel, a laughing group strolled out from one of the corridors led by the Emperor with Princess Agnes on his arm. Was I surprised? Not at her! Agnes was liable to turn up anywhere she took a notion.

Maximilian held up a long slim hand and called in English, "You come late, my friend Berrien, I have despair of seeing you. Baby, too, she despairs, eh, little one?" He picked up the spaniel and cradled her affectionately as she licked his luxuriant golden beard.

"Isn't he wonderful?" Beau whispered. "Now aren't you glad to be here?"

I didn't reply, for Agnes, having caught sight of me, gave a shriek and rushed up and whisked me away. The Emperor and Beau joined the group playing croquet.

Later, in her bedroom, as her maid sewed my long feet into short red satin slippers and tightened a taffeta sash around the waist of one of her delectable white muslins, Agnes told me why this party today was important and why the Emperor was so relieved when Beau appeared.

"Your husband and Luis Blasio and old Dr. Billimek will be the only ones left in Mexico with whom the Emperor can truly relax. This is a farewell party for the Emperor's most trusted advisers, Count Zichy and Charles de Bombelles, and for the Empress's most faithful ladies-in-waiting, Countess Paola Kollonitz and the Marchesa Coria." Agnes fastened a string of blood-colored corals around my throat. "You can return them when *I* return. It will be soon. The Emperor wants Salm to come quickly. He knows all of Salm's family. I think they are cousins on his mother's side. Where was I? Oh, anyway, having foolishly listened to various whisperers, Maximilian is sending his courtiers, his real friends, home to Austria, replacing them with Mexicans."

I fixed a pair of matching coral earrings in my ears. They were startlingly becoming. My eyes shone like silver in my sunburned face. "However did you manage to get here today?"

"Despite his Juarist connections, Herr Hube is a friend of the Zichys. He nosed about and heard of this little house party, so he arranged for me to travel this far with the Zichys on my way to Vera Cruz."

"This isn't on the way to Vera Cruz."

Agnes laughed. "You're such an innocent, Angelica. One rarely reaches one's destination except roundabout. I'm taking a steamer for Havana in three days and carrying all the information Prince Salm needs to make up *his* mind to offer his services to Maximilian."

"Where is Count Thun and where is the Empress? Why aren't they here since the party is for their special friends too?"

"Count Thun fortunately ate some spoiled meat and 'clever little Charlotte' had a business meeting concerning the Carlota Colony with your friend, Maury. She hates Cuernavaca. It's too hot and humid and this old castle *is* full of snakes and scorpions. Walk across the room and let me look at you. You have gorgeous legs. No one but Frau Kuhacsavitch will object to your wearing such a short dress. Maximilian will be delighted. He appreciates beauty. Didn't you notice the way he looked at the exquisite face of that Indian girl, the gardener's wife, as she sucked an orange and watched the Countess del Valle knock the Emperor's ball through the waiting wicket?"

"Is Maximilian fickle?"

"Test him. You're lovelier than the Indian girl."

"I can't. I'm too worried about Beau today to flirt, even with an Emperor."

"You take things too seriously. Some men can slip easily from one way of life into another; from one country into another; from one woman into another. Others, like certain trees, can never be transplanted. Look at the Emperor: for all his heroic attempts to be more Mexican than the Mexicans, he remains a homesick dreamy Austrian."

"What about Prince Salm?"

"Ah, that one!" Agnes's big brown velvet eyes sparkled. "Prince Salm is the third son of his father; fortunately a born adventurer; a soldier with all his soul, and war is his element. Wherever there is action and danger he *is* at home. So am I, really. I shared Salm's tent in all his campaigns during the Civil War!"

"You couldn't have; they'd not let you."

"But I did." Agnes's rippling laughter was water-soft.

"Even when it rained and snowed?"

"Tents are natural to me. I love them."

Angus had been correct. I hadn't believed him.

"Beau would never have let me."

"Your Southern Beau is different from my Prussian Prince. You must be patient with him. If he can't, in time, settle happily in Mexico you'll just have to return to South Carolina and be hung."

PART II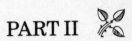

Miramontes

JUNE 1865

*From the house of flowering butterflies
was born the song:
I hear it come to life, I the singer;
It wanders in aquatic flower beds,
Wanders, flying, the peerless firefly
of the gods.*
ANCIENT NÁHUATL

16

In the dining room hung with faded Chinese paper, we sat from three until six o'clock at a long refectory table pyramided with fruits and flowers and ate and drank from heavy silver plates and goblets. Rather *they* ate. I don't like smoked salmon or herrings in sour cream or weiner-schnitzel or apple strudel or cold potatoes in vinegar, nor do I speak French or German. From time to time the Emperor would call charmingly down the table in English commanding me to play a waltz or a *lieder*. Willingly, I would retire to the piano in the grand salon that opened into the dining room.

José Luis Blasio had put out piles of Maximilian's favorite tunes and songs. But so many hours! A young gentleman, Don Anselmo Zurutuza, whose Hacienda Atlacomulco was near Miramontes, often came and sat beside me, chatting in Spanish about a lovely mare he wanted to lend me to ride and how much he missed his wife, who was spending the summer in Madrid. My only other diversion was Maximilian's little Hungarian cook who was fascinated by my playing and kept running in from the kitchen to listen.

Sometimes he directed me with a long wooden spoon. Had it not been for those two and the little spaniel who barked at Tudos and howled at the high notes, I would have gnawed my handkerchief to shreds as Carlota did at Puebla.

Beau was loath to leave at six but "clever" Agnes was on my side, so by six-fifteen Beau was teasing me about how virginal I looked in white muslin with red silk roses in my hair, trotting out ahead of the escort soldiers in my eagerness to reach Miramontes first.

As we came out onto the main road leading to Atlacomulco our guide and the escort soldiers suddenly closed in around me, drawing out their pistols.

"Señora, order your husband to pull his sombrero down further on his head to hide his fierce hair," the guide said. "Every tree on each side of the road hides one of Porfirio Díaz's guerrilla soldiers. In his gray *charro* clothes they may mistake the señor for the Emperor and not harm us."

I translated as he spoke. Instantly Beau pulled down his white and silver sombrero, shot his pistol in the direction of the woods and, leaning forward as if General Grant himself were on his tail, gave a Rebel yell and led us, galloping, past the grove into open country.

In about half an hour we came to a high wall and an open gateway with "Miramontes" painted over the masonry arch. The word "Heaven" would have looked the same to me. For twenty more minutes we ascended through a beautiful young green coffee plantation. Below we saw great fields of waving sugar cane and spreading grazing lands full of cattle. In a low place, giving an impression of vastness and solitude, was the hacienda itself, walled like a medieval village. Eagles, vultures and hawks wheeled and cried above us in the sky now rosied with the last sunlight of the long hot summer day. I hardly remember the frantic final galloping, but I'll always cherish the patriarchal cross and the three bells of the Trinity over the massive stone gateway silhouetted against the pink cloud-strewn sky.

For just a minute we halted at the entrance to the cobbled courtyard full of people. No one was aware of us. They were listening to three men leaning lazily against a graceful carriage, playing guitars. Some Indian women wearing garlands of poppies were dancing monotonously and singing so softly and sleepily that despite my excitement I felt as if I were in a blissful half-dreamy state of contentment. Squatting in front of the smoking sugar factory four men were playing at cards and in front of the coffee mill a group was betting on a chicken fight.

By the well, under a spreading ash tree, stood a fiercely mus-tachioed *mestizo* with a red sash and bow tie, looking down ador-ingly at a beautiful little round Indian girl seated on a stone bench. And she was looking up adoringly at Phillip Berrien!

"We come!" called the guide.

"Phillip!" I cried.

"Well, I'm Billybedamned!" shouted Beau.

The checkered sunlight played tricks with Phillip's sun-browned face and laughing black eyes. His soft white Mexican shirt with flowing sleeves was open revealing his hard chest softened with silky black hair. Always the handsomest of the Berriens, now there was an air of the pirate, the rogue, about him that shivered me pleasantly as he lifted me down from my horse and gave me a tingling kiss.

Beau kept beating him on the back and saying, "What the hell are you doing here ahead of us? We thought you were in New Orleans! What's going on? What's going on?"

"First, Bubba, you must greet your administrator, your overseer, *el* Señor Fidencio Carrisosa, known as Lencho. Lencho, may I present to you your *hacendado!*"

"All right all right," Beau said, brusquely acknowledging Len-cho's greeting. "Get on with your story, Phillip."

Ignoring Beau's impetuousness Phillip gave me a hug. "You look like a bride in that outfit, Angelica. This is Elsie Garcia, your personal maid. How lucky you are! Old lady Escandon left her behind when she took off for Madrid."

Elsie bobbed a quick curtsy and showed delightful dimples.

The peons in the courtyard crowded curiously around us. Phillip held up his hand, saying first in English to Beau, then in Castilian Spanish, "These are our workers from the village nearby. They have earned many extra reales in helping save the hacienda from vandalism. I too."

The Indians lifted their straw hats and bowed politely to Beau. He made a great effort to respond properly but he was irritated by Phillip's lengthy formalities and showed it. I was surprised at Phillip's easy courteous manner. England had done much for him.

Taking Beau's hand I whispered, "The people expect you to say something."

"You say it," he grumbled. "I'm going to kill Phillip for putting me through all this."

"*You* must speak. Even in English."

"Howdy-do, folks. Thank you for whatever you did to help. Get this thing over with, Phillip, you son of a gun."

"And this is your lady!" Phillip gaily announced.

The good humor of the workers overflowed as I made a nice little speech in Spanish about how glad I was to be here and tomorrow every one of them must tell me their names and all about their families.

After the hat-waving and *oles* Lencho stood up in the carriage and invited the workers to gather in front of the brandy house where long tables held pottery jugs of pulque and drinking gourds. Their wives were laying out earthen bowls of chili and avocados and piles of roasted goat, tortillas, mashed beans, sliced pineapple and melons. Oh, those women! Shining black hair and white teeth dazzling in smiles, dresses blending with the colors of the fruits and flowers on the table, they carried their babies within a wide rebozo wrapped around their soft bodies like a gentle womb, making my longing for *my* baby hard and sharp.

"You arrived just in time for our fiesta," Phillip said.

"In our honor?" Beau asked.

"No, Bubba, in appreciation of our peons not running away when the guerrillas occupied the hacienda. If only you'd come sooner! The hacienda is a perfect fortress. We could have—no, it's just as well you weren't here. You would have defended your castle with your life and lost both. I, being me, leaned with the wind and saved both."

"For God's sake, Phillip, stop pontificating. What guerrillas and why were they occupying my house? Also when did you appear on the scene with your heroics?"

Phillip laughed and so did I. Beau was more like himself than he'd been since we came to Mexico.

Phillip told us about receiving Beau's telegram in Vera Cruz, inquiring about the location of Cuernavaca, hiring a guide and riding cross-country from the coast. He arrived the day before the guerrillas moved in to spy on the Emperor in Cuernavaca.

"We passed them near the palace," Beau said.

"They won't be back. They're on their way to report to Juárez in Chihuahua. I wish you could have seen this place before. The silver and paintings they took away are worth more than you paid for the whole estate."

"I'll only pay for what's here today."

"Sorry. I paid the Escandon administrator the day *I* took over."

"Count on you to be a jackass," Beau said, but not unkindly.

Lencho brought a tray of orangeade. "The house servants have done what they could, Señor Felipe. Can come in now, the *hacendados*."

"This way," Phillip said, taking my hand, "into what this morning could only have been called an Augean stable."

An old wrought-iron *cancela* with heart- and rose-shaped motifs screened the major courtyard from the covered corridor of the dwelling. Lencho opened an intricately carved cypress door beside it. Beau rushed curiously ahead of everybody.

"Aren't you going to carry Angelica over the threshold of her new home?" Phillip called to Beau's retreating figure.

"Leave him alone, Phillip. He's been in a state ever since Vera Cruz."

"But not I, my sweet." Phillip swooped me up and carried me through the door into a seemingly endless vaulted and arched corridor that ran around the great oblong stone house.

Barefooted Indian maids and men were walking around with buckets and mops. Piles of broken chairs and tables and pottery *jardinières* littered the crushed flower beds of the enclosed patio that looked like the Garden of Eden to me. I could envision my baby and Button playing in the shady fish pool.

"This house was built when Queen Elizabeth sat on the throne of England," Phillip said. "It's been fancied up a bit since but not much. I'm in love with it."

"Come here quick," Beau called from somewhere above.

I followed Phillip up a stone staircase with a carved balustrade leading to a gallery almost identical to the one below. High windows looked out over the patio on one side and the glorious mountains on the other. There were lots of low-swung chairs covered in cowhide along the corridor and interesting painted benches and tables filled with pyramids of fruit and flowers in bright pottery stands.

"The only damage the guerrillas did up here was to steal everything made of silver and gold," Phillip said, guiding us along the big rooms, some holding vestiges of luxury, others entirely empty. "If you all had taken possession a week ago—"

Beau was walking through a pair of carved double doors. His head touched the wide-spread *concha* above it. He turned back. "So far I haven't made too many correct decisions since I left the ship but blame it on my having to look at these damn snowcapped mountains all the time. I'd never have bought this place if I'd known Popocatépetl would be blowing his evil smoke down at me."

"Close the shutters on that side. The volcano is at least twenty-five miles away. You'll not smell his smoke. The guerrillas were decent fellows, Bubba. All they are after is to rid Mexico of that foreign Emperor and bring back their own President. They don't steal for themselves, only to supply Juárez's army."

"To hell with Juárez and his army!" Beau said, stumbling on a loose board.

"Look, Beau! This is my room!" I had entered the grand salon dominated by a concert-sized grand piano, several Queen Anne-type painted cabinets, and a few gilt French chairs and sofas. A magnificent silver chandelier with pierced galleries and brackets and a delicate wrought-iron chain hung from the ceiling. A big window looking out on the patio gave a mothlike effect with white gauze wings hanging from the elegantly molded *concha* above.

Beau reached up to touch the chandelier. "How'd the devils happen to leave this beauty?" He ran his fingers around the pierced silver gallery.

A group of house servants had trailed along with us pointing at this and that for us to exclaim over. Suddenly one of them cried out, "Take down the hand, *hacendado!*"

But it was too late. A scorpion was clinging to the freckled white hand.

"He got me!"

The servants surged forward to help. With a curse Beau shook his fist, flinging the scorpion in their direction and started toward them. It was too much. They fled in terror from the raging giant with the flaming hair and wild green eyes. Only little Elsie had the wit to capture the scuttling scorpion under an orangeade cup as it made for the doorway. Lencho rushed off to prepare the antidote for the poison sting.

17

Hours later I was propped on a pile of down pillows between lavishly embroidered cool cotton sheets. Beau was lying beside me, totally drunk, or in a coma, after forcing down a pitcher full of strong brandy infused with guaicum, boiled milk and ground scorpions, including the one that had stung him on the wrist.

"Dear God," I prayed, "make the antidote work." Beau's frantic struggle to breathe had lessened but his pulse was barely discernible. Was he going to die? I touched his heart. It beat unevenly and very slowly.

Elsie was tying a heavy rope all the way around the bed. "Scorpions will not walk across the rough surface of the rope, Señora Angel, I promise you."

"I believe you. Goodnight, Elsie, truly I think God has sent you to me. I will never forget your help."

"Nor I my joy in serving you. Already I prefer waiting on you to the drippy-nosed Doña Luisa, though she once gave me one of her torn lace petticoats at Easter when we lived in Yucatán."

"Go now to your rest. It is after midnight."

"Nevertheless I will sleep in a hammock in the corridor outside your door. Señor Felipe and Lencho are also there in case the *hacendado*'s heart does not beat. Shall I leave burning one of the candlesticks?"

"Both. The light will comfort me."

By candlelight I saw the enormous painted wood bed reflected in the large tin-framed mirror across the room. On the silver-blue headboard white doves and swags were intermixed with oleander-like flowers in dark blues and orange-pinks. A swag floating between two larger flying doves carried this verse;

> *Give me your wings, sweet dove, to fly into your nest*
> *If last night you slept alone, tonight you will sleep with me.*

It should read the other way round! For myself and, since tonight I was living like one, it would be good to be like one of those Spanish nuns who came soon after the conquest, who suffered neither fears nor reactions, who remained calm and impervious to everything throughout the most trying times. Tonight I felt the need of such dedicated stoicism.

I heard Elsie giggling and a man whispering. I could imagine the circle sliding over the waiting hook. Lencho must be putting up her hammock. Lencho? Or was it Phillip?

If the antidote did not work, tomorrow there would be a funeral for a *hacendado*. The brightest star of the Berriens would be extinguished. Phillip would be the heir to all this.

To my overwrought imagination everything in the room suddenly appeared to have a symbolic meaning. Even the unglazed pottery five-branched candlestick on which Eve was giving a bowed-head Adam an apple while looking up at a merry red devil with a great bushy pink tail who was handing another apple into her uplifted hand. The branch of the unusual tree on which the devil was perched—

"Angelica, I've fetched the doctor."

Startled, I opened my eyes. Bright sunlight was pouring into the room. A haggard Phillip and Dr. Billimek were standing beside the bed. They were talking in French. Dr. Billimek was shaking his head.

"It's all right, Angelica," Phillip said. "Unaccustomed to a redhead's coloring Lencho was worried because Bubba looked so white. He thought he had died. He went to the Borda Palace and fetched this delightful gentleman who declares that Beau's heart and breathing are now quite normal. He'll just have to sleep off that magnum of brandy he drank and digest all those repulsive scorpions. Hey—don't cry! All our bad times are over."

Later, in the dressing room leading off our bedroom, Elsie was teaching me how to arrange a lace fichu on a new flowered muslin dress.

"You must wear the shoes, señora."

"They are too tight. I prefer going barefoot. The floor tiles feel good."

"If you walk barefoot it will make you low in front of the house servants; a dreadful happening when Señor Felipe stands so high."

"Come with me, Angelica, there is a present in the patio for you," Phillip said from the doorway.

"I'll look in on Beau first."

"No. Come now." There was about him an air of urgency. It confused me.

We met Lencho on the wide stairway carrying a basin and a pile of towels. With him was a very old Indian with a round shaved head and lizard eyes who smiled coldly and maliciously at me.

Phillip pulled me aside to let the two continue up. "Lencho thinks Bubba's wrist should be lanced and the poison let out while he can feel no pain because of the brandy."

"But Dr. Billimek said—"

"Dr. Billimek understands butterflies but not scorpions. The medicine man is saying to Lencho that if you stay he goes. I'll find you as soon as possible."

Lencho turned back. "Señora, our neighbor, Don Anselmo Zurutuza, who assisted me in finding the German doctor, has sent you a bird. Don Anselmo heard of the guerrillas loosing all of ours. The new bird sits on a perch by the fountain. He is not happy."

There were three of them and one of me. These past few years have taught me when I must retreat and to do so as gracefully as possible. I hoped Beau would not suffer. I had pressed the inflamed and swollen wrist a few minutes ago and he had not winced. And I longed to be alone in the garden.

The morning was not yet too hot. As my miserable feet touched the pebble- and stone-paved walk leading into the flower gardens I was filled with sudden rapture. Ripping off the ridiculous satin slippers I began to run joyously and freely under arches formed by blooming roses that led to an orange walk through the orchard.

As I came back into the flower garden a coral snake with its black viper head twisted in front of me. Hummingbirds emitted sparkles of colored light from their brilliant wings. Little green parrots and gold satin warblers took turns eating black seeds from a burst papaya hanging from the branch of a tree under which sat *my* big blue and red parrot on a bamboo perch. I tried to talk to it but every time I came close it started screaming, so I walked around the tree to look at a great tank of clear water that was the focal point of the patio. I sat myself down on the rim of the pool by the fountain which was topped with the stone figure of a mythical mermaid spilling water into a carved black marble shell that overflowed into the pool.

I laved my hot dusty feet in the water and I looked up at the house—*my* house. I looked around at the beautiful mountains and volcanoes and I looked back at the dark green orchard through which I had come the roundabout way to here and I thought: This is not a dream. I have been here before. I have lived here in these mountains in another life. Everything is familiar to me—the smells, the light, the birdsongs. I belong here. I am going to be happier here than I have ever been anywhere before in this life.

My bird said plainly, "Jesus and Mary! Jesus and Mary!"

Phillip sat down beside me, took off his boots, and dangled his feet in the water beside mine. "Bubba is over the hill. He would have lost his arm if Lencho hadn't taken charge. I never saw such black stuff as poured out. Don't look at me like that. You aren't going to faint, are you?"

I laughed. "I've only fainted once in my life, when Frederick Pierce read me a telegram saying Beau had been lost in the war."

"The war I ran away from. Do you hate me, Angelica?"

"Of course not."

"What a cad I was, leaving you and Button alone on Hilton Head. And yet—"

"You were young and bitter." I touched his knee affectionately.

"Only a year younger than you. Whatever happened to old Pierce?"

"Button shot him."

Phillip moved my hand angrily.

"That's another mark against me. I should have killed him with the carving knife that first Christmas we spent alone on the island."

"Why didn't you write?"

"I did, over and over. You never answered my letters."

"I never received them. I knew you had hired on a ship bound for Liverpool. What did you do when you got there?"

"I worked in the Cotton Exchange for a year; then on a whim looked up one of Mother's Barnwell cousins, Cousin Bess, the Lady Melancourt, in London. She took a fancy to me and set me up at Oxford for a term after which I sowed a few interesting oats on the Continent. Then I returned to Liverpool to make my fortune. Not a very pretty picture but I've no regrets at having bypassed a war I didn't believe in. I was glad to come back this way when Beau sent me word in care of Cousin Bess. I prefer Southern belles to British ones."

"How did you learn Spanish?"

"The same day Bubba's letter arrived I hunted a Spanish teacher. On the voyage over I was lucky to draw three priests from Castile as cabin mates. Now catch me up with you."

"I will tomorrow. I'm too happy today."

With that he purposely fell into the tank with all his clothes on, coming up from the bottom, laughing, with a fall of feathery green waterweeds in his black hair. "I'll make you even happier. I know a secret and if you will meet me under the ash tree by the well in half an hour I will share it with you," he called, swimming lazily around and around the pool.

I picked a red dahlia and tossed it to him. He caught it, turned a backward somersault in the water, came up at the edge and grabbed one of my ankles.

"Jump in. The cool water will refresh you more than an afternoon of resting."

"I'd drown."

"I'd not let you."

"Señora Angel!"

Lencho and Elsie were standing together on the upper corridor watching Phillip and me. "The *hacendado* has waked and is asking for you."

I had wings! I could fly! "Turn loose my ankle, Phillip. Beau wants me. Let me go!" I reached out with my other foot to push his head under water but I knew he'd not hesitate to pull me in with him. I drew it back. "Please, Phillip. Wonderful Phillip!"

"If you'll promise to meet me in the courtyard. He'll be asleep when you get there anyway. Promise?"

"Yes, I'll be there." I ran lightheartedly along the path to the lower corridor, then up the stairs and along the upper one.

Someone had closed the shutters. The big blue bed was dim. Beau's face was ghostly in the half-light; his wide-open eyes tormented, his voice a frail whisper.

"I had a dreadful dream. You were walking around the rim of that evil volcano. Come close, Angel, kiss me. Come—"

He was asleep again before my lips touched his clammy forehead. His right arm was swathed in bandages.

Lencho touched my shoulder. "Permit the *hacendado* to sleep. Look only to make you know that all is well with him, then leave quickly. The priest of our people insists on no spirit but his and the *hacendado*'s in the room until all poison has drained away."

With a strange feeling of excited fancy I thought: I can spend all day in the garden!

But Elsie insisted on my sitting down while she sewed another pair of those dreadful satin slippers on my restless feet. As she stitched she sang a song of verses of the *Jota Aragonesa* that seemed to have no end nor any beginning.

> *"The woman who loves two at once*
> *Knows what is discreet and right*
> *Since if one of her candles goes out*
> *Still the other remains alight . . ."*

My cheeks flamed. How dared she misconstrue Phillip's brotherly teasing? Sternly I sat up straight to put her in her place once and for all.

"Please, Señora Angel, may I talk first?"

My instinct was to say no, jerk my foot from her gentle hands and rush away.

But she was already talking.

"I must marry with Lencho. I have promise that. My heart is with him, yes, but my eyes fly too easily to Señor Felipe. Since you bring no trunk I know you return to Mexico City. Will you take me with you so my heart alone can say what I do?"

What a fool I am at times!

"That will be wonderful, Elsie. But I hope never to return to the city for long."

18 🌿

The courtyard at noon was a deserted blazing square. The workers had vanished into the shady orchard to eat their lunch and have a siesta until the fierce part of the day passed. The only movement on the burning cobbles was an occasional lizard and the lacy shadows of the ash tree, zagged now and then by the deeper shadow of a flying vulture.

Phillip was standing by the well under the tree when I came hopping along, trying not to feel the burning stones through my silly satin slippers. In a black sombrero, white cotton trousers and a loose white Mexican blouse sashed in black, he could easily have been taken for a brigand but never for a Southern gentleman.

I stood beside him while he explained the buildings surrounding the main courtyard: the carriage house, the stables, the great coffee mill for sorting and bagging the beans, the house for boiling sugar, the house for making brandy, the machine shop, the fowl house, the feed house and on and on all the way around to the exquisite sixteenth-century chapel.

"Let's go inside the chapel."

"Lencho says there are three hundred workers on the hacienda and one hundred and fifty horses and mules, not counting burros. The workers are paid three to four reales a day, the more skilled six or seven reales a day."

"What is a real worth? It's too hot out here."

"Eight reales equal a peso; a peso is worth about a dollar. A

Yankee dollar, not a Confederate one." Phillip jumped to his feet. "Since you're not interested in finance, we'll visit the chapel."

"Isn't that where the secret is?"

"You've caught me! You always do. But you really must show a little interest in the affairs of the hacienda."

"I will. But today I only want to face up to beautiful things. It's the first chance I've had to be myself all to myself since I left home. Yesterday was too full of surprises."

"This will be a good surprise."

Small blue and cream and rust and black Puebla tiles encased the baroque façade of the chapel. The cypress double doors were intricately carved. As Phillip pushed them ajar, sunlight raced ahead of us to touch six twisted gilt-encrusted Solomonic columns holding up a vaulted gilt and stucco ceiling, giving a mosquelike appearance to the small jewel of a structure.

Inside the doors were two recesses outlined in colorful tiles. In one was a carved olive wood figure of the Archangel Gabriel decked in red and gold satin robes. In the other was a black St. Christopher in a darkly smeared costume of silver tissue with his pants rolled up, looking up at a black Christ Child on his shoulder. Phillip picked up a sharp stone lying beside the statue and scraped the cheek of the Child. It glittered.

"One of the workers had the sense to paint this statue black when the soldiers came. St. Christopher is made of silver and the Child of solid gold."

"How beautiful! Did you know I have a little son?"

"Stephen Elliott wrote Cousin Bess the news of Edward's arrival when her brother, Uncle Billy, died. Do you miss your baby?"

"So much—so much—"

"Hush—not today."

In the midst of the golden grotto, the backdrop of plain painted wood with a primitive image of the Virgin of Guadalupe seemed tawdry and mediocre. On the dark refectory table that held the host stood an array of tin lustre shields pierced so that a lit candle in a holder behind them made feeble filigrees of light.

"The altar is the least interesting part of the chapel. I'm disappointed."

I noticed six Indians standing beside the marble baptismal font. Lencho was with them.

"We wait, Lencho," Phillip called.

Quickly the Indians ran to the sacristy and adroitly, as if in a theater, began to fold the rear panels of the backdrop to reveal an overwhelming, ultrabaroque altar worked in pure shining silver!

The sunlight from the open door struck it blindingly. Phillip let out a low whistle. I dropped to my knees. I couldn't help it.

"You can see better standing up. Save your prayers for later. This is a miniature duplicate of the altar of the cathedral at Taxco. Lencho's grandfather created this after working at Taxco for old Borda whose artisans built that one. But the altar is not the marvel. The marvel is that all this silver came off this estate! Lencho himself was taught the art of silverworking by his father and his grandfather. Angelica, Bubba doesn't know it, but when he reactivates the old silver mine he's going to be so rich he can buy up the whole city of Charleston! I'm so jealous of him I could die."

As Phillip and I were finishing supper on the starlit corridor, a ghostlike Beau appeared from the shadows looking to have lost half his weight. Phillip jumped up and supported him to a chair beside me.

"Don't either of you dare say a sympathetic word," Beau said slowly, managing a pale simulacrum of a grin. "If you do, I will burst into unbridled cursing."

Phillip's eyes met mine over the candles. Both of us realized that Beau was not only weak and debilitated from his ordeal but in a nervously emotional mood that could easily dissolve his rationale. The memory of the first night I met him flashed across my mind. We were at dinner at Cedar Grove. Having stood as much Virginia etiquette as he was able, Beau had grasped a slender wine glass so hard it shattered, saying, "Whenever I am out of sight of my ocean and smell of my marsh I am homesick, but *if ever* I were doomed to stay away from them long I would surely die."

"Phillip has discovered a silver mine on the hacienda!" I said quickly.

"Figuratively it can be a gold mine," Phillip added. Beau looked distracted and did not respond. Phillip tried another topic. "Tell me how you wangled a royal invitation to lunch yesterday. I couldn't believe my ears when Lencho told me."

Beau looked Phillip straight in the face with a superior if feeble smile. "I always sit at the head table wherever I find myself."

"Better choose your table carefully in Mexico. I sailed from Europe with Napoleon III's envoy. He made no secret of his mission: to inform Marshall Bazaine of Napoleon's orders to begin removal of French troops from Mexico at once. Old Seward has shaken the United States flag in Nap's face and told him to dust out of Mexico."

"Napoleon will never desert Maximilian."

"If France supports the Emperor in remaining on the throne of Mexico a year longer, things will have gone too far and Washington will declare war on Paris. Napoleon won't risk that."

"Then Vienna will step in."

"Never. All London knows that Austria faces a hostile Prussia."

Beau pulled his slinged arm against his chest as if it pained him. "The Mexican people are happy with the Empire. You should hear them hail the Emperor when he rides down the Alameda."

"If you had been here and heard the guerrilla soldiers speaking of Juárez as if he were Jesus Christ, of the disposal of a foreign Emperor as a holy crusade, you'd think twice before you follow another lost cause."

"Have you seen a brighter light?" Beau asked sarcastically.

"Not yet. From what I've heard I don't like either one. I thought you came here to help Maury develop a Confederate colony, not to get involved in Mexican politics. Why ever did you?"

"I don't know—" Beau paused. "I really don't, unless being in the company of fellow sufferers did not suit me."

The heartrending wail of a *flamenco* being played on several guitars was heard in the patio below. I rose from the table and sat on the balustrade trying to shut out the conversation between the brothers, longing to run down into the patio and wail along with the guitars.

It was as if, not yet having heard, I knew exactly what Beau was going to say next. And he said it:

"Nothing—nobody—could persuade me to live here at Miramontes. Oh, from time to time Angelica and I will visit, especially in the winter or when the Emperor is in residence at the Borda Palace. But last night made up my mind. You can be the *hacendado*, Phillip. With my whole heart and in another's hearing I this minute present you with half the ownership and half the fantastic silver profits and all the glory of administering Miramontes until your life's end. So help me God!"

Clearly startled, Phillip didn't try to hide his astonishment as Beau continued wearily: "We'll go to the city as soon as I'm able— tomorrow or the next day. I'll have partnership papers drawn up legally for the two of us to sign. Never trust family. That's one good lesson Papa taught me."

Through the *cancela*, from the courtyard, floated another song and a different guitar.

"*Flores negras del destino—*"

I put my hands over my ears and closed my eyes, desperately

willing Phillip to reject Beau's impulsive offer. For this was my home. I could never share it with that other woman who would be Phillip's wife. I didn't move a muscle. But I knew that my beautiful day was over.

"What about Angelica's wishes? She loves it here." Phillip spoke very fast.

"But I don't." Beau closed his eyes. His head sank down on his chest as if he suddenly slept.

Phillip came over and stood beside me. "Now I will show him."

"What will you show your big brother?" I whispered.

He put his lips against my ear. "How to run a plantation. I'll show Bubba and everybody. Especially you. And Miramontes will like me."

Phillip was happy and excited. It was strange to hear him say this, not about Cotton Hall in South Carolina, but about Miramontes. Miramontes near Cuernavaca in Mexico.

Beau's head popped up. He looked scarily around for us. Quickly we sat back down with him.

"Angelica's wishes?" His voice was weak and petulant. "I've accepted a position in the Imperial Guard. Angelica may be invited to become a lady-in-waiting to the Empress. That will solve everything."

Phillip touched his sandal warningly to my instep.

"I'll not be a lady-in-waiting to anybody!"

I jerked away my foot and fled. Fled down the corridor to the lamplit bedroom. I sat down and stared at the painted doves flaunting their silly verse:

> Give me your wings, sweet dove—to fly into your nest
> and listened to the singer below in the courtyard:
> "Flores negras del destino—"
> listened—

PART III

Maximilian

JULY 1865

*...You give your heart to one thing after
another.
Carrying, you do not carry it.
You destroy your heart on earth.
Are you not always pursuing things aimlessly?*
ANCIENT TOLTEC

19 🌿

On June 26, 1865, the Zocalo was packed with carriages interlaced with beggars and thieves of every sex and age and ragged costume. The barracklike National Palace, which had been so hastily refurbished by the Emperor into a semblance of a royal place, was packed with foreign ministers, émigrés, silver barons, French officers and jeweled Creoles mingling with Mexican officials, all here to watch God join together the French marshall and the Mexican girl in holy matrimony.

Beau enthusiastically pointed to Napoleon's latest gift to Maximilian, a pair of fabulous Sèvres vases he'd personally placed at the entrance to the throne room. But there was no chance for leisurely appreciation. Everything was noise and jostle for position. The whole affair was so international, so un-Mexican, it was as if Maximilian meant to put on a tremendous show to bluff Europe and America with a display of splendor and importance. But there was something frantic, something unsolid, something of the garish atmosphere of a carnival about the whole affair.

I would have given anything for Agnes. She would have been beside herself. I wasn't. I clung to Beau and Phillip through the marriage ceremony in the palace chapel presided over by the ever-smiling Bishop Labastida and through the wedding banquet, hosted by the Emperor. Maximilian toasted Bazaine as if he were his beloved brother. I saw Bazaine look at Maximilian with contempt, then light up like a fire when the Emperor presented him with Buenavista, one of the richest haciendas in Mexico, as a wedding gift. When Bazaine sat down, he looked around furtively to see if he had betrayed his greedy disloyalty to anybody else.

After the banquet, which lasted four hours, Maximilian and Carlota went into the throne room to formally receive the wedding guests.

"I will present Phillip now." Beau was wearing the scarlet and gold jacket of the Austrian Hussars. Phillip was darkly elegant in a gray cutaway coat and a high starched collar softened by a wide silver cravat. They were the handsomest men there. They really were, despite my prejudice!

"Be careful of your hand. It's still enflamed," I said.

"I'll keep it on the hilt of my sword. People will take me for royalty. I should have bought a monocle. I've always wanted one."

Phillip mumbled his disapproval. "Bubba looked more natural playing Massa on the piazza at Cotton Hall than he does here playing Austrian."

"I love my lady and my king." Beau's voice held a tenderness that made me want to nestle him.

Maximilian's face was all smiles and charming affability as he greeted people gracefully. He stood in front of a gilded throne while Carlota sat in a similar one with her hands folded. She was staring straight ahead with half-closed eyes, hardly noticing her swarming, bowing guests. Suddenly she caught sight of me. The eyes opened and she smiled, not sweetly but imploringly.

Come and help me, said her big sad eyes. We kept looking at each other.

"Take your place in line." Beau gave me a push. "We must speak to Their Majesties and then I can introduce Phillip to the people he should meet."

"And who are they?"

"Angus McLeod," he laughed.

"That's all?"

"He runs Mon Real, doesn't he? Angelica, get out of line, the Empress is beckoning to you!"

At Carlota's request I took my place between two ginger-faced ladies-in-waiting standing behind her. Towering over the short Mexican ladies I remained as unhappy as Carlota for the next two hours until Don Carlos approached with Doña Teresa and the McLeods.

Flora's petulant expression as she jealously took note of me, so close to the Empress while she was standing with a mere Mayor of Jalapa, did not become her. Nor did her immediate complaints about the tacky little house she was living in near the mine endear her to Carlota.

Angus, to my amusement and relief, cleverly manipulated all of us. Within minutes Flora was in my place, her prim Scotch bonnet between the two black lace mantillas where my blue, floppy-brimmed Eugénie hat had been. Beau was arm in arm with Maury, Early and Magruder talking to General Jo Shelby, who had arrived with his Iron Brigade from Missouri the day before. Phillip and Angus were touching heads with Sir Peter Campbell-Scarlett, the British Minister. Doña Teresa, happily eating *dulces*, was gossiping in the dining room with other Creole cousins of the bride. And I was standing in one of the long windows leading to a sunlit balcony with Don Carlos.

"I am impressed with your husband's brother."

"You've only just met him."

"Earlier, while you, the blue flower, protected the so-haughty Empress, I have been with him and the wily Señor Angus for much conversation during which I promised Señor Angus to be his faithful slave if he would arrange for me to tell tales to you for half an hour."

"I hope they will be scandalous," I said with a pleasant feeling that there was something scandalous itself in the slight rustle of my taffeta petticoat underneath the blue organdy flounces of my dress. Then, aware of Don Carlos's eyes on my breasts, I wished to diminish their effect, but could not think of a way.

"How lovely you are! I have quite forgot all the wicked tales I planned to tell you."

I turned and looked over my shoulder, seeking Beau.

Don Carlos took the hint. "No, stay. I am about to burst with trifles, I promise you."

He was witty and sarcastic, revealing more than mere polite party conversation, commenting on everything.

"It's like standing in a theater watching a corrupt but breathtaking play," he said.

"My husband and I don't belong in the play."

"Your husband joined the cast of characters too late. The scenery is already out of place, the actors are swapping leading roles in midscene and the curtain master is confused about the ropes."

"My brother-in-law will hate to miss playing a part. He is fascinated with Mexico."

"He belongs in the play. He and Señor Angus will make excellent actors. I listened to them as they cornered the world silver market and settled the political future of Mexico. We need their kind in Mexico."

"Did you also talk with my husband?"

"No. He speaks only French and English. I neither."

"A pity. You could have asked him about his day in Jalapa."

"I know on whose head the roses rained, Señora Angelica. It is a dangerous game your husband plays. Better that he should have accepted the challenge of Córdoba than the illusion of Cuernavaca."

"You sound as if you have been spying, Don Carlos."

"I look and listen. Regard how the Frenchwomen as well as the French soldiers have been deprived of their most valuable possession by their sojourn in Mexico."

"What do you call their 'most valuable possession'? They're covered with jewels and gold medals."

"Their dignity. To test a person's or an animal's ability to maintain its dignity in spite of any temptation is a game at which I excel."

"I believe you. I saw you with the yellow cat."

"Which I discarded immediately."

"How dreadful of you."

"The cat was overproud; then it lost its dignity, thus my interest. I am a very wicked man, Señora Angel, is it not true?"

Don Carlos laughed disarmingly but I knew he planned to play his little game with me if he ever got a chance because he said, "I have never been close to a North American lady before. Your proudness is unique and challenging as is your personal dignity compared with that of the Frenchwomen and the Scotch Señora. But we must continue our spying. I want you to tell me what strikes you sharpest this afternoon."

We were on the periphery of the crowd. I noticed French officers behaving badly toward the Mexicans, speaking to and about them insultingly. I saw Captain de Courcy, a high officer on Bazaine's staff, watching Madame de Courcy dance a quadrille with General Almonte, who was of mixed blood. Captain de Courcy said loudly, "I never thought I would see my wife partnered by a nigger." The ugly scar on General Almonte's swarthy face flamed angrily, he too having heard. A tune later I saw the child bride, Josefina de Peina y Bazaine, spill a glass of champagne all over the Marshall's wedding coat in scandalized astonishment as Madame de Courcy and another French officer's tipsy wife joined in a wild cancan and showed their underdrawers.

"I can't bear the Imperialist atmosphere. Let's walk outside on the balcony and breathe some fresh air," said Don Carlos.

As I stepped over the threshold I saw Phillip advancing, pushing his way roughly past the high-kickers, knocking one off her stride. I knew he was looking for me in particular. I lifted my hand and he his to indicate we'd found each other.

"I admire the way Señor Phillip treats those Frenchwomen. I wish I had his courage," Don Carlos yelled in my ear as the music grew even madder and the palace was overwhelmed by the wild singing of the "Marseillaise."

"Bubba, aren't you jealous of Don Juan?"

"Don't know him. Why would I be jealous of a half-breed?"

Our carriage was passing down the Alameda on the way to Maury's house. It was almost dark. The wide avenue was practically empty, all available pockets having been picked earlier in the day.

"It's not Don Juan, Phillip. It's Don Carlos Miranda," I said, fitting myself comfortably between the brothers.

"Oh, him!" said Beau. "Don't trust him a minute, but why should I be jealous of his flirting with Angelica?"

"Because—" I bit my lips, wanting to say: Because he's too attracted to me. Because when he took my arm I felt his fingers tighten and then tremble loose the way yours do.

"Because what?" Phillip insisted wickedly.

"Anyway his heart wasn't in it," I said.

"He is a malicious sensual hedonist."

"Gracious heavens!" I said, "what big words you have, Señor Felipe."

"Angus has heard things about Don Carlos you wouldn't believe."

"Oh, yes, I would."

"Tell me. I love evil gossip." Phillip was in high spirits.

"Hush, you two," Beau said sternly. "It tires me just to listen to your nonsense."

He lifted my hand and kissed it and began singing "Beautiful Dreamer Waken to Me."

"You've played like an ostrich all day," Phillip said. "I know what a strong spell Angelica can cast, especially on shady characters. Remember Frederick Pierce?"

Beau stopped singing but didn't answer Phillip.

"Don't be mean, Phillip. For Don Carlos compliments are only a Mexican formality," I insisted.

Someone in the street shouted "Viva Juárez! *Viva el cinco de mayo!*"

"Don Carlos is Juárez's heir apparent. They complement each other: one has money; the other power; together, everything needed to succeed in Mexico. Don Carlos can be dangerous."

"A mere Mayor of Jalapa? You're crazy, isn't he, love?" Beau said, gently touching my breast with his elbow.

"I think he's more than a *mere* anything. I never knew anybody like him before."

And Phillip tossed his head upward, saying, "Angus thinks the mayor title is a bluff to fool the Moderates into leaving Don Carlos alone. That way he can spy and still remain on the public scene. Should Juárez topple the Emperor, Don Carlos will be his number-one minister; eventually President of Mexico. At the moment he's like an actor in a play. I for one consider him to perform his part perfectly."

"That's funny." I laughed. "He said the same thing about you."

Beau kissed my hand again but didn't comment. Phillip began humming "Beautiful Dreamer." Lamplighters with glowing torches were lighting the gas lights in front of the houses. It was beginning to rain and many of the lamps went out.

20 ❧

The following Sunday we were the guests of the old Countess Corbina for a day in the country at her summer place, Hacienda

Contenta, four miles out of Mexico City. Colonel Alfons von Kodolitsch and his Bavarian wife, Lisa, came for us in an open carriage. Beau was at his best but, not speaking French, I spent the hour quietly admiring the way while they discussed whatever interests Bavarians in Mexico.

The fine road was paved and divided by a stone aqueduct with 900 arches built by the conquistadores to bring fresh water to the city from a source on the hill of Chapultepec. We drove under the cliff of Chapultepec Castle through a grove of stupendous cypresses which had been old when, our driver carefully explained and I translated, Montezuma and his young lords used to lie under them and smoke pipes of tobacco mixed with amber.

Fingering a long thin cigar and looking dryly regal in a high turban of pink velvet with a diamond the size of a quail egg pinned in the front, Countess Corbina welcomed us excessively. Long diamond earrings came to her shoulders and though her dress was black taffeta it was blazoned with so many rubies, diamonds and emeralds it sparkled gay as a Roman candle.

The house was stonily enormous with lines of empty rooms running after each other around the ubiquitous corridor. Countess Corbina explained to me in excellent English that she had twice furnished this, her summer palace, but in two revolutions all her furniture and everything else had been tossed out the windows and destroyed. She now confined herself to strict necessities, such as the huge billiard table and the Broadwood grand piano, the only pieces of furniture in the drawing room!

The day began with a champagne breakfast on the sunlit terrace looking out over the Valley of Mexico, the volcanoes and Chapultepec Castle. After breakfast we danced Mexican folk dances accompanied by guitars; then came a champagne feast in a vaulted dining hall; then an orchestra of fiddles and horns led us into polkas, reels and mazurkas interspersed with bowls of brandy punch. We rested in hammocks hung in cool empty rooms and ended the day with four lengthy quadrilles, made possible by more brandy, champagne, squeaky fiddles, guitars and horns.

That's the bare bones of the day. The substance was that during the last dance the very tipsy Countess announced loudly in English that she was traveling to Europe for an indefinite stay and, having taken a fancy to the American major, offered to let him her house during her absence. Beau had been holding her body up during the quadrille. I was dancing with a foolish little Austrian with a monocle.

I nodded vigorously in Beau's direction. He leaned down and

began whispering in her diamonded ear. I watched her amusedly tap him on the top of his head with her fan as he kissed her hand to seal the bargain.

A country place of our own a few minutes from Chapultepec Castle and the Emperor; dozens of house servants and a panoramic view that Beau could look away from and I at. What good fortune!

We laughed and sang "Dixie" all the way back to the city to the curiosity of the von Kodolitsches, who had never heard that lively melody before but who soon joined in German with their own homesick words.

21 🌿

The memories of the year and a half we spent at Tacubaya are fantastic and lucid, like the afterglow of a long confused dream which, under its apparent disorder, is clearly and fatally symbolic and on course toward a target.

Tacubaya was a sprawling little village made interesting by the summer houses of rich Mexicans and foreign ministers and exploiters. I rarely encountered them. It wasn't because I was too busy. I had nothing in the world to do. The multitude of the Countess's house servants and gardeners were lazy and shrewd. Six of them did the work of one. Elsie put up with them for a week before returning to Miramontes to "marry with Lencho." I missed her but made no effort to change the pattern of the hacienda because the cook was excellent and the two old soldiers who guarded the gate, though seldom sober, were ever smiling and in their places. I enjoyed saying good morning and good evening to the three of them.

The fact that the air was always soft, except a little while in winter, the sky always blue, the flowers always blossoming, the birds always singing, and fountains ever-playing made Hacienda

Contenta a spiritual sanctuary, a physical refuge and an emotional protection. But I never thought of making it my nest. It was a branch on which I'd lit to plume my wings after a long migration.

And then there was this: We had just unpacked our trunks when a letter came from our lawyer, Joab Pritchard, bluntly stating that, since the assassination of President Lincoln, the North was so hellbent on punishing the South, whom it blamed as the murderer, he wouldn't be so foolish as to bring my case to the attention of a scalawag court lest they send a whole brigade down to Mexico to catch me. And as for Beau—the feeling in the South was presently bitter against those who had run away rather than remain to help reconstruct their homeland. He might be lynched if he came riding into St. Luke's Parish with a sackfull of silver money.

"Leave the children in Virginia where they are safe. I will write your uncle often and telegraph you in care of Commodore Maury if an emergency arises. Within a few months I promise you will be free to come home where you and my dear cousin Beau belong."

So I continued pluming my wings and became adept at keeping a tight grip on myself in terror of my real danger: Beau's erratic behavior and overinvolvement in the Emperor's life.

Every morning he galloped away to quest at Chapultepec or wherever Maximilian happened to be, returning in the evening with tales of Empire in which Maximilian was always good King Arthur, he Sir Lancelot and Juárez the evil dragon.

In July, for the second time since I'd been in Mexico, Matthew Fontaine Maury became my savior. Lonesome for his wife and eight children, and waiting for his oldest son, Dickie, to arrive at Córdoba with his family, Maury had frequent missions and meetings at Chapultepec, so he visited us often. He enjoyed the cool, fresh air, the enthralling view from the terrace and long walks with me about the countryside.

My lively exuberance, that every day in this rarefied air made even livelier, never seemed to weary him. He talked to me and wasted his time on me with free-hearted generosity. Somehow I wasn't at all astonished. At twenty-three you accept admiration from great men naturally as if you had earned it in some mysterious way.

Carlota was the only one at Chapultepec for whom Maury had any respect. Maximilian's wavering loyalties and volatile opinions disturbed him.

I had a suspicion that he kept the habits of his navy days and drank too much rum, but it never dimmed him. I am sure that the affection and compassion he felt for me as much as his unfailing good humor sustained me through that first long summer. I never discussed my anxiety about Beau. I didn't need to. Maury's fatherly gentleness toward Beau was evidence that he shared my concern!

In the evenings his big round head glistened in the lamplight as he bent over his scientific work. Beau was able to understand his diagrams for a prospective transatlantic cable, but my only comment was that it looked like a chain of snakes on gray rocks. Punishment for such malapertness was the pleasure of playing Chopin on the piano until bedtime, or a game of billiards, at which *he* excelled.

Maury's attitude toward Phillip was quite the reverse of his softness for Beau! Phillip fascinated him. I don't know which of us was more pleased at the sight of that dark dashing caballero in his *charro* riding clothes and jingling silver spurs.

Phillip was like a breezy wind from the mountains as he told of the progress of his exciting silver venture at Miramontes; his trips to Pachuca to study Angus McLeod's *modus operandi* and to learn where to obtain the so necessary quicksilver. The success he had in training the double pink roses of the garden on curved trellises and teaching the big bird to sing spirituals delighted him. He was enthusiastic about the way Elsie kept all the rooms and corridors full of fresh flowers and had taught him to dance a flamenco as wildly as the young Mexican boy who trained the fighting cocks.

When he did tell of failures in boiling sugar, finding worms on the young coffee plants and accidents in the silver mine, his very way of telling them was a refusal to acknowledge their existence. He had a gesture of his hands that seemed to solve them, whether pointing skyward to the Lord or outward to a curl that had escaped and fallen down against my neck.

"Now tell me what's happening to you and Bubba. Tell me ... " His eyes would study me with frightening insight.

I would go stiff and inattentive, allowing nothing to burst out from me except a mumble of feigned nonsense. Often I would be lucky, for just as Phillip started "Tell me ... " I would hear those familiar beloved footsteps and that marvelous voice calling "Angelica—I'm here," and I could turn and run away and believe that the world was still the circle of Beau's arms.

22

I agreed to become a lady-in-waiting to Carlota on September 17. It happened because Beau and Maury and I took dinner at Chapultepec Castle on Mexican Independence Day, September 16.

We clung to each other in the best soft-cushioned and fringe-shaded Corbina carriage as the four fat brown mules struggled up the steep ascent of Chapultepec—"the Hill of the Grasshopper." Everything looked bright and sparkling green, indescribably fresh after a hard morning rain. The Peruvian trees with their bending green branches and red berries glittered with raindrops and the deep green branches of the hoary cypresses sparkled.

Maury had just finished telling Beau that Maximilian had reluctantly given Prince John Magruder a hacienda at Córdoba as a sop for not keeping a more important promise, when we came on a group of filthy prisoners, chained together, hacking a clearing in the trees. In time to their chopping they were singing, to the tune of "La Paloma":

> "We saw you, Mama Carlota
> We saw you, soiled dove
> When you were at Lake Chalco
> With your secret love
> Mama Carlota is barren
> Mama Carlota is a whore."

I expected the slouching guards in Imperialist uniforms to strike the singers but they laughed and shrugged, whistling the tune themselves along with the prisoners. They continued whistling as they waved us along.

Beau and Maury admitted to having heard "Mama Carlota" sung on the streets in the city during the past summer.

"The Juaristi have found a way to wound her," Maury said. "Tell me the words."

"They are making fun of Carlota for having no children."

"It is a strain between them," Beau said. "It is the one thing I don't understand about Maximilian. He blames her entirely for their childless marriage. I don't like her very much but I know she wants an heir even more than he, Imperial-minded as she is."

"She's only twenty-five," Maury said. "Give her time."

And one of the prisoners shouted, "Give me a kiss, señorita!"

I put my hands over my ears.

*"Dame tu caja dulce!"** another called and laughed so hard as I ducked my head into Beau's shoulder that he fell in his irons before the guard's gun butt struck him in the face.

"What did he say?" Beau and Maury demanded simultaneously.

"Silliness."

"Why would that song about Carlota upset you?" Beau asked.

"Because it's a mean song."

"The prisoners are probably captured guerrillas or Juaristi. What harm could be in their song?"

"The harm is in the guards permitting them to sing it right on the castle grounds."

Maury said, "I don't like it either. The poor girl is in trouble enough at home."

"With whom?" Beau bristled forward, already defensive.

"Everybody. Surely you know about the decree she pushed through this summer while many of the ministers and the Emperor himself were away?"

"I was away too. Tell me."

"The decree having to do with the rights of the peons on the big haciendas. They are to be paid a living wage and all corporal punishment is to be abolished."

"Isn't that a good decree?" I asked.

"Wasn't freeing the slaves in the South a good law from the Northern view?" Smiling, Maury handed me a red flower he had picked from a hanging vine. "Of course the decree is good—from the idealist's point of view—but it has backfired on Carlota. The *hacendados* are dismissing the peons who insist on their rights and have closed the hacienda stores where they have bought on credit from generation to generation. The starving Indians blame their Emperor for their plight. Maximilian blames Carlota for the criticism he is receiving from the *hacendados*. Remember the *hacendados* are the ones who voted *for* an Empire. Another heartache for little Carlota, who felt she was making history."

Sighing I looked up at the fortress castle perched like a huge stone grasshopper on the basalt crag. The castle appeared even more formidable and cold gray close up than it did from our terrace, where distance lent it an element of enchantment.

---

*"Give me your candy box!"

"I wish we were going anywhere but to Chapultepec today."

"You will have a wonderful time," Beau said, "as you did in Cuernavaca."

"You will disappear with the Emperor as *you* did in Cuernavaca."

"But not I," said my precious Maury. "Won't I do as a sweetheart, Angelica?"

I laughed, more at myself than at my champion.

"Smell the wet cedars; the rain has brought out their pungency." Beau was so electric that when he put his big warm hand over mine and locked our fingers together I said I was thrilled to be on the way to Chapultepec and I meant it!

The dinner was not at all what I had expected. It was more like one of Mrs. Meriweather's Sunday dinners in Virginia than a royal feast.

Assembled in the great hall were the French Minister Dano, with a gaunt, sorrowful-eyed Mexican lady-in-waiting, Señora María Pacheco, General Count Thun, the Kuhacsavitches (she, poor thing, had to deal with the Mexican servants), the aristocratic Creole Count del Valle and his elegant Countess (they arranged all the royal functions), and the very rich del Barrios. Maximilian's favorite local courtier, Don Carlos Sanchez de Navarro was there as well with his protégé, Father Fischer, a sensual-looking, tonsured German priest with thick fingers and hypnotic pale blue eyes.

It was mail day for Europe. Everybody, including ourselves, had brought letters to travel in the Emperor's mail sack. We were comparing destinations when Maximilian, immaculate in a white linen frock coat, hurried from the garden trailed by a panting Luis Blasio.

The Emperor was waving a handful of letters he'd written this morning. "You did come!" He took my hand and kissed it after I'd curtsied, then made the rounds of the others, charmingly pleased that each one had honored him by coming today. Finally he invited Beau, Maury and me into a sitting room that joined Carlota's chamber. He opened the door without knocking and said in English in his rather high voice, "Carlota, here is your Mr. Maury and the Berriens."

She came out immediately, fanning herself with a sandalwood fan. She was dressed in a pale silvery silk that clung to her superb figure. Perspiration was running down the creamy magnolia skin of her throat.

"Sit on that sofa, Mr. Maury."

We both sat. Beau and Maximilian went over to a long window where a spider had woven an interesting web around a green moth. Baby ran around them in circles, barking. Señora Pacheco came to the door and motioned me to get up. Maury started to rise too but Carlota touched him gently with her plump little hand.

"The Emperor wishes you always to be seated. Now, about New Orleans—"

So far she hadn't even nodded to me. I should never have let myself in for this charade. While they discussed General Sheridan arresting Confederates in New Orleans who were attempting to board ships for Mexico, I remained standing, wondering how to feign a heart attack. No, typhus, I decided, as a furry rat ran behind a Chinese screen. "Eek!" it went as a trap snapped sharply.

I giggled nervously.

"You spoke, Mrs. Berrien?" Carlota's lips smiled but not her eyes.

"I apologize, Your Majesty. I was thinking of how my Aunt Dell would—"

"She is funny, that Aunt Dell?"

"Most Virginians are queer, Your Majesty. I wish you could meet my sister-in-law, Lucy Ellen, in Fredericksburg," dear kind Maury said. "But I guess I'm the queerest of them all."

"Never you, Mr. Maury," Carlota said softly and I realized she felt the same daughterly way toward him as I. My dislike for her lessened, but not much.

Dinner was announced. Carrying his little spaniel, the Emperor led off and we followed single file. Massive double doors opened into the long dark dining room with three beautiful Viennese chandeliers holding lighted candles, even at half-past three in the afternoon. An aide, Baron von Pelt, whispered in my ear, "On the left of Count Thun," and in Maury's "On the Empress's right."

A bewigged, liveried Mexican servant waited behind each chair. Beau had told me what a time General Almonte had had training them in Hapsburg etiquette. They had not quite learned. The room sounded like the tower of Babel: French, German, Spanish and English being spoken in broken and pure accents. Occasionally little Tudos ran in to inquire, in Hungarian, if his goulash pleased His Majesty and Maximilian nodded fondly. The dinner was heavy, the wines light. I didn't eat much. Beau sat near Maximilian and Father Fischer.

The priest was just back from Rome. He had stopped in New York and been appalled at the intensity of the pro-Juárez feeling there. We could expect the U.S. Army to lay siege to Chapultepec any day!

In German he told all sorts of shady stories of goings-on in the Vatican. José Luis Blasio translated a few. I thought them coarse and vulgar. Maximilian appeared to consider them funny. And so did Beau when Maximilian repeated them in English to him. And so did Señora Pacheco and Countess del Valle.

Count Thun made an effort to entertain me first in German, then in French. I responded in Spanish and English. We gave up and turned to the person on our other sides. I was sorry, for even though Agnes had not cared for him, he was a handsome magnetic man with whom Beau spent much time.

José Luis Blasio was on my right. "I'm sorry you and the Count can't communicate. I know he wants to express his gratitude to you for allowing your husband to take dangerous expeditions with the Emperor."

"I don't understand. Major Berrien speaks of his duties as pleasures."

"In a way they are. The Emperor loves his rides into the country, especially to Cuernavaca. He enjoys supervising the construction of his flower gardens at the Borda Palace, and going to the little village of Acapazingo, where he is building an Indian chalet with a water garden. These excursions are his favorite forms of relaxation. General Bazaine frowns on them, for the Emperor insists on traveling without a military escort and there is always the danger of his being kidnapped. As you can see I wouldn't be much help, but Major Berrien—ah, there is a man, *mucho hombre!*"

I choked on my wine making a great sputter. I knew Beau was frowning at me but I wouldn't look at him for I was frowning too. To think—he had been that close to Miramontes and not taken me! I would fix him when we got back to the Hacienda Contenta, which would be renamed Hacienda Furiosa!

Count Thun was speaking directly to me in German, Blasio interpreting as he spoke: "The army should present Major Berrien with its highest medal for protecting our Emperor when our troops are badly needed elsewhere. Even the fact of the two often being mistaken for each other is a shield for my sovereign."

"*Danke schön*, Count Thun."

He clicked his heels under the table and kissed my hand over the mango sherbet.

After dinner I called to Beau, who was vanishing with the men into the Emperor's study for brandy and cigars. Surely he heard but he pretended not to. Or maybe he really didn't. Blasio had commented at dinner on the mesmerism in Beau's eyes whenever he was in the presence of His Majesty.

So I went walking in the garden along with Señora Pacheco, behind Carlota. In a black dress with a high jabot of black lace and a string of heavy gold beads Señora Pacheco seemed shy and absent as a young nun. The dinner had been a sort of penance and ritual combined to the withdrawn, stiff soul. The conversation around her had seemed to float above her consciousness, never penetrating or disturbing her dutiful inner self. She told me she had been widowed five years ago when she was eighteen. We were the same age! Cloisters having been done away with in Mexico, Chapultepec became her retreat. She spoke in a plaintive, faded voice. It was clear that she revered the Empress and was blind to any fault in her.

Under the largest cypress tree in the garden Carlota turned around. "I have been listening to you and Señora Pacheco, Mrs. Berrien. I am pleased at your knowledge of Spanish. When I decided to ask you to become one of my ladies-in-waiting it was to help me understand American customs better. Now you can be of real help to me."

Señora Pacheco squeezed my hand pleadingly.

"Not for anything," I murmured to the señora; and to the Empress, "I have no training for such a position, Your Majesty."

"You play the piano beautifully. None of my other ladies can so entertain me. I would only require your services one full day a week. There is a vacancy. The unfortunate Señora Lucas de Alemán has just announced her pregnancy. I have a special wish for you, having heard so many excellent remarks about you from Mr. Maury."

"I will consider it, Your Majesty, but I am not suitable. My heart and mind are too often heavy with longing for my baby son."

Standing behind Carlota, Señora Pacheco shook her head at me and put her finger on her lips.

I leaned down, pretending to remove a pebble from my slipper. Straightening up I noticed a black butterfly fluttering over the center part on top of Carlota's head. It gave a bad feeling, the black butterfly on the small dark head. I was about to blow it away when Maximilian came down the path waving a gilt-banded cigar.

"Oh, wonderful! Oh, stand still, Charlotte. Don't even breathe."

She must have felt a tickle on her scalp. She slapped at the plait wound on top of her head like a crown. The gauzy wings lifted themselves out of reach onto a purple orchid hanging from a branch.

Maximilian threw down the cigar and stamped on it with a narrow shining boot, speaking harshly to Carlota in German.

110

Carlota put her hand on the top of her head as if to recapture the butterfly. Again I thought, she has the saddest eyes I have ever seen.

"Forgive me," she said in Spanish.

He collected himself and took her hand in his. "The black butterfly was one I've been seeking ever since we came here. Forgive *me*, little dove. Now, Mr. Maury says he cannot proceed with any more colonial business if it is handled by the Mexican ministers. He insists on transacting all business with me directly. Nor must the Mexican ministers have any say in his plans or affairs. It poses a problem for us. He plans to travel on the steamer leaving on November the thirteenth for France."

"No." Carlota pressed her handkerchief against her teeth. "He must not go. He is my friend."

"It is only to visit his wife," I put in, aware I was not supposed to speak out but she needed comfort. "He hasn't seen her for three years. He will come back."

Ignoring me, Maximilian said, "I told Mr. Maury to continue the conversation with you. You will make notes and give me a verbal explanation and have it all ready for me by four o'clock in the morning. Mrs. Berrien will remain with you. The major and I have something pressing to attend."

"What is more pressing than losing our plan for colonization?"

"You will understand later. *We* are not going to lose anything."

Señora Pacheco and I went with Carlota to her sitting room where Maury was waiting, sipping a large goblet of brandy. This time I was invited to sit. Carlota made notes as fast as he could talk. He spoke of his frustrations with the Emperor's broken promises and about prices and titles for land; protection against guerrillas; and of Bazaine putting Confederates in the French Foreign Legion who had come to Mexico expecting to be attached to the Emperor's Troops. He mentioned a proper Office for Immigration headquarters. His son, Dick, and his family were on their way from Virginia. Dick's help would be invaluable. The Soulés were letting him their house in the city for $150 a month. It could be a dwelling as well as the Immigration office. Dick would need a salary of $2,500 a year and he, Maury, should have $5,000. It would allow him to support his wife and other children in England. He had found that his cost of living, including servants, in Mexico City was 28 cents a day.

Carlota was clever, practical and businesslike. Despite his wanderings she kept him on the main issues: the bona fide offers of the Mexican government to the Confederate exiles as were related to land and taxes.

At half-past four he said, "You can execute more business in an afternoon than all the ministers can in a week."

"I believe I can," Carlota said enthusiastically. While Maury rose and refilled his goblet from a decanter on her desk, she told him about recently receiving a letter from her dearest friend, the Empress Eugénie of France, enclosing a copy of a long letter from the French Admiral Chabanne about Maury's "New Virginia" which commended the plan as a grand idea.

"The Decree of Colonization has been injured in the translation. It is not as good as I drew it or promised the immigrants." Maury shook his head and put his nose over the brandy.

Carlota had been sitting straight as a rod for over an hour. She appeared fresher and more relaxed than she had when we arrived. Weary, I drooped and slouched in my chair as I used to do when I was a too-tall adolescent. Had Beau walked in at that instant I would have murdered him for involving me in this scene. Don Carlos's wicked face flashed across my mind and his words echoed in my consciousness: "You and your husband don't belong in this play."

"Still," Carlota was saying positively, "the newspapers proclaim the Decree of Colonization to be the most important act of the Empire so far. Now, you must excuse me for a little while, Mr. Maury. Pacheco, call Martha Doblinger to rearrange my hair. I undid it when I mistook the butterfly for a mosquito. Pacheco, where are you?"

Poor Pacheco was sound asleep on a hard stool by the small fireplace in the corner. Carlota went over and poked her cheek with the pencil she had been using. Any wavering I had had about agreeing to become one of her ladies completely vanished. Never would I.

"What newspapers did Carlota mean?" I asked Maury, who was fast following Pacheco's example on the sofa after the Empress's boudoir door closed. "Wake up and talk to me."

"Go along!" He carefully set the empty goblet on a shaky gilt table. "It's time for my nap."

"No—I'm interested. Will the news of the Decree of Colonization be carried only in the Imperialist controlled papers—*The Mexican Times* and *El Diario del Imperio*? What will the Liberal *El Pájaro Verde* say of it? Or the French *L'Estafette*?"

"I didn't think you read the newspapers."

With difficulty I managed not to say anything caustic, as Maury, mellowed by brandy, proceeded to answer my question with no reference to its meaning.

"Well," he said, stretching out his legs and balancing his big head on the soft high back of the sofa, "just see how much more honorable and desirable my position is here than it would have been in Russia or France!"

"Are you talking to me?"

"No, honey, I was talking to Mrs. Maury. Now, you just sit still a while."

Carlota, wearing a swallow-tailed gold and white taffeta afternoon costume, her hair redone into glossy side curls and covered by a blond lace mantilla, joined the Kuhacsavitches, the del Valles, the del Barrios, Count Thun and Father Fischer along with my half-awake Confederate scientist and me in the darkening entrance hall where José Luis Blasio had summoned us. As if by prearrangement, the Imperial coach, drawn by six white horses, drew up in front of the castle at that exact moment.

Poor Pacheco, *her* hair in wisps down her perspiring cheeks, came running up with a beautiful little sandalwood fan which she handed the Empress.

"I had no idea the Emperor had driven out on an affair of state," Carlota murmured, leading us onto the terrace. It had gotten cloudy again, like the morning. Popocatépetl was shrouded in mist. The fields of maguey spreading out on either side stuck up like sharp black swords. The flat-roofed city was a jumbled pile of dark blocks; even the far towers of the cathedral, usually rosy red in the sunset, looked cold and gray.

The Imperial coach had several occupants. Curiosity was apparent on all our faces. Maury stood very close to me. His breath smelled awful. "The Emperor is sly," he whispered. "This is one of his tricks."

"Sh-h-h!" I held Maury's arm so he wouldn't lean on Count Thun. The Count's expression portended a thundercloud about to clap in our faces. Why had Blasio called everybody here on the terrace at the same time? Why were we huddling so silently? I remembered Beau's mischievous eyes in the cedar forest this morning.

The footman standing beside the coach turned the handle too quickly. The door flew open. His Majesty stepped out like a jack-o-box. We ladies collapsed in curtsies. The regal snap of Carlota's fan encircled us. Maximilian held out his arms. A pair of big freckled hands with a scorpion-shaped scar on one wrist put a little boy about two years old into them. Maximilian's blond beard rested on the curly hair of the child who kicked out at the footman's white wig. Gently Maximilian pulled back the child's foot, then looked up at Carlota.

"Before you read it in the newspapers—and they have all been given complete details—I want you to hear that I have formally adopted Augustin Iturbide, grandson of the former Emperor of Mexico, as my legal heir."

Carlota flinched as if he had struck her with a whip and, while Beau and a lady in black got out of the coach, she tore at her handkerchief with her teeth as she had done in Puebla when the Emperor left her alone at the Birthday Ball.

Maximilian steadied little Augustin on the flagstones and, in Spanish, bade him run to Carlota. "Go and kiss the lady in white."

"His mother is an American. She was not included in the agreement. Augustin Iturbide was born in the United States," I heard José Luis Blasio whisper to the Countess del Valle.

I caught Father Fischer's cat-that-swallowed-the-canary smirk and the slight but positive glance of recognition that passed between him and the child's aunt, the Princess Iturbide.

"We have long desired a child in the palace," Maximilian said to us, clustered about Carlota.

Augustin picked up a shell that was part of a flower arrangement and threw it at Baby which had run out to welcome her master.

Propelled by his gloating aunt, the chubby little boy in black satin and point lace approached Carlota.

She had a strange look in her eyes. It sent chills down my spine. I didn't know what I'd do if she hurt him. Coldly she looked down at the impish, rosy little face. Her fingers clenched tight around the fan for a moment, then she handed the fan to Augustin and with a royal rustle of silk petticoats marched decisively back into her sitting room and slammed the door.

23

Like the sun god in the early morning light, Beau suddenly appeared on the terrace from the darkness of the orange grove.

"I thought you were at Chapultepec." I tried to stifle the excitement his unexpected presence fires in me, but I could feel pink color flaming my cheeks. I must have had a premonition he would return to have put on my most becoming lilac muslin morning gown and left my hair hanging loose around my bare shoulders.

"I went, but the routine orders had been changed. Maximilian is riding into the city with Carlota instead of me this morning. He hasn't done that in a long time."

"They must have made up in the night." -

"Boy, was she furious! I didn't know he hadn't told her about Augustin."

"Why didn't he bring the mother instead of the aunt of the poor little thing?"

"Father Fischer advised him against it. The aunt won't compete with Maximilian for Augustin's affection. Don't feel sorry for the brat. He's spoiled as the devil."

"Carlota asked me to become one of her ladies yesterday but I refused. Now I am writing an acceptance because I felt sorry for her."

"Why would you feel sorry for her? She has a compulsion for perfection that would drive any man away."

"It's probably just her own need for protection, her fear of letting her crown slip even a teeny bit. Pacheco says she's pathetically taken up with herself. She's like a sensitive plant grown in the shade suddenly transplanted into a sunny place. She tries hard but she'll never be able to adapt to Mexico. Nor to little Augustin. That's really why I've accepted her offer. Who knows? I may be able to encourage her to enjoy the child."

"That will solve everything. Knowing you are at the castle will make my heart easier about you while I am away."

"If you're off for Cuernavaca I insist on going too."

"This is quite different. The Emperor is sending von Kodolitsch and me, under a white flag, to the northern frontier to find Juárez's headquarters. Our mission is to invite Juárez to meet with the

Emperor and work out an understanding between them for the good of the Mexican people."

"Juárez is a horrid man. He won't consider receiving you and he might shoot you on sight. Don Carlos says Juárez would never, under any circumstances, agree to a rapprochement with the Emperor. I refuse to let you travel on such a dangerous assignment."

"Oh, come on, Angel. The time is now. My being an American bringing the olive branch may tip the scales. Juárez's legal term of office will terminate at the end of November. The Mexican Constitution says that if no fresh election is possible the power will temporarily go to the President of the Supreme Court, Gonzalez Ortega. That is why the situation is so immediate. Ortega has taken refuge in the United States. This gives Juárez a chance to prolong his presidency, as the United States trusts the Indian himself, not the country. So long as *he* is President, they'll probably fight the Empire. Maximilian desperately needs Juárez's ruthlessness and intelligence. He can't count on Bazaine. Since he married the rich Creole, he would love to see the crown fall off Maximilian's head so he could pick it up and put it on his own. Better to share the Empire with Juárez than Bazaine, and better to be under Juárez's influence than that of the German priest, Fischer."

"You laughed louder than anyone at his remarks yesterday at dinner."

"He's witty as hell. I couldn't help laughing at those evil stories of monks and nuns at the Vatican."

"You can't go! Maury left at dawn to meet his son at the Carlota Colony. There's no telling when he'll come back. I won't send my letter to the Empress! I'll stay with Phillip at Miramontes."

"He's not there. He's with Angus at Pachuca."

"Elsie and Lencho will take care of me."

"Our link with the children is Maury's address in the city. It's vital for you to drive there every day and check for a telegram from Joab Pritchard while I am away."

"We've never had a telegram from Joab Pritchard."

"If anything happened to Edward wouldn't you want to know it immediately?" Beau was up to his old tricks. He sat down on the bench beside me and began running his fingers through my hair as he does before we make love. I liked it but I pushed his hand aside.

"All right," he said, grabbing a handful of hair and twisting it tenderly about my throat, "if you must have the truth—I want to know you are waiting right here in case we finish sooner than von Kodolitsch thinks possible. Suppose I am wounded or killed or taken prisoner? The Emperor would be able to notify you instantly."

A fuzzy-haired maid in a white *huipil* fetched a tray of melon and pineapple and orange slices laid in a pattern on fresh green leaves. She was followed by the head house man in a gay red shirt, balancing a tray on his head. It held a silver coffee pot, a basket of tortillas and buns, and an earthen pot of honey.

"Are you ready for breakfast, señora?"

"Yes, thank you. Please bring another cup and plate for the señor."

"Immediately, señora, and eggs perhaps?"

"Would you like some boiled eggs, Beau?"

"Yes, ten, soft, with butter. God, for a plate of hominy! I hate those limp tortillas."

As the sun rose higher, and the eggs came, boiled perfectly, things were cozier between us than they had been in months.

"Beau, tell me your real thoughts about the Emperor. I can't understand him."

"Maybe I don't either. When I am with him things seem clear and sensible that, when I am with you, take on quite a different meaning. But he's a charming, delightful companion who spirits me into his world and shuts out this one."

"We can still go to South America."

"The Amazon would have intrigued me, Mexico doesn't. But when we were in Havana, Mexico seemed so much nearer the children. I know you think I don't talk about Edward and Button enough but when I do it tears me apart inside. I've been Button's only real father since he was a baby and our little one—"

He dropped the egg he was cracking. It spattered all over the silver tray.

I handed him another egg and started on a different subject to quiet his agitation.

"What does Carlota think of Juárez?"

"She has nagged the Emperor constantly against making any overtures to Juárez. He doesn't pay her much attention anymore. But I repeat, better lean toward Juárez than Father Fischer or the French."

"Doesn't Maximilian love Carlota? They seemed so happy in Puebla last June."

"He loves her. I don't think he is *in* love with her. He respects her mind and he depends on her. She simply doesn't fascinate him as you do me. Her rejection of little Augustin yesterday has prompted him to go against her in this at once, as a punishment.

"Now—kiss me. None of the damned servants are looking. Suppose they are. Don't think of them as real people—"

"I wish you wouldn't talk like that."

"I won't if you will come into the orchard with me. There's a lovely double hammock slung under a special tree full of the sweetest blossoms—"

PART IV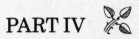

Carlota

NOVEMBER 1865

Then gather the fairest flowers from thy gardens
To bind round thy brow
And seize the joys of the present
Ere they perish....

EMPEROR NEZAHUALCOYOTL
(THE HUNGRY FOX), 1450

24 🌿

In early November a sudden crisis of state saved me from going completely crazy waiting for Beau to return from the north. The emergency had to do with a new financial wizard, Monsieur Langlais of Paris, sent by Napoleon to attempt to straighten out the Empire's money matters.

Having no intention of "roaring like a sucking dove" (to quote Aunt Dell), Langlais immediately set about putting a stop to the Emperor's beautification projects, ruthlessly dismissed dishonest Treasury officials and demanded strict economy measures which so antagonized the Conservative Mexican ministers that the lot of them threatened to resign and go over to the Liberal Juaristi.

To avert such a showdown Maximilian was forced to cancel a long-cherished goodwill visit to the Yucatán Peninsula and remain in Mexico City. He decided to send the Empress in his place. Yucatán was important, being the only state left in Mexico whole-heartedly anti-Juárez and dedicated to the Empire.

I was overjoyed at the prospect of leaving the gloomy old castle.

The gloom had started a month ago on the very day I arrived to begin my new career.

"You couldn't have come at a worse time." María Pacheco had been standing at the head of the terrace steps, shading her eyes with her hand, for she wore no hat and the reflection of the October sun on the window panes bothered her.

"How did you know I was here? I've just dismounted," I called up to her.

"I heard you laughing."

"The horse groom and little Augustin were making faces at Father Fischer."

"So, you arrive with laughter. Good luck to you, that you may not depart in tears."

I was about to ask why today was a bad time for me when Carlota came from the hall and began pacing up and down the terrace, talking agitatedly to herself.

"Sh-h-h." María Pacheco caught my arm. "A very bad time."

"She behaves as if she doesn't see us or hear us," I whispered, drawing my riding skirt up on my arm.

"She is like this often since the coming of La Prima and the little boy; morose is she and filled with dark thoughts; indifferent to everything she was once interested in. Before the boy she always sat by the Emperor's side in council meetings and participated in decisions. Now, when she does attend a meeting she is sent out if an important matter comes up. She ran out here from the council room. I heard the door slam. Oh-oh-oh—and look who sees her—"

The sour-faced Princess Iturbide rose from a wrought-iron bench at the far end of the terrace and motioned Father Fischer to fetch Augustin to her.

Carlota swept past them as though they were invisible, though the child waved at her and held out a pretty stone he'd picked up in the driveway.

General Bazaine marched out, his handsome face beaming with excitement. He didn't see Carlota.

"It's a *fait accompli*," he said to Father Fischer. "My description of our defeats in Sonora and Chihuahua frightened the pants off him. It's kill or be killed now. There never was an alternative but he refused to believe it."

Princess Iturbide waved her fan at Bazaine. "*Ole!*" she cried.

The "*Ole*" reached Carlota, whose pacing had brought her face to face with Bazaine.

"He didn't sign the decree, did he? He wouldn't. I know he wouldn't."

"Your Majesty!" Embarrassed, Bazaine bowed to the Empress and ran down the steps ignoring her question.

"Father Fischer, come and tell me what Bazaine said to you."

Light as a cat, large though he was, Father Fischer had vanished.

Voices of ministers and officials were heard in the hall. Liveried Mexican servants came with silver trays. They bowed first to the Princess and then to the Empress.

Something tickled my nose. I sneezed three times—loudly.

Carlota tightened her mouth into an ugly straight line.

"And who are you?" she asked coldly, inescapably confronted by my physical presence.

"I am your new lady-in-waiting, Your Majesty." Beau would have been proud of my stiff curtsy.

"Yes, yes, I know that and I seem to remember having seen you somewhere before, but I have forgotten your name. . . . I am sure the signing was not important. It never is."

It was in all the newspapers the next day. The October Decree, signed into law by Maximilian, Emperor of Mexico, pronounced the death sentence on anyone found or captured with arms in his hands or known to belong to a guerrilla band. No right of appeal would be given to the accused and he would be executed without trial within twenty-four hours. Should an enemy soldier be captured in battle the officer in command would preside over a routine court-martial, empowered to hand out sentences of life or death to the prisoner.

At noon the Emperor rode to the National Palace in an open carriage with little Augustin and Baby. But the Zocalo was so packed with angry people he ordered his coachman to turn around and take him back to Chapultepec.

María Pacheco and I were playing cards by the window. Maximilian's full lower lip looked loose as he spoke to Carlota rapidly in German. She was embroidering a yellow lily on a square of white silk, but as he talked her fingers trembled so much the embroidery hoop wobbled as she held it and she had to stick the needle in the heart of the lily, put the hoop down and clasp her hands in the lap of her dress.

"*Nein*," she said, shaking her head.

Maximilian repeated the same German words. Again she said, "*Nein*," and shook her head while the little spaniel danced happily around the room jumping at a large fly that buzzed in the ominous silence. Finally, exasperated, Maximilian turned to us, fretting in his rather poor Spanish.

"Ladies, it is important the Empress cancels her drive to the *paseo*. None of you is to leave the palace. I have performed our duty for today." Fingering the part in the middle of his beautiful beard he waited for Carlota to say something.

"If you had listened to me instead of to Bazaine and refused to disband the original Mexican Army, the guerrillas would not have had a chance to form into such a formidable force." Carlota spoke in Spanish and told the Emperor to continue the same so no one could accuse them of plotting anything.

"I make the effort to arrange an efficient native army but Bazaine demands the money and matériel for his own French soldiers. I write a long letter to Napoleon. I am blaming Bazaine for this bad situation," Maximilian said plaintively.

Carlota realized her strength. This was the first time her husband had sought her counsel in weeks. Without looking up, stitching steadily, she said firmly, "Bazaine also wrote Napoleon a long letter blaming you for everything. I heard of it through my father. Especially Bazaine blamed you for sending away your two strongest Mexican generals on a holiday at your expense."

"Marquez was overcruel; Miramon overreligious. They play into Juárez's hand. Go home they do one after another the soldiers."

"You sent Miramon away because he was too priestlike; yet you have permitted a lecherous German priest to influence you to sign this draconian October Decree that is turning the people against us. And, Maxl, you really must take more trouble with your verbs."

Pacheco whispered to me, "The decree is no different from the way it was when Santa Anna ruled and fought. Shall I say it to comfort him?"

"Don't dare," I whispered back.

Maximilian gave a sigh that almost took him down onto the carpet. "What will be our next move, Little Charlotte?"

Carlota jabbed the needle once again into the lily's heart and stood up straight as an arrow.

"We must show the people we are not afraid. I will drive out in the open barouche with my ladies as usual. Are you sure you comprehended what was happening in the Zocalo? Perhaps you were overcautious." In her voice was fear, but also an overriding sense of assertive stubbornness.

"I will discuss it with Father Fischer. Perhaps I was." Maximilian left the room quickly, followed by his merry Baby.

She turned to us. "Go at once and dress in bright colors. It is nearly three o'clock. Before we drive to the Viga we will attend a program of Spanish dancers at the theater."

Despite our crinolines we fitted comfortably in the clumsy open barouche. Handsome, blond Colonel Alfred van der Smissen of the Empress's own guard, considered the bravest fighter of them all, and three other mustachioed Belgians rode escort.

It was a breezy afternoon. Scarlet poinsettias blazed like cheerful fires in the cypress grove below the castle, but as soon as we reached the Alameda we were aware of hostility: averted faces, turned backs, the absence of any *Oles* or *Vivas*.

There was an ominous crowd in front of the theater. They were listening to a speaker who had been hoisted up on a pair of brawny shoulders. I recognized him at once: the outrider, Paco! He stopped in the middle of a sentence as I stepped down from the barouche after the Empress. Everyone stared at Carlota but no one removed his sombrero. Van der Smissen jerked out his big pistol and knocked off the sombreros of those nearest the Empress; then he pointed the pistol at Paco, who instantly removed his sombrero and spun it through the air onto the ground at my feet.

Carlota clutched van der Smissen's sleeve and looked pleadingly up at him. "What should I do, Alfred?"

For a split second it appeared as if he were going to put his arm around her. Then he snapped to attention. "Ladies, get in the barouche quickly." Though there were four armed guards, there were hundreds of *them* threatening. He was a soldier, not a martyr. "Head for Chapultepec as rapidly as possible," he ordered the coachman.

As we clattered off I couldn't resist looking back. Someone had handed Paco his hat. He was wiping the dirt from the rolled white brim and singing so loud the crowd easily joined in, for his voice was clear and powerful:

> *"Fly away, Mama Carlota*
> *Fly away, cruel dove*
> *We will set snares and nets*
> *To capture you and him."*

You would have thought that would have ended our sallies into the city. Not so. Carlota insisted on our continuing our daily drives to the *paseo* or to the cathedral, but never again in an open vehicle. We traveled in a curtained coach drawn by six white mules with bells on their harness so that there would be no doubt who was passing.

Count del Valle and Miguel López said that when the Emperor rode out with them on horseback or in the carriage with little Augustin, people responded courteously to his pleasant waves and smiles, occasionally even throwing a rose or a kiss in his direction.

Evil tongues whispered that Carlota and General Bazaine had influenced the gentle Emperor to sign the cruel decree and the Mexican people believed them, for they had never liked those two disdainful ones—the Empress and the French marshall.

The castle had been dull enough before the October Decree, now it was deadly. The Emperor was frequently ill with dysentery or malaria. State dinners and dances and soirées were more often canceled than held. The del Valles and the Kuhacsavitches never knew from one day to the next what orders to expect or to give. The isolation in the gloomy castle was a hundred times worse than my isolation on Hilton Head during the Civil War. And then, on the very night I decided to write my resignation, I saw the Empress smile for the first time since I came to Chapultepec.

I was walking in the cypress grove planning what I would say in my letter when Carlota passed by. I slipped behind a giant tree out of sight. She was riding a splendid gray thoroughbred. She had a white dust mantle tossed over her dark, beautifully fitting riding habit. A feathery white hat with a long gauze veil floating behind changed her into a fairy queen racing through the gloaming pursued by Alfred van der Smissen, his yellow hair blowing. He had on a scarlet uniform and was expertly handling a spirited white stallion. Carlota turned her head to look at him and her eyes glowed like dark jewels. Her usually tight lips were parted in a gay smile.

"I simply couldn't believe it," I told Maria Pacheco later.

Pacheco was polishing her long fingernails with pink paste that matched the sudden color that flared in her cheeks. "He's been in Michoacan. They often ride out together when he is on duty here at the castle. He is her countryman. He makes her less lonely."

"Where do they go?"

"Here and there. She said they were going to Lake Chalco tonight. Will be a full moon. They haven't been there in a long time."

I remembered the prisoners singing last summer:

> "We saw you, Mamá Carlota
> With your secret love,"

but I didn't tell María Pacheco that. Nor did I deliver my resignation.

The next morning Carlota invited me to accompany her to Yucatán, I being the best horse rider among her ladies.

Carlota made no effort to hide her delight at the prospect of getting away from Chapultepec and the sour Princess Iturbide and the lively little boy who wasn't her little boy, nor her pleasure that the arrogant super-soldier, Alfred van der Smissen, was to be in charge of our journey to Vera Cruz.

25 ❧

Sending a message to Phillip to come and take me to Hacienda Contenta to get my summer clothes was easy. Maximilian's gardeners constantly traveled back and forth between the Hill of the Grasshopper and Cuernavaca.

"You simply can't go to Yucatán," Phillip blustered. "I want you entirely removed from court circles. Stay at Miramontes where I can look after you. Last week a Mexican officer in the Imperial Army, Raoul Mendez, a cruel and vindictive man, murdered two Republican generals—Ateaga and Salazar. They had been leading the anti-Imperialist forces in Michoacan but neither could be classed as bandits. Their execution has further fired the hatred of the people against the government. Since the October Decree no one close to Their Majesties is safe. The decree has given fuel to the anti-Imperialist propaganda in the United States. I am convinced that there is no hope of peace in Mexico now."

Phillip was a realist. And the most interesting kind of realist— the kind with broad shoulders. He was one of the few men I knew who could hold two completely opposite concepts in his mind at once such as Plato's Dialogues and why if you put an eagle's feather on a man's head while he is artfully carving a leg of lamb into wafer-perfect slices he will start to tear the meat apart in greedy chunks. He stood before me now in skintight trousers and a loose chamois shirt, and his eyes roamed all over me as if he was thoroughly familiar with every part.

Suddenly I was enveloped in his arms. It wasn't a thrilling kind of embrace but it was wonderful to be enveloped totally. It made me realize what a stranger's wilderness Chapultepec had been for me—how lonely.

I slept well that night but the next morning Phillip persisted. "Stay with me at Miramontes till Bubba returns. Elsie will pamper you like an Empress and I will show you our silver mine."

"I promised Beau not to leave Carlota while he was away. She has made a point of my accompanying her. Yucatán will be a diversion for me. I need a diversion, Phillip."

We were drinking coffee in the long dining room by a small fire, for the November wind had turned chill and the terrace was a shroud of mist.

"When does she start out?"

"In three days."

"So do I."

"To Miramontes?"

"No, to Pachuca. I would have returned to Miramontes had you not been so stubborn. Angus is in big trouble."

I closed my eyes. I didn't want to hear any disturbing news this morning. Drinking coffee with Phillip in front of a cheerful fire had given me the illusion of home. Suddenly the coffee tasted bitter.

"I hate to bring bad news to you," he was saying.

I stood up and walked over to the window that looked out toward the volcanoes, dissolved in clouds. "Oh, well," I said wearily, "so long as it isn't about Beau I can survive it."

"It concerns Flora."

I was ashamed of my feeling of relief. I turned, fiddling with the satin bow at the waist of my pink velvet morning robe.

"When you saw her at Bazaine's wedding she had changed, hadn't she?"

"Not really. She was jealous because I was standing close to the Empress. Angus fixed everything, though. That was almost five months ago. What's wrong with her?"

"She's covered with sores and most of her hair has fallen out. She's determined to leave Mexico at once. Angus is going with her."

I thought of the bright-eyed Angus who could "do anything" and was on his way to becoming the richest "mon" in all Mexico.

"Close your mouth, Angelica."

"Poor Angus."

"I expected you to say 'poor Flora.' You never do what I anticipate."

Our talk was interrupted by the arrival of breakfast during which Phillip explained that Angus had requested the Emperor to accept Flora as a lady-in-waiting to the Empress when the first symptoms of hives and falling hair appeared. The English doctor in Pachuca blamed everything on Flora's distaste for the primitive little mining village and the climate. Maximilian turned Angus's request over to the Kuhacsavitches who carelessly tossed it aside. Two months later they handed it to Colonel Miguel López to attend.

"I know López. He's one of the Emperor's favorites. He's always looking at himself in the mirror. The servants say he has two faces!"

"He was very high-horse with Angus. Ironically *you* had just been appointed to the only vacant post. López's rudeness to Angus came on a day when your admirer, Don Carlos, approached him with an offer from Juárez to represent the Liberals as regards future Mexican trade with Great Britain."

"Angus will be good at that—but I thought he was on the Emperor's side."

"Angus says it's easy to adore Maximilian but impossible to respect him. And, prepare yourself—"

"Couldn't you wait until we are alone to tell me?"

"The servants don't understand English. You just don't want to hear what you know I'm going to say. Well, being realistic—"

"You've joined the Juaristi."

He lifted his head. His eyes opened very wide. And he burst out laughing. "Not the army, just the party. You know I'd never put on a soldier's uniform."

"Why did you?"

Phillip started telling about going with Angus and Don Carlos to Chihuahua but paused as I frowned disapprovingly.

"No," Phillip murmured, "you couldn't possibly understand what I learned from that good, just man."

"If Juárez is such a good just man why does he refuse to talk with the Emperor who, even his enemies concede, is a good just man too?"

"There is no way anyone could persuade Juárez to come to terms with an Austrian Emperor of his Mexico."

"Beau is convinced he can persuade him."

"Don't tell me that's the mission Bubba has hared off on! Of all people to send! Is he alone?"

"With Colonel von Kodolitsch and a platoon of Horse Guards."

"Prussians! I can see Juárez now taking their measure and cocking his pistol."

"Oh, Lord, I'm so confused. I'll do what you wish, Phillip, I won't go to Yucatán."

Phillip was apparently fascinated with the bow I had managed to untie completely. He reached out and deftly retied it across my stomach—very tight.

"Would you like me to make a trip to Virginia and bring you your little baby?"

The tenderness in his voice undid me. My throat felt dry and tight. A tear rolled down my cheek but he wasn't watching. He was putting a spindly stick of wood on the little fire.

"I daren't compare this with the great logs and all that juicy fat lightwood we used to burn at Cotton Hall." He laughed, sounding very young. "You didn't answer. Do I head for Virginia or the north, searching for Bubba to make sure he doesn't get his head knocked off by Benito Juárez?"

"You know the answer. But bless you for saying what you did. Edward and Button belong at Miramontes, not here at Tacubaya. And they need a father. So be careful of yourself and Beau, dear Phillip."

He took my face in his hands and looked at me, long and hard. He was two inches taller than I. He had to bend down a little to kiss the tip of my nose.

"Some people," he said, "are very fortunate in their relatives. Though you didn't choose me, here I am saving your credulous spouse. You will proceed to Yucatán knowing all will be well and I will drink another cup of coffee and ride north, stopping in Pachuca. Angus will know how to pick up Bubba's trail. I'll follow Herr Berrien straight to Juárez's headquarters. If necessary I can always turn to Don Carlos for help. He's the most influential of all the secret hierarchy."

26 ❧

On November 4 our entourage trotted down the Hill of the Grasshopper toward the Valley of Mexico en route to Vera Cruz. We were led by the Empress in a black velvet riding dress, mounted on her beautiful gray thoroughbred, just a step ahead of Alfred van der Smissen and another gold-braided officer. I was comfortably mounted on a strong American gelding, having declined a swansdown seat in the royal coach with Felix Eloin (who was to be the Empress's adviser), both the del Barrios, María Pacheco and Carlota's maid, Martha Doblinger. I squirmed a bit in my wide side-saddle just to remind my backsides of the punishment they had taken six months ago on the same dreadful road to the coast.

Foreign Minister Ramírez and General Uraga rode on either side of me, but the Ambassadors of England and Belgium, their eyes sharpened for prospects of trade in Yucatán, sat in a wide-bodied coach with José Luis Blasio and the royal chaplain and young Dr. Basch, the Emperor's new personal physician.

No sun shone. The wind blew down from the mountains with ice in its teeth. The helmets of the Guards and the Hussars made a parade before us and bright birds flew up and down like flags above our heads. Wrapped in furs, Maximilian stood between Father Fischer and Miguel López, waving a kid-gloved hand until Carlota's horse rounded the first curve.

Ramírez called across me to Uraga, "Ten pesos he'll be at Cuernavaca by night."

And Uraga answered, "She waits patiently, his *querida*, for him and the old woman who brings *los niños!*"

What a change from their obsequious attitudes in the hall where we gathered. They couldn't have heard the Emperor's final instructions to Carlota but they had stood with bowed heads, their hats in their hands.

Standing close behind Carlota I *had* heard, though the Emperor spoke very low in English, "Be wary of Eloin and Uraga who always want to be so aristocratic, which will get you nowhere in Yucatán, where the people are very democratic and have no use for pomposity and etiquette. Dress simply, which in any case is more becoming to you. Invite the local landlords and Indian leaders to your gatherings, for the more these people are invited the more they will be won over. That will impress the foreign ambassadors and we need their support. Above all never keep people waiting. Mérida and Campeche are the oldest European cities in the New World. I will not be beside you to soften any of your snobberies. Remember, the manner in which you handle this mission could mean much to the Empire. You will be accorded all honor as the sovereign. I have no doubt of your behaving as one. You were born a queen, little Charlotte."

When we arrived in Puebla on November 6 it was a shock to ride through the threateningly silent, shuttered streets, despite banners proclaiming the Empress's arrival, and compare it to the flower-decked "*Viva*"-shouting city of her birthday fiesta in June.

"Puebla is embittered by the cost of the French occupation and the fact of the October Decree," Labastida explained, in his sonorific voice as he welcomed us into his palace, bristling with armed guards and sullen servants.

After a disastrous banquet to which nobody who was invited came, we went to the theater. Seated in red leather chairs, we watched a pantomime about brigands entering a house. We were actually frightened when we realized that the audience was not hissing at the brigands on stage but at us!

We were supposed to rest in Puebla for two days. But the unfriendly atmosphere and the vulgar remarks in Spanish (which few of the Austrian or French understood and which the Mexicans in our escort ignored) decided Carlota to proceed at once with the dreaded ascent of the Cumbres.

It was awful. At least in June the weather had been fine, now at the end of the rainy season the roads were full of holes, the torrents swollen and terrible mud was everywhere. The royal coach stuck fast and the one carrying the chaplain, the doctor and the secretary turned over. Poor José Luis Blasio lost his glasses and Dr. Basch fell on his nose and broke it. By the time we reached Jalapa I was crazy with exhaustion.

We stayed in the fine house of a rich family. A bed was never so welcome, even shared with Pacheco, who lay holding herself together stiff as a pine pole, lest our toes or our arms should accidentally come in contact.

In the middle of the night, Martha Doblinger, her head shrouded in an enormous nightcap, her eyes red from weeping, ran in with a candle and told us to get up and come at once to the Empress. She was having one of her spells.

Not wearing a corset, my riding skirt was easy to step into. Leaving Pacheco struggling with strings, I followed Martha to the big shadowy room where Carlota, her eyes wild, ordered me to ring for a carriage to take her to the house of the Mayor of Jalapa. She would demand of him why he hadn't met her on her arrival at the city gate and why there had been no reception or ball in her honor for tonight.

There was no reasoning with her. I couldn't find van der Smissen. He was at the garrison. At last, I don't know how, I managed to get us into a carriage.

The guard at Don Carlos's gate told us that the house was empty. The Mirandas y Faggoagas were in the south.

Carlota insisted on entering.

I remembered the majordomo's name. "Call Joaquin," I said.

The guard, terrified of the madwoman who claimed to be the Queen of Mexico, rushed away and returned with the majordomo, Joaquin, muttering in his nightshirt. Joaquin curtly explained that the house was empty. Don Carlos and Doña Teresa were not at home. Nobody was at home. We must go away and come again on a Friday; any Friday.

"Light the candles," Carlota ordered shrilly, and, preceded by Joaquin, followed by me, wandered through the large empty rooms as if looking for something she could not find.

I struck a table and stepped on a live chicken. Thinking my candle was a strange daybreak he began crowing ardently. I stepped back and realized that I was alone. Carlota and Joaquin had vanished. I could hear her running along the tiled floor of the long gallery and Joaquin clumping after, begging her to stop, oh, stop, and depart, at least until the day-dawn.

I was in the salon in which I had paid my first miserable Mexican visit. I touched my hot candle to five tapers in a branched silver candlestick. I replaced the glass dome over the bouquet of wax flowers, displaced when I bumped into the table. Beside the dome were two pipes. I touched one. It was warm. I peered down. It was smoking. Picking it up I put it to my lips and drew in a delicious essence. I pulled deeper, speculating on the way the candlelight shone on various objects, especially the beautiful *cancela* at the far end of the room. It was then I heard the voice—

"Señora Angel!"

It wasn't the Empress. It wasn't Joaquin. But it *was* familiar!

"Here! Bring the pipe."

A long bare arm thrust itself through the openwork spindles of the *cancela*. A tapered ivory hand beckoned. "Come," wheedled the voice, "exquisite, absolute Angel, bring me the pipe."

Holding tight to my candlestick with one hand and the pipe with the other I forced my feet to tiptoe the length of the room to the openwork screen. I put my face against the spindles. Candlelight immediately picked up the statue of the Virgin. But suddenly she was blotted out as a dark object moved in front and put itself up against my face. Instead of into the Virgin's sweet smiling eyes I found myself staring straight into a pair of shining jaguar eyes.

I shut my eyes. I screamed. I know I screamed. But no sound was heard except soft laughter from behind the screen.

"Her Majesty has taken me by surprise."

Bare hands lifted up a papier-mâché head covered in jaguar skin revealing the melancholy priestlike face of the Mayor of Jalapa. His eyes lit up gleaming momentarily, with the quickly veiled, sly cunning of a wild animal.

"Is Doña Teresa back there with you?" I whispered.

"We, my wife and I, are not in the city, having been notified of the coming of the Empress." Clearly visible behind the openwork design, Don Carlos's well-formed body was entirely naked.

I wanted to laugh—to cry—to scream again—this time out loud. I lifted the candlestick higher, nearer the screen. There was another form crouched on the floor at his bare feet, a naked skinny female, wearing a dog's head covered in coarse white hair.

He grabbed my wrist. My arm went limp, helpless to pull itself away. The touch of his clammy fingers started me shuddering all over. His voice begging me to give him the pipe was low and intimate. I held the pipe behind me where he could not snatch at it. But it was as if the beam of candlelight was tying us together in a jesting, teasing travesty. It was as if we were merging in a ghastly, wavery way. And I couldn't find the strength to move. I just kept watching his animal eyes coming closer and closer. If that face had touched mine, I would have fainted, for suddenly I could feel his panting breath spray orgiastically into my eyes and mouth.

"Señora! Señora! Are you in the salon?" Joaquin and the Empress were standing in the doorway leading to the gallery. I must not have screamed aloud. Not caring what I bumped into or turned over, I ran straight out onto the gallery in front of the Empress and I did not excuse myself. I rushed blindly down the stairs and climbed into the carriage ahead of her.

Joaquin put his knotty worried face in the carriage window. "What happened to you back in there?"

"Nothing," I moaned, feeling deadly sick, "nothing. Here, take this pipe. It's not tobacco. What is it?"

"Opium," he said brusquely. "Doña Teresa will be unhappy and hurt if she should hear that you had come to her house and she not here to receive you courteously. She is a true lady."

"She will not hear." I laid my head back and clenched my fists. The jaguar and the she-dog! Surely it was a horrible fantasy? Surely such things didn't actually take place—

"Even that bird-brain Pacheco has more courage than you. Move over and stop shaking. You are occupying more than your share of the seat as usual," Carlota said, grinding her elbow into my side. I hated her.

27 ❧

Yet I admired Carlota two days later as she stepped out from a hastily erected tent at Paso del Macho, looking composed and immaculate, holding her riding crop high as if it were a scepter. None of the hundreds of Paris-bonneted ladies and frock-coated gentlemen of Vera Cruz who had ridden out on the train to escort the Empress the rest of the way had any inkling that less than an hour earlier she had been draggled, dusty and bone-weary from days in the saddle and nights in uncomfortable lodgings. Martha Doblinger was a wizard!

Wearing an olive silk taffeta traveling suit pinstriped in yellow and trimmed in black silk frogs, and a small yellow feather hat, Carlota was a perfect picture of royal fortitude as she stepped aboard the train.

After the threatening silences, lewd songs and mean remarks she had been subjected to ever since leaving Chapultepec, it was a pleasure to be part of her reception in Republican Vera Cruz (which had prospered excessively, tradewise, under the Empire). The whole city was a fiesta of flags, bunting, flowers and white doves flying. All the church bells pealed at the same time. *Viva*'s and *Ole*'s and *Bienvenida*'s came from every throat. Our steps were jaunty and light as we kept time to happy music and followed the gilded chariot, made by local craftsmen especially to carry the Empress, through the friendly streets.

The sight of Mount Orizaba soaring and shining on the horizon rekindled my soul, somewhat dimmed by the disgusting episode at the house of Don Carlos in Jalapa. I determined never to speak to Don Carlos again even if, on some official occasion, we found ourselves face to face. Fortunately he took no part in our two festive days in Vera Cruz where we were banqueted and serenaded and delighted with habaneras and waltzes.

Carlota was her most appealing self: "I realize the cheers are not for me, but because I am the Emperor's wife," she said in her formal speech to the town council.

"Van der Smissen is advising her well," Sir Peter Campbell-Scarlett commented to me. "A pity he isn't accompanying us to Yucatán."

I agreed. Seeing her as she was in Vera Cruz made it hard to believe she had that other dark side I had seen in Jalapa.

At the mayor's ball for her the night before we sailed she was radiant. She wore her most becoming ball gown of white mull embroidered with cattails in Turkey work and lilies of the valley in pearls and satin. After having properly begun the dancing, partnered by the mayor, she danced only with Alfred van der Smissen the rest of the evening. He was a powerful waltzer, often lifting her from the floor, turning and twisting her around as if both were in a rapture of flying. And once I saw him kiss the top of her head and heard her happy laugh.

Angus McLeod showed up midway through the evening. He made a beeline for me. He and Flora were in Vera Cruz en route to England. Being Angus, he heard of the ball and came, leaving frigid Flora sulking in their hotel room.

"Ye owe me this evening," he said, "because 'twas ye became a proper lady-in-waiting to Her Majesty and not Mrs. McLeod. It broke Mrs. McLeod's heart."

"I wish she had. I feel no need of being close to royalty," I replied testily, moving away from him.

He swayed on his feet and caught hold of my arm, slurring, "Ne'er mind. 'Twouldn't have changed the outcome."

Unaccustomed to being at a ball without a partner to come to my aid when someone annoyed me, I longed for Beau—or Phillip. Dared I leave the ballroom before Her Majesty? When I made mistakes in Creole etiquette the del Valles and the del Barrios looked at each other and raised their eyebrows. (After all, what can one expect from an American?) I decided to leave anyway.

As if he read my thoughts, Angus let his restless fingers clench tighter around my arm and said, "What's happening to ye is like what's happening to me. It's like—what's it like? It's like being on a horse that's bolting."

"Let me go, Angus." I struck his wrist hard with my fan.

"Don't be so fussy. If ye don't come outside and listen to me for ten minutes, I'll make a scene right here in front of the Empress, I will."

A look at his distraught eyes convinced me. What was he so agitated about? Was he afraid Phillip had told me of his Juarist activities? What did he want of me? To hear something scandalous about Carlota he could use in England to prejudice Disraeli against trade with the Empire? I don't like turncoats and I resented his pushing his way into this happy party for the Empress.

The hot torchlit patio was filled with heavy-scented night-blooming flowers and swarms of bats and mosquitos.

I was wearing my blue flounced organdy and hated to sit on a dark bench, not knowing what birds had roosted on it. Angus lurched down beside me, spilling oozy chocolates in my lap, worse than birds. I said nothing, realizing he was very drunk as well as very garrulous.

"Old Bustamente said he knew that Santa Anna passed the days of 1822 and 1823 in cockfighting and gambling, yet if they *were* his main occupations he found time to overturn an Empire as a sideline. He was a hero with a touch of brutality was Santa Anna. Juárez isn't heroic like him at all but he'll overturn the Empire as a sideline too. Then he'll call me back from England to step up into my proper place—he will—"

Sir Peter Campbell-Scarlett came out onto the *galería*. He was smoking a cigar.

"I have promised Sir Peter the mazurka. He is looking for me. Don't dare pull me back or I'll be the one to make a scene. You can tell Flora goodbye for me."

I left him laughing senselessly. How changed he was from the interesting, enthusiastic young Scotsman of our first encounter in Puebla. "Mexico has a mysterious effect on some people," I said to Sir Peter as we danced, "it is as if the old gods still rule invisibly."

"You refer to young McLeod, whom you cruelly left weeping on the bench in the patio?"

"Angus was laughing."

"Perhaps he was when you left him, but I heard him weeping when I stepped out onto the gravel to toss my cigar into the fountain."

I was having a troubled dream about being alone on a lake in a little rowboat with endless flocks of wild geese passing overhead flying lower and lower and lower when a steady knocking roused me. Carrying a candle, Pacheco and Martha Doblinger entered.

"Her Majesty has locked her door on the inside. We are afraid she is having a spell, as in Jalapa. Shall we waken the del Barrios?"

"Is she alone?"

"I don't know."

"Ask Martha."

"I have tried. She shakes her head and moans, only understanding German."

"The del Barrios don't speak German. Do you know which is Sir Peter Campbell-Scarlett's room?"

"Yes."

I dressed hastily and followed Pacheco along the corridor, trailed by Martha.

Sir Peter answered my nervous knocking, his mouth an *O* of shocked surprise on seeing me. Trying not to laugh, I was as dignified as possible under the circumstances. "We can't communicate with Martha. She is the only one who can tell us if it is indicated for someone to break open Her Majesty's locked door. You do speak German, don't you?"

He spoke rapidly. Martha nodded her head and shook her head and nodded again. She tried not to let me but I heard and so did Pacheco: "Van der Smissen."

Repressing a smile, Sir Peter ran his long fingers swiftly through his rumpled hair and said briskly, "It is not for us to interfere. Go back to your beds, ladies. I have ordered la Doblinger to continue to sit quietly in the hall. When Her Majesty's guest leaves, Martha will enter and attend her as usual. The Empress and the colonel are in all probability working out her approach and her speech to the Yucatecans she will face in Mérida."

28

After her unexpectedly positive reception in Vera Cruz Carlota declared, "A Mexican Empress can only travel in a Mexican transport!" So we sailed from Vera Cruz on a miserable Mexican packet steamer instead of the trim Austrian corvette, *Dándalo*, which was supposed to take us to Yucatán.

The stormy voyage battered and tossed us around like jumping beans. Carlota, the del Valles and Pacheco remained below the whole time, emerging in Progresa looking like picked birds, while the rested ambassadors, who had sailed in the *Dándalo*, waited for us on the scorching shore, fresh and eager.

Carriages fetched us over the goose-colored sandy road, winding among henequen fields and bush, to Mérida, where we were revived by flutters of doves, deluges of flowers and thousands of Republican Yucatecans filling the roofs, doorways and balconies of the fascinating sixteenth- and seventeenth-century houses. But during the long pronouncements of loyalty to the Empire, Carlota listened with half-closed eyes. It was obvious that the journey was taking a toll of her endurance.

The vast clay-colored stone house in which we were entertained was built in 1530 by one of the first of the conquistadores. He used two molded plaster figures of Spanish soldiers, each standing with one foot on the back of a prostrate Indian, as the overdecoration for his massive double front doors. The house was built around so many courtyards one felt as if one were in a little town all by itself.

My high-ceilinged room was cool but roosters crowed constantly and cathedral bells clanged and clanged every hour all over Mérida.

"Have you slept well, Señora Angel?" a pitiful female voice asked. Countess del Valle, white as a spook, was standing by the mass of mosquito netting shrouding my *reredos*-type bed. Dawn had not come, but in the street below my shuttered window I could hear Yucatecans going back and forth singing and talking.

"Listen, I am ill. You must help me. All in the Empress's suite have ptomaine, especially María Pacheco, who is a weak woman in all ways," she moaned.

"It was the turkey. It was rotten, though the *mole* sauce concealed it at first," I remarked, snuggling comfortably in my soft pillows. "I was able to rid myself of it before it poisoned me."

The Countess nodded wretchedly. "One did not expect such food in so important a house filled with more gold and silver treasures than I saw in our whole year in Paris. Fortunately Her Majesty ate the pompano. Now she insists on riding to the Mayan ruins at Uxmal today, having been invited on a picnic by the aristocracy of Mérida. I choose you to have the honor of waiting on her. You will, won't you?"

I had planned to explore Mérida with Sir Peter that morning. We were both fascinated with the colonial architecture and the massive cathedral with its uneven towers. But the Mayan ruins would be even more exciting to me. And I knew Sir Peter would prefer meeting with the rich henequen *hacendados*. "I've always done as you requested, haven't I, Countess?" I asked, springing out of bed and stretching like a pleased cat.

"You and Her Majesty are the only ones who have surmounted the past three days. It is strange that you foreigners would be stronger than we who have lived here always; very remarkable. And you have a glow about you which I do not understand at all."

Carlota's exhaustion was even more apparent as I watched her walking slowly along the marble arcade of the Montejo house in the warm, humid darkness of *madrugada*. A servant was holding a lamp high over her head. It pointed up dark circles around her eyes and accented the pure whiteness of her skin. She had on her tightly fitted black riding dress over which she had tossed a white dust mantle.

I thought of the other time I saw her dressed like that. I wished that Alfred van der Smissen had not waved goodbye to her at Vera Cruz, for he was the only one at whom she smiled and his was the only advice she ever heeded. But the fascination of van der Smissen naturally must have gnawed at her nerves and terrified her by threatening the precarious preciousness of her crown. It had gashed two furrows between her dark brows until at times she looked almost maniacal.

"Your Majesty," I began, "do you think it wise—?"

Close behind her, the Count del Valle, his ascetic face drawn and drained, said, "The day will be too hot, Your Majesty. You are pushing yourself unreasonably. Don't go. I promised His Majesty to take care of you."

"We must hurry," she replied mechanically, halting a minute to decide which way to pass around the wrought-iron *cancela*, ignoring him and me as if we were shades in the shadows. "The Emperor said I must never keep these people waiting."

"People? What people? Who are they? Wait, Your Majesty, where are your Guard? The Dragoons? You are making a mistake—"

A surge of horses and most of the young bloods of Mérida, gaily dressed, were gathered in the cobbled courtyard to accompany her to Uxmal.

The holiday spirit was contagious. The Empress joined in the racing, if not in the singing of merry Mexican tunes (no "Mamá Carlota" here). But when the sun rose, the heat grew so fierce that even the heartiest began to lag and languish. We reached Uxmal before noon where a picnic was spread on sweet-smelling grass mats under spreading ash trees. Afterward, everybody was ready for a siesta, but Carlota would have none of it.

"Don't attempt to dissuade me, Berrien," she said firmly. "I am determined to be the first European woman to set foot in this ancient city."

You are very stubborn and foolish and thoughtless of the way others feel, I said to myself.

As if commenting, she faced her sleepy escorts. "I am accustomed to doing what I wish. And this afternoon I wish to go alone into the Mayan ruins with my American lady-in-waiting and this nice priest who has volunteered to explain all."

The priest was a sturdy, weathered *mestizo* who had been sent out to meet us from the nearby hacienda at which we were to stop the night.

"It is perfectly safe, is it not?" she asked.

"Oh, very safe," cried the thinly shod caballeros of Mérida. "There are no guerrillas, no bandits in Yucatán. And the Indians of Mayan descent are gentle people. We will stand guard at all the ways in and out of the ruins and wait for you most heroically."

She and I had on thick-soled boots. The priest wore rope sandals but his feet looked hard as horn.

"Those ones—those gay caballeros—will be sleeping the minute we step from this thicket and stand before the Temple of the Dwarf," he said, striding along, crushing blue convolvulus and red-berried vines with his splayed toes.

He pointed out the mysterious magnificence of the entire classic Puuc City that had been abandoned in the year 1000.

"Where did the Maya go?"

"*¿Quién sabe?*" He shook his head. "To their gods, I presume."

The architectural gem was the House of the Turtles. The Nunnery and Las Palomas were the most difficult to make a guess as to what they really had been. But the grandest, stateliest and best preserved stone structure was the Governor's Palace, faced with undulating lines of masks of the rain gods imposed on bold *grecques* and latticework. Hundred-foot-long writhing rattlesnakes complete with rattles crawled from end to end.

"And the Spaniards came four thousand miles to teach the Maya baroque!" Carlota marveled. "This building alone is worth the journey. I feel at home in palaces however desolate. It's shady on this step. I will sit down. Hand me my pencil and pad, Berrien. I will make extensive notes, for I must describe everything that passes or has passed to the Emperor. He has desired to come here all of his adult life. Go, girl. Don't stand there watching me."

I was accustomed to her ways by now. Today I felt more of a comradeship with her than I'd thought possible. I smiled and dipped a little curtsy to please her. She nodded formally. The priest laughed out loud and we winked at each other as I walked away.

My blue linen riding habit was soaked with perspiration. I pulled off the jacket and let the strong south wind blow through my sheer muslin shirtwaist. Had the priest not sat down on a stone ledge nearby I'd have taken it off and flapped it in the wind to dry. My breasts might have dried too. Poor things they were covered with prickly heat rash from hot sweat.

There was a platform across the grassy terrace on the very edge of the high hill on which the palace stood. The priest joined me there. Between the platform and the palace was a gigantic stone shaft plunging into the ground.

"It's taller than a pine tree! I wonder how far down it goes? How did it get here?"

"No one knows that answer. What is known for a fact is that it is the penis of the Rain God fertilizing the good earth. The Maya worshiped symbols. Everything is symbolic in this place."

Tenderly I touched the great column penetrating the earth. It was warm and hard. I laid my cheek down on it. It felt good. I could imagine it pulsing with vibrant life. I let the illusion pour into me as a cloud of flycatchers whirled overhead like a golden net against the pale blue sky. I could look down into the flaming crown of an African tulip tree below. Two iguanas moved lazily together in the sun on the platform. A blue motmot bird, over a foot long, flew from one sapling to another, pulling at his racket-tipped tail. "Poot poot!" he cried, "poot poot!" A white-winged dove called from a banana tree, "My lover called to me, my lover called to me!" A fiery, hooded oriole lit on the shaft close to my face. Symbols of Beau were everywhere. The oriole's eyes and my eyes met as if he were bringing me a message and then he lifted his wings and vanished. For a moment I was transported into a dreamy world of relaxed languor. Then I had another feeling—a weird sense of departed spirits—infinite emptiness, somberness, loneliness, cruelty.

There was a statue the priest called Chac Mool resting in the center of the priest's platform. The stone man was lying on his back, holding up his knees to balance a basin into which the living hearts of beautiful warriors, hallucinated with magic mushrooms, once were tossed. Eagles would swoop down and bear the beating hearts heavenward. Chac Mool's face was fixing me now with his witless stone statement of mortality. And beyond him were the jungle and the bristling henequen fields stretching toward the sea.

"Berrien!" called the Empress, shaking her trailing skirt, "come here—I'm covered in ticks!"

The priest had taken shady refuge in the doorway of one of the dark rooms of the Governor's Palace, into and out of which small swifts flew. "Immediately we go to the Hacienda de Ponce," he said. "The Indian women there make ointments that will shrivel and loosen the ticks."

Intoning some kind of incantation against ticks and devils, he made haste ahead of us, beating at the prickly underbrush with his stick. Halfway down the hill, near where the priest had just walked, I saw a rattlesnake coiled up a foot and a half high. Its eyes were fixing Carlota as if she were a bird. Its forked tongue flicked in and out. "They won't bother you, if you don't bother them," Beau had said.

"Your Majesty," I said softly, "stand very still. Look back at me."

"No. I must get rid of these ticks. I hate them." She stepped forward kicking loose a shower of little stones.

I grabbed her, jerking her back against me as the powerful serpentine body hurtled past her so close it almost knocked her arm off.

There was a moment of total silence. Then the priest began rushing about, beating bushes again with his stick. "What have I done? What have I done?" he kept saying in despair.

Carlota was screaming hysterically, tearing off her sleeve. "Look at my arm. Where did the fangs go in? How can you say it didn't strike me? Oh, oh, I can feel the poison pouring through me."

The priest collected his senses first. He took her bare arm and ran his hand all over it. "I am a doctor as well as a priest," he said. "You've been lucky. Not a mark. Ask this beautiful lady who has been so brave and saved you. She will tell you—not a mark."

Making a superb effort despite her almost convulsive trembling, Carlota wrapped the torn-off sleeve around her arm and said, "This is the second time you have saved me, Berrien."

"I don't recall ever having saved you before, Your Majesty," I said through chattering teeth.

"Oh, yes, the first time was the night of my Birthday Ball when you played a waltz and the Emperor and I waltzed together—" Her voice broke off. She started running back up the hill. "Who are those men down there? Who are they after? I know—they are waiting to kill me."

Before I finished explaining that they were our merry escort she was herself again and able to nod haughtily at the young caballeros flying up to assist us the rest of the way down.

All of us realized that Carlota was breaking down. And I saw something new in her eyes. I know now it was fear. The Count del Valle insisted that she return to Mexico City.

"We will see," she answered, looking little and lost and sad amid the swaths of red velvet draperies held back by ornate marble cupids, and the plethora of immense carved sofas and chairs. "We will see how my visit goes in Campeche, and whether it is wise for me to stay there. I am not in the least bit nervous, only one must not tempt Providence too much. It is strange for me to be here at all."

Stranger for me, I reflected as sometimes, after a day of total lassitude in Campeche, I suddenly thought of Beau as vividly as if he were before me and wept with longing and the sharpness of missing him. My imagination played tricks on me. I would hear him calling "Angel!" from the gallery outside my room and I would run up and down, searching.

A week later, having completely run out of tincture of opium and quinine, Dr. Basch at last convinced Carlota that she must be sensible. If she wished to kill us all, surely she could find a less painful way than diarrhea and malaria. It was time for us to end this pilgrimage.

That same morning Carlota's front tooth began to throb. In the evening she was to address a gathering of all the notables of Campeche. For hours we pressed first warm, then cold, cloths against her face. The pain grew more rather than less.

"Forget about the speaking," our hostess, a niece of Gutierrez d'Estrada, urged. "They will come back tomorrow."

"Campeche is not important," said Count del Valle.

"You are worn out," I put in.

But she reminded us that this was our last stop before returning to Mexico City. Republican Campeche was as important to the Empire as Mérida. She represented the Emperor of Mexico. Her appearance here was one of the main objectives for this whole tour.

"I long more than you know, Count, to go home," she said.

"It is but two weeks until the most sacred and holy night of the year," María Pacheco mourned. "Her Majesty dreams of winter snow and ice."

"December? It can't be—not here in this scorching heat!"

An hour later an enormous crowd had assembled in the plaza outside of the salon in which Carlota paced up and down. The mayor and dozens of dignitaries were on the balcony. Bands were playing, soldiers marching and flags flying. As in Mérida, the ancient house in which we were staying was right on the plaza.

Carlota was sobbing.

Dr. Basch sat with his head in his hands. "I have no more ideas. The tooth must be pulled."

"I refuse. It is my front tooth. I will not stand up in front of those people without a front tooth. They would laugh and point at me,"

Carlota said, stamping both her feet, one after another.

It was at that moment Martha Doblinger entered with the cup. She didn't know what was in it. One of the Indian housemaids had put it in her hand.

Our hostess sent for the maid who explained that it was a cup of very potent but exceedingly rare mushroom broth. Her father, a medicine man as well as a priest, had brewed it to cure the dear little Empress with whom the Indians of Campeche had fallen in love.

"See," the maid said, "I drink some first. *Totoache* will not harm, only help."

Everyone agreed the *totoache* was worth a try. Only I begged Carlota not to drink it. When, hesitantly, she reached for the cup I was bold enough to take it away from her.

"So, Berrien, you are determined to save me three times instead of two?" She smiled bitterly, and snatched the cup away from me. She drank thirstily, then handed me the empty cup. "See, Berrien—I am quite all right—I can feel the pain disappearing. I will go out on the balcony. Countess, is my hair quite neat—my crown straight? Accompany me, Berrien. Your tallness makes my smallness more appealing."

Through the opened shutters of the French doors leading out onto the wrought-iron balcony we could see the plaza packed with people and hear them crying "*Viva! Viva! la Emperatrice.*" In the center, some of them were holding up a banner with *Viva! el gran Leopoldo* written on it. In the foreshortened view through the shutters the banner appeared to be gliding on the air like a large white bird.

Carlota's eyes had a madness in them. We all saw it and remembered it. She spoke with flushed cheeks and hot eyes. Not in a steady stream, just tossing out platitudes, but with so much animation I felt I had never seen her so taken out of herself. The crowd roared its appreciation.

During the cheering Dr. Basch tried to direct her inside, but she clutched at the arm of the man standing behind her and shouted, "How could I not have made every effort to address these sweet simple people? They give me back my belief in human nature. Do you see the banner, Señor Mayor? There is nothing weak or vacillating about *el gran Leopoldo*. He chooses his ministers for their intelligence and skill not for their graceful looks or cunning guile. He is in all ways a man, *mucho hombre*, as you say in Mexico. He on the banner, *el gran Leopoldo*, is my father, the King of Belgium, Señor Mayor."

When we landed back in Vera Cruz, Carlota received a telegram saying her father was dying.

Maximilian met us in Puebla. The King of Belgium was dead. Carlota was in such an hysteria of grief she could not tell Maximilian of her triumphs in Yucatán and Campeche. On Christmas Eve in Cuernavaca she learned that King Leopold had died on December 10, the very same day of the banner in Campeche!

29

I arrived from the long journey at Miramontes on December 23.

"The Emperor's courier stopped by an hour ago and told us to expect you. Bubba is having his bath after a hard day overseeing the transplanting of petunia plants at the Borda Palace. I'll send Lencho for him immediately," Phillip said, helping me down from my horse.

"Let me surprise him. Do I look all right?"

"You look wonderful, if a shade darkened by the Mayan sun. Aren't you going to kiss me as a reward for having ridden my backsides off so that your wandering husband would be eagerly waiting for you on your return home?"

The mocking devil was in his eyes. His lips were smiling. He smelled of fresh hay.

I threw my arms around his neck. Oh, how wonderful everything is, I thought; then I realized it was Phillip not Beau waiting eagerly for me and was finding me a little too wonderful. One didn't kiss one's sister quite like that.

Elsie called from the second-story gallery, "I have marry with Lencho, Señora Angel, and a baby comes! I am so happy with seeing you I could die!"

Giving me one more hug, Phillip said, "We're adding mercury and salts to the wet silver ore this afternoon. It's the most important part of the mining process. I shouldn't have left the workers, but I had to see you come riding through the gate."

"Why isn't Beau helping you?"

"Silver mining doesn't interest him. Sometimes the crops do, especially our tiny stand of sea island cotton. Ah, here's Lencho—he knows where Bubba is at this time of day. Oh—" he called back over his shoulder as he untied his horse from the post by the water trough, "I have put you in a different room than the one you chose the other time. I live in the one with the blue bed now. Bubba says it reminds him of those nightmares he had after the scorpion sting. See you at supper."

I would miss the big blue bed:

> *Give me your wings, sweet dove, to fly into your nest*
> *If last night you slept alone, tonight you will sleep with me.*

Shivering with anticipation, I walked side by side with Lencho, he talking volubly about how improved all was, here at Miramontes, under Señor Felipe's careful administering.

"A new ceiling over the patio by the pool similar to one Señor Felipe saw at Lake Como." Lencho pointed to a pink and white striped canvas awning at the far end of the garden.

He continued to take pride in the newly painted frescoes around the walls of the lower colonnade; cages of singing birds in every arch; well-tended plants set at regular intervals in Puebla pottery tubs; fresh flower arrangements on every table and highly polished mahogany and cane benches and chairs grouped between gay sisal hammocks. Heaven or Home? Both.

I took a deep breath and prepared myself for the ultimate pleasure: to see Beau coming toward me with open arms. But I saw only neat little Indian girls mopping the floors and straw-hatted gardeners making intricate designs with their brooms in the gravel walks.

As if he read my thoughts, Lencho said, "*El gran señor* does not like to be disturbed during the hour of his bath. But I know he will welcome such a disturbance as you, Señora Angel. What a surprise this is going to be for both of you."

As we walked on along the airy upper gallery he described his wedding and how Señor Felipe danced a flamenco so rapidly that not even the deer-heeled girl from the cantina in the village could keep up with him.

He stopped in front of closed double doors with a carnelian colored plaster shell molded above them. He knocked. The walls were too thick for us to hear anything from inside. My heart was in my throat. I could hardly breathe.

Lencho opened one of the doors. Beau didn't notice. He was sitting at a shaving stand, studying himself in an ornate silver mirror hanging from a silver chain. The sun, shining in from the mountain-view windows, cast a light only on his flaming hair. His forehead, which was all I saw reflected in the glass, was wrinkled in absorption.

I stepped inside. The wind was banging a shutter against one of the windows. The collar of Beau's loose white shirt was open. A white cotton towel was around his neck. He lifted his razor and, leaning toward the mirror, gently tipped an unfamiliar mutton-chop sideburn flourishing on his left cheek.

I took off my hat and veil and handed them to Lencho, who was standing very still as if waiting for something unusual. I was so keyed-up with excitement I was afraid I might faint. But even if I did it didn't matter now. I was at last within reach of Beau's arms.

"Beau," I said softly, "dear husband . . ."

At the sound of my voice he jumped up, turning over his chair and knocking his head so hard against the mirror he sent it flying on its chain like a pendulum. "I'm Billybedamned! Angelica!" He came toward me. Involuntarily I covered my face in my hands and stepped back against Lencho.

No! My heart warned, oh, no! But Beau was laughing. Lencho was laughing. I couldn't help laughing too.

Beau had grown a beard and a mustache! Both were the color of ripe wheat. The mustache was nicely waxed and turned and the beard, carefully parted in the middle, was identical to the Emperor's, though not nearly so long.

"Does it tickle?" he asked between kisses.

"Yes, especially when you kiss me like that."

"Then prepare to be tickled to death. Lencho, what the hell are you doing standing there staring at us?"

"What says he, Señora Angel?" Lencho asked, delighted to have been part of such a big surprise.

"He says, 'Please say to the *hacendado* we will join him at supper.'"

The door closed. I sat in Beau's lap and we both looked at the ornate iron-poster bed as hotly as if we were in Richmond on the snowy December night after we were married over five years ago.

"First, you must tell me how you like my beard and then—"

If I told him the way I felt when I first saw him it would spoil everything. How had he not noticed my instant recoil?

"It isn't red as I thought it would be. It's gold," I said, stroking his throat and letting my fingers run up and around the back of his neck.

He kissed me again. His mustache felt silky and wet. "My Angelica," he began, unbuttoning my shirtwaist. "I can hardly wait—"

The door was flung open without knocking. I sprang away from him, pulling my shirtwaist together. In the doorway stood a beaming Elsie.

"Not to unpack for you now, eh? Lencho stands outside with all your cases and boxes which have just arrived."

"No, Elsie, not now. I'll call you."

We heard her and Lencho giggling as the door closed.

At least the interruption had spared me the temptation of telling Beau what I really thought of his growing a beard like the Emperor's.

"I knew you'd love it," he said, breathing hard as he finished unbuttoning my waist and tenderly took my bare breasts in his hands and kissed them.

The sound of his voice brought back the first night of our love story in the hotel in Richmond, Virginia, and so intense were my memories that at first I did not hear him say as he picked me up, saying, "And so to bed, to quote dear old Pepys."

The linen sheets were smooth and cool but for just a moment I was uncomfortable. The beard changed him. I missed his strong chin, the carved outline of his mouth. He balanced himself on one elbow, circling me with the other arm, lifting me to meet him. As I arched my back, he dropped me and sat up looking agitatedly around the room.

"Luggage? Did she say your things had arrived? How could they—only an hour after you?"

"What are you talking about? What's happened to you?" I sat up and reached out to touch him, but he was on his way to the armoire. Snatching a kimono he hurried onto the gallery. "Your things *are* here, by damn," he called back in to me. "Elsie! Lencho! Where are you? Come quickly!"

I could hear bare feet running along the gallery. "What passes, señor? What is wrong?"

"Tell me how did these things get here? Who brought them? In what? When?"

"No understand, señor," Elsie said as he fired questions at her so rapidly even I found it difficult to keep up.

There was another kimono in the armoire which I wrapped

wearily around myself. It took the last ounce of my strength to trail outside.

Elsie announced that the boxes and the valise had come perched on the top of great quantities of luggage in a big wide coach belonging to the Empress. Their Majesties had decided not to remain in Puebla, covered in black crepe with the sadness of her father's death, but to drive at once to Cuernavaca to spend the feast of the Epiphany. The driver of the coach had told all these things to Lencho who, in turn, had given them to her to explain to the *hacendados*.

Standing miserably in the doorway after I translated this to Beau, I watched him rummaging in the armoire. He jerked out a gold embroidered uniform jacket. "Bad timing," he muttered as he pulled on his trousers. "But I must be at the palace when they arrive in case there's something I can do for the Emperor. She'll be harder to live with now than ever."

"You are leaving me to go to the Borda Palace the first afternoon I've seen you in almost two months?" I still couldn't take in what was happening.

"If I don't, old Fischer or Pretty Boy López will get ahead of me." He sat down in front of the mirror and began combing his golden beard.

I wanted to pull every hair of it out by the roots. A sob I couldn't swallow burst from my throat, though I tried very hard not to in my sudden fierce pride that, until this afternoon, had never shown itself in anything that had to do with him.

He gave one final twirl to his mustache, came over and put his arms around me. The gold braid of his coat scratched my cheek. I pushed him away.

"Don't be angry. I didn't plan this. It's not my fault. You're exhausted. It's probably all for the best that this came up. Climb back in bed and have a nice long rest and then Elsie will fix you a nice long hot bath. By suppertime I'll be home. I'm sure I will. Nitey-bye—my Angel."

I let the kimono slip down onto the floor, got in bed and pulled the embroidered sheet up over my chin so Elsie wouldn't see it quivering. She placed a cotton cloth soaked in eau de cologne across my forehead but mercifully didn't say anything. I was glad she stayed in the room, quietly unpacking, going comfortably back and forth across the tiled floor on bare feet, every now and then stopping to touch my shoulder or rub the soles of my feet with camphor water.

Try not to mind so much, I thought, only let him come back tonight and so long as he does come back he will, I know, show me how much he really loves me.

30 🌿

He didn't come back for supper. Phillip and I waited to eat until ten o'clock. Afterward we sat under the pink and white striped awning by the pool until midnight listening to night birds singing and little frogs and cicadas talking in the leaves.

I told him the highlights of the trip to Yucatán. He was fascinated with my description of Uxmal.

"I have been reading everything I can get my hands on about Mexico from the time of the Maya right up to Juárez. I wish Bubba would try and understand this country."

"I don't think he ever will."

"He's too absorbed with Maximilian—too flattered when people in the street mistake him for the Emperor. Watching the way he tends his beard—his manner—his walk—his thinking—all scare the hell out of me."

I took a deep breath. With Phillip I never had any desire to be anything but honest—to face up to whatever was ahead. "I guess I've been frightened ever since the day of the picnic in the forest. The escape door to enchantment opened and he rushed right in. As soon as we can go back to South Carolina he'll be himself again. I believe it, Phillip. And I love him so much I can protect him—even from himself."

"I hope so," he said. "But from which self?"

I drank a little glass of the brandy he'd made from his first cane crop. "When the children come to be with us here, things will be different," I said helplessly.

He reached for my hand and kissed it. "You look tired. I *am* tired and tomorrow is Christmas Eve. Can you imagine it in this tropical setting? I see Lencho hovering on the gallery. Go to bed like a good girl and get your beauty sleep."

But it wasn't Lencho. It was Beau who stepped out into the torchlight. How long had he been there? Had he been listening? Evidently not, for he looked so fresh and happy that all of my pride and most of my worries went flying away as if they had never been.

31

The next day was a holiday so Phillip invited us to take a look at the silver mine. "You can see its potential better when everything is quiet."

Beau insisted he'd promised Maximilian to help decorate a Christmas tree at La Borda with ornaments his mother the Arch-duchess Sophia had sent him from Vienna.

"I've worked a miracle and found a wandering friar who has agreed to perform Holy Mass in our little chapel this evening. You'll be back for that, won't you, Bubba?" Phillip said.

No answer. Beau frowned.

"Please, Beau. Christmas Eve night means a lot to me. I will miss our baby especially tonight," I said.

Beau cocked his thumb and forefinger like a pistol, aiming at a little green warbler whisking through a waving palm tree. "Bang! Bang! Of course I'll be back. What do you take me for?"

Phillip and I drove to the mine in a small red buggy pulled by a flop-eared mule. Then we rode little burros down a cliff to the narrow opening where I climbed down a steep rickety ladder into the mine itself. For hours we went down dark mazelike passages and into the big vaulted rooms that were the refining works. Phillip explained how the ore was broken up and separated from the refuse by hand-hammering at the mine head. This was then loaded into leather sacks onto burros and mules and carried to a stone, fortresslike compound where the pure silver was extracted. Great water wheels furnished the power that reduced the ore into wet mud into which the vital mercury and salts were added. Little mules trampled this for three weeks as if they were making a vintage wine. When the quicksilver had entirely merged with the raw silver it was refined by being put in huge kettles and fired for twelve hours during which the mercury vaporized.

"Feel this." Phillip handed me a heavy metal chunk. "This bar of pure silver will be worked into shapes designed by Lencho. He can copy anything; but his own designs are fantastically beautiful."

"What if the silver gives out? This mine looks as if it had been worked over pretty thoroughly."

"There is enough that has been wasted in the past lying around to keep us millionaires for generations if we are clever. I've already invented some marvelous machinery that will simplify the whole process."

"I wish Beau had come."

"Leave him playing toy soldier. I work better without worrying about all his nonsense," Phillip said tersely. "Frankly, he bores the hell out of me."

"But it is important for him to be involved in this," I said. "He would be better off. And so would I."

"He's made his choice. I've made mine. Don't try and smooth things between us. Remember we've been brothers longer than you have known us. We always kiss and make up our differences eventually though we may sound like the worst enemies in the world while we're fighting it out. Hey, your skirt is covered in mud. You've seen it all except the best part—Lencho's workshop. Let's get out of here."

Lencho's workshop was shuttered and barred. A gathering of workers said he was arranging the altar in the chapel for tonight's mass. He had left word that the *hacendado* was not to interfere but to remain on the outside so that he might be happily surprised when the Holy Night celebration feast was ready.

"Lencho makes a specialty of surprises," Phillip laughed. "I know what to do. We're hot as hell and your frock could do with a washing. Let's jump in the pool and cool off. I'll teach you to swim."

Sitting on a cushion under the pink and white canopy I took off my shabby black leather boots and wiggled my toes excitedly. "You mean literally jump in the water with our clothes on?"

"Unless you're wearing all your corsets." He laughed shamelessly.

"You promise not to let me drown?"

"Of course I won't. I can't imagine anybody not knowing how to swim."

The water was clear and delightfully refreshing. My short muslin dress swished around my bare legs.

I have always been afraid of water but I was ashamed to show it. I clenched my teeth and thrashed my arms and legs obediently as Phillip guided me with one hand under my stomach to give me confidence.

"Pretend you're a dog—just let yourself go and paddle. You're doing fine. Keep it up."

I could feel Phillip take his hand away. There was nothing under me but water. I didn't even try to swim. An ugly memory flashed in my mind: Don Carlos behind the *cancela* with the she-dog. Terror engulfed me. I sank toward the bottom of the pool feeling my lungs fill with water as I opened my mouth to scream.

I was dragged up choking and sputtering. Scolding, Phillip began hitting me on the back as I struggled to find my breath.

"What the hell's going on here?"

Beau was standing on the edge of the pool, glaring furiously at Phillip, who kept beating me on the back.

"I'm trying to teach Angelica to swim." Phillip laughed. "I had no idea she was made of solid rock."

"Get out of there, Angelica." Beau's voice was cold and harsh. "Cover yourself with a towel. How dare you go in the water without a proper bathing costume?"

"What?" I pushed my soaking wet hair out of my face. I felt my breasts thrust darkly against the slight film of sheer material that revealed my entire body.

"Golly—I'm sorry." Phillip's face was scarlet. His body was as revealed as mine and it was beautiful. "I'll begone, sweet maiden." He vanished leaving me standing alone in the middle of the pool while Beau pulled down a strip of canvas and held it out.

"Come, walk to the edge. Don't be afraid. Your feet are on the bottom. You can't sink, unless you do so from pure mortification. Hell, don't cry. It doesn't matter, really it doesn't. That's it—give me your hand. Up you come. Now run and let Elsie dry you off while I go and whip the devil out of Phillip—"

"Please, Beau, he didn't mean—"

"I'm not. I was just talking. You really should know how to swim. He's quite right. No harm done—run on now. I'll fetch your shoes. Hey—you need new ones. These are awful."

For a moment he was like his old self. And I thought: If I play my cards right this afternoon, maybe I can persuade him to shave off that dreadful beard!

Phillip had sent colored cards lettered in gilt inviting all the nearby *hacendados* and their families to the Christmas Eve Mass:

> *The Berrien family requests that you will honour them with your presence and that of your family, in the solemn function of Kalends and Mass, with which the Marquesa Escandon formerly made a humble remembrance of the Birth of the Saviour, which festivity will as usual take place on the evening of the 24th of this month, at ten o'clock in the silver chapel of Miramontes. This will be the last night of the Posadas.*
>
> *Miramontes, December 1865*

Elsie explained the posadas. They were a combination of religion and fun, very pretty. They were inspired by these events: When the decree came from Caesar that "all the world should be taxed" the Holy Mary and her husband Joseph came to Bethlehem but could not find a room in any inn. So they wandered about for nine days being turned away by everybody. Then on the ninth day an innkeeper lent them a stable where Jesus the Christ was born.

About ten our guests arrived. The men had on their finest velvet brocade waistcoats and ruffled shirts. The ladies and children were weighted down in silks and jewels. Bearded Beau was striking in his scarlet and gold-braided Imperial uniform and Phillip looked exactly like Lord Byron in his London full dress suit and flowing black silk tie.

Lencho blew a cow's horn to mark the beginning of the ceremony and a lighted candle was given each guest. We formed a line, two by two, and marched, singing litanies, all through the decorated house. When we had visited and been turned away from eight rooms, we crossed the courtyard to the chapel hesitating before the closed doors while a shower of fireworks exploded over our heads.

"It is the descent of the heralding angels," Doña Margaret Zurutuza explained to me. "Listen and you will hear—"

Elsie was singing the "Gloria." She had a lovely true soprano voice; full of power and sweetness. And then came Lencho's surprise.

First a group of Indian women dressed like shepherds appeared from behind the chapel. Then came the voices of Mary and Joseph begging for admittance saying that it was cold and dark, that the wind blew a hurricane and they must have shelter from the night. Elsie was singing the part of Mary. I didn't recognize the rich baritone of Joseph.

I reached out for Beau's hand, wondering how he was feeling on this holiest of nights under a thousand tropical stars shining.

"I had forgot what a fine voice Phillip has," Beau said. "Hearing him in this weird, wretched place makes me too homesick. You'll have to excuse me for a little while."

A chorus from inside the chapel sang, refusing to open the doors.

"Wait—"

"Sh-h-h—" Doña Margaret hissed and tapped me reprovingly with her fan.

Phillip was singing again; again begging to be let in from the night.

And again the voices inside the chapel refused.

And then Phillip sang, low and oh so movingly, entreating those on the inside, saying that, before their doors, she who was wandering in the dark of night and had no place to lay her head was in very truth the Queen of Heaven.

At this name Lencho dressed as the innkeeper threw open the doors and the Holy Family, followed by our procession, entered the chapel into a dazzle of light and beauty. The silver altar glittered with dozens of wax candles and lustre lamps set in front of it.

Moss-covered platforms had been set around the body of the chapel, like small stages, holding papier-mâché figures from the New Testament: the Annunciation, the Salutation of Mary to Elizabeth, the Wise Men of the East, the Shepherds, the Kings of the Orient, Herod, the flight into Egypt. There were tubs of green trees and flowering plants and flocks of paper sheep and a little gilt cradle to lay the baby Jesus in.

One of the papier-mâché angels held an exquisite baby, molded of wax and beautifully painted, in her arms. Roses and orange blossoms and poinsettias were everywhere. And, I almost forgot, there was a sinister-looking live priest in scarlet and gold vestments. He took the baby from the angel and laid it in the cradle.

"That is the end of the posada," Doña Margaret said, handing me a lace handkerchief.

I wasn't aware that I was crying, but she said the candlelight made my tears appear to be made of crystal. It concerned her. I was too beautiful not to be able to weep human tears.

The mass lasted only a short time. Once when I rose from kneeling with the others I caught a glimpse of Beau frowning in front of the Angel of the Annunciation. And once I looked over at Joseph, I mean Phillip, standing by the gilt cradle. He was looking at me with such tenderness and adoration I felt the pulses beat like hammers in my throat. He was in love with me! I guess I had known it for a long time. Tonight I admitted it, to myself anyway. I only hoped Beau, in his usual fashion, was not paying any attention to his younger brother.

When mass was over we returned to the big salon—angels, shepherds and everybody—and danced until a most elaborate champagne supper was served. While outside in the courtyard gay *piñatas* were broken and children scrambled about for little gifts, dozens of guitars and fiddles played, quantities of pulque and rum were drunk and the Indians danced and shot fireworks until the daydawn.

At Christmas breakfast Phillip presented Beau and me with a

dozen solid silver dinner plates that Lencho had made. Beau gave me a snuffbox that had belonged to Catherine the Great. The Emperor had presented it to him. As if that weren't bad enough, he then left to spend the whole day at the Borda Palace.

Beau came home at sundown with the news that the Empress was returning to Chapultepec after New Year's. The Emperor had been so pleased with the accounts of Carlota's personal triumph and success in Yucatan and Campeche he had requested her to handle all the affairs of state with the ministers during the winter while he regained his health in Cuernavaca. Carlota had requested that I continue serving her as a lady-in-waiting. He had accepted the honor.

"For I am going with Colonel van der Smissen to once again seek out Juarez and arrange a meeting between him with the Emperor. I may be away a long time."

"Why Alfred van der Smissen instead of Alfons von Kodolitsch?" I asked miserably.

"Oh, I imagine Maximilian finally intercepted one of van der Smissen's moony glances in Her Majesty's direction."

He *had* noticed Phillip looking at me last night! I knew it and I knew that his mouth, under that awful beard, was not smiling but drawn tight in a hard unlovely line.

PART V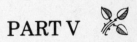

The French Withdrawal

1866

*when everything—in fact—that walks or creeps
and everything that flies or swims; everything
shrinks in a crackle of butterflies;*

JOSÉ GOROSTIZA
Muerte sin Fin

32

The next morning, on waking, I snuggled closer to Beau, thinking with warm, moist joy of the night, happy in the knowing I had regained complete possession of him.

"Once more," Beau murmured sleepily. He was surprised and showed his annoyance when Lencho came to inform him of van der Smissen's arrival. The soldiers waited in the courtyard, booted and spurred, impatient to be on the way before the sun grew fierce.

We dressed quickly. He did not let me bind his sash but rushed out with it hanging on his arm. He looked back and almost turned but he changed his mind. His face flushed and he ran quickly along the colonnade toward the stairway. I followed, catching up with him at the top step. He took me in his arms, looking not in my eyes, but above them, at my forehead. No, he was looking at Phillip, who had come from his room and was standing behind me.

"I'll miss you so."

"I leave you in my brother's tender care." He laughed a cold, stiff laugh and pushed me away. "You will escort her to La Borda today, Phillip?"

"If that's what she wants."

"The Empress is expecting her. Why do you always set out to aggravate me?"

"I don't mean to. Of course I'll take her today. Go with God, brother."

Impulsively Beau hugged Phillip. "I don't know what's wrong with me. Take my lady when she gives the word."

"Wait," I begged, "let me tie your sash. It is my blessing."

The black horse, which Lencho had ordered to be saddled, was brought up to the border of the flower bed. Beau kissed me again, said goodbye to Phillip and Lencho, and rode north with van der Smissen to find Juárez.

At breakfast, which Lencho brought to us on little rattan tables on the upper colonnade, Phillip ate practically nothing.

"Bubba can't run away forever. He can't spend his life fighting. He's a brilliant classical scholar, a fine planter and businessman. But he's becoming nothing but an unpaid professional soldier. When he returns, you and I must persuade him to go to Brazil—Colombia—anywhere but here."

"I've tried every way I know. He won't leave Maximilian."

"And I hate your toadying to the Empress. I find it degrading."

"Not if I won't permit it to be degrading. From the day I fell in love with Beau everything changed in my life. Carlota's imperious ways don't really touch me. I am too proud—too proud—" I burst into tears.

Phillip was on the edge of weeping too. I knew it was because there was no way he could help me.

The sound of Elsie's fast, light footsteps forced me to myself, and, hiding my face from Phillip, I called, "Well, Elsie, we must begin to repack. I will be leaving this afternoon."

"Oh, no, please, señora, not ready are the ruffles on your petticoats nor ribbon strung in the camisoles."

"Sorry, Elsie, but she insists on leaving us," Phillip said quietly, in a tone as natural as though it had never entered his head that I meant anything more to him than a pleasant Christmas guest.

I left for Mexico City with the Empress on New Year's Day. In her absorption with doing what she enjoyed most—running things —Carlota almost forgot to grieve for her father. Then, late in January a letter came from Napoleon III bluntly announcing that, heeding the wishes of his *corps législatif* in Paris, he was withdrawing his financial support of the Mexican Empire. He would bring all French troops back to France within the year! He was sure the Empire could stand on its own feet now. An Austro-Prussian war was imminent and Washington was up to the same tricks as Napoleon had been up to in 1862—snatching Mexican gold.

That brought Maximilian out of the double hammock at his Indian chalet to Chapultepec in haste. I was in the room when he read the next letter from Napoleon aloud to Carlota:

" 'The departure of the French troops may cause a temporary embarrassment but it will have the advantage of removing all pretexts of interference from the United States.' "

"What are we going to do?" Carlota asked, chewing on her handkerchief.

Maximilian turned to proud ice. "I will write and propose that he withdraw his troops immediately from the Mexican continent, while I, for my part, guided by my honor, will try and defend my Empire with the help of my new countrymen."

In an uncontrollable fit of rage, Carlota sat down immediately and wrote an insulting letter to the Empress Eugénie, one to the Emperor Napoleon, one to the Pope and whomever else came into her mind. I know she did because she had me make copies of them from Spanish into English. She said I had better penmanship than Luis Blasio.

In February, Beau, van der Smissen and von Kodolitsch returned from Paso del Norte where they had finally found Juárez. But Juárez had refused to receive them, saying he was too busy entertaining General Lew Wallace and General Philip Sheridan. He would not interrupt any of his plans and projects, in which the Emperor played but a small part.

I definitely resigned my post as lady-in-waiting when Beau returned. He said he was glad I did, and he pretended to take an interest in silver mining. We spent the cold months at Miramontes. To my surprise he never left the hacienda, not even to join the Emperor in Cuernavaca on Maximilian's frequent visits there. "I don't care for Indians parading as ladies," he sniffed.

In March we returned to Tacubaya and the Salms arrived in Mexico.

That made all the difference in our lives. The Prince and Beau, in Aunt Dell's words, "took to each other" immediately. We were a congenial, gay foursome. Our life assumed an air of normalcy I'd forgot existed.

Prince Salm was very aristocratic and brave-looking with a beautifully turned and waxed-brown mustache and keen brown eyes. He wore a monocle. People stared and he loved it. He adored

Agnes. She said she rode him with a tight rein because he was so hotheaded, liable to bolt on impulse. Inactivity was as impossible for him as it was for Beau. They got each other all fired up and before I knew it they rode off together to fight somewhere in the west with General Mejía.

Beau being away, I had no excuse not to substitute for Pacheco at Chapultepec when she came down with measles in March.

"But only for two weeks," I reluctantly told Miguel López, who brought the request to Hacienda Contenta.

Carlota looked twenty years older than she had in Campeche or in January. She wore nothing but shapeless black clothes hung with black mourning ribbons for her father. The sadness and depression that had always been strong in her had given way to a kind of sullen rudeness toward everybody. She was sick at heart, anguished. I did not know how to help her. I hoped Mexican measles didn't last as long as American ones. It was an unhappy time, culminating in a short bitter incident that determined me never to act as her lady-in-waiting again.

It was a blowy, bright day. I was walking on the terrace when Maury arrived unexpectedly in a wide black *volante* that looked like an oversized beetle. He was very red in the face, his tie was crooked and his hat mashed in at the crown. We walked happily into the castle arm-in-arm. Carlota was standing in the doorway of her apartment watching us. Her eyes were deep pools of dull shadow contrasting gloomily with the masklike pallor of her skin.

"Has she been ill?" Maury whispered.

"Not that I know of."

Unsmiling, Carlota greeted him, listening impatiently as he jubilantly announced news, printed in the *Mexican Times* that very day, of the landing of 250 Confederates in Tampico.

"They will be the last. I promise you."

Forgetting to take off his hat, Maury mumbled something about his having come to say goodbye.

A chill ran through me as Carlota proposed going through her study into her boudoir where nobody could spy on her. Thinking she meant me I stepped back into the entrance hall.

"No, no, you must be with us at all times, Berrien, so that Mr. Maury will not misquote me," Carlota said in a cold impersonal way.

Maury was dumfounded. He mumbled again that his real purpose in calling today was to bid Her Majesty goodbye before he sailed for England to visit his wife. He was leaving the next day for Vera Cruz. It was a sudden decision.

"What difference does that make?" Carlota's mouth didn't change its tight hard expression.

Maury looked questioningly at me. He got quite flustered. Drops of sweat popped out on his big nose.

"I think it's wonderful he's going to visit his wife," I said, much too loudly. How could anybody hurt gentle Maury's feelings as she was doing? I wanted to pull her hair out by the roots.

"We are not interested in your thoughts, Berrien. Mr. Maury, I sat in a meeting this morning with the ministers. All, including myself, voted to abolish the Colonization Commission. It is a farce. Mexico is for the Mexicans, not the Americans."

"But surely," his voice shook with agitation, "if it was a good idea less than a year ago, it is a good idea now."

As if he had not spoken, she continued rudely, "I will arrange a position for you in the observatory or as an adviser in one of the museums."

"Neither, Your Majesty." Proudly Maury rose and pulled me up beside him.

"You are not free to choose. You are a failure." Carlota appeared oblivious of Maury's indignation.

"Oh, yes, Your Majesty. I may not understand you or your sudden change in policy. But I am free to choose and always will be. I will never come back to Mexico."

I knew that this confrontation was not a mere matter of words. Suddenly, there was a deep and uncrossable gulf between them. Neither had any comprehension of the other, nor ever again could.

She didn't even walk to the door with him. "She is angry and sad and frightened," I said to him as we stood, hand in hand, by his *volante*. "She's not been the same since Campeche."

"It's all for the best," he sighed. "I came to Chapultepec wondering how to tell her goodbye. She always seemed so small and vulnerable; so fond of me. I've felt protective toward her. It's hard to understand..."

I knew what he meant. A door had shut. Should he reopen it he would find no enchanted garden. He had come to the surface, into the light of day. He knew now that there would never be a successful Confederate colony in Mexico.

"I gladly leave behind my illusions," he said. "I'd almost forgot that I still have important contributions to make... the transatlantic cable I've been working on, for instance. I will write you from London and you must write me often, for you know what your affection has meant to a lonely man. I wish you and Beau would get out of Mexico before it's too late. It's a bad country."

"I don't think it's a bad country, Mr. Maury. But I know it's bad for Beau."

As the *volante* rattled off down the hill I almost ran after it calling to Maury to take me away with him. Instead I went inside to formally say farewell forever to the Empress. This time not even Beau could change my mind.

In August Maximilian honored Maury with the Grand Cross of the Order of Guadalupe when the news of the success of the laying of his transatlantic cable flashed over the world.

True to his word, Maury never returned to Mexico. He blamed the Empress entirely for the failure of the Carlota Colony. Apparently he overlooked General Early's vicious criticisms of the venture in the *New York Times* and General Magruder's collaborating with Marshall Bazaine, when he became disillusioned at the manner in which the Empire played false with the Confederates.

Maximilian was being forced more and more to renounce his Liberal principles and submit to reactionary Mexicans like Gutierrez de Estrada and Miramon. He told the French Minister Dano that if France abandoned him he would personally defend his realm from the mountain fastnesses to the sea. His nice but ugly little Indian General Mejía had taught him how an army could operate without money. I could imagine Monsieur Dano's snorting laugh.

Inside himself Maximilian was desperate and frightened. He continued to send his officers to make overtures from him to Benito Juárez. They were totally ignored.

Then, guerrilla fighting increased. A French officer told Agnes that the French soldiers were running like crazy people after an enemy that could not be caught. And Juárez began moving south from Chihuahua, taking town after town with hardly a struggle. No one was surprised when Napoleon sent another letter. This time it was an ultimatum to Maximilian. "You abdicate. I get out."

Maximilian decided to renounce his crown, rumor had it, but Carlota had such violent prolonged hysterics he wearily agreed to dig into his diminished treasury and send her to Europe to implore Napoleon not to remove his troops from Mexico. Carlota knew the Empire could never survive without the French. This time Father Fischer and Miguel López were on her side. Beau and Prince Salm and van der Smissen were fighting in Tulancingo, but even if they'd been on the scene, I don't think their powers of persuasion would have made any difference.

The same faithful group that had gone with her to Yucatán, except me, accompanied Carlota to Europe.

Pacheco wrote to me from Rome:

> We Mexicans are stranded in Italy not knowing whether to remain here or return to Mexico until we hear from our Emperor. In the meantime if what we all suspect secretly and only to ourselves, never aloud to each other, is true, it is tragedy—sin coming home to roost. It has destroyed her for she will not admit her pregnancy, even to her own bitter heart.
>
> Once I heard her cry out in the night "If he had never come to Mexico! Or if I had never gone to Mexico! But things working as they have I could not help loving him."

Pacheco's letter went on to describe how seasick Carlota was on the ocean voyage from Mexico to France; how in Paris Eugénie and Napoleon evaded her; the cruel indifference of the Austrian Hapsburgs after learning of Carlota's condition; their not even answering her frantic telegrams for help; the bankers' and statesmen's rudeness and unavailability. All these things added up, culminating in one final frenzy in the Vatican, when Carlota insisted on spending the night in the Pope's bedroom to keep from being murdered.

> El Papa said, "I have been spared nothing in this life. A woman even chooses to go mad in the Vatican!" You should be with us, dear Berrien, for at least you would have been courageous enough to have physically restrained our poor little Empress from attacking El Papa's person. At last her brother, the King of Belgium, came on the railway cars and took her home.
>
> With felicitations I remain the friend of your bosom, Maria Pacheco.

Was I surprised? No. Shocked? Yes. Sorry for Carlota? I suppose so. In any event I knew I would never forget her. I rummaged in a special box and put on the lace shawl the Empress had tossed on my bare shoulders the night of her Birthday Ball. I sat a long time looking over at Chapultepec Castle, forgetful of all the petty unpleasantness, absorbed in a vague sense of sorrow for the unfortunate, over-ambitious young woman.

When Maximilian learned of Carlota's breakdown, he realized what she had meant to him. On November 24 he called together his council of Conservative Ministers to abdicate. But they voted 19–2 to support the Empire if he continued on his throne, and to raise $2 million for military defense. That wouldn't have influenced him but when they appealed to his honor he agreed to stay for a time.

Then things got much worse. Juárez now controlled so much territory that when Beau (recently home from Tulancingo) and I accompanied the Emperor for Christmas with the Bringas family in Orizaba, Maximilian announced that he would abdicate immediately after the feast of the Epiphany. No one was surprised when Father Fischer, along with General Márquez and General Miramon followed him to Orizaba.

Beau was present when the two generals promised Maximilian that the Conservative party would pour troops and money around his head if he would rely exclusively on his Mexican subjects. They offered all sorts of golden impossibilities if he would stay. But, Beau said, it was Father Fischer's appeal to Maximilian's noble spirit, saying that all of his friends in Mexico would be destroyed if he left the country, that broke him down.

"The Emperor hasn't been to Cuernavaca since last September," Beau added, "I don't think he will ever go there again. Guerrillas have looted and ransacked the Borda Palace and totally torn up and destroyed his flower gardens and his Indian chalet. No one knows where his Indian sweetheart and her baby son are living."

Phillip came into the city to tell us about the destruction of the Borda Palace. He warned Beau not to show up at Miramontes in his Imperial uniform or he'd be murdered along the way. Beau said that suited him just fine. He had no desire to travel in or to enemy territory.

"Are you safe there, Phillip?" I asked.

"I'm a Juarist, remember?" he answered lightly, but not happily. And then he told about the Juaristi burning the lovely hacienda at Atlacomulco and stealing all the fine Zurutuza race horses and talking birds.

"What more do you expect of peons?" Beau asked.

"I hate violence, even in the name of righteousness," Phillip said.

The Juarist glorious "mission" grew more revolutionary every day, pushing itself with a steady flow of violence. When Maximilian returned from Orizaba after Christmas he found Chapultepec Castle vandalized and looted by his own servants and soldiers! Fortunately he'd taken Tudos and Baby with him to Orizaba or they'd have been the first to be killed, since everybody knew how he treasured them.

He moved to Mexico City to live with no pomp or circumstance or court surrounding him. He felt the three of them were safer that way until he could honorably set sail for Europe, where now he knew he had always belonged.

33 ❧

February 5, 1867, was a momentous day. We were crushed together in high-backed chairs on the Iturbide Hotel balcony waiting for the first glimpse of Marshall Bazaine on his big sorrel horse leading the French Army of Occupation out of Mexico City en route to Vera Cruz to embark for France.

Wrapped in shawls and cloaks, Maximilian was inside the grand salon, shivering with an attack of chills and fever.

"It's just nerves," Agnes said bluntly, straightening her chic New York tam-o-'shanter on rows of brown side curls. In a lilac, many-bustled gown she was straight out of Godey's latest fashion book. In a flounced white wool skirt with a red rebozo tossed over one shoulder à la Mexicaine, at least I was warm.

The sun rising behind Popocatépetl glinted fiery white as it penetrated the cone of the volcano. It was the kind of morning one expected to hear church bells pealing joyously and bands playing merry music. Flowers should have been flying down from balconies. But they were not. Not even a red dahlia or a marigold.

I took Agnes's gloved hand and held onto it. With her I had a sense of security and friendship I'd not had in Mexico with anyone except Phillip, who seldom visited us in Tacubaya now except to bring Beau an accounting of the silver mine.

I could look down the Calle Francisco and see the Alameda and the Zocalo, covered with tens of thousands of figures in holiday dress.

A muffled drum was heard. Instantly everybody was silent. Two men who had been fighting in the street below our balcony suddenly embraced and kissed each other. And then we saw the soldiers.

"It is precisely nine o'clock," declared the elegant Prussian Minister, Baron Magnus.

Led by silver-helmeted Marshall Bazaine and his brilliantly uniformed staff the French went marching past the Alameda, through the Calle Francisco and Calle Plateros, over the Plaza de Armas, past the Imperial Palace and on out the Garita San Antonio headed for Vera Cruz.

There was the sound of feet and drums; just feet and drums. The silence that hung over every street and alley, balcony and rooftop was so heavy one felt as if the bright blue morning sky was about to collapse like a circus tent and smother us.

The French Count and Countess Seguier, uninvited, joined our Imperial group on the hotel balcony. The Bringas from Orizaba and the Adalids of the city, all in black velvet and diamonds, were on the adjoining balcony. The men had on their most formal uniforms and frock coats and tall silk hats.

Beau, Prince Salm, Father Fischer and the slippery-eyed Miguel López were inside the hotel salon drinking champagne with the Emperor.

"Hold Jimmy for me. Don't let him bark." Agnes slipped her long-legged terrier's leash around my wrist. "I'm going in and drag Salm out here to watch the show. He's as ready to explode as a firecracker. He and López had words yesterday. He swears he's going to pull his nose today."

Countess Seguier tossed a rose in the direction of Bazaine, but Baron Hammerstein leaned out, caught it and crushed it under his boot heel. She waved her handkerchief and went into an ecstasy. "What a brilliant army! With such soldiers the world may be conquered. And that will do. Let them only return to *la belle* France and they will march against Berlin and take it *à la bayonet!*" Finally she was hustled away by her red-faced husband who, Agnes told me later, had received a tearing bite on the trouser from Jimmy, at her whispered command.

The little Jewish physician, Dr. Basch, came out and sat in the chair left empty by the French Countess's disorderly departure. "Princess Agnes and Prince Salm have mercifully carried their menace home," he said.

"At least Her Majesty was spared hearing La Seguier." I pulled my rebozo up around my neck.

"But little else," he answered dryly. "She took her royal duty far too seriously."

José Luis Blasio said, "I wished for you many times in Paris and Rome, Dr. Basch. The trip was a nightmare from beginning to end. Her Majesty was never totally rational after Campeche."

"I blame myself for permitting the Empress to drink that broth in Campeche from what the Indians call magic mushrooms. I've been reading up on induced hallucinations among the Mayans and Aztecs. There is no doubt in my mind but that the *totoache* hastened her breakdown," Dr. Basch said.

"Carlota showed many signs of instability before we went to Yucatán," I commented.

"But knowing her temperament, I feel guilty all the same. She never spared herself," said Dr. Basch.

The ones on the balcony went in and out. Sometimes I caught a glimpse of the Emperor parting the lace curtains at the window and peeping out at the marching soldiers and the rich Creoles fleeing in heavy coaches piled high with jewels and money. I hoped Maximilian would come and stand on the balcony and let the people see what a true king he was. But he had been drinking heavily. He held onto the curtains to steady himself. The French soldiers wheeled and turned coquettishly, trying to flirt with the señoritas filling the overhanging balconies. But the black-eyed beauties looked down with insolent indifference.

Every now and then an explosion of ammunition being destroyed in the arsenal shattered the silence. It was rumored that Bazaine had offered to hand the city and all the stores of supplies to Juárez's top general, Porfirio Díaz, but that Díaz refused, saying he chose to take the city by force when he was ready.

Agnes was now on the street below our balcony persuading Prince Salm into a carriage. He appeared very unhappy. She looked up at me and waved jauntily. A coach filled with jeweled Mexicans locked wheels with their carriage. It took forever for the two vehicles to free themselves. I knew I should go inside and drag Beau away too but I didn't want to make a scene. He would not be as easy to handle as Prince Salm, who made no fuss at all when Agnes finally pushed him bodily into the carriage.

José Luis Blasio pointed over the balcony. Bazaine's pregnant young wife was being carried by on a litter. She was weeping. Wagonloads of her servants and treasures followed. From the quiet onlookers, someone threw a firecracker at the litter. The cracker was one of the kind they sell on Good Friday in the shape of Judas. It exploded under the lead mule. The mule heehawed and jumped up and down. But no one laughed. The police began hitting whoever was nearby with the butts of their guns. I felt sick and depressed.

"Do you think you could persuade Major Berrien to take me home?" I asked Blasio.

"No." He angled my parasol to keep the sun out of my eyes.

Sadly, I thought, Carlota wouldn't believe the way Maximilian looks today—so sad and untidy, wearing casual embroidered Mexican house slippers, his beard not properly combed.

A raucous song suddenly fractured the steady tramping sound of boots and the snapping of French flags in the rising February wind. The two erstwhile antagonists under our balcony were singing:

"Goodbye, Mamá Carlota!"

I hoped the doors behind me were tightly closed and the Emperor couldn't hear.

"Goodbye, my little dove,
When the French go
The Emperor goes too."

One of the policemen down the street shouted, "The Emperor is leaving the city. The Emperor is among the rich ones deserting Mexico. The Emperor is leaving the city!"

The cry ran along the crowd like a lit fuse. Even the marching soldiers joined in the tumult and shouting. "The Emperor is fleeing—"

General Count Thun jumped up. He looked over the rail and called back to José Luis Blasio, "Go inside and request His Majesty to step out and show himself on the balcony at once. He must make the effort. It is vital."

Fists were raised like torches. I remembered Dickens's story of the French Revolution. Inflamed people were running in all directions.

"Down with the Emperor! *Abajo el emperador!*"

The doors to the balcony opened.

Beau, wrapped in the Emperor's gray cloak, stepped out. I giggled nervously. He was wearing a soft black slouch hat. It hid his hair. His now luxuriant beard shone golden in the sunlight. He strode to the rail and lifted up his hand in greeting as he looked sardonically down on the French soldiers. Suddenly someone pointed up to Beau. The mob yelled and screamed:

"The Emperor! *El emperador! Viva! Ole! Abajo!*"

I could have murdered Beau. He swayed on his feet. He had drunk much too much champagne. Baron Magnus motioned him to sit down beside me. I suppose so no one would comment on his being too tall to be the Emperor.

Miguel López came out and stood behind Beau's chair. His thin fair hair was cleverly arranged to cover his bald spots. I hated his handsome supercilious face a thousand times more than the unctuous red one of Father Fischer, who joined him, lending credence to the masquerade. And Beau just sat there looking down on the melodrama and laughing foolishly as the surging mass continued to shout and cheer, both for, and against.

Part VI

The Chieftain

FEBRUARY 1867

There the Eagle-Tiger is fresh and in
flower
There the chieftain's fire opens like
a flower.
ANCIENT AZTEC WARRIOR SONG

34 ❧

A week later Agnes and the Prince were taking tea with Beau and me on the terrace of Hacienda Contenta. Beau and the Prince had just been notified that they had been transferred from the Emperor's staff into Colonel Count Khevenhuller's Cazadores. They were outraged.

"General Márquez is determined to maneuver all foreigners out of the Mexican Army," Prince Salm said angrily. "I can understand Márquez's aversion to Prussians—they know so much more about the science of war than he does. But my God, a draper's assistant posing as a general!"

"And that scoundrel, Father Fischer, has kept me away from the Emperor since the day the French left town," Beau growled.

"Only José Luis Blasio and Dr. Basch have seen him. I ran into Luis at the Hotel Iturbide where I stopped for a brandy yesterday. He was in a state because Fischer either cancels or postpones every audience scheduled for His Majesty with foreign ministers and envoys. Nobody is allowed to see him."

Agnes laughed. "Márquez is not as bad as Juárez's pet, General Escobedo. He is being raised to the number-two spot in the Liberal command. He was a mule trainer."

"He's the one you flirted with in Vera Cruz just after you landed, isn't he?" The Prince smiled broadly as Jimmy nuzzled his knee, begging for a bite of cake from a silver basket.

"To get you the horse you'd set your heart on. It worked, didn't it!"

They laughed, lighthearted as children.

I was about to call the houseman for more tea when he appeared, bringing a note to Beau from, of all people, Father Fischer.

The note requested Beau and me to come at once to the Hacienda La Teya where a group of Confederates waited impatiently to see the Emperor on a matter that they claimed to be of importance to the Empire. José Luis Blasio was not to be found. There was no one else at La Teya except His Majesty who spoke English. His Majesty did not wish to be disturbed this afternoon.

"By all means, go," urged Prince Salm.

"Felix and I will wait here for you," Agnes said, settling herself comfortably in a hammock hung in an arch in the colonnade.

"Yes," Beau said eagerly, "it is my chance to get behind Father Fischer's back and find a way into Maximilian's presence. I will insist that he reinstate Salm and me as his aides-de-camp. It's strange he wouldn't wish to be disturbed if the matter *does* concern the Empire."

"He's already disturbed. I imagine he's heard the news that Agnes's friend, General Escobedo, has outflanked his General Miramon and cut his soldiers to pieces in that savage battle at San Jacinto. Everybody at the Hotel Iturbide was talking of it yesterday."

"He was informed on the morning the French left that Miramon had captured Juárez's seat of government at Zacatecas and practically had the old fox himself in his clutches," Beau muttered.

"Is he ever told the truth?" I asked.

"Not by Father Fischer or Márquez," the Prince answered.

"Why doesn't Father Fischer send the Confederates away as he does everybody else?" Agnes asked, handing Jimmy a tomato sandwich which he gobbled greedily.

"He probably doesn't realize they're non-Americans. He is being very careful to woo anybody he thinks is marked 'Made in USA' these days," the Prince said.

"Except me," Beau said, shrugging his broad shoulders.

"Even you today," I said. "I'll get my bonnet while you order the carriage."

Hacienda La Teya was a large, if unimpressive, stone house belonging to a rich Swiss merchant. Beau and I spent an hour talking with a group of angry Confederate expatriates who had come from Córdoba bringing rooted quinine plants, grown from seeds Maury had ordered from India. Rather I spent the hour talking. Had the Swiss merchant or his wife spoken English it would have been wiser had we not been present. Beau behaved in such an unnatural and stiff manner he antagonized everybody. I clearly heard one of the gentlemen, a Mr. Talcott, say to another as they left in a huff:

"Who was that unpleasant gentleman with the big beard? He didn't make sense. When I asked him what regiment he fought with he said the Cazadores! There was no such outfit in the Confederate Army. He is an imposter. And I'm through with this Emperor fellow. Cinchona can be a miracle crop for Mexico and he wasn't even interested or courteous enough to listen. I'll be glad when Juárez chases him out."

I went storming back to tell Beau how mortified I had been by his behavior but he had disappeared. I walked through an open door into another room and then into another. I found him standing in front of a velvet curtain hanging from a wide *concha*, eavesdropping. He put his finger to his lips and motioned me to come and stand beside him. We could hear José Luis Blasio reading aloud in German. Then the Emperor's voice:

"Now let me hear how the letter is sounding in Spanish. My mother always hides many meanings in her words. Perhaps I will be receiving her message more clear in the Spanish."

" 'When the whole family was gathered round the Christmas Tree, Papa and I and our four grandchildren with their parents, suddenly the big clock struck, the one with *your* works from Olmutz, and it seemed to me like a greeting from you, chiming in the family circle from afar. Tears came into my eyes. The Emperor noticed them I think and guessed the cause, for he turned hastily away and yet I am BOUND to want you to stay in Mexico so long as it is possible and can be done with honour.' "

"We've no right to listen like this," I whispered. Beau let me lead him back through the two rooms to the one where we'd visited with the insulted Confederates.

Beau said, "I'm not going back to Tacubaya until I talk with him."

After a while Maximilian entered. He was surprised and pleased to see us.

"I have had good news of your Empress, Madame Berrien. She

has times now when she is cheerful. She wrote my mother, the Archduchess Sophia, a rational letter thanking for the presents my mother arranged to be put in her room at Miramar on Christmas Eve. Keep your seats—both of you. I've missed you, Colonel. But you know the reason I've had to let you and Salm move into another assignment. I'm trying to please too many people. Now I'll tell you something. I've made a decision. Five minutes ago I made it from a letter of my mother. It is my only escape from the ministers and the priests and generals who are my jailers.

"This is it: Tomorrow I take supreme command of the Mexican Army and ride out at the head of my troops for Querétaro which the Imperialists have chosen as their citadel. Too bad you and Salm won't be going along as my aides-de-camp. You mean a great deal to me."

Father Fischer and General Márquez came hurrying in. After glaring at us they managed to sweep the Emperor away to solve some silly, trumped-up crisis with his cabinet. We could hear the little spaniel barking as the Emperor went shuffling through the hall in embroidered house slippers to meet with his Mexican ministers and generals.

Beau didn't say a word on the drive back to Tacubaya nor did I, because I couldn't think of anything to say. I was thankful to see Agnes and the Prince still there.

Prince Salm could think of much to say. Mainly ideas as to how he and Beau could manage to get themselves reattached to the Emperor's staff, and ride for Querétaro with him.

Beau was easy to convince. Before suppertime, excited as rascals, they left to visit the Secretary of War.

They hadn't returned by the next morning. Phillip came in time for lunch. When we finished eating our usual chicken and rice and mashed beans and tortillas, Phillip said, "Dress up in your most becoming riding habits, ladies. We'll ride into the city and watch the Emperor take command of his troops. The whole town is on fire with excitement. The streets will be packed with people. Flags will be waved and speeches made from balconies. We mustn't miss history."

Agnes said she'd wait here. The Prince knew she was at Hacienda Contenta. Eventually he'd get word to her here. Anyway she hated seeing the Emperor the way he looked today—so sad and unelegant.

It was a pity she didn't come. A miracle had happened to Maximilian since the day before. Riding in an open carriage, the Emperor joined his troops outside of the city gates. There were supposed to have been 10,000 Mexicans in uniform ready to march with him but only about 1,600 were assembled. As usual, the ministers had promised mountains and produced mice.

Still, I'll never forget Maximilian that afternoon nor the wonderful reception he received from his troops as he got out of the carriage and gracefully mounted a handsome piebald horse with a fancy Mexican saddle and bridle. He wore a general's coat without epaulets, dark trousers, over them shiny black boots reaching up to his knees, and a large white sombrero.

"I can't decide whether he is playing the part of El Cid or Don Quixote. Were I convinced he is a modern counterpart of El Cid I might be persuaded to switch sides. Lately I've been afflicted with the unfamiliar itch of patriotism in strange places in my selfish soul. But look! He's even fetched his Sancho Panza along!" Phillip said.

"That's little Tudos, his Hungarian cook, on the white mule. Tudos follows Maximilian everywhere. And there goes the Emperor's heartstring—his Baby. He's the little King Charles spaniel sitting on the front seat of the carriage with Maximilian's Mexican servants."

"Were His Majesty wearing a silver helmet with flying plumes I'd definitely say El Cid. The whole of Mexico City is adoring him today. However, in that unwieldy white sombrero he reminds me too much of Bubba. So I am forced to continue to pronounce for the Liberal side and keep me and my fortune safe."

The Emperor was armed with a saber and had two revolvers attached to his saddle. He was holding a little field glass in his hand, through which he scanned the troops and the city walls. He sat erect and appeared strong, physically as well as spiritually. Gone was the stooped, weak-voiced Maximilian of yesterday. Today he was the man on horseback, in the heroic sense of the phrase.

Beau would have loved being a part of this. But we never saw any sign of him or the Prince. Phillip searched for him all night. By midmorning next day, Agnes's friend, Herr Hube, told her that Count Khevenhuller sent word he had seen the Prince and the giant with the golden beard riding out of Mexico City with General Vidaurri, one day's marching behind the Emperor.

Had Agnes not taken the disappearance of Beau and the Prince so casually I would have died of worry. She laughed at my hysterical relief when a messenger fetched a hastily scrawled note from Beau a week later:

Quiclican—

Precious Angel,

With Baron Magnus's help the Prince and I persuaded a most remarkable man, General Vidaurri (he reminds me of Stonewall Jackson in looks and manner) to take us with him to Quiclican, where the Emperor and his troops had halted. We galloped all night. There was no way to get word to you. We had barely arrived when the Emperor rode out in front of his troops. As he passed along the line on his wonderful piebald horse in the morning sunshine, the Prince and I were standing on the right wing with General Vidaurri. Seeing us Maximilian shook his little field glass at us and called in English:

"Zounds! Salm and Berrien! How did you come here?"

"Your Majesty would not take us with you," Prince Salm said, grinning impudently, "and as we would not remain idle in Mexico we requested General Vidaurri to take us with him."

"I am glad to see you here." Maximilian shook hands with us in a warm friendly way and rode on.

We will continue on to Querétaro with him. Keep Agnes with you at Hacienda Contenta so I will not fear a furtive lover creeping through your casement window and stealing you away from your constant

Beau

35 ❧

We didn't hear again from Beau or the Prince until April 10 when a half-drunken courier left letters with my own two tipsy soldiers at the gate. They took their time delivering the letters to us on the terrace where we were drying our hair in the sunshine.

A dusty wind was making the canvas awning crackle over the corner where we sat. Black vultures, their feathers ruffling, were skittering up and down along the edge of the red roof. Below, cornfields were blowing their green flags sideways in the wind and the windmill that drew water from a nearby lake was spinning gaily. The cliff, baked and yellowish, reflected the sun and the harsh dryness and gave off the peculiar decayed odor of Mexico, as if the ground had sweated itself dry.

I snatched the letters, crumpled and smudged from weeks in a dirty leather sack.

"Let's read them aloud," Agnes said, tearing hers open. "You first." Her hazel eyes looked at me with a wicked challenge. Her cheerful voice took all my will away. Gingerly I tore open the envelope. Suppose the Prince said sweeter things to her than Beau did to me? Back in South Carolina I would have been sure of Beau. Here—well—and it hurt me to admit it to myself—I was never sure of Beau.

"Hurry," she said, "or I'll think you're afraid."

So in a low voice I read:

Querétaro
March 20, 1867

My Lady Angel,

> *My Emperor is grand beyond belief. He bivouacs in the open and sleeps beside me and Salm, wrapped in a plaid on ground from which we've often just cleared the cacti. He still speaks of his desire to come to an honorable agreement with Juárez and if not to die gallantly on the battlefield. Army life agrees with him. His face once again glows golden and his beautiful blue eyes are no longer sad and weary, but bright and eager for a fight.*

> *Often it is I, wearing my white sombrero, who rides the grand piebald horse (thinking wishfully of my Teaser) into battle. It is a game the Emperor and I play, this change of selves. Our soldiers wave their sabers and rally round me shouting "El emperador!" And the enemy aim their rifles and charge toward me, and my big horse laughs Ha! Ha! amid the trumpets, as in the days of the Old Testament. What a wonderful life! I can't properly describe the exaltation of it.*

> *Last week, 13 March to be exact, Maximilian presented medals for valor to his officers and men. The soldiers' were of gold and silver but ours were bronze. As he stepped back, General Miramon stepped forward and pinned a bronze medal on his uniform saying, "Your Majesty has deserved this more than any of us."*

> *That night, as we lay side by side under a canopy of stars, Maximilian told Salm and me that that gesture from an ex-*

Republican President of Mexico, who had been against a monarchy, made him feel that at last he truly belonged to Mexico.

Though I could never feel that way, I know I belong to the Emperor. Yet sometimes I fancy I hear you calling in the night, "Maxl! Maxl!" And I hear myself answering: "Angel, where are you? And when are you coming to Querétaro?"

Assure the lively Princess Agnes that her Prince has distinguished himself in every battle in which the Cazadores have fought as has your devoted husband.

General Baynard Berrien of His Majesty's
Imperial Mexican Army

"What does he mean, General?"

"My letter was written three days later. Maybe Felix will explain. Unless—"

"More fantasy?" I murmured.

"Listen—

Querétaro
23 March 1867

My beloved wife,

I trust you and Jimmy are well and snug at Hacienda Contenta. When I left you on the terrace that afternoon the best part of me remained with you, as always.

The next day the Emperor invited me and Colonel Berrien to ride on either side of him. Almost at once an enemy force attacked us. Maximilian suddenly and unexpectedly let out a wild warcry and with a look of savage joy, gave his first military command! From that day on he has exulted in every skirmish and battle with the enemy. He told me, as we rode into Querétaro, that he was happier than he had been in years and, believe me, my dear, he looks it.

Querétaro, alas, is full of dissension among the generals. Márquez undermines every reckless plan of Miramon's; Mendez hates Miramon and Márquez. Only the little ugly Indian, General Mejía, is loved and respected by everyone, even this tough German cadet!

We were welcomed to Querétaro with flowers and speeches. But at a council of war yesterday, the three Mexican generals finally admitted our weakness, and the fact that we haven't won a single battle. They gave in to Maximilian, agreeing to send Márquez to Mexico City to order the Austrian regiments to proceed at once to our relief here in Querétaro. We are running out of food, money and ammunition; only our morale remains steadfast and strong.

But I'll make you a wager that money, from the sale of the Emperor's treasures which was handled by Father Fischer, will not be forthcoming. Nor will Fischer.

Now—back to here. Our headquarters are on the Cerro de las Campañas looking over the lovely colonial town of Querétaro, surrounded by orange groves and cornfields and white-washed haciendas. But evil Márquez, who is laughingly labeled Chief of Staff, hasn't had sense enough to occupy these haciendas. Anyone experienced in strategy has only to stand on the cerro to realize that Querétaro is the worst place in the world to defend, as every house can be reached by gunfire from the surrounding hills, and can only be protected if there are sufficient troops to occupy those hills.

Unfortunately my hero is consulting too many people and listens to everybody's advice. He waits for things to happen and waits and waits and waits.

Tell the beautiful Mrs. B. that I have great trouble restraining her big battle-bemused husband. I've never seen but one fighter so fierce and brave: Captain Rodríquez. I can comprehend Rodríquez; after all Mexico is his country. But Berrien deals in delusions so obscure and impossible I have difficulty comprehending. And he wears his new bronze medal as if it were a crucifix. I, being a simpler soul, merely wax and turn my mustaches and tighten my monocle at a prouder angle because of mine.

Márquez, whom Berrien and I call Don Leopardo, left for Mexico City yesterday. He is taking 1,000 horsemen to break through the enemy's lines. That leaves us here with only 7,000 men! He is to collect the money and the Austrian regiments and reinforcements and return at once to Querétaro. This is our only hope of survival, believe me.

Run around Mexico City and listen with your keen ears to find out if Márquez has obeyed orders and if General Escobedo is coming this way with 16,000 troops from the North and if Regules and Corona are advancing on us from the west with 10,000, as we have heard rumored. Yourself bring the news. I cannot be parted from you any longer, my love. See to it.

This letter should reach you within hours. The corporal who is carrying the mail sack swears he must pass Herr Hube's house on the way to his own home near Tacubaya.

I love you, sweet Princess. You and that rascal, Jimmy, completely fill up the heart of your General Prince

Salm

P. S. I forgot to mention that the Emperor has made Berrien and me generals. López is darkly angry and refuses to speak to us. The Emperor was persuaded by Miramon not to raise López because of something ugly in his past when he was attached to Santa Anna's staff.

36

"Márquez has betrayed the Emperor!" a shocked Agnes cried.

Márquez had arrived in Mexico City with the thousand Imperial horsemen on March 27. Balls, dinners, fiestas and fireworks had acclaimed him the hero of the hour after hearing him brag of stupendous victories he had won over the Juaristi at Querétaro. I had cried "*Viva!*" and "*Ole*" to the traitor louder than anybody. I had even led a quadrille with him at the Adalid's mansion on April 1. That was the very night before Márquez left the city, headed for Puebla, not Querétaro, to stage his own campaign. He was accompanied by the Austrian regiments of unsuspecting Count Khevenhuller, Baron Hammerstein, von Kodolitsch and von Kollonitz (the foreigners he'd insisted the Emperor leave behind in February!).

"We must go at once to Father Fischer, and tell him the truth," I said indignantly.

And at this moment Phillip announced himself.

His sunburned face seemed darker than usual as he strode proudly in. He was very erect and his expressive voice more resonant than I'd ever heard it. He looked at me with his glinting brown eyes, very much the man to the rescue.

"I've come to take you ladies away. The Liberal soldiers will be here within the hour. Díaz has totally routed Márquez and the Imperial forces at Puebla. It is a terrible calamity. The news has spread through Mexico like a whirlwind. The entire Imperial Infantry went over to the Liberal side; the paid conscripts hid in the sugar cane and cornfields; the artillery cut their horses loose and rode off on them."

"And Márquez?"

"He abandoned his army and fled the Empire. Only the Austrian brigade stood firm. Colonel von Kodolitsch and his Hussars are bringing the remnants back to Mexico City. But this is the end of their usefulness to the Emperor. Have you had word from Querétaro?"

"Yes—here are two letters."

My heart was beating so fast I could scarcely breathe. I tried to imagine what it was going to be like: Mexico City taken over by the Liberals. Attacked by the Liberals! And Díaz marching into Tacubaya at that very minute!

Jimmy bounded in, followed by Agnes's maid, Margarita. In her haste she'd buttoned her dress wrong. It bulged out over her bosom. "Has something happened? The other servants have run away."

"Yes and no . . ." I said, completely distraught over Phillip's horror story.

"Pull yourself together and make up your mind to leave here at once. The Hacienda Contenta will be one of the first targets when the Liberals get here." Phillip reached for my hand; protectively his fingers gathered mine inside. Drums and bugles were sounding close and closer. "Listen! Díaz has already occupied Tacubaya. We may be too late."

"No, we aren't," said Agnes positively. "I know a back lane to Herr Hube's. We'll be safe once we're there. He's a friend and colleague of Díaz. Where did Jimmy go? Jimmy! Come to Mamá quick! Follow me, Angelica."

I wanted to take time to snatch up a tintype of Edward standing by his rocking horse that Aunt Dell had sent and one of Button on a bicycle, but Phillip had an iron grip on my arm and propelled me along the gallery and down the stairs. At the entrance doors three dusty Juarist soldiers were shoving each other inside. Others crowded behind them.

We ran swiftly through the kitchen. Phillip's carriage was hitched in the courtyard. Margarita was already sitting on the front seat. We jumped in. The driver cut the horses with his whip. I looked up at the gallery. In every arch there were bunches of soldiers with curious faces and heavy guns.

Jimmy growled and started to bark but Agnes silenced him with a raised finger. "By the way, Phillip, tell me how you always manage to turn up at Angelica's at precisely the crucial moment?"

"Oh, I have a hidden alarm bell where she's concerned," he laughed.

All the way to the Hube house nobody said another word. But Phillip kept his hand with its strange strong warmth and weight on my knee. My heart stilled and grew soft.

Had General Don Porfirio Díaz not hesitated for two days in Tacubaya and Chapultepec, but followed up his victory at San Lorenzo, he could have taken Mexico City without difficulty. But by the third day Márquez surfaced in the city and was gathering his demoralized troops. The Austrian regiments returned. Preparations for the siege of Mexico City commenced.

Once again I was an exile without a home or possessions; only the clothes I stood up in. Phillip gave me fifteen golden onzas for a new wardrobe. Frau Hube had a quick little German sewing lady who copied some of Agnes's fashionable dresses for me. Herr Hube did even better—he knew an English tailor who cut me the most becoming riding habit I've ever owned; and an Italian bootmaker fitted my feet into the most comfortable riding and walking boots I'd had in years.

And yet life at the Hubes was unpleasant. I didn't dislike them, it was just too much a skeleton life—desiccated—lifeless, despite Agnes's vibrancy. Knowing Beau's attitude I didn't consider moving to Miramontes, but I had almost made up my mind to ride the diligence to Vera Cruz and take a ship for Norfolk, Virginia, when Agnes began having nightmares.

PART VII 🌿

Don Porfirio Díaz

APRIL 1867

Only he who wears bells on his ankles
Shall hear my song.
Only she shall hear my song
Whose face is masked.
SONG OF XOCHIPILLI
LEGEND OF THE SUNS
(ANCIENT *Cantares Mexicanos*)

37 ❧

For three nights, one after another, Agnes dreamed that she saw the Prince, covered in blood, dying on the battlefield. Horses and men screamed in agony, cannons roared, and always the Emperor was leaning over the Prince begging him not to leave him, while the Prince kept calling, "Aggie! Aggie!"

"Felix is wounded or in terrible danger."

"What can you do?"

"I can go to Chapultepec. I know Colonel Léon who is in command there. He was in Felix's company in the United States for two years. He will give me permission to enter Mexico City and talk to the commanders of the foreign troops. If I know what is happening, I will know what to do."

After breakfast Herr Hube sent for Agnes. "What is this that Margarita has told the cook? I hear that you are planning to do something foolish."

Herr Hube spoke softly as he always did when talking to Agnes, knowing he had no chance of persuading her to anything against her will.

Agnes assumed a false, submissive air and said she wished to go to Mexico City and talk to Baron Magnus, Colonel von Kodolitsch and Count Khevenhuller to learn if they would surrender if Porfirio Díaz would promise life and liberty to the Emperor and his officers.

"And do you also propose to order the great General Díaz how to deal with the foreign commanders?" he asked sarcastically.

"No—merely to suggest it to him."

"You are impossible," moaned Herr Hube.

"It's the Prince's only chance!" Agnes said, loudly, as if he were deaf, dropping her timid manner entirely.

Flourishing his arms in despair Herr Hube fumed and quarreled, saying, "I forbid it. The Prince has left you in my care. I myself am taking the carriage to talk with General Díaz about the Prince. Restrain yourself and continue with your embroidery."

As soon as he was gone, Agnes chuckled merrily and took my hand. "We're wearing our prettiest dresses today. Let's walk to Chapultepec!"

"But Agnes—"

"Don't you believe in dreams?"

"Of course I do. I can't understand why I never dream of Beau anymore. During the Confederate war I did so much. Once his spirit actually came and stayed with me for hours. Now, no matter how hard I try, I can't touch his spirit. I am desolate because of it. I am going to leave Mexico."

"What a thing to say!" Agnes exclaimed. "All the more reason to save him." She looked critically at me. "You're too pale. You need to get out of this house and I need you as my interpreter with Díaz."

But Frau Hube had locked the door! She knew Agnes better than Herr Hube did.

"Oh, well, let's make haste and save our husbands." Agnes laughed but her words brought me to my senses. What had I been thinking of? Me run away in a diligence and leave Beau lying wounded on a battlefield? It was so preposterous that involuntarily I began laughing too. In no time at all we had climbed out of the window. We ran past the gatekeeper into the dusty street where the April sun poured warmth on my head like balm.

The soldiers along the way had seen Agnes before, driving out with Herr Hube, so there was no difficulty between Tacubaya and Chapultepec. Colonel León was eating lunch in a restaurant. Jimmy and I sat on the castle terrace while Agnes went to see him. I was glad it was midday and full of brightness. It kept me from seeing the dark little ghost of Carlota, the tall golden ghost of Maximilian, the grape-eyed ghost of Father Fischer or the ghosts of flushed General Bazaine and dove-shy Pacheco; all of whom I knew were lurking in the shadows. Even the gentle ghost of Maury would not have been welcome today. And the darling, impish ghost of little Augustin would have undone me completely.

In their places tramped short, earth-faced Indians and *mestizos* in white cotton uniforms of the Republic. From the barracks Indian and *mestizo* prisoners, in the uniforms of the Empire, clamored feebly against the rising wind in Montezuma's cypress trees.

"Angelica darling, forgive me for being so long. It wasn't easy to convince Colonel León but he has finally written passes for us to enter the city *and* a letter to Díaz. Were you asleep?"

"No," I said, jumping up and shaking the wrinkles out of my rose muslin skirt. "I was daydreaming. Shall we walk the rest of the way? I could walk forever."

"It's only two more miles," she said blithely. "Colonel León says Querétaro cannot hold out much longer. We must get there quickly."

It was late afternoon when we rang the bell at the residence of the Prussian Minister. Baron Magnus greeted us stiffly. I couldn't, of course, understand what he and Agnes said to each other in German, but gradually his hostility to us lessened and he ordered a carriage to take us to see Colonel von Kodolitsch and Colonel Count Khevenhuller.

When we were in the carriage Agnes put her arm around me and began to cry.

"I'm silly enough to believe that God is taking care of us," she whispered.

"He has to be," I said, feeling that some influence, far beyond us, was showing its power and arranging all the marvelous events that were taking place. At least I considered them marvels.

When Agnes finished three more sobs she blew her nose and said gaily, "I never could stand Baron Magnus, but you would have been proud of me could you have understood what I said. I made him think all this was entirely his idea."

"Then why doesn't he make the overture to Díaz? Why you?"

Agnes tapped her front tooth with her forefinger. "Because he knows how persistent I am and that no insult Díaz might offer could in any way make me betray myself. I'm no Prussian. My pride is not unbending. I can close my eyes and do anything, can you?"

Can I? I hope I am never put to the test. I know I can do anything that requires courage if someone I love is in danger. But anything? "I don't know, Agnes, I really don't."

"Well, you'd better think about it because before this adventure is over you will probably have to decide. Being a spy or a go-between forces you to do many things you wouldn't do if, as Herr Hube suggested, you stuck to your embroidery."

The conversation was in German. Agnes translated everything quickly to me as it progressed.

Haggard and exhausted, Count Khevenhuller wanted to surrender at once, but stiffly controlled Colonel von Kodolitsch insisted on first learning of the Emperor's will. Count Thun had returned to Austria. The new Austrian Minister was a fool. He could not even make a simple decision.

They were still shocked and horrified at what they had done: obeyed Márquez and gone with him to fight at Puebla instead of to the relief of their beloved Emperor at Querétaro.

To my wonder, they hung on Agnes's words. I suppose she was their last straw. After all there was no one else. Everyone else had gone.

"Which of you will meet with Díaz and discuss the matter?" Agnes asked.

The two great commanders fidgeted at her bluntness and looked at their toes. They said that regrettably Márquez was still Chief of Staff of the Imperial Army and had, this very morning, issued an order to shoot any officer or soldier communicating with the enemy.

"Well then," she said positively, "give me a writ allowing me to treat in the name of the foreign officers and soldiers. I must have something to show Don Porfirio Díaz except my face."

"It is too dangerous for us to put our signatures on anything until we know how His Majesty would have us act. Go on your own account. As the Princess Salm you will carry enough clout with the general for him to at least listen," Count Khevenhuller said.

"It's the best we can do," von Kodolitsch sighed. "Márquez is draining every drop of Prussian pride out of our souls."

The colonels decided that Agnes should request Díaz to permit us to travel to Querétaro to inform the Emperor of the true state of affairs and to know his will.

Should Díaz refuse to give us a pass, the Princess was to offer Díaz the surrender of all foreign troops in Mexico under condition that Díaz give his word of honor that he would guarantee the life of the Emperor and the foreign troops if they should ever become his prisoners.

We drove back to Baron Magnus's and asked him to give us proof that we were in truth agents of the foreign officers. Although he would not sign his name either, he did promise to pay all our expenses and introduce us to a Madame Baz, whose husband was a Liberal general, and who had often acted as a go-between for Magnus with Juárez. Perhaps she would go with us to Díaz tomorrow.

It was growing dark. We were very tired but we called on Madame Baz. She said her husband had himself been ordered to go to Escobedo in Querétaro. She gave us a note to Díaz saying that Princess Salm really was deputed by the Prussian Minister and the foreign officers to act in their behalf. "Tell Herr Hube what has gone on. Perhaps he will escort you to Díaz. He is greatly indebted to Prince Salm's family."

It had been the longest day. Agnes slept with her head hanging out of the carriage window all the way back to the Hubes'. I think she could curl up in a foxhole and be perfectly comfortable, so long as she knew she was in the middle of whatever was going on. And she doesn't worry like I do. I had a terrible time getting to sleep, even after Margarita had bathed me and helped me climb into Frau Hube's big ugly bed. And then—I guess it was because I was overtired—I had the most awful nightmare about Beau.

A storm had blown up. I went to pull in the windows but the cool damp air felt so good I pushed the gauze curtains aside and lay back down on the foot of the bed. I watched the lightning stab back and forth across the sky and listened to the thunder boom and crash across the courtyard.

Suddenly above the thunder I heard a familiar whicker. I jumped up and ran to the window. A flash of lightning revealed the white stallion, Teaser, reared on his hind legs, pawing the slanting sheet of rain aside as if it were a glass curtain. Directly under his hoofs Beau sat, stark naked, seemingly made of gleaming marble. He was throwing a little ball from one hand to another. His red hair was plastered down around his temples. Another stab of lightning tore the dark apart and showed his face—white and shining, beardless and beautiful—

Beau, I screamed—Beau—

Again the whicker—no, this time it was a neighing, a horse scream. The thrashing hoofs were coming straight down on that marble face—that smooth beloved face. Beau was looking up at me oblivious of the murdering hoofs.

"No—Teaser—down—Teaser!" I sobbed.

But the thunder kept booming, drowning out my voice. The lightning stopped flashing. Darkness descended. I started running but there was a curtain hanging between me and the gallery. A curtain made of bristly blond whisker-hair. The curtain was in the shape of a beard—Maximilian's beard. It was parted in the center but fastened together with sharp white teeth. The teeth moved. A voice called softly, "Maxl! Maxl!"

I screamed and I screamed until I woke up lying under the window. I knew I had not seen Teaser or Beau. I knew I had only dreamed of my love. And I also knew that tomorrow I was going to do anything in my power to charm Díaz into giving me a pass to Querétaro. There was nothing he could ask of me I would not do.

38 ❧

To our surprise fat, red-faced Herr Hube was so pleased with what we had done, he called us *liebchens* and fixed us a guacamole of avocados and tomatoes to eat with our breakfast of potato cakes and bacon.

"Dress up," he said, beaming through his round spectacles, "the general has an eye for pretty ladies."

Herr Hube rode a fat pacing mule along with us to Díaz's headquarters. Agnes and I vied with each other to see who could make our prancy horses step the highest along the hedges of spikey maguey and through the wide pools of water in the muddy road.

Liberal soldiers were everywhere, lounging, playing cards or marching. Because of Herr Hube we were ushered into the Archbishop's Palace at once and our cards taken away on a silver waiter that a little brown-faced boy of about eight held out to us.

General Don Porfirio Díaz was very handsome, of medium height with brilliant black intelligent eyes, a full sensual mouth and enormous ears with tufts of black hair growing out of them. He was wearing a blue cutaway coat with brass buttons, blue trousers and high boots. For a second my heart stood still, burningly aware of his physical presence, his hard male body inside his thin blue clothes. His black eyes shone appreciatively as he took my hand. My whole body grew tense in an effort to excite this dark glistening man, for I knew deep inside me that he was the key.

"*Es muy flaca y alta y blanca como Ixtaccihuatl. Me gusta,*" he said in a low dangerous voice.

"He says I am very thin and like the white woman volcano," I told a curious Agnes.

"*Linda.*" He still held my hand, studying it with a sort of wonder at the contrast with his dark brown one.

Herr Hube cleared his throat. Díaz instantly clicked his heels, dropped my hand as if it seared his fingers, and turned his back, addressing himself entirely to Agnes, though I had to interpret everything he said.

He'd heard from Colonel León that the Princess Salm had an offer from the foreign troops in Mexico City for surrender. He would listen. Not to promise. Only to listen.

I watched myself in a mirror. My black riding habit fitted my body like a glove. My magnolia skin glistened as much as his brown skin did.

I could hardly believe my ears when that earthy, darkly glowing man, his eyes flashing, turned to me and said harshly, "I do not believe a word you or the Princess Salm says. You only wish to go to Querétaro to carry messages from the garrison in Mexico City that could end with a plan for Márquez to attack the Liberals. Márquez! That old fox will use the seven days it will take you señoras to go to Querétaro and return, to fortify the city against me. All this I know, do you comprehend?"

"Please, General Díaz, let me explain our position as regards the Emperor."

"No! Never! In addition it is beyond my power to make any promises with reference to the Emperor. I command only one-half of the Liberal Army and I can only treat about Mexico City which I will take when I am ready. Juárez will in the end decide for the Emperor. As for Márquez: he should be hung not dealt with. But, if the foreign troops will come to me personally and surrender, I will grant them life and liberty and all they can carry with them except their guns. For example: I will take them at government expense to any port they choose in order to return to Europe, or, Señora Angel in your case, the United States."

Shocked, I translated this to a shocked Agnes.

"I was sure your riding vest had undone him. Nag him about our passes."

But his glowing face had changed to a mask, crude and half-savage. He closed his eyes as Herr Hube stood up and spoke with tears of Prince Salm and his countrymen so far from home. He implored the general to trust Princess Salm as their emissary. "All bloodshed will cease and the country will bless you as its savior, Herr General."

"The country or these señoras, Herr Hube?"

"General Díaz," I said as softly as I could, "we have taken too much of your time. Will you give me a pass only to visit my husband, an American, who I have reason to believe is wounded?"

"Yes," he snapped impatiently, but coming very close to me. So close his dominant maleness exuded like incense. I could understand all I had heard about his power to lead men. He had the gift of demon power. The oldest, darkest gift of all.

I had a power too. I had almost forgotten my own power in my blind proneness to Beau. I moved closer to Díaz.

"Now?"

Again Herr Hube rebuked us with a cough. And again Díaz clicked his heels, acknowledging.

"Tomorrow, señora. No, not tomorrow. Tomorrow is Good Friday. I never do anything but pray on Good Friday. Come Saturday. I will also give you a letter to Escobedo. I will leave it to him whether or not he will permit you to enter Querétaro."

"Would *you* permit us, General?" I was not about to give up my advantage.

"No, Señora Angel, even though you are so thin and tall and the color of the moon. And let me say that for your sake it is good that it is you who speak the Spanish and not the Princess; she has an evil glint in her eye that I do not trust, is it not so?"

He laughed and sent for a tray of coffee.

"Until Saturday." He lifted his cup to me and I mine to him, smiling.

"What a siren *you* have turned out to be," Agnes said as we cantered home. "We do make a pair of rascals, don't we?"

Good Friday was on April 19. No horse or mule or carriage of any sort was permitted to enter Mexico City so Agnes and I walked the four miles from Tacubaya, knowing how necessary it was for us to inform Baron Magnus and the colonels about what had gone on at our meeting with Díaz. We felt terribly important; as if the fate of Mexico rested entirely on our lively backs. We talked quite pompously all the way to Baron Magnus's.

The colonels were with him, waiting for us. Over lovely glasses of rum and orange juice, everybody agreed that the immediate move should be for Agnes and me to procure the passes from Díaz and to travel to Querétaro. There we could learn the Emperor's feelings about Díaz's promise.

We ate lunch with the Baroness in the garden. It was cool and shady. The banana trees made swishing sounds that harmonized with the splashing fountain. It was so relaxing, I had to force myself to rise and say it was time for us to leave. But Baron Magnus said no, we must remain at the Prussian Embassy until after Easter. It was not safe for women to be walking on the road. Good Friday was a holiday. Two elegantly dressed foreign ladies would be to the soldiers and the workers, full of pulque and carnal appetites, like an open gate to a bull.

"And also I am afraid of Márquez. He is perfectly capable of arresting you as you approach the city gate to leave. He holds a special spite for Prince Salm and Colonel Berrien after they disobeyed him and went to Querétaro with the Emperor," said the Baron.

I tried to explain how vital it was for me to visit Díaz in Tacubaya tomorrow. Márquez could as easily arrest us tomorrow as today. But Agnes wanted to watch the Good Friday evening celebration in the city. She pooh-poohed my warnings about Díaz's nature. She had sensed nothing strange about General Díaz but I suspected his powerful ego. Agnes teased me about having fallen under the spell of the long line of Díaz's nose and brow that dashed backward proclaiming his Aztec heritage; his dark lips so smooth and savage.

I am no match for Agnes unless I can show proof. That Díaz had sensuously called me thin and tall and very different from Mexican women was hardly proof that he would wreak vengeance on me if I didn't keep my appointment with him. Nobody in Mexico ever keeps appointments on the appointed day. Especially during the Holy Week finale.

So I mingled uneasily in the noisy, colorful throng that filled the Zocalo and I bought a Judas firework. It was interesting that the grotesque pot-bellied figures always had gringo or Creole faces— never Indian or Mexican ones.

The celebrating people seemed unaware that there was a death struggle going on in Mexico; that their Empire was being crucified and their Republic resurrected.

"This is better than a circus parade," Agnes squealed, throwing out streamers of red and blue paper someone had handed to her. "Listen to the music! Have you ever heard such grand disharmony?"

It came from all directions—sometimes a miserere, sometimes a march, more often a habanera or a mariachi chorus of horns and violins. But most surprising were the drunken groups of Imperial troops laughing their heads off and singing dreadful versions of "Mamá Carlota."

"I am studying the Spanish just so I can understand the words to that song," the Baron said slowly. "Continue please, the telling of the words. I am not liking to miss anything."

I sat for hours with the interested Baron, the bored Baroness and the reckless Agnes in a plaza watching the long retinue of mitred priests with banners and crucifixes walk the stations of the cross. The Virgin in mourning, prostrate at the foot of the cross, was so lifelike I wanted to run and comfort her. I wondered if Maria and Ignacia Miranda had dressed *their* Virgin in black for today. I remembered the night the cat-face of Don Carlos had blotted out her lovely face behind the *cancela*.

A precognition grabbed my heart and turned it over in my chest. "We have made a horrible mistake. Díaz will be furious *and* insulted." I cried out in Spanish, "I have lost my finest ally."

People around us hissed and pointed two fingers at me as if I'd blasphemed. Their faces were further reddened by the glare of hundreds of candles mingling their little fires with the scarlet, black and purple of an amazing sunset so garish it appeared to have been spewed up by a whole hell full of devils. My resistance shriveled. I went with the tide.

On April 22, Easter Monday, Baron Magnus decided it was safe for us to drive through the Liberal garrison at Chapultepec and sent us home in his carriage. Frau Hube met us at the door in tears.

Yesterday Díaz had issued an order: All persons who proposed to leave the area of Mexico City under pretext of negotiating would be shot.

Herr Hube had been to General Baz. He and the general were at the Archbishop's Palace this minute attempting to secure a meeting with Díaz. Yesterday they had also tried and the day before. Oh, why had we remained so long in the town?

General Baz had told Herr Hube that on Saturday Díaz came to headquarters dressed in his finest uniform covered with all his medals. He had been so heavily perfumed that the guards had nudged each other and winked knowingly. Even French champagne he had ordered, iced, placed in his office.

All this, said General Baz, was for the Señora Berrien, who had wounded General Díaz deeply by disgracing him in front of his officers.

"How?" I asked, knowing quite well the answer.

"By not keeping your appointment." Frau Hube's red eyes glared accusingly at me.

"It wasn't Angelica, Frau Hube. It's my fault; but we must take time to change our clothes and start all over. Your new white muslin with the big bustle will tame the lion, Angelica. Bustles become you more than anyone I ever saw. They make you look like a swan."

"It won't work, Agnes. Díaz is not like most men."

"Of course it will. No man could resist you in your swan costume."

"Díaz is not a cob with fiery eyes. He's a stone god with stone eyes."

"Let's hurry and change anyway."

As we were tying on our bonnets, a carriage drawn by four mules drove up with an officer sent to take us immediately to Díaz.

We were received by a small, wiry adjutant who told us we were to leave Mexico at once. He handed us passports and asked from which port we wished to sail. An escort would take us there this very day.

Agnes began shouting in English that they might shoot her or put her in irons but they could not compel her to leave the country. Hearing her from a nearby room, where he waited hoping to see Díaz, Herr Hube ran out. He begged Agnes to sit quietly.

And then a door opened. It was Díaz himself. "No, I will not leave Mexico!" Agnes rushed toward him crying.

He brushed past her rudely, grabbed my arm, pulled me into his office and shut the door.

His glistening face, in which the Spanish and the Indian had melded so perfectly, was hard as iron.

"You broke your word," he said. "Now I have no use for you, tall thin woman."

I tried to explain to him that Baron Magnus had refused to allow me to travel the road on Saturday. His expression never changed.

My power over him had gone limp. In his eyes was only the black stare of reproachfulness.

"I wish you to go away."

"I will if you will give the Princess and me passes to travel to Querétaro."

"I have to fight for my way in Mexico and you will have to fight for yours. So well now then go and do it. I will have nothing more to do with you."

"I can't leave the country until I hear from my husband. I am frightened for him." I felt my spirits sinking, my head going around. Beau was the stuff of my life. Whatever courage I had in my spirit was all for him; even the courage to pretend weakness and to lie. I let my tears rain down.

It didn't work. General Baz entered. *"Se permite?"*

Díaz turned on him with volcanic violence but General Baz was more like a Frenchman than a Mexican. He was able to wheel and bend and plead until finally Díaz shrugged his beautiful shoulders and said very well the Princess and the white woman who was a breaker of promises could go to Querétaro but he would not give us an escort. Escobedo might do with the women as he liked, permit them to enter Querétaro or send them on to Tampico or Vera Cruz or cut their heads off. Anything so long as it took place where he, General Díaz, was not.

As I left I looked back at him, pleadingly. He marched over to the window, leaned out and began complaining to someone below. "This whole palace stinks," he bellowed.

By the next day General Baz had written thirty-seven letters to *hacendados*, postmasters, innkeepers and officers to help us along the way to Querétaro. Herr Hube furnished four good mules and his own coachman. Agnes bought a rickety yellow fiacre; and a noted Liberal, Mr. Para, who had been sitting beside Agnes and Herr Hube during the time I was humbling myself to Díaz, offered to escort us part of the way. He had a mounted, armed servant as well as a hideous coachman who, I was positive, was a murdering bandit.

I didn't mind the way Agnes flirted with Mr. Para. She said we needed him to escort us the whole way and asked if I had any other brighter suggestions. I shook my head. All I could think of was that within four days I would touch hands with Beau. All the rest was nothing.

40 ❧

On the second day a platoon of Liberal soldiers galloped up to the sun-scorched post where we were changing mules. Agnes and I were cooling off in the shade by the well.

"Where are those soldiers headed?" I wondered.

Agnes dropped the gourd from which she had been drinking. "They're after us! Díaz has changed his mind and is going to prevent our reaching Querétaro. Let's hide!"

We slipped quickly into a nearby thicket of thorny bushes and flowers behind the well.

"Get farther down. Ouch! Everything is sticking into me," Agnes whispered.

Despite a prickly cactus under my knee, I managed to keep still while I peeped through a clump of poinsettia petals.

"I see Phillip!" I cried, jumping up and pointing at one of the officers in a gray uniform, mounted on a flashy brown nag with strong hindquarters and wide haunches.

"That's not Phillip. That's a Mexican. No! It *is* Phillip!"

He saw us and waved an envelope, shouting, "It's over, Angelica, you're free, free, free as a bird!"

After we'd hugged each other, Phillip read Joab's message aloud: " 'Angelica's case was thrown out of court in Columbia, S.C., April 19. Hooray for the Bonnie Blue flag. Pritchard.' "

The telegram crackled in my hot hands. It felt flimsy and of no substance. It had come too late. I didn't care anymore. That part of me and my life was too far away. It was as if I had just listened to a marvelous message concerning somebody else entirely.

While he watered his horse Phillip pulled me very close.

"It is terribly important for you to hurry on to Querétaro, lure my brother away from there and head out for Vera Cruz. This situation between the Emperor and Juárez is in its last days. Bubba must not be caught in the finale. He would never be able to handle it unexplosively."

"You know he will never leave Maximilian. I have no influence over him anymore."

"I never thought I'd hear you say it."

"You wouldn't have six months ago."

"You're free to go to your little boy now. It lifts a big load off my mind even if it doesn't seem to matter to you."

I reached out and caught his strong sensitive hand to me and kissed it on the knuckles. "Matter to me? You know it matters. Don't say things like that."

"It's no time for sentiment," Agnes interrupted. Her face and her manner were serious. "I recognize that uniform, Phillip. It's worn by Díaz's crack regiment."

"General Díaz has made me one of his captains because I speak three languages."

"I don't believe you've joined an army," I said, pushing Jimmy's rump off my foot.

"On the very day you left Tacubaya I came to Herr Hube's house and picked up your letter telling me where you were headed. I also learned that Díaz had signed a writ ordering all foreigners to leave Mexico at once unless they were in the Republican Army or employed by the Republican government of Benito Juárez.

"So I went to call on Díaz. I was never so impressed with anyone before in my life. He's the coming man in Mexico."

I nodded my head in agreement, remembering how strongly I'd felt Díaz's power. "But how did even he persuade you to put on a uniform?"

"Rumors are circulating that he will soon supersede Juárez as President. I decided to get on the bandwagon. Actually, it's not that simple. The truth is I finally met the man I can truly look up to and follow."

Agnes gave a wicked chuckle. "Angelica had the same effect on Díaz as Díaz had on you."

"Tell me about it." Phillip was gazing sternly at me, waiting for what Agnes would say.

Agnes gloried in telling Phillip the story of Díaz's interest in me and our foolish bungling of it. "If Angelica had only been willing to wiggle her bustle a little bit," Agnes laughed, "Díaz would have given in to her slightest request."

Sighing, Phillip took my hand and bent over it, pretending to brush away a mosquito that wasn't there, trying to hide his emotion, which he knew he must not show.

"I should never have offended him. That has turned out to be worse than had I encouraged him."

"It's dangerous to offend an ambitious man like Díaz." Phillip bit his lip. He lifted his head. "Now, your other conquest, Don Carlos, is powerful because he has control of his wife's riches. Insult him all you please—he would never recognize it."

"A woman should never offend any man she might be able to use in some way," Agnes said, smiling and pulling Jimmy over onto her feet.

"Your next conquest must be Juárez, Angelica." Phillip said.

"You have no heart to wish me such a fate," I answered playfully.

His face grew radiant as if I'd said I love you. "I'd not be jealous of Juárez."

"But you would of Don Carlos or Díaz?" I teased.

"Don't even speak of it."

"Juárez will be *my* conquest," Agnes said, unaware of the little drama taking place between me and Phillip.

"That he must," Phillip agreed, smiling.

I just stood there with gnats and mosquitos whining in my ears and black ants stinging my legs. I didn't care. Everything was going to be all right. For the first time I fully realized how much Phillip meant to me. How lost Beau and I would be without him.

"I don't understand how you, an American, could get past Díaz's dislike of foreigners," said Agnes.

"General Baz and Herr Hube vouched for me. I am now Captain Don Felipe Berrieno de Miramontes. My regiment thinks I am a privileged Creole. Don't give me away. If you do, I won't have a chance to help you all. Things are bad at Querétaro. A jubilant telegram from General Escobedo came to Díaz just before I left. You must be very careful of yourselves."

"We will behave as if we know nothing about anything," Agnes said, as we walked back to the fiacre.

"I almost forgot! I brought a letter for you, Agnes. Frau Hube said someone pushed it under the door and vanished. Wait and read it when you stop for the night. That Para fellow is one of Díaz's spies. I don't think he speaks English but he wouldn't hesitate to shoot you if you did anything suspicious in his opinion."

"Where are you headed?"

"San Luis Potosí, with the writ ordering all foreigners to leave the country. The minute Juárez signs the writ, it becomes law."

The soldiers, with whom Phillip was riding, and Mr. Para, came out of the post house and began mounting up. I continued to lean out of the fiacre smiling at Phillip for as long as I could make out his erect graceful figure on the dusty road in front of us.

41 ❧

We stopped for the night at a large hacienda belonging to a cousin of General Baz. The *hacendado*, an Imperialist, did not invite Mr. Para inside so Agnes and I were free to talk. We read the Prince's letter over and over.

My sweet Princess,

I had hoped to give you in person the abrazo *I send in this letter. Very soon now I will, for a plan has finally been made. You must pray that it is successful. The Emperor's health and spirits are failing dangerously.*

But recently when Beau and I (we have dispensed with formal names, my friend and I) had fallen asleep in the trenches I woke to see the Emperor standing beside us with that kind benevolent smile which warmed the heart. He had his little dog with him and he would stop and talk with the soldiers. This show of interest was so unusual and so flattering to the poor simple men that they adored the Emperor, who treated them not as cannon fodder, but as human beings. He is ready to share with them all their dangers and privations.

It is more the privations than the dangers that are depleting our strength and morale. The Liberals have occupied all the outlying haciendas (we could have so easily done this when we arrived) and food is almost impossible to come by. Little Tudos cooked us a feast last night: roast mule which had lain in vinegar! Tudos is our mascot. I recall one particular instance in which he made quite an impression on everyone. It was during one of our early, successful battles. I was close to His Majesty when I heard someone blubbering. I looked around and saw it was poor Tudos, clinging to his mule's mane. A spent ball from the height had passed right through Tudos's upper lip and knocked out his front teeth. The bullet was still in his mouth. Tudos spit the bullet out along with some more teeth. He still complains of his food tasting like lead! He follows the Emperor into the thick of any fighting without any sort of weapon.

Miguel López's regiment has been put in charge of the defenses of La Cruz where we are now holed up. Again Maximilian's heart has made a decision that your Prussian Prince considers a great blunder. López is weak and spiteful and eaten up with jealousy of Beau and me who are now Maximilian's closest confidants and companions.

We have accepted the fact that Querétaro is indefensible and that it is vital for the Emperor to leave; to make his way to the coast. It could all be so simple except for Miramon's stupidities and the Emperor's unbreakable habit of believing Miramon and López instead of Mejía and me.

We attack and win a hill; then retreat and lose two, over and over. We pack to leave the Cruz and then the Emperor listens to some foolish idea of Miramon's and we unpack and do not leave. It is all so maddening and foolish. Not Quixotic—just foolish.

Now for our plan: Mejía says that he can organize 3,000 of his Indian tribesmen who will slip into the Cruz at night and take the places of our men who will then march away silently with the Emperor. Why didn't we do this at Easter? Only God can answer that.

Yesterday, having agreed to the plan, Maximilian divided his personal treasures among Beau, Dr. Basch, Luis Blasio, Miguel López and myself. As Maximilian was pinning a decoration on López's jacket, Baby suddenly went into a frenzy and attacked López. Had the Emperor looked at López's expression instead of bending down to pick up the little dog he would have seen his enemy plain. I do not trust the man nor ever will.

Maximilian asked López to send him a black sombrero and some black thread with which to tie his beard back. Impersonating the Emperor, Beau will march out first, wearing a white sombrero, and allow himself to be captured. He will be taken before Escobedo who will have no interest in a bearded American in a white sombrero. Meanwhile, we will be safe away among the hills en route to the coast where the Austrian corvette, Elisabeth, is waiting to take the Emperor aboard. Beau and I will then make our way to Mexico City and our darlings.

Felix

On arriving on the *Cuesta China* looking down on Querétaro, Mr. Para guided us straight to Escobedo's headquarters in a little tent propped up with sticks. Phillip had been correct. Mr. Para was a Juarist spy, especially deputed to report on Agnes's and my every move and conversation.

General Escobedo was a round-nosed, heavy-faced man in his middle thirties. He had crinkly eyes that gave an illusion of geniality. His uniform was similar to Díaz's but with more lace, incongruous against the backdrop of the primitive tent.

Agnes explained to Mr. Para, who was acting as Escobedo's interpreter, that she had heard the Prince was wounded and wished to see him. Smiling, Escobedo shook his head and sat down on a raw wooden chest beside Agnes. Very close. He said he did not think the Prince was wounded. He himself could testify to the Prince's skill in battle. But if the Prince fell into his hands he would treat him kindly. More so than he would the red giant with the yellow beard who shouted as he fought and who had killed too many of Escobedo's brave soldiers ever to be treated kindly.

Later when I asked Agnes how she could bear to sit there and let Escobedo touch her hand and her thigh she shrugged and said she was experienced in dealing with horse trainers; mule trainers were no different. It was merely a question of understanding their preferences and not expecting them to be any more than they were.

"Remember it is I who want something of Escobedo, not him of me."

Even so he refused to give us a pass into Querétaro. "Take the diligence to San Luis tonight. I will give you a letter to Juárez. He knows both your husbands. Let him say whether or not you may enter Querétaro. I do not have the power to say."

"I go with the señoras." Mr. Para bowed.

Agnes jumped up and gave her hand to Escobedo.

"I will also send one of my officers to look after you." Escobedo rose too and kissed Agnes's hand boldly on the palm.

"But, sir." I stepped forward, but stopped suddenly, noticing the instant hostility on Escobedo's heavy face.

Agnes caught my arm and whispered reproachfully, "What's the matter with you? We've got what we came for."

I could feel the top of my head pressing against the hot canvas roof of the tent. It was not humanly possible for me to leave Querétaro without seeing Beau.

In faltering tones, but in Spanish, I threw my pride in the dirt. "For the sake of the holy head of Jesus, General Escobedo, and for the bloody wound in his side, permit me to look upon my dear husband's face just one single minute before we depart for San Luis."

"Señora, what are you thinking of?" he asked harshly.

"I am thinking of what is the honorable thing for a general to do."

This remark infuriated Escobedo. Whatever possessed me to be such an ass? I'll never know.

"There is no question of it," he said. "Señor Para, escort this woman out."

Realizing things were going wrong, though not understanding what was being said, Agnes begged Mr. Para to tell the brave general to forgive the silly señora who apparently had lost her wits from the hotness of the long drive in the Mexican sun.

Furious, I let Agnes lead me away and push me into the rickety fiacre. We were driven to the railroad station where, weary hours later, a pleasant English-speaking officer, Colonel Aspirez, brought us tickets to San Luis Potosí, paid for by Escobedo!

In San Luis Potosí Colonel Aspirez went to Juárez's headquarters first to explain why he had brought two foreign ladies, one a German Princess, the other a North American, to request an audience with His Eminence the President of Mexico.

"We can't have a repeat of the Escobedo fiasco," Agnes said positively. "Let me do the talking to Juárez."

"Suppose he prefers me?" I couldn't resist saying, and we both laughed. "But don't worry, I'm in control of myself this morning. I'll gladly remain in the background."

One of Juárez's ministers, a Mr. Iglesia, introduced himself as our interpreter.

"*Vámanos*," he said, perambulating like a stringy old turkey-cock ahead of us into an immense marble and gold-leaf salon.

A pure Indian, Benito Juárez was rather short and very dark, with hard black eyes. A jagged scar across his lined face made it even more sinister. He was dressed in ill-fitting black clothes. His hands behind him, he stood rocking a little on his wide feet.

"Which is the Princess; which the North American?"

"The American is the very tall beauty; the Princess has the many side curls and the bouncy backsides." Mr. Iglesia had no idea either of us spoke Spanish.

Juárez motioned to Mr. Iglesia. "Ask the American if she is from New York or Washington."

"Neither," I answered in Spanish. "I am a Confederate exile."

"One of those!" Juárez spat out the words scornfully, fixing me with his malicious snake eyes.

For a few minutes I just stood there towering over the squat square man who did not glisten; who had a power, certainly, but not the mysterious demon power of Díaz—rather the cold black power of the man of law without mercy. Yes, I looked down on that shaggy head and Juárez, aware, oozed the malice short men feel for tall women they are forced to look up to. My usefulness here was at an end. I retreated behind a potted palm while Juárez turned to Agnes, who had magically managed to shrink herself down shorter than he.

"And you, Princess, what can I do for you?"

"Change the mind of General Díaz, sir."

Juárez said he'd had no details from Don Porfirio Díaz but the two of us must have done something very dangerous to the Liberal cause for him to have suddenly ordered all foreigners to leave the country.

Agnes and I looked at each other. I reddened. Juárez noticed and nodded as if he'd known all along I was the real villain, not sweet little Agnes, to whom he had obviously taken a great fancy.

Agnes gushed all that had happened with the colonels and Baron Magnus in Mexico City. "But first I need to meet with the Emperor and learn his will."

Patting Jimmy with one hand and Agnes with the other, Juárez said, "I can't give you an answer until I am better informed. You must remain in San Luis for the present. Querétaro will fall within a few days."

"What of the Emperor, Mr. President?" Agnes insisted in her blunt way.

"Already I have too many such questions, Princess. From England they come and Germany and Austria and France and Belgium and from the United States. I am weary of foreign interference in the affairs of Mexico, especially Mr. Seward and the United States. As for those high-headed Confederates who came rushing into Mexico two years ago, thinking to take over our lands and silver mines while looking down on me and my people as if we were less than black slaves, I think I hate them most of all. Each request that I spare the life of one of them or the Usurper makes me only more determined to see that justice is done."

"You'd never shoot Maximilian, would you?" Agnes's big brown eyes went soft and sad with tears.

"I will never forgive him the months I have spent as a fugitive running from one frontier town to another. Or for calling himself a Liberal! Besides, he is not of Mexico. He is a foreigner."

Then to my horror, Agnes fell on her knees and grabbed Juárez around his thick legs. Juárez tried to raise her. Jimmy began growling. I started toward her, but out of the corner of her eyes she saw me, shook her head and clung even more convulsively to Juárez. Strangely Juárez looked more moved than angry. He, as well as Mr. Iglesia, had tears in their eyes.

"Have pity, Mr. President," Agnes sobbed.

Juárez answered in a sad voice, "I am grieved, Princess, to see you on your knees before me; but if all the kings and queens of Europe were in your place I could not spare that life. It will not be I who takes it, it will be the Mexican people and the law; and if I should not do its will, the people would take it and mine also."

I had to bite my tongue to keep it from shouting what a happy day that would be for Mexico!

Agnes let Juárez raise her up and comfort her as if she were a little girl. Then he gave her his arm and led her, while Jimmy and I followed, through the customary progression of big reception rooms to the head of the stairs where he said, "Until soon," and sent us to stay in a luxurious house belonging to an Imperialist banker who had recently become a Liberal.

On May 15, we were wakened by a ringing of all the bells in the city and heard that Querétaro had fallen. Our host told us at breakfast that Querétaro had been sold to the Liberals for 3,000 gold onzas by a certain Imperial Colonel López.

I was not surprised. But I was too worried about Beau to waste rage on López, for the banker continued:

"The Emperor and the Prince and the big General Berrien have all been captured. They are prisoners of war. Oh, dreadful day! Escape is the Emperor's only chance. If only someone had the daring to manage his escape!"

Agnes jumped up from the table and flung a rebozo around her shoulders. "Daring! Yes, that's the word! and I have it."

"Are you going to plead further with Juárez?" I asked.

"I will satisfy any scruples Juárez may raise. We may not be able to save Maximilian but I'm damned if I stay here and let them hurt Salm. You pack. I am going to get permission for us to return to Querétaro today!"

The morning deepened hour after hour. My thoughts ran like this: Perhaps Agnes is a prisoner now herself. Juárez didn't look like a man with any tenderness in his heart. And where is Phillip? I am so accustomed to his popping up when I need him, it is a shock when he doesn't. Is he still in San Luis or has he gone back to Tacubaya? If only the someone I hear running along the corridor outside is Agnes.

"Please, God, let it be Agnes."

The door flew open. "Juárez is at a celebration dinner. I can't get near him. The diligence for Querétaro leaves in a few minutes. I stopped and bought our tickets and secured seats. Where is Jimmy? Sitting on Mama's portmanteau like a good boy. Wouldn't you know—"

And we were off.

PART VIII

Querétaro

MAY 1867

Rivers, torrents and streams move onward
to their destination.
Not one flows back to its pleasant source.

EMPEROR NEZAHUALCOYOTL
(THE HUNGRY FOX)
FROM THE MANUSCRIPTS
DE IXTLILXOCHITL

43 ❧

As the diligence topped the final hill and I looked down over the tiled domes and baroque steeples of Querétaro sheening in the black and silver sunset I breathed a prayer that this would be the last time I came here.

It was quite dark when the coach steps clattered down at the Hotel de Diligencias. The streets and *pulquerías* were pandemonium. Liberal soldiers in dirty white and gray uniforms were drinking and singing scurrilous versions of "Mamá Carlota" and shouting obscenities at any woman who dared walk the night. There wasn't a chance for us to venture out seeking General Escobedo.

The pleasant pot-bellied manager of the hotel, himself once an Imperialist, knew the Prince and the huge, blond-bearded officer well. They had often eaten there and always paid their *cuenta*. Caballeros they were, is it not so, compared to the guerrillas and bandidos parading as soldiers of the Republic who were gobbling his tortillas and mule meat and swilling his rum and grumbling about the price.

Yes, he knew where the poor gentlemen were. Unfortunate to be prisoners but fortunate to have been locked in the Carmelite Convent of Santa Teresita rather than in that of the Capucines.

The manager rented us a room for the night and said that he knew a rich widow who had recently lost her husband, an Imperialist officer, in the fighting. He himself would take us to her hacienda tomorrow where we would be more suitable than women alone in the hotel.

The next morning we went to find a carriage to take Agnes to the Hacienda Hercules where Escobedo now had his headquarters. The streets were deserted. Everyone must have been sleeping off the drunken revelry of the night before. There wasn't a vehicle to be seen except a few pushcarts and wheelbarrows; nor a person except the vendors of *dulces* and bread and one fishman.

But someone had left a saddled horse at the hitching rail of the hotel.

"Don't stop me!" Agnes cried suddenly and ran and untied the horse. She caught her skirt up somehow and jumped—yes—that is what she did—into the saddle. I caught Jimmy's collar and held him while she galloped off, her skirts billowing like a cloud around her.

Someone was laughing behind me. It was the manager of the hotel, dressed in his Sunday clothes to escort us to the widow's hacienda. "I would pay many pesos to see that performance any day," he said, giving me his arm.

The widow, Doña Pepita Vicentis, was a slight dark woman in black muslin with black satin shoes and stockings. Her pretty little face, ruled by huge round black eyes, looked curiously saffron in contrast. Her black hair worn low over her ears was drawn into a smooth chignon on her proud neck. She welcomed us with shy effusiveness.

Her hacienda was a museum of velvet draperies, fine paintings, marble tables, pier-glass mirrors, dazzling chandeliers, spindly French chairs and countless glass domes covering artificial flowers and birds. Most had been collected by her father who had been banished twice; once for having too Liberal opinions and the second time for not being Liberal enough.

Our rooms opened into a lovely little chapel with paintings of saints and virgins holding lilies. Mass, Doña Pepita said, was held secretly here each morning. We were welcome to pray with her and take the sacrament if we promised not to tell.

In front of the hacienda was a jewel of a flower garden filled with roses, peculiarly fine dahlias, pomegranate trees and violets which had the sweetest fragrance. I had just finished picking a bunch when Agnes rolled up in a carriage with Liberal Colonel Villaneuva.

"General Escobedo was in a fine humor. He gave us permission to go to the convent!" Agnes said.

Suddenly, faced with the reality of seeing Beau, I came to my full senses. I had felt and acted like a sleepwalker for a long time. Could I control myself when I faced my husband shut up in a cell, waiting his sentence of life imprisonment or death?

Agnes went inside to change her dress while, tormented, I walked up and down the garden paths and senselessly flung my sweet violets into the fishpool.

The convent was built in a quadrangle with vaulted corridors going around a courtyard planted with orange and lemon trees. In the center was a pretty fountain that would have sounded sooth-ing if it could have been heard above the yelling soldiers, the barking dogs, and a man walking around banging senselessly on a drum.

A guard greeted Villaneuva and pointed to some narrow stairs at the far end of the arched walkway. Agnes and I picked our way up filthy steps, smelling of privy and covered with the slatternly wives and ragged children of the guards. Sweat and pulque exuded from the pores of the soldiers' dark, grimy skins. I wished I had kept my violets to put to my nose.

Colonel Villanueva said reassuring things to us as, shocked and frightened, Agnes and I clung to each other like little lost girls.

"Here is the place." Villanueva bowed and stood back, motioning us to precede him into a small foul room where several neglected-looking officers were lying about on coconut mats. One raised his uncombed head. It was Luis Blasio! He jumped up, looking as if he'd popped from a dustbin, and ran and took my hand. His were clammy and hot.

"The Prince is in the Emperor's room. His Majesty is not feeling well. But wait, I will fetch the Prince."

Prince Salm's mustaches, usually standing straight out at the sides in waxed and turned perfection, hung limp around his mouth. His cheeks were covered with unshaven stubble. Only his monocle still defied physical disorder. Agnes fell into his arms. He leaned to kiss her but she sagged like a broken doll.

"We've been trying to see you for weeks," she sobbed.

"Quiet!" the Prince said, cradling her. "The night we were captured, a Liberal officer, a German-American, rode up to me. He had been a first lieutenant of artillery in my company in the Civil War. He told me you had come to Querétaro weeks ago and, being refused permission to see us, had gone on to San Luis. I didn't believe him. He also told us that López sold the Emperor for gold; also that López came in and looted the Emperor's room while we were being taken to General Escobedo, before being locked in here."

"López also stole the Emperor's silver washing pitcher and chamber pot," an officer from behind Blasio hissed hoarsely.

And then I saw my Beau. My heart went cold. Black spots swam before my eyes as, rough-bearded, dirty and pale as a ghost, he rose from a cot in the corner of the room. He brushed his hands across his sunken eyes and staggered toward me, his arms outstretched.

Above the frenetic drumbeats, above all the hideous sounds that came from every direction, I heard his hoarse whispering, "My love—my Angelica! I told them you would come and take me home to my mother. She has kept the Christmas tree green for her Maxl all winter. She has kept—"

I ran to him as he fell. Dr. Basch and Blasio and the Prince caught him. Together we dragged him back to his cot.

"How long has he been like this?" I asked, choking back a flood of desolate tears.

"Since the night he impersonated the Emperor. General Berrien has been through much. I have just given him morphine. He is not dying. It is the disorder in his eyes and the rumpled whiskers that most alarm. Later today the barber comes. The general will look and feel very different this afternoon. Go now, greet His Majesty." Dr. Basch forcibly propelled me onto the flat roof over which we could walk to the Emperor's room.

Agnes murmured, "It's hard to realize that this dreadful place may be where our lovely dream will end."

It was such a big bare room. Thin and pale, the Emperor was lying on a narrow bed. His beautiful blue eyes were very sad. He greeted Agnes first, then he took my hand in one of his thin translucent hands and pressed it and kissed it. He said Carlota had loved me, that he was glad I had come. "How did you ever manage to get here?"

He sat up and drank some sugar water while Agnes told him of her negotiations with Díaz, of the colonels and Baron Magnus, about our trip to San Luis Potosí and the way Márquez was behaving like a dictator in Mexico City.

"If Juárez should unexpectedly offer to let me personally shoot one traitor I would choose Márquez over López," he said bitterly.

Tudos and Grill, the Emperor's valet, entered with basins of hot water and soap. Dr. Basch suggested we return later in the day.

"What can we bring you when we come this afternoon?" I asked Maximilian.

"That, my dear, you must inquire of the doctor," he replied. Then making an effort to be cheerful, he said, stroking his beard with a thin finger, "Drawers! Clean underlinen and sheets! They will do us more good than medicine."

On our way out I stopped by the cot where Beau was now apparently sleeping soundly. A sob burst from my throat. He opened his eyes and with a stern cold look he asked, "Who are you to presume to weep in here?"

"I am Angelica. You called my name not fifteen minutes ago."

"No, I never called your name. That was the other me. He has been gone a long time. I thought you knew."

Dr. Basch touched my arm. "Don't look so shattered. When you come later, he will be himself. It is the drug that speaks. Go now. Let him rest."

Agnes insisted we drive from the convent straight to Hacienda Hercules. "We must entreat Escobedo to give them a more comfortable prison; at least for the present."

"I'll go in and beg with you."

"No. You make Escobedo feel like a muleteer. I make him feel like a Chief of Staff."

Even Colonel Villanueva laughed at this. While Agnes was inside, he told me about López's patriotic exposing of Maximilian's escape plan.

It had taken place on May 14, while we were in San Luis Potosí. López showed up early in the day at Escobedo's headquarters. For a heavy sack of gold he revealed the intended escape plan. López told Escobedo he must act quickly. The next day would be too late. Mejía's Indian friends would have occupied the Cruz taking the places of the prisoners. The big bird would have flown. Escobedo eagerly accepted all of López's conditions.

When he left Liberal headquarters, López went straight to the Cruz and requested the Emperor to turn the Hussars over to him for a mission. Naturally López sent them away on a fool's errand. At black of dark the Liberals slipped into the Cruz. López had been very thorough. There wasn't a single Imperial soldier on guard. Even the Emperor's personal guard at his door had disappeared.

Had López not thoroughly informed them, the Liberals would have captured the big man with the golden beard, wearing a white sombrero, who walked out first, and that would have been the end of the story.

"Yes, without the warning of López we would have never suspected an imposter. So much like the Emperor he looked and acted. *Mucho hombre*, that one! He lit a cigar and coughed a few times to make sure that if anyone were lurking they would mistake him for the Emperor and capture him and take him at once to Escobedo. All alone by himself was the big man in the night while we, the Liberal soldiers, hid ourselves in dark doorways and waited. We could even hear him bravely singing a little."

"What was he singing?"

"An unlikely song for such a dark time. It was about a lady sweet and kind. Oh, señora, I am making you sad. Please forgive me while I tell something beautiful: such as his white sombrero shining like a moon eclipsing in the distance as he walked away into the night, walked and walked . . ."

When I am most moved sometimes I am my calmest. Inside I had turned myself to protective stone. "Did he not suspect your presence?"

"Who can tell? He should have sensed something. It was all too easy. If only the German Prince hadn't snatched the pistols from the Emperor's hand as His Majesty came out of the Cruz with a little dog running at his feet!"

"If only what?" I was consumed with horror and curiosity.

"We could have mercifully shot the Emperor then and there. He would have been armed."

Villanueva evidently saw nothing shameful in this.

"Shot him?"

"He would have been spared much, señora."

"Is that all that happened? What of Mejía's Indians?"

"As is the way with Indians, they confused the escape day. Many other strange things took place. The plaza was deserted and black but suddenly a big piebald horse was standing there saddled and waiting."

"Did López mean for the Emperor to escape?"

"I am not sure. It wasn't he, but the Indian Mejía who begged the Emperor to mount and ride for Cerro de las Campañas, taking his chances."

"The Emperor must have thought it was too late."

"The Emperor is an unwise man. He told Mejía no, he would wait for the Hussars."

Villanueva went on to describe how the Hussars had been stopped on their way back to the Cruz and ordered to surrender to

López. They were so furious they either shot their horses or drove them away to keep the Liberals from getting them.

"Did no one make any effort to resist?"

"When the Emperor realized that the plaza was full of Liberal soldiers he cried, 'We will cut our way through.' Mejía was standing beside him and said, 'No!' Then a volley roared from the left and flares blazed everywhere. The little dog must have felt a bullet whiz past. She ran away."

"Oh, no—not Baby!"

"The Emperor called '*Bébé! Bébé!*' but she ran on. So he said to the Prince who wears a piece of glass in his eye, 'Now Salm, pray for a lucky bullet to touch me.' In three languages he repeated that!"

"Do you know where the little dog is?"

"One of our officers caught her and took her home."

"Will you buy her back for me? I'll pay anything."

"It is not possible. The one with the glass in his eye has tried. But the officer has taken a fancy to the little bitch. He has renamed her Empress."

"And the man in the white sombrero?" I asked, knowing the answer but wanting to hear Villanueva's explanation.

"When he realized that nobody was coming with him to the hills, he, the crazy one, turned around and walked straight back into the trap. López tried to keep him out, saying to Colonel Miguel Palacios that your husband was not an Imperial general but merely an American expatriate. Being *estúpido*, Palacios made the error of ordering one of his captains to prevent the man in the white sombrero from joining the Emperor inside.

"*El gran hombre* went berserk when the captain merely touched him with his sword to motion him to go away from the prison. That one's neck he snapped with his bare hands. However, he broke up many more soldiers before the rest of the company, led by Palacios, literally fell in a pile on top of him, forcing him down on the stones. They then tied him up and dragged him as carelessly as if he had been a dead bull over the cobblestones into the convent and threw him in a cell without straw or water."

The sudden fit of trembling that took me frightened Villaneuva and he caught me by the arm, but I pulled abruptly away from him.

"What you tell me is too horrible, too cruel to be true. No! It can't be true."

"You must enlighten me, señora. Why would any man so sacrifice himself merely to be with another?"

A strange quiet of mind fell upon me, knowing instinctively that it was easy to reconcile the story Villaneuva had told me with my understanding of Beau's character.

"To understand why, you would have to know the man," I said proudly.

Colonel Villanueva shrugged and lit a cigar. "Never could I know such a man. So easy for him it was to be free. But he did not choose to be free."

Beaming, Agnes came out of the Hacienda Hercules waving her pink parasol.

"General Escobedo says he will move them! He has already arranged for a big comfortable hacienda to be used as a prison for the Emperor and the generals. And he's invited me to bring the Emperor, the Prince, Beau and you to visit him this afternoon. I have a hunch Escobedo intends to enter into some negotiations with the Emperor."

"We must make haste to find clean underdrawers for His Majesty!" I said woodenly.

Sitting at a long, rickety table in the center of the convent cell, fully dressed, wearing a wide black felt hat, his luxuriant beard beautifully arranged, Beau was writing by the light of a candle in a tall silver stick when Agnes and I returned with practically all of the gentlemen's drawers in Querétaro.

Carefully I put down my armful and hastened to hug Beau.

Everybody in the room laughed as I planted a passionate kiss on Maximilian's full soft lips!

A former Swiss barber, who was now also a Liberal corporal, on duty at the prison, had been summoned and had worked miracles on the Emperor. Beau and the Prince, who came in when they heard the laughter, had also felt the barber's skillful touch. Felix's mustaches had never been stiffer or better turned. Beau's beard was a twin of the Emperor's, washed, scented and beautifully parted in the center. He was terribly thin and appeared even weaker than when he'd been bitten by the scorpion. But he was in command of himself.

My having mistaken the Emperor for him tickled Beau more than anybody else. He continued laughing while I told him about Joab's telegram, but I don't think he listened.

"Our afternoon has begun well," the Emperor said, rising and giving Agnes and me each an arm. He was wearing his most formal

222

uniform and high black boots. Beau and the Prince, in gold-braided scarlet jackets and white trousers, followed us out into the yard. As we passed, the other prisoners all saluted the Emperor with great respect and love. We were just stepping into a beautiful carriage sent for us by Señor Rubio, the banker who owned Hacienda Hercules, when Beau bent over, moaning.

"You must go without me. The cramps have come back. Worse than ever."

I was wearing my bustled white muslin—my swan dress—and a white satin bonnet faced with tiny white rosebuds. Not caring if I tore my dress to shreds I started to jump out of the carriage, but the Emperor restrained me, saying, "Please come. Dr. Basch will take care of my dear friend. I need you."

"And I don't, for I go with you." Beau took my hand and kissed it with cold lips, and off we drove to the Hacienda Hercules in the Fabrea, escorted by twenty-five men of the Cazadores de Galeano in their showiest uniforms.

44

Near a fountain in a marble basin in the front garden of the Hacienda Hercules a crowd of Liberal officers and expensively tailored dignitaries and ministers were gathered. They bowed very low to the Emperor. They all wore pastel kid gloves, tall silk hats, black frock coats and highly polished, pointy French shoes. The thin black lines of their Spanish beards and their lush Prince Albert beards and their drooping military mustaches were perfumed and oiled. The smell was heavier than the full-blown roses shedding red, yellow and white petals on the gravel walks.

General Escobedo's blue uniform was so covered in lace, gold medals and braid that he was forced to come forward very slowly, his hand extended stiffly, to the Emperor.

Introductions and formal greetings over, he led us down a shady path to a rose-rimmed patio where heavy mahogany chairs were arranged in a circle. We sat and began speaking of the weird El Greco quality of the sunset last evening and the scarcity of corn and whether the harbor of Vera Cruz should be enlarged to take care of the shipping that was sure to increase in this new age of steam. Everybody nodded but nobody heard because two brass bands, playing different loud tunes at the same time, drowned out everything else.

The noise and the long-winded conversation confused the Emperor. He grew paler and paler. At last he told General Escobedo that he wished to make some propositions regarding his abdication.

Escobedo said the Emperor and the Prince could make the propositions to Colonel Villanueva who, later, would translate them to him. He, General Escobedo, would in turn propose them to Juárez, if it seemed to him the suitable thing to propose.

Reluctantly, I was about to follow Agnes and Escobedo through the garden maze when I heard a light step behind me. Turning, I saw Don Carlos Miranda. I shall never forget his expression. No longer melancholy he, but triumphant, gloating, excited in his strange, unnatural way.

"So—" he bowed gracefully—"fate continues to bring us together in the most unlikely places, is true?"

I tried to speak coolly, calmly, and could not.

"I have surprised you too quickly," he said, coming nearer. I backed away from him into a thick rosebush. The thorns snatched the bustle of my dress and held me. Don Carlos's sweet breath caressed my face.

"Not at all, Señor Mayor," I said, managing a pathetic smile, "I did not expect to see you here this afternoon."

"Don Carlos, not Señor Mayor, Señora Angel. Stand still and I will loosen the thorns that hold you. Such a pretty costume. Like a swan you are; or a white gazelle; perhaps even a snow leopard. Wait, you are almost free."

I could feel his hands pulling at the rose branches. "Now you are no longer a captive. You must come with me for refreshments and let me show you everything."

He put my hand on his arm and held it there while he propelled me toward the house. I could not resist him. The touch of his pale blue, kid-gloved fingers on mine was a caress. His voice was intimate and soft.

The dining room was safely filled with uniforms and mantillas and top hats. All bowed to Don Carlos. His importance was obvious.

He insisted I eat a pineapple sherbet and drink a glass of champagne. Smiling all the while, he watched my eyes. "Who would have thought we could come together at last in Querétaro? Querétaro is the deck from which the trump card of this game of destiny will be drawn. And I hold that card."

"What do you mean, Don Carlos?" Suddenly I realized how foolish I had been behaving. I knew I could get vital information out of this man. I was "dropping my candy in the sand" as Maum Hannah used to say. I had done that accidentally with Díaz. I must be more careful not to lose Don Carlos's interest in me. The champagne was steadying. I clicked my glass lightly against his.

"To destiny!"

"*Our* destiny!" he repeated.

"Where is Doña Teresa? I would like to pay my respects to her." I mustn't be *too* encouraging.

"She is not here. Being full of religion she has taken the girls to Rome to be blessed by the Pope and to be forgiven for having such a wretch for a father." He put on his melancholy expression and touched his nose, his eyes never leaving my face.

Did he suspect my sudden change in attitude? Or was he remembering the midnight in Jalapa when Carlota and I had stormed into his house and I discovered him behind the *cancela*?

"I know that you miss your girls."

"Ah, but this grand excitement of what to do with a captured Emperor takes my mind off all else. Or almost all else."

I put my empty champagne glass down on a silver tray that an ornate servant was carrying and picked up a full glass. Touching my lips to the cool crystal I lowered my eyelids provocatively, looking at him through the thick, black fringe of my eyelashes.

"What to do with the Emperor? Of course you will banish him to Europe as soon as he abdicates, which he plans to do immediately."

I had shocked him.

"Abdicate? There has been no such talk."

"It's going on right now. You can hear it from Escobedo himself, if he chooses to tell you."

For a moment he left a silence. "Escobedo choose? That nobody brags that he alone captured the Emperor. Escobedo a hero? What a joke! I am in charge in Querétaro, not Escobedo. Don Porfirio Díaz must hear of this at once, of course, but it is I who will control the trial. Juárez has arranged everything."

"Surely the Emperor will not be subjected to a trial?" We had not considered that. If what Don Carlos said was true then immediate escape *was* the only answer. And it would be up to Agnes and me to pull the strings.

I drank the whole glass of champagne at a gulp so Don Carlos would not notice my agitation. I felt myself being drawn toward a strange landscape and did not like the feeling.

"Escobedo is captivated by the Princess Salm but she is not quite so clever as she thinks she is. She overestimates her fascination for him as much as she does his power. Other than I, only two men have power: Juárez and Díaz. Escobedo is no soldier. At San Jacinto he shivered in his tent while the hundreds of foreign soldiers and officers were routinely slaughtered. Escobedo is accustomed to dealing with mules not massacres or court-martials. Like his mules he will balk when the Princess tries to lead him away from the path we have schooled him to follow."

"She has persuaded him to move the Emperor to more comfortable quarters."

"Has she indeed!"

I lowered my head and forced a light tone of voice. "What did you mean when you spoke of your control at the trial?"

His parchment-textured skin stretched smooth and tight across his aquiline features. "I talk in riddles." He laughed. It sounded sharp like a bark. "You have too much effect on me. I give in to your every smile. So now to please you we rejoin the ones suffering on the patio under the big bassoon. But I would be happy if, when we meet the Salms and His Majesty, you will ride home in my carriage." The smile of his face was false but perfect. "I know your husband is ill. I know all that goes on in the convent. Only I do not know where you are staying. If you will drive with me I will send my physician to visit your husband."

Thankful to have Dr. Basch as an excuse for Beau not seeing Don Carlos's doctor, I nevertheless made myself tantalizingly agreeable on the drive with him back to Doña Pepita's. It was of the essence for all of us that I learn how in the world he, Don Carlos Miranda, was going to control the destiny of Maximilian and of—oh, horrible thought—my wonderful, my disturbed, my own beloved Beau.

45

On my breakfast tray the next morning was a silver basket of pink roses from Don Carlos along with a letter in a gilt-edged envelope. I read it aloud to Agnes. Don Carlos regretted that he must travel immediately to San Luis Potosí. A hint I had dropped during the party at the Hacienda Hercules made an immediate meeting between him and President Juárez essential. But I must not forget my promise to play the piano for him one evening. A matching silver basket of identical pink roses would arrive on the day of his return which, pray the Holy Virgin, would be soon. He would expect me to keep my word.

"What so important a secret could you have divulged to send Don Carlos flying to Juárez?"

"We spoke mostly of Escobedo. I said very little." I certainly wasn't going to repeat Don Carlos's caustic opinion of her charms. "After he mentioned a trial I was so stunned I began chattering away about nothing like my Aunt Dell."

"When I told Salm about the trial, he was horrified; so was the Emperor. Now even the Emperor agrees that escape is the only answer. But it must take place before Don Carlos returns from San Luis, unless—?"

Suddenly the air tingled all over my skin like cold water. I tried but could not hold myself still while Agnes ran her eyes curiously over my lacy shimmy. Up went her eyebrows. Her meaning was as clear as if she had shouted it.

"Oh, no. Never. I wouldn't and I couldn't; not with him."

"What about with Díaz?"

I wished she hadn't asked me that. For I liked Díaz. I liked him so much that his crudities hadn't offended me, not his bragging, nor his savage insolences. I remembered Phillip rationalizing that unique man's fascination for him: Díaz had been a boy brought up in the midst of soldiers, in camps among illiterate peons and lazy Indians. His only education, by dissolute priests, had been in the drunken fiestas of civil war. And look at him—soon to be the most powerful leader in Mexico!

"Well," persisted Agnes, "what about with Díaz?"

"I refuse to think about it."

Three days later I was forced to think about it.

Agnes had spent the night with the Prince at the convent, just as she had managed to share his tent during our War Between the States: by unobtrusively outwitting the authorities. I was taking an afternoon siesta in a hammock on the lower colonnade near the fish pool. Suddenly Agnes burst around the *cancela*, her unbrushed hair down on her shoulders, her face paler than I had ever seen it.

She slumped into a chair, put her elbows on the marble-topped table and rested her trembling chin in her cupped hands. "Oh, it's awful, awful. This morning Escobedo received a scathing telegram from Juárez forbidding him to move the prisoners to more comfortable quarters. He is to cease treating them as prisoners of war. They must be shown the utmost severity and restraint until the day of the trial and, the telegram said: Maximilian, Mejía, Miramon and the murdering general—who claims to be an American, but who is not an American, only a Confederate exile from America—are to be singled out for especially harsh treatment."

"It's my fault," I cried, scrambling out of the hammock. "I told Don Carlos about moving the prisoners *and* about the Emperor's abdication plans."

"Don Carlos would have gone to Juárez anyway. When he saw the Emperor and the Prince, in their dress uniforms, at the party at Hacienda Hercules with the two of us, he was livid."

"How did Escobedo react to the telegram?"

"It scared him to death. He rushed the Emperor and the rest of the prisoners out of the Convent Santa Teresita and marched them in the broiling sun to the terrible Convent of the Capucines. I walked with them. I've never been that hot in my whole life. Salm was so concerned over Beau not having on a hat he never told me when the new escape plan is to take place, and I've already bargained for horses. The military commander wouldn't let me inside the Capucines. He's an illiterate Indian. None of my tricks worked on him at all. My head is in a whirl. I can't think what to do."

"Well, I can," I said, taking a parasol from a nearby stand. "I'm going to the Capucines this minute. You rest and have a bath. I'll be back before sundown."

At first, luck was with me. Colonel Aspirez, the fiscal in command, was standing at the wrought-iron entrance gates. I knew Colonel Aspirez. He was an educated gentleman, a friend of Doña Pepita's late husband. He came often to her house for a glass of wine and to bring her news of the town.

"May I visit my husband, Colonel Aspirez?"

"The rules have been changed, Señora Berrien. But I will bend them since your husband's sickness has returned. He has given the guards much trouble today. Perhaps you can quiet him."

A bulky, bald-headed officer in a dirty white uniform was standing laughing in the center of the treeless courtyard. He was shaking a plaited leather quirt at the upper gallery.

"That is Colonel Palacios. He is in military command here. It is most unfortunate."

Beau was up there on that gallery. Naked to the waist he was shouting curses and shaking his fist at Palacios.

"Paco! Paco! Paco! Paco Dodo is your name."

"Mi nombre es Colonel Miguel Palacios. Le diga prontissimo!"

"I will not say it, you squint-eyed hyena. Paco Dodo is your name."

"Colonel, my husband has mistaken you for Paco Dudas, the chief of the outriders who first brought us to Puebla," I called from the safety of Colonel Aspirez's shadow. If Palacios heard me he gave no sign.

"Hush that big ugly mouth, General Donkey." Palacios cracked the quirt toward Beau's face.

"I'm not afraid of you, you damned, bald-headed buzzard." Beau spat down on the cobbles. The spittle fried on the scorching stone. "All day the sight of you has stuck in my craw. Now the time has come when I am going to kill you."

"What says he?" Palacios called to Aspirez.

Aspirez whispered, "You translate, Señora Berrien. That one would think I made it up to insult him in front of you."

I did, literally.

Palacios looked first puzzled then shocked, then he snarled, "Colonel Don Miguel Palacios *un zopilote*? Now it is certain that it will be I who will do the killing; here or on the Hill of the Bells. I care not which."

Beau burst out laughing, his huge chest rising and falling with his uneven breathing. His fiery hair was standing on end like a torch. His skin was blistered. He threw back his head and in doing so staggered and fell against the spiked iron railing and kept on laughing and laughing. The laughter seemed to increase his weakness. When he laughed he put his hand to his chest and head as if they hurt. It was hard to tell whether he was laughing or groaning or doing both at the same time. His wedding ring shone on his finger. I couldn't stand it any longer. "Loose my arm, Colonel Aspirez. I must get to him quickly."

"Not now, señora. No."

Beau had lowered his head like a bull making ready to charge.

Palacios was the red rag and he sensed it. His mean squinch eyes held a comical expression like those of a cat which had missed his pounce.

"Follow me, you two," he said rudely, turning and hastening through the doorway of the *zaguán*.

"Beau, I'm on my way up. Beau, I'm coming."

He was roughly forcing the two guards beside him closer to the rail. Was he going to throw them over? Prince Salm appeared and pulled Beau's hands away from the guards. Beau threw his arms around the Prince and began to laugh some more.

The Prince saw me. "Don't come up, Angelica. I will take care of Beau. Tell Aggie the birthday is to be the second of June."

"Colonel Palacios is motioning for us. We go now," Colonel Aspirez said loudly; then he whispered in my ear, "Palacios locked the Emperor in the mausoleum—the crypt of the convent—to punish him for his sins. He is a brutal man is Palacios. There is no light, no bed, no chair in the crypt. Only tombs are there and darkness. I cannot fight Palacios."

"I must see my husband." Tears were running down my cheeks.

"You would only be permitted to see not to stay. In addition I do not think the big General knew it was you who waved at him. For two days he has been delirious with the high fever. The march in the sun was bad for him too. He needs not to be here at all. He will be shot along with the others. I believe it. What a joke! He is far from a Mexican and not even an Austrian."

I finally began to understand that my goal could not be reached except through a maze of deception. Without a qualm I accepted lies as part of my life's business, saying to myself that it was wrong to deceive and to lie, most of all to gentle Aspirez, but to swerve in going after the only thing in the world worth fighting for was wrong too.

"I will not insist to visit, Colonel, not anymore."

Escape! Flight! Those were my only thoughts. When I gave Agnes the Prince's message she said she had enough time before the second of June to go to and come from San Luis. She would plead with Juárez to postpone the trial in case something went wrong with the escape plan.

I borrowed one of Doña Pepita's grandmother's black mourning dresses and Doña Pepita's thickest black crepe veil and widow's bonnet to wear on the diligence to Mexico City.

Fortunately, her grandmother had been taller than Doña Pepita. I looked the part I was playing. My Spanish was correct; my grief genuine. No one questioned me. All the dry, sunbaked, dusty way I perfected my plan. It was a simple one: to inform Baron Magnus and the Austrian Minister immediately of the Emperor's perilous situation; from there to call on the Hubes in Tacubaya and beg to stay at their house. Then I would put on a pretty dress and lots of perfume and go to Díaz. Find Phillip? Not until after Díaz. He might stop me.

46 🌿

As the diligence clattered past the National Palace and through the Zocalo, people were thick as sparrows but strangely quiet. No afternoon band played; no flags were fluttered nor flowers flung; no rich carriages filled with jeweled occupants dashed past the Alameda. The only seeming life was the brilliant sunlight and the fanged shadow of the cathedral on the dusty stones. Lariats of glare, thrown by the late May sun, lashed the shufflers along Maximilian's beautifully created boulevard.

Massive and handsome as a medieval Teuton knight, the cards carefully fanned out in his exquisitely tended hand, Baron Magnus was sitting at a gaming table in the vaulted salon of the seventeenth-century stone mansion owned by the Prussian Embassy. When his manservant announced me, the Baron carefully folded the cards and laid them in a neat pile on the tabletop so he could resume his play against himself exactly where he left off when he was disturbed.

He took my hand, led me to a soft sofa and called for rum and fresh fruits. The salon was in shadow, except for a shaft of sunset piercing a silver-lustre mirror on the far wall.

"Frau Berrien! I am not knowing of Colonel Berrien's death.

What tragedy today to be seeing you in a black veil. Please be saying all that is passing in Querétaro."

To my relief he had learned to speak Spanish, if only in the present tense.

It was good to hear the rum splashing into the silver goblet. The smell of lemon and pineapple was good too. I had traveled steadily for two days and two nights.

"My husband is not dead, Baron. He is a very ill prisoner in the Convent Capucines where the Emperor has been moved. I wore these weeds for my safety. Listen—"

While I told him everything—the threatened trial, the Emperor's offer to abdicate and Juárez's fury at Escobedo's concern for the Emperor's comfort—the Baron kept pacing to the window then back to me. When I finished giving the details of the Emperor being locked in the crypt, with little Tudos crouched like a faithful hound on the hot stones outside, the shaft of sunlight had left the cloudy mirror.

In the falling darkness, the Baron sat down beside me and said wearily, "I send the Baroness to Prussia for I am knowing all is being at the end. But today, because of your friend, Commander Maury, all of Europe is seeing and condemning Querétaro. Italy, France, United States, Belgium, Holland, Austria too, are sending messages on the ocean cable to Juárez imploring him to free Maximilian, but he will not be doing that. Nothing is bringing mercy or pity to Juárez. I am meeting him once. What else is there for me to be knowing?"

I knew I could trust him. "Prince and Princess Salm have planned an escape for the Emperor and the generals to take place on the night of the second of June."

"Then why are you being here instead of being there to be helping?"

"My husband is too ill. He would complicate the escape. I came to beg Díaz to use his influence with Escobedo to transfer my husband from Querétaro to the prison at Chapultepec. General Berrien has been singled out for special punishment as an accomplice of the Confederate States of America."

"That is hard to be believing."

"Juárez thinks it will make a good impression on the President of the United States."

"How are you knowing this thing?"

"Juárez himself told Princess Salm."

"You think an escape from the Capucines can be taking place?"

"The Princess and the Prince have worked themselves to death to arrange it. I hope and pray."

"On the third of June we will be knowing on the telegraph. In between I hire the best lawyers in Mexico to go with me to defend the Emperor if the escape plan fails and he comes to a trial. Also I take the Austrian and Belgian and Italian Ministers who have not yet do with courage their duty. But it is difficult to be having travel passes. Márquez refuses to give them to anyone for Querétaro. It is as if he is wishing only harm to his Emperor."

"I am on my way to Tacubaya to the Hubes'. Tomorrow I will beg Díaz for passes."

"You are my guest here in Mexico City tonight. In the morning you go."

"No. Once before I made a mistake and went too late to Díaz."

"As then, it is not safe for you to be on the road in the dark. But if you are demanding to go, my coachman and outriders and I myself accompany you with pistols and swords. First you are to eat a supper here with me. Are you not?"

"With pleasure, Baron. I have never been so hungry for Prussian food. I've had enough chiles and tamales and enchiladas to last me a very long time."

Torches and flares lightened the outside of the Bishop's Palace in Tacubaya. Within, candles and gas chandeliers squared every window into a four-sided star shining in the dark hulk of stone masonry.

"We go in together and ask for Díaz now tonight." The Baron leaned out of his ornate glass-enclosed coach, calling directions in German up to his coachman.

I smelt of days of sweating and gathering grime and dust. My perfume bottle and my rouge pot were in my portmanteau. Díaz mustn't see me like this. My whole scheme to save Beau would be doomed. I knew it. "I am overweary, Baron. You visit Díaz tonight. I'll come tomorrow."

"No, it is on you I am placing my bet to win this card game. Here, I help you down and out. Is good?"

"No," I said crossly, "is not good." Then, seeing his handsome face grow downcast and worried, I wanted to kick myself for being selfish. "I am nervous about what Díaz might say if we intrude without permission."

"The talking I do; the smiling you. Yes?"

"Yes . . . There he is now!"

Had he been standing there in the *zaguán* all the time we were arguing on the steps? His hair gleamed like black feathers. His dark lips, so softly savage, parted in a gloating sort of smile as his sharp eyes absorbed my mourning clothes.

Baron Magnus said, "Frau Berrien is this day from Querétaro. We come to you to be asking passes back to Querétaro."

"Márquez is in charge in Mexico City until I throw him out—maybe tomorrow, maybe next week or the week after. Go to him."

I tried to excuse myself but my legs refused to carry me away. I gripped the handle of my reticule and leaned toward Díaz. Immediately his expression changed and he assumed his former air of insolent hauteur, asking the Baron a long question in French.

I couldn't understand it, but the Baron was so relieved not to be forced to plod any further in his poor Spanish that words gushed out of his mouth like a geyser. Díaz nodded his head every now and again, but continued looking straight at me, not at my face, but at a point where a pulse fluttered under my chin. After a few minutes his proud mask softened and he appeared almost gentle and abstracted. Finally he said in Spanish, "I have great sympathy for the Emperor and pity for his brave soldiers so far from their homes. I will send telegrams to San Luis and Querétaro to condemn the crypt. Come with me inside from the night and I will listen to your reasons to go to Querétaro."

But he continued dominating the conversation, even when we were seated, facing him behind the immense mahogany table that served as his desk.

My attention wandered impatiently, but the Baron listened closely, though he was obviously more interested in the man than in what he was saying. Díaz spoke of how and when to begin his showdown for power with Juárez. First he must enter Mexico City in triumph, he said, with flags and bands and flowers and an endless parade of troops, ahead of Juárez. His next image would be that of miracle-maker. He would build factories and shipyards and spin all the different kinds of wheels that had made the United States great in half a century of spinning. While Juárez spoke only of bringing law and justice, he, Díaz, would promise prosperity and pesos.

I nodded, for I could feel how powerful Díaz could become through his glistening gift of charisma and eloquence, rare in one so intelligent.

"Márquez is a worm I will crush with no trouble. But for the time being I must bow to Juárez because he is the President. Still I will do what I am able in my present power to help the Emperor and let the world see me as his savior. However, once you are in Querétaro I can't offer you or this lady my protection."

"But you must understand, General Díaz, that I want nothing. I am not needing protection. The King of Prussia protects me," the baron said stiffly.

"I understand, I understand," Díaz interrupted, reaching for a form that lay on a pile of papers on the desk. "How many passes do you ask from me which I will fill out and give when Márquez refuses you?"

"Seven, General Díaz: myself, two lawyers, the Ministers of Belgium, Italy and Austria, and this brave lady."

"Six passes I give." Frowning doubtfully, summoning back his cocky conceit, Díaz continued, "Is the widow a spy that she comes one day and returns the next?"

And then I knew I had to lose the advantage of my widowhood if I wanted to lose the suspicion of being a spy. "I came on my husband's behalf. I am Angelica Berrien. We have met before."

"I recognize you, so tall and thin like a sleeping white volcano, Señora Angel, and I still do not trust you. Yet come tomorrow and I will decide whether to give you a pass to return to Querétaro or send you away from Mexico as a foreigner."

The next morning Herr Hube was so determined that Phillip be told I was in Tacubaya I reluctantly agreed.

Herr Hube returned at teatime in a fluster. Phillip had left before dawn for Querétaro and San Luis on a special assignment for Díaz.

"Yes, Frau Berrien, I saw Díaz. He refused to discuss Herr Phillip's errand with me. Díaz was in an irritable humor. He cut me short when I requested an appointment for you. He said, 'Let her come herself and wait her turn.'"

"He's never forgiven me for breaking our appointment at Easter."

"I'll go with you. He can be very rude."

"No, Herr Hube, but thank you for your kindness."

"It is that I am so sad for all of you. Especially your unfortunate husband."

"Don't, Herr Hube. You'll make me cry and if I break down I won't be able to fight for General Berrien. I'll fall to pieces; tiny sharp pieces."

For six days, in a freshly ironed flounced muslin costume, I went to the Bishop's Palace and sat in the crowded *zaguán* on a hard cane bench watching soldiers coming and going. Sometimes I caught a glimpse of Díaz in his showy uniform standing in the doorway studying me. Once he waved and walked back toward his office. Taking it for a signal I jumped up and ran through the *sala*. The door to his office was open. I burst in. It was empty. There was no other door, nor open window. He had to be in here somewhere. I even looked under the massive table, in a ponderous armoire, behind the draperies. "I'm going to kill him," I muttered. I was so furious that I tipped over a marble stand and upset a jar of white roses. I left them lying in a puddle of water by his red velvet and gold-leaf throne chair.

I didn't go back after that, having decided, on Herr Hube's advice, to wait until Phillip returned to storm the palace again.

47

Sounds of Frau Hube quarreling with one of the little maids about not properly sweeping the patio reached me in my room. There had been a whirling sandstorm all week. The sand had stung the delicate blooming flowers mercilessly, leaving brown spots on their satin petals. It had sifted in hills all up and down the colonnade.

I thought: I must dress up and force myself to go again to Díaz's headquarters even though I dislike him now. But beyond my dislike is fear and beyond fear dark fascination and an awareness that if I humble myself properly he will do anything I ask. But first I will write Beau a love letter—

I sat down at a table by a window, closed against the needling sand, and wrote: "*I am doing everything that I know to persuade Díaz to remove you from Querétaro. If he won't—*"

Suddenly I stopped writing, thinking: Tomorrow will be June third. Beau may have escaped safely by tomorrow, but if he hasn't I must not burden him with my wretched fears. If what Baron

Magnus hints at—Beau to be executed along with the Emperor and Mejía and Miramon—should be true! But it cannot be true. All that is happening is too terrible, too unreal to be true. It can't happen. It can't. It is the Baron's Prussian pessimism. That is all. Is anyone in the world so miserable as I?

"No, there is no one," I told myself, and opening the window to the sound of birdsongs, I called down to the little maid, sweeping the patio, to come and help me with buttons and strings for I was ready to put on my best dress and go at once to Díaz.

I knew something terrible had happened the instant Díaz approached me with a dark surging flow of male tenderness.

He talked rapidly, telling me that time had run out for the Emperor. No escape plan, however brilliant, could work now.

"Wait until tomorrow," I said, cold with wanting, yet not wanting, to listen to what he was saying.

"Nothing tomorrow. No escape. Day before yesterday the new fiscal at the Capucines, Colonel Villaneuva, overheard the Prince Salm begging on his knees to the Emperor not to abandon his part in an escape plan, for all was perfectly arranged. But the Emperor insisted he must wait for the arrival of his lawyers and Baron Magnus. He is a foolish man, the Emperor."

"What of General Berrien?" I gathered my courage and forced myself to say, then suddenly stopped because my breathing was too quick and painful.

"He is closely guarded, along with the Emperor and Mejía and Miramon—those four—in the Convent Capucines. Prince Salm and Luis Blasio and the other officers were marched away from the Capucines back to the Convent Santa Teresita on the order of Juárez himself when Villaneuva told of overhearing the escape plan."

"Was my husband left at the Capucines because of his illness?" I asked in a shaking voice. I could feel the pallor spreading over my face; the cold sweat; the weak trembling.

Díaz lifted his shoulders and spread out his hands. "No," he said.

"Princess Salm was more successful in San Luis than I have been in Tacubaya," I said bitterly.

"Not so," said Díaz.

"Every move of the Princess Salm had been spied on in San Luis. Soldiers marched in front of and behind her wherever she went. Juárez had taken quite a fancy to her and being such a conniver himself had outguessed her at every turning. But it was the talk of the Mexican guerrilla army how two seemingly helpless foreign ladies had undertaken single-handedly to rescue the Emperor and his generals and had almost succeeded!

I laughed with him at that and looked helpless, for I was determined not to further reveal any of myself and my doubts and fears to Díaz.

He waited for me to say something, but I forced myself not to. The silence became so intolerable and irritating that Díaz himself broke it.

"I am surprised to find you did not ride away with Baron Magnus that first night but remained here totally alone."

I had to say something. "I'm surprised myself."

He looked at me with a strange intimate sort of pity and I felt the time had come for me to take over, so I began telling Díaz about my baby boy and why we had come to Mexico, of Beau's dislike of Miramontes and the grand flight of flamingoes the Empress and I had watched one day-dawn in Campeche, till Díaz couldn't stand it any longer and interrupted, saying that although he was interested in my past life he must bring me back to the matter at hand which was the decision of what price I was willing to pay for General Berrien's freedom?

"We have money."

"You or your brother-in-law, my friend, Don Felipe?"

So he knew all about the three of us! "We—my husband and I."

"Then I will tell you the price in Querétaro. I will be there next week before the trial. It may be money. It may be a favor. *Quien sabe*? Don Felipe sent the courier from San Luis Potosí with all the bad news I have just given you. But for now: I expect within the hour, Baron Magnus and the two lawyers, Señor Martínez de la Torre and Señor Riva Palacios. Señor Riva is no relation of the evil colonel, who is in military command at the prison. You must be ready to accompany them to Querétaro tonight. I am arranging a comfortable coach and an escort of soldiers for you. Márquez refuses to grant a pass to anyone attempting to assist the Emperor. He it is who is the enemy, not I. I am definitely for banishing the Emperor, not execution. I will state my position to Juárez and then to his crony, Don Carlos Miranda, who rules the trial."

By now I had recovered enough calm of mind to speak in an ordinary voice. "Why do you, a Liberal, extend courtesies to the so-called enemies of the Republic?"

"When I look at you I remember that I felt like this sometimes when I was a little boy in church and used to kneel to the beautiful Virgin with the long white hands. I felt her moon power. Oh—power—yes—I have always had a desire for power. I give the good things because in the future I want the world to trade with my Mexico. Here, take my handkerchief—don't cry—"

I turned and ran blindly toward the *zaguán* holding his scented handkerchief against my heart.

48

On the travel back to Querétaro I managed to hide my forebodings from Baron Magnus, who steadfastly refused to accept an unfavorable verdict as inevitable.

"See," he explained to the lawyers over and over, "it is in these documents I am bringing from the King of Prussia: Guarantees if the Emperor is being banished not executed. To San Luis I take them when we arrive, if Don Carlos Miranda is granting me an audience to say impossibles."

"Do you know Don Carlos?" I asked.

"I am meeting him, as you, at the wedding of Bazaine. The man of ease Don Carlos is seeming then. He fools everyone."

They put me down at Doña Pepita's. A long carriage with four mules was standing in front of the gate flanked by two guards and a swarthy, tough-faced little captain. I could hear Agnes calling me as she came running from Escobedo's headquarters which had been moved a short ways down our street before I left.

"Be careful what you say to me," Agnes warned, "but please comfort me."

As I put my arms around her she buried her face in my shoulder and began to talk fast.

My heart was a crazy bird, beating its wings and pricking me with its beak. I did not know what to say and could hardly make out what Agnes was gasping. All I could think of was: What to do now, Lord? Oh, what to do?

"I tried to bribe Palacios."

"Not that common brute? How could you?"

"Hush. This is my problem. You're in the clear so far."

"So far? What do you mean?"

"Palacios is a fool. I sent him a message and he brought me home from Santa Teresita last night. I invited him into my bedroom to continue talking business. Silly me—I locked the door and began unbuttoning my shirtwaist. He jumped out of the window and ran straight to Escobedo and told him about the bribe and the plan."

"You're going too fast for me. What bribe? What plan?"

The tough captain approached. "Is too long an *abrazo*," he snarled. "What passes?"

"The Princess has a woman sickness. Please permit us to talk in private."

"If you remain here on the street where I can look at you at all times and you speak only of woman sickness."

"I promise, Captain."

There was a spreading tree near the gate leading through the wall that separated the street from Doña Pepita's house. Agnes and I leaned against the trunk and talked freely, confident none of the surrounding soldiers understood English.

"Well, you know the Mexican's weakness for bribes. When I came home from San Luis and learned that the Emperor refused to take part in the June second escape plan, I couldn't believe it. I was determined to try one more time to convince him. I told him how the number of telegrams coming from all over Europe had only hardened Juárez's resolve, as a descendant of Montezuma, to revenge Mexico for the centuries of foreign oppression. That didn't seem to matter, but when Maximilian learned that his brother, the Austrian Emperor, had reinstated him as his successor to the Austrian throne, he agreed to my bribing Palacios to leave the gate open tonight." Agnes's voice had become lively and animated. Her cheeks reddened and her expressive hands couldn't keep still.

"Do try and look sick," I said, feeling Agnes's forehead as if for fever. "The captain is suspicious."

"Maximilian agreed to give Palacios Bills of Change, for one hundred thousand pesos, on the Royal Family of Austria, signed by him and the European diplomats, to help him reach the street where a horse would be saddled and waiting. Two horses. I would be there."

"A piece of paper for Palacios?" I asked incredulously.

"It would have been worth every penny."

"You know Palacios can't read. A sack of gold onzas would have made sense to him."

"You're right as usual, but I couldn't believe it when Escobedo sent for me this morning and told me that the air in Querétaro does not seem to agree with me, that it is indeed very bad. I assured him that I felt fine, but he repeated that I did not look at all well. He is sending me to San Luis Potosí where I will feel much better. I told him I did not choose to go again to San Luis. He exploded and accused me of having no gratitude or honor because I had tried to bribe his officers and to put him in an embarrassing position."

"Is that all?" I had to smile at her indignant expression.

"All? I am being sent away this very instant. Escobedo won't even let me say goodbye to the Emperor or to Salm. I am to go to Juárez under a guard where I can plead and grovel for their lives. He is through with me and all foreigners. The Austrian Minister was given the same order. All the ministers left Querétaro last night. Baron Lago took away, unsigned, the Emperor's codicil to his will directing Salm to write the account of the Emperor's last days. Oh, it's awful, awful. Everything depends on you now. Come inside, and help me pack."

As we were about to enter the gate, the captain grabbed Agnes's arm.

She jerked away, but said nothing, as if too amazed that he should touch her.

Again he took her arm. She went pale with anger and to everyone's amazement, quick as a flash, pulled a little pistol from under her dress and pointed it at the captain's chest.

"If you put your little finger on me again you are dead."

Dazed, the terrified Indian whimpered that he meant no harm. General Escobedo had threatened him with the firing squad if he let her out of his sight.

"Oh, well," she said, dropping the pistol and twirling it on her forefinger, "come in and help me pack or go back to your master."

He flew. And so did the next half-hour as I helped Margarita fold Agnes's dresses and Agnes brushed her tousled hair. Tudos came with a message that the Emperor wanted to see Agnes immediately. She sat down to write to him but the captain burst in with an escort of six soldiers. We were outnumbered. Our time was up.

Promising to get word to Prince Salm and the Emperor, I helped Agnes step into the carriage, followed by Margarita and Jimmy. Colonel Villanueva rode up as they were about to leave.

"Villanueva has the Emperor's check," she told me brusquely, "make sure he returns it to the Emperor."

I wanted to ask her why she continued to trust this handsome, forked-tongue colonel, but he was too close and I depended too much on his goodwill to anger him, for I would see Beau by this time tomorrow or I would kill someone.

"Drive the Princess to General Escobedo," Villanueva said to the captain.

Agnes didn't hear him but she did hear the captain direct the coachman. She jumped right over Margarita and Jimmy into the street. "I refuse to be exposed to Escobedo's sneering remarks," she shouted. "If he wishes to see me, let him come here." Her eyes were narrow knives of rage.

Villaneuva whirled about and ordered the coachman to take the Princess to Santa Rosa to wait for the diligence to San Luis Potosí.

The captain, his mouth agape, incapable of uttering another word, merely rumbled the command in his throat to the coachman.

Villanueva laughed. "General Escobedo said he would rather face a whole Imperialist battalion than an angry Princess Salm. I know what he meant."

Agnes and I kissed each other. "I wonder if we will ever meet again," she said. "I know I won't be allowed to come back here. Juárez has assured me that no harm will come to Salm. But Beau is in great danger. Promise me you will count on Díaz. A telegram from him came to Escobedo's headquarters when I was there. He'll be here in Querétaro before the trial. Díaz is our final hope for mercy. You know that, don't you?"

"Yes, I know it. And I know you and I will meet again. I have loved you, Agnes."

Villanueva was issuing instructions. The coachman would go at a gallop to Santa Rosa so the Princess would not be able to change her mind and again jump out of the carriage.

"If we're going, let's go," she shouted hoarsely. Tears were running down her cheeks and mine too.

We hugged each other one more time before she got back into the carriage.

The escort soldiers were already mounted. Villanueva spurred his horse and they were off. The tattoo of hoofbeats filled the street.

I ran a ways after the carriage calling, "Find Phillip in San Luis! Tell him to hurry, hurry—"

"You're the only one who can save Beau or the Emperor now. You're all by yourself—all by yourself." Agnes's voice floated ghostily through the cloud of bitter dust raised by the galloping horses and the grinding wheels.

49

Before I had time to bathe away the travel dirt and put on a cool loose gown to join Doña Pepita on the shady colonnade I was called to the *sala* to speak to Baron Magnus, who had just come from Escobedo's headquarters, where he had gone to pay his respects on arrival.

"Escobedo is promising you one visit to the Capucines, but only one and that with me. I am swearing on my honor you do nothing at the prison except speaking and looking at your poor husband. Do you come?"

"Of course I'm coming," I said, rebuckling the belt of my skirt and putting on my hat.

The Capucines was hot as an oven. Colonel Palacios and the Baron accompanied me to Beau's cell and, leaving guards at the door, went on to find the Emperor. Beau was lying with his face turned toward the light. His cheeks were hollow, but flushed scarlet. His eyes were closed and his hands were clenched together on his bare chest. His lips were moving. He was talking in his sleep. "Is Maximilian still inside the crypt? Or am I in here by myself?" He kicked out with both feet and turned over on his back. I realized he was deeply sleeping.

My nervousness had been building up ever since we left Doña Pepita's and had by now come to such a pitch I stopped fighting it. A pure wonderful love for this man flooded all over me. I knelt down and put my cheek softly against his burning cheek. "Lie still, my heart, I'm here."

I knew the Emperor's plight was worse than Beau's. The effort I had made on the way from Tacubaya to Querétaro to impress Baron Magnus that I was a capable, level-headed person seeking the Emperor's good had made the Baron willing to bring me here with him today, vouching for me with his honor. I should have felt guilty, for all I was really seeking was Beau's release from this place. My Beau whom I would follow to the pit of Hades rather than exist in paradise without him. The sweetnesses of love that we had shared had been so joyful. Suppose—oh, suppose—it turned out that in the end Beau *would* actually be shot along with the Emperor.

Hearing slow footsteps approaching I jumped to my feet.

"Angelica."

It was the first time he had ever called me by my first name. I had forgot how luminously blue his eyes were, how graceful his every move. Maximilian was holding a fan in one beautiful hand and his white sombrero in the other, spinning it around like a pinwheel. He was wearing a rumpled gray silk dressing gown and blue silk slippers.

"He will need this before I do," he said, hanging the sombrero on a hook by the door. "Dr. Basch will keep us both from the trial. They have only to look at my poor general; and I will take a purgative for proof. My so royal mother would never believe such a thing could happen to her Maxl. Never. Come, walk with me along the gallery. This is my time for the exercise. We talk English and the guards do not understand. If they say speak Spanish we talk in riddles. Did Beau know you?"

"In his sleep he asked if you were still inside the crypt."

"How could he have been aware of that, ill as he was?"

"Is your present cell comfortable?"

He laughed shortly. "A clean bed, a washstand and two chairs, two candles in lovely silver sticks, my books and papers and a chamber pot. It was more than Charles II of England was permitted."

"Don't think of him."

"He died well. Come—walk faster and tell me if anyone has ever seen my Baby in the town?"

I told him what I had heard—that she was well looked after and rechristened Empress. I felt him shiver from the inward horror of this whole nightmare, which must have grabbed him with fresh force as a double wound was opened with the words: Empress and Baby.

"Señora Mejía and her children are with the little general. She weeps. The young Señora Miramon does not weep but I think she is even more grieved. The sight of her tenderness desolates me. But come, we must speak of other things, such as the incomparable Princess Salm who has risked her life for me so many times."

"She was much disappointed that you refused to go along with the escape."

"Neither she nor the Prince believed me but it was not possible. I hadn't the physical strength and I didn't have much confidence in the plan. I didn't trust the Liberal officers Prince Salm believed were friendly. I feared they were luring me into a trap which would give Juárez a chance to kill us all and then tell the world that

Maximilian of Hapsburg and his generals were shot while trying to escape from prison. I am a sick man, my dear. I have only enough courage left to die."

His eyes glittering, Beau was sitting up on the bed when we went back to his cell. The Emperor sat beside him and fanned him. Beau seemed unaware of my presence and I knew it was best not to agitate him, for Baron Magnus had returned. He was standing in the doorway, motioning me to come with him.

"Go. We will speak of cool things—he and I," Maximilian said soothingly. "I will tell of the Vienna winter carnival. Next year, when you are part of my household, we will all attend the carnival. The dances last till the dawning and the day's festivities are like the night. Wearing scarlet and silver we will waltz on the ice in the snow. Confetti will mingle with the snowflakes and colored paper ribbons hanging in garlands from the winter bare branches of the linden trees.

"I'll never forget a particular night during a ball in Liechtenstein Palace. A snowstorm was howling outside. Suddenly the palace windows blew open and the room was awhirl with snowflakes and waltzers. Charlotte's dark hair and flushed cheeks shone in snow-crystals as if dusted with stars—" His high voice broke. Beau's huge skeletal hands took Maximilian's slim tapered fingers in his. Their fingers interlocked.

I wept on Baron Magnus's shoulder all the way back to my own prison.

50

"Please, not to be annoying Escobedo by insisting on visiting the other prisoners of the Capucines or Santa Teresita. Still he hurts from his dealings with the Princess Salm," Baron Magnus counseled, when he came the next morning. He was on his way to San

Luis Potosí in one last attempt to plead with Juárez to banish, not execute, the Emperor. "Not going on the street either, for too obvious a foreigner are you. Returning before the bad day I am, surely."

He promised to seek Phillip and urge him to come to me in Querétaro, whatever the consequences. And I promised him to be good, to stay in the house, and not to be worrying.

Not to worry! What a laugh.

The week passed by in a gloom of despair. I felt as if the bottom had gone from my spirit. I hovered in nothingness. The menace of the trial hung over me. Bewildering cruelty was becoming too much for me. I longed to feel the clean cool fog of a Blue Ridge morning in Virginia; to hear the belling of hounds and the sound of the horn; to smell the fresh pink apple blossoms. I wanted to hide from Mexico itself. I hated the wind that was either a chilling draft or a scorching sting; the massive rains that sluiced away the planted earth and the hostile sun that burned and sucked the land dry. The odors, overpowering with sweetness or nauseously fecal, revolted me. I forgot the vision of Mount Orizaba, the magnificence of the Cumbres and the serenity of Miramontes. I was choked with rage and resentment and frustration. I had never spent my days in such stretches of emptiness; so inert, so without desire.

On June 13 I persuaded Doña Pepita to walk with me to see where the trial would be held. It was the first time I had passed through her gate since my one terrible visit with Beau in the Capucines the week before.

We walked down to the Iturbide Theater which was decorated with bunting and flags and wreaths of bright dahlias, roses and zinnias as if for a fiesta or a grand opera. Vendors were selling *pulque* and *meringues* and firecrackers. One held out a particularly repulsive papier-mâché replica of a very white-faced man with a yellow paper beard parted in the middle. It resembled Beau more than it did the Emperor.

The crowd was noisy and restless waiting for ten o'clock.

"These people are from other places," Doña Pepita said disapprovingly, "I don't see a single Querétarono. We are on the Emperor's side. Our shutters are closed against this sad carnival."

An open carriage drove up with the prisoners. Mejía slumped dejectedly, but the young Miramon, his head still bandaged from a wound he'd got at the battle of San Jacinto, waved jauntily at his beautiful wife and three little children huddled under a tree watching, as he stepped down and walked proudly into the theater.

"Neither the Emperor nor my husband is with them! The Emperor must have followed Dr. Basch's advice."

"Thanks be to God. Let us return home quickly," Doña Pepita said. "We should not have come."

After lunch I sat in the patio. I just sat. I could not read or sew or even care. Suddenly Doña Pepita rushed out, saying that General Don Porfirio Díaz was here, to find out if it was my wish to leave Mexico without my husband.

"Am I to see Díaz now?"

"Yes, do you wish me to stay with you?"

I rose and walked slowly toward the *zaguán*, stopping every now and then to decide how to answer the question I knew Díaz was going to ask me. Doña Pepita ran along beside me saying that if I was not certain of myself she would go inside the little chapel and offer many prayers.

"Yes. Pray for me now."

I passed into the dim vaulted *sala* where Díaz paced the marble floor. He was weighted down with medals and clanking with a too-long sword. I had determined to be still and very proud when we came together, but he gave me such a flash of his black eyes, in a sort of happy deference, that I held out my hand and when he took it I felt a gush of hot blood flow between us. When he let my hand go I looked down curiously to see if it was red. I felt inertia drain away and a power surging through me, a blossoming of spirit. For the first time since I had been back in Querétaro I smiled and I faltered a bit as I said, "I had not expected you."

His glistening black eyes held mine with a rather terrible challenge and his rich dark voice was soft. "You are too pale and thin. The strain of this tragedy tells in your eyes."

"Oh, but I am feeling much stronger now."

Then, no longer boyish, Díaz boldly touched my hand, as if to test to see if hot darkness would flow between us once again. "Will you sit while I explain what goes on, and the price?"

The price! I looked closely at him. The fierce brightness of his eyes seemed to hold something like tenderness for me. But his savage assurance looked far beyond me into his own destiny. I lowered my eyes, murmuring, "It is kind of you to offer me a chance to leave Mexico, but I would never leave my husband."

"Not even for your baby boy?" he asked wonderingly, sternly.

I hung my head. "No. There is a great love between my husband and me."

Conflicting feelings showed in his eyes. He hated being thwarted even in the smallest matter and showed it. Then the dark distant look came back, and with it the gleam of daring and power which gave him his masterfulness.

He wanted me, this savage, godlike general. He was not in love with me but he wanted me. And I? I refused to answer that—even to myself.

"You will never break your word to me again?"

"No. I promise."

"Then I will do all possible with Juárez and Escobedo to have set free the General Berrien."

Then he laughed as he explained that in any event he had already promised his fine friend and officer, Don Felipe de Miramontes, that he would act in behalf of his brother the general. He had gone to Escobedo's headquarters this morning where Colonel Villanueva had described to him the night of the surrender, when the Emperor and his generals had failed in escaping from La Cruz. The General Berrien had not been captured with arms in his hand as had the others who were thus automatically condemned to a court-martial and ultimate sentencing by the general who did the capturing. No, the General Berrien, unarmed, had of his own will returned, walking in the moonlight, to the Cruz.

"So you see, there is much I can do." Díaz grinned, relishing catching Escobedo at fault.

A bell rang joyously in a nearby church. "I am so deep in debt to you, Don Porfirio, I will never be able to repay you."

"When I ride back through here, Doña Angel, on June the fifteenth, you will have supper with me. Today I run to San Luis to finalize the details of the Liberals entering into Mexico City which is mine. Also I will explain to Juárez that if he agrees to banish, not execute, the Emperor, His Majesty will be a forgotten man in two months. If he kills, the ghost of Maximilian will ride up and down his wide beautiful boulevards of Mexico forever."

"Go with God, Don Porfirio."

"Goodbye until I am in Querétaro again," he said. Our eyes met. We both knew we were playing for high stakes. He for his future. I for Beau.

When Díaz left I slipped into the chapel. I knelt beside Doña Pepita and tried to pray. Doña Pepita believed in heaven and was afraid of hell, but I had no thoughts for these simple faiths, less now than ever.

It is three more days until everything will be resolved, I told the Lord. I can live until then, but if I must endure one day beyond that, I know I will do something foolish and reckless, for I cannot be longer than that in this state of desperation.

Doña Pepita must have known much grief in her life, for she allowed me the privilege of solitude the rest of the day. In the evening after supper I played for her on the piano. Afterward she came up and timidly asked if Díaz was going to help me or was he merely here for the trial. Stopping in the middle of an air from *Norma* I said to myself: The time has come for me to tell this dear kind person exactly what is facing me.

"Díaz is on his way to Juárez to decide which of them will lead the victory parade into Mexico City. He will be back on the fifteenth and has invited me to spend the evening with him."

"But suppose the other basket of roses from Don Carlos comes on the fifteenth?"

"Then," I said bitterly, "you will have to pray harder and longer for me to make the proper choice."

"I would take Don Porfirio," the little dark bit of a woman said quickly and positively, almost gaily.

"But suppose Don Carlos is the one who holds the key?"

She shrugged. "Then him I would take. But it would be a pity. The priest would not like hearing what I would be forced to confess."

She fascinated me. I had thought Doña Pepita would roll her huge deep dark eyes upward in saintly horror yet here she was approaching the problem as calmly as if it were a choice between which red rooster's neck to wring for Sunday dinner.

"You mean you would have committed adultery to save Don Rafael's life if you had been given the chance?"

"Many adulteries, Señora Angel."

"Wouldn't it have burdened you at prayer?"

"God would have found me unworthy of his love had I not done what was indicated to save my Rafael. He was much a man, my Rafael. Pater Soria says that I must remember he died fighting for Mexico and that we shall meet in Heaven. But it is hard in the night for me to think that way."

Colonel Aspirez came twice a day to report to Doña Pepita on the progress of the trial; or, I suspected, to begin (or continue?) a bit of sly courting on the side.

I would listen avidly when he spoke of the trial then excuse myself. It boiled down to this: the trial was a morass of travesties. All the foreign envoys had been ordered to leave Querétaro. The two lawyers from Mexico City argued and defended the Emperor with brilliance and integrity, but they might just as well have been blowing dandelion fluff on the wind, for they were countered with such accusations as the fact that Maximilian Hapsburg epitomized foreign intervention in Mexico and had usurped her sovereignty. He was responsible for the 3 October Decree of 1865 by which hundreds of innocents had been killed etc., etc., etc. In all thirteen accusations were made. There was no chance for the Emperor, unless the assessor, who was Don Carlos Miranda, was called in to break a tie, should the six judges so vote, and declared a verdict of banishment, not execution.

"Is Don Carlos in Querétaro?" I asked.

"Oh, yes, he sits there in the theater wearing pale-blue kid gloves, smoking his cigar and smiling as casually as if he were watching a boring bullfight."

I sighed with relief. Perhaps I would be spared making a choice after all.

51 🌿

There was one blackbird that always sang higher and sweeter and shriller than the others in the fig tree that kept tapping against the shutter closed against the morning sunstream.

"I'll fix him," I muttered sleepily, jumping out of bed and opening the shutter, "Get! Fly!"

The tapping continued. Someone was knocking at the door of my bedroom. No breeze was blowing the fig branch against the opened shutter.

Thinking it was the maid with my breakfast I put on a pink India muslin wrapper and called, "Is permitted to enter."

Phillip strode in. His boots were caked with dirt. His face was black with unshaven whiskers. I'd not realized before what a heavy beard he had. But more than all that was the look in his eyes. Once before I had seen such a grief in Phillip's eyes. It was the afternoon of the day of the battle of Port Royal, when he had stood in the doorway holding parts of his brother Eddie, wrapped in a gray velvet lap robe.

I knew in a flash what he was going to tell me. Beau was dead. Unable to speak, arms outstretched, I ran toward him. Without warning he caught me and began kissing me full on my mouth.

Shocked, I tried to push him away. "Is Beau—?"

In answer he pulled me closer and kissed me again and again. He kissed me as if he had never kissed anyone else before, as if he would never kiss anyone else again. It was the longest kiss I'd ever had. Helpless, stupefied, I waited until the onslaught ended and then I pulled my filmy wrapper tight across my breasts and said coldly, "What has come over you? Tell me—has something happened to Beau?"

"No." He looked at me pleadingly, almost compassionately. "Don't be angry with me. I've been in the saddle for thirty-six hours and spent an hour at the prison with Bubba and am quite unbalanced."

Still angry, but not quite as angry, I answered, "That's no excuse."

He walked over to the open window, turned, and said, "The rest of this day is the most important day in our lives. If I shock you and weep from time to time, blame it on exhaustion and the feeling that you always awake in me, and the way Bubba looks."

"Let me ring for some coffee. You need it."

"No. I'll breakfast later." Phillip's voice broke.

My mouth was dry. I swallowed a few times. It didn't help.

"Díaz is eight or ten hours behind me. The verdict will come tomorrow." Phillip had got his voice under control and he spoke very rapidly. "Díaz wishes you to have supper with him tonight. Did you promise him a visit?"

I nodded.

"Suppose he asks a favor of you in return for removing Bubba from the Capucines to Santa Teresita?"

My chest was closing. I had to gulp to breathe. "Not to Santa Teresita. Díaz must get him away from Querétaro entirely."

"That was the most *I* dared ask of Díaz. You see, the reason Bubba was left at the Capucines with the Emperor and the two generals is that Escobedo thought he, too, was a general."

"He is. So is Prince Salm."

"Escobedo declares Prince Salm is a colonel. There is no piece of paper saying he was ever made a general. Bubba swore so violently that *he* was a general no one disputed them. Instead, they let him sign his own death warrant by insisting on calling himself a general. How ironic everything is," he said bitterly. "Now he can unsign it if Escobedo demotes him to colonel. But the foreign prisoners in Santa Teresita are to set out on foot for Vera Cruz as soon as the trial is over tomorrow."

"If Escobedo moves Beau from the Capucines to Santa Teresita and he is sent on the march to Vera Cruz he will die anyway."

"I know. Maximilian's doctor told me."

"Oh, what am I to do?"

Phillip's eyes had that unbearable pain in them again. "You must save Bubba," he whispered.

There was another knock at the door. It was the housekeeper bringing my breakfast. She talked loudly to herself as she poured me a cup of coffee from a silver pot and spooned a boiled egg into a china cup.

"A brothel this hacienda has become since the North American whores have occupied it. Princesses they call themselves. A Princess in a pig's eye! Each day I beg Doña Pepita to throw this one out but Doña Pepita won't listen, poor, pretty little bird."

"Good morning, Señora Angel." A grim-faced Doña Pepita was standing in the doorway, holding a silver basket.

The housekeeper ducked her head and scuttled away.

"They have come, the matching roses," Doña Pepita said sympathetically. "This time with a difference."

A single red bud pointed and sharp like a cat's tongue stuck up vibrantly in the center of the pale pink roses.

"Who sent them?" Phillip asked sharply. "And what is the meaning of the red rose?"

"They are from Don Carlos Miranda," Doña Pepita said. "Your sister will explain the rose. Eat your breakfast quickly, my dear. Pater Soria is here. So I am going into the chapel for the whole morning to pray about the choice."

Phillip came forward. He put his finger under my chin and lifted my face so that my eyes looked straight into his. My throat was on fire, my heart felt as if it were struggling to leap from my mouth. Phillip's unshaven face burned by wind and sun was tense and tight. He stood tall and strong; no weakness anywhere anymore; only an aggressive rigidity. There was a note on heavy parchment tied to the silver handle of the basket.

"Read it aloud," he said.

"Senora Angel,
Tonight you will come to my house. You have promised. I will expect you to play for me enough preludes to fill two hours, no more, for I am having supper with the six judges who will complete the trial tomorrow. It pleases me this idea of a little

prelude to the main play which will continue on the next night. I
hope it pleases you also. My carriage will come for you at six en
punto *this evening.*

With esteem
from Don Carlos Miranda y Fagoagas."

"So—the beautiful Angelica will have a chance to save not only her husband but also the Emperor," Phillip said bitterly. "It galls me to the very pit of my soul and body."

"What do you mean?

"Díaz won't expect you until after eight at the earliest. So will it be Don Carlos or Don Porfirio or both?"

"I don't know. I truly don't know. Don Carlos repulses me. Díaz doesn't."

Phillip shook his head slowly as if all this was too bizarre to actually be taking place. His lips were trembling. "I don't want you to have anything to do with either. But you must. Neither can hurt you, not really. We'd never forgive ourselves if we didn't do everything in our power to save Bubba, perhaps even the Emperor! You must keep both appointments." He grasped my shoulders and ran his fingers through my hair pulling it a little, then gave me the silver dagger that he wore at his belt and rushed from the room without another word.

52

Doña Pepita insisted I carry her tiny white lace parasol and put on her small white kid gloves to perfect my costume after I had reluctantly let her maid hook me into my bustled white muslin dress.

"Your bustle wants setting straight, but go with God," Doña Pepita called sadly as I opened the parasol and waved a lace handkerchief to indicate that I was securely settled in Don Carlos's open barouche.

Joaquin helped me down at a towered hacienda not too far away from Doña Pepita's. He did not look at me but I thought I heard him say in a low voice, "You have only to call for me, señora, and I will come. Only very loud you must call, for I am a little deaf."

Don Carlos was standing in the vaulted stone corridor. A tall gilt clock behind him said six o'clock. He was wearing a white frock coat and slim white trousers, strapped tightly under pointed black patent leather slippers.

I felt like a rabbit which had just caught the cry of a hawk in the clouds above it. I looked imploringly back at Joaquin, wanting to hurl myself in a frenzy at the grillwork gate through which I had just stepped. Yet Don Carlos had not even touched my hand, had only opened his moist red lips and said, "Good! You have come at last!"

His close, shiny black hair and thin line of beard smelled pleasantly of limes. His face almost touched mine as he insisted on untying the strings of my white satin bonnet before guiding me through marble and velvet rooms to the music room, dominated by a grand piano and three gilt harps.

"In here we will begin our prelude," he said in his soft, sinuous voice. "I remember the night you played so brilliantly in Puebla for the Emperor and Empress to waltz. I anticipate transcendence."

"What would you like to hear?" I asked, pulling off the short-fingered kid gloves that had made my hands look like monkey paws.

"Are you familiar with Liszt?"

I knew the Gretchen interlude of the Faust opera. I would have preferred playing a less poignantly passionate piece, but I was determined to please him.

When I had finished there was a pause. "You have achieved perfection. Anything that might follow would be second best. Let us go into the garden and have an aperitif—our beginning ceremony."

That my visit would last only another hour and forty-eight minutes couraged, even boldened, me. I determined to sparkle, fooling him with my lightness.

The dark garden was hemmed in by thick tall trees on one side and the yellow-red mansion on the other. Sitting in the center of a tiled patio, beside a small fountain of spouting nymphs and dolphins, felt like being in the depth of some flowery part of Purgatory. From a bush behind my chair, mystic white datura bells hung heavy and silent, like ghost bells, their scent thick and smothering. A drum was beating with a pounding powerful note, and an earthen flute with a shrill sound shaped a monotonous melody, on the other side of a high brick wall that separated the garden from the street.

Don Carlos clapped his hands. Two servants came. He ordered one to go into the street and stop the noise. The other set down a tray holding two small crystal glasses and a green bottle.

"General Bazaine presented me with this liqueur the day before he left Mexico for France. He said it was for a very special occasion."

"Is it more festive than champagne?" I asked, fanning myself, for the heat was stifling.

"I hope so." He looked cool and aloof. "I frown on pouring from a tradesman's bottle, but Bazaine warned me against decanting absinthe. I will obey him faithfully."

"I have never tasted absinthe. Have you?"

"No. We will be children, experimenting with a delicious secret."

He was so natural, so human, I began to relax. Phillip had been right. He couldn't hurt me. How foolish I had been.

He handed me a glass. I took a small sip and shivered with pleasure. Don Carlos took a sip, his feral eyes locking mine intimately.

"Bazaine assured me in the name of the Most Holy Toe of St. Peter, that absinthe was magic. It will intensify all things—stars—skies—music—fragrance—laughter—joy—hopes—"

"Enough, Don Carlos." I laughed at his exuberances. "I'm not sure I could cope with such excitements. Perhaps I should insist on champagne."

"Oh, no," he said easily, "you have come here to humor me and share this magic elixir. If you do I will humor you, though in all probability what you will demand of me will destroy me."

He refilled our glasses and I commented on the unusual brilliance of the first stars and the amazingly deep blue of the evening sky. Two cats came trotting from the garden down a gravel path toward the twilight patio.

The drum shuddered and grew still. Or was it I? The clay flute wavered into muteness. Or was it I?

The gray cat in the lead leapt on my knee then scrambled over my breast, squatted on my shoulder and pushed its nose under my ear. I knocked it away.

Then the black cat, a slinking, snaky cat, raised itself on its hind legs and began licking the slim hand Don Carlos had left dangling by his chair. It jumped onto the table to get nearer his face and rubbed herself on his cheek. All this with such a roar of purrs that, when I leaned forward holding out my empty glass to be refilled, Don Carlos's own chest seemed on fire with purrs.

I heard myself talking about Beau and the Emperor, telling Don Carlos that I knew he controlled their fate. Begging him to spare them.

"Fly, Angelica." Oh, so gently he lifted the black cat to the stones. Both cats scampered away. "Fly! It is not too late. We'll meet in another pit somewhere." His clear voice was growing slurry.

Mine was steady. I have never felt sharper or more alert. I was determined that he not change the subject. I grew garrulous in my begging, or was a macaw squawking?

Don Carlos shrugged and emptied his glass. "Well, I gave you a chance to fly away. You didn't fly. Now you must humor me and play a game. It will only be a game. If you play I will swear on my Christian honor that the silly young judge will vote to banish the Emperor, not execute him. Do you believe me?"

"Yes, I believe you. But before I agree to play your game you must write down your promise to vote for banishment of the Emperor."

He clapped his hands. The same servants came and then went for paper and ink and a pen. Don Carlos wrote what I asked him and threw the pen into the fountain. The servants giggled and slipped away. I took the crisp paper he'd signed and held it tight in my hand so that it could not fly away from me. By the strong thudding of my pulses I knew the absinthe was making me drunk in a strange way and that it was making Don Carlos drunk in a different way. He spoke of the old Serpent, of Moloch, of demons and devils.

The coming of night darkened the green of the palm trees. They were darker now than the absinthe. Parrots swung to and fro on their branches with an air of discontent. They were noisy. The fountain clattered and surged.

"So now that I have destroyed myself, is true? You must take off your clothes, depersonalize yourself. You must become a palm tree. I have always envisioned you, so tall and slim, as a palm tree."

He unhooked my dress. The night wind caressed my hot body. It felt cool and welcome. I laughed merrily as I ripped off my white satin slippers with high red heels.

"There—" He tossed my dress onto a bunch of ripe bananas hanging on a near tree. "You reminded me of a swan in that dress. I particularly do not enjoy swans. One chased me when I was a boy."

I hissed like an angry swan. He slapped me. I had hidden Phillip's silver dagger inside my reticule. I found it and went for Don Carlos's throat. He snatched the dagger and slapped me again. I wept. He threw the dagger in the fountain. It cuddled the pen. He comforted me with absinthe from his glass and retrieved the dagger.

His movements had got very slow and suggestive. A wind was blowing the palm fronds around. He unloosed my hair. It swished around me like a crown of dark palm fronds. Back and forth. Back and forth. It was very exciting.

Later we went into the house. I carried our glasses and he the absinthe bottle which was now less than half-full. Then we were in a huge empty room full of mirrors and animal heads made of papier-mâché. A cathedral candle, lit, was in the middle of the room. It reflected in all the mirrors making a whole cathedral of lit candles.

"You must be careful not to let me outsoar you and drive your woman image out completely. So far you are safe with me. I mean you no harm. I adore you. I signed the paper, didn't I?" Don Carlos muttered, lurching into a mirror.

My mind was totally awake. Never had I been more aware, more conscious of every shade and shadow of everything. Even the sparkles in the mirrors were pricking me like ice-points all over. Everywhere. The slip of paper crackled loudly in my hand. Could he hear it? Slyly I peeped sideways at him. He was taking a monkey head from one of the hooks on the wall. He fitted it over my head. My long hair clung to my body as the monkey neck covered mine. Cleverly I slipped the paper safely inside the mask against my ear. What was he saying?

"But should I fall prey to all that is pagan in myself—you must run away as fast as you can and hide."

I could see easily through the monkeymask eyeholes. I giggled at my image in all the mirrors. The room was full of monkey women and lit candles.

The black cat scampered in. Don Carlos said, "Watch me exorcise the demon spirit of the cat."

He took off his clothes and placed a jaguar head over his head. His body was like old ivory, beautiful. He lifted his arms and, as though in front of an altar, danced and prostrated himself, touching the floor with his forehead and at last grabbing up the cat and pretending to devour it, uttering moaning cries.

Fascinated, I watched his eyes, his fixed demoniacal eyes—his evil, wanton eyes. He even purred so convincingly that I began to pray desperately, that he, as the cat was doing, would close his cat-eyes and sleep. For it was that or the moment was near when all

257

that would be left for him to do was yowl and scream and slash open his erectile body or penetrate mine!

Danger thrashed around me like a windblown garment. It was choking me. I must get it off. Instinctively I bent down and jerked the jaguar head off the human head—the vulnerable head—of my enemy. Candlelight licked the shining black hair. His anguished cry was that of a wounded animal, not a person, who was collapsing as if death itself had snatched at him. For without the big cat head to sustain him Don Carlos was only a limp twitching object.

Only a limp object! Laughing I pushed him with my foot. Strengthless softness!

"I won the game!" I said loudly to make sure he heard me far away down there in purgatory. "I stripped you of your dignity. Look at yourself in all these mirrors. You are the exorcised tomcat. I have destroyed your demon spirit."

Miserably, he raised himself and looked in the mirrors. I shrugged my shoulders and went out into the cool moonlit corridor. It was time for me to go home now. I had an appointment to meet someone. Who? Never mind; Doña Pepita would tell me; or Agnes; or Phillip. I heard Don Carlos howl. He must have seen how ridiculous he looked. I laughed. I didn't care. I heard him hush. Then I heard him running. I turned around. He had put the jaguar head back on. He had Phillip's dagger. He was running very fast. But I was faster.

I made a dash for the nearest open door. I screamed and screamed for Joaquin. The house was dark, but I knew I must do what Don Carlos had told me earlier to do. I must run and hide from him; hide under chairs, wrap myself in velvet draperies, crouch behind doors, shrink inside cabinets. Through room after room I ran and hid myself until I crashed into a standing harp. The jangled shrieks of strained harp strings ripped the silence around me. I grabbed hold of the harp's cold upright body. I held tight to it. It would save me. I would ride on it to Díaz. He was waiting in the next room for me. The dying echo of the mangled strings was the only sound left in the world.

No one was running after me. I was alone. No one had ever been following me. How long had I clung to the harp? "Joaquin!" I cried, "Joaquin!"

This time he came quickly. "The barouche is waiting to take you home," he said, helping me steady myself and carefully removing the papier-mâché monkey head.

"Home? I'm going for a late supper with General Díaz." I made a heroic effort to gather my dignity. "Do you mind if I hold your arm on the way out?"

"No, señora, but first it is best that you put on your clothes; unfortunately I could not find your shoes."

I was stark naked from my toes up. The risen sun splashed rosy fingers across my bruised breasts.

There was no use for me to say anything. Docile as a child I let Joaquin dress me and lead me into the vaulted corridor. The gilt clock was gathering itself to strike and it struck six times. I had been here for twelve hours! I leaned heavily on Joaquin all the way to the barouche.

"Did you commit?"

"No. He served something to drink that crazed me; him too."

"My prayers were answered. An angel guarded you."

"Angels do not guard drunkards," muttered the warty housekeeper, pouring freshly scented warm water into an oblong glazed pottery bathing tub.

Doña Pepita ordered the housekeeper to shut up and wash me, which she did, but muttering in my ear as she bent over me, in a voice too low for Doña Pepita to hear: "Angels do not guard whores. The devil himself it was, more likely, judging from the red scrapes and scratches in such strange and secret places."

She was nearer the truth than Doña Pepita with her gentle visions and constant faiths, for later, restless in my bed, it flashed through my consciousness that I'd left, inside the monkey head, the slip of paper Don Carlos had signed, promising on his honor to vote against the sentence of execution for Maximilian and his generals that I'd planned to take to the trial this very day.

He had won the game after all!

53

The harp strings had scraped and cut me cruelly despite the protection of my heavy hair. Everything hurt—the soft linen sheets, my thin cotton nightgown, the morning light filtering through closed shutters, the small puffs of breeze that sent a sudden rumpling of the mosquito netting cascading cloudily down around the bed.

The flame of my heart had gone out. I turned restlessly from side to side. The room was too large—the ceiling cathedral high. I fancied I could hear bats flitting and chittering among the bending beams.

I cared about nothing except to be alone; for no one to speak to me; no one to come near me. My spirit and my soul had been stolen away. I would never be able to live in the world of people again. The very thought of explaining to Phillip was painful and sickening. I couldn't do it. Not ever.

I pushed open the shutters and sat by the open window in my nightgown, contemplating the pool. Was it deep enough for me to drown myself in? Red hibiscus drooped from burning bushes. Withered roses scattered scentless petals on the gravel walks swept into tortured patterns. The scent of crushed gardenias wavered nauseously. In my mind I knew I was still under the effects of the absinthe, but that didn't lessen my shame or the magnitude of the mistake I had made. I and I alone would be responsible for the death of the Emperor and possibly Beau and Prince Salm as well. For there would be no mercy in Díaz for anyone connected with me now. I'd broken my promise to him again.

The sound of a carriage stopping in front of the house made as much noise as a parade of cannons. A knock thundered at my door.

"The trial is over," Doña Pepita said in a little voice, wearily removing a black mantilla from her small head. "All the ladies of Querétaro were invited to attend but none did. We knelt in the church from ten o'clock until the finish. One of my cousins, Don Antonio Zorro, sat through it all. Three of the very young jurors wearing yellow kid gloves voted for banishment and three wearing baby blue ones voted for execution before a firing squad. The stupid young judge, a minor official, wearing pink kid gloves, gave the deciding vote for execution of Maximilian and his generals instead of banishment.

"Was Don Carlos there?"

"Yes. Don Antonio said the face of Don Carlos was green and sick, yet he wore a wicked smile throughout the reading of the sentence to the Emperor in absentia and to Mejía and Miramon in person. They are to be executed on the Hill of the Bells at three o'clock this afternoon."

I heard the words, but I did not comment. I was shattered. I could not have spoken without shrieking. I pulled my hair, like a black mourning veil across my face and turned to the wall. "I will never forgive myself."

Doña Pepita began plumping up my pillow and smoothing the covers I'd wrestled into a tangle. "Perhaps God will forgive you. But you must begin to think of someone beside yourself. The poor Emperor had double bad news today."

I sat up, pushing my hair out of my eyes. "What could be worse than a death sentence?"

"Señora Mejía told that a telegram had come to the Emperor with news of the death of Carlota."

"Will Maximilian be spared nothing? Everything has been taken from him. But I know how he feels. My broken world can't be put back together either. Díaz will ruin Phillip out of vengeance for me. And my husband will die on the march to Vera Cruz."

"Why would Díaz have vengeance for you? He's gone out of his way to help you."

"Did Díaz himself come for me last night?"

"He never came at all. Haven't you read your letter? He sent it by courier shortly after you went to the house of Don Carlos. I put it on the table by your bed. Here it is, unopened, little friend. On top of everything else, you've been worrying about Díaz?"

Doña Pepita remained standing by the bed while I tore open the letter and drank it in as thirstily as if it had been the cup of salvation itself.

Estimada Doña Angel,

This letter is being written in haste to say that this time it is I, Don Porfirio Díaz, who breaks the appointment. I, Don Porfirio alone wear the blame. The tall thin woman, the sleeping volcano, the all lovely things white and shining, thou, Doña Angel, must forgive. It is because nothing good was accomplished of that man Juárez in San Luis Potosí that I must hurry to take the lead in a triumphal entry into Imperial Mexico City which will then become my Liberal Mexico City and so remain.

I have ordered General Escobedo to release the Colonel Berrien into my custody immediately. He dare not refuse for he will appear a clown before the world if I tell that he mistakes a

*colonel for a general and accords him the same honor, even the
sentence of death, side by side, equal in importance to the
Emperor. I have also given the order that thou, Doña Angel
Berrien, are to be permitted to visit thy husband in the Convent
Capucines as often as thou choose until such time as he is
brought safely to me in Tacubaya or Mexico City.*

I kiss thy white white hand with regret and esteem

Don Porfirio Díaz

*Escobedo's Headquarters
Seven hours less ten minutes of the evening
15 June 1867*

Despite weakness and fits of trembling I dressed and started for
the Capucines, ignoring Doña Pepita's advice to walk slowly in the
fiery sun. On the way I recognized the reddish mansion of Don
Carlos. I would be forced to pass it, running the risk of being seen
by him. Such shame crawled over my body that I almost turned
back. I tried to ease my guilt by saying: No one would have believed
me if I had waved the paper signed by Don Carlos in the courtroom.
Besides, Don Carlos was not the ultimate judge. He may have
controlled the ultimate judge, but I could not have proved it. And I
won't ever have to tell anybody about last night; especially not
Phillip or Beau.

The thought of Beau—free—all mine forever—wherever—revived me so that I found myself running, light-footed as a deer, the
rest of the way to the grim gate of the Capucines, and singing my
own loving words to the notes of "Jesu Joy of Man's Desiring."

Beau was surprisingly rational and appeared strong. He knew
about the trial. It had been inevitable. When the guard at his door
refused to permit us to visit the Emperor, he merely sat back down
on his bed beside me and put his arms around me. I felt his flesh and
the even beat of his heart. He said nothing, but pushed my hair
back from my forehead, as he does when he loves me most.

"I dreamed last night of our baby son. He was looking everywhere for you, calling your name."

"Angelica?"

"No. 'Mother.' You didn't get hurt last night?"

"No, I wasn't hurt." How did he know?

"I must leave here at once. I am no longer safe."

"Phillip is coming back for you within a week."

"Where will he take me?"

"To Díaz in Tacubaya."

"Home?"

"You mean Hacienda Contenta?"

"No—I mean Cotton Hall. I want to go home. I want to see Edward and Button. Have I been ill long?"

"Many weeks."

"Where is Prince Salm? God, I love that man."

"He is in the Convent Santa Teresita."

"Have you talked with him?"

"No, but I plan to visit him when I leave you this afternoon."

"Not until after three o'clock. Promise to wake me when the Emperor is summoned," he murmured sleepily. "I am going with him."

We waited silently for three o'clock to strike. Only Dr. Basch and Father Soria and the wives of Mejía and Miramon were permitted on the upper story.

At four o'clock Colonel Palacios came with a telegram from Juárez. The execution was postponed for three days in order to give Baron Magnus time to reach Querétaro and attend the Emperor's last wishes and to the embalming of his body.

I woke Beau to tell him but the fever had come back, higher than ever and he was delirious.

On June 18, the morning before the last morning, Maximilian bribed a guard with a gold piece and came to Beau's cell. Beau was asleep in a hammock. Maximilian leaned over and kissed him on the mouth. As the two blond beards melded I felt a wind pass through the cell.

When Maximilian left I touched Beau's forehead. It was cold and he was sweating. He opened his eyes and smiled weakly at me, repeating what he had said two days earlier, "Remember, you are to wake me when the time comes for him to leave. I am going with him."

"Did you realize he was in here just now?"

"Yes. I told him everything."

PART IX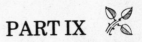

The Hill of the Bells

JUNE 1867

*Who could foretell the song that hailed
the sun
Would be the accomplice of the singer's
doom?*

To a Linnet
SOR JUANA (THE BEAUTIFUL NUN)
17TH CENTURY

54 ❧

It was a soft summer day. From the cell windows you could see the cloudless blue sky outside. Sunlight glittered on the lemon trees in the cloister garden. Baron Magnus came to visit Beau.

Baron Magnus said the Emperor told him that hearing of Carlota's death had been a great consolation. The Baron had not had the heart to contradict it nor to inform him of her incurable madness. "The Emperor is saying also, 'Is strange that from my earliest youth I always have this feeling I will not be dying a natural death, and for a long time I am knowing I am not leaving this country of Mexico alive.' "

"Aside from my husband and the Prince, you have been Maximilian's best friend," I said.

"He is a wonderful human being as well as an Emperor. If Juárez and the Emperor could ever be meeting face to face all would be different. But Juárez is always refusing to believe in His Majesty's Liberal aspirations for Mexico; or in his magnificent standard of honor and his dedication to duty."

"How could Father Fischer and the Austrian and Belgian Ministers have behaved so cowardly? Everyone has deserted him."

"But not his friends. Not the Salms nor you two, nor Luis Blasio nor Dr. Basch, nor Tudos, von Kodolitsch, Count Khevenhuller, von Kollonitz—I can be naming hundreds who are loving him and not deserting him."

"I deserted him. I could have saved him."

"You are having no proof of that."

The Baron was so sincere and handsome and fine. I had an urgency to confess my sin and be forgiven. I needed help, oh, how I needed help! It came out in a rush—the evening I'd spent with Don Carlos.

"You see—I could have saved the Emperor if I'd not lost the paper with Don Carlos's signature on it."

He laughed. "Oh, come now, Juárez alone is controlling the outcome of the trial. Don Carlos is being an aristocratic figurehead with much money, blowing himself up to impress the political parties. The whole trial is a light opera put on only for the benefit of the foreign newspapers. My dear lady, the verdict is when Maximilian puts himself under the influence of Father Fischer and Bazaine in signing the October Decree. It is his death warrant he signs that day. Nothing you do changes the outcome of the mock trial though I am thinking you are the most loyal and courageous lady I am ever meeting."

"Don't forget Princess Salm."

"That one! As you Americans say, 'What a bird!' "

Beau sat up.

"Look! With the beard, it is amazing. Almost—"

"Almost what?"

The Baron lowered his voice and said half playfully, half confidentially, "We can never be pulling it off—"

"You mean have my husband climb the Hill of the Bells tomorrow in the Emperor's clothes?"

Baron Magnus shook his head in vehement negation. "I do not think of what I am saying."

"If he were well, Baron, he would insist on doing exactly what you are thinking of. So while I weep for Maximilian, I thank God for the Mexican dysentery."

Later in the day I requested permission to take a basket of peaches to the Emperor, but the convent was crammed with soldiers and guards searching every turret and corner for a chance sympathizer who might be attempting a rescue.

Colonel Palacios sneered at my request and said rudely, "You will never fool me again. I do not trust you any more than I would trust the whorish Princess Salm. Juárez alone can deal with that kind. Go home. I am tired of seeing you always around. You can return after the prisoners leave in the morning at six promptly. After that your big man will be marched out with those of Santa Teresita on the road to Vera Cruz. And I will have seen the last of you and that crazy one."

I would not stoop to argue with Palacios. I was very tired and Dr. Basch had given Beau a strong sleeping potion.

I was waiting at the gate of the Convent of the Capucines before half-past five the next morning. The streets were empty; all house windows shuttered.

As church bells clanged and all the clocks of the town struck six, Maximilian, dressed in a black frock coat, black trousers and a black felt hat and accompanied only by little Tudos, came down a staircase into the courtyard. He walked with steady steps, his head high, his face just a little paler than the last time I'd seen him. He was followed by Mejía and Miramon, also in black civilian clothes. As he passed through the iron convent gate in the fresh morning sunshine, the Emperor turned to Mejía and said, "What a wonderful day! I have always wanted to die on a morning like this."

I caught his eye as he climbed into the first closed black carriage. He lifted his finger toward me and nodded. I never saw any face with such a wonderful spiritual look. The carriage rolled away with Tudos trotting behind it like a little dog.

Mejía had to be lifted into the next carriage. His wife, sobbing and screaming, with their new baby at her breast, ran after the carriage. She tried to grab hold of the wheels and stop it but soldiers prevented her with their bayonets. Miramon was different. He even carried an air of bravado about him as if he were going to a ball. His wife was not present. She was in San Luis Potosí pleading with Juárez.

In an open buggy following the three closed carriages I recognized Baron Magnus. I had always admired him and been somewhat in awe of his grand presence but at this moment I loved him. I hurried inside the empty courtyard and up the steps to Beau's cell.

Dr. Basch was coming out. "I couldn't go to the Hill of the Bells with His Majesty. I simply couldn't." He burst into hard gulping sobs and ran down the long empty gallery.

Beau had slept through the commotion. I touched his forehead. It was cool; his pulse regular. He had on a pair of white cotton trousers, nothing else. He had recently been washed. The red hairs on his chest were still damp. That must have been what Dr. Basch was doing in his cell: vicariously performing last rites. From somewhere not too far away I heard a dog howling as dogs do when someone is dying. I knew it was Baby. It had to be.

What a terrible day. What an awful day. Would I be able to hear the volley from the hill on the upstairs gallery? I went out and sat on the balustrade, leaning against one of the stone arches. I don't know how long I sat there before the great iron gates swung open and eight soldiers entered the courtyard. They were carrying an open coffin. It was too short for the body inside. The long narrow feet dangled pitifully over the end. Tudos was holding on to one of the feet. He was crying out loud. The Emperor's black felt hat was on his head. It came down over his ears.

The firing squad marched behind the coffin. They were laughing and joking, their footsteps clanging gaily on the cobblestones.

Baron Magnus was scuffling with the loutish Palacios at the gate.

"Coming in, I am," he demanded loudly.

"Not coming in you am," laughed Palacios, lifting his pistol.

Pushing him against the iron bars, Baron Magnus felled Palacios with his powerful fist, grabbed Palacios's pistol and hastened after Maximilian's body toward the crypt of the convent.

Someone came up beside me. It was Beau, wearing the Emperor's white sombrero. His eyes were cast down, receiving in full force the sight of the dead king. For an instant he seemed dazed. "*Qué pasa* down there?" he shouted.

I could feel the sensations that must be going through him, the anguish, the wish to kick out, to break heads, smash ribs and distribute death right and left.

One of the firing squad soldiers looked up. I recognized him. It was Paco. Puzzled he pointed up at Beau and spoke rapidly to the others.

"It is the Emperor! See his white sombrero and golden beard! We shot an imposter on the Hill of the Bells."

"Paco!" I called. "You remember el Señor Berrien! This is he— not the Emperor."

Beau had a pistol. I don't know where he had got it. He aimed at Paco.

I pushed his wrist. "Go back into your cell."

He pulled the trigger. The bullet zoomed across the courtyard, hit the cloister bell and set it clanging.

There was a curious smack behind me. Shards of stone and stucco hit the nape of my neck.

"Go back in your cell," I screamed as Paco fired again.

Beau's eyes were glazed with a terrible fury, the fury of death. He stared past me without seeing me, a cold flame consuming him. Still without seeing me, he ran along the gallery and up the staircase at the far end. I stood watching him, transfixed. The daylight seemed to darken though no cloud passed the sun.

"Pigs! You down there!" His voice was above me.

In answer, several shots and confused noises came from the courtyard as more soldiers filled it and dispersed, running up various staircases to head Beau off from every direction.

I stumbled up the stairs in the nearest corner to a stone turret with seats around the inside. I sank on one of them looking up in terror at the roof, waiting for Beau to appear.

Soldiers were now filling all the vaulted cloister galleries. Only Paco, gun pointed, still stood in the courtyard below, waiting, his mean little eyes squinted upward. For a time all was quiet. Then Beau appeared on the rampart of the roof. Stooped, he was running along the edge to the corresponding turret across from me. This turret was roofless.

Everybody was screaming and shouting. Something stirred far down inside of me. I had to be with him. I didn't mind dying so long as I died with him. The roof was glaring with sunlight. It was flat, but different levels made it uneven. I ran straight out into the light toward the turret where Beau had taken refuge.

He must have seen me. He couldn't have missed seeing me. I watched in horror as he stepped from the turret shouting, "*Viva* Maximilian! Long live the Emperor of Mexico!" He aimed his pistol down at Paco and pulled the trigger.

"Beau!" I screamed.

There were explosions from many guns. The white sombrero leapt into the air and Beau hovered a moment as if undecided whether to fly upward or downward, then dropped like a great bird on the stones below.

55 🌿

On June 20 Colonel Count von Kodolitsch, Colonel Count Kheven-huller, Colonel Alfons von Kollonitz and Baron Hammerstein assembled in the palace in Mexico City and hoisted a white flag. Márquez and Father Fischer had disappeared. Colonel Phillip Berrien acted as interpreter between these officers and General Don Porfirio Díaz, who accepted their surrender and arranged all difficult points with the greatest chivalry and delicacy.

The next day Mexican soldiers headed by General Díaz entered the city under a rain of flowers and cheers and happy songs.

Thus expired the Mexican Empire.

On June 22 Phillip set out for Querétaro to take his brother home.

Three weeks later, at the William Elliott house in Beaufort, S.C., Phillip wrote invitations to the funeral in his flowing script. The notorious colored madam of the town, Livia Berrien, carried some of the invitations in a basket to the proper ones in Beaufort; Cudjo Manigo, riding the white stallion, Teaser, delivered the rest to the plantations still owned or occupied by Carolinians.

The invitations were on cheap white paper with a black margin. They read:

> Angelica Burwell Berrien and Phillip Elliott Berrien with deepest sorrow inform friends and relatives of the death of their beloved husband and brother, General Baynard Elliott Berrien, of the Mexican Imperial Army, who was killed in the service of his adopted country on 19 June. The funeral will take place this afternoon at three o'clock at Cotton Hall Plantation on Hilton Head Island.

PART X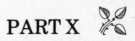

Hilton Head

JULY 1867

The horrors of the tomb are but the cradle of the sun
And the dark shadows of death are brilliant lights for the stars.

EMPEROR NEZAHUALCOYOTL
(THE HUNGRY FOX)
FROM THE MANUSCRIPTS
DE IXTLILXOCHITL

56 🌿

"I am the resurrection and the life. . . ."

I hope I never hear those words again. The spreading live oak tree among whose roots Beau will lie, is bending down to gather him into itself. A bull alligator bellowing in the creek beyond the piney woods drowns out the next sentences. A mosquito is buzzing inside Cousin Annie's voluminous black mourning veil that shrouds me. I dare not scratch, for everybody is pitying me, expecting me to weep. But I am able to hold back the tears for my wild, proud love, now lying between his brother and the little grandfather in the gold coat.

" *. . . whom I shall see for myself and mine eyes shall behold, and not another."*

I wonder if the little grandfather's gold coat has rotted away? I wish somebody had knocked down those stark house chimneys. What once appeared a medieval castle from Port Royal Sound is now nothing but eight tall blackened chimneys soaring meaninglessly against the mass of cumulus clouds threatening the sky.

"We brought nothing into this world and it is certain we can take nothing out . . ."

Livia must weigh over three hundred pounds. She loved her mistress's baby, Beau, more than she did her own baby, Pharaoh. He was her white baby at her young black breast.

"When thou with rebukes dost chasten a man for sin thou makest his beauty to consume away . . ."

But Maum Hannah and Masai loved him more. They huddle forlornly together, moaning. Maum Hannah and Masai loved him almost as much as I did. Without his presence this plantation is nothing but burnt-out chimneys and unplowed fields and gardens choked with briars.

"In the morning it is green, and groweth up: but in the evening it is cut down, dried up, and withered."

The gray Spanish moss dripping funereally from the live oaks makes ragged mourning streamers. How different from the fragrant flowery vines that hang from the trees at Miramontes. Phillip will never agree to be a farmer here.

"For one star differeth from another star in glory."

Everybody looks so poor and shabby in their old worn-out clothes. Even their eyes are passive, overwhelmed with defeat. In comparison Phillip glows with a fresh pure look, vibrant and full of energy.

"As is the earthy, such are they also that are earthy."

Carlota was spared standing by Maximilian's grave. But she also missed seeing him play the part of a strong man at the end. She worshiped strong men. They say Maximilian looked at the seven men who faced him with lifted guns and said, in a clear voice, "Mexicans! May my blood be the last which shall be spilt for the welfare of the country: *Viva* Mexico!" and he fell, whispering slowly the word Carlota loved, *"Hombre."*

"Now this I say brethren, flesh and blood cannot inherit the Kingdom of God."

I think I am going to fall down, but not slowly. I am tired from the long journey from Querétaro. I wish I hadn't promised to stay the night with Stephen and Charlotte Elliott at Parris Island. What do I wish? To sleep here in the cemetery beside Beau on the briary ground? Or in Maum Hannah's little cabin with her and Masai? To go to Virginia on the night train from Charleston and live there the rest of my dry, withered life with little Edward and Aunt Dell and Uncle Jim?

"Thou knowest Lord the secret of our hearts; shut not thy merciful ears to our prayers . . ."

Beau's gentlemen friends and cousins are taking turns throwing shovelfulls of dirt on the coffin. It makes a horrible empty sound.

"... *earth to earth, ashes to ashes, dust to dust*";

I sway against Stephen. He steadies me with the stump of his right arm. The odor of the salt marsh floods my nostrils and revives me. Oh, Beau darling, can you smell it?

"... *those who sleep in him shall be changed and made like unto his glorious body* ..."

No one ever had such a glorious body as Beau. Will Button want to stay with me in Virginia, or go to Mexico with Phillip? Mount Orizaba would fascinate him.

"... *and grant him an entrance into the land of light and joy.*"

Will the grave never be filled? Will Maum Hannah never raise the final song? People open their gold watches every few minutes. If the tide ebbs before the priest pronounces the benediction they will be forced to wait here in the cemetery for it to rise again. They are afraid to go home in the dark. They are afraid of the restless Yankee soldiers who occupy the island and of armed former slaves who prowl the night.

"*Grant to us who are still in our Pilgrimage* ... *that we may be joined with thy blessed saints* ..."

The service is endless. He didn't have to put in that particular prayer, did he?"

"... *be with us all evermore. Amen.*"

They are hurrying up to kiss me and go away. Phillip stands beside me, graciously thanking everybody for coming. How different he appears from them. He is spirited and unafraid.

The Negroes are singing as they steal away:

Moonlight Starlight Moonlight Starlight
Lay the body to the tomb—Oh, lay the body to the tomb.

The tide is rising. A cool breeze is pouring in from the ocean. Phillip and I are alone now in the cemetery.

"Will you come back to Mexico with me? If you say yes, I will go to Virginia with you to pick up the boys. They will thrive at Miramontes. If you say no, you must ride the night train to Virginia alone."

Close to the grave a sapling is twisted into a circle. A redbird is sitting in the bend of the circle forming a lit lantern. The redbird is singing an afternoon song of pure glorious joy.

"Which will it be?"

Redbirds have always reminded me of Beau. "You know I can never love anyone but Beau."

Phillip puts his forefinger to his lips, and extends his hand. It is a warm, strong hand. I take it and follow him willingly to the little steamboat waiting at the dock to carry us to Charleston to take the Virginia train together.

AFTERWORD

Explanatory words concerning three children:

1. In a book about his famous father, General Weygand of World War I, Jacques Weygand states in a chapter called "La legende" that when the Empress Carlota died in 1927, General Weygand received several letters all saying 'your mother just died. Further information is available.' The General was not present at Carlota's funeral as it was often insisted, but no one can deny his amazing physical resemblance to pictures of that super-soldier, Alfred van der Smissen, who never married and eventually committed suicide.

2. Rumor also whispered that Maximilian and his Indian sweetheart, Concepcion Sedano, had a son who was taken to Europe by the Adilid family after Maximilian's execution. He was shot as a German spy during World War I in a small French village.

3. Little Augustin Iturbide was given back to his mother and lived a long, rich unpolitical life in Mexico.